International Finance

International Finance

Edited by **Rupert Fry**

Willford Press

New York

Published by Willford Press,
118-35 Queens Blvd., Suite 400,
Forest Hills, NY 11375, USA
www.willfordpress.com

International Finance
Edited byRupert Fry

International Standard Book Number: 978-1-68285-184-5 (Hardback)

Printed in China.

Contents

Preface

International finance, also known as international macroeconomics, deals with monetary exchange across national borders. The discipline focuses on global capital markets, currency exchange rates and foreign investments. This book aims to analyze various facets of this field and highlights some of its key concepts and applications. The topics included in this book on international finance are of utmost significance and bound to provide incredible insights to the readers. It emphasizes on understanding different aspects of financial markets, institutions and international syndications. This book will prove to be immensely beneficial to students and researchers engaged in this field.

The researches compiled throughout the book are authentic and of high quality, combining several disciplines and from very diverse regions from around the world. Drawing on the contributions of many researchers from diverse countries, the book's objective is to provide the readers with the latest achievements in the area of research. This book will surely be a source of knowledge to all interested and researching the field.

In the end, I would like to express my deep sense of gratitude to all the authors for meeting the set deadlines in completing and submitting their research chapters. I would also like to thank the publisher for the support offered to us throughout the course of the book. Finally, I extend my sincere thanks to my family for being a constant source of inspiration and encouragement.

Editor

Behavioral governance, accounting and corporate governance quality

Ronald Chibuike Iwu-Egwuonwu

Department of Business Administration, University of Abuja, Nigeria.
Managing Partner Stride Associates Consulting, Nigeria. E-mail: owenbrucelyn@yahoo.co.uk.

The article explores the concepts of behavioral governance and behavioral accountability both of which look at the quality of the behavior of organization members, especially directors, as the foundation for sound corporate achievement. This author posits that the effectiveness of governance in general and corporate governance in particular is dependent on the behavioral effectiveness of those who govern and manage. That governance fails is often because more effort is devoted at creating and sustaining structures and processes while almost no meaningful attention is given to genuine institutionalization of behavioral and ethical accountability which are accomplished by the hands of genuine integrity. The quality of corporate performance is hinged on the quality of behavioral performance and accountability with which members of the organization are associated. But given that the elevation of human animality in our organizations has tended to diminish the moral value of organizations, directors should adopt the concept of behavioral governance and behavioral accountability, to raise the quality of behavior and accountability in our organizations, as the route to genuinely raising the quality of performance in their organization.

Key words: Corporate governance, behavioral governance, behavioral accountability, ethical behavior, human animality, moral tone at the top, core organizational values.

INTRODUCTION

Behavioral accountability is deeply rooted in what this author refers to as behavioral and ethical governance. It is a form of accountability that should precede financial accountability because without it, no accountability is meaningful. This is buttressed by the number of corporate malfeasance, distresses and celebrated corporate failures in recent times, some of which were thought unbelievable. In almost all of these cases, a common factor that cuts across is the use of financial accountability, expressed through cooked accounting figures, to deceive the investing public into believing that these organizations were being run well.

Unfortunately, while robust pictures of corporate performance were being painted, the internal control mechanisms of such organizations had been eroded by corporate executives and directors who exist without what can amount to even a modicum of sustainable good character (Iwu-Egwuonwu, 2004). So, what is ordinarily referred to as corporate malfeasance, distress and failure is actually an indictment on the moral character of executives and directors of our organizations.

It is a settled issue that no organization succeeds as a long-lived going concern without proper governance, just as no nation succeeds without the proper governance of its political and economic institutions. Since governance is the act of human beings who are subject to and products of vicissitudes of character, its quality and the success of organizations are dependent on the behavioral quality of those who govern and manage. This is why behavioral and ethical concerns are issues in any attempt to raise the quality of corporate and public institutions' governance. This fact is predicated on the well rehearsed wisdom that nothing works well unless human behavior aligns it to the path of success, and no organization fails, suffers fraud or becomes distressed except by the behavior of its executives and directors. Thus, organizations as human devices tend to be imperfect in the ways they work because of the imperfections and failings of human behavior (Bello J.A, 1988). Organizations therefore, succeed only to the extent to which the efforts of directors and managers to align their behaviors and those of other organizational members with the intentions of stakeholders succeed. This author holds the strong view that effectiveness of governance in general and corporate governance in particular, is dependent on the behavioral effectiveness of those who govern and manage. That governance fails is often because more effort is devoted at creating and sustaining structures and processes while almost no meaningful attention is given to genuine institutionalization of behavioral and ethical accountability, which are accomplished by the hands of genuine integrity. There is a long list of corporate casualties across international divides on account of behavioral misalignments or diminished behavioral governance and accountability.

In Nigeria alone, 54 banks have either failed or been forced to close between 1994 and 2005. Then there were the cases of the then Lever Brothers Nigeria Plc and Cadbury Nigeria Plc, who overstated their earnings through the cooking of accounts and were appropriately sanctioned by the Securities and Exchange Commission (SEC). In other climes, especially in the United States of America, corporate distress and eventual failure are gradually gaining the status of a national culture and this has been a great concern to regulators. A complete listing of such corporate distresses and failures is impossible here but suffice it to underscore the following: Enron, Arthur Andersen, AIG, Tyco, WorldCom, Qwest, Global Crossing, Vivendi *et cetera*.

What is behavioral governance?

Behavior is said to consist of “activities, interactions, sentiments and performance of individuals and groups”, and observable behavior is of interest when it depicts a pattern (Bello, 1988). This author conceptualizes behavioral governance to mean the direction and control of organizations by directors and managers who would display behaviors that are consistent with higher values and eliciting same from other organizational members, in such a way that doing just the right things, as defined in the immortal values of higher existence, becomes automatic in the conduct of every organizational member, thus aligning the organization to self-perpetuating success.

While not neglecting the structures and processes of good governance, behavioral governance breathes life into them by building the patterns that are receptive to genuine corporate accountability, corporate justice, transparency, genuine disclosures, accounting processes that have integrity and a genuine foundation of high performance as opposed to cooked performance.

What is accountability and accounting in relation to governance?

First, it is important we define corporate governance briefly in order to take our bearing on accountability and accounting, as they affect corporate governance behavior. The Guardian (August 25, 2010) argues that, the simple idea of corporate governance is about building confidence in your product, erected on the foundation of transparency and accountability, good corporate governance flowed from practices that involved fairness, accountability, responsibility and transparency on a foundation of intellectual honesty. In its simplest definition, corporate governance is a system by which corporations are governed and controlled with a view to increasing shareholder value and meeting the expectations of other stakeholders.

Of course, poor corporate governance was a major factor in almost all known cases of distress of financial institutions. In a report that also evaluates the management of paper accounting records by the government of Namibia, Barata et al. (2001) noted that governments are investing heavily in introducing new financial management systems as a means of improving accountability and managerial efficiency. This is a development that underscores the laying of a sound foundation for behavioral accountability because if the behavior of executives and boards of directors is not properly checked by accounting accountability, which in itself is a subset of behavioral accountability, the quality of governance that will become evident is such that was prevalent at Enron.

But O'Donovan (2003) in her paper titled “Change Management- A Board Culture of Corporate Governance” defines corporate governance as 'an internal system encompassing policies, processes and people, which serves the needs of shareholders and other stakeholders, by directing and controlling management activities with good business savvy, objectivity, accountability and integrity. She further posits that sound corporate governance is reliant on external marketplace commitment and legislation, plus a healthy board culture which safeguards policies and processes. Furthermore, O'Donovan argues that 'the perceived quality of a company's corporate governance can influence its share price, as well as the cost of raising capital.

Accountability and accounting are both instruments that promote high quality of good governance. Sheng (2000) admits that an important theme of corporate governance is to ensure the accountability of certain individuals in an organization, through mechanisms that try to reduce or eliminate the principal-agent problem. A related but separate thread of discussion focuses on the impact of a corporate governance system in economic efficiency, with a strong emphasis on shareholders' welfare. Accountability and accounting are defined and explained as follows:

Accountability: accountability has to do with the opportunity to perform or have an oversight over a subject, which may include an institution, the liability to be called upon to render an account and the obligation to bear the consequences for failure to perform as expected. In leadership roles, accountability is the acknowledgment and assumption of responsibility for actions, products, decisions and policies including the administration, governance and implementation within the scope of the role or employment position and encompassing the obligation to report, explain and be answerable for resulting consequences. The Institute of Social Accountability also reports that accountability is expressed in terms of accounting, reporting and assurance: how management is to report to its shareholders. Stone et al. (2010) have listed eight types of accountability to include:

1. Moral accountability
2. Administrative accountability
3. Political accountability
4. Managerial accountability
5. Market accountability
6. Legal/judicial accountability
7. Constituency relations accountability and
8. Professional accountability (Yu, 2010; Singh, 2009).

Accounting: Snyder (2008) sees accounting as the art of recording, summarizing, reporting and analyzing financial transactions. An accounting system can be a simple, utilitarian check register, or, as with Microsoft Office Accounting, it can be a complete record of all the activities of a business, providing details of every aspect of the business, allowing the analysis of business trends and providing insight into future prospects. The five account types are denoted under two broad accounting areas as follows:

a) Balance sheet accounts

Assets: Things of value that are owned and used by the business.
Liabilities: Debts that are owed by the business.
Equity: The owner's claim to business assets.

b) Profit and loss accounts

Revenue: The amounts earned from the sales of goods and services.
Expenses: Costs incurred in the course of business.

Each of these areas of accounting supports both the need and requirement for accountability in organizations. But when the quality of accounting is poor in any organization or country, then not much can be said of what is normally regarded as accountability in such systems. That is probably why Wu Zhong (2009) says that there is "No Accounting in China's Accountability".

Emphasizing the need to improve accountable accounting, Watkins (2002) notes that although the "threats" to the accounting profession do not seem so ominous, they are present all the same. One starting point in addressing them, is to better understand the role of accounting information. To accomplish this, one must consider the unique competencies accounting comprises. One could, for example, select from among the elements of decision usefulness, stewardship, control, fairness, attestation, relevance, reliability, representational faithfulness, and accountability for the grounding norms for both accounting information and accountants' competencies. She also quotes Yuji Ijiri to have underscored the importance of accountability, as the foundation of accounting and contrasts this view with one of simply supplying quantitative information for economic decision-making. She notes that Ijiri has further developed the notion of an accountability view of accounting and offers additional distinctions between it and a decision-usefulness orientation, for understanding the purpose of accounting and accounting systems.

"A primary difference speaks of the tensions that are always present, when attempting to provide information that is both relevant and reliable. A decision-usefulness orientation of accounting, places greater emphasis on the relevance of information provided to decision makers". Watkins continued by noting that 'if accounting systems are to facilitate accountability, then the goal of accounting is to construct a "reality" of organizations, which facilitates a fair representation of its activities. This is a concept that the profession seems to once have recognized and yet has lost sight of.

Foundations of governance behavior

Given the nature of man, the effective management of the characteristics of individual members of the organization becomes a very crucial matter in effective behavioral governance. Omoregie (1993) affirms that human nature includes both rationality and animality. The rational value in human beings is reason while the animal aspect, consists of the numerous passions and desires generally referred to as lower emotions. Much of the behavioral misalignments that have diminished the worth of so many organizations in our corporate community today are traceable to human animality or the overriding effects of the lower emotions of members of such organizations. This human animality which is often the source of injustice in human behavior (Rawls, 1972), also tends to bring human beings down to the animal level which manifests in lack of self control exacerbated by the urge for primitive acquisition, fraud or inclination to defeat internal control systems for personal gains, manipulative behaviors in employment matters and dealings with others, injustice and all forms of inclination to grow rich within the dreams of avarice, *et cetera*.

The lower emotions of man are raw and need to be controlled. By their raw nature, these lower emotions are not bad but the interpretations we give to their presence in our thoughts or minds, is what determines the effect or hold they have on us. Thus, when people are not disciplined, the raw emotions that define the animal in them would push up to prominence, to seize the entire human being, by subduing all senses of reason and elicit behaviors that may shock the unsuspecting world. All manner of evil in our corporate world, as well as in our society are traceable to man's inability to sustain self discipline by allowing the animal in us to dictate our approach to life, as well as the interpretations we give to material things and the manner of their acquisition.

The rational aspect of man or the "reason" component of man, tends to raise him to the rational, spiritual level where higher values of life are considered beyond personal gratifications. Rationality in corporate governance is thus defined by man's ability to suppress lower emotions, see clearly, make right and selfless judgments, reach sound decisions and generally bring self discipline to bear in all his actions. Thus, a man who is rational is a man whose self discipline is sustained and whose reasoning capacity successfully keeps his animal nature in check. Genuine achievements are the hallmark of people who have attained high rationality in their official and personal affairs by succeeding in the control of their passions, their desires or appetites and their entire emotionality. Such are the people governance today and tomorrow needs, in order to minimize unsought consequences and become clothed in best practice and excellence.

Behavioral governance in the composition of the board

Good boards go bad when directors appear to have lost their values. In this regard, Rechtman (2002) advises that what needs to be done is to prevent them from getting so terribly off-track by leading them back in the right direction. But in my view, the easiest way to get a board "going on the right direction" all the time, is to compose such board with behavioral accountability as the bedrock. A so called good board can only go bad, if it was in the first place constituted for other reasons than the sound behaviors of the board members, underscored by the hands of integrity.

In the composition of corporate boards, the concept of behavioral governance requires that the appointers of directors rely not only on the paper qualifications and experience of those to be appointed but more crucially on their built-out character and how this aligns not only with the intentions of the organization but also with the high level of trust and morality built into the position of director which the role occupant must exemplify at all times. The same goes for every management level staff and all other organizational level staff, whose behavioral output must indeed reinforce the pillars of behavioral governance. Behavioral governance concept aims at the inner core of the person and thus focuses on the proper development of the positive aspects of the character of directors and managers, in order to enhance their behavioral output and the probability that in all circumstances they would be completely led by higher values and not the lower ones underscored by the weaknesses of man and the ills of society. The content of behavioral governance is broad as it encompasses all the tools, issues, subjects and processes that mould and sustain sound behavior in society and in organizations. A partial list includes: integrity of directors and the entire human resources of the organization, strong disposition to transparency, a well developed sense of true justice and the genuine disposition to dispense this justice fearlessly, ability and readiness to meet disclosure requirements instead of seeking to defeat them, a high capability for moral behavior, honesty, reliability for doing the right things, fairness in dealings with the organization, its members and stakeholders; the disposition to ask for genuine accountability and support it, self discipline, proper personality management, having a strategic focus *et cetera* (Iwu-Egwuonwu, 2004).

We earnestly should get concerned with the elevation of behavioral governance in our organizations, primarily for the need to redefine our highly distorted moral values the application of which has tended to diminish genuine corporate performance in favor of "cooked" performance. We need behavioral governance to rejuvenate the human conscience which presently appears dead on the altar of greed, avarice and the urge for primitive acquisitions in our organizations. We also need it to rejuvenate in us the behavioral prerequisites for becoming good custodians of the resources held, on behalf of wider interests and to govern and manage for the general good. These are the backbone of behavioral and ethical governance.

Behavioral accountability

The principal characteristics of effective corporate governance are accountability, transparency, protection and guarantee of the rights and privileges of all stakeholders and the extent of genuine checks and balances in the organization. These are the issues subsumed by what this author refers to as behavioral accountability. The past, present and future of corporate governance, like any other human system, have always hinged and will continue to hinge on the behavioral quality of owners, directors and managers of the corporation. It is the individual and collective behaviors of these people that sum up into the behavior an organization is associated with. They set the tone of how jobs are parceled to units or departments that do them and they influence the behavioral quality of other employees of the organization. Behavioral accountability thus summarizes the moral, functional and righteous obligations of corporate managers and directors to the corporation and society in the conduct of their governance cardinal roles of directing, decisioning, supervising and accountability, especially through the accounting process.

Two types of accountability are discernible in human organizations. These are behavioral and financial/accounting accountability. The quality and reliability of the latter is greatly influenced by the quality of the former. Behavioral accountability is predicated on the effective development of the human conscience and the development of the self inhibitory and shame attack mechanisms in directors, managers and employees of the organization. The success or failure of organizations is never because of poor financial or managerial accountability but primarily because of the quality of behavioral accountability. This is because the quality of behavioral accountability is the basis for relying on the financial figures presented by any organization. When we ask the question "who are behind these figures", we are ultimately exploring to reveal the behavioral quality of the managers and directors who have authored and endorsed the accounts or financial statements presented to the organization. No such financial statements can be reliable if the behavioral accountability of those behind them is not reliable.

Financial figures are created and painted by human beings who are influenced by the quality of their conscience or moral development. Since human beings are what they create, the financial accountability of management should be taken with little seriousness until the behavioral quality of those behind the figures (that is, the directors, managers and auditors) are known. This much has been buttressed in the case of the unfortunate overstatement of corporate earnings by Lever Brothers Nigeria Plc some years ago and Cadbury Nigeria Plc in 2008, as well as in the collapse of several banks in Nigeria in which shareholders' funds were totally wiped out. Nearly all other cases of corporate distress, collapse and stock value manipulations across the corporate world go further to buttress this fact. All these cases may have appeared to have been occasioned by poor financial accountability but the real cause is acute moral or behavioral dysfunctions in the management and boards of these organizations.

The need to watch the moral tone at the top

Companies would often present rosy financial pictures of their operations but reliance on this can often lead to cataclysmic outcomes. What is safe to rely on to determine whether these figures are likely to be the true reflections of actual performance, is to try to determine what Ed Harper (2001) refers to as "The Tone at the Top". The tone at the top refers to the quality of the behavioral accountability of directors and management. This dictates both the tone of ethical behavior the organization may be associated with and the quality of financial accountability accommodated and delivered in that organization. A major truth is that, many top corporate executives and directors in whose hands the quality of the accountability seen in their organization resides, are not often what they want the public to believe they are. If they were, the corporate financial mess which we have witnessed in recent times, courtesy of the ten banks whose executives and boards, the Central Bank of Nigeria sacked, would not have existed in the first place. Some of the directors were pastors in churches, who used the banks' money to walk their way into pastoral positions. As the investigations by the Police unfolded, we were shocked to note in disbelief the number of houses and other properties worth hundreds of billions of Naira and Dollars, being associated with a single Managing Director of a bank alone. Yet some of these CEOs got into their banks from the top by the instrumentality of either bringing investors together to form such banks or a family member's position in the bank, paved the way for them. So, do not let your judgment of who is a behaviorally sound CEO or board director, be again fooled by the excessive or overt religiosity and the aura of "moral role models" which they appear to surround themselves with. The veil has already been lifted and we can now see that they were never the saints they appeared to be. Not many of these corporate lords live within their means. Ed Harper notes that "whenever you have an officer of the company who is going to receive personal gain beyond his official compensation, something is wrong with that system".

When the high-up officers of an organization have problems of behavioral accountability, both sides of the audit effort (external and internal auditors) must be on their guard, in order not to trade in their professional conscience and code of best practice. Thus, to ensure proper reporting of accounting information and the true financial state of an organization from financial records, Ed Harper cautions that auditors should always be interested in finding out what the moral tone at the top is like. They must find out if the top people of the organization condone "petty conniving and cutting corners on ethical issues; or if they try to hide things". They must also find out if these top organizational people "attempt to go outside normal channels of due process when it comes to making decisions about money", and whether their tone is conducive to the effectiveness of a good internal control system. It must also be found out "if the CEO is willing to be questioned".

Ed Harper further notes that the poor behavioral accountability of top corporate officers is particularly captured in situations where, "they would rather have the company pay for what are clearly personal/family items which sometimes are outrageous" and "where there is conspiracy among a small group of people in the organization, even the best internal control systems will be hard pressed to defeat it because the control systems are usually built on having two people sign the check or two people sign an approval. If you have a conspiracy of those two people, it's not going to be revealed easily". Executive fraud is a particularly disturbing dent on the behavioral accountability of corporate officers. This fraud is captured in so many ways and in different shapes and sizes, depending on the organization and the sophistication of the internal control systems it has installed for itself. Executive fraud is broadly defined as an act of deliberate deception, trickery or cheating by an executive or officer of a company (including outside directors), through which the gaining of a personal or group advantage is intended or achieved by an executive. The nature and types of executive fraud are discussed in the next two paragraphs.

Many have argued that problems of behavioral accountability in organizations arise principally from the pressure on corporate executives to succeed in generating profits, even short term profits. Consequently, these executives are said to indulge in sharp practices to declare spurious profits. It is however this author's informed view, that pressure alone is not the problem as pressure is distinguishable from the inclination for immoral behavior. That an executive has behavioral accountability problem is a fundamental issue which may not necessarily arise from immediate environmental problems or pressure. Most behavioral problems originate from deep seated inclinations for dysfunctional behavior, either arising from uncontrolled ambition occasioned by the malfunctioning of the self-inhibitory system in the individual or earlier environmental influences that have helped to mould the individual's personality or both.

So, it appears to me that issues of behavioral accountability problem, border more on the nature of the individual, which can be corrected by the individual himself nurturing a good self-inhibitory and shame attack psychological system. Both are developed through good upbringing, self discipline and the internalization of values that impact positively on the superego. The ways results are achieved in an organization therefore, hint on the moral background of its directors, CEO and the body of the management staff. Shareholders can press for good results and the CEO can further imprint this on the minds of the management staff, but "it is the duty of those who handle the figures to do so in a professional manner and to offer the professionally sound advice and stick to it".

Nature of executive fraud

As stated earlier, executive fraud is broadly defined as an act of deliberate deception, trickery or cheating by an executive or officer of a company (including outside directors), through which the gaining of a personal or group advantage is intended or achieved by an executive or director. Broadly speaking, executive fraud can be classified into two major groups as next discussed.

Fraudulent manipulation of accounts not involving defalcations or abstraction of money

This usually takes the form of inflation of assets or omission of liabilities with the intention or purpose of making the company appear to be performing better than it truly is. This kind of fraud is at times difficult to find out, not necessarily because it is less frequent but mainly because those that perpetrate it often try to leave no clues for immediate detection. This is because such people are often trusted to be high performers whose stewardship can therefore not be doubted. It is a fraud mostly prevalent in organizations quoted on the stock exchange who would also want to paint rosy pictures not merited by them in order to make themselves and their stocks attractive to unsuspecting investors. Cases of "sudden" failure or insolvency of organizations whose published performance remained attractive to the end include the celebrated Enron case, National Bank of Nigeria, Intercontinental Bank Plc, Oceanic Bank Plc and so many such organizations. The broad reasons for this kind of fraud which arises from poor behavioral accountability include:

i) To enhance the performance of a business with unearned profit and thus show that the management of the organization has been successful, with the possible implication of increasing the commission on results or performance bonus payable to the chief executive and other concerned officers of the organization. The reported cases of Enron, Tyco, and Global Crossing, and even Vivendi, as well as the 54 banks that collapsed in Nigeria between 1994 and 2005, come in here as clear examples.

ii) To "shore up" or "bolster" a business which is in an insecure performance position, in order to earn or maintain the confidence of shareholders, creditors, prospective investors and the public. The cases cited in (i) above also apply appropriately here.

iii) To enable directors pay dividends which considering the true position of the organization would otherwise not have been possible. In this case, the reported profit is bogus, dividend and company tax will be paid from capital and this further depreciates the company by the amount of such payouts.

Fraudulent manipulation of accounts not involving defalcations or abstraction of money is often very ingeniously and skillfully concealed and is in many cases carried out by persons holding positions of the highest trust and having the entire confidence of directors and shareholders. A common way it is perpetrated, is through the manipulation of cut off procedures in an organization.

Cut off procedures are procedures in operation aimed at ensuring that an accord exists between purchase records and stocks and between sales and stock at the end of an accounting period. Thus, all goods received prior to the date of closing the books should be included in purchases. If they are included in stock but omitted from purchases, profit will be overstated to that extent. This is where the fraud occurs. Similarly, goods sold and included in sales in the trading account must be omitted from stock even if they are still on the premises.

The popular English case, re: Thomas Gerard and Sons Limited (1967), is a good example of the fraudulent manipulation of accounts, especially cut off procedures, by the Managing Director of a limited liability company. For the financial periods ended in March, from 1957 to 1962, the company paid dividends out of capital or otherwise irregularly to the extent of 26,254 pounds (net tax) and made payments of profits in excess of its liability, to the extent of 56,659 pounds. The case was heard on a summon by the liquidator of the company. Further details of the case include as follows:

"The company was a private company of longstanding. It carried on business as cotton spinners. Its accounts had for some years shown steady profits as a prosperous business. The Managing Director was a man of good repute, one autumn the crash came. The company's financial position was investigated and it was found to be insolvent; in the recent years in which profits had been, there had not in fact been profits. The fault was falsifications by the Managing Director in relation to stock. He was prosecuted and convicted. In the creditors' winding-up, the liquidator proceeded against him for misfeasance and the sum of 7,100 pounds was paid by him in settlement. The apparent profits had been shown as the result of the manipulation of stock. Purchases at the end of an accounting period had not been brought into that period; this had continued increasing over the years. Sales or receipts had been wrongly attributed at the end of periods. For these purposes, dates on invoices had been altered and top copy invoices had been torn out of the invoice books by the Managing Director. The auditor conducting the audits had asked for an explanation, and the Managing Director had said that these were end of period transactions and it was more convenient not to include them in the period in question.

In addition to the manipulation of year-end purchases and sales invoices described above, the Managing Director had also caused the half-yearly stock valuations to be considerably inflated by the inclusion of non-existent stock. This is also the pattern of fraudulent manipulation of accounts reported at Lever Brothers Nigeria Plc, on the one hand and Cadbury Nigeria Plc, on the other. In the case of Lever Brothers Nigeria Plc, now Unilever Nigeria Plc, the Managing Director, who also held the combined position of CEO and Chairman of the board (CEO duality), was forced to resign and in the case of Cadbury Nigeria Plc, both the Managing Director and Finance Director were sacked. In both cases, the accounts were overstated by more than 1 billion Naira (N1 billion) of unearned income and in both cases the Securities and Exchange Commission intervened by reversing the position of the accounts thereby exposing the level of losses both in the dividend paid out which ought not to have been paid, the corporate tax paid which ought not to have been paid and the real loses the companies recorded.

Defalcations involving the misappropriation of either money or goods

This involves the misappropriation of assets by executives, assets which they hold in trust. This fraud occurs more in companies where executives are seldom subjected to internal checks, as in most cases where the CEO is also the chairman of the board of directors. The methods employed by these executives to conceal such frauds are usually simple, when compared to fraudulent manipulation of accounts not involving defalcations or abstraction of money. Frauds under this category may take the following forms:

i) Outright stealing of cash: Here, executives steal cash and use an assortment of schemes to cover such stealing. Methods commonly used in perpetrating this type of fraud include arranged break-ins leading to loss of cash by the organization; and the executives who successfully arrange such stealing would normally get a fat share of the booty. Another method is the careful or skilful removal of money by tricking the custodian of the money out for the "operation" to take place and a scapegoat is made of him later, over something he knew nothing about, *et cetera*.

ii) Cheque fraud: Executives with diminished self inhibitory and malfunctioning shame attack mechanisms, who have access to unused company cheque leaves, can defraud the company by forging the signature(s) to the account. Fraud executed this way can be easily covered, especially if the perpetrator has as his schedule the maintenance of the company's bank accounts and the reconciliation of the bank statements. Cheque fraud can also be perpetrated via the fraudulent alteration of an already authorized and signed cheque, for an amount higher than what was authorized. Payment documents such as suppliers' invoices and payment vouchers, can also be forged and routed through proper channels to effect payment. It is also possible to effect payment on the same document/invoice/received goods or purchases more than once, especially if that document was not stamped at the time of first payment.

iii) Imprest account fraud: Imprest accounts are kept for a lot of purposes such as petty cash expenses and purchases. An imprest may be kept in cash or in a bank account specially meant for that purpose. A common imprest account fraud, involves "borrowing" from the imprest. Borrowing in this way is fraudulent because the so called loan may have been unauthorized in the first place and the amount borrowed may not be returned. Opportunities for this type of fraud are enormous in a system where imprest account balances are not counted and reconciled to relevant records, at regular and random intervals by independent persons. Some imprest account systems do not provide for independent prepayment checks on expenditure. Payments are only checked independently at the time of reimbursement. Such systems make it relatively easier to forge payment documents such as receipts and invoices while reducing the possibility of discovering such forgeries.

iv) Accounts receivable fraud: A major type of accounts receivable fraud is as "teeming and lading". Money received from a debtor can be misappropriated and in order to prevent that debtor's account from appearing to be overdue in accounting records, cash received subsequently from other debtors is credited to him/her. This process can continue indefinitely. In service companies, one common fraud is to bill a client for services rendered to another person. For example, employees of a telephone company can bill clients for call they (employees) made. If the client does not complain of inordinately high bills, such fraud is concealed.

v) Bad and doubtful debts cover-up: Most organizations have a policy of making provisions for debts that are overdue. Such provision may be specific, general or a combination of both. Debts long overdue may be written off as bad, especially where specific provisions have been made. Executives in charge of accounts receivables may connive with debtors, making it possible for the accounts of such debtors to remain outstanding without investigation until they are considered doubtful of recovery, provided for and eventually written off.

We often hear of banks for which non-performing loans constitute a significant proportion of loan portfolios. Some of these loans were properly advanced to associates of the executives of these banks. Often such loans are written off and the banks lose. Another ingenious method devised by bank executives to defraud the bank is to talk some people or fictitious companies into coming to get loans, on the arrangement that the total sum is shared in a manner that will give the bank executives organizing it about 80% while the company or person fronting the loan receives 20% free. Fictitious collaterals are arranged as well as fictitious office addresses and it will be recorded that the proper investigations and search on such persons, companies and the collaterals they presented are made. The loan is granted and year-in, year-out interests are calculated on such loans which have no traceable person or company in the banks' records. A preponderance of this practice will leave the bank making huge book profits/positive balances out of "loans" that will never be repaid. This is the way, the defunct National Bank of Nigeria Plc went under.

vi) Utilities and expense fraud: This type of fraud concerns the abuse of services or funds provided to executives to assist them to function properly and effectively. A good example of the abuse of utilities is the use of vehicles meant solely for official functions for private and sometimes domestic purposes. Often, we see official vehicles, especially in the public sector in Nigeria; being converted to taking "madam" to the market and children to school while the owner organization will suffer losses in the cost of gasoline, maintenance of the wear and tear and sometimes accidents that permanently demobilize such automobiles.

Traveling expenses fraud is another common fraud in corporate entities. In many organizations, executives scheme to be sent on tours because going on tour has become an avenue for making quick money by fleecing the organization. There was a case of one executive who took a touring advance of N100,000 for an assignment from Abuja to Lagos. He put up with his senior brother in Lagos and upon returning to Abuja after 5 days he retired the money he took and claimed that he spent N85,000 on accommodation and feeding and of course "manufactured" receipts from nearby hotels to back it up. He further claimed to have spent extra N20,000 of his personal purse and ended up being reimbursed the N20,000.

vii) Contracts and supplies fraud: Kickbacks and the 10% syndrome fall under this heading. Purchase orders and contracts are inflated by the amount of gratification expected to be received from the suppliers or contractors, by those who awarded the contracts or the purchase orders, after the payment has been approved. Specie of this fraud is to request for the supply of substandard items as a pass-off for standard items. The amount approved will be for standard items but monetary difference between what was approved and what was supplied will be shared by the conniving executives.

viii) "The P.R syndrome" fraud: The public relations or PR syndrome is an attempt by individuals to alter, rationalize and even glorify the concept of bribery. Words and phrases such as "settlement", brown envelopes and seeing officials "at home" fall under this form of bribery and corruption. Bribery is now the order of the day among executives and there are instances that the society even frowns at refusal by their working sons and daughters, to be "settled". Such officials who refused to be "settled" are among those who remain old fashioned about trust and this should be the bottom-line behavior expected of accountants and auditors.

Procurement fraud

Another area that will be touched in this paper concerns procurement fraud, a practice that is executed so carefully to deceive auditors. Every organization is expected to have clear operational procedures for all activities, including the procurement of goods. Akintola Williams (AW), an International Firm of Chartered Accountants and Consultants (1995), advises that the best approach to handle the procurement assignment to minimize fraud is to describe procedure for procurement and to highlight along the line, points where fraud is highly probable. The procedure includes the following:

Storekeeper raises purchase requisition;
Purchasing Manager examines and ensures that the requisition was approved by the head of department;
Purchasing Manager asks for quotation;
Quotation box and the quotations opened at the same time;
Purchasing Manager initiates the raising of Local Purchase Order (LPO);
LPO is approved by the two recognized signatories who must be senior managers but the Financial Controller must be one of the signatories;
Goods are delivered by the supplier to the goods inspection unit;
Inspection unit raises goods inspection report form to accompany the goods to the store (if found suitable and meets LPO specifications);
Store raises GRN;
Accounts department receives copies of LPO and GRN and attaches supplier invoice to the other documents;
Upon maturity the invoice is paid to the suppliers.

Notwithstanding that appropriate procedure is in place as laid out above, purchasing fraud can still be perpetrated by ingenious evil minds in the following ways:

Storekeeper can raise false requisition. This is more likely if suppliers often "dash" or gratify the storekeeper or if the supplier wants to dispose the item with a view to replenishing his stock. The supplier can connive with the storekeeper or the purchasing manager who will initiate purchase requisition under flimsy excuse. Once the supply is concluded, payment is effected and the palms of the collaborators have already been greased.

Quotation is processed. The purchasing manager can manipulate the quotations to favor his candidate (that is the favored supplier) because there is always room for "a thank you" under that operation or arrangement. Over-invoicing can be initiated at this point. Fraud at delivery point: The inspection unit and the storekeeper could connive with the supplier to do the following:

i) Short-supply
ii) Supply inferior goods

Payment of suppliers

The accounts department can manipulate the supplier's invoice for early payment before the due date. There will be a commission payable to the accounts staff for such service. Furthermore, under cash rationing, the accounts can pay their favored customer in defiance of laid down rules. The less favored supplier will be made to suffer late payment. Since management is aware of cash rationing, detection of such fraud is not very easy.

Using the same document to pay twice

Fraudulent payment is equally possible where the same document is used to pay twice. Another approach is to connive with the supplier by asking the supplier to submit another invoice, a second invoice, with spurious reasons given, for the same goods earlier paid for. The earlier payment might be debited into stores account while the subsequent invoice can be expended.

Using the same document for cash and credit sales

Some local suppliers have no separate document for cash and credit sales. Under that circumstance, the purchaser might advise against the use of stamp. Upon the retirement of the cash advance taken to buy the goods, the same invoice can be drawn out later for payment. Cash purchase is equally prone to abuse. The production of receipt from third party/supplier is not a conclusive evidence of the amount paid for stated goods purchased. In most cases the vendor often asks from the purchaser how much to state on the receipt. The balance between the actual cost of the goods purchased and the overstated difference is the fraud against the purchasing company.

Pilferage of the purchased stock from the store

This can take various forms. One way of doing this in a service workshop, for instance, is to requisition for spare-parts required for the job in excess of the real need. The excess, though charged to the job, will be withdrawn and sold. More especially, in the workshop, already completed and closed job card number can be used to requisition for spare-parts. Furthermore, requisitioned parts may never be used on the job; instead, the allegedly damaged part may be repaired and used. In an electronic workshop, for instance, damaged parts removed from the job might be returned to the store to cover for excess requisition or false requisition earlier made. This accounts mostly for the accumulation of damaged stock in the store.

Management can approve the sale of damaged items at give-away prices, but the storekeeper can release good stock to the buyer in exchange for gratification. This is always at a huge cost to the organization. This is very common in the case of expensive and difficult to source parts or items. It happens also where a company being aware of the scarcity of some products or items and due to increasing need for such items, buys more stock for the store.

Uncommon ways auditors can uncover procurement fraud

There is fraud at nearly every stage of the procurement process. The uncommon ways by which auditors can uncover some of the frauds include the following:

i) Ask for schedules of suppliers and hand-pick (randomly) some of these suppliers and visit them. Pose as a prospective buyer for a company and try to strike a deal or bargain. Then proceed to have informal discussions with the suppliers as to the honesty of their business transactions. You may discover by how many internal storekeepers and purchasing managers fleece their organization.
ii) Visit another and pose as a vendor of certain items or parts from a company. This method is used to discover those who are not true suppliers of such items or parts but who are fronted by the stores people and the purchasing manager to fleece the company. Here, if the alleged supplier you have visited is not truly in that business, you will know easily.
iii) Propose a deal with some accounts staff.
iv) Visit some suppliers of latest supplies to verify the price.
v) Deliberately delay the payment of some of some supplies under the pretext of an investigation going on. Ask the accounts department to refer such a supplier to you for discussion.
vi) Be friendly with some security officers who may reveal some malpractices.
vii) As an auditor, recommend an unscheduled transfer of staff from one duty to another or from one location to another.

All these issues have great implications for governance as a whole, whether in the private or public sector and both.

Fraud sheltering

Another angle to explore executive behavioral accountability problem is fraud sheltering. This is a behavioral dysfunction underscored by the covering up of frauds or commercial crimes by executives, who should ordinarily be protecting their organization from harm. It occurs in several ways that may include the following:

a) When executives pretend that they do not know that the organization is losing money and assets through carefully planned and concealed leakages which feather the nests of their own paddies and allies in the organization.
b) When an executive's mentees, relations, friends or "boys", working with or having anything to do with the organization, clearly fleeces the organization of money and assets but are protected by their high-up mentors to the detriment of the organization. Some of these mentors or executives may share in the booty or may have actually been the very sponsors of the fraud but shelter those who are used to execute it.
c) When an executive abets or deliberately facilitates the perpetration of frauds and does everything to cover it from prying or curious eyes.

Fraud sheltering may be a consequence of deficient psychological stabilizing factors in a person. It is thus, a direct offshoot of diminished conscience and this makes it a deadly practice, since those with diminished conscience can perpetrate any commercial crime and proceed to cause morbid harm to perceived threats on their way to sheltering their crimes. This is probably why Ojo (1995) maintains that "since the sheltering of fraud further breeds more frauds or encourages more people to indulge in fraudulent acts, sheltering could in fact be viewed as even a worse corporate crime than the direct act of fraud". So, all boils down to the moral character at the top which sets the behavioral tone of what happens in other layers of the organization.

Faithfulness to core organizational values

Accountability is an all-pervading and permeating issue in corporate governance. It summarizes the need for faithfulness to the core values of the organization including accountability of the self, financial/managerial accountability and accountability to wider stakeholders. Our treatment of behavioral accountability summarizes what is referred to here as accountability of the self; financial/managerial accountability is subsumed under accountability of the organization but much more in this regard, is faithfulness to other non-financial core organizational values which define the pillars of organizational consistency, longevity, sanity and proper functioning. The third, not the least, is accountability to wider stakeholders which includes faithfulness to societal level ethics as well as the shouldering of corporate social responsibility. Corporate directors and managers have a duty to remain faithful to organizational core values and central purposes, defined in the "memorandum" and "Articles of Association" of the company.

The governance importance of faithfulness to core organizational values is mentioned by Heinz Weihrich in his work titled "How to Achieve Excellence by Managing the Culture in your company" which summarizes the fact that faithfulness to core values that include internal organizational processes results in corporate excellence. To excel is to be "superior to others and to be outstandingly good or proficient". Therefore, excellence means being imbued with great value; being very good in a high degree and surpassing others in some good quality. "Applied to corporate objectives" therefore, excellence can be achieved in various forms that include profit, customer satisfaction, cost efficiency, staff welfare, product quality, organizational stability, organizational respect, integrity and faithfulness to so many other core specific and broad organizational values. Amplifying the fact that accountability of the organization goes beyond sound internal financial controls, to include faithfulness to shared core values, Peters and Waterman (1982) found that "Companies whose articulated goals were only financial, did not do nearly as well financially as those that had broader sets of values, to which they are faithful and which are shared by all employees as the dominating business idea". They thus noted that, the dominance and coherence of core values (that is corporate culture) proved to be an essential quality of excellent companies". In many organizations, the basis for stability and success embodied in corporate values has been destroyed by the unfaithfulness of management staff and board members to these values. This is exacerbated by their inconsistency and selfishness, in the application and observance of these values. This selfishness resulted in a lot of unwholesome practices and insider dealings in a preponderance of Nigerian banks, most of which have failed, liquidated or are presently managed by the Central Bank of Nigeria appointed intervention Management team. Insider dealings were exacerbated in these banks with a consequence that, boardroom squabbles that led to physical fights got elevated in some of them. A comprehensive listing of the content of corporate values, to which directors and managers must be faithful, is not possible in this work. But suffice it to discuss at least two of such value areas.

Integrity of the organization

It is said that when salt has lost its savor, it cannot again be salted by anything. Integrity is the salt of the organization which summarizes into its self worth. Integrity is a core corporate value and a critically perishable one for that matter, simply because its diminished nature can negatively affect the quality of the organization's image and worth and vice versa. Directors and management, as custodians of this value, should thus be accountable for whatever quality of integrity the organization becomes associated with. Vogle (2002) captures the need for integrity in organizational behavior by pointing out the growing and persistent decay in American business, that led to "the U.S business scandals". Vogle notes that "the challenge of CEOs is to get their sights on the inevitably long road to rebuild confidence in the honesty of their stewardship". Integrity got shunted aside by a booming stock market, mounting pressure for short term profit improvements and the lure for quick multimillion dollar personal gains.

Integrity of an organization is the entireness or wholeness of that organization; it is the unimpaired state of the organization, its uprightness, honesty and purity. It is the garb of honesty and incorruptibility that underscore the entirety of corporate vision and activities with which an organization is identified. The board of directors is the ultimate organ by which modern organizations are directed and controlled. Therefore, the integrity of the board of directors defines, to a large extent, the integrity by which the organization is associated with. It is the board of directors whose duty it is, to curtail the excesses of the management team to give the organization the ultimate image of integrity, outsiders and wider stakeholders may identify it with. Consequently, the image an organization is associated with is the image which the board of directors has earned for that organization. This is buttressed by what happened at Cadbury Nigeria Plc in 2008. When the management misbehaved by overstating the accounts of the company, it was the board of directors through the then Chairman of the board that blew the whistle. This was an act of courage that was aimed at preserving the hard earned integrity of the company over decades of its existence. Integrity is a scarce resource and a compass that should guide organizations in choosing whoever they want to appoint into the board as a non executive director, officer director, managers and employees.

The human resource system

An organization's human resource system is another critical core value to which directors and managers must remain obedient and faithful. The effectiveness and the undisturbed quality of the human resource system, lend great value to the success of an organization because the human resource system is the engine room and soul of every organization. Directors approve policy along key human resource values and systems which management should respect, observe and deliver. These policies reinforce the human resource culture of the organization. Policies may cover such issues as recruitment, selection, compensation, maintenance, promotion, discipline, separation and so on. There is need to preserve these value areas in the human resource function because any attempt to manipulate them to suit personal or group whims will flush down to the whole organization with unpleasant consequences. So, being obedient to core human resource values within the organization is both a major test and an important beacon of accountability for corporate directors because accountability also defines how consistent directors are in safeguarding such corporate resources. A practice where directors would want to bend HR rules in order to, for instance, hire their own person or manipulate well laid out processes or systems in order to promote their own candidate, may open up behavioral and performance gaps that may render all other subsystems within the system dysfunctional.

Consistency in the observance of laid down processes and systems within the organization, is part of a disciplined culture with which directors and managers must identify. Directors are thus accountable for the quality of respect and discipline accorded core value areas in their organization. The foundation of core accountability values is laid, when directors maintain exemplary behavior in all issues that relate to major or minor policies, rules and regulations within the organization as well as standards, procedures and operating plans.

Conclusion

This work explores the concepts of behavioral governance and behavioral accountability both of which look at the quality of the behavior of organizational members, especially directors, as the foundation of sound corporate achievement. This author posits that the effectiveness of governance in general and corporate governance in particular, is dependent on the behavioral effectiveness of those who govern and manage. That governance fails is often because more effort is devoted at creating and sustaining structures and processes while almost no meaningful attention is given to genuine institutionalization of behavioral and ethical accountability, which are accomplished by the hands of genuine integrity. The quality of corporate performance is hinged on the quality of behavioral performance and accountability with which members of the organization are associated. But given that the elevation of human animality in our organizations has tended to diminish the value of organizations, directors should adopt the concept of behavioral governance and behavioral accountability, to raise the quality of behavior and accountability in our organizations, as the route to genuinely raising the quality of performance in their organization.

REFERENCES

Allfreeessays.com (2010). Accountability is Synonymous with Responsibility (Electronic version). Retrieved August 25, 2010 from http://www.allfreeessays.com/essays/ Accountability -Is-Synonymous-With-Responsibility/22155.html.

Consultants AW (1995). Purchasing and Stores Fraud. In R. Egwuonwu (ed.), Corporate Financial Risk Exposure Management. Ikeja, Lagos: Stride Associates Ltd, pp. 345-352.

Barata, B, Bennett R, Cain P, Routledge D (2001). From Accounting to Accountability: Managing Financial Records as a Strategic Resource Namibia: A Case Study (Electronic version), [infoDEV 257-980121]. Retrieved on August 25, 2010 from http://www.irmt.org/documents/research_reports/accounting_recs/IRMT_acc_rec_namibia.PDF.

Bello JA (1988). Organizational Behavior in Nigeria. In O. Iyanda and J.A Bello (ed.), Elements of Business in Nigeria Akoka, Yaba, Lagos. University of Lagos Press, pp. 237-239.

Harper Ed (2001). The Tone at the Top (Electronic version). Christian Science Sentinel., pp. 5-6.

Iwu-Egwuonwu R (2004). Institutional Governance: Behavioral and Ethical Issues. Ikeja, Nigeria, Stride Associates.

O'Donovan G (2003). Change Management – "A Board Culture of Corporate Governance" (Electronic version). A Mondaq Business Briefing. Retrieved August 25, 2010 from http://www.accessmylibrary.com/article-1G1-108655592/change-management-board-culture.html.

Ojo A (1995). Fraud Sheltering. In R. Egwuonwu (ed.), Corporate Financial Risk Exposure Management. Ikeja, Lagos: Stride Associates Ltd, pp. 358-371.

Omoregbe J (1993). Ethics: A Systematic and Historical Study. (3rd Edition), Maryland, Lagos: Joja Educational Research and Publishers Ltd., 20(8-9): 112-115, 249-260, 267-269.

Peters TJ, Waterman RH (1982). In Search of Excellence: Lessons from America's Best Run Companies; New York, Warner Books, 1-2: 8-9.

Rawls J (1972). A theory of Justice. Electronic version) Retrieved on September 12, 2009 from http://en.wikipedia.org/wiki/John_Rawls.

Rechtman JE (2002). When Good Boards go Bad: How can Well Meaning Boards get so Terribly Off-track? And How can You Lead Them Back in the Right Direction?" Board Member, II(9): 5.

Sheng A (2000). Transparency, Accountability and Standards in Global Markets". A paper presented at the OECD Second Asian Roundtable on Corporate Governance Luncheon Address (Electronic version). Retrieved on August 25, 2010 from http://www .oecd.org/dataoecd/6/30/1930855.pdf.

Singh N (2009). Thoughts on Types of Accountability (Electronic version). Retrieved on August 25, 2010 from http://accountabilityindia.blogspot.com/2009/11/ thoughts-on-types-of-accountability.html.

Snyder S (2008) What is Accounting? (Electronic version). Retrieved August 25, 2010 from http://office.microsoft.com/en-us/support/what-is-accountingHA010102445.aspx? Redir=0.

Stone B, Dwivedi OP, Jabbra JG (2010). Accountability is Synonymous with Responsibility (Electronic version). Retrieved August 25, 2010 from http://www.allfreeessays.com /essays/Accountability-Is-Synonymous-With Responsibility/22155 .html.

The Guardian (August 25, 2010). Good Corporate Governance as Change Agents for Banks (Electronic version). Retrieved on August 25, 2010 from www.guardiannewsngr .com/ index.php?option=com_content&view=article&id=21099:good-corporate-governance-as-change-agent-for-banks&catid=30:money watch&Itemid=p.593.

Vogle F (2002) The U.S Business Scandals: Perspectives on Ethics and Culture at Home and Abroad (Electronic version), Retrieved July 29, 2009 from www.ethicsworld.com, pp. 1-5(12): 16-17.

Watkins AL (2002). An Accountability View of Accounting (Electronic version). Retrieved August 25, 2010 from http://www.allbusiness.com/technology/computer-software-management/4065927-1.html.

Zhong Wu (2009). No Accounting in China's Accountability (Electronic version). Retrieved on August 25, 2010 from http://www.atimes.com/atimes/China/KD22Ad01 .html).

Yu F, Kennedy E, Teddlie C, Crain MA (2010). Comparison of Four Generic Types of Accountability Model (Electronic version) Retrieved on August 25, from http://www.learningpt.org/sipsig/Yu_Kennedy_Teddlie_Crain.pdf.

Doing business with China: Is China keeping its legal WTO obligations?

Isola Oluwabusuyi

4370 Peachtree Road N. E. Atlanta, Ga 30319, USA. E-mail: oluwabusuyi5@yahoo.com

Is China keeping its legal world trade organization (WTO) obligations? On December 11, 2001, China became the 143rd member of the WTO after 15 years of negotiations. The accession package approved in Qatar for the People's Republic of China includes commitments on transparency and predictability, tariffs, trading rights and distributions, service agreements, TRIPS, import licensing importation and investment approvals, technical barriers to trade, taxes and subsidies. On September 15, 2010, MarketWatch reported the filling of two new trade cases against China by the United States at the WTO. The two cases were related to China's legal WTO obligations under the 2001 agreement. While these two fillings were not the first since the agreement was signed in 2001, one would only hope they will be the last. This paper attempts to examine China's performance under the agreement since it was signed in 2001.

Key words: International trade, international business, global management, world trade organization.

INTRODUCTION

On Tuesday, September 19th, 2010 the Chinese Yuan strengthened to a new high of 6.7057 against the U.S. dollar as the People's Bank of China fixed the Yuan's daily mid-point rate at a new record high for an eighth straight trading day (rttnews.com, 2010).

The U.S. president Barack Obama had just criticized the Chinese government the day before claiming the Chinese leaders are not doing all they said they would do to strengthen the Yuan, thereby gaining unfair trade advantages.

The question here is; is China keeping its WTO obligations? This paper would examine China's obligetions under the 2001 WTO agreement. The paper would also examine the extent of China's compliance with the obligations. Attempts would also be made to understand the dichotomies if any between China's obligations and its fulfillment. The implications of the study's findings would be analyzed for countries doing business with China.

What are the obligations?

On December 11, 2001, China became the 143rd member of the WTO after 15 years of negotiations. The accession package approved in Qatar for the People's Republic of China includes the following commitments.

Tariffs

China committed to reducing most industrial tariffs from 1997 average of 25 to 8.9% by 2005. However, all the parties involved agreed that some tariffs would continue through 2010.

Service commitments

China agreed to eliminate market access restrictions to a broad range of service sectors, including banking, insurance, telecommunications, professional services, accounting, legal and management consultancy services.

Trading rights and distribution

China agreed to allow Chinese enterprises to have full trading rights within three years of accession to WTO, subject to certain minimum registered capital requirements. This is in contrast to the pre-accession condition in which China restricts the number of companies that can import and export products. China also had restrictions on products that could be imported or exported. China also agreed to grant product-distributing rights to foreign companies to distribute their own products in China within three years of accession to WTO. Foreign companies could not distribute their own products in China before 2001.

Trade-related intellectual property rights

China agreed to implement the TRIPS (Trade-related aspects of intellectual property rights) agreement in full from the date of accession. China was notorious for serious Intellectual property rights' infringement before the accession.

Taxes

China agreed to ensure that its laws, regulations and other measures relating to internal taxes and charges levied on imports comply with WTO rules and are applied in a nondiscriminatory manner.

Subsidies

China agreed to eliminate, upon accession, all subsidies on industrial goods that are prohibited under WTO rules, that is export and import substitution subsidies.

Did China fulfill her legal obligations?

The answer to this question seems to be an emphatic number. On September 15, 2010, MarketWatch reported the filing of two new trade cases against China by the U.S. at the WTO (marketwatch.com, Sept 2010). While the Chinese side has made several claims to the contrary, observers are of the opinion that China has failed woefully in meeting its WTO obligations. Overall most of the articles from the Chinese side seem to emphasize the establishment of new rules and regulations designed to satisfy the commitments made to the WTO. Outsiders on the other hand are saying that the various legislations are mere cover up for lack of willingness on China side to implement any of the rules promulgated by the country. By November 11th, 2010 China has participated in a total of 98 WTO cases either as complainant, respondent or third party. In 20 of those cases, China was the respondent. Although the number of cases in itself maybe a misleading factor in assessing China's compliance, the severity and the number of countries that participated in most of the complaints against China would serve as a better measure of China's performance under its WTO legal obligations.

A critical examination of trade statistics also seems to support the opposing view. A very good example is piracy statistics for the last few years. In 2009, Japan had a low piracy rate of 21%, about the same as the United States at 20%. On the other hand, China had a rate of 79% (Japan Today, September, 2010) According to US customs statistics, counterfeits seizure from China was worth $87.3 million in 2004 and $62.5 million in 2003. In 2002, 49% of all counterfeit goods seized came from China compared with 46% in 2001. The percentage for 2003 was 66. Despite all the promises made by China to stamp out piracy, the problem seems to be growing in leaps and bounds. The list of WTO consultations associated with these commitments as well as the current state of the commitments is discussed in the subsequent paragraphs.

Tariffs

On 30 March 2006, Canada, European Communities, and the United States requested consultations with China regarding China's imposition of measures that adversely affect exports of automobile parts from the European Communities, Canada, and the United States to China. The measures according to the United States penalized manufacturers for using imported auto parts in the manufacture of vehicles for sale in China by imposing tariffs on auto parts that are essentially equal to tariffs on complete vehicles. On 11th February, 2009 at the DSB meeting, China informed the DSB that it intends to implement DSB recommendations on the matter and that it requires a reasonable period to do so (DS342). China's average tariff rate currently stands at 9.8% (People's Daily, September 2010). This represents a substantial drop from the 15.3% that existed before it dropped to 12% on the first day of 2002. The rate saw a further drop to 11% in 2003, with some duties on information and technology imports canceled (Xinhua News Agency, 2003).

Service commitments

The Chinese government made amendments to its laws, regulations and other policies concerning service trade. 14 sets of laws were modified, 37 sets of administrative regulations were modified or formulated, and 1,000-plus pieces of departmental regulations were formulated, rectified or repealed according to Chinese sources. However, China used unreasonable capitalization and other requirements to restrict foreign access to the service sectors. The requirements stipulated by China exceeded international norms according to USTR. When US complained about the practice, China began to take steps to reduce capitalization requirements in the insurance sector. The most recent case filed by U.S. against China with the WTO involved credit cards services in China. The other product involved in the case was Steel.

On 15 September 2010, the United States requested consultations with China with respect to unfair treatment of foreign companies providing financial services in China. The United States claimed that certain restrictions and requirements maintained by China pertaining to electronic payment services for payment card transactions involving Chinese renminbi restricted the ability of foreign financial service providers to participate in the system and that this is inconsistent with Articles XVI and XVII of the GATS (DS413). This dispute is still in the process of being resolved.

Trading rights and distribution

The United States Trade Representative (USTR) accused China of having fallen behind in its implementation of its commitment to ensure the unrestricted rights of Chinese and foreign businesses to engage in importing and exporting by 11th December, 2004. On 3rd March, 2008, the United States requested consultations with China concerning measures relating to restraints of trade in financial services of foreign companies in China (DS373). European communities requested to join the consultation on 14th March, 2008 and the request was subsequently accepted by China. China later signed a memorandum of understanding with the United States on this issue and informed WTO of the same on 4th December, 2008.

Trade-related intellectual property rights

China made important adjustments to its major intellectual property right laws, including laws concerning patents, trademarks and copyright, the report says. Relevant provisions have met the demand from Trade-Related Intellectual Property Rights agreement, it says. On one hand, China has enacted much legislation to improve Intellectual property rights situation but on the other hand, China has done almost nothing to enforce the legislations.

Sources from inside China claimed that the Chinese government did little to control the copyright violation situation. According to annual statistics of Chinese State Administration of Industry and Commerce, of the 22,001 cases registered in 2000, there were 45 criminal prosecutions and the average fine was $794. The situation has not improved much since then.

On 10th April, 2007, the United States requested consultation with China concerning measures relating to the protection and enforcement of intellectual property rights in China. The complaints covered China's lack criminal procedures and penalties for commercial scale trademark counterfeiting and copyright piracy as well the subsequent release of infringing goods to commerce channels in China. Canada, Japan, European Communities, and Mexico later requested to join the consultation. China and the United States notified the DSB of agreed procedures under Articles 21 and 22 of DSU on 8th April, 2010 (DS362)

Taxes

China continued to use value-added tax (VAT) policies to encourage domestic production in a number of industrial and agricultural sectors. VAT rebates were provided to domestic semiconductor producers to create disadvantages for United States exports of semiconductors to China. On 18th March, 2004, the United States requested consultations with China concerning China's preferential value-added tax ("VAT") for domestically produced or designed integrated circuits ("IC"). Both parties later agreed to resolve the issue privately.

On 2 February 2007, the United States requested consultations with China concerning measures aimed at rewarding enterprises in China for buying domestic rather than imported goods thereby placing imported goods at disadvantage to domestic products. The measure gave b refunds and exemptions from taxes to enterprises in China for buying domestic rather than imported products. Australia, Canada, Chile, European Communities, Turkey and Chinese Taipei joined the consultation and on 19th December, 2007, China and the United States informed the DSB that they had reached agreement in relation to the dispute (DS358).

Subsidies

The USTR also claimed that China continued to use subsidies to promote some agricultural exports. On 19 January 2009, Guatemala requested consultations with China about certain measures considered to have the effect of granting subsidies for agricultural products. These measures include offering grants, loans and other incentives rooted in export performance to enterprises in China. Guatemala contends that these measures are inconsistent with Articles 3, 8, 9 and 10, of the Agreement on Agriculture in that the measures benefits products of Chinese origin and not imported products. DS390 is still in process.

Why did China fail to meet the obligations?

The dichotomy between China's obligations and its performance of those obligations cannot be easily ignored. In 2008, US exports to China was $69 billion while Import from China was $337 billion thereby creating a trade deficit of $268 billion. In 2009, the situation was not much better as indicated in the Table 1 (Table 1 data is also illustrated graphically in Figures 1 and 2. Trade deficit also stood at $226 billion according to the US Census Bureau. The first step in solving this hydra

Table 1. US China Trade data for 2006 to 2010.

Year	Export	Import	Balance
2010	48,551.1	193,918.2	-145,367.1
2009	69,496.7	296,373.9	-226,877.2
2008	69,732.8	337,772.6	-268,039.8
2007	62,936.9	321,442.9	-258,506.0
2006	53,673.0	287,774.4	-234,101.3
Total	304,390.50	1,437,282.00	-1,132,891.40

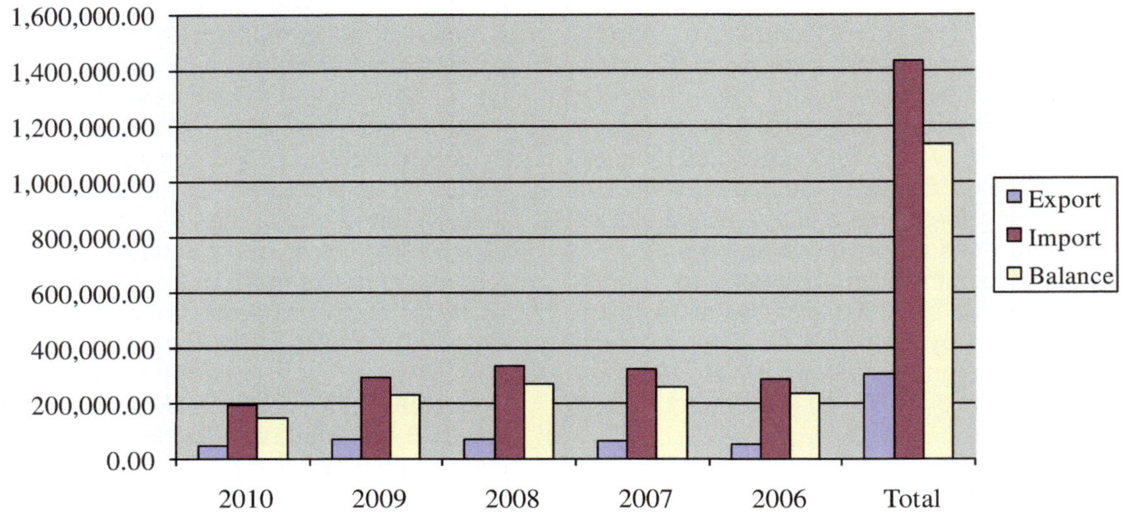

Figure 1. US Export and Import to China from 2006 to 2010.

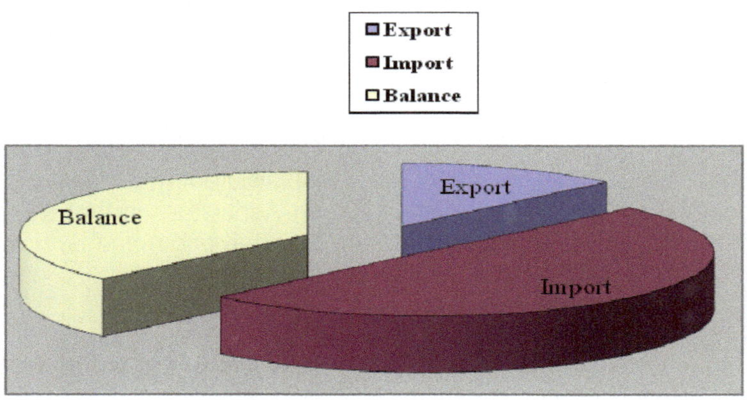

Figure 2. US Balance of Trade with China from 2001 to 2005

headed threat is to diagnose the problem. Scholars should ask such questions as why these people are behaving this way. It is only when the reasons behind China's double standards is fully understood that there can be any serious attempt at arriving at solutions. One of the methods used in the past to try to understand groups of people is culture study.

Did China underperform because of culture?

Culture can be defined as the way of life of a group of

people. Damen (1987) also defined culture as learned and shared human patterns or models for living. These patterns and models pervade all aspects of human social interaction. Why would China commit to certain obligations and not fulfill them, two, three, even four years after making those commitments? Is it something in their culture or outside the culture? This paper would examine the Chinese culture to see if explanations for the dichotomy could be found in the ways of life of the Chinese people. In studying the Chinese culture, Chinese proverbs would be used as a window into the mind of the Chinese culture. The book of Analects is one of the most revered sources of information on Chinese culture. The book contains most of the sayings of Confucius and other highly respected Chinese teachers. Using proverbs or sayings to understand the cultures of a people is a well-known method in Anthropology and that technique would be employed in this paper. The emphasis would be on the value placed on forthrightness in the Chinese culture. Is the Chinese culture favorable to saying one thing and doing something else? This is the question; the proposed study of the book of Analects would try to answer.

A careful look at the book of Analects revealed two sides of the coin. On one hand are tons of sayings that exhort forthrightness and on the other hand are a few sayings that qualified forthrightness. A few of these sayings are enumerated in the following paragraphs. In Chapter 7 verse 24 of the book, the master taught trust. This seems to be contrary to the news coming out of China. How can we trust China, if the engineering department of one of Chinese major Universities is actually in charge of a serial cracking website? However, in verse 18 of the same chapter (7) the master seems to be discouraging people from exposing the evil deeds of their relatives. The sayings in the following paragraphs are different versions of the two sides of the coin.

[1:4] Tseng Tzu said: "Each day I examine myself in three ways: in doing things for others, have I been disloyal? In my interactions with friends, have I been untrustworthy? Have not practiced what I have preached?" This particular saying seems to be teaching loyalty and justice.

[1:5] Confucius said: "If you would govern a state of a thousand chariots (a small-to-middle-size state), you must pay strict attention to business, be true to your word, be economical in expenditure and love the people. You should use them according to the seasons." This saying also emphasizes trustworthiness. [1:13]Yu Tzu said: "When your own trustworthiness is close to rightness, your words can be followed. When your show of respect is according to propriety, you will be far from shame and disgrace. If you have genuine affection within your family, you can become an ancestor." This saying seems to encourage Chinese to keep their words.[2:22] Confucius said: "If a person lacks trustworthiness, I do not know what she or he can be good for. When a pin is missing from the yoke-bar of a large wagon, or from the collar-bar of a small wagon, how can it go?" This saying is an outright condemnation of the use of double standards.

[7:24] The Master taught four things: Culture, correct action, loyalty and trust. This is also an emphasis on trustworthiness.

[13:4] Fan Chih wanted to ask about agriculture. Confucius said, "Why don't you ask an old farmer?" Fan Chih then said that he would like to learn about gardening. Confucius said, "Why don't you ask an old gardener?" Fan Chih left. Confucius said, "Fan is really simple, isn't he? If the men in charge love propriety, the people cannot stand to be disrespectful. If the men in charge love Rightness, then the people cannot stand not to follow them. If the men in charge love trust, then the people cannot stand not to respond with their emotions. If you were to govern in this way, the people would come flocking to your kingdom, carrying their babies on their backs. Why do you have to worry about agriculture?" This was a direct message to leaders to cherish trustworthiness.

[4:16]Confucius said: "The Superior Man is aware of Rightness, the inferior man is aware of advantage." This saying is one of the few that seems to say that the end does not justify the means.

[7:18]The Duke of Sheh told Confucius: "In my land, there are Just men. If a father steals a sheep, the son will testify against him." Confucius said, "The Just men in my land are different from this. The father conceals the wrongs of his son, and the son conceals the wrongs of his father. This is Rightness!" This is one of the few sayings that seem to qualify trustworthiness. If there is anything in Chinese culture that can explain the current attitude of Chinese leadership towards its WTO obligetions, it is this saying. The saying actually encourages people to hide the wrongs of their relatives.

[17:24]Tzu Kung asked, "Does the superior Man also have things that he hates?" Confucius said, "He does. He hates those who advertise the faults of others. He hates those who abide in lowliness and slander the great. He hates those who are bold without propriety. He hates those who are convinced of their own perfection, and closed off to anything else. How about you, what do you hate?" This is another saying that seems to encourage wrongdoing.

[2:10] Confucius said: "See a person's means (of getting things). Observe his motives. Examine that in which he rests. How can a person conceal his character? How can a person conceal his character?" [Comment] People think that they are successfully hiding the devious plots that are going on in their minds. But as the Doctrine of the Mean teaches, "The sincerity on the inside shows on the outside." When someone is deceitful, everyone knows it. When someone is good and honest, everyone knows it. This is also in favor of loyalty and trustworthiness. [4:5 Confucius] said, "Riches and honors are what all men desire. But if they cannot be attained in accordance with the Tao they should not be kept. Poverty and low status are what all men hate. But if they cannot be avoided while staying in accordance with the Tao, you should not avoid them. If a Superior Man departs from humaneness, how can he be worthy of that name? A Superior Man never leaves humaneness for even the time of a single meal. In moments of haste he acts according to it. In times of difficulty or confusion he acts according to it." This is another saying in favor of trustworthiness.

[4:10] Confucius said: "When the Superior Man deals with the world he is not prejudiced for or against anything. He does what is Right." This is also another saying in favor of justice.

[4:14] Confucius said: "I don't worry abut not having a good position; I worry about the means I use to gain position. I don't worry about being unknown; I seek to be known in the right way." This saying, also emphasize the fact that the end does not justify the means.

Trustworthiness is encouraged by ten out of the thirteen sayings quoted in this paper. Only three of the sayings seem to be saying the contrary. With this kind of picture, one wonders why the leadership of such a nation would choose to pitch their tent with the minority rather than the majority. Why would the Chinese leadership ignore all the good admonitions of great leaders like Confucius and focus on some minor exhortations in the book of analects? Many have tried to give different explanations for the disturbing condition. This paper would now focus on one of the theories that seem to be the most sensible of them all. The morality abandonment theory proposed by many Chinese insiders claimed that the Chinese Communist party abandoned the golden elements of the Chinese culture long time ago. The proponents of this theory claims that the current leadership of the party is now working with a different principle. The new principle is “the end justifies the means”. If the assertions of this group of people are true, we are all in big trouble.

End justifies the means

Morality: The problem is that so many Chinese now have become victims of this principle, “The ends justify the means” (Man-Yan Ng, 2005) As far as Mr. Ng is concerned; the problem is not with the religion or faith. He further reiterates that all the faiths (Confucianism or Buddhism or Taoism) can be considered to have relatively high moral and ethics. He claimed that it was the Chinese Communist Party, who systematically destroyed all religions and faith-groups since they took power in 1949. As far as he is concerned, the current behavior of the Chinese leadership is a reflection of this new state of mind. They have destroyed all religions and faith groups along with the morality they represent. “A few years ago some Hong Kong Chinese tried to transport about 30 000 bibles of the original version into China. They were sentenced and jailed” (Ng, 2005) Mr. Ng and the group he represent have made many other assertions that nations doing business with China need to consider carefully. Some of the assertions are presented in the following paragraphs.

Legal system: Mr. Chow and his other Chinese colleagues claim, “The Chinese legal system is a joke”. When a Chinese official shows you the legal system, he will show you that they have local courts, provincial high court, Supreme Court; they have the law and so on. However, they will not show you the last step, the last thing: on top of this system- the Chinese Communist Party. One single telephone call from a party boss can decide on the contents of a sentence in a court” How can you do business and feel safe in a country that does not have a functioning legal system? (Ng, 2005) This seems to be in agreement with most of the stories coming out of China about legal nightmares. In the highly publicized Beijing McDonald's case, the Chinese government took back from Mc Donald a piece of property they had actually purchased and developed.

Thick and thin rule of law

The rule of law can be understood as a legal-political regime under which the law restrains the government by promoting certain liberties and creating order and predictability regarding how a country functions. In the most basic sense, the rule of law is a system that attempts to protect the rights of citizens from arbitrary and abusive use of government power (Yu and Guernsey, 2008). Some scholars have tried to approach the China legal issue from a language perspective. They opined that nations sometimes work with different definitions of the rule of law. Scholars in this group are of the opinion that China might be working with a definition of rule of law that is different from the one we work with in the West. These legal theorists have proposed multiple definitions for the rule of law, which can be categorized into two general types: "thick" and "thin". The "thin" version of the rule of law is "a vision of judging that celebrates the systemic virtues of regularity, predictability and certainty over the concern with substantive justice in particular instances: formal rules are the most efficacious and legitimate way to protect substantive values."(Wang, 2004) Arguably, the implication is that "it is possible for a legal system to comply with the rule of law and still be undemocratic and/or unjust in general... and in particular instances." A "thick" version, on the contrary, holds that "the existence of pre-announced, objectively-knowable and impartially applied rules must be supplemented by tying such formal virtues to a substantive account of democratic justice." Law as such becomes inseparable from values and politics (Wang, 2004).

The inconsistencies found in the administration of law in China are being explained by these legal theorists as manifestations of the thick rule of law, which is flexible. The problem with this approach however, lies in the fact that the Chinese legal environment does not seem to fit into this classification. Some of the other facts coming out of China seem to be too out of the norm to be easily explained by this dichotomy. One of the assertions of Mr. Ng and his colleagues is that the Chinese government could enforce laws that they actually want to enforce. The Tiananmen crackdown and the Fa Lung Goon movement crackdown are examples of the might of the Chinese government and their ability to enforce whatever they want to enforce. What seems to be lacking is the political will to enforce rather than the ability to enforce the legislations. Maybe it is because enforcement would hurt local economy.

Implications for trade partners

Piracy will grow

The bad news is that the amount of seizures of pirated products is increasing," said Jon W. Dudas, under secretary of Commerce for Intellectual Property. "The percentage is growing. In addition, the dollar figure is rising,"77% of the aggregate value of goods seized in the United States between 2004 and 2009 came from China (Dobson, 2010). Shipments from China accounted for 66% in 2003, or $62.5 million, 49% in 2002 and 46% in 2001.

A recent study by the Business Software Alliance found that 79 percent of all software used in China was pirated. Altogether, software vendors claim that they suffered $3.5 billion in losses last year due to Chinese piracy. It is even alleged that the Chinese government strongly supports piracy (Ng, 2005). In a surprise move by the Chinese Academy of Engineering Physics they are now hosting one of the largest crack sites in the world - 0daycn.net.

The web site is quoted as boasting of creating cracks within 1 day of a software title being released. They achieve this by monitoring download websites, publisher's exes and pad files. The Chinese Academy of Engineering Physics, also known as the Southwest Institute, is the primary design laboratory for Chinese nuclear weapons, located in Mianyang (Sichuan). Mian Yang city lies on the northern tip of the Chengdu Plain.

Trade deficit will continue to grow

U.S.-based Wal-Mart was responsible for 11% of the growth of the total U.S. trade deficit with China between 2001 and 2006 (Scott, 2007) If Wal-Mart continues to expand the way it is right now and if the Yuan continues to exchange at a fictitious rate, US trade deficit with China would continue to grow. Innovation, which is the strength of the American economy, would not be able to bail the country out of her predicament. The likes of Mr. Ng and Mr. Chow keep claiming that the Chinese government is behind piracy in China. The trade of a nation is defined by what he is able to offer in return for what he takes from the International market. America is currently in a bad situation with respect to its trade with China. On one hand, the country is encouraged to keep taking from China because of the artificially cheap Yuan and on the other hand, the country cannot pay for what it is taking from China with innovation because of piracy. It is a perfect recipe for trade imbalance. If the claim that a Chinese University Engineering department is involved with illegal software piracy is true, the future of US trade is in big trouble.

China will continue to manipulate the Yuan

On Monday September 20th, 2010, the US President complained about the Chinese leader's refusal to do what they promised concerning the value of the Yuan. On December 12th, 2005, bloomberg.com reported on China's Premier's response to the criticism that the Yuan did not adjust properly in value since. Finance ministers and central bankers from the Group of Seven industrial nations had complained that the Yuan's appreciation against the dollar since its revaluation in July 21st, 2005 is not acceptable. In responding to that complaint made on December 3rd, 2005 Premier Wen Jiabao said the rate was adjusted to a reasonable level. US lawmakers have threatened trade sanctions against China, if the country does not make amends. This cat and mouse game would continue for as long as China can afford to keep it going. What the Premier was saying, was we would continue to keep the Yuan at a rate that would allow us to get all the trade surplus we can get. The implication of this type of attitude is scary. It can only mean one thing; China would continue to bleed America until there is no blood left. The only reason people are buying products from China is because they are cheaper and one of the reasons they are cheaper is because of the exchange rate. Since China has refused to play by the rules thus far, it can be safely inferred that the country would continue to manipulate the Yuan to keep Chinese imports cheap. Until the world can find a way to make the Chinese government allow the Yuan to yield to the natural forces of demand and supply, we would continue to be at a disadvantage. Japan used similar strategy in the past.

Some of us would have to go and work in China

Unemployment rate in the US now stands at 9.8% for adult men according to the Bureau of labor statistics report released on August 2010. On November 21st, 2005, General Motors announced its new plan to cut 30,000 jobs by 2008 to the associated press. The news published by news.yahoo.com was later followed on December 7th, 2005 by Ford Motor Company's announcement to cut another 30,000 jobs in North

America within the next five years. Announcing the loss of 60,000 jobs in less than two months within the same geographic zone is not a good sign. Why did those companies and several others reduce their work force? One of the obvious reasons is that they are not competing well. In 2005, General Motors came 3rd on the list of the best 500 companies in the world. Ford placed 4th on the same list. In 2010, the picture was even more dismal General Motors came in 15th and Ford Motors was 8th on the list. Going by those figures alone would be misleading, the fact of the case is that it is costing those companies far much more to produce in North America, than it is costing them to manufacture elsewhere. In 2004, every GM car sold had additional $1400 health care cost tagged to the price. Global competitors could no longer afford these costs. Japanese car manufacturers are not burdened with such costs, neither are Chinese car manufacturers. On the same fortune 500 list, Wal-Mart came first. On November 29, 2004, China Daily news reported that Wal-Mart is the eighth largest importer from China after U.S., Russia and others.

The newspaper claimed that 70% of what is sold in Wal-Mart is made in China. The paper also claimed that Wal-Mart alone is responsible for a lion share of the trade deficit between US and China. In 2003, Wal-Mart imported over $15billion dollars worth of goods from China. The implication of all these is that the work of the future would be in China, except things change drasticcally. Once all the companies close down in America, we would all have to go to China to go and find job. $15 billon worth of investment in a single economy would sure create many jobs in that country.

One of the major problems facing General Motors is counterfeiting of one of the companies products in China. On September 6, 2004, alwayson-network.com reported that Deputy Commerce Minister Zhang Zhigang claimed that General Motor has not provided enough evidence to prove that Chery Automobile Corp. copied one of its car models. The main point of the whole argument was that General Motors did not register that particular model in China. The smart Chery Automobile Corp. has successfully added more to American job problems by stealing that car model from General Motors.

CONCLUSION

The consensus seems to be that China has not fulfilled its obligations under the WTO agreement that it signed in 2001. Out of ten major categories listed in the agreement, reports from the Chinese side emphasized performance on only three. The excuse so far is that China has put in place many laws, but as far as enforcement is concerned, all we can see is lip service. In the report published by Xinhua News Agency, TRIPS, service sector access and Tariffs were the three major areas emphasized. The Chinese side did not say much about Import licensing, tax and subsidy protection, use of technical specifications, full trading rights and the like in their progress report. Moreover, even in the areas emphasized, we all know that performance is not up to par. With 77% of the aggregate value of goods seized in the United States between 2004 and 2009 coming from China, one can hardly say that China has lived up to its commitment to TRIPS. The whole scenario is fast becoming pathetic and the only hope is that someone would soon figure out what should be done to arrest the situation. The pattern that seems to be emerging is that the Chinese leadership waits for others to complain about what they are supposed to do and then try to do a little bit of it after serious complaints. In the case of using VAT to subsidize national companies, US had to report China to WTO before they finally did something about it. This was an obligation that they agreed to when they joined the WTO.

The reasons for lack luster performance could be found in many things. There seems to be a tiny part of the Chinese culture that condones disloyalty but the general tendency found in Chinese culture studies is the promotion of trustworthiness. Other attempts to explain the behavior also include the "end justifies the means" theory proposed by some insiders that feel that the Chinese communist party is no longer committed to morality. This group of people believes that the Chinese communist party has destroyed the conscience of China. They believe that it is the only possible explanation for how China is treating the rest of the world. The final theory is that of thick and thin definition of the rule of law. This theory proposes that China is only trying to practice the thick rule of law, which is flexible in nature. However, the facts coming out of China could not support this last theory.

The implications of this state of affairs to countries doing business with China are enormous. If all the findings of this study are true, it only implies that many of us would have to go and work in China one day. With 9.8% unemployment rate for adult men according to the Bureau of labor statistics report released on August, 2010, the future of employment around here does not seem to be rosy. Trade imbalance between US and China would also continue to worsen as the Chinese leadership continues to manipulate the Yuan. Piracy, according to many is the mainstay of many local economies in China. Some people claim that stopping piracy would actually make many local economies collapse in China. As more well established institutions in China get behind piracy, the situation would only worsen. If there were, any lesson to be learnt from all these, it would be the fact that the rest of the world is not interested in playing the game according to our rules. If we are going to successfully compete against these people, we might have to learn a lot more about them.

RECOMMENDATIONS

The following recommendations are aimed at eroding the

unfair advantage that China has successfully created for itself by consistently violating the conditions of its accession to WTO.

Yuan manipulation

The use of International Institutions and the US congress to put pressure on China has been advocated by many although critics has argued that the US trade deficit problem is too deep to be solved by these measures. The goal of these measures is to get the Yuan to appreciate to such a level that Chinese products would no longer be as cheap as they currently are. The most recent release of $600billion to the US economy might be a stealth approach to solving the currency imbalance problem. IMF's global responsibilities include monitoring global exchange rate manipulation. Interest groups also hoped that a meeting of finance ministers of the Group of Seven (G7) most industrialized countries in London in late November 2005 would be used as a venue to deal with the Chinese currency issue on a global scale. Their hopes were not dashed during the meeting. It was in response to the issues raised during the meeting that China's Premier Wen Jiabao claimed that Yuan's appreciation of less than 0.37 percent since its revaluation in July is reasonable.

On the other side of the spectrum however, are the likes of Mr. Greenspan who said that a violent revaluation of the Yuan would create chaos in the global trade arena. In a letter to the US Senate in March 2005, Mr. Greenspan said that floatation of the Yuan, a move wanted by many in the US, could cause a heavy flow of capital out of China, which would in turn undermine Chinese banks and destabilize the world economy (Greenspan, 2004; China Daily, 2005). However, on September 25, 2010, Ben Bernanke (the new Fed chairperson) expressed a contrary opinion to that of his predecessor. Ben Bernanke said one solution to the current financial crisis in the United States is greater exchange rate flexibility. This essentially implies that certain developing countries, like China, should let their currencies appreciate (International Business Times, Sept. 2010) Others have said that such a move would not solve the trade balance problem, and that it would only make investments flow to other ASEAN countries.

Some have also suggested that the US Congress get tough on China. "Congress should take action immediately," said AFL-CIO Secretary-Treasurer Richard Trumka. "It's time they slapped back. There is a solution in Congress." Labor groups say that Congress should use the Hunter-Ryan bill, World Trade Organization compliance legislation that defines currency manipulation, declares it an illegal subsidy and empowers other agencies of government to act. The 1994 GATT Agreement on Subsidies and Countervailing Measures (SCM) also provide measures for addressing Subsidy related issues. U.S. Senator Charles E. Schumer, a leading critic of the Chinese currency policy and author of the China Free Trade Act, a bill that would impose 27.5% tariffs on Chinese imports, said that Beijing's "refusal to acknowledge reality and take the necessary corrective actions hurts every American"(IPS, 2005).

The problem with these measures however is that of effectiveness. A recent study by the Asian Development Bank showed that Chinese exports account for a relatively small share of U.S. imports (about 13.4 percent in 2004) while U.S. exports to China constitute an even smaller share of about 4.3 percent of total U.S. exports. This implies that even if the revaluation were to shrink imports from China by half and double U.S. exports to Beijing, it would cut the US trade deficit by only about 29 billion dollars, or 0.24% of GDP (China Daily, 2005).

In summary, uncontrolled Yuan appreciations would most likely harm, rather than help, the sustained development of the Chinese economy. Such a move would create very little benefit for Japan and US.

Piracy

In China, piracy is so entrenched that even the pirates complain about it.

According to an article by Anne Stevenson-Yang and Ken DeWoskin in the March issue of the "far eastern economic review", Chinese storekeepers who sell fake DVDs for 10 Yuan gripe about street vendors selling them for seven. Moreover, the street vendors complain about competitors offering two-for-one specials (Blodget, 2005). Piracy is a problem that would not go away soon however, some concerned citizens have tried to come up with a few solutions, some of which are discussed thus.

Redesign business processes to make it more difficult to steal stuff, and consider what you do lose as cost of doing business. Pay for your own enforcement raids. Do not do China joint ventures, which function as a siphon tube through which local entrepreneurs suck out ideas, technology, and products.

Design your products to have shorter life cycles, thus leaving pirates stuck with warehouses full of outdated stuff. Cut prices, making piracy less profitable. Give away technology in hopes of establishing a standard that you can control. Offer local pricing: Do not force people who make $1,000 a year to pay $250 for an office suite. Shift to a service/support model, and give your products away for free (Blodget, 2005).

REFERENCES

Blodget H (2005). How to Solve China's Piracy Problem: A dozen ideas. Maybe one will work. Retrieved from http://www.slate.com/id/2116629/

Damen L (1987). Culture Learning: The Fifth Dimension on the Language Classroom. Reading, MA: Addison-Wesley.

Dobson C (2010). China: World's 'Single Largest Source' of Counterfeit Goods Retrieved from http://www.theepochtimes.com/n2/content/view/35528/ Greenspan A (2004). RMB free floating could be risky. Retrieved Dec11, 2005

fromhttp://www.chinadaily.com.cn/english/doc/2004 03/04/content_311683.htm
Japan Today (2010) Cutting software piracy can create $142 bil in economic gains Retrieved September 25, 2010 from http://www.japantoday.com/category/technology/view/cutting-software-piracy-can-create-142-bil-in-economic-gains
RTT News (2010). Chinese Yuan Climbs To New High Against Dollar, Retrieved from http://www.rttnews.com/Content/CurrencyMarket.aspx?Id=1423919&SM=1
Scott RE (2007). The Wal-Mart effect: Its Chinese imports have displaced nearly 200,000 U.S. jobs Economic Policy Institute Retrieved November 24, 2010 from http://www.epi.org/publications/entry/ib235/
Wang J (2004). The Rule of Law in China: A realistic view of the Jurisprudence, the impact of the WTO, and the prospects for future development. Singapore Journal of Legal Studies. 347-390
Xinhua News Agency (2003). Report Summarizes China's Implementation of WTO. Retrieved Dec 11, 2005 from http://www.china.org.cn/english/MATERIAL/61603.htm
Yu H, Guernsey A (2008). The Rule of Law as a Goal of Development Policy Retrieved Nov 24, 2010 from http://www.uiowa.edu/ifdebook/faq/Rule_of_Law.shtml

Analysis of risk among agribusiness enterprises investment in Abia State, Nigeria

Nto P. O. O.*, Mbanasor J. A. and Nwaru J. C.

College of Agribusiness and Financial Management, Michael Okpara University of Agriculture, Umudike, Nigeria.

The study analysed risk among agribusiness enterprises investment in Abia State of Nigeria. Specifically, it examined types of risk and the degree of influence on the agribusiness enterprises. The study also examined common risk reducing strategies among the agribusiness enterprises in the area. Primary data collected from 40 formal agribusiness firms were used in the study. The data were analysed with w-statistics and validated with Pearson criterion (χ^2). The result indicated a w-statistics of 0.79. The result was verified by Pearson criterion and this gave χ^2 calculated value of 4.81 which is lower than table value of 11.07 at 5% significant level. The result revealed that risk sources affecting agribusiness investment were financial, marketing, currency and production in that order. The common risk reducing strategies were diversification, integration, forward contracting, and insurance, among others. Based on this, it was recommended that government should make policies that will encourage investors adopt the highlighted risk reducing strategies in risk management.

Key word: Analysis, agribusiness, investment, Abia State, Nigeria.

INTRODUCTION

Risk analysis among agribusiness investments has become increasingly popular in recent years. This is obvious considering that agribusiness investment depends on vagaries of the environment and nature. Hence, there has been scepticism about the realisation of Millennium Development Goals (MDGs) most especially, cutting of people living under food insecurity by half in 2015 (Moss et al., 2003; Drollete, 2009; NIPC, 2006; Chaddad et al., 2010; Kuyrah et al., 2006).

Nigeria being prone to a lot of environmental inconsistencies requires high degree of risk aversion strategy to break the circle of poverty which engulfed over 70% of its population and also to achieve increased food production to meet 3.18% population growth (NIPC, 2007; Ojo, 2003; FRN, 2009; Alimi and Ayanwale, 2005; FOS, 1996).

Risk which investment economists describe as the variation from expected outcomes due to imperfect knowledge of investor in decision making is inherent in every form of enterprise but is more intensive in input-output relation among agribusiness productions (Kuyrah et al., 2006; Odii, 1998). Alimi and Ayanwale (2005) opined that a situation of imperfect knowledge is more common in agribusiness enterprises. Hence, investors in agribusiness enterprises face the danger that what they expect ex-ante may not be realised ex-post (Ndugbu, 2003). For instance, each time an investor borrows money for investment in agribusiness enterprise, there is the possibility that return on investment is less than cost of borrowed fund. Also, in this era of global climate change, an investor cannot predict with certainty the degree of fluctuation in prices of input and output.

According to Njavro (2009), NIPC (2006), CN (2008), Dercon (2002) and Mikhaylova (2005), risk sources to agribusiness enterprises can be grouped into social, market, political, financial, production and foreign exchange risk. Social risk is suggestive that the risks or hazards have their origin from man. The risk could be due to fire outbreak, burglary or theft, kidnapping of investors/workers for ransom, embezzlement, strike, civil commotion and changes in social structure e.g. divorce and dissolution of partnership which can lead to unexpected decline in efficient operation of enterprise.

Market risk arises due to fluctuation in input and output prices. Political risk is due to changes in government machineries and policies. The use of debt in financing agribusiness investment exposes the firm to financial risk. Foreign exchange risk is borne out of the firm's dependence on foreign currency. Production risk occurs

*Corresponding author. E-mail: nto2015@yahoo.com.

because agribusiness enterprise is affected by many uncontrollable events that are often related to weather, drought, physical hazard to the factory site and technological failure of the firm. This risk affects the efficient conversion of input to output (Barry and Frazer, 1984; Bauer and Bushe, 2003; Aneke, 2007). Thus, empirical studies have produced varieties of sources of risk. According to Alimi and Ayanwale (2005), in a study conducted on risk in onion production in Kebbi State, Nigeria, reported that the most important sources of risk are technical-drought, market and financial. Mikhaylova (2005) noted that the most important risk sources among agribusiness marketing firms in Central and Eastern Europe are currency and del credere in that order.

The literature on risk cannot be complete without a brief discussion on the issues of risk measurement. According to Macaver and Ehimare (2010), risk measurement has been a challenging issue among sectors and industries. Risk being the probability of adverse outcomes associated with an action or decision according to Njavro (2009), Akinsuhre (2006), Chandra (2006), Macaver and Ehimare (2010) and Ndugbu (2003) is measurable in empirical and quantitative manner using three major statistical tools such as expected value, variance/standard deviation and coefficient of variation. Expected value (EV) is the sum of the probabilities that different outcomes will occur multiplied by resulting payoffs (Martin and Markus, 2000; Hardaker, 2000). For instance, if the possible outcomes of the investment decision are X_1, X_2...Xn and the corresponding probabilities of the investment decision are P_1, P_2...P_n then the expected value is stated as

$$EV = P_1 X_1 + P_2 X_2 + \dots + P_n X_n \quad \dots\dots\dots\dots\dots\dots\dots \quad (1)$$

Where; the sum of $P_s = 1$

Despite the simplicity in the use of expected value method in risk measurement, it collapses information about the likelihood of different outcomes into a single statistic. This is a very convenient way of economizing on the amount of information needed to make decision; therefore there is need for caution (Macaver and Ehimare, 2010). Also, the expected value only provides information about the average value of a random variable but does not indicate the degree of risk associated with the random variable, hence the need for standard deviation (Hardaker, 2000).

Standard deviation is a statistical measure of absolute dispersion from the mean value. It measures variability around an expected value (Akinsulire, 2006). Following Chaddad et al. (2010) and Macaver and Ehimare (2010) standard deviation is computed thus:

$$\delta = P_1 (X_1 - EV)^2 + P_2 (X_2 - EV)^2 + \dots + P_n (X_n - EV)^2 \quad \dots\dots(2)$$

where δ is the standard deviation.

Akinsulire (2006) held that the higher the standard deviation of a project, the riskier it is. The weakness of standard deviation as a measure of risk arises when choice has to be made between enterprises having the same standard deviation but different expected value .Hardaker (2000) added that neither variance nor standard deviation tells anything about the location of the distribution of outcomes on the x-axis. Pandey (2006), Chandra (2006), Alimi and Anyawale (2005) opined that coefficient of variation becomes a better tool for handling the issue of difference in size or scale among agribusiness enterprise. Coefficient of variation is defined as the standard deviation of the probability distribution divided by its expected value.

$$\text{Coefficient of variation (CV)} = \delta / EV \dots\dots\dots\dots \quad (3)$$

Hence it is a useful statistics for comparing the degree of variation from one set of outcome to another, even if the expected values are drastically different from each other. The decision rule is that, the lower the ratio of standard deviation and expected value, the better the risk-return trade off. The flaw with coefficient of variation is that it may give unreliable result when the expected value is negative or zero. For instance, an investment with a zero expected value will also have a zero standard deviation, implying non-risky investment. The ratio will make no sense hence limits the usefulness of coefficient of variation in risk measurement. Besides, it cannot be used to construct confidence intervals (Hardaker 2000 and Chaddad et al., 2010).

However, there is need for an econometric model which will take care of the limiting factors associated with the discussed models. This becomes necessary now that Abia State and Nigeria in general is brainstorming on the possibility of achieving economic growth and food security in line with vision 20, 2020 projects and MDGs blueprint. Though, similar studies may have been conducted in other areas, the findings of which may not be relevant for policy formulation in Abia State. Therefore, the need for the study with the following specific objectives: (1) Examine sources of risk and the degree of influence on agribusiness enterprise investment, and (2) Examine risk reducing strategies in the agribusiness investment.

RESEARCH METHODOLOGY

Study area

The study was conducted in Abia State of Nigeria. The state is approximately within Latitudes 4°, 41′ and 6°, 14′ North of the Equator and Longitudes 7°, 10′ and 8° East of the Greenwich median. It has seventeen local government areas that are divided along three agricultural zones namely Ohafia, Umuahia, and Aba (ABSEEDS, 2005; Balogun, 2008).

The state is selected for this study from many others because of numerous agribusiness enterprises, some of which have either formal or informal status. The formal agribusiness enterprises are predominantly found in the urban areas of the state (Marchet et al., 2001).

Sample selection and data collection

The following sampling technique was adopted in the selection of the agribusiness firms that were used for the study. The first stage was a fact finding visit to the Ministry of Commerce and Industry as well as Aba Chamber of Commerce, Industry, Mines and Agriculture from where a list of all the companies and factories (registered with the above agencies) in the State was obtained. The second stage involved a purposive sampling technique to select the agribusiness firms in the list and the population guided in knowing the number that was selected. The population of the agribusiness firms in the list was 300 which formed the sampling frame for the study.

The third stage was a preliminary visit to some of the agribusiness firms by the researcher and an enumerator appointed from the Ministry of Commerce and Industry. The reasons for the visit were to validate the list of agribusiness firms from the Ministry of Commerce and Industry and eliminate moribund enterprises. Another visit was conducted on three agribusiness firms purposively selected from each of the agricultural zones. The visit paved way for the pretesting of validity and reliability of the research instruments that were used so as to enhance successful data collection.

Data for this study were generated through cross sectional method using survey instruments administered on the management team of each of the agribusiness firms. The survey instruments were responded to by the investors or their representatives in the firms who are in positions to provide the necessary data. The services of enumerators were used to obtain the data. To ensure reliability of data, the enumerators were drawn from the members of staff of Abia State Ministry of Commerce and Industry. The Ministry was also chosen because of the existing statutory relationship (that is, as Supervisory Ministry) with the agribusiness firms. The enumerators were given little training to enable them carryout effective data collection through the use of the survey instrument. After which, random sampling technique was used to select forty viable agribusiness firms which were functional for a period not less than ten years . The distributions of the firms were as follows: Twenty firms were selected from Aba zone while fifteen were selected from Umuahia zone and five from Ohafia zone. The inequality in the sampling spread was due to clusters of most of the agribusiness firms in Aba and Umuahia zones (Marchet et al., 2001).

Objective (1) was realized through simple descriptive statistics while objective (2) was analyzed through ranking risk factors by experts (staff that are well informed on risk management) as well as verification of concordance and probability of judgments with econometric model namely W- statistics and Pearson criterion. This involved ranking the degree of risk by the way of "experts' judgment". The following procedures were taken. In the first place, expert judgment method means to collect as many as possible experts evaluations of each risk factor influence upon the production economic indicator (which are the firms selected). Each risk factor would be put in order of descending influence. As a rule, the most important risk factor is given the rank one, the rest are given ranks two, three, four etc., in order of descending influence. Expert appraisal from each of the 40 agribusiness firms was carried out following Mikhaylova (2005).

1. Selection of experts among 40 firms who are competent to know issues regarding the various risk factors
2. Ranking factors by the experts
3. Information (expert judgments) processing
4. Verification of concordance and probability of expert judgments
5. Use of estimation results for working out the econometric model.

It is important to state that during ranking, some kinds of risks were given the same rank. Experts were requested to specify the positions given to such kind of risks in the process of general ranking; the risk factors in order of ranks decrease. We assumed that weight of position varies from 1 to 6. The factors which were given the same risk weight were equal to arithmetic middling of corresponding positions. Position and weights given to risks and the result of experts' judgments processing were presented in Tables 2 and 3. The next was the determination of the coefficient of concordance to verify concordance of expert judgments

$$W = \frac{S}{\frac{1}{2}m^2(n^3-n) - \frac{m}{12n}\sum_{j=i}^{M} Tj} \quad (4)$$

Where; S = Sum of deviation squares (derived from processing of expert judgements); M = number of experts (40); n = number of risk, and Tj = Indicator that allows taking into consideration coincidence of ranks and was estimated by the formula;

$$Tj = \sum_{K=1}^{n} (t_k^3 - t_k) \quad (5)$$

Where; tK = number of rank K coincidences while ranking factor by expert j. Thus, coefficient of concordance varied within the range o ≤ w ≤ 1. The decision rules were that if w ≥ 0.5 then the concordance may be regarded as satisfactory, if w ≥ 0.7, then concordance is considered as good. W = 1 means entire coincidence of expert judgments. (that is, execellent and more reliable result). The probability of concordance coefficient was verified by Pearson criterion. This criterion was calculated thus:

$$\chi^2 = \frac{S}{\frac{1}{12}*m*n*(n+1) - \frac{1}{n-1}*\frac{1}{12}*\sum_{j=i}^{M} Tj} \quad (6)$$

Calculated value χ2Calc was compared with table value χ 2 Table. If χ2Calc exceeds χ2table, then the null hypothesis about concordance of 40 experts judgments on the risk factors ranking may be rejected, that is, we may assert that concordance of experts judgments is non-random. So in accordance with expert's judgments, we determined the factors which have extreme influence upon the profitability of agribusiness operation. Following Alimi and Ayanwale (2005) and Mikhaylova, (2005), the risk factors for consideration were:

X1 = Currency risk
X2 = Political risk
X3 = Production risk
X4 = Market (price) risk
X5 = Financial risk
X6 = Social risk

Table 1. Distribution of risk sources affecting agribusiness enterprises.

Risk source	Frequency	Percentage
Currency (X_1)	40	100
Political (X_2)	40	100
Production (X_3)	40	100
Market (price) (X_4)	40	100
Financial (X_5)	40	100
Social (X_6)	40	100

Source: field survey data 2010;*Multiple responses were recorded.

RESULTS AND DISCUSSION

Here, the various sources of risk and their degree of influence on the agribusiness enterprises were discussed. This was done with the use of simple descriptive statistics, w- statistics and Pearson's criterion (x^2).

Sources of risks

As presented in Table 1, the risk sources identified to be affecting agribusiness enterprises in the study area were currency risk, political risk, production risk, market risk, financial risk, and social risk. Though 100% of the sampled firms identified the six risk sources but their degree of influence may not be the same on the productivity or profitability of the enterprises. The result is in line with the findings of Mbanasor and Nwankwo (2001), Nwaru et al. (2007) Alimi and Ayanwade (2005) as well as Mikhaylova (2005) who reported that the identified risks were the major sources of risk in agribusiness operations.

The six risk sources were also split into their various components as to determine the ones that are important to the investors.

Ranking of risk sources and their components

The identified risk sources and the ranking by staff (who were well informed on risk management) in their order of importance are presented in Table 2.

The table indicated that none of the firms considered such risk components as government instability, government interference and repatriation of earning, physical hazards in the factory, war and civil commotion/disturbances, changes in social structure, death and sickness as components of risk sources in the area. The risk components are considered inconsequential as NIPC (2007) noted that since 1999, a lot of policies have been put in place to encourage foreign investors to come to Nigeria.

Table 2 further indicated that the firms stated that meteorological, technological failure, input and output prices, high interest rate, and accessibility to credit as important risk components. Sixty (60) percent of the firms considered kidnapping of workers important while 50 and 42.5% of the sampled firms viewed poor management, theft and burglary, respectively, as other important risk components. More so, 27.5% ranked translation as a major risk component in currency risk source. Akinsulire (2006) opined that translation exposure has effect on the translation of multinational firms' financial statements.

The table also indicated that 22.5% of firms recognised transaction, policy shock, and technological success of competitors respectively as important risk components of agribusiness firms in the area. The result on policy shock is good especially when related to that obtained by Dercon (2002) which reported that policy shock such as changes in taxation, and ban on migrants, are sources of risk to agribusiness operation.

The risk sources identified cause adversity in return to investment. Each or any combination of the outcomes, of the risk sources leads to low productivity and income to the firms.

However, ranking by simple descriptive statistics may be misleading as the tool cannot be tested econometrically. So the analysis of ranking of the degree of influence was further conducted using W – statistics and Pearson criterion (x^2). This starts with the processing of ranking by the experts. The experts who formed the assessment team were of the same rank across the different agribusiness firms that is, managing directors of the 40 sampled firms) so they all have equal weight of 1. Each expert's judgement was multiplied by 1 to give the weight of the risk variable. The weights given to risk and the results of the expert's judgement were calculated and presented in Table 3.

Table 3 indicated that the central tendency is 191, that is, total weight divided by the number of risk sources (1146/6) while the sum of deviation square is 664. The table also indicated that the sum of mean of rank is 28.645. It was based on this that coefficient of concordance was determined to verify concordance of experts judgements.

Coefficient of concordance using W – statistic was calculated to be 0.792. Hence, Mikhalova (2005) held that if W > 0.50, then concordance may be regarded as satisfactory, but if W > 0.7 then concordance is considered as good. W = 1 means entire concordance of experts judgements. Since the result is 0.792, it means that the concordance should be regarded as good. The probability of concordance coefficient of expert judgments was verified by Pearson criterion, following, Mikhalova (2005) and this gave x^2 (Pearson criterion calculated) 4.81. At a degree of freedom of 5 (that is $y = 6 - 1 = 5$, where 6 is the number of risk sources) and 5% significance level (that is, probability P = 0.95), the table value of Pearson criterion is $x^2_{table} = 11.07$. The decision

Table 2. Firms' ranking of risk sources and components in Abia State.

Risk sources and component	Rank						Frequency	Percentage
	1	2	3	4	5	6		
Currency								
Transaction	2	1	3	1	1	1	9	22.50
Translation	1	2	5	1	1	1	11	27.50
Economic	3	4	1	-	-	-	8	20.00
Political								
Policy shock	4	3	2	-	-	-	9	22.50
Government instability	-	-	-	-	-	-	-	-
Government interference	-	-	-	-	-	-	-	-
Repatriation of earning	-	-	-	-	-	-	-	-
Production								
Meteorological	6	8	10	6	5	5	40	100.00
Technological failure	40	-	-	-	-	-	40	100.00
Technological success of competitor	1	2	3	-	-	-	9	22.50
Physical hazard in factory	-	-	-	-	-	-	-	-
Market								
Input price	2	2	7	9	5	15	40	100.00
Output price	1	4	6	8	6	15	40	100.00
Financial								
High interest rate	40	-	-	-	-	-	40	100.00
Accessibility of credit	15	3	2	4	3	13	40	100.00
Social								
Theft and burglary	-	-	-	-	-	-	-	-
Poor management	3	5	4	-	8	-	20	50.00
Strike	-	-	-	-	-	-	-	-
War/civil commotion	-	-	-	-	-	-	-	-
Kidnapping of workers	12	1	3	6	1	1	24	60.00
Death and sickness	-	-	-	-	-	-	-	-

Calculated from field survey data, 2010.

Table 3. Result of experts' judgement processing of agribusiness firms in Abia State.

Sources	Total weight	Deviation of sum from the central tendency	Deviation squared	Mean of rank
Currency	192	1	1	4.80
Political	200	9	81	5.00
Production	195	4	16	4.88
Market	180	-9	81	4.50
Financial	174	-17	289	4.40
Social	205	14	196	5.12
Total	1146	2	664	28.65

Calculated from field survey data, 2010.

rule is that if calculated ^{2} exceed the x^2_{table}, then the null hypothesis about concordance of 40 experts' judgements which ranked 6 risk factors may be rejected as non-random. So in accordance with experts' judgements, we

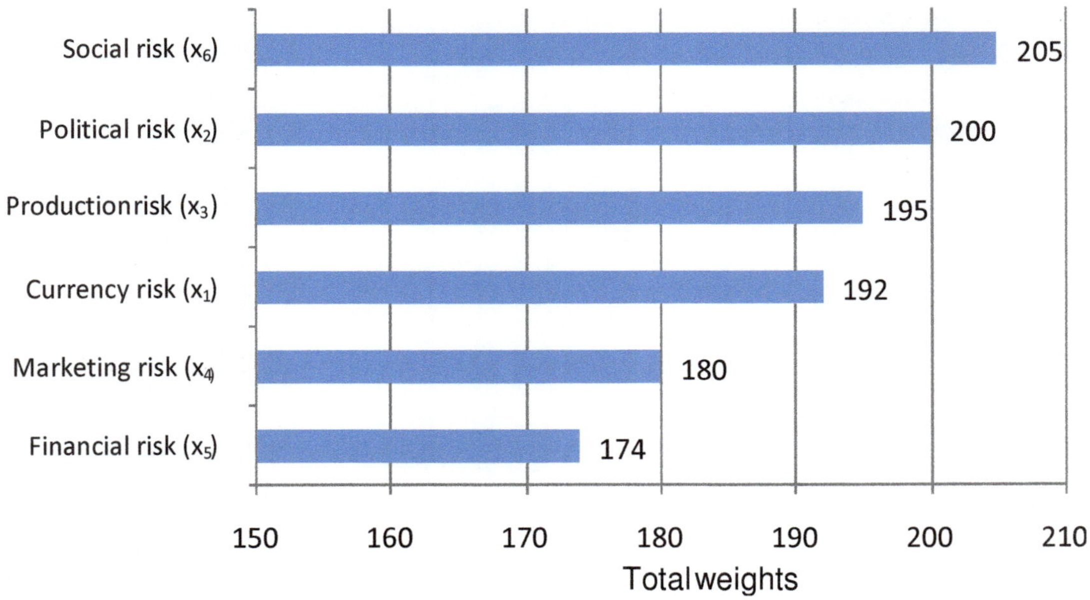

Figure 1. Decreasing influence of risk factors.

Table 4. Firms optimal risk reducing strategies in Abia State.

Risk aversion strategy	Frequency	Percentage
Diversification	34	85.00
Integration	32	80.00
Insurance	20	50.00
Forward contracting	22	55.00
Sequential marketing	10	25.00
Cooperation marketing	8	20.00
Foreign exchange hedging	13	32.50
Borrowing	6	15.00
Savings	6	15.00

Source: Field survey, 2010 *Multiple responses were recorded.

may determine and isolate the risk factors which have extreme influence on investments and productivity in the selected agribusiness enterprises. After ranking the factors, that is, placing factors in order of decreasing impact upon the agribusiness operations, experts' judgements on the risk could be positioned as shown in Figure 1.

Figure 1 show that the four most important risk factors selected were financial, marketing, currency and production risks. They appeared in order of decreasing influence. Since the weights assigned to the variables ranged from 1 to 6 with 1 being the highest, it means that the higher the total weight assigned, the lower the influence of the variable. Hence in selecting the most significant risk factors in order of decreasing influence a target of four most important risk factors was set. Using the aforementioned criterion therefore (order of decreasing influence), as shown by the bar charts based on the total weights of the risk variables previously mentioned, it could be inferred that, among the risk factors considered, financial risk had the highest influence, followed by marketing risk, currency risk (exchange rate) and production risk in that order. This result is satisfactory, especially when compared with that obtained through ranking of risk factors in Table 2. This result is in conformity with a 'priori' expectation considering the difficulty involved in securing credit, fluctuation in price of inputs and outputs as well as that of exchange rate.

However, Alimi and Ayanwale (2005) reported that financial risk was not a source of risk in agribusiness operation. This could be due to the fact that investors in their study area never employed debt financing.

Risk reducing strategies

A number of the optimal risk reducing strategies adopted by the sampled firms are summarized and presented in Table 4.

A majority (85%) of the firms adopted diversification strategy as a way of reducing risks. This involves investment in more than one portfolio. Some of the agribusiness operators also engaged in non agribusiness activities. Engagement in and earning of non agribusiness income lowered the variants of incomes from agribusiness operation. Some of the agribusiness investors engaged in diversification of products produced, that is, they are involved in the production of two or more agribusiness products or output simultaneously. Alimi and Ayanwale (2005), Akinsulire (2006), Pandey (2004) and Van Horne (2004) noted that diversification served the best by spreading risk across a number of enterprises. Diversification acts as a strategy to stabilise firms' incomes.

Table 4 also revealed that significant proportions (80%) of the firms used integration to reduce agribusiness risks. Integration is a contracting agreement between different actors in agribusiness chain. Integration helps to overcome the disruption of the supply of inputs or evacuation of output in the agribusiness chain. This result is consistent with several studies (Ndugbu, 2003; Akinsulire, 2006). Hence, integration is used to reduce risk associated with fluctuation in input and output supply through the encouragement of backward and forward integration.

Fifty five percent of the agribusiness firms adopted forward contracting as a strategy to reduce risks. In this case, the firms reduce price risk by allowing agribusiness firms to agree and be sure of the price they want to sell their commodities in future before they are ready for disposal. The essence of such arrangement being a commitment to provide agribusiness commodity of a type, at a time and a price and in quality required by a known buyer. Alimi and Ayanwale (2005) and Varangis et al. (2002) added that forward contracting also involves entering into forward contract for the exchange of one currency for another at a specific future date and at a specific exchange rate by multinational firms. Hence, forward contracting is used to reduce foreign exchange related risk by multinational agribusiness companies. Though the result is contrary to the report of Nwaru et al. (2007) that forward contracting is virtually non-existent for most agribusiness firms except brewery and flour mill industries, because of weak legal system to enforce contract. Furthermore, the results (Table 4) indicate that 50% of the firms used insurance strategy to reduce their risk. This involves payment of premium to an insurance company which indemnifies the insured investor against losses recorded in the business. However, this result is not in consonance with Alimi and Ayanwale (2005) who reported that investors never used insurance as a means of reducing risk because of their unavailability. The table also revealed that 32.5, 25, 20 and 15% used foreign exchange hedging, sequential marketing and borrowing/ saving, respectively, as optimal risk reducing strategies. The result is however, satisfactory when compared with that obtained by Alimi and Ayanwale (2005) and Varangis et al. (2002).

Conclusion

This study makes a significant contribution to the existing literature on risk analysis among agribusiness enterprises. It provides a new practical perspective on the issue of ranking the degree of risk on agribusiness investments and how there could be managed. The study revealed that the major risk sources in the area are financial followed by marketing, currency,and production in that order while the risk aversion strategies are diversification, integration, forward contracting and insurance. Drawing from the findings of the study, efforts should be geared towards the development of agencies and institutions that would reduce financial and market risks that have been found to be critical among agribusiness enterprises. This is fundamentals to the growth and development of agribusiness enterprises in Nigeria.

REFERENCES

Abia State Economic Empowerment Development Strategy ABSEEDS (2005). Abia State Planning Commission Blue Print, Mbeyi and Associate Nig. Ltd, Lagos

Akinsulire O (2006). Financial management (4th edition) Ceemol Nigeria Ltd, Lagos.

Alimi T, Ayanwale AB (2005). "Risk and Risk Management Strategies in onion Production in Kebbi State of Nigeria" J. Soc. Sci. 10(1).

Aneke JI (2007). "Agricultural Insurance" In Reading in Agricultural Economics and Extension, Akubuilo CJC, Umebali EE, Mgbada JU, Ugwu DS, Egwu WE, Awoke MU (eds). Computer Edge Puplishers. Enugu. pp. 221-244.

Balogun O (2008). Nigeria Atlas of Electoral Constituencies Independent National Electoral Commission (INEC) Abuja.

Barry PJ, Baker CB (1984). "Financial Response to Risk in Agriculture", In Barry PJ (eds), Risk Mgt Agric., IOWA State University Press, Ames. pp. 183-198.

Bauer L, Bushe D (2003). Designing Risk Management Strate, Managing the Modern Farm Business, third edition, university of Alberta.

Chaddad I, Al-Husni M, Chen BF (2010). "Risk Analysis in Agricultural Enterprises", Revne Des economies nord Africaines. p.16

Chandra O (2006). Project Planning, Analyaia, Selection, Financing and Implementation and Review (6th edition), Tata Mcgraw – Hill publishing Company Ltd. New Delhi

Corporate Nigeria (CN) (2008). The Business, Trade and Investment Guide. Corporate Guides International Ltd. www.corporate –Nigeria net

Dercon S (2002). "Income Risk; Coping Strategies and Safety Nets" The World Bank Research Observer, 17(2): 141-166

Drollete SA (2009). "Management Production Risk in Agriculture" AG/AGCO/RMA

Federal Office of Statistics (FOS) (1996). Population Figures FOS publication.

Federal Republic of Nigeria official Gazette (FRN) (2009) "Legal Notice on Publication of 2006 Census final result" 2nd February, 96(2).

Hardaker JB (2000). "Some Issues in Dealing with Risk in Agriculture." Working paper series in Agricultural and Resources Economics, Austr.

Kuyrah JN, Obare G, Herrero M, Waishaka M (2006). "Agricultural Income Risk and Rural Poverty Dynamics Strategies of smallholder producers in Kenya" Contributed paper, presented at the international Association of Agricultural Economics Conference; Gold Coast, Australia, August., pp. 12-16.

Marchet JM, Nasir J, Ramachandra V, Shah MK, Tyler G, Zhao I (2001). "Results of the Nigerian Firm Survey; Regional Program on Enterprise Development, African Region", The World Bank, Draft for Review.

Martin P, Markus D (2000). "Risk in Agriculture As Impediment To Rural Lending- The Case of North-Western Kazakhstan." Discussion paper, Institute of Agricultural Development in Central and Eastern Europe.

Mbanasor JA, Nwankwo OO (2001). "An Economic study of Palm Oil Marketing in Akwa Ibom State," J. Applied Chem. Agric. Res. JACAR., 7: 120-126.

Mikhaylova LI (2005). "Risk Management in International Agricultural Markets" IAMO-Forum, Agricultural and Food Markets in Central and Eastern Europe, Seminar Paper 16-18 June, Halle (Saale).

Moss C, Schonkwiler J, Schmitz A (2003). "The Certainty Equivalence of farm land value: 1910 – 2000". In Moss, C.B and A. Schmitz

(editors).Goverment Policy and farmland markets: The maintenance of farm wealth, IOWA State University press: Ames.
Ndugbu MO (2003). Foundation of Project and Investment Analysis, Barloz publishers Ltd, Owerri.
Njavro M (2009). "Risk Management in Agribusiness." Paper presented at Zagreb School of Economics and Management, June 5.
Nigerian Investment Promotion Commission (2007). Newsletter. The Nigerian Investment Promotion Commission (NIPC) Publication October.
Nigerian Investment Promotion Commission (NIPC) (2008). Newsletter; A Quarterly Publication, 6th Edition, July- September.
Nigeria Investment Promotion Commission (2006). Consolidated Annual Report (2004-2006), Nigerian Investment Promotion Commission, Billy Comms and Co Ltd, Abuja
Nwaru JC, Onyenweaku CE, Njoku SC (2007). Rural Risk management Strategies in Imo State of Nigeria: The case of Insured and uninsured Arable Crop Farmers. Int. J. Agric. Rural Dev., 10(2): 18-24.
Odii MACA (1998). Modern Farm Management; Techniques; Alphabeth Nigeria Publishers, Owerri.
Ojo SO (2003). "Productivity and Technical Efficiency of Poultry Egg Production in Nigeria", Int. J. Poult. Sci. 29(6): 459-464.
Pandey IM (2004). Financial Management (9th ed). Vikas Publishing House PVT Ltd New delhi.
Van-Horne JC (2004). Financial Management and Policy (12th edition). Pearson Education (Singapore Pte Ltd.) Delhi.
Varangis P, Larson D, Anderson JR (2002). Agricultural Markets and Risk: Management of the Latter, not the Farmer," Paper Presented in a Seminar Held to Honour Ronald C. Duncan on the Occasion of his Retirement as Executive Director of the National Centre for Development Studies and Director, Asia Pacific School of Economics and Management, Australian National University, Caribbean in July 2001.

4

The impact of fiscal policies on consumers' spending

Matthias Nnadi

School of Management, Cranfield University, Bedfordshire, UK. E-mail: Matthias.nnadi@cranfield.ac.uk.

The economic impasse experienced in the UK is being counteracted by aggressive fiscal policies geared toward encouraging spending on consumables. Using the retail price index and data obtained from the Office of National Statistics, this paper assessed the effectiveness of the government's fiscal measures to stabilize the economy through spending. The article developed a consumer spending model (CSM) and assessed its impact on intrinsic fiscal policies such as bank rate, inflation, percentage earnings increase and mortgage rate. The study finds bank rate and annual inflation as most significant factors affecting consumer spending and suggests that fiscal measures targeted at reducing bank lending rates and controlling inflation should be the government's policy priority.

Key words: Bank rate, spending, mortgage rate.

INTRODUCTION

The recent slowdown in the economic activities of most countries left some ripples in the consumers spending pattern and the fiscal policy of the United Kingdom. The retail price index shrank as most shops suffered liquidation. The Government consistently revised the interest rates to cushion the economic crunch on consumers and encourage a spending rather than a thrift economy. For instance, at the onset of the recession, the major central banks introduced inertia in their interest rate targets relative to the cyclical decline in economic activities. The European Central Bank was not left out as it focused on higher wage settlements in parts of EU including Germany, Italy, and the Netherlands (Hetzel, 2009). Whether these measures produced the expected results have remained an issue of debate.

Inflationary targets have been used as a mechanism of reducing inflation rate volatility, interest rate and hence inject a transparent monetary policy in the economy. The United Kingdom, like many other countries had adopted this policy since 1992 and had maintained a target of 2%. This arguably had been used in mitigating the exchange volatility on the economy.

Lee (2009) outlined that 26 countries comprising of Canada, Peru, Chile, Sweden, Australia and Israel have also maintained inflationary targets. The adoption of inflation targets could have a significant impact on the stock market especially if it falls below the expected level. Conversely, interest rates provide alternative source and uses of fund which affect bank credit. Ezeoha and Amaeshi (2010) support this preposition and argued that the expectations theory of interest rate posits that banks invest in assets with higher rates as to maximise their returns. This could impact on inflation as the quantity theory suggests that inflation is caused by increase in money supply which exceeds the growth rate.

This paper examines some intrinsic variables that are predatory on the consumers spending. The consumers spending level on goods, as measured by the retail price index (RPI) can be affected by a range of factors. The consumer spending model (CSM) developed in this study uses 4 variables namely: Bank or interest rate (BR), annual inflation (AI), annual earnings increase (AEI) and mortgage rate (MR) respectively to explain the consumers spending and behavioural pattern particularly during economic melt down.

LITERATURE REVIEW

Economic and financial studies have produced different models to explain effects of interest, mortgage, inflationary rates and earnings on spending. Ward (2008) expanded on the Hedonic pricing model to generate quality adjusted price indices and cautions against the removal of mortgage interest repayments from macro-economic inflationary target measures in the UK. Cansino et al. (2007) used the simple accounting matrix (SAM) model to estimate the impact of tax on retail sales and on the prices indices in Spain. Others such as Llop and Manresa (2004) developed the computable general equilibrium (CGE) model to analyses indirect taxes on spending.

The retail price index (RPI) had been a very popular standard of measurement of inflation, household spending on consumables and includes mortgage interest repayments. Ward (2008) adds that the RPI in the UK is also considered as a suitable benchmark in assessing the cost of living and thus used as a reference point in wage negotiations. In this respect, it is more acceptable than the consumer price index (CPI) or the harmonised index of consumer prices (HICP) as introduced among EU countries.

The fiscal characteristic of inflation is anchored on the assumption that central banks determine the inflationary trends based on the inflation targets. This doctrine defies the exogenous strength of the market forces that influence market prices (Hetzel, 2009).

The extend of control of inflation by regulatory banks has been tested by Friedman (1969), using the natural rate hypothesis (NRH) who posit that while the unexpected inflation can stimulate economic activities, expected inflation cannot. The interest rate must also provide incentives for individuals to change their contemporaneous demand for resources relative to their future demands.

The UK introduced some fiscal policies including quantitative easing technique to ameliorate the harsh economic impasse. The bank lending rate including LIBOR was drastically reduced, as well as the VAT from 17.5 to 15%. These policies perhaps were in compliance with the suggestions of the European Monetary Union (EMU) on member countries to initiate fiscal measures that will facilitate a speedy adjustment to the macroeconomic shock (Colciago et al., 2008).

The focus was to encourage spending on goods as a measure of stimulating the economy. Some analysts believe that increase in bank rates and fall in fuel prices would help in stabilising inflation (Kirchhoff, 2008).

A key central policy of most countries is focused on addressing the imbalance in the fiscal policy, particularly the budget deficits.

Therefore, knowledge of the causes of fiscal imbalances offers vital information to domestic fiscal authorities in their efforts to either achieve fiscal balances.

Kollias and Paleologou (2006) outlined two alternative hypotheses of government spending and tax revenue; the spend tax and tax-spend hypotheses. While the former describes spending decisions prior to changes in tax, the latter explains how changes in government tax revenues lead to changes in expenditure.

These hypotheses have consistently produced mixed results. Payne (2003) attributes this to difference in the methodology, model specification and the time frame of the studies.

However et al. (1992) posit that the lack of causality between revenue and expenditure is because of the government structure.

CONSUMERS SPENDING MODEL

This study develops a consumers spending model (CSM) to examine the impact of some intrinsic variables on consumers spending. The retail price index (RPI) is applied as a proxy for consumers' spending, which is an acceptable standard for measuring the amount spent by households on consumables. The model is developed using the Hodrick and Prescott (1997) filter with a parameter lambda (λ) as the smoothing coefficient. The filter sets the potential component of output to minimise the loss function, *L* and represented in the function:

$$L = \sum_{t=1}^{s} (y_t - y_t^T)^2 + \lambda \sum_{t=2}^{s-1} (\Delta y^T_{t+1} - \Delta y^T_t)^2$$

The λ vector had all its elements equals to zero and therefore a non- negative scaler. The value of λ = 100 (for annual observations) and s = sample.

The assumption is that the RPI is dependent on bank rate, inflation, earnings increase and mortgage rate. The intrinsic potentials of these variables signify that they exert influential impacts on spending. The CSM therefore takes the following specifications:

$$RPI_t = \beta_0 + \beta_1 BR_t + \beta_2 AI_t + \beta_3 AEI_t + \beta_4 MR_t + \varepsilon_t$$

where *RPI* is the retail price index at any time *t*, β is the constant term, *BR* is the bank rate, *AI* is the annual inflation, *AEI* is the annual earnings increase percent, *MR* is the mortgage rate while the ε is the error term.

Hetzel (2009) maintains that sustained money creation by the central banks such as the ECB (European Central Bank) and BoE (Bank of England) will revive the spending of the public through a portfolio rebalancing mechanism. Thus the bank rate will rise with no increase in expected inflation as the increase in spending restores and revamps the confidence in the economy.

The decline in the annual earning increase had been less contentious. This is due largely to the fall in the demand for goods and services to the extent that profits from businesses cannot be further squeezed. Pay freezes which initially started with small firms particularly in housing related industries in the early quarter of 2008, gradually affected even the big firms (Hackworth, 2009).

EMPIRICAL FINDINGS AND CONCLUSIONS

The means of the variables and there standard deviations are shown in Table1.The means of BR,AI,AEI and MR are 4.49,3.07,3.60 and 6.24 respectively with standard deviations show that the mean of the variables are similar with a marginal value in their standard deviation.

Table 1 shows the mean of the variables with a marginal value in the standard deviation. First, the study established the correlation between the *RPI* and the other intrinsic consumer spending variables. The correlations in Table 2 shows that the bank rates and annual inflation have significant correlation with the *RPI*. While the *BR* has a negative correlation with the *RPI*, the *AI* had a positive correlation.

This implies that an increase in bank rate depletes

Table 1. Descriptive statistics.

Variables	Mean	Min.	Max.	Standard deviation	Obs.
RPI	177.67	144.14	214.83	22.38	16
BR	4.49	0.50	7.25	1.54	43
AI	3.07	-1.60	5.00	1.46	66
AEI	3.60	-2.00	5.70	1.25	53
MR	6.24	3.50	7.75	1.09	28

Table 2. Correlation matrix.

Variables	RPI	BR	AI	AEI	MR
RPI	1.000				
BR	-0.705**	1.000			
AI	0.791**	-0.416**	1.000		
AEI	-0.212	0.310*	-0.398**	1.000	
MR	0.035	0.257	0.289	0.165	1.000

**significant at 0.01 level *significant at 0.05 level.

Table 3. OLS cross sectional regression.

Variables	Model 1	Model 2	Model 3
Constant	13.955 (0.000)**	15.985 (0.000)**	18.313 (0.000)**
Bank rate (BR)	-0.705 (0.002)**	-0.491 (0.003)**	-0.452 (0.011)*
Annual inflation(AI)		0.668 (0.000)**	0.722 (0.001)**
Annual earning increase percent (AEI)		0.205 (0.144)	0.230 (0.128)
Mortgage rate (MR)			-0.095 (0.529)
Adj. r square	0.461	0.788	0.778
R square change	0.497	0.334	0.006

The bank rates (BR) and the mortgage rates (MR) comprise of the 2001 to 2009 rates regimes determined by the Bank of England (BoE) and the commercial and mortgage institutions. The annual inflation (AI), the percentage annual earnings increase (AEI) and the retail price index (RPI) comprise of data obtained from the UK Office of National Statistics (ONS) and other economic gazettes from 2004 -2009. Each model contains the beta value of the variables and their correspondent significant values in brackets. The constant depicts the standard error of the unstandardised coefficient values. Dependent variable: Retail price index (RPI). **significant at 0.01 and *significant at 0.05.

consumers spending while inflationary trend has an effect on spending. The table indicates that *RPI* has a significant correlation of -0.705 with *BR* and 0.791 with *AI* respectively.

The result of the OLS cross sectional regression shows that both *BR* and *AI* are significant factors in encouraging spending. The result in Table 3 contains 3 models to test the significant effect of the variables in stimulating consumers spending. The bank rate had a significant negative coefficient across the three models. Its significance tends to reduce with the introduction of other variables. The variable had a high coefficient of -0.705 and the R-square change indicates that it makes a 49.7% contribution to the consumers spending model. Arneric et al. (2009) admit that bank interest inadvertently affect economic activities.

Annual inflation showed the highest significant positive coefficient of 0.722. The R-square change in model 2 indicates that the variable makes a contributory impact of 33.4%. The various studies undertaken on the inflationary effect on retail prices accentuate its crucial role. Yet researchers are open to admit that much remains to be investigated about inflation (Hausman, 2004; Wynne and Rodriguez-Palenzuela 2004). This study however leans support to Colciago et al. (2008) that inflation has a stimulatory effect on spending.

Hunt (2009) highlights that the current UK inflation rate is not only a result of the globalisation, but a result of the foreign imports and appreciation of the pounds sterling. The study warns that caution must be exercised on over reliance on the trend of past interest rate as the guide for estimating future rates.

Both the annual earnings increase and mortgage rate showed no significance and are thus less forceful in stimulating spending. However, their inclusion is essential for the model regression to be significant. Infact, both the AEI and MR are integral elements of the RPI.

Conclusion

The study had established intrinsic factors in the retail price index. The result had shown that while bank rate has a significant negative impact on spending, annual inflation exerts a positive impact on spending. Therefore, to stimulate the economy through consumer spending, the government fiscal policy should be geared towards stabilising the inflationary trend.

The annual earnings increase and mortgage rate showed no insignificance in stimulating consumer spending. This is not surprising as the UK Office of National Statistics also incorporates bank interest rates in the estimation of mortgage rate matrix (ONS, 2005).

The consumer spending model (CSM) highlights the importance of the intrinsic spending variables used in the study. Both the bank rate and annual inflation are highly correlated with the retail price index, which is a measure of consumers spending on consumables.

REFERENCES

Arneric J, Jurun E, Kordic L (2009). Empirical Study of Real Trade Turnover. Proceedings of World Academy of Science, Engr. Technol., 37: 2070-3740.

Colciago A, Ropele T, Muscatella VA, Tirelli P (2008). The Role of Fiscal Policy in a Monetary Union: are National Automatic Stabilizers Effective? Rev. Int. Econ., 16(3): 591-610.

Cansino JM, Cardenete MA, Roman R (2007). Regional evaluation of a tax on the retail sales of certain fuels through a social accounting matrix. Appl. Econ. Lett., 14: 877-880.

Ezeoha AE, Amaeshi K (2010). Banking System Development, Small Businesses and Minority Lending. Int. J. Financial Services Mgt. 4(4): 285-295.

Friedman M (1969). The Monetary Studies of the National Bureau. (In) The Optimum Quantity of Money and Other Essays, edited by Milton Friedman, Chicago: Aldine Pub. pp. 261-84.

Hackworth C (2009). Recent developments in pay settlement. Bank England Q. Bull. Q4, 293-296.

Hausman J (2004). Sources of bias and solutions to bias in the CPI. J. Econ. Perspective, 17(1): 23-44.

Hetzel RL (2009). Monetary Policy in the 2008 -2009 Recession. Econ. Q., 95(2): 201-233.

Hodrick R, Prescott EC (1997). Postwar U.S. Business Cycles: An Empirical Investigation. J. Money, Credit, and Banking. 29(1): 1-16.

Hoover KD, Sheffrin SM (1992). Causation, spending, and taxes: sand in the sandbox or tax collector for the welfare state? Am. Econ. Rev., 82: 225-48.

Hunt BL (2009). UK Inflation and Relative Prices over the 1997 -2006 Period: How Important was Globalisation? Global Econ. J., 9(3): 1-29.

Kollias C, Paleologou S (2006). Fiscal policy in the European Union. J. Econ. Stud., 33(2): 108-120.

Kirchhoff S (2008). Inflation swells in July. USA Today, August 15,02b.

Lee U (2009). The Impact of Inflation Targeting on the Relationship between Stock Returns and Inflation: International Evidence. Int. J. Finance, 21(3): 6124-6141.

Llop M, Manresa A (2004). The General equilibrium effects of social security contributions under alternative incidence assumptions. Applied Econ. Lett., 11: 847-50.

ONS (2005). Consumer price index: technical manuals. Office for National Statistics, London.

Payne JE (2003). A Survey of the international empirical evidence on the tax-spend debate. Publ. Finance Rev., 31: 302-24.

Ward D (2008). An assessment of mortgage interest inflation measurement bias in the UK. Int. Rev. Applied Econ., 22(3):373 -386.

Waynne MA, Rodriguez P (2004). Measurement bias in the HICP, what do we know, and what what do we need to know? J. Econ. Surveys, 181(1): 79-112.

5

Hedge funds and their interaction with market parameters

Samet GÜNAY[1,2] and Gökberk CAN[1,3]

[1]Anadolu BİL Vocational School, İstanbul Aydin University, Florya Campus, İstanbul, Turkey.
[2]İstanbul University, İstanbul, Turkey.
[3]Marmara University, İstanbul, Turkey.

The performance of hedge funds and other financial institutions has been carefully studied during the last financial crisis. In our study which spans through a time period of 31 December, 1999 to 21 June, 2011, the relationship between global hedge fund indice and Federal Reserve's effective interest rate, and the relationship between the 10 year-term Treasury bill and the M2 monetary supply variables as the United States' economy indicator was tested with vector autoregression analysis (VAR). Based on the results obtained, the indices stastistically and significantly reflect the developments guiding the U.S. economy and then became effective on our present variables.

Key words: Hedge funds, vector autoregression analysis (VAR).

INTRODUCTION

The term, hedge funds, was first used by a journalist, Carol Loomis, to describe an innovative investment structure created by Alfred Winslow Jones. He set up hedges by investing in securities that he determined as undervalued, funding these positions partly by taking short positions in overvalued securities, creating a market-neutral position (Lee et al., 2001). Although, there is no set definition for a hedge fund, it usually refers to an actively managed investment pool that does not advertise, and is privately organized to be exempt from the Securities Acts of 1933 and 1934 (Frumkin and Vandegrift, 2009). Bloomberg defines a hedge fund as "a fund that employs a variety of techniques to enhance returns, such as both buying and shorting stocks according to a valuation model" (Bouges, 2004). Today, the term hedge fund encompasses investment philosophies that are far from the original market- neutral strategy of Jones, and include the global macro styles of people like Soros and Julian Robertson (Brown and Goetzmann, 2003).

Hedge funds are really no different from any other for profit business enterprise, owners provide capital to managers who seek to deploy and manage that capital and turn a profit for the benefit of the owners (Earle, 2010). As private entities, hedge funds are not allowed to advertise, but they are exempted from disclosure requirements facing traditional investment funds (Hedges IV, 2005). Hedge funds differ from traditional investments in many respects including benchmarks, investment processes, fees, and regulatory environment (Dopfel, 2005). Under the US Securities Act 1933, funds offered for sale have to be registered with, and be regulated by, the Securities and Exchange Commission (SEC). But in 1982, the Reagan Administration introduced Regulation D, which allowed funds to escape SEC control if they were not sold through a public offering and were instead sold to 'accredited investors' – individuals with net worth over $1 million or income over $200,000 – and to banks, corporations and pension funds with assets over $5 million (Chapman, 2010). Hedge funds are in general exempted from securities regulations that dictate internal controls that managers must implement and maintain, fees that managers can charge investors, and disclosures that fund managers must make to investors (Cassar and Gerakos, 2010). Setting up as offshore funds, many hedge funds are able to avoid further scrutiny or tax requirements imposed in the USA (Hedges IV, 2005).

Mutual funds' typical long-only and-hold-type strategy

*Corresponding author. E-mail: gokberkcan@aydin.edu.tr.

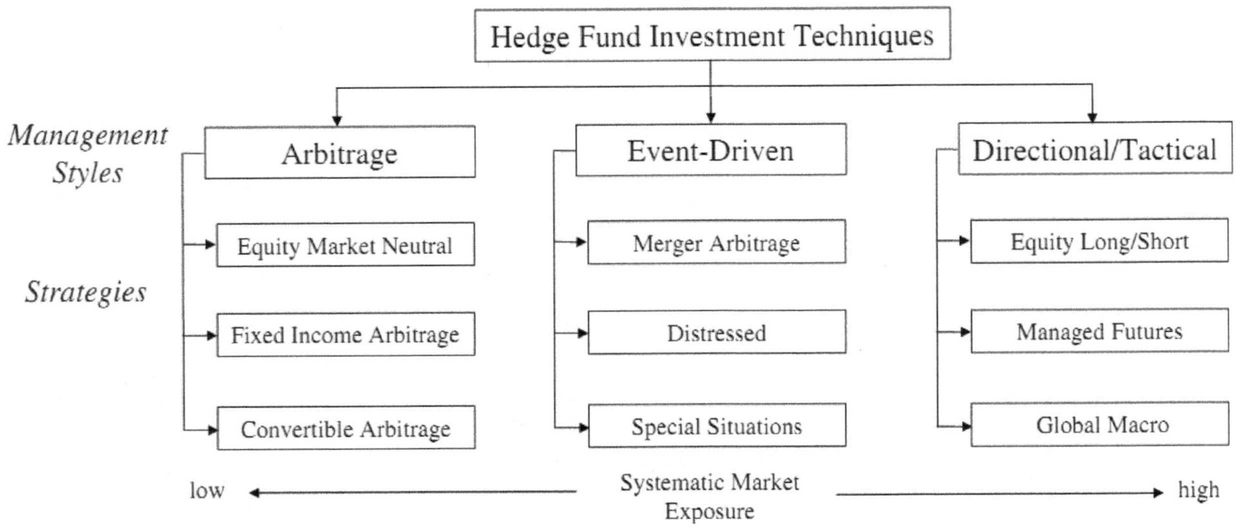

Figure 1. Hedge fund investment techniques (Fuss et al., 2007).

on standard asset classes with minimum risk is not enough in capturing risk premia associated with dynamic trading strategies or spread-based strategies. This is where the hedge funds get the starring role with their more dynamic trading strategies (Agarwal and Naik, 2003). The structure of hedge funds exposes the investor to numerous risk factors such as volatility, counter- party, or liquidity risk. Exposure to these risk factors is not only a source of a superior risk-return trade-off but also the very essence of hedge funds' extensive diversification possibilities compared to traditional investments (Christory et al., 2006). Hedge funds also suffer from opaque reporting; short track records of low-frequency returns, loosely defined investment styles, high minimum investment requirements, high fees, and low liquidity (Beckers et al., 2007). Due to their ability to short-sell and the extensive use of leverage, hedge funds have often outperformed many traditional benchmarks. This is often accredited to the ability of the hedge fund manager (Cerrato and Iannelli, 2006).

Hedge funds employ a wide array of dynamic, event driven, and relative value trading strategies to access statistical arbitrages in financial markets (Eberlein and Madan, 2009). Hedge funds can invest in the distressed debt of a foreign country; can buy equities "long" and/or "short"; can invest and trade using a complex computer-driven algorithm; can speculate in foreign currencies; can arbitrage commodity futures, etc. In other words, they can do anything sufficiently profitable to justify the fees they charge to investors (Donaldson, 2008) (Figure 1). Within the alternative asset universe, hedge funds are increasingly popular as possible investment opportunities for wealthy investors who possess long time horizons (Darius et al., 2002). A key determinant of hedge fund risk is the degree of similarity between the trading strategies of different funds (Adrian, 2007).

LITERATURE REVIEW

Studies on hedge funds can be diversified in many classes basically on regulation requirement for hedge funds and fraud, audit, internal control and corporate governance issues, alpha (manager skills) and beta (market exposure) components (Brunel, 2007), and return analysis.

The fact that hedge funds cease reporting because of unfavorable results implies extremely high failure rates for hedge funds. While some hedge funds have provided generous returns, investors are at high risk of buying a poorly performing fund or, even worse, a failing one (Grecu et al., 2007). Under this condition, performance of audited funds should be reviewed; audited funds have much smaller return discrepancies than non-audited funds and there is a significantly positive correlation between the auditing and fund size and funds listed on exchanges and unlevered funds have better data quality than others (Liang, 2003). Taxation and transparency is another problem about hedge funds. Hedge fund managers intentionally block transparency for strategic reasons and deny information to their own investors and to the government in order to guard their strategies from theft (Donaldson, 2008). In practice, voluntary reporting and the backfilling of only favorable past results can cause returns calculated from hedge fund databases to be biased upwards (Malkiel and Saha, 2005).

The findings on managers' skills show that practicing internal control in hedge funds reduces fraud and misstatements (Cassar and Gerakos, 2010); information asymmetry due to geographic location (distance) creates differences on return (Teo, 2009) and managers' education and work experiences' have important effect on funds' performance (Maxam et al., 2004). Another study based on hedge funds' location-manager skill relationship shows that Australian hedge fund managers do not have the skills to time market volatility (Do et al., 2009). Hedge fund managers do employ leverage; they seem to be leveraging their value added rather than simply modulating market or other factor risk exposures (Brunel, 2007). Some managers do not consistently follow a pre-specified investment style due to the hard clusters analysis and hedge funds with more than 36 months of tracking record that are more consistent do not usually generate higher future performance (Gibson and Gyger, 2007). While equity fund managers are exposed to three dominant style strategies, 'market', 'value' and 'momentum', managers vary their exposures to the 'market' in time to exploit favourable market moves. However, a similar pattern is not observed for their 'value' or 'momentum' exposures (Dupleich et al., 2010). Projected performance due to market moves and/or manager skills are the questions that investors want and need the answers of (Clark and Winkelmann, 2004).

There is a clear performance difference between live and dead funds resulted by using four models (single index market model, stale prices, Fama-French, Harvey-Siddique (2000) two-factor model) (Ding and Shawky, 2007). Results show that hedge funds' age and size have an effect on their performance; age has a negative relationship with hedge fund returns. As a fund's age increases, its managers suffer from style drift, leading to lower returns (Frumkin And Vandegrift, 2009). If an investors wish to maximise returns, they should start their hedge fund screening with younger, smaller funds, but those who wish to maximise capital preservation should begin their hedge fund screening with larger, older funds (Jones, 2007). The performance of funds is very volatile; funds with the highest return last period are generally no-alpha funds and best and worst performing funds tend to switch their places often (Manser and Schmid, 2009).

Risk components of the hedge funds are one of the key issues that need a deep review. When absolute or total risk-adjusted returns are used, Hedge funds are unable to consistently beat the market (Ackermann et al., 1999). The identification of systemic risk factors inherent in hedge fund strategies is the key input to important questions such as optimal contract design between buyers and sellers of hedge fund products (Fung and Hsieh, 2006). The volatility risk is related to returns of most hedge fund strategies in a nonlinear way. Further, the use of volatility risk as a factor in hedge fund analysis suffers from asymmetry that is similar to the impact of price risk (Peltomaki, 2005). Although, there is a beta puzzle for very specialised strategies, like the distressed securities and the short sellers one, with the help of a conditional version of the Fama and French model, there does not seem to be a beta puzzle in the hedge fund industry (Racicot and Théoret, 2007). Increases in hedge fund covariances tend to precede elevations in volatility. This result suggests that comovement measured in dollars is a more relevant indicator of risk than comovement measured in correlation, that is, covariance normalized by volatility (Adrian, 2007). Statistical properties of the 70 Asian hedge funds were tested and it showed the inappropriateness of the traditional mean-variance optimizer to form optimal hedge fund portfolios. In this study, a practical heuristic approach was used with the semi-variance as a better measure for downside risk (Fang et al., 2008).

Conditional correlations between hedge funds and other investments are generally symmetric, and therefore find no evidence supporting contagion between hedge funds and other investments in extreme down versus extreme up markets (Li and Kazemi, 2007). On a risk-adjusted basis, the average hedge fund outperformed the average mutual fund in the period January 1992 through December 1996; this performance difference cannot be explained by survivorship bias (Liang, 1998). By applying stacked cross-sectional regression and quartile portfolio approach methods for detecting the performance persistence of five different hedge fund styles; the results showed that both the degree and existence of performance persistence vary among hedge fund styles (Pätäri and Tolvanen, 2009). Using active currency management was beneficial to an international equity portfolio for Japanese investors from 2001 to 2006, especially when used with hedge funds; while the trading model adopted from Reinert works well for the JPY portfolio, was not effective on the various European currency-based portfolios (Tee, 2009).

ECONOMETRIC ANALYSIS

The volume of discussions on the United States' financial system started increasing with the mortgage crisis which started in 2007. Corporations working in audit-free markets and many financial institutions went bankrupt and some has been publicized. Along with corporations gone bankrupt like banks and insurance companies another concern was about the hedge funds. Their secrecy, active structure and levered transactions with investments in high-risk sectors and instruments created a concerned and careful audience about the future of these funds back in the '90s until now. With their position in most risky tranche in complex instruments like Collateral Debt Obligation, hedge funds' interaction with the markets, the attentions were drown to these institutions again.

The objective of this study is; to determine hedge funds' relation with the parameters of United States' financial markets containing the leading indicators in the global finance markets during the period lodging the previously mentioned developments. Ultimately this interaction and results are becoming determinant on global markets in terms of liquidity and risk perception. The variables used in our study are presented in Table 1 with their codes in the model as the vector auto-

Table 1. Data codes table.

Data	Code
Eurekahedge fund of funds index	Infohf
Monthly effective fed interest rate	Infedrate
Market yield on U.S. treasury securities at 10-year	Intbond_10
Components of non-M2 M3 / RPS Total (Billions of dollar)	Inm2

regressive model is preferred as the econometric analysis.

The time interval of variables' used in our study is December, 31 1999 to June, 21 2011. Our variables have a monthly frequency and in total, 140 months of time period is in subject. While Lnfohf variable was obtained from Eureka Hedge, other variables are downloaded from Federal Reserve's (Fed) web site.

VAR model

We often want to model the dynamic relationships among several timeseries variables. A simple way to do so without making many assumptions is to use what is called a vector autoregression, or VAR, model, which is the multivariate analog of an autoregressive model for a single time series (Davidson and Mackinnon, 1999). As a matter of fact, in our study a relation between more than one variable is desired to be determined. The direction of interaction in economic and financial variables is not fully known. In VAR model, in question there is no constraint to discriminate between fixed and independent variable. Therefore the most suitable model for our study is VAR analysis.

Given a set of K time series variables $y_t = (y_{1t}, \ldots, y_{Kt})'$, the basic VAR model is of the form

$$y_t = A_1 y_{t-1} + \ldots + A_p Y_{t-p} + u_t \quad (1)$$

where $u_t = (u_{1t}, \ldots, u_{Kt})$ is an unobservable zero-mean independent white noise process with time invariant positive definite covariance matrix $E(u_t u_t) = \Sigma u$ and A_i are $(K \times K)$ coefficient matrices. This model is often briefly referred to as a VAR(p) process because the number of lags is p (Lütkepohl, 2003).

Prior to going over to the VAR analysis Dickey Fuller and Philips-Perron unit root tests will be realized aimed at our variables' stationarity. Ahead of unit root tests, every variable's logarithm was derived and examined unit root test by doing so to level up the variables. Studying on non- stationary time series might backfire in producing misleading results as showing substantial relations as existing.

Unit root test

In some studies, interest rates, foreign exchange rates, or the price series of an asset are of interest. These series tend to be nonstationary. For a price series, the nonstationarity is mainly due to the fact that there is no fixed level for the price. In the time series literature, such a nonstationary series is called unit-root nonstationary time series (Tsay, 2005).

$$Y_t = {}_{\rho}Y_{t-1} + u_t \qquad -1 \leq \rho \leq 1 \quad (2)$$

This model resembles the Markov first-order autoregressive model. If ρ = 1, becomes a Random Walk Model (RWM) (without drift). If ρ is in fact 1, we face what is known as the unit root problem, that is, a situation of nonstationarity. If, however, $|\rho| \leq 1$, that is if the absolute value of ρ is less than one, then it can be shown that the time series Y_t is stationary in the sense we have defined it. In practice, then, it is important to find out if a time series possesses a unit root (Gujarati, 2004). Results obtained from unit root tests are presented in Table 2 and 3.

The lag value in ADF models are picked in accordance with AIC criteria. Both in two tables values are reflected as if, between paranthesis the test statistics values, values marked with (*) test statistics' probability value and finally numbers between the square brackets optimum laglevel for every test. Accordingly, given MacKinnon critical values under the tables for variables are not stationary both fixed and trend, and fixed and both not fixed and not trend. All variables as seen in the fourth row have become stationary series with their first differ-ences. As one can see from the results in the table all of our variables have become stationary in their first difference. There in after, all tests have been examined with stationary variables. I(0) and I(1) form graphics of variables are shown in Figure 2.

A critical element in the specification of VAR models is the determination of the lag length of the VAR. The importance of lag length determination is demonstrated by Braun and Mittnik (1993) who show that estimates of a VAR whose lag length differs from the true lag length are inconsistent as are the impulse response functions and variance decompositions derived from the estimated VAR (Ozcicek and Douglas, 1999). For selection of the lag length of the VAR, we consider the VAR Lag Order Selection Criteria. Obtained results are as shown in Table 4.

Variables must be stationary as they should be indivually and also as whole. Therefore, inverse roots of the AR characteristic polynomial's should be examined.

Table 2. Augmented Dickey- Fuller (ADF) test.

Variable	ADF (Intercept)	ADF (Trend and intercept)	ADF (None)	ADF stationary series	ADF stationary level
Infedrate	(0.316155) 0.9183* [3]	(-1.210863) 0.9038* [3]	(0.714449) 0.4056* [3]	(4.485041) 0.0003* [2]	I(1)
Infohf	(1.694508) 0.4318* [1]	(-1.483692) 0.8307* [1]	(2.032527) 0.9899* [1]	(8.162819) 0.0000* [0]	I(1)
lnm2	(1.504963) 0.5283* [2]	(-2.375994) 0.3904* [2]	(4.399679) 1.0000* [2]	(5.153254) 0.0000* [1]	I(1)
Lntbond_10	(2.532002) 0.1102* [1]	(-3.756723) 0.0219* [1]	(1.247038) 0.1946* [1]	(9.756374) 0.0000* [0]	I(1)

MacKinnon critical values (for 1%): 1st row: -3.478911, 2nd row: -4.026942, 3rd row: -2.582076, 4th row: -3.478911

Table 3. Determination of effective lag level.

Lag	LogL	LR	FPE	AIC	SC	HQ
0	1150.223	NA	2.95e-13	-17.49959	-17.41180	-17.46392
1	1210.528	116.0050	1.50e-13	-18.17599	17.73703*	-17.99763
2	1240.039	54.96759	1.22e-13	-18.38227	-17.59214	18.06121*
3	1257.472	31.40639*	1.20e-13*	18.40415*	-17.26286	-17.94039
4	1267.058	16.68424	1.33e-13	-18.30623	-16.81376	-17.69978
5	1278.993	20.04228	1.42e-13	-18.24416	-16.40052	-17.49501
6	1285.153	9.969977	1.66e-13	-18.09394	-15.89914	-17.20209
7	1299.430	22.23269	1.72e-13	-18.06764	-15.52166	-17.03309
8	1311.892	18.64550	1.85e-13	-18.01362	-15.11648	-16.83638

As can be seen from Figure 3, the AR characteristic polynomial's inverse roots' dispersion in the circle shows the model does not have a problem in terms of stationary. As a consequence of that, it validates VAR model in a consistent structure.

Granger causality test

Let's approach to a VAR model as the following

$$y_t = \delta_0 + \alpha_1 y_{t-1} + \gamma_1 z_{t-1} + \alpha_2 y_{t-2} + \gamma_2 z_{t-2} + \ldots \quad (3)$$

This equation allows us to test whether, after controlling for past y, past z help to forecast y_t. Generally, we say that z Granger causes y if

$$E(y_t | I_{t-1}) \neq E(y_t | J_{t-1}) \quad (4)$$

where I_{t-1} contains past information on y and z, and J_{t-1} contains only information on past y. When (4) holds, past z is useful, in addition to past y, for predicting y_t. The term "causes" in "Granger causes" should be interpreted with caution. The only sense in which z "causes" y is given in (4). In particular, it has nothing to say about contemporaneous causality between y and z, so it does not allow us to determine whether z_t is an exogenous or endogenous variable in an equation relating y_t to z_t (Wooldridge, 2002).

Interaction trend

Granger causality test informs about the interactions' direction of variables on the VAR model. Based on the results, graphics on the interactions' direction are presented as shown in Figure 4. On the graphics, it can be seen that changes in hedge funds' performance has an effect on Fed interest rate, 10 year-term treasury bond and M2 monetary supply. Theoretically, although it is not easy to say hedge funds' performance affects these three variables, on the grounds of results we can tell hedge funds have effects on Fed's and other policy-makers' decisions by accepting hedge funds' managers, as of the

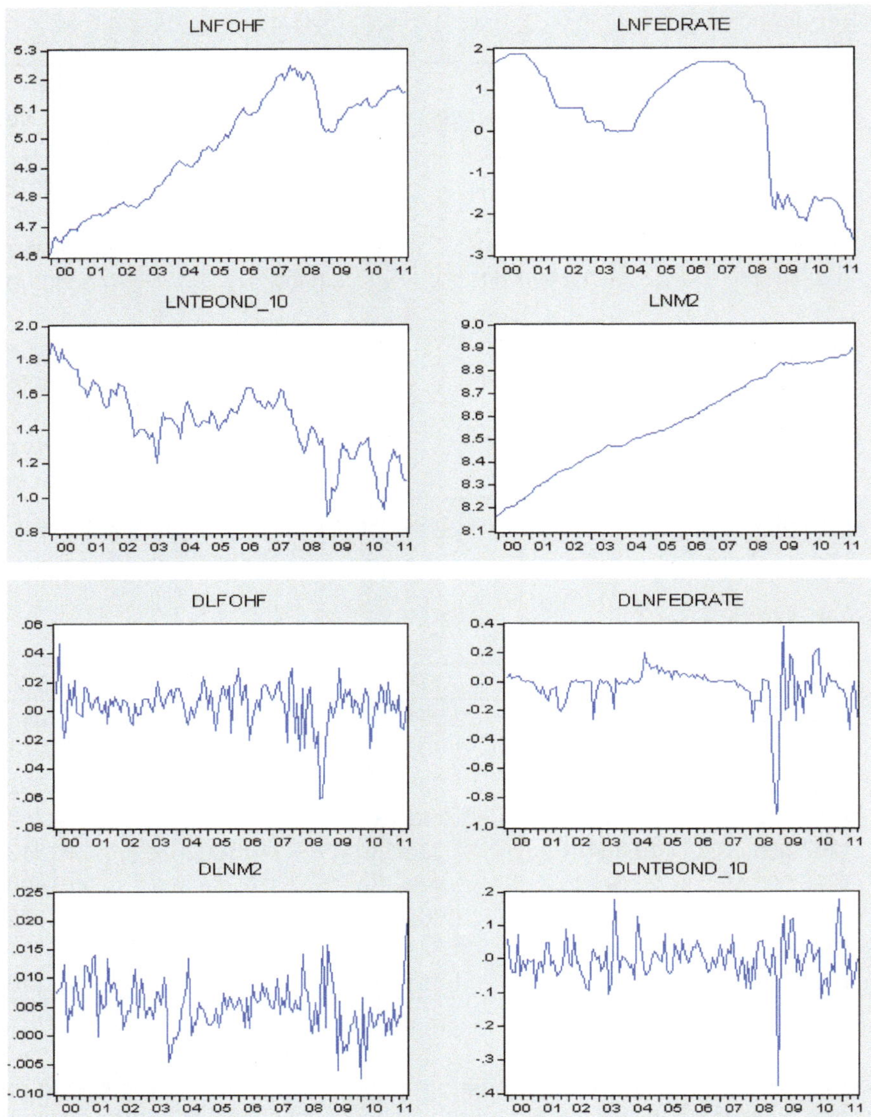

Figure 2. I(0) and I(1) series graphs.

Table 4. Granger causality table.

Null hypothesis	FStatistic	Probability
DLNFEDRATE does not Granger cause DLNFOHF	0.24001	0.86830
DLNFOHF does not Granger cause DLNFEDRATE	11.1330	1.5E-06
DLNM2 does not Granger cause DLNFOHF	0.68483	0.56288
DLNFOHF does not Granger cause DLNM2	3.64523	0.01451
DLNTBOND_10 does not Granger cause DLNFOHF	0.13842	0.93688
DLNFOHF does not Granger cause DLNTBOND_10	6.65055	0.00033
DLNM2 does not Granger cause DLNFEDRATE	0.91971	0.43338
DLNFEDRATE does not Granger cause DLNM2	2.22602	0.08825
DLNTBOND_10 does not Granger cause DLNFEDRATE	2.9 1228	0.03696
DLNFEDRATE does not Granger cause DLNTBOND_10	2.08266	0.10569
DLNTBOND_10 does not Granger cause DLNM2	8.64022	2.9E-05
DLNM2 does not Granger cause DLNTBOND_10	1.23751	0.29886

Model's Cholesky ranking based on the data gathered from Granger causality test is: fohffedrate tbond_10 m2.

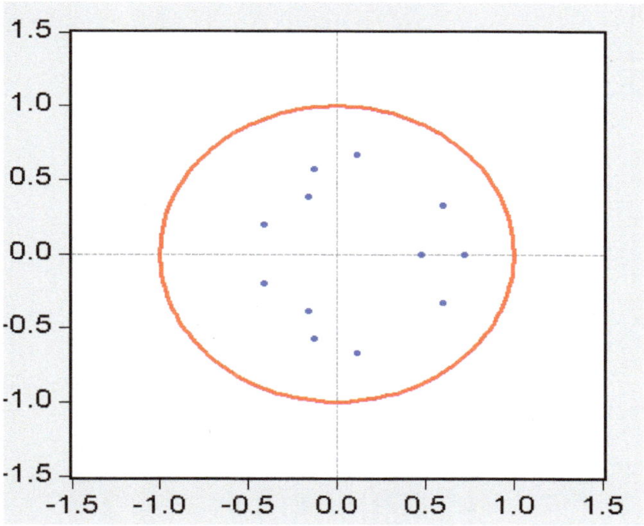

Figure 3. Inverse roots of AR characteristic polynomial. One common use of vector autoregressions is to test the hypothesis that one or more of the variables in a VAR do not "Granger cause" the others.

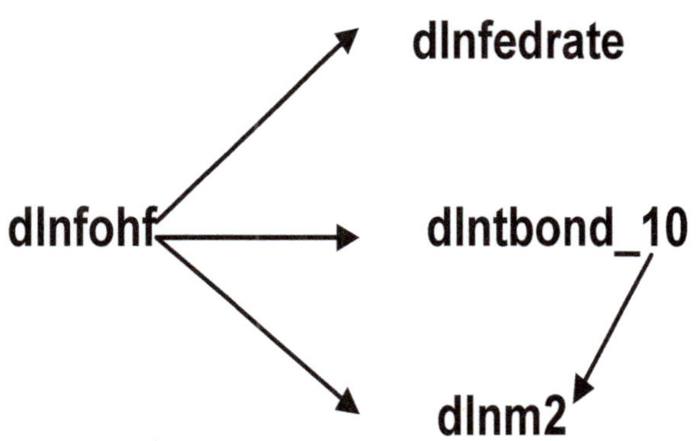

Figure 4. Interaction trend graph.

markets' most professional players,risk-return performance is an important indicator on the market's general trend.

Block F-tests and an examination of causality in a VAR will suggest which of the variables in the model have statistically significant impacts on the future values of each of the variables in the system. But F-test results will not, by construction, be able to explain the sign of the relationship or how long these effects require to take place. Therefore, throughout performing financial evaluations on the model, model's residulas considering impulse responses analysis and variance decomposition analysis is benefited instead of interpreting parameters of model. Variance decompositions determine how much of the s-step-ahead forecast error variance of a given variable is explained by innovations to each explanatory variable for s = 1, 2, . . . Impulse responses trace out the responsiveness of the dependent variables in the VAR to shocks each of the variables (Brooks, 2008).

As is shown in Table 5, all changes in DLNFOHF variable is explained by its own shocks; more details of variance decomposition analysis are given in appendix. 34% of variance of estimation error in DLNFEDRATE variable is explained by DLNFOHF variable; variance fluctation in DLNTBOND_10 and DLNM2 variables explained by other variables in both long and short term which remains in low level.

Results obtained in impulse-responses analysis confirm the ones gathered in variance decomposition. As shown in Figure 5, in the first row, the most important reaction happens to DLNFEDRATE variable in the face of a standart deviation shock to DLNFOFH variable. A decrease is observed after increases in DLNFEDRATE variable in every two-month period. It can be said that the effect of the shock is totally removed on the tenth month. Another attention-grabbing interaction is the volatility occuring in DLNFEDRATE variable when a standart deviation shock is given to DLNTBOND_10 variable. We observed that DLNM2 variable has no effect on other parameters. In respect of existing variables, DLNM2 is an exogenous variable.

Conclusion

As previously mentioned in our study's literature review, different results were obtained from analysis by several researchers on the performance and interaction of hedge funds and other financial instruments. Due to the difficulty encountered during the research period and the high volatility in the global financial system, a chaotic stage was created. Generally, Fed's changes in policy interest cause incidences in other countries' money and capital markets. Stock exchanges react to these changes on the instant. The interactions' in the parities volatility definitely creates return opportunities for investors like hedge funds. In our study, instead of Fed policy interest rate, we exercised effective Fed interest rates used by banks lending to each other and in pricing daily developments much faster.

Our study's results reveal Fed interest rate, the United States' M2 monetary supply and 10 year-term Treasury Bonds' returns are affected by the global hedge funds' performances. Of course, the point to notice is the variable we used as the global hedge fund performance is an index formed by the result of the most professional investors' positions' returns and losses. Over here, opened and closed positions guide the markets in the light of returns or losses. A change in the short-term affects the Fed's effective interest rates and the rates in turn change dependently in long-term treasury bonds as a result of the market players' positions. Fed serves the

Table 5. Variance decomposition.

Period	DLNFOHF	DLNFEDRATE	DLNTBOND_10	DLNM2
1	100.0000	0.000000	0.000000	0.000000
10	97.24690	0.522814	1.021505	1.208785
1	2.116337	97.88366	0.000000	0.000000
10	33.95163	59.64281	5.206976	1.198583
1	3.319119	2.547136	94.13374	0.000000
10	16.24260	4.631515	77.20123	1.924654
1	2.223214	4.241441	1.812861	91.72248
10	15.17407	6.341919	14.14115	64.34286

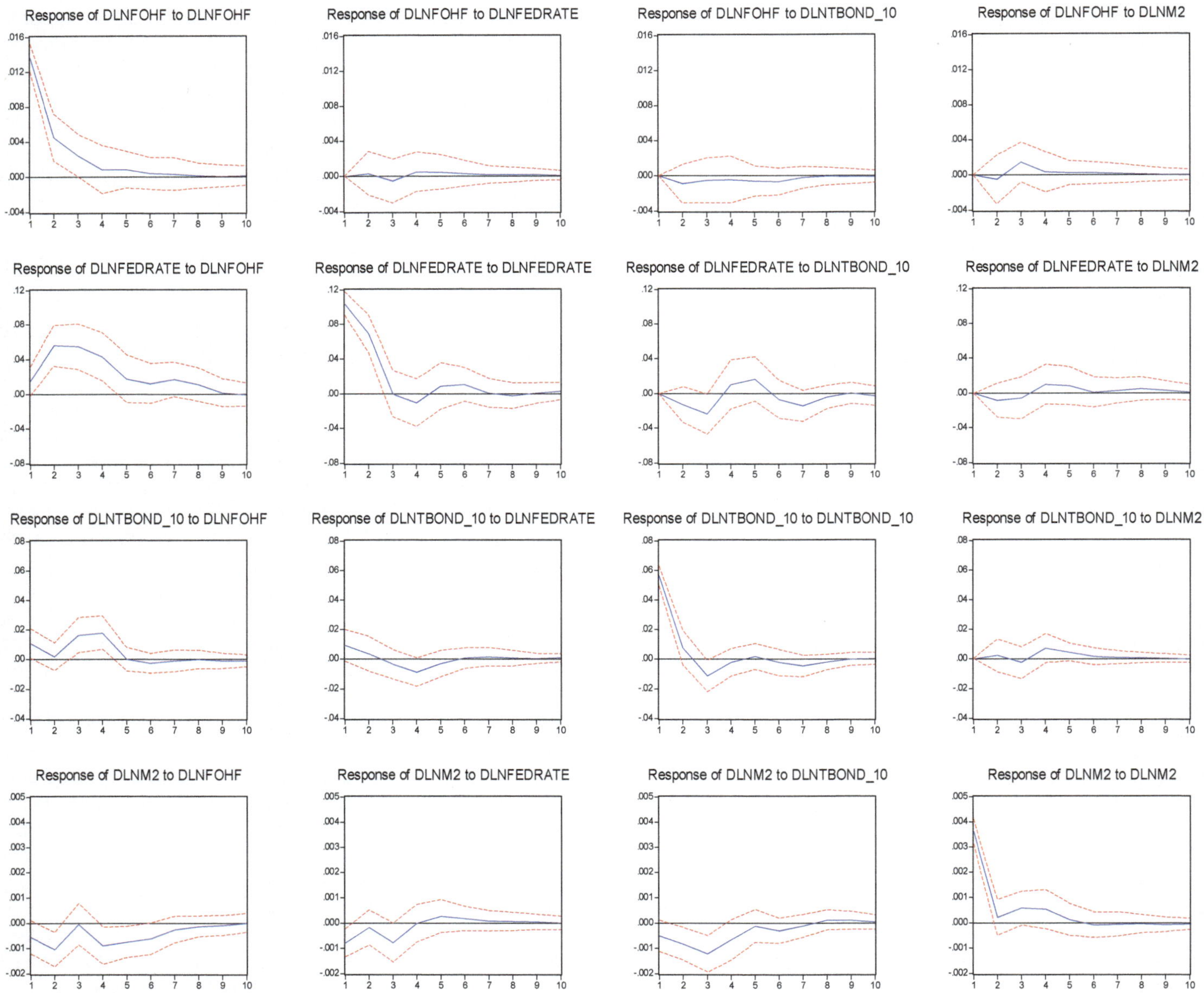

Figure 5. Impulse responses analysis (Response to Cholesky One S.D. Innovations ± 2 S.E.).

purpose of liquidity within the frame of its goals in inflation, unemployement and economic growth. As a consequence within both the U.S.A and the global market frame, hedge fund indices are vulnerability reflecting index.

REFERENCES

Ackermann C, McEnally R, Ravenscraft D (1999). The Performance of Hedge Funds: Risk, Return, and Incentives. J. Financ., 54(3): 833-874. doi:10.1111/0022-1082.00129.

Adrian T (2007). Measuring Risk in the Hedge Fund Sector. Current Issues In Economics and Finance, 13(3): 2-7.

Agarwal V, Naik N Y(2003): Risks and Portfolio Decisions Involving Hedge Funds. Rev. Financial Stud., 17(1): 63-98. doi:10.1093/rfs/hhg044.

Beckers SE, Curds R, Weinberger S (2007). Funds of Hedge Funds Take the Wrong Risks. J. Portf. Manag., 33(3): 108-121. doi:10.3905/jpm.2007.684758.

Bouges JC (2004). Alternative Hedge Fund Product Performance: The Impact of Regulation on Performance. J. Altern. Investments, 7(3): 70-80. doi:10.3905/jai.2004.461459.

Brooks C (2008). Introductory Econometrics for Finance, Second Edition, Cambridge University Press.

Brown SJ, Goetzmann WN (2003). Hedge Funds with Style. J. Portfolio Manag., 29(3): 101-112. doi:10.3905/jpm.2003.319877.

Brunel JLP (2007). Are Hedge Fund Strategies Just About Leverage? J. Wealth Manag., 10(3): 40-51. doi:10.3905/jwm.2007.698895.

Cassar G, Gerakos J (2010). Determinants of Hedge Fund Internal Controls and Fees. Account. Rev., 85(6): 1887-1919. doi:10.2308/accr.2010.85.6.1887.

Cerrato M, Iannelli A (2006). Testing For Random Walk and Structural Breaks in Hedge Funds Returns. Int. J. Theor. Appl. Financ., 9(3): 341-358.

Chapman J (2010). Phasing out hedge funds. Public Policy Res., 17(1): 36-41. doi:10.1111/j.1744-540X.2010.00599.x

Christory C, Daul S, Giraud JR (2006). Quantification of Hedge Fund Default Risk. J. Alternative Investments, 9(2): 71-86. doi:10.3905/jai.2006.655938.

Clark KA, Winkelmann K (2004). Active Risk Budgeting In Action: Understanding Hedge Fund Performance. J. Alternative Investments, 7(3): 35-46.doi:10.3905/jai.2004.461456.

Darius D, Ilhan A, Mulvey J, Simsek K, Sircar R (2002). Trend-following hedge funds and multi-period asset allocation. Quant. Financ., 2(5): 354-361. doi:10.1088/1469-7688/2/5/304.

Davidson R, Mackinnon JG (1999). Econometric Theory and Methods. Oxford University Press, UK.

Ding B, Shawky H (2007). The Performance of Hedge Fund Strategies and the Asymmetry of Return Distributions. Eur. Financial Manag., 13(2): 309-331. doi:10.1111/j.1468-036X.2006.00356.x.

Do V, Faff R, Veeraraghavan M (2009). Do Australian hedge fund managers possess timing abilities? Appl. Financial Econ., 19(1): 27-38. doi:10.1080/09603100701735987.

Donaldson T (2008). Hedge Funds Ethics. Bus. Ethics Q., 18(3): 405-416.

Dopfel FE (2005). How Hedge Funds Fit. J. Portfolio Manag., 31(4): 9-20. doi:10.3905/jpm.2005.570144.

Dupleich R, Giamouridis D, Mesomeris S, Noorizadeh N (2010). Unbundling Common Style Exposures, Time Variance and Style Timing of Hedge Fund Beta. J. Asset Manag., 11(1): 19-30. doi:10.1057/jam.2010.2.

Earle JE (2010). Compensating Hedge Fund Managers with Stock Options: A New Path to Alignment of Interests with Investors. Benefits Law J., 23(3): 80-94.

Eberlein E, Madan D B (2009): Hedge Fund Performance: Sources and Measures. Int. J. Theoretical Applied Financ., 12(03): 267-282. doi:10.1142/S0219024909005282.

Fang V, Phoon KF, Xiang VYD (2008). A Heuristic Approach to Asian Hedge Fund Allocation. J. Wealth Manag., 10(4): 42-52. doi:10.3905/jwm.2008.701850.

Frumkin D, Vandegrift D (2009). The Effect of Size, Age, Beta and Disclosure Requirements On Hedge Fund Performance. J. Derivatives Hedge Funds, 15(3): 241-251. doi:10.1057/jdhf.2009.12

Fung WKH, Hsieh DA (2006). Hedge Funds: An Industry in Its Adolescence. Econ. Rev., (4): 1-35.

Fuss R, Kaiser DG, Adams Z (2007). Value at risk, GARCH modelling and the forecasting of hedge fund return volatility. J. Derivatives, 13(1): 2-25. doi:10.1057/palgrave.dutr.1850048.

Gibson R, Gyger S (2007). The Style Consistency of Hedge Funds. Eur. Financial Manag., 13(2): 287-308. doi:10.1111/j.1468-036X.2006.00355.x.

Grecu A, Malkiel BG, Saha A (2007). Why Do Hedge Funds Stop Reporting Performance? J. Portf. Manag., 34(1): 119-126. doi:10.3905/jpm.2007.698041.

Gujarati DN (2004). Basic Econometrics, Fourth Edition, The McGraw−Hill Companies.

Hedges IV JR (2005). Hedge Fund Transparency. Eur. J. Financ., 11(5): 411-417. doi:10.1080/1351847042000286685.

Jones M (2007). Examination of fund age and size and its impact on hedge fund performance. Derivatives Use, Trading Regulation, 12(4): 342-350. doi:10.1057/palgrave.dutr.1850052.

Lee DKC, Lwi S, Phoon KF (2001). An Equitable Structure for Hedge Fund Incentive Fees. J. Altern. Investments, 4(2): 43-48. doi:10.3905/jai.2001.319009.

Li Y, Kazemi H (2007). Conditional Properties of Hedge Funds: Evidence from Daily Returns. Eur. Financial Manag., 13(2): 211-238. doi:10.1111/j.1468-036X.2006.00352.x.

Liang B (1998). On the Performance of Hedge Funds. J. Financ., 54(3): 833-874. doi:10.2139/ssrn.89490.

Liang B (2003). The Accuracy of Hedge Fund Returns. J. Portfolio Manag., 29(3): 111-122. doi:10.3905/jpm.2003.319889.

Lütkepohl H (2003). Vector Autoregressions: A Companion to Theoretical Econometrics, Blackwell Publishing, USA.

Malkiel BG, Saha A (2005). Hedge Funds: Risk and Return. Financial Anal. J., 61(6): 80-88. doi:10.2469/faj.v61.n6.2775.

Manser S, Schmid MM (2009). The performance persistence of equity long/short hedge funds. J. Deriv. Hedge Funds, 15(1): 51-69. doi:10.1057/jdhf.2008.28.

Maxam CL, Nikbakht E, Petrova M, Spieler AC (2004). Manager Characteristics and Hedge Fund Performance. J. Appl. Financ., 16(2): 57-70.

Ozcicek O, McMillin WD (1999). Lag Length Selection in Vector Autoregressive Models: Symmetric and Asymmetric Lags, Applied Economics, Taylor Francis J., 31(4): 517-24.

Peltomaki J (2009). The Asymmetric Impact of Volatility Risk on Hedge Fund Returns. J. Appl. Financ., 17(1): 88-95.

Pätäri EJ, Tolvanen J (2009). Chasing performance persistence of hedge funds – Comparative analysis of evaluation techniques. J. Deriv. Hedge Funds, 15(3): 223-240. doi:10.1057/jdhf.2009.11

Racicot F-É, Théoret R (2007). The beta puzzle revisited: A panel study of hedge fund returns. J. Derivatives Hedge Funds, 13(2): 125-146. doi:10.1057/palgrave.jdhf.1850062.

Tee K-H (2009). Is active currency management effective for international equity portfolios involving managed futures and hedge funds?J. Derivatives Hedge Funds, 15(2): 137-148. doi:10.1057/jdhf.2009.7.

Teo M (2009). The Geography of Hedge Funds. Rev. Financial Stud., 22(9): 3531-3561. doi:10.1093/rfs/hhp007.

Tsay RS (2005). Analysis of Financial Time Series, Second Edition, John Wiley & Sons, New Jersey.

Wooldridge J (2002). Introductory Econometrics: A Modern Approach, Second Edition, South-Western College Publishing.

Appendix. Variance decomposition (All periods).

Period	DLNFOHF	DLNFEDRATE	DLNTBOND_10	DLNM2
1	100.0000	0.000000	0.000000	0.000000
2	99.42357	0.052746	0.404381	0.119308
3	98.17373	0.190202	0.528048	1.108017
4	97.91381	0.314313	0.617729	1.154152
5	97.61369	0.423583	0.787755	1.174968
6	97.33868	0.472241	0.993605	1.195468
7	97.29141	0.488378	1.015231	1.204977
8	97.27216	0.502438	1.016897	1.208509
9	97.25516	0.516945	1.019147	1.208752
10	97.24690	0.522814	1.021505	1.208785
1	2.116337	97.88366	0.000000	0.000000
2	1.748964	81.30543	0.849708	0.355229
3	2.781920	68.53818	3.211359	0.431257
4	3.280326	63.02231	3.368499	0.805932
5	3.309041	61.50531	4.343448	1.060830
6	3.326994	61.20719	4.469808	1.053069
7	3.373445	60.03981	5.162265	1.063472
8	3.398187	59.67213	5.190553	1.155441
9	3.397271	59.64220	5.189279	1.195816
10	3.395163	59.64281	5.206976	1.198583
1	3.319119	2.547136	94.13374	0.000000
2	3.322913	2.841190	93.69294	0.142960
3	9.858333	2.864814	86.95776	0.319093
4	1.625555	4.417034	77.86835	1.459068
5	1.613968	4.616946	77.36859	1.874783
6	1.626204	4.606143	77.21138	1.920431
7	1.619515	4.625224	77.26029	1.919337
8	1.617836	4.625326	77.27171	1.924606
9	1.621232	4.624312	77.23837	1.924995
10	1.624260	4.631515	77.21230	1.924654
1	2.223214	4.241441	1.812861	91.12248
2	8.821149	3.933925	5.852948	81.39198
3	7.678583	6.657326	13.11716	72.54693
4	11.08961	6.151441	14.31436	68.44459
5	13.40731	6.320579	13.92918	66.34292
6	14.85402	6.321914	14.05108	64.77298
7	15.09895	6.331547	14.04922	64.52028
8	15.15316	6.340633	14.09605	64.41015
9	15.17673	6.342596	14.13515	64.34552
10	15.17407	6.341919	14.14115	64.34286

6

Training and utilization of staff and job performance in post primary education board, in North Senatorial District of Delta State, Nigeria

E. D. Nakpodia

Department of Educational Administration and Policy Studies, Delta State University, Abraka, Nigeria.
E-mail: edwardnakpodia@yahoo.com.

This is an empirical study which examined the relevance of training and utilization of staff for job performance in Post Primary Education Board, in North Senatorial District of Delta State, Nigeria. To guide this study, three null hypotheses were formulated. The design of the study was survey. The sample of the study was 20 (13.24%) schools / offices and 200 (3.5%) staff, drawn from 5,734 staff of Post Primary Education Board and 153 public schools / offices, through stratified sampling technique. The major instrument used for data collection was a questionnaire which was validated and found reliable at 0.75 reliability coefficient. The results revealed that there is a high significant difference between the performance of NCE graduates and University graduates; the work reveals that there is a significant difference between full-time and part-time graduates. Also, the study exposed that there is significant difference between deployment of staff according to sex

Key words: Training, utilization, staff, job performance, post primary education board, Nigeria.

INTRODUCTION

The Post Primary Education Board and the public schools have become so complex that the administration cannot be left in the hands of those who have no formal training. The educational system needs those who can harness the human, physical and materials resources available to achieve the set objectives. Hence, there is a widespread acceptance of the argument that more training needs to be provided, but there is a lack of enthusiasm to make the provision. The significance of this for personnel managers is substantial. Training and staff utilization is a major feature of the personnel function and makes up one third of the course for professional membership of any establishment, yet apathy towards training by other managers causes personnel specialist themselves to lose interest and to advocate the need for training of staff with insufficient vigour.

It has been suggested that the most significant features of employment package offered by recruiters to new graduates is the extent of training and utilization of staff that is promised in the offer. There is no obvious need to offer training in order to recruit the next people; and this will become more acute as the effect of the single Nigerian market develops.

In fact, training is not, however, a separate authority that can be limited to training school. It must be closely connected with the work places of those that are to be trained. Hence, a saying that:

"With the increasing range both of areas in which training is needed and of ways in which this training can be provided, specialists have a major role to play."

However, they are unlikely to be playing that role effectively if they are operating in isolation from the line managers of those trained.

The training officer also has to maintain contacts with potential external providers of training. Training is the area of personnel work in which there is the greatest use of consultants and other external providers. These range from colleges, universities, commercial consultants, government agencies, to suppliers of do-it-yourself training facilities, like computer-based training. Figure 1 shows the training officer's basic network of contacts.

There are a number of advantages to be drawn on outside sources for training, as it provides a range of

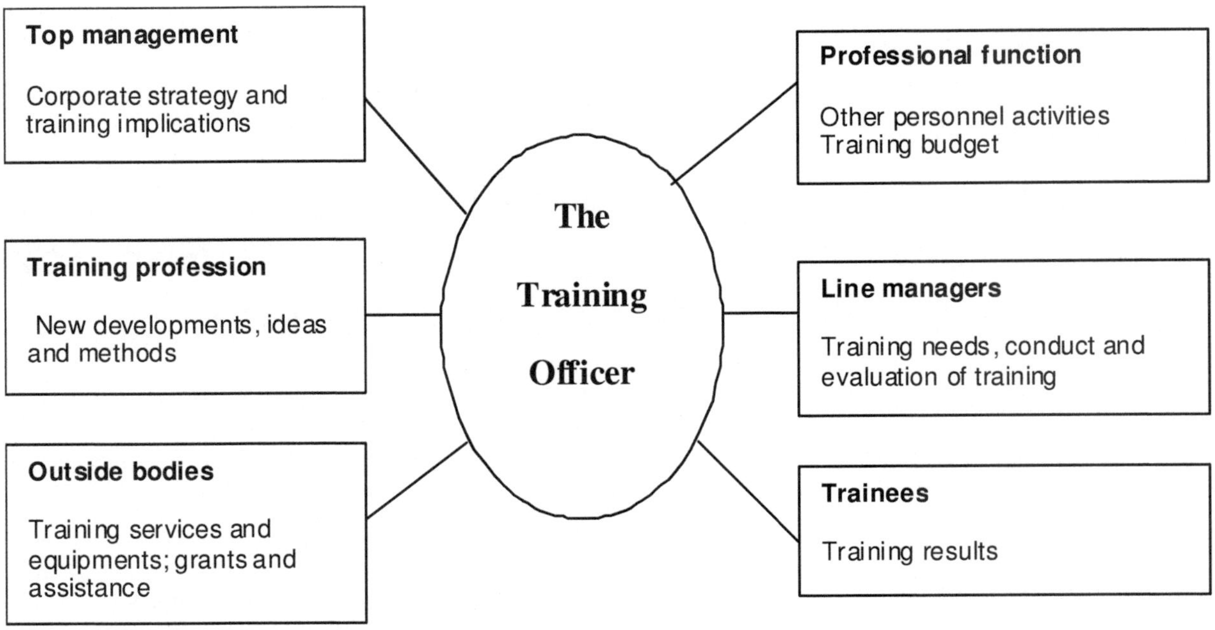

Figure 1. The training officer's network.

skills that very few organizations can maintain in-house, and means that the commissioner of training need only think of what is needed to provide good training, without any concern about keeping trainers occupied. It also provides the opportunity of saving in costs overall as there are not the continuing month-by-month employment costs of training personnel.

Furthermore, there is the tendency for the external supplier to provide nothing but courses even though the training need might be better served by some other strategy, and are external supplier will be tempted to diagnose a problem that needs a training solution rather than a different type of solution

In fact, the success of any organization depends on the quality and quantity of its factors of production human and materials resources. Of all the factors, the human resources appear to be the most important because, according to the human resource theorists, without human effort all other factors are inept. For instance, land, machines and money cannot be useful except they are managed and coordinated by human resource. Itedjere (1995) believes that the quality and efficiency of staff that perform functions necessary for the achievement of organizational goals and objectives determine the success of such an organization.

The quality and efficiency of staff are the functions of the level of training and utilization of such staff. The staff of a system may become obsolete if they do not update themselves with new knowledge, skills, and new work methods for the progress of the organization in which they work. The entire system may become rustic and obsolete also, if it lacks, the systematic means of continually developing and renewing the systems' capabilities. Nakpodia (2006) reported that "engineer's knowledge of his field is cut into half every ten years because of the advancement of the field unless he or she continues to work". Training is a planned programme of both staff and the system.

According to Peretomode and Peretomode (2001), training is a planned organizational efforts concerned with helping an employee to acquire specific and immediately useable skills, knowledge, concepts, attitudes and behaviours to enable him or her perform more efficiently and effectively on his present job.

Also, training is a specialized process through which one learns to perform directly tasks of varying complexities and acquires expected job behaviours, Obadan (2000) opined that training personnel cannot be said to be effective or even be of any importance unless the trained personnel are utilized to the advantage of the individual in the system.

In addition, utilization is development of staff to his area of specialization. If a staff is not developed in his or her area of specialization, he will not be efficient or effective in job performance. So, it is necessary to ensure that the right peg is in the right hole.

The Delta State Post Primary Education Board recognizes the importance of training and utilization in the achievement of its goals, hence, over the years a good amount of its budget has been invested in staff training.

Statement of the problems

A look to any established educational institution will confirm that various resources are usually allocated to schools. Even though the resources allocated may vary depending on the system, location and population of the school, resources are usually allocated to schools and their different management depends on training and institution, especially on the human aspect. The human resource includes the staffing of teachers, the arrangement of non-teaching staff to existing position and role of the principal. Each of these classes of people has roles to play in the running of the school. The proper utilization of each of these people becomes very necessary in order to ensure school effectiveness. This is because effectiveness can be classified as the harmonization between performance and the set of objectives which cannot be of value judgment, reveal what is causing the problem or failure within the system in terms of training and utilization of the staff for effective job performance.

Many organizations have increased their quality training because of the need for product to meet high standard in customer satisfaction.

The general staff shift towards a market orientation in some organizations has partly replaced the external stimulus that was previously provided by training board. Although, that type of stimulus carries with it the inevitable concern with the immediate and short term and only a limited range of training objectives can be quickly satisfied.

Furthermore, an increase in training is usually the fruit of success rather than its cause; although continue training may be seen as a essential to sustaining that success as it is said that:

"High performances of jobs attracts as it is likely to train, and train twice as many employees as low performance business, and high performance jobs increase their training by 25% over the last five years, with low performance reducing their training by 20% (Sloman, 1989)."

The Post Primary Education Board is an office charged with the responsibilities of training, and utilizing their trained staff in their areas of specialization in the various secondary schools in the state.

This office sees that its staff which are secondary school teachers and non-teaching staff are trained through seminars, conferences and workshops. Staffs are also granted study leave with or without pay for programmes in higher institutions such as in-services training, sandwich, weekend, part-time and regular programmes.

Some of these trainings are done through the best person for the job and training him thoroughly in the best tasks and procedure to be followed and giving him jobs for which he is best suited physically as well as intellectually.

The researcher tries to find out the extent to which training affects the job performance of staff through proper utilization in secondary schools in Delta State, Nigeria.

Research hypotheses

The following null hypotheses were formulated to guide the study:

1. There is no significant difference between NCE graduates and university graduates in their job performance in Post Primary Education Board.
2. There is no significant difference between the staff trained under full-time and part-time programmes in their job performance in Post Primary Education Board.
3. There is no significant difference between male and female staff trained in their job performance in Post Primary Education Board.

LITERATURE REVIEW

Training and utilization of staff

Training as defined by Peretomode et al. (2001) is the planned organizational efforts or activities conceived with helping an employee acquire specific and immediately usable skills, knowledge, concepts, attitude and behaviours to enable him or her perform more efficiently and effectively on his present job.

Also, Obadan (2000) saw training as "a specialized process through which one learns to perform direct tasks of varying complexity and acquire expected job behaviours"

These definitions implies that training is an organized procedure by which people learn and acquire knowledge and skills for a definite purpose; and a continual process of helping employees to perform at a high level (Donnelly, 1995).

Training is a process of increasing human efficiency through which people are offered the opportunity to acquire new skills and current knowledge required in carrying out various specialized tasks in their place of work.

In fact, training is defined as the teaching of vocational or practical that relate to specific skills.

Although training of personnel is important but training without utilization of trained staff is a waste because without the application of acquired skills to the task that is to be performed, there cannot be progress or advancement (Nwagwu, 1992).

Hence, Obadan (2000) sees utilization as "useful engagement of staff in his area of specialization for effectiveness and efficiency". To him, utilization as an active involvement of people in their area of specialization through out the organization; and that whatever basket of skills knowledge, ability and experience is available, it is only a part of the larger system and requires a deliberate alignment of effective human utilization to achieve an effective goal.

Utilization of Staff

Most NCE and first degree holders are employed as secondary school teachers. Holders of post graduate degrees such as M.Ed., M.Phil. and Ph.D. are appointed as lecturers in tertiary educational institutions such as colleges of education and universities. Some educations are employed in Local Government Education Authorities, Teaching Service Commission, University Registries, and so on.

Banks also employ a number of graduates of educational management. Such people are utilized in personnel, training and development, etc. A number trained education managers have established private consultancy outfits providing valuable service to educational organizations. Holders of post graduate degrees can also tap job opportunities international agencies such UNESCO, UNICEF, World Bank, African Development Bank and so on. Lectureship appointments in universities abroad are also available holders of Ph.D. in education management. One potential avenue of utilizing education managers is their participation in the Technical aid Corps programme. Under this programme, Nigerian professional are posed to some African countries to assist them in their national development efforts, since shortage of human capital is a major problem of development in most African countries. Trained Nigerian education managers can assist such African countries in the management of their education systems to achieve national development objectives.

One of the major problems of utilizing trained education managers is the recruitment into principalship based on years of teaching experience. Most graduates of educational administration are appointed as classroom teachers. Their full potentials are therefore not harnessed in this circumstance. When a teaching subject is not indicated on the certificate, graduates find it difficult to get teaching appointment. As suggested earlier, there is the need to place less emphasis on the undergraduate programme.

When graduates of educational management are to be appointed as supervisors in Local Government Education Authorities, teaching experience may still be required in spite of their professional training in instructional supervision. One will recommend that selection interview should be conducted when such supervisors are to be employed. The abilities of candidates can be determined at this stage.

Features of job performance

Job performance is a commonly used, yet poorly defined concept in industrial and organizational psychology, the branch of psychology that deals with the work place. It is most commonly refers to whether a person performs his/her job well. Despite the confusion over how it should be exactly defined, performance is an extremely important criterion that relates to organizational outcomes and success. Coming from the psychological perspective, Campbell (1990) describes job performance as an individual level variable. That is, performance is something a single person does. This differentiates it from more encompassing constructs such as organizational performance and national performance which are higher level variables.

Performance is a multidimensional phenomenon whose elements include effectiveness, efficiency, economy, productivity, quality and behaviour. (Obadan, 1999). The sub-concepts of job performance are explained as follows:

1. Effectiveness measure the extent to which an employee achieve the output requirements of his position, with the emphasis not so much an "how" it is achieved but on organization or employee is therefore effective when the results attained are the same as those initially intended.
2. Efficiency is a measure of how well resources are being used to produce output or result. It is a comparison of actual achievement during a given period.
3. Quality –refer to the desired characteristics of the achieved output or result. These could be timeliness, reliability, accuracy frequency accessibility, convenience, mating time and response time.

Assessing organizational or school performance is, however, a particular challenge for organizations such as Post Primary Education Board where human resources are used for impacting knowledge on students. In such a case, all elements of performance are requiring; and having known the various elements should be evaluated to achieve the required goals and objectives of the system.

Another key feature of job performance is that it has to be goal relevant. Performance must be directed towards organizational goals that are relevant to the job or role. Therefore, performance does not include activities where effort is expended towards achieving peripheral goals. For example, the efforts put toward the goal of getting to work in the shortest amount of time, is not performance, except when it is concerned with avoiding lateness. Despite the emphasis on defining and predicting job performance, it is not a single unified construct. There are vastly many jobs each with different performance standards. Therefore, job performance is conceptualized as a multidimensional construct consisting of more than one kind of behaviour. Campbell (1990) proposed an eight factor model of performance existent (to a greater or lesser extent) across all jobs:

1. The first factor is task specific behaviours which include those behaviours that an individual undertakes as part of a job. They are the core substantive tasks that

delineate one job from another.

2. On the other hand, non-task specific behaviours, the second factor, are those behaviours which an individual is required to undertake which do not pertain only to a particular job. Returning to the sales person, an example of a task specific behaviour would be showing a product to a potential customer. A non-task specific behaviour would be showing a product to a potential customer. A non-task specific behaviour or a sales person might be training new staff members.

3. Written and oral communication tasks refer to activities where the incumbent is evaluated, not on the content of a message necessarily, but on the adeptness with which they deliver the communication. Employees need to make formal and informal oral and written presentations to various audiences in many different jobs in the work force.

4. An individual's performance can also be assessed in terms of effort, either day to day, or when there are extraordinary circumstances. This factor reflects the degree to which people commit themselves to job tasks.

5. The performance domain might also include an aspect of personal discipline. Individuals would be expected to be in good standing with the law, not abuse alcohol, etc.

6. In jobs where people work closely or are highly interdependent, performance may include the degree to which a person helps out the groups and his or her colleagues. This might include acting as a good role model, coaching, giving advice or helping to maintain group goals.

7. Many good jobs also have a supervisory or leadership component. The individual will be relied upon to undertake many of the things delineated under the previous factor and in addition will be responsible for meting out rewards and punishments. These aspects of performance happen in a face to face manner.

8. Managerial and administrative performance entails those aspects of a job which serve the group or organization but do not involve direct supervision. A managerial task would be setting an organizational goal or responding to external stimuli to assist a group in achieving its goals. In addition, a manager might be responsible for monitoring group and individual progress towards goals and monitoring organizational resources.

NCE graduates and trained University graduates

Among the staff of Post Primary Education Board are graduates with National Certificate in Education (NCE). They are trained specifically for teaching. This is because their main course of study comprises of education courses, since the aim is for them to be specialists in the teaching field.

This certificate is acquired after a period of three years studies. During the programme they are usually sent out on teaching practice for a period of time, exposing them to the job ahead. This class of staff are now restricted to teaching in Junior Secondary School (JSS1-3). They are also teaching the Senior Secondary where there are no enough university graduates teaching to teach in the senior secondary classes and up till today, and still used where there are lack of teachers.

The NCE graduates are made to teach the junior students because; the level of their studies is to be able to teach such students. They do not have in-depth studies of the courses as it is done in the degree programme, that is why their performance should be lower than that of the trained university graduates, who can teach in Junior and Senior secondary schools.

Also, among the staff of Post Primary Education Board are another class of staff, the trained university graduates. This class of staff is trained specifically for teaching and is specialists in the teaching field. They have in-depth study of their subject areas; this certificate is acquired after a period of four years studies. Their main area of specialization is done along with education courses and that qualify them as specialists in their areas as teachers. The trained graduate teachers are qualified to teach in both junior and Senior secondary schools. Infact, it is expected that the subjects will be better taught in all the classes by them because of their in depth knowledge of their courses. The performance of trained graduate teachers can in no way be compared with that of an NCE graduate staff in terms of all standards. They should be regarded as a more qualify staff to NCE graduates and as a result, should perform more effectively and efficiently and assist in the co-ordination of the performance of other staff within the system. Some of these university graduates in the system are not trained.

Forms of staff training programmes in post primary education board

There are various forms of training programmes available to staff of Post Primary Education Board. The staffs in this system are offered training programmes that enables them acquires new and improved skills and knowledge that help them to perform better thereby enhancing their level of productivity.The formal of training programmes as discussed by Oder (1995), are equally applicable to Post Primary Education Board. They are thus explained.

Full- time programmes

Full-time programmes could be for both academic and non-academic staff, they fall into three categories:

I. In-Service Training: This is where by the trainee receive his monthly salaries, the cost of the training (that is, School fees, accommodation fees, books allowances, projected allowances etc). It could be long or short term

courses. Population benefits from such trainings are usually selected by the Board according to laid down criteria to study courses relevant to the system.
II. Study leave with pay: unlike the in-service training, the trainee receives only the monthly salaries for periods approved by the Board. He pays for the cost of training. The beneficiaries are expected to have serviced for a stipulated period of five years before they are granted the offer. They are usually absorbed immediately after the training, but must have studied course relevant to the system.

Part- time programmes

This form of training is becoming one of the comment training programmes for obtaining further qualifications after employment, it is usually done in the evenings after the day's work. It is very popular because it is conversant for the trainees who could not obtain study leave, with or without pay. Non- teaching staff could utilize such programmes because they are not usually free always the long vacation.

Sandwich programme

This form of training has also become one of the commonest programme for obtaining further qualifications after employment, certificates such as OND, NCE, HND, B.Ed, B.Sc, B.A. M.Ed, M.Sc and P.hD, these certificates are relevant to Post Primary Educations Board.

Week-end programmed

This programmes again is a very common training programme among the staff for obtaining higher qualifications after employment to be able to acquire some skills, knowledge and attitudes to be able to meet organizational needs and developed one' self. The relevant certificates are same with those seen above.

Training and utilization of staff by staff

The pattern of development in Post Primary Education Board does not lay emphasis on sex, but gives some consideration to the married women, who in one way or the other should be with their husbands. But development in the system has taken a different shape, since the political reality and other factors, like God fathers and God mothers among the government high officer. These requests have diverted the sense of direction from what the system is set up to achieve to pleasing the individuals. As a result of these alarming requests vacancies are no more considered in relationship with the subjects. The staff are developed indiscriminately especially the female staff, the relevance of neither the subject nor withstanding. There could be ten English teachers in a school for instance; where only five English teachers are needed, same thing applies to almost all the subjects taught in the urban secondary schools, over staffing the urban secondary schools. In this situation, the staff will not have normal periods and as a result they learn about.

Egwunyenga (2000) pointed out that one of the scientific management principals of Frederick Taylor is "a large daily task: A clearly defined daily task should be assigned to every workers". The same principle was explained in another way that each person in the organization high or low, should have a clearly defined daily task that requires a full days effort complete (a large daily task), and should be given such standardized conditions and appliances as will enable him to accomplish his task with certainty (Peretomode, 2001). In a situation where a staff/teacher does not have enough work/period to occupy him/her for the period/school/office hours, then the management has failed in its duties.

In the case, these staff they should be regarded as not being adequately utilized. This drift of staff from the rural secondary schools to urban secondary schools is leaving the rural secondary schools with inadequate staff.

The situation becomes worse especially on the rural schools where among the few staff; some female staff would have to go on maternity leave for a period of three months. The performance of the remaining staff will be ineffective and inefficient as they will be over laboured. And in other to cover the scheme of work will be rushing the students, thereby giving them have measures the average manpower expert should be interested in the utilization of skills by developing them in their areas where the skills are most needed. It is through adequate can be achieved. In deployment, sex should not be considered or favoured, otherwise, the system will not achieve the aim and objective of training and utilization which is aimed at improving job performance.

METHODOLOGY

The design employed for the study was survey. This design was most appropriate and suitable for the study since questionnaire was the major instrument used for collection of data from the sampled schools and offices.

Population of the study

The population of this study includes one hundred and fifty three (153) schools / offices and five thousand seven hundred and thirty-four (5,734) staff of Post Primary Education Board in Delta North Senatorial District as shown in the Table 1.

Table 1. Population size of schools, offices and staff of Post Primary Education Board in the North Senatorial District according to Local Government Area of Delta State, Nigeria.

S/n	Delta North Senatorial District LGAS	Number of Schools and Offices	Number of Staff	% of Schools	% of Staff
1.	Aniocha North	18	547	11.8	9.5
2.	Aniocha South	19	635	12.4	11
3.	Ika North East	21	846	13.7	14.8
4.	Ika South	19	978	12.4	17
5.	Ndokuna East	17	269	11	4.7
6.	Ndokuna West	20	450	13	7.9
7.	Oshimili North	10	462	6.5	8.1
8.	Oshimili South	14	841	9.2	14.7
9.	Ukwuani	12	386	7.8	6.7
10.	PPEB H/Q	1	306	0.7	5.3
11	Zonal Offices	2	14	1.5	0.3
		153	5734	100	100

Source: Post Primary Education Board Department of Planning Research and Statistics, Asaba March, 2009.

Table 2. Size of simple random sampling of school/offices staff in the pubic secondary schools in Delta North Senatorial District of Delta State, Nigeria.

S/n	Delta North Senatorial District LGA	Number of School	Number of sampled School	% Number of sampled School	Number of Staff	Number of sampled Staff	% Number of sampled Staff
1.	Aniocha North	18	2	10	547	20	10
2.	Aniocha South	19	3	15	635	25	12.5
3.	Ika North East	21	3	15	846	35	17.5
4.	Ika South	19	3	15	978	40	20
5.	Ndokwa East	17	1	5	26 9	5	2.5
6.	Ndokwa West	20	2	10	450	10	5
7.	Oshimili North	10	1	5	462	10	5
8.	Oshimili South	14	2	10	841	35	17.5
9.	Ukwuani	12	2	10	386	10	5
10.	PPEB H/Q & Zonal	1	1	5	306	10	5
11	Zonal Offices	2	-	-	-		0
	Total	153	20	100	5734	200	100

Source: Post Primary Education Board Department of Planning Research and Statistics, Asaba March, 2009.

Sample and sampling technique

The researcher sampled 20 schools and offices representing (13.24%) and 200 staff representing 3.5% from the target population of 5,734 staff of Post Primary Education Board and 153 public secondary schools/offices in Delta North Senatorial District through stratified random sampling technique because local government areas trained and untrained staff, including male and female staff strata were considered in the study Table 2.

Instrument

The research instrument titled "training and utilization of staff and Job performance questionnaire (TUSJPQ)" was used in the study to generate information on the basis of the research hypotheses formulated for this study. The questionnaire is made up of two sections, which consist of thirty (30) items.

Validity of the Instrument

Two types of procedures were adopted by the researcher to establish the validity of the instrument. These include face and content validity. The researcher presented the instrument to experts in the field of discipline for moderation and approval. Their comments and advice were used to review the instrument to ensure its face value. Also, in terms of its content values, items in the questionnaire were scrutinized by experts to ensure that they adequately cover the areas of training and utilization of staff and to eliminate items that tend to repeat themselves. The highest score of 4 was scored for each response, indicating the most positive

Table 3. T– test analysis on training and utilization of staff of NCE and university graduates.

Source	N	X	SD	Df	t-cri	t-cal	Decision
Trained	120	287.2	71.8	198	1.96	7.29	Significant
Untrained	80	227.4	25.3				

*P≤ 0.05 level of significance.

Table 4. T – test Analysis on Training and Utilization of Staff of Full-time and Part-time trained staff.

Source	N	X	SD	Df	t-cri	t-cal	Decision
Trained	120	282.8	11.6	198	1.96	7.94	Significant
Untrained	80	220.4	8.3				

*P≤0.05 level of significance.

training and utilization of staff and a score of 1 of the response, indicative of the most negative.

Reliability of the Instrument

The reliability of the battery of test was determined by conducting a split half reliability test in which case, only one test is administered to eliminate measurement errors such as differences in testing conditions. The data of the two scores were correlated by employing the Spearman Brown Prophecy Formula to estimate the reliability of the instrument which yielded 0.75 reliability coefficient. This showed that the reliability coefficient has a high internal consistency.

Administration of Instrument

To ensure high percentage return of the research instrument, the researcher administered the questionnaire personally to the respondents in the sampled schools and offices, and retrieved them instantly.

Method of data analysis

The study made extensive use of tables for the presentation and for analysis of data. In testing for the significant difference of the null hypotheses formulated, a t-test statistic was employed.

RESULTS

The results of this study were presented and discussed accordingly with respect to the hypotheses formulated.

Hypotheses testing

H_1: There is no significant difference between NCE graduates and university graduates in their performance in Post Primary Education Board.

The Table 3 shows a t-critical value of 1.96 and a t-calculated value of 7.29. The t critical value of 1.96 is less than the t calculated value of 7.29; hence, the null hypothesis was rejected which means that there is a significant difference between NCE and University graduate. These findings could be justified as most of the University graduates are acquainted with new approaches in solving both educational and administrative problems.

H_2: There is no significant difference between the staff trained under full-time and part-time programmes in their performance in Post Primary Education Board.

The Table 4 shows a t-critical value of 1.96 and a t-calculated value of 7.94. The t critical value of 1.96 is less than the t calculated value of 7.94, hence, the null hypothesis was rejected which means that there is a significant difference between Full-time and Part-time trained staff. These findings could be justified as majority of the subjects believed that staffs trained in Full-time and Part-time programme do not perform equally.

H_3: There is no significant difference between male and female staff trained in their performance in Post Primary Education Board.

The Table 5 shows a t-critical value of 1.96 and a t-calculated value of 12.5. The t critical value of 1.96 is less than the t calculated value of 12.5, hence, the null hypothesis was rejected which means that there is a significant difference in the deployment of staff according to sex. This may be justified as most of the subjects believed that deployment according to sex, influences staff performance.

DISCUSSION

Hypotheses 1 revealed that there was a significant difference between NCE and University graduates as shown in Table 3. These findings may be accepted as

Table 5. T – test Analysis on Training and Utilization of Staff of staff according to sex.

Source	N	X	SD	Df	t-cri	t-cal	Decision
Trained	120	314.2	23.7	198	1.96	12.5	Significant
Untrained	80	210.8	7.4				

*P≤0.05 level of significance.

University graduates have in-depth study of the courses and are acquainted with better skills and approaches in solving both educational and management problems. This is in consonance with Nakpodia (1998) who opined that training is often organized for staff to upgrade and update their knowledge and skills.

Hypothesis 2 showed that there was a significant difference between full-time and part-time trained staff as shown in table 4. The findings may be accepted as majority of the respondents responded that staff trained in full-time programmes performs better than part-time trained. This finding supports the work of Odor (1995) who opined that job performance of the full-time trained staff is higher than that of part-time trained as the former is usually highly coordinated, because of the relaxed manner in which the course was studied.

Hypothesis 3 showed that there was a significant difference between deployments of staff according to sex as shown in table 5. These findings may be accepted as majority of the respondents responded that deployment of staff according to sex influences staff performances negatively, as many teachers have very few periods or schedule of work to do in the urban areas while those in the rural areas are faced with so much loads. This study supports the work of Peretomode (2001), which pointed out clearly that each person in an organization, high or low, should have a clearly defined daily work that requires a full day's effort. The study further revealed that there was a significant difference in the deployment of trained and untrained staff as shown in table 5. These findings may be accepted as majority of the respondents agreed that deployment of staff affect effective performance of staff. This is in consonance with Peretomode (2001), who believed with the scientific management theory of scientifically selecting the best person for the job and training him thoroughly in the tasks and procedures to be followed and giving him jobs for which he is best suited physically as well as intellectually.

Findings

The following findings were made in the study:

1. There is a high significant difference between the performance of NCE graduates and University graduates.
2. The work reveals that there is a significant difference between full-time and part-time graduates.
3. The study exposes that there is significant difference between deployment of staff according to sex.

Conclusion

As a result of the findings, the following conclusions have been drawn that this paper dealt with training and utilization of staff and job performance. Some improvements needed in the quality of staff training and utilization and the associated problems were also highlighted. The study revealed that the performance of the university graduate staff is far above that of NCE graduate staff as a result of the in-depth knowledge of the course studied. The researcher also reached the conclusion that graduates who had full-time studies performed better than part-time graduates. This is because the former had the studies in a relaxed manner and more in-depth knowledge of the course than the part-time graduates. In addition, the research has shown that the deployment of staff according to sex affects performance adversely. The female staffs are mainly deployed to the urban areas while the male staffs are mainly in the rural areas.

In fact, the quality of training received by staff will go a long way in determining the employment opportunities available to staff and their competence on the job.

RECOMMENDATIONS

The researcher has advanced the following recommendations:

1. The staff should be encouraged to go on further training through any form of training that is available in the interest of the staff and the organization which he/she serves.
2. Full-time studies are recommended for staff who are qualified for better performance at the end of their studies. Although part-time is not ruled out since it's one of the ways staff can train themselves.
3. Deployment of staff according to sex congests schools and offices in urban areas, leaving the schools in rural areas with just a few staff to handle both subjects studied and the ones not studied. Staff should be evenly distributed for effective job performance in the interest of the school system.

REFERENCES

Nakpodia ED (1998). Relationship Between Principals and Teachers perceptions of principals' performance of certain Administrative tasks in Delta State secondary schools, Unpublished Ph.D. Thesis, Delta state university, Abraka.

Nwagwu (1992). Training and Utilization of Educational Planners and Administrators in Africa, Owerri: The Nigerian Association for Educational Administration and Planning (NAEAP).

Obadan (2000). Improving Productivity in Nigeria Economy Through Effective Planning and Research, Ibadan: National Centre for Economic Management and Administration.

Sloman M (1989). On –the- Job Training : A Costly Poor Relation . Personnel Management, 21(2) February.

Campbell FR, Edwin MB, Nystrand OR (1990). Introduction to Educational Administration 6th edition, Allyn and Bacon, pp. 23

Donnelly CK (1995). Fundamentals of Management 9th Edition; Texas:Business Publications Inc. p.16

Egwunyenga JE (2000). Essential of School Administration, Benin-City:Justice – Jeco Publishers, p.40

Nakpodia ED (2006). Educational Administration- A New ApproachWarri: Jonakase Publishers, p.60

Odor GO (1995). Administration of schools in Nigeria: Theory and Practice. Benin City: Monose Amalgamates, p.25

Peretomode VF (2001). Educational Administration Applied Concepts and Theoretical Perspectives, Lagos. Joja Educational Research and Publishers LTD, p.87

Peretomode VF, Peretomode O (2001). Human Resources Management Lagos: Obaroh and Ogbinaka Publishers LTD, p.102

Analysis of fiscal deficits and interest rates in Nigeria

Vincent N. Ezeabasili[1]* and Joseph N. Mojekwu[2]

[1]Department of Capital Market Studies, Anambra State University, Igbariam Campus, Anambra State, Nigeria.
[2]Department of Actuarial Sciences and Insurance, Faculty of Business Administration University of Lagos, Nigeria.

This study investigates the effect of fiscal deficits on nominal interest rate in Nigeria. Cointegration techniques and structural analysis were adopted for the study. Empirical evidence emerges that the coefficient of fiscal deficit variable is positive and statistically significant. This indicates that the elasticity of fiscal deficit with respect to income is 0.114, an indication that large deficit causes higher interest rates. In addition, money supply has an inverse relationship with interest rates in Nigeria, but there exist a positive and significant relationship between inflation and interest rate. The coefficient of government expenditure is positive with a short run effect of 0.229. It is recommended that government should consider the option of bond financing of budget deficit as an alternative to monetary financing.

Key words: Fiscal deficit, nominal interest rate, cointegration, Nigeria.

INTRODUCTION

The rate of interest is the reward for parting with liquidity for a specified period. In a sense, it is seen as a measure of the unwillingness of those who possess money to part with their liquid control over it. It is the "price" which equilibrates the desire to hold wealth in the form of cash with the available quality of each that is the price of credit. Interest rate as the price paid for the right to borrow and use loanable funds, are the costs of holding money (Anyanwu and Oaikhanem, 1995). There are two types of interest rates; the nominal and real interest rates. The market rate of interest is roughly equivalent to the sum of the two forms of cost of holding money, that is: the market or nominal rate of interest equals (approximately) the real rate of interest plus the rate of increase in the price level. The nominal rates of interests are the rates of interest actually paid. They are the sum of expressed inflation and a real rate of return (Edward, 2004). The real rates are the nominal rates minus the expected rate of inflation (Anyanwu and Oaikhenam, 1995; Jhingan, 2004).

The persistence of fiscal deficits in developing countries which are mostly financed by government borrowing from the banking system has been blamed for much of the economic crises that beset them, since the 1980's, including debt overhang and the accompanying debt crises, high inflation, poor investment performance and growth (Anyanwu, 1998; Onwiduokit, 1999). According to Anyanwu (1998) large fiscal deficits being financed through creation of money have, or will soon produce high interest rates, thus hindering capital formation and economic growth in developed and developing countries. The views held by the popular press on fiscal deficit interest rate relationship is "deficits are the major reason that an interest rate stay close to record high levels" (American Banker, 1982). Again, a trade group asserted that "more than anything else, it is the spectre of an overwhelming volume of deficit financing which haunts housing and financial markets" (Wall Street Journal, 1982). Edward (2004) posits that since nominal interest rates are the sum of an expected inflation component and a real interest rate of return, a non-accommodative monetary policy stance not only implies that the expected inflation component of nominal rates will be unchanged in the face of higher deficits, but that monetary policy will not resist any upwards pressure on real interest rates that arise from greater government borrowing.

Fischer and Easterly (1990) argues that when debt is used to finance government expenditures, consumers' income will be increased as more money is injected into the economy. In the short-run, given that resources are not fully utilized, crowding out of private investments by

*Corresponding author. E-mail: jnmoje@yahoo.com.

high interest rates would not occur. If on the other hand, the economy is at full employment, the Keynesian School views deficit financing to be identical to the classical view, which entails reduction in private capital formation, increased interest rates and consumption. This according to Ubogu (1982) will lead to inflation if not accompanied by a reduction in money stock.

Over thirty seven years, between 1970 and 2006, the fiscal operations of the Nigerian government resulted in deficits in 33 years. This is as a result of the volatile revenue base which combines with increasing expenditure profile of government, thus making the incidence of fiscal deficits inevitable. In Nigeria, fiscal deficits were generally financed from the banking system and external sources (NCEMA, 2004; CBN, 2006). However, a number of studies have attempted to examine the relationship between fiscal deficits on interest rates. Such studies (Evans, 1998; Perrotti, 2004; Abderrezak, 1987; Feldstein and Eckstein, 1970; Plosser, 1982; Elmendorf, 1996; Cebula, 2005; Easterly and Schmidt-Hebbel, 1993; Aschauer, 1989; Blejer and Khan, 1984; Khan and Reinhart, 1990; Easterly, 1990; Govannini and De Melo, 1990; Anyanwu, 1998; Adams and Bankole, 2000; Ariyo and Raheem, 1991) etc, are replete in the literature. Most of these works were done in countries different from the Nigerian context. Again, the time frame considered in these works is short. Also is the fact that the results in these studies are conflicting. These shortcomings have somehow contributed to the knowledge gap in the literature, thus warranting a more systematic examination of the relationship between fiscal deficits and interest rates in the Nigerian context. This study seeks improve on the past studies by, using a broad data set spanning 1970 and 2006, such data is far more than those used in previous studies. The period also covers all the periods of economic reforms in Nigeria. Using recent developments in time series econometrics as provided by Engle and Granger (1987), Andrews (1991) etc, this study is able to distinguish between long and short run effects of the variables in the model adopted.

LITERATURE

Macroeconomic theory posits that financing budget deficit by increasing the supply of government securities *citeris-paribus* reduces its prices and raises the real interest rates, thus crowds-out private investment. This phenomenon can lead to a debt problem. Thus, if interest rates are not controlled, high fiscal deficits are correlated with strongly negative real interest rates, and the loss of access to external borrowing for financing fiscal deficits often leads to higher taxes on domestic financial intermediation. This phenomenon can even lead to stagnant or declining economic growth. Overall, the literature on the relationship between fiscal deficit, and interest rate has always been concerned with more reliance on domestic financing of fiscal deficits as external finance declines sharply in highly indebted countries (Wijnbergen, 1989).

Many studies such as (Evans, 1988; Plosser, 1982; Feldstein and Eckstein, 1970, etc) have examined the effect of fiscal deficit on nominal interest rates or some measures of interest rates. However, conclusions reached by these studies are mixed and inconclusive. Three views are upheld. The first indicates that interest rates are an increasing function of fiscal deficit. The second argument suggests that budget deficit negatively affects real interest rate. The last view holds that changes in fiscal deficit have a neutral effect on interest rates, thus, rejecting the crowding-out hypothesis.

Evans (1988) rejected the argument that nominal interest rates increases as a result of large fiscal deficits. Perroti (2004) studied five OECD countries between 1960 and 2001 and came to the conclusion that only in the 1980 period is there some evidence of (small) positive effect of government spending on long run interest rates. Abderrezak (1987) postulate that large fiscal deficit causes increases in nominal interest rates. Feldstein and Eckstein (1970) explained interest rates by combining standard liquidity preference theory with the assumption that nominal interest rates reflect the expected rate of inflation. They argue that market interest rates depend on the real quantity of money, real income, inflation, and outstanding government debt. Their finding suggests a statistically significant positive effect of government debt on nominal interest rates. Plosser (1982) assumed that the financial markets are efficient and postulated that only unexpected changes in privately held government debt, monetary authority holding of government debt, and government purchases of goods and services would result in changes in interest rates. His findings suggests that unexpected increase in government spending will lead to an increase in interest rates, and that the method of financing the higher spending has some effect on interest rate. These result tends to suggest that the amount of government debt the public holds has little influence on interest rates and that this depends on the method of financing the debt which according to him heavily affects interest rates.

In the United States, the financial market development following news reports about the deficit reduction laws are consistent with the prediction of economic theory. Higher expected government spending and budget deficits raised real interest rates and the value of the dollar, while lower expected spending and deficits reduced real rates and the value of the dollar (Elmendorf, 1996). Further empirical evidence by Cebula (2005) argue that primary deficits raises the nominal interest yield on bonds in the United States of America. Easterly and Schmidt-Hebbel (1993) argued that debt financing of deficits lead to higher real interest rates or increased financial repression of the financial markets, with fiscal gains coming at an increasingly unfavourable terms.

Domestic borrowing in the form of issuance of domestic debt instruments intermediated through the banking system has its own dangers as its effect on the economy depends entirely on whether there is financial repression or financial deregulation (Easterly, 1990; Govannini and De Melo, 1990). In their separate studies of some developing countries, the authors concluded that excessive government borrowing from the banking system leads to credit squeeze through higher real interest rates when the financial market is deregulated and when in financial repression through credit allocation. Subsequently, this leads to crowding out of credit that would otherwise, be available to the private sector. Similarly, since real interest rate determines how investors and consumer schedule there investments and consumption, assuming they have access to credit, has some salutary effects on investment and consumption. Easterly (1989), Govannini and De Melo (1990) argues that an increase in real interest rate resulting from higher government domestic borrowing could lower private investment and consumption. Nevertheless, this relationship depends entirely on the degree of complementary effects between public investment and private investment. Where the degree of relationship is low, then borrowing by the government could crowd out private investment and then lower growth (Aschauer, 1989; Blejer and Khan, 1984; Khan and Reinhart, 1990). For Nigeria, the empirical work of Anyanwu (1998) has not revealed a significant positive association between overall fiscal deficits and its foreign financing and domestic nominal deposit interest rates, but there appears to be evidence for a significant positive association between domestic financing of fiscal deficits and domestic nominal deposit rates during the period 1987 to 1995. Specifically, the work posits that, domestic financing of fiscal deficits, the level of real income, and foreign interest rates play important roles in the determination of deposit rates in Nigeria, Ghana, and the Gambia.

The study by Adam and Bankole (2000) revealed a positive relationship between interest rate and fiscal deficit. They argue that increasing reliance on domestic financial markets for financing government deficits is likely to lead to steep increases in interest costs. However, Ariyo and Raheem (1991) cited in Tchokote (2004) suggests that fiscal deficits has a significant impact on interest rate in Nigeria.

In conclusion, most of the studies reviewed in the literature have shown inconclusive conclusions on the effect of fiscal deficits on interest rates. Even the results of the extant works conducted in the Nigerian context also shows conflicting results in their conclusions. The observed differences in these conclusions have some how contributed to the knowledge gap in the literature thus warranting a more systematic examination of the relationship between fiscal deficits and interest rates in Nigeria.

THEORETICAL FRAMEWORK

Under the fiscal approach to the balance of payments; the current account balance is defined as the difference between monetary value of domestic output and the aggregate demand (absorption). The budget balance is consequently defined as the gap between government revenues and expenditures. The above definition derives from the national income identity, as:

$$Y = C + I + G + (X - M) \quad (1)$$

Where Y represents GDP, C is private consumption, I stands for private investment, G is government consumption, X and M stand for exports and imports respectively.

Assuming the aggregate demand $A = C + I + G$ then Equation (1) can be rewritten as follows:

$$Y - A = X - M \quad (2)$$

Equation (2) reflects the behaviour of the external sector of the economy. The direct interpretation is that, external imbalances always trigger a series of developments in the economy, which in this case is budget deficit. Therefore, any attempt to restore the balance must include effort to align revenue with expenditure.

In order to isolate the disposable income, tax (T) and international reserve (R) (the latter is introduced basically on the assumption of the fixed exchange rate regime) are introduced into the national income identity. It follows that Equation (1) will become:

$$Y + R - T = C + I + (G - T) + (R + X - M) \quad (3)$$

In the following equation, S (savings) is the disposable income minus private consumption. That is:

$S = Y + R - T - C$, the private absorption capacity is represented by $(C + I)$, $(G - T)$ is for budget deficit, while the current account balance CAB is represented by $(R + X - M)$, R represents international transfer receipts and T stands for taxes. Substituting S and CAB by their respective components, we get:

$$(S - I) + (T - G) = (R + X - M) \quad (4)$$

It is often argued that deficit in the current account occurs when aggregate investment outweighs aggregate savings. However, if investments equals savings and government expenditure is greater than its revenue then, the current account deficit becomes inevitable. The literature on the current account is quite obvious when it indicates the degree at which the domestic economy interacts with its external assets. Thus, $(X + R - M)$ would also be equivalent to the increase in net official assets plus the rate of capital outflow that is ΔNFA.

$$\text{Hence } CA = \Delta NFA \quad (5)$$

The links between net savings of the private sector and the public sector deficit is easily appreciated through the following illustration.

$$(S - I) + (T - G) = \Delta NFA \quad (6)$$

The direct interpretation of the above equation assuming $S = I$ is that:

(i) a budget deficit will be financed through a reduction in external net claims, which can be done through increase in external public

debt or reduction of international reserves in the case of a fixed exchange regime.
(ii) Budget deficit could also be financed domestically, through increase in government debt held by the private economic sector. The relationship in the banking system provides a clear understanding on how domestic borrowing is applied in financing a budget deficit and the balance sheet is given as follows:

$$\Delta NFA^{b} = \Delta M_2 - (\Delta DC^{g} + \Delta DC^{nb}) \quad (7)$$

The liability of the banking system is represented by M_2, that is the broad money, ΔDC^{g} is domestic credit of the banking system to government and ΔDC^{nb} is the credit of non-banking sector (private sector) to the government. Equation (7) expresses the difference between money expansion and credit expansion and, which works as follows. An increase in money relative to credit expansion will reflect as an increase in the net foreign asset.
In countries where the capital markets are not advanced (such as Nigeria), budget deficit is usually financed through domestic and external borrowing. This expression can be simplified as follows:

$$G - T = \Delta DC^{g} - \Delta NFA^{g} \quad (8)$$

By substituting (8) into (7), the relationship between the financing of the budget deficit and the banking system is brought to the fore. Thus:

$$G - T = \Delta M_2 - \Delta DC^{nb} - (\Delta NFA^{b} + NFA^{g}) \quad (9)$$

Equation (9) illustrates the sources through which government deficit can be financed. First, by an increase in money (ΔM_2). Second, borrowing from non-banking sector. Lastly, by a reduction in international reserve or external borrowing. In all, increased budget deficit will translate into increased current account deficit which precipitates new external borrowing or draw down of external reserves. However, all the three means of financing a deficit may lead to appreciation of real and nominal exchange rates under flexible exchange rate regime and capital mobility.

The specification of the interest model mirrors the works of Ariyo and Raheem (1991), cited in Tchokote (2004). The specification of the model considers the following variables: Interest rate (INT) is the independent variable; while Government expenditure (G), fiscal deficit (FD), money supply (MS), and inflation rate (INF) are the, dependent variable; U_t is error term.The model is represented as:

$$INT = f(G, FD, MS, INF, INT_{t-1})$$

The equation for the above relationship becomes:

$$INT = b_o + b_1 G + b_2 FD + b_3 MS + b_4 INF + b_5 INT_{t-1} + U_t \quad (10)$$

b_o is the intercept and, b_1, b_2, b_3, b_4, are the coefficients of the regression equation.
A priori, it is expected that the following relationship will occur;
$b_1, b_2, b_4, b_5 > 0$; $b_3 < 0$;

The secondary data for the period 1970 to 2006 which were used as the macroeconomic variables in this study were obtained from the statistical bulletin of the Central Bank of Nigeria (CBN). (2006)

Estimation technique – Cointegration and error correction model (ECM) estimation technique

We investigated the time series characteristics of the data to test whether the variables are integrated. The Augmented Dickey-Fuller (ADF), as specified in Dickey and Fuller (1979), and Phillips-Perron (Phillips and Peron, 1988) was employed. For the ADF, the null hypothesis is that the variable being considered has a unit root against an alternative that it does not. The model for the ADF is as specified as:

$$\Delta y_t = \alpha + \beta T + \gamma y_{t-1} + \sum_{i=1}^{P} d_t \Delta y_{t-1} + \varepsilon_t \quad (11)$$

Where y_t is the variable being considered, T is the time trend (which is only allowed if significant), and ε_t is a random error term. The Akaike Information Criterion is used in selecting p (the lag-length) after testing for first and higher order serial correlation in the residuals. The lagged variables serve as a correction mechanism for possible serial correlation. The Phillips-Peron (PP) test uses models similar to the Dickey-Fuller tests but with Newey and West (1994) non-parametric correction for correcting possible serial correlation rather than the lagged variables method employed in ADF. Also Bartlett Kernel (Andrews, 1991) is used as an automated bandwidth estimator for lag truncation of the Newey and West nonparametric correction. The test statistics of the PP have the same distribution as those of Dickey-Fuller with critical levels as provided by MacKinnon (1996). The fact that two series are unit roots can be an indication of a long run relationship between the two series.

Error correction model

To test for the long run relationships between the variables, we apply the Engle-Granger (1987) two step cointegration test which uses the residuals from the long run equation estimated with the non-stationary variables, and then test for the existence of unit root in the residual using the ADF regression and compare the value to an appropriate asymptotic null distribution. If two time series y_t and x_t are both integrated of order d (that is I(d)), then, in general, any linear combination of the two series will also be I(d); that is, the residuals obtained on regressing y_t on x_t are I(d). If, however, there exists a vector b, such that the disturbance term from the regression ($e_t = y_t - bx_t$) is of a lower order of integration I(d-b), where b>0, then Engle and Granger (1987) define y_t and x_t as cointegrated of order (d,b).

The economic interpretation of cointegration is that if two or more series are linked to form an equilibrium relationship spanning the long run, then even though the series themselves may be non-stationary, they will move closely together over time and their difference will be stationary. Their long run relationship is the equilibrium to which the system converges over time, and the disturbance term can be interpreted as the disequilibrium error or the distance that the system is away from equilibrium at time t. In order to estimate the long run relationship between yt and xt it is necessary to estimate the static model:

$$y_t = \beta X_t + e_t \quad (12)$$

Although the equilibrium long run relationship can be estimated directly using Equation (12), it is also important to consider the short run dynamics of the variables under consideration, since the system may not always be in equilibrium. A simple dynamic model of short run adjustment can be written as:

$$y_t = \alpha_0 + \gamma_0 X_t + \ldots + \gamma_1 X_{t-1} + \alpha_1 y_{t-1} + u_t \quad (13)$$

Reparameterising and rearranging Equation (13) gives the error correction formulation (ECM):

$$\Delta y_t = \gamma_0 \Delta X_t - (1 - \alpha_1)[y_{t-1} - \beta_0 - \beta_1 X_{t-1}] + u_t \quad (14)$$

where β_0 and β_1 are coefficients estimated from equation.

The ECM incorporates both short run and long run effects. When equilibrium holds, $[y_{t-1} - \beta_0 - \beta_1 X_{t-1}] = 0$. But in the short run, when disequilibrium exists, this term is non-zero and measures the distance that the system is away from equilibrium during time t. Thus $(1-\alpha_1)$ provides an estimate of the speed of adjustment of the variable y_t. For instance, if $[y_{t-1} - \beta_0\ \beta_1 X_{t-1}] < 0$, that is, y_{t-1} has moved below its equilibrium level, since $-(1-\alpha_1)$ is negative, it will boost Δy_t, thereby forcing it back to its long run path. Engle and Granger show that two or more variables are cointegrated of order I(1,1) if and only if an ECM exists.

The first stage in the Engle-Granger framework is to test whether the variables are cointegrated. This is accomplished by testing the residuals of Equation (9) for stationarity. That is, the null hypothesis of it being I(1) is tested against the alternate of it being I(0). Although any unit root test can be used, Engle and Granger advocated the use of Augmented Dickey Fuller tests on the residuals. The second stage of the EG procedure comprises of estimating the short run ECM itself from the residuals of the regression of the first stage. That is, having obtained $\varepsilon_{t-1} = y_{t-1} - \beta X_{t-1}$, we estimate Equation (14) to determine the dynamic structure of the system.

We expect that there is a long-run relationship between money supply, economic activity, domestic interest rates and foreign interest rates. We therefore test for the existence of a cointegrating relationship. This is done using the above ECM methodology. In the first step we estimate the coefficients by OLS and test for the existence of a unit root in the residuals. The analysis is also supplemented by testing for the number of cointegrating relationships using the Johansen procedure. The deviations from the long run path are captured at the second stage. When the coefficients of the lagged residual term from the first stage is negative, it suggests that the system comes back to the long run path or adjusts. Therefore, there exists an error correction mechanism. The parsimonious error correction mechanism (ECM) can be specified as:

$$\Delta INT_t = \alpha_1 + \Delta G_{t-s} + \Delta FD_{t-s} + \Delta MS_{t-s} + \Delta INF_{t-s} + \Delta INT_{t-1} + ECM_{t-1} + \mu_t \qquad (15)$$

Where the variables are defined in Equation (10).

The Johansen cointegration specification

The finding that many macro time series may contain a unit root has spurred the development of the theory of non-stationary time series analysis. Engle and Granger (1987) pointed out that a linear combination of two or more non-stationary series may be stationary. If such a stationary linear combination exists, the non-stationary time series are said to be cointegrated. The stationary linear combination is called the cointegrating equation and may be interpreted as a long-run equilibrium relationship among the variables. The purpose of the cointegration test is to determine whether a group of non-stationary series are cointegrated or not. Consider a VAR of order *p*:

$$y_t = A_1 y_{t-1} + \ldots + A_p y_{t-p} + Bx_t + \varepsilon_t \qquad (16)$$

Where y_t is a -vector of non-stationary I(1) variables, x_t is a -vector of deterministic variables, and ε_t is a vector of innovations. We may rewrite this VAR as :

$$\Delta y_t = \Pi y_{t-1} + \sum_{i=1}^{p-1} \Gamma_i y_{t-i} A_p y_{t-p} + Bx_t + \varepsilon_t \qquad (17)$$

where :

$$\Pi = \sum_{i=1}^{p} A_i - I, \quad \Gamma_i = -\sum_{j=i+1}^{p-1} A_p + Bx_t + \varepsilon_t \qquad (18)$$

Granger's representation theorem asserts that if the coefficient matrix Π has reduced rank *r* < *k*, then there exist *k* < *r*, matrices *α* and *β* each with rank *r* such that $\Pi = \alpha\beta'$ and $\beta' y_t$ is I(0). *r* is the number of cointegrating relations (the cointegrating rank) and each column of *β* is the cointegrating vector. The elements of are known as the adjustment parameters in the VEC model. Johansen's method is to estimate the Π matrix from an unrestricted VAR and to test whether we can reject the restrictions implied by the reduced rank of Π.

Forecast error variance decomposition

A shock to any variable in the vector error correction (VEC) model not only directly affects the variable but is also transmitted to all of the other endogenous variables through the dynamic (lag) structure of the VEC. An impulse response function traces the effect of a one-time shock to one of the innovations on current and future values of the endogenous variables. While impulse response functions trace the effects of a shock to one endogenous variable on to the other variables in the VEC, variance decomposition separates the variation in an endogenous variable into the component shocks to the VEC. Thus, the variance decomposition provides information about the relative importance of each random innovation in affecting the variables in the VEC. The general form of the VECM for estimating the variance decomposition is therefore expressed as:

$$Ln\Delta INT_t = \sum_{k=1}^{r} \alpha_{1k} v_{k,t-p} + \sum_{s=1}^{p} \phi_{1,s} Ln\Delta G_t + \sum_{s=1}^{p} \phi_{2,s} Ln\Delta FD_{t-s} + \sum_{s=1}^{p} \phi_{3,s} Ln\Delta MS_{t-s} + \sum_{s=1}^{p} \phi_{4,s} LN\Delta INF_{t-s} + \sum_{s=1}^{p} \phi_{5,s} LnINT_{t-1} + \mu_t \qquad (19)$$

where: *p* ̃*l*(is the optimal lag length of the VAR), $\alpha_{i,k}$ = the adjustment coefficients

$v_{k,t-p}$ = is the cointegrating vector, μ_i = intercepts

The amount of forecast error variance of variable *j* accounted for by exogenous shocks to variable *k* is given by $\omega_{jk,h}$:

$$\omega_{jk,h} = \sum_{i=0}^{h-1} (e_j' \Theta_i e_k)^2 / MSE[y_{j,t}(h)] \qquad (20)$$

Where MSE is the mean square error (MSE) of an estimator and is one of many ways to quantify the difference between values implied by an estimator and the true values of the quantity being estimated. MSE is a risk function, corresponding to the expected value of the squared error loss or quadratic loss. MSE measures the average of

Table 1. Summary statistics of variables applied in the regression analysis.

	Mean	Median	Maximum	Minimum	Std.Dev.	Obs
LFD	0.111193	0.066115	0.50274	-0.37609	0.182012	37
LINF	1.198114	1.147584	1.862203	0.538775	0.326202	37
LGEXP	10.67595	10.44326	12.26543	8.95612	1.019011	37
LMS	10.7536	10.5844	12.42014	8.990916	1.059701	37
LINT	0.913497	1.004665	1.366273	0.425974	0.289786	37

Source: Author's computation with data derived from CBN statistical bulletin using econometric views 6.0.

the squares of the errors. The error is the amount by which the value implied by the estimator differs from the quantity to be estimated.

The variance decomposition is displayed in a table format which displays a separate variance decomposition for each endogenous variable. A column in the Table gives the forecast error of the variable at the given forecast horizon. The source of this forecast error is the variation in the current and future values of the innovations to each endogenous variable in the VAR. The remaining columns give the percentage of the forecast variance due to each innovation, with each row adding up to 100. As with the impulse responses, the variance decomposition based on the Cholesky factor can change dramatically if you alter the ordering of the variables in the VAR. For example, the first period decomposition for the first variable in the VAR ordering is completely due to its own innovation.

PRESENTATION AND DISCUSSION OF RESULTS

The characteristics of the data series used in the regression analysis are presented in Table 1. The table reports the summary of statistics used in the analysis. It provides information about the means and standard deviations of the main variables. The mean value of log of interest rate stood at 0.913 while the mean of the log of fiscal deficit and monetary supply stood at 0.111 and 10.75 respectively.

The variables for our analysis were subjected to two types of unit roots test to determine whether they are unit roots or stationary series. The tests employed were the ADF test and the Phillips-Perron test (PP) test. For the ADF and PP tests, two models are considered viz, with constant, with time trend. The null in both the ADF and PP test is the presence of unit root.

The ADF results in Table 2 show that 99% of the variables are integrated of order one in the two models of unit root test considered. Only one variable was found to be significant at its level and a reasonable number of the other variables were at the 5% level. One exception was however observable, log of government expenditure (LGEXP). The LGEXP was found to be stationary and significant at 5% level in the model that includes a constant and a linear time trend at levels but insignificant in the model that includes only a constant. One interesting feature noted in the results was that all the variables were stationary in model with constant as well as constant and linear time trend at the first difference level.

The PP test statistics reported in Table 3 reinforces the result in the model that include only constant in the ADF test and also supported those models that include a constant and a linear time trend. The PP test supports the presence of unit roots in nearly all the series. The LGEXP were found to be stationary and significant at 5% level in the model that includes a constant and a linear time trend at levels but insignificant in the model that includes only a constant. It is evident from Tables 2 and 3 that the variables become stationary series when appropriately differenced. From the two types of integration tests carried out (above), it could be concluded that all the variables in our models contain unit roots. Therefore, we can safely proceed to use the co-integration method in analyzing our models as conventional regression models will generate spurious results due to the integration level of the series. Following the findings that the data series are by nature, mostly non-stationary stochastic processes, econometric developments regarding the concepts of cointegration are particularly opposite in testing for equilibrium. Accordingly, the long run properties of the variables in the behavioural equations were examined using the Engle-Granger two-step procedure.

Presented in Table 4 are the results of the unit root tests of the residuals of the static long run models. The regression residuals have zero mean, and as they are not expected to have deterministic trend, the unit roots exercise were conducted by excluding both the models that includes constant and constant with time trend. The ADF test statistics and the Phillip-Perron statistics suggest that the disequilibrium errors are mostly I(0), and as such, the variables in the static equations are cointegrated.

In view of the problems with the Engle-Granger framework for testing cointegration, the results were validated using the Johansen (1991, 1995) approach. The Johansen's framework provides the number of cointegrating equations and estimates of all cointegrating vectors in the multivariate case. The Johansen cointegration test results are presented in the Tables. The trace test and the max-eigen test were conducted to establish the number of cointegrating relations in each of the equations. The trace test results are presented in the

Table 2. Table of the observed result of the augmented dickey fuller test (ADF)*.

Variables	Level		First difference	
	Model 1	Model 2	Model 1	Model 2
LFD	-3.20642	-4.67947	-5.84943	-5.86981
LGEXP	-0.77383	-4.30895	-7.14852	-7.07677
LINF	-3.54217	-3.52697	-6.36578	-6.30673
LINT	-1.98285	-1.95053	-2.84996	-3.08591
LMS	-1.34321	-2.44379	-3.38974	-3.40472

*The Null hypothesis is the presence of unit root. Model 1 includes a constant while model 2 includes a constant and a linear time trend. Lags were selected based on Schwarz Information Criterion. *, **, *** indicate significance at 1, 5, and 10% respectively. Econometric views 6.0 was used in the derivation.

Table 3. Table of the observed result of the Phillips-Perron Test (PP)*.

Variables	Level		First Difference	
	Model 1	Model 2	Model 1	Model 2
LFD	-3.17008	-4.54522	-13.1983	-14.133
LGEXP	-0.66233	-2.14895	-7.12546	-7.05476
LINF	-3.29075	-3.27206	-13.7516	-13.3734
LINT	-1.42665	-1.52242	-6.96867	-7.09702
LMS	-0.78309	-1.90896	-3.42703	-3.42266

The null hypothesis is the presence of unit root. Model 1 includes a constant, model 2 includes a constant and a linear time trend. The Bandwith was chosen using Newey-West method with Barttlet Kernel spectral estimation, **, *** indicate significance at 1, 5 and 10% respectively. Econometric views 6.0 was used in the derivation.

Table 4. Table of observed result of the unit root test of residual of ECM variables.

Equation	Augmented dickey fuller test	Phillips-Perron test
Interest rate equation	-5.2106	-5.2115

(1) Lags were selected based on Schwarz Information Criterion in the ADF test (2) The Bandwith was chosen using Newey-West method with Barttlet Kernel spectral estimation in the Phillip-Perron test (3) *, **, *** indicate significance at 1%, 5%, and 10% respectively. Econometric views 6.0 was used in the derivation.

first part of the table while the max-eigen results were presented in the second part of the table. Test results indicate the existence of one cointegrating equation in the equations at the 1 and 5% significance level. In addition, the normalized cointegrating coefficients show that the variables in the equations are relatively important. The consistency in the test results confirms the existence of long run relationship among the exogenous and dependent variables in the model. As the data series are non-stationary and the vector of variables in the equations appear to be cointegrated, execution of the second phase of the Engle-Granger technique led to the estimation of error-correction forms of the stochastic equations. The equations represent the short-run behaviour and the adjustment to the long run models. The residuals from the cointegrating regressions lagged one period were used as error correction mechanism in the dynamic equations. The ordinary least squares (OLS) estimation method was used as it is an essential component of most other estimation techniques. In addition, the OLS remains one of the most commonly used methods in econometric investigations involving large models. Estimates of the preferred specifications obtained using general-to-specific method are presented in Table 5 and discussed below. The results were evaluated using conventional diagnostic tests.

The general discussion of the error correction models is useful here. All the diagnostic test statistics are quite satisfactory. The magnitude of the coefficients confirms the absence of redundant regressors. Judged by the significance of the t-statistics, the coefficients are well determined. The disequilibrium error term, ECM_{t-1}, is statistically significant and negative (as expected) in the equations. The significance of the error terms confirms

Table 5. Table of observed result of the johansen multivariate cointegration test results for the interest rate equation.

Sample(adjusted): 1971 2006				
Included observations: 36 after adjusting endpoints				
Trend assumption: No deterministic trend (restricted constant)				
Series: LINT LGEXP LFD LMS LINF				
Lags interval (in first differences): No lags				
Unrestricted cointegration rank test				
Hypothesized		**Trace**	**5 (%)**	**1 (%)**
No. of CE(s)	Eigenvalue	Statistic	Critical value	Critical value
None **	0.809525	109.727	76.07	84.45
At most 1	0.501973	50.03044	53.12	60.16
At most 2	0.30273	24.93483	34.91	41.07
At most 3	0.23501	11.95387	19.96	24.6
At most 4	0.062144	2.309734	9.24	12.97
*(**) denotes rejection of the hypothesis at the 5%(1%) level				
Trace test indicates 1 cointegrating equation(s) at both 5% and 1% levels				
Hypothesized		**Max-eigen**	**5 (%)**	**1 (%)**
No. of CE(s)	Eigenvalue	Statistic	Critical value	Critical value
None **	0.809525	59.69652	34.4	39.79
At most 1	0.501973	25.09561	28.14	33.24
At most 2	0.30273	12.98097	22	26.81
At most 3	0.23501	9.644132	15.67	20.2
At most 4	0.062144	2.309734	9.24	12.97
*(**) denotes rejection of the hypothesis at the 5%(1%) level				
Max-eigenvalue test indicates 1 cointegrating equation(s) at both 5% and 1% levels				

Source: Author's computation from cointegration test using econometric views 6.0.

the existence of long run relationship between the variables in the error correction model. Of particular interest is the coefficient on the lagged ECM in the interest rate equation. The ECM induces about 83% adjustment per period in these equations. In addition, the equation is statistically significant and the overall statistical fit is good. The marginal significance level of the F-statistics for most of them is zero. Hence, the null hypothesis of the F-statistics is rejected for all choices of significance level. Therefore, the conclusion is that, as groups, the regression coefficients are significantly different from zero. The high value of the Durbin-Watson (DW) in each case indicates absence of autocorrelation. Finally, the relatively low value of the standard error of the regressions is a clear evidence of the goodness of fit of the equation.

In the interest rate equation result presented in Table 6, the coefficient of government expenditure is positive in the second lag, indicating a short run effect of 0.229, with a further adjustment after a one year lag of 0.344. The coefficient of the fiscal deficit variable is positive and statistically significant. The result indicates that the elasticity of fiscal deficit with respect to interest rate is 0.114. This result is consistent with Cebula (2005) and Abderrezak (1987) that large deficit causes higher interest rates. In addition, money supply in the second period lag has an inverse relationship with interest rate in Nigeria. A 1% increase in money supply is capable of decreasing interest rate by about 0.48% in Nigeria during the study period. In addition, there exist a positive and significant relationship between inflation and interest rate in Nigeria. A 1% increase in the level of inflation is capable of stimulating interest rate by about 0.092% at the 10% level of significance. The sample goodness of fit measure, the adjusted R^2, indicates that 55.9% of the variation in interest rate in Nigeria is attributable to the regressors.

Impulse response analysis and forecast variance decomposition

Figure 1 (Appendix) shows that the effect of fiscal deficit, government expenditure and inflation impulse, on interest rate are negative for the period under study. Only the impulses from money supply on interest rate generates positive impulses with it making full impact from the 7th period. In the variance decomposition of the interest rate result presented in Table 1 (Appendix), the estimates of

Table 6. Parsimonious model of interest rate equation.

Dependent Variable: D(LINT)				
Method: Least Squares				
Date: 09/09/08 Time: 13:07				
Sample(adjusted): 1974-2006				
Included observations: 33 after adjusting endpoints				
	Coefficient	Std. Error	t-Statistic	Prob.
C	0.009581	0.029643	0.323204	0.7499
D(LGEXP(-2))	0.229169	0.137899	1.661865	0.1121
D(LGEXP(-3))	0.344331	0.148266	2.322391	0.0309
D(LFD(-3))	0.114707	0.086903	1.319934	0.2018
D(LMS)	-0.345192	0.218833	-1.577425	0.1304
D(LMS(-2))	-0.479093	0.265719	-1.803011	0.0865
D(LINF)	-0.092771	0.048222	-1.923840	0.0687
D(LINF(-2))	-0.088251	0.044615	-1.978051	0.0619
D(LINF(-3))	-0.122812	0.040798	-3.010268	0.0069
D(LINT(-1))	1.065569	0.427115	2.494805	0.0215
D(LINT(-2))	0.304673	0.162757	1.871951	0.0759
D(LINT(-3))	0.660788	0.138171	4.782406	0.0001
ECM2(-1)	-0.821744	0.463875	-2.655337	0.0152
R-squared	0.724483	Mean dependent var		0.019110
Adjusted R-squared	0.559174	S.D. dependent var		0.101117
S.E. of regression	0.067136	Akaike info criterion		-2.277082
Sum squared resid	0.090145	Schwarz criterion		-1.687549
Log likelihood	50.57185	Durbin-Watson stat.		1.994232
F-statistic	0.001808			

Source: Regression results from analysis using econometric views 6.0.

the future changes in the variables reveal that fiscal deficit explains about 15.54% in of the future changes in the interest rate in Nigeria. This is followed by government expenditure which explain about 4.88% of the future changes in the interest rate in Nigeria. The interest rate variable was however, found to explain about 74.57%.

SUMMARY AND CONCLUSION

This study was done to determine the fiscal deficits-interest rates relationship in the Nigerian context from 1970 – 2006. After establishing the unit root status of the variables in the structural equation and the existence of cointegration, the OLS two-stage approach as suggested by Engle-Granger (1987) was utilized in deriving the short run and long run estimates. The structural analysis was done using the impulse response analysis and forecast error variance decomposition to trace the one-time shock to one of the innovation in current and future values of the endogenous variables. Empirical evidence emerges that the coefficient of government expenditure is positive in the second lag, indicating a short run effect of 0.229, with further adjustment after one year lag of 0.344. The coefficient of fiscal deficit variable is positive and statistically significant. This result indicates that the elasticity of fiscal deficit with respect interest rate is 0.114, indicating that large budget deficit causes higher interest rates in Nigeria. A 1% increase in money supply is capable of decreasing interest rates by 0.48% during the study period. In addition, there exists a positive and significant relationship between inflation and interest rates. A 1% increase in the level of inflation is capable of stimulating interest rate by 0.092%. It is recommended that monetary financing of government deficits should be de-emphasized, since is accentuates the problem of inflation. In the alternative, bonds should be used to finance government extra-budgetary expenses. It is also important for government to budget in line with resource availability.

REFERENCES

Abderrezak A (1987). The Impact of Government Deficits on Interest Rates. Doctoral Dissertation, Department of Economics, Kansas State University, U.S.A.

Adam JA, Bankole AS (2000). The Macroeconomics of Fiscal Deficits in Nigeria. Nigerian J. Econ. Soc. Stud., 42(3): 263-289.
American Banker (1982). Mc Gilliaddy Deficits Do Matter. March 11
Andrews DWK (1991). Heteroske Desticity and Autocorrelation Consistent Convenance Matrix Estimation. Econometrica, 59: 817-858.
Anyanwu JC (1998). Do Large Fiscal Deficits Produce High Interest Rate?: The Case of Nigeria, Ghana and The Gambia, 1987:3 – 1995: 4. CBN Financial Econ. Rev., 36(1): 51-84.
Anyanwu JC, Oaikhenam H (1995). Macroeconomics: Theory and Applications. (1st Ed), Onitsha, Joane Publishers,
Ariyo A, Raheen MI (1991). Effects of Fiscal Deficits on some Macroeconomic Aggregates in Nigeria cited in Tchokote (2004). Macroeconomics of Fiscal Defices in Cameroun, Doctoral Dissertation, University of Ibadan, pp. 72-81.
Aschauer D (1989). In Public Expenditure Productivity. J. Monetary Econ., 23: 177-200.
Blejer MI, Khan MS (1984). Government Policy and Private Investment in Developing Countries. IMF Staff Papers, 31(2): 379-403.
Cebula RT (2005). Recent empirical evidence on the impact of the primary budget deficit on nominal longer-term treasury note interest rate yields. Glob. Bus. Econ. Rev., 7(1): 47-58.
Central Bank of Nigeria (2006). CBN Annual Report and Statement of Accounts. (Lagos: Central Bank of Nigeria).
Dickey DA, Fuller WA (1979). Distribution of the Estimators for Autoregressive Time Series with a Unit Root. J. Am. Stat. Ass., 74: 427-431.
Easterly W (1989). A Consistency Framework for Macroeconomic Analysis. Working Paper Series 324 World Bank, Country Economic Department, Washington D.C.
Easterly W (1990). How much adjustment in enough? The case of Columbia. Working Paper Series 626, World Bank Country Economics Department, Washington D.C.
Easterly W, Schmidt-Hebbal K (1993). Fiscal Adjustment and Macroeconomic Performance Outreach 10 May (World Bank Policy Research Department).
Edward N (2004). Budget Deficits and Interest Rates. Monetary Trends, The Federal Reserve Bank of St. Louis, March, pp. 22-28
Elmendorf DW (1996). The Effects of Deficit Reduction Laws on Real Interest Rates. Federal Reserve Board, October pp.1-31.
Engle RF, Granger CWJ (1987). Cointegration and Error Correction Representation, Estimation and Testing. Econometrica, 55: 251-276.
Evans P (1998). All Consumers Ricardian? Evidence for the United States, J. Polit. Econ., pp. 983-1004.
Feldstein M, Eckstein O (1970). The Fundamental Determinants of the interest rate. Rev. Econ. Stat., 52: 363-375.
Fischer S, Easterly W (1990). The Economics of Government Budget Constraints. World Bank Observer, 5(2): 23-41
Giovannini A, De Mello M (1990). Government Revenue from Financial Repression. World Bank Country Economic Department, Washington D.C. Processed. Working, p. 533.
Johansen S (1991). A Statistical Analysis of Co-integration Vectors. J. Econ. Dyn. Control, 12: 231-254.
Johansen S (1995). Estimation and Hypothesis Testing of Cointegration Vectors in Gaussian Vector Autoregressive Models. Econometrica, 59: 1551-1580.
Khan MS, Reinhart CM (1990). Private Investment and Economic Growth in Developing Countries. World Development 18, January, pp. 19-27.
MacKinnon JG (1996). Numerical Distribution Functions for Unit Root and Cointegration Test. J. Appl. Econ., 11: 601-618.
NCEMA (2004). Macroeconomic Effects of Deficit Financing in Nigeria. National Center for Economic Management and Administration(NCEMA) Workshop, Ibadan, pp. 5-21.
Newey W, West K (1994). Automatic Lag Selection in Covariance Matrix Estimation. Rev. Econ. Stud., 61: 631-653.
Onwioduokit EA (1999). Fiscal Deficits and Inflation Dynamics in Nigeria: An Empirical Investigation of Causal Relationships. CBN Econ. Fin. Rev., 37(2): 1-16.
Perotti R (2004). Estimating the effects of fiscal policy in OECD countries. IGIER – Universita: Bocconi and Centre for Economic Policy, pp.1-43.
Phillips PCB, Perron P (1988). Testing for a Unit Root in Time Series Regression. Biometrika, 75: 335-346.
Plosser C (1982). Government Financing Decisions and Asset Returns, J. Monetary Econ., 9: 245-252.
Ubogu RE (1982). Deficit Financing and the Nigerian Economy. Nigerian Economic Society Workshop on Deficit Financing, University of Ibadan, pp. 3-4.
Van WS (1989). External Debt, Inflation and the Public Sector: Towards Fiscal Policy for Sustainable Growth. World Bank Econ. Rev., 3(3): 297-320.
Wall Street Journal (1982). Thryst Industry urges cut in U.S. Deficit. The Wall Street Journal, March 4.

APPENDIX

Table 1. Variance decomposition of the interest rate equation.

	S.E.	LINT	LGEXP	LFD	LMS	LINF
1	0.095527	100	0	0	0	0
2	0.116672	96.99737	0.549945	2.322163	0.066551	0.063975
3	0.148542	87.9227	0.474082	9.028925	0.359462	2.214829
4	0.170078	85.49625	0.741728	10.62883	0.284111	2.849081
5	0.182297	83.10019	1.663729	11.96825	0.331526	2.936303
6	0.191019	80.34623	2.760788	13.2731	0.684418	2.935468
7	0.197446	78.03286	3.725898	14.19015	1.149527	2.901565
8	0.202053	76.36234	4.356228	14.83125	1.563315	2.886862
9	0.205325	75.26015	4.705028	15.26842	1.869597	2.896802
10	0.207579	74.5748	4.883998	15.54655	2.079549	2.915099

Source: Regression results from analysis using econometric views 6.0.

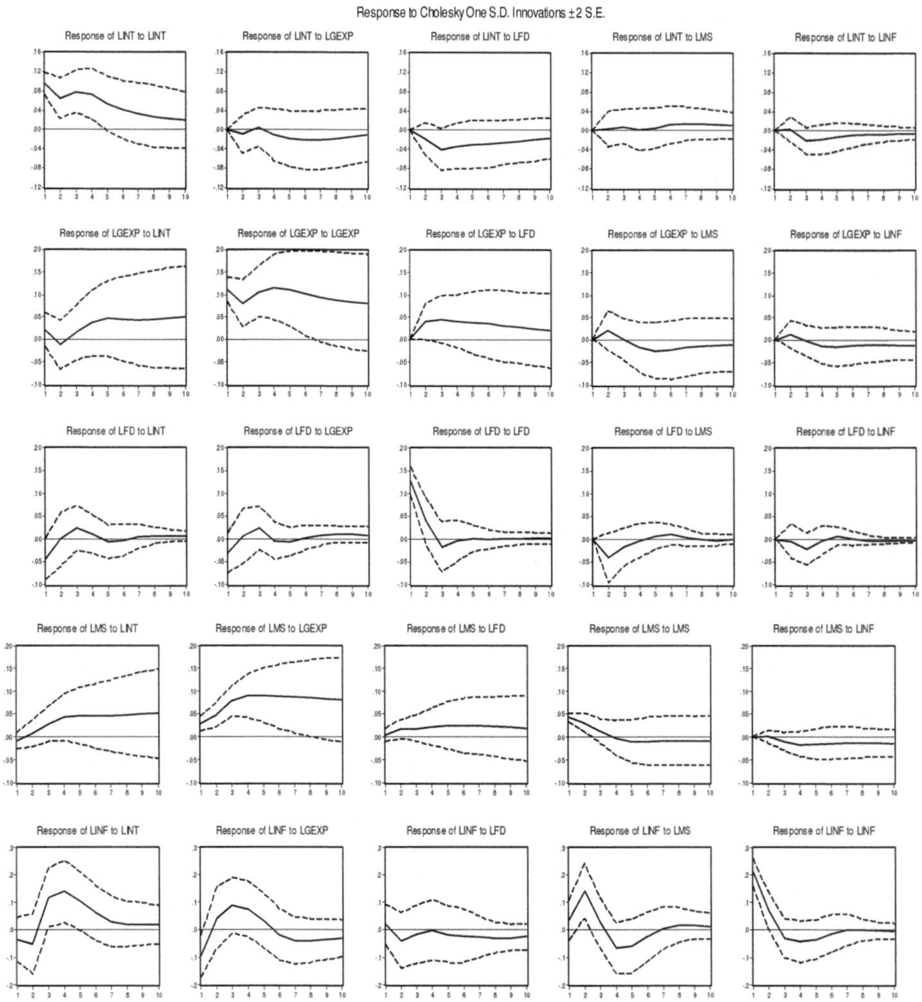

Figure 1. Accumulated impulse response functions for the interest rate equation. The dashed lines are 95% bootstrap confidence bounds. The effects of fiscal deficit, government expenditure and inflation impulses on interest rate are negative for the period under consideration. Only the impulses from the money supply on interest rate generate positive impulses on the interest rate with it making its full impact from the seventh period.

Causality analysis among electricity consumption, consumer expenditure, gross domestic product (GDP) and foreign direct investment (FDI): Case study of Malaysia

Hussain Ali Bekhet* and Nor Salwati bt Othman

College of Business Management and Accounting, Kampus Sultan Haji Ahmad Shah, UniversityTenaga Nasional, Pahang, Malaysia.

The current paper attempts to examine the causal relationship between electricity consumption (EC), consumer price index (CPI), gross domestic product (GDP) and foreign direct investment (FDI). Time series data were used for these variables for 1971 to 2009 period. The vector error correction model (VECM) was employed to estimate the causal relationship between electricity consumption with respective independent variables. All variables were found to be co-integrated indicating the existence of long run relationship among them. Furthermore, the result for long run causality from electricity consumption to FDI, GDP growth and inflation was found to be significant. The results suggest that electricity consumption is an important element determining economic growth in Malaysia and a powerful tool in executing government policy for energy saving. Policy makers should be aware of the importance of stable electricity supply in order to achieve sustainable economic growth.

Key words: Electricity consumption, unit root test, co-integration, vector error correction model, Malaysia.

INTRODUCTION

Over the past two decades, the topic of causal relationship between energy consumption and macroeconomics variables has been analyzed by many researchers. Numerous studies have examined the causal relationship between energy or electricity consumption and several independent variables such as economic growth, price, employment and foreign direct investment (FDI). However, the empirical finding was found either inconsistent or conflicting not only across countries but also across the methodologies used within the same country. Masih and Masih (2007) pointed out that there was no causal relationship between energy consumption and gross domestic product (GDP) in Malaysia. Chen et al. (2007) revealed that there was unidirectional causality from electricity consumption to GDP in Malaysia, while Tang (2009) showed that there was bidirectional causality between electricity consumption and income in Malaysia.

Moreover, the majority of previous studies have focused on the causal relationship between electricity consumption (energy consumption) and economic growth (Masih and Masih, 2007; Yoo, 2006; Ho, 2007; Chandran, 2010; Bekhet and Yusof, 2009). Hondroyiannis, et al (2002) used energy consumption (in general), real GDP and price development. Halicioglu (2007) used residential energy, income, price and urbanization. From the best of our knowledge, only Tang (2009) investigated the causal relationship between FDI and electricity consumption. He also examined the causal relationship between electricity consumption and other independent variables. Based on the above reasons, the current study attempts to re-examine the causal relationship between electricity consumption and real GDP. Also, the relationship between electricity consumption, total expenditure, GDP and FDI, will be investigated.

Historically, results from previous studies can be categorised into three types (Akinlo, 2008); unidirectional causality, second bidirectional causality, and finally, no causality. The causality results are very useful in

*Corresponding author. E-mail: Profhussain@uniten.edu.my.

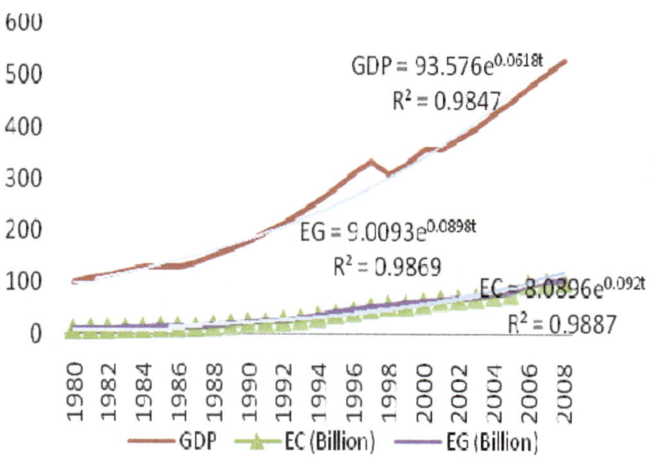

Figure 1a. Electricity consumption, electricity generation and GDP of Malaysia (1980 to 2009).

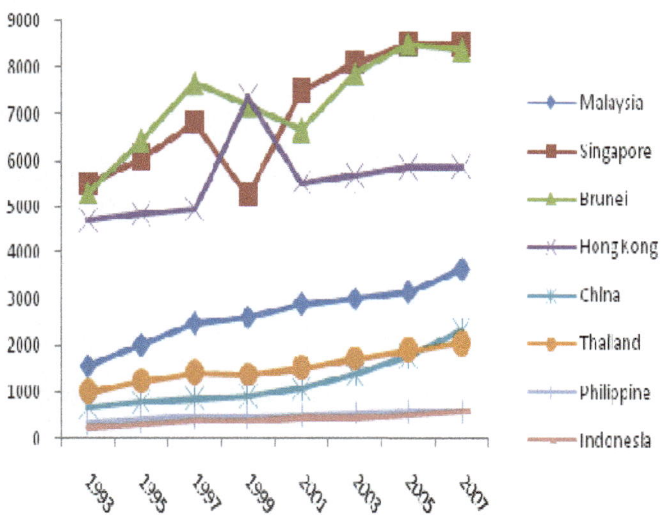

Figure 1b. Electricity consumption in kilowatt hour per capita in ASEAN countries.

determining the appropriate strategies to stimulate growth and to control the level of consumption of the respective countries. For example, if it is found unidirectional causality exists, running from energy consumption to real GDP, it may be implied that the economy will grow if policy makers increase the amount of energy consumption in a country. On the other hand, if unidirectional causality is found to run from real GDP to energy consumption, this would imply that any strategy to increase or decrease the energy will not affect the economic growth. The aim of this paper is to carry out causality tests among electricity consumption, and total expenditure, CPI, GDP and FDI in Malaysia for 1971 to 2009 period. Based on the finding, it would then be possible to determine, which policy is the most appropriate for Malaysia scenario. Furthermore, this can be decided either by concentrating on electricity generation or controlling the electricity usage. In other words, this study will enable us to better understand the role of electricity towards Malaysia economics.

OVERVIEW OF ELECTRICITY SECTOR IN MALAYSIA

In the past three decades, the role of electricity sectors has been viewed as a vital concern in accelerating Malaysian economy. Several studies have found a positive connection between electricity consumption and the economic growth (Ghosh, 2002; Hondroyiannis, et al, 2002; Yoo, 2006; Tang, 2008; Athukorala and Wilson, 2009; Chandran, 2010 and Bekhet and Othman, 2011). These studies reached the conclusion that there was a causal flow from electricity consumption to economic growth. Figure 1a shows the growth rate of the electricity consumption and GDP in Malaysia. The total electricity consumption recorded a growth rate of 9.2% for 1980 to 2009 period. Meanwhile, the GDP recorded RM100.29 million in 1980, increasing by 6.2% per year for 1980 to 2008 period. The main reason for the growth of electricity demand was due to the development of transport sectors such as the railway system, particularly the light rail transit in Klang Valley and inter-city commuter train service and tremendous development of Information Communication Technology, ICT (National Energy Balance, 2007).

The strong growth in manufacturing activity (which is 4.5% within the year 2006 to 2008), supported by the increased in export (which is 4% within the year 2006 to 2008), strong domestic demand, higher tourism activity (it's growth is 33.5% within the year 2006 to 2008) and the opening of new retail outlets have also contributed to the growth in electricity consumption (National Energy Balance, 2007). To this point, electricity consumption per capita in Malaysia was found to be among the highest in ASEAN countries (Figure 1b).

Besides the appearance of positive trend for electricity consumption and GDP in Figure 1a, the same trend was also found for total consumption expenditure made by the Malaysian population, consumer price index (CPI) and FDI. The total consumption expenditure consists of aggregate expenditure for electricity and non electrical goods and this witnessed an increase by 5.4% per year for 1980 to 2009 period. The FDI and CPI increased by 4.3 and 2.8% respectively for the same commencement period.

Unfortunately, the growth in electricity consumption was found to be higher than the growth in electricity generation for the 1980 to 2009 period (Figure 1a). In order to meet the demand of electricity from various sectors, the government invested hugest amounts of money in mega projects such as Bakun hydroelectric project. In this way, the government invested RM41.1

billion in electricity supply industry (8th Malaysia plan). This project is expected to be completed by 2010 with a capacity of 2400 megawatt (Oh et al., 2010). The completion of Bakun project will accelerate the growth in electricity generation and the hydroelectric is expected to account for about 30 to 35% of the generation mix by 2030 (Oh et al., 2010). In addition, there are more projects that have been identified for increasing the generation of the electricity (for more details, (Oh et al., 2010).

LITERATURE REVIEW

The relationship between electricity consumption and economic growth has been widely discussed by many researchers around the world. Unfortunately,the empirical finding was found to be inconsistent across countries and including the methodology used. Jumbe (2004) studied the causality between electricity consumption, agriculture income and non agriculture income. He used error correction model (ECM) and Granger causality analysis for 1970 to 1999 period in Malawi. The Granger causality analysis results showed that agriculture and non agriculture income cause electricity consumption and at the same time the electricity consumption causes the total income. The ECM analysis results showed unidirectional causality from agriculture and non agriculture income to electricity consumption. Narayan and Smyth (2005) used the same methodology with Jumbe (2004) to Australia and found that the growth affected electricity consumption and employment in the short run. Mozumder and Marathe (2007) used the Granger causality analysis to analyze causality direction between GDP and electricity consumption. He found that GDP affected electricity consumption and no causality was found from electricity consumption to GDP.

Asafu (2000) studied the causality between energy consumption, income and price for a number of Asian developing countries such as India, Indonesia, Philippine and Thailand. He used Granger causality analysis data for 1971 to 1995 period. The results showed that the directions of causality were different for different countries in Asia. He found a unidirectional causality from energy consumption to income in India and Indonesia whereas a bidirectional causality between energy consumption and income was found in Philippine and Thailand.

Similarly, Masih and Masih (2007) studied the causality between energy consumption and GDP in Asian countries using vector error correction model (VECM) and VAR analysis. They used annual data over 1955 to 1999 period. They drew the conclusion that there was no causal relationship between energy consumption and GDP in Malaysia, Singapore and Philippine. They also found that there was bidirectional causality between energy consumption and GDP in Pakistan, unidirectional causality from energy consumption to GDP in India and unidirectional causality from GDP to energy consumption in Indonesia.

Ciarreta, et al. (2010) used a panel data from 1970 to 2007 to analyze the causality relationship between electricity consumption, real GDP and energy price. They revealed the long run equilibrium relationship between variables. The causal relationship running from electricity consumption to GDP is revealed. Also, they found a bidirectional relationship between energy price and GDP. Apergis et al. (2011) also used a panel data from 1990 to 2006 for 88 countries. They found a bidirectional relationship between electricity consumption and growth in the short run and long run.

Chen et al. (2007) used different types of energy consumption (electricity) to test the causal relationship with GDP in Asian countries. They used data for 1971 to 2001 period to conclude that there was a unidirectional causality from GDP to electricity consumption in the short run in Malaysia. Furthermore, they found different results as compared to Masih and Masih (2007) and Chandran (2010). They also found unidirectional causality from electricity consumption to GDP in Indonesia. The result in Philippine was conflicting with Masih and Masih (2007). However, they found a unidirectional causality from GDP to electricity consumption. Causality relationship between electricity consumption and other variables in Malaysia was found conflicting with Lean et al. (2010). They found bidirectional causality between aggregate output and electricity consumption. Lang (2010) found bidirectional causality among total electricity consumption, industrial electricity consumption and real GDP in Taiwan for 1971-2006 period.

Yoo (2006) used different types of methodology (Granger causality) to test the causal relationship between electricity consumption and growth in Asian countries for 1971 to 2002 period. He found bidirectional causality between variables. This result is consistent with Tang (2009) who used a similar methodology for 1970 to 2005 period. Furthermore, he found unidirectional causality from growth to electricity consumption in Indonesia and Thailand, which is consistent with Masih and Masih (2007) results. Ho (2007) investigated the causal relationship between electricity consumption and GDP in China. He used ECM analysis for 1966 to 2002 period and found unidirectional causality from electricity consumption to GDP. Shiu and Lam (2004) used the same method in China and also obtained the same result. Tang (2009) used ECM and Granger causality analysis to test causality relationship between electricity consumption, income, population and FDI. He used data for 1970 to 2005 period. He found bidirectional causality between electricity consumption, income and FDI in the short run. On the other hand, Chandran (2010) used ARDL analysis to measure the causality relationship on the same variables which he found the same result. In appendix 1, we summarize the results of the previous causality studies.

DATA AND VARIABLES

In this paper, time series data of electricity consumption (EC), CPI (P), total consumption expenditure (C), real gross domestic product (Y) and FDI for the 1971 to 2009 period for Malaysia will be used. CPI (P), total consumption expenditure (C), real gross domestic product (Y) and foreign direct investment (FDI) as the independent variables will be employed. All of the data were obtained from World Bank and have also been cross-checked with the Department of Statistics of Malaysia (DSOM) and Energy Information administration-EIA (www.eia.doe.gov). Below are more details including its definition:

(i) Electricity consumption (EC) which was measured in million kilowatts.
(ii) Consumer price index (P) was used as a proxy of price. It was used to measure the reaction of electricity consumption towards the changes in price level.
(iii) Total consumption expenditure (C) consists of total expenditure made by the government and private sectors on goods and services. It was used to clarify the role of electricity consumption as a major contributor to total consumption or not.
(iv) Real gross domestic product (Y) was used as a proxy of income. It was used to measure the elasticity of electricity consumption towards the changes in income.
(v) Foreign direct investment (FDI) which is outflow and inflow of FDI. In this analysis, we considered the net value of inflow FDI. The positive value indicated that the value of inflow is greater that the outflow value and vice versa.

All variables are expressed in logarithmic form in order to obtain more stationary behaviour (Vogelvang, 2005). Total consumption expenditure (C), GDP (Y) and FDI were measured in US dollar million and using 2005 as the based year.

METHODOLOGY

The electricity consumption (EC) can be expressed in general as a function of GDP, total consumption expenditure (C), CPI and foreign direct investment (FDI). The electricity consumption is the dependent variable and the rest are the independent variables which expected to influence the level of electricity consumption. The function of electricity consumption can be expressed in Equation (1).

$$EC_t = f(Y_t, C_t, P_t, F_t) \tag{1}$$

where EC, Y, C, P *and* F represent electricity consumption, GDP, consumption expenditure, CPI and FDI respectively. We can represent this function in a mathematical model as shown in Equation (2):

$$EC_t = Y_t^{\rho_1} C_t^{\rho_2} P_t^{\rho_3} F_t^{\rho_4} \tag{2}$$

To apply this model, we transformed it to be linear as shown in Equation (3):

$$lec_t = \rho_0 + \rho_1 lY_t + \rho_2 lC_t + \rho_3 lP_t + \rho_4 lF + e_t \tag{3}$$

where, ρ_0 is a constant and ρ_1, ρ_2, ρ_3 *and* ρ_4 are the coefficients estimate. The above model (3) provides the information on long run effect.

The analysis of Granger causality will involve the process of examining the stationarity of the time series and verifying the order of co-integration by using the Engle-Granger test. In order to conduct the Engle-Granger test, the series of variables are required to be stationary. This is done by testing for unit root test by using ADF and P.P tests at level $I(0)$. If we failed to reject the null hypothesis $[H_0: Y_t \sim I(0)]$, we have to proceed with stationarity test at first difference $I(1)$ (Studenmund, 2006). If once again we failed to reject null hypothesis $[H_0: Y_t \sim I(1)]$, we will proceed to test stationarity at second difference. Usually, the macroeconomics data will achieve stationarity at first or second difference. The function of stationarity is to avoid from spurious regression results.

The co-integration can be capture by analyzing the stationarity of the residual for estimate model by OLS method. If the residual is stationary, this indicates that there is long run equilibrium among variables (Vogelvang, 2005) and all the variables are accepted by macroeconomics theory to analyze the elasticity of electricity consumption. If the variables are not co-integrated at level [failed to reject null hypothesis $H_0: ect_t \sim I(0)$] we ought to test for co-integration at first and then second difference until they are co-integrated. The decision whether to reject or not is depended on the value of ADF statistic for residual. If this value is smaller than the critical value of ADF we have to reject the null hypothesis which means there is no co-integration (Hamilton, 1994; Fuller, 1976; Volgelvang, 2005). This procedure is crucial because the elasticities are valid only if the variables have the same order of integration. ADF and P.P tests for co-integration will be used to investigate the degree of integration.

In order to examine the direction of causality between EC and the respective macroeconomics variables, the dynamic Granger causality test is used. Granger causality was employed due to it's ability to response for both large and small sample size (Odhiambo, 2009). The multivariate Granger causality model between EC, GDP, CPI, C and FDI based on the ECM is specified as follow:

$$\Delta lec_t = \alpha_0 + \sum_{i=1} \alpha_1 \Delta lec_{t-1} + \sum_{i=1} \alpha_2 \Delta lY_{t-1} + \sum_{i=1} \alpha_3 \Delta lP_{t-1} + \sum_{i=1} \alpha_4 \Delta lC_{t-1} + \sum_{i=1} \alpha_5 \Delta lF_{t-1} + \alpha_6\, ect_{t-1} \tag{4}$$

$$\Delta lY_t = \mu_0 + \sum_{i=1} \mu_1 \Delta lY_{t-1} + \sum_{i=1} \mu_2 \Delta lec_{t-1} + \sum_{i=1} \mu_3 \Delta lP_{t-1} + \sum_{i=1} \mu_4 \Delta lC_{t-1} + \sum_{i=1} \mu_5 \Delta lF_{t-1} + \mu_6\, ect_{t-1} \tag{5}$$

$$\Delta lP_t = \beta_0 + \sum_{i=1} \beta_1 \Delta lP_{t-1} + \sum_{i=1} \beta_2 \Delta lY_{t-1} + \sum_{i=1} \beta_3 \Delta lec_{t-1} + \sum_{i=1} \beta_4 \Delta lC_{t-1} + \sum_{i=1} \beta_5 \Delta lF_{t-1} + \beta_6\, ect_{t-1} \tag{6}$$

Table 1. Conditions for causal relationship.

Causal flow			Condition	
			Short run	Long run
Economic growth	→	Electricity consumption	$\alpha_2 \neq 0$	$\alpha_6 \neq 0$
Electricity Consumption	→	Economic growth	$\mu_2 \neq 0$	$\mu_6 \neq 0$
Electricity consumption	→	Inflation	$\beta_3 \neq 0$	$\beta_6 \neq 0$
Inflation	→	Electricity consumption	$\alpha_3 \neq 0$	$\alpha_6 \neq 0$
Electricity consumption	→	Consumption expenditure	$\varphi_4 \neq 0$	$\varphi_6 \neq 0$
Consumption expenditure	→	Electricity consumption	$\alpha_4 \neq 0$	$\alpha_6 \neq 0$
Electricity consumption	→	FDI	$\theta_5 \neq 0$	$\theta_6 \neq 0$
FDI	→	Electricity consumption	$\alpha_5 \neq 0$	$\alpha_6 \neq 0$

Table 2. The results of the unit root test.

Stage	Variables	ADF	P.P
		Trend and intercept	Trend and intercept
At Level	lec	-5.4916*	-2.1007
	lY	-2.2431	-2.4363
	lP	-4.0329	-2.7867
	lC	-2.6001	-2.6001
	lF	-3.2940***	-3.3473***
At 1st difference	Δlec	-3.9796**	-3.9965**
	ΔlY	-4.8261*	-4.7499*
	ΔlP	-4.2282*	4.2282*
	ΔlC	-5.2989*	-5.2704*
	ΔlF	-8.0860*	-8.1108*

*, **, *** Represent the stationary at 1, 5 and 10% significant level, respectively. Source: Output EViews 6.0.

$$\Delta lC_t = \varphi_0 + \sum_{i=1} \varphi_1 \Delta lC_{t-1} + \sum_{i=1} \varphi_2 \Delta lY_{t-1} + \sum_{i=1} \varphi_3 \Delta lP_{t-1} + \sum_{i=1} \varphi_4 \Delta lec_{t-1} + \sum_{i=1} \varphi_5 \Delta lF_{t-1} + \varphi_6 ect_{t-1} \quad (7)$$

$$\Delta lF_t = \theta_0 + \sum_{i=1} \theta_1 \Delta lF_{t-1} + \sum_{i=1} \theta_2 \Delta lY_{t-1} + \sum_{i=1} \theta_3 \Delta lP_{t-1} + \sum_{i=1} \theta_4 \Delta lC_{t-1} + \sum_{i=1} \theta_5 \Delta lec_{t-1} + \theta_6 ect_{t-1} \quad (8)$$

Where lec, lY, lP, lC and lF represent the natural log of electricity consumption, CPI, consumption expenditure and foreign direct investment respectively. ect represents error correction term. The ECM enables us to estimate the long run and short run Granger causality. The coefficient $\alpha_i, \mu_i, \beta_i, \varphi_i$ and θ_i (i=1,….,5) indicate the short run causality if the value is not equal to zero. However, if these coefficients equal to zero, this will indicate that there is no short run causality among respective variables. Furthermore the coefficients $\alpha_6, \mu_6, \beta_6, \varphi_6$ and θ_6 indicate the long run causality if the coefficient is not equal to zero and vice versa. These causal conditions among above variables can be summarized as shown in Table 1.

RESULT ANALYSIS

Table 2 shows the results for the ADF and P.P unit root test for electricity consumption (lec), GDP (lY), CPI (lP), consumption expenditure (lC) and FDI (lF). In this test, we include intercept because it is more appropriate with economic practice (Vogelvang, 2005). The results indicate that electricity consumption and FDI at $I(0)$ are stationary at 10% significant level while the remainder variables contain unit root or non stationary. However, the first differences of study variables lead to stationary at least at 5% significant level. These results are consistent with the notion that most of the macroeconomics variables are non-stationary at $I(0)$, but they will become stationary after the first or second difference (Nelson and Plosser, 1982; Tang, 2008).

In order to examine the long run relationship among variables, the co-integration test was conducted by using Engle-Granger Augmented Dickey-Fuller test. The result showed that the value of ADF statistic for residual is smaller than ADF critical value at 5% significant level. The results revealed that there was an evidence of long run relationship among the study variables and it also indicated that all of the variables were accepted by macroeconomics theory to analyze the causal relationship. Likewise, the existence of a co-integrating relationship among electricity consumption, and explanator variables suggested that there ought to Granger causality in at least one direction. The result of long run co-integration relationship between electricity consumption and independent variables showed in Equation (9). It indicated that GDP, total consumption expenditure and FDI have a significant effect to electricity consumption in the long run at 1% significant level. However, it did not indicate any causal flow from one variable to another.

$lec_t = -5.82 + 1.91 lY_t - 0.47 lC_t + 0.11 lP_t - 1.91 lF_t$

p.value (0.00) (0.00) (0.31) (0.00)

t= (15.40) (-3.50) (1.03) (-4.57)

R^2 = 0.99 DW = 1.51

F- test = 5896 (0.00) (9)

Since all of the variables were co-integrated, the causality relationship can be examined by using VECM. If equation (9) provides us with the information of long run relationship, the VECM would provide us with the evidence of short run and long run causality relationship as shown that in Equations (10 to14).

$\Delta lec_t = 0.04 + 0.52 \Delta lEC_{t-1} + 0.02 \Delta lY_{t-1} - 0.18 \Delta lP_{t-1} + 0.12 \Delta lC_{t-1} + 0.12 \Delta lF_{t-1} - 0.32 ect_{t-1}$

p value (0.02) (0.97) (0.44) (0.52) (0.23) (0.14)

t=(2.54) 0.04) (-0.79) (0.65) (1.20) (-1.50)

R^2 = 0.37 DW = 1.90

F- test = 2.89 (0.02) (10)

$\Delta lY_t = 0.04 + 0.72 \Delta lY_{t-1} - 0.01 \Delta lec_{t-1} - 0.19 \Delta lP_{t-1} - 0.22 \Delta lC_{t-1} - 0.01 \Delta lF_{t-1} + 0.99 ect_{t-1}$

p value (0.06) (0.97)(0.40) (0.23) (0.45) (0.02)

t = (1.98) (-0.41) (-0.86) (-1.18) (-0.77) (-2.49)

R^2 =0.25 DW = 1.90

F- test = 1.69 (0.16) (11)

$\Delta lP_t = 0.02 + 0.40 \Delta lP_{t-1} + 0.17 \Delta lY_{t-1} - 0.11 \Delta lec_{t-1} + 0.09 \Delta lC_{t-1} - 0.01 \Delta lF_{t-1} + 0.22 ect_{t-1}$

p value (0.01) (0.32) (0.30) (0.41) (0.22) (0.00)

t= (2.97) (1.02) (-1.06) (0.83) (-1.26) (-3.27)

R^2 = 0.57 DW = 1.62

F- test = 6.53 (0.00) (12)

$\Delta lC_t = 0.04 - 0.32 \Delta lC_{t-1} + 0.77 \Delta lY_{t-1} - 0.06 \Delta lP_{t-1} - 0.11 \Delta lec_{t-1} - 0.003 \Delta lF_{t-1} + 0.004 ect_{t-1}$

p value(0.32) (0.16) (0.87) (0.70) (0.89) (0.98)

t = (-1.02) (1.45) (-0.17) (-0.39) (-0.14) (0.02)

R^2 =0.10 DW=1.80

F- test = 0.54(0.77) (13)

$\Delta lF_t = - 0.16 - 0.10 \Delta lF_{t-1} - 4.49 \Delta lY_{t-1} + 2.54 \Delta lP_{t-1} + 2.76 \Delta lC_{t-1} + 2.79 \Delta lec_{t-1} - 0.59 ect_{t-1}$

p value (0.68) (0.33) (0.47) (0.31) (0.36) (0.05)

t = (-0.41) (-0.99) (0.74) (1.02) (0.93)(-2.06)

R^2 = 0.24 DW = 2.17

F- test = 1.61 (0.18) (14)

However, it can be seen that the F statistic for Equation (10) and (12) were significant at 5% significance level, while F statistic for the remainder equations were found to be insignificant. The short-run effects of the past values of electricity consumption was significant at the 5% level (Equation 10), but neither GDP, price, consumption expenditure and FDI was significant. This result indicated that the previous electricity consumption effect the current electricity consumption. Moreover, Equations (11 and 12) showed the same pattern. The results showed that the past values of income growth (price) effect the current income growth (price).

The coefficients for "ect" in Equations (11, 12 and 14) were found significant at 5% level. So, the information of long run causality provided. Equation (11) shown that the unidirectional causality running from electricity consumption to income growth which is consistent with previous studies (Akinlo, 2009; Bekhet and Yusof, 2009; Chandran, 2010) and contrast with Mozumber (2007). However, it was inconsistent with Jumbe (2004), Oh (2004), Yoo (2006) and Tang (2009), where the bilateral causality between electricity consumption and growth were found.

Equation (12) showed the unidirectional long run causality running from electricity consumption to inflation. Meanwhile, Equation (14) showed the long run causality running from electricity consumption to FDI and no short run causality. FDI is the engine for growth and the long run causality was inconsistent with Tang (2009).

POLICY IMPLICATIONS

The results show unidirectional causality running from electricity consumption to growth in FDI. This indicates that electricity consumption may increase the inflow of foreign investment in Malaysia and thus improves the balance of payment (reduce deficit). The growth in FDI and real GDP was seen as a positive indicator. However, the growth in electricity consumption can be seen as a negative indicator as well. The results show the causality running from electricity consumption to CPI. This indicates that the increase in electricity consumption will lead to inflation and as a consequence it will reduce consumer purchasing power.

Also, the results provide us with evidence that Malaysia is an energy dependent country. Thus, the energy policies should aim to increase electricity generation by sustaining the current electricity supply and at the same time exploring the possibilities renewable for electricity generation. Policy makers ought to ensure that the growth of electricity supply is greater than the growth of electricity consumption to boost the economic growth. In other words, better management on energy growth policies is vital in order to ensure sufficient electricity supply to support the Malaysia economic development. Meanwhile, energy saving policy could be inappropriate for economic growth in the long run.

CONCLUSION AND RECOMMENDATION

In current paper, we analyzed the causal relationship among electricity consumption, CPI, total consumption expenditure, GDP and FDI by using VECM. The time series data for 1971 to 2009 period was employed in order to meet those objectives. The co-integration test has proven that there was a long run relationship between the studied variables. Then we proceeded with analyzing the causal relationship among the variables using VECM. But, the result for long run causality from electricity consumption to FDI was found to be significant. This result is inconsistent with Tang result's (2009). Moreover, the result for long run causality running from electricity consumption to inflation was found to be significant at 1% level. This indicates that the increase electricity consumption will affect the major macroeconomics problem (inflation). This result is consistent with the observation in Thailand and Philippine but inconsistent with other developing countries (Asafu et al., 2000).

Furthermore, current paper proves that the electricity consumption is a vital component to stimulate economic growth in Malaysia. Also, the results showed that there was a long run causality running from electricity consumption to economic growth and it is consistent with Chandran (2010), Ho (2007), Yoo (2006) and Jumbe (2004). Unfortunately, economic growth cannot be simply achieved if there is a shortage of electricity supply. In addition, it is a crucial challenge to the policy makers to ensure a sufficient amount of electricity supply within a country. For future research, it is suggested to analyze and explore the possibility of energy sustainable and renewable in a country since it is a necessity in order to ensure smooth implementation of development projects and to stimulating country's economic growth today and thereafter.

REFERENCES

Akinlo AE (2009). Electricity consumption and economic growth in Negeria: Evidence from cointegration and co-feature analysis. J. Policy Model., 31: 681-693.

Apergis N, Payne JE (2011). A dynamic panel study of economic development and the electricity consumption-growth nexus. Energy Econ., (in press)

Asafu-Adjaye J. (2000). The relationship between elasticity consumption, electricity prices and economics growth: Time series evidence from Asian developing countries. Energy Econ., 2: 615-625.

Athukorala PPAW, Wilson C (2009). Estimating short and long term residential demand for electricity: New evidence from Sri Langka, Energy Econ., pp. 44-46

Bekhet HA, Yusof NY (2009). Assessing the relationship between oil prices, energy consumption and macroeconomics performance in Malaysia: Co-integration and vector error correction model (VECM) approach. J. Int. Bus. Res., 2: 152-175.

Bekhet HA, Othman NS (2011). Assessing the Elasticities of Electricity Consumption for rural and urban areas in Malaysia: A Non-linear approach. Int. J. Econ. Fin., 3(1).

Chandran VGR, Sharma S, Madhavan K (2010). Electricity consumption-growth nexus: The case of Malaysia. Energy Policy, 38: 606-612.

Chen ST, Kuo HI, Chen C (2007). The relationship between GDP and electricity consumption in 10 Asian countries. Energy Policy, 35: 2611-2621.

Ghosh S (2002). Electricity consumption and economic growth in India, Energy policy, 30: 125-129.

Halicioglu F (2007). Residential electricity demand dynamics in Turkey, Energy Econ., 29: 199-210.

Ho CY, Siu KW (2007). A dynamic equilibrium of electricity consumption and GDP in Hong Kong: An empirical investigation. Energy Policy, 35: 2507-2513.

Hondroyiannis G, Lolos S, Papapetroa E (2002). Energy consumption and economic growth: assessing the evidence from Greece. Energy Econ., 24: 319-336.

Jumbe CBL (2004). Cointegration and causality between electricity consumption and GDP: Empirical evidence from Malawi, Energy Econ., 26: 61-68.

Lang YC, Lin HP, Chang CH (2010). Linear and nonlinear causality between sectoral electricity consumption and economic growth: Evidence from Taiwan. Energy Policy, 38: 6570-6573.

Lean HH, Smyth R (2010). Multivariate Granger causality between electricity generation, exports, prices and GDP in Malaysia. Energy, 35: 3640-3648.

Masih AM, Masih R (2007). Energy consumption, real income and temporal causality: Result from a multi study based on co-integration and error correction modeling techniques, 18: 165-183.

Mozumder P, Marathe A (2007). Causality relationship between electricity consumption and GDP in Bangladesh. Energy Policy, 35: 375-402.

Narayan PK, Smyth R, Prasad A (2005). Electricity consumption, employment and real income in Australia evidence from multivariate Granger causality test. Energy Policy, 33: 1109-1116.

Odhiambo NM (2009). Electricity consumption and economic growth in South Africa: A trivariate causality test. Energy Economics, 31: 635-640.

Oh W, Lee K (2004). Causal relationship between energy consumption and GDP revisited: the case of Korea 1970-1999. Energy Econ., 26: 51-59.

Shiu A, Lam PL (2004), Electricity consumption and economic growth in China. Energy Policy, 32: 47-54.

Studenmund AH (2006). Using econometrics: A practical guide, 5th Edition, Pearson International Edition.US.

Tang CF (2008). A re-examination of the relationship between electricity consumption and economic growth in Malaysia. Energy Policy, 36: 3077-3085.
Tang CF (2009). Electricity consumption, income, foreign direct investment and population in Malaysia. J. Econ. Stud., 36: 371-382.
Vogelvang B (2005). Econometrics: Theory and applications with EViews, 1st Edition, Prentice Hall.UK, pp.14-16
Yoo SH (2006). Electricity consumption and economics growth: Evidence from Korea. Energy Policy, 33: 1627-1632.
Yoo SH (2006). The causal relationship between electricity consumption and economic growth in the ASEAN countries. Energy Policy, 34: 3573-3582.
Yoo SH (2006). Electricity consumption and economic growth: A cross-country analysis. Energy Policy, 34: 3573-3582.
Zachariadis T, Pashourtidou N (2007). An empirical analysis of electricity consumption in Cyprus, Energy Econ., 29: 183-198.

APPENDIX

Appendix 1. Results of the previous causality studies.

Country	Empirical work	Study period	Methodology	Variables used	Results
India	Asafu-Adjaye (2000)	1971-1995	G.C	Energy Consumption (EnC), Income and price	-EnC causes income
Indonesia					-EnC causes income
Philippine					-Bilateral causality between EnC and income -EnC, income and price are mutually causal.
Thailand					- Bilateral causality between EnC and income - EnC, income and price are mutually causal.
Melawi	Jumbe (2004)	1970-1999	Granger causality (G.C) and ECM	Electricity consumption (EC), Agriculture income (GDP) and non Agriculture income (NGDP)	-EC causes GDP -GDP causes EC -NGDP causes EC -GDP and NGDP causes EC
Korea	Oh and Lee (2004)	1970-1999	VECM and VAR	Energy consumption and GDP	- Bilateral causality between EC and growth in long run. - EC causes growth in short run.
China	Shiu et al .(2004)	1971-2000	ECM	EC and real GDP	EC causes real GDP
Australia	Narayan and Smyth (2005)	1966-1999	GC and ECM	EC, employment and income	- Growth causes EC in short run - Growth causes employment in short run.
Indonesia	Yoo (2006)	1971-2002	G.C	EC and Growth(g)	-g causes EC
Malaysia					-Bilateral causality between EC and g
Singapore					-Bilateral causality between EC and g
Thailand					g causes EC
Bangladesh	Mazumder et al. (2007)	1971-1999	G.C	GDP percapita and EC percapita	-GDP causes EC
India	Masih and Masih (2007)	1955-1991	VECM and VAR	Energy consumption (EnC) and GDP	-EnC causes GDP
Pakistan					- EC causes GDP, GDP causes EC.
Indonesia					- GDP causes EC
Malaysia					-No causal relationship
Singapore					- No causal relationship
Philippine					-No causal relationship
China	Chen et al. (2007)	1971-2001	VECM	GDP and EC	-No causality relationship

Appendix 1. Contd.

Hong Kong Indonesia India Korea Malaysia Philippine Singapore Taiwan Thailand					- EC causes GDP -EC causes GDP (LR) -GDP causes EC -GDP causes EC, and EC causes GDP GDP causes EC in Short run (SR) -GDP causes EC -GDP causes EC, and EC causes GDP -No causality relationship -No causality relationship.
Hong Kong	Ho et al. (2007)	1966-2002	ECM	EC and GDP	-EC causes GDP
Malaysia	Tang (2008)	1972-2008	ARDL ECM	EC and growth	- EC and growth are not co-integrated -Bilateral causality between EC and growth.
Malaysia	Tang (2009)	1970-2005	ECM and GC	EC, Income, population and FDI	-Bilateral causality between EC, income and FDI in the short run. -Income, FDI and Population causes EC
Nigeria	Akinlo (2009)	1980-2006	ECM	EC and growth	- Unidirectional causality from EC to growth.
South Africa	Odhiambo (2009)	1971-2006	Co-integration ECM	EC, growth and employment	-Bidirectional causality between EC and growth in long run. -EC causes growth in long run.
Malaysia	Chandran, et al. (2010)	1971-2003	ARDL	EC and growth	-EC causes growth in the short and long run.
Malaysia	Lean et al. (2010)	1970-2008	Granger causality	Economic growth Electricity generation Export Prices	-Unidirectional causality from economics growth to electricity generation -No causality between price and economic growth.
Malaysia	Lean et al. (2010)	1971-2006	Granger causality	Electricity consumption Aggregate output Export Labor Capital	-Bidirectional causality between aggregate output and electricity consumption.
Taiwan	Lang et al. (2010)	1982-2008	Granger causality	Total electricity consumption Real GDP Residential electricity consumption Industrial electricity consumption	-Bidirectional causality among Total electricity consumption, Industrial electricity consumption and real GDP. -No causality between Residential electricity consumption and Real GDP.

Appendix 1. Contd.

Europe	Ciarreta et al. (2010)	1970-2007 (panel data)	Co-integration VECM	Electricity consumption Real GDP Energy price	-The long run relationship between 3 series (Electricity consumption, real gdp and energy price). -Negative short run and strong causality from electricity consumption to GDP. -Bidirectional relationship between energy price and GDP.
88 selected countries	Apergis et al. (2011)	1990-2006	Granger causality	Electricity consumption Real GDP Real fixed capital formation Total labor force	-Bidirectional causality between electricity consumption and economic growth in short run and long run. -Unidirectional causality from electricity consumption to economic growth.

GC = Granger causality; ECM = error correction model.

Social and financial performance of microfinance institutions: Is there a trade-off?

BEN SOLTANE Bassem

Faculty of Economics and Management of Sfax-Tunisia. E-mail: bensoltane.bassem@laposte.net.

The simultaneous achievement of financial and social objectives assigned to microfinance institutions is a challenge. Showing good financial performance (good profitability) and having a high depth of outreach (serving the poor) may be contradictory. Therefore, these "banks for the poor" are facing a trade-off that can lead to mission drift. To verify the existence of this fact, we have analyzed the relationship between financial performance and depth of outreach from a sample of 64 microfinance institutions of the Middle East and North Africa (MENA) region, from 2008 to 2010. Our results showed that the relationship is neutral, but we were able to confirm the presence of a trade-off that stems from the desire of microfinance institutions to reduce their portfolio at risk. However, we did not find that a higher portfolio at risk is associated with poorer clients, and hence a not justified mission drift. We can therefore conclude that microfinance institutions can well and truly achieve their double objective (social and financial) and thus fulfill their "ultimate promise".

Key words: Microfinance institutions, social performance, financial performance, depth of outreach, trade-off, mission drift, panel data, Middle East and North Africa (MENA) region.

INTRODUCTION

The boom of microfinance, the hope it raises as a catalyst for sustainable economic development as well as the extent of resources invested in this sector, deserve our attention. Microfinance means the provision of financial services such as savings, loans and insurance to low-income persons carrying out productive activities, and excluded from the standard banking system because of their socio-economic profile (Labie, 1999). These low-income people are not employees, they do not offer required guarantee and are often illiterate, so they would not be profitable for the microfinance institutions (MFIs).
According to the definition, microfinance is somehow a response to the debt problems and economic crisis in most developing countries. In this sense, it is seen as one of the tools intended to reduce the poverty. In addition, in contrast to the development aid policies conducted previously maintaining the poor in a state of dependence on handouts and on the provision of free social services, the experiences to empower poor to break the ties that bind them to their precarious conditions were seen by the good eye.

Therefore, the challenge of microfinance institutions (MFIs), commonly known as "bank for the poor", consists in putting in place systems that allows the greatest number of poor people, to access to financial services and on a sustainable basis. These institutions have often found their origin in the development projects and nearby non-governmental organizations (NGOs) and their success can be attributed to the introduction of non-traditional methods of hedging against default risk such as joint liability, social pressures or personal guarantees. Indeed, it is often decentralized financial systems, aiming at providing, in an efficient and financially sustainable way, small loan without collateral to the poorest segments of the society. These microcredits are often used to finance self-employment activities for low-income people and urban and rural micro-entrepreneurs who have limited or no access to formal financial services. To achieve their objectives, MFIs need to be as competitive as possible and financially viable, that is, profitable.

Thus, in their quest to obtain additional and required financial resources to meet an increasing demand for microcredits, MFIs still face some problems such as the need to reduce operating costs to a minimum, improving the performance of financial management and administration. In order to negotiate resources from commercial banks and receive assistance from donors, they must inspire confidence and trust, ensuring their own financial sustainability, and develop appropriate financial mechanisms to capture financial resources, allowing them to make economies of scale.

Financial performance becomes the watchword in the governance of MFIs. Everything is done to show good financial results. Nevertheless, paying too much attention to profitability is likely to move away the institution from their primary objective of delivering financial services to the poor by a too strict selection of clients (move away from their social objectives). On the other hand, an overly social vision could lead to the application of very low interest rates threatening the viability of the institution. Financial intermediation and social intermediation, double mission of MFIs, can therefore be subject to divergent priorities and expectations and therefore can easily lead to conflict.

Therefore, one wonders if the MFIs face a trade-off between achieving good financial performance (financial target) and a high depth of outreach (social objective). Many "banks of the poor", given the high risks of poorest, attempt to abandon them to the detriment of wealthy belonging to the middle class and move away from their primary objective of delivering financial services to the poor. We seek to know whether the pursuit of financial returns by microfinance institutions conflicts with their desire to provide financial services to the poorest of the poor. In other words, we want to determine whether the targeting of the poorest prove to be obstacle to the achievement of good financial performance or rather these two goals can be achieved together. To reach this purpose, we will rely on the case of some MFIs in the Middle East and North Africa (MENA) region.

The rest of this paper will be structured as follows. Subsequently, the study provides a brief overview of the microfinance schism. Thereafter, it presents the research framework, sample (data collection) and variables followed by the research methodology. The study then presents its results and discussions. Finally the study was concluded.

THE MICROFINANCE SCHISM

Microfinance is a mean of poverty alleviation in developing countries through the financing of the activities productive of incomes for poor households. However, the best way of helping the poor to have access to the financial services leads to an opposition between two approaches (Welfarist and Institutionalist) which Jonathan Morduch refers to as the "microfinance schism" (Armendáriz and Jonathan, 2005). Though they all share the objective of poverty alleviation, these two paradigms put microfinance at the crossroads Each position differ on how to provide microfinance services (NGO vs. commercial banks), the technology to be used (financial service approach or minimalist providing financial services only vs. integrated service approach), and finally the performance evaluation methods.

Protagonists of the welfarist approach (also called the direct credit approach) perceive the microfinance as an effective tool in the fight against poverty and vulnerability and improve the well-being of the poor. In addition to providing financial services, this approach favors the granting of non-financial services such as training and technical assistance to micro-entrepreneurs, literacy and so on. It is this vision that prevailed in the 80's.

The welfarist approach focuses on creating solidarity institutions such as NGOs or cooperatives which regard microfinance as a major tool for reducing the poverty of poorest (Hamed, 2004). The best-known example of the welfarist approach is the famous Grameen Bank winning the Nobel Peace Prize 2006, along with its founder Muhammad Yunus. Another example is the village banking programs developed by Foundation of International Community Assistance (FINCA) in Latin America and more recently in Africa and Asia.

Based on the logic of subsidization (interest rates were even lower than market rates), this approach led to high unpaid rates and transaction costs, resulting in the failure of many microcredit programs (Von Pischke et al., 1983; World Bank, 198; Yaron, 1994).

Partisans of the welfarist approach use "welfare studies" (also called "Household Studies") to evaluate the effectiveness of microcredit programs. The purpose is to measure the impact of microcredit on the living conditions of the targeted populations, that is, the change in terms of well-being and quality of life of the beneficiaries. They want to assess the situation before and after accession to the MFIs. Thus, they are interested about the changes in the level of income, nutrition and education of the poor as well as the access to health care services and insurance. However, institutionalists reproach this type of studies to be too subjective and lead to excessive costs in addition to the methodological difficulties that may encounter.

Supported by international organisations such as the World Bank, the United Nations, United States Agency for International Development (USAID), Consultative Group to Assist the Poorest (CGAP), the institutionalist approach (or financial market approach) try to put the microcredit programs within the logic of market. Aware of the limited capacity of donors to meet the huge demand for microcredit, protagonists of this approach insist on the will of the setting up of a sustainable microfinance system as well as the will of rendering loans within the reach of the majority of the population (De Briey, 2005). Each MFI should aim at financial sustainability by maximizing its effectiveness and its productivity, in order to reach financial self-sufficiency. As a consequence, they require from its clients very high interest rates in order to cover transaction costs related to any microcredit. The objective is not focused on improving the welfare of the very poor in general but rather on serving on clients very close to the poverty line, geographically concentrated, having highly profitable activities with short production cycle. This approach can be observed through two great trends: We find the upgrading process of microcredit programs: process of creating certain regulated MFIs in countries (such as Peru, Bolivia) offering a regulation process of the specialized institutions in microfinance. These MFIs are NGOs moving away from their status as "Non-Profit Organization" to regulated financial institutions having the status of limited companies and which come clearly within the scope of profitability logic (De Briey, 2005). On the other hand, we find the downgrading process of microcredit programs where certain traditional commercial banks which are looking for new markets and new clients can directly grant loans to the micro-entrepreneurs or can acquire shares in the MFIs.

As regards the evaluation of microcredit programs, the protagonists of the "institutionalists" approach prefer to use proxies and carry out "institutional studies". They are interested in market variables such as the number of poor people affected, financial self-sufficiency, financial sustainability, profitability, quality of service, etc. (Otero and Rhyne, 1994). Institutionalists emphasize the performance evaluation from the standpoint of the institution to the detriment of its customers. They consider financial autonomy as a criterion that better fulfills the social mission (Cornée, 2007). The welfarists, in turn, criticize the failure of the institutionalists to take into account the effect of microcredit on the poor people.

As we can see, the debate between welfarists and Institutionnalists is far from over despite their common goal of reducing poverty "to include the excluded" (Bhatt, 1997). It looked like two nations divided by a common language (Woller and Dunford, 1999). While the welfarists, anxious to serve the poorest people focus on the depth outreach, the institutionnalists, seeking for financial viability, will prefer instead the breath of outreach.

Thus we wonder whether this dichotomous view of microfinance has its reason for being. Is the "best practices" recommended by the institutionalists camp are the only and unique methods for managing these microfinance institutions. According to Otero and Rhyne (1994), practitioners of microfinance, both approaches are the two ends of a spectrum within which different forms of microcredit programs fall. Therefore, there is not a single model of microfinance able to solve the various problems of development of the poor people around the world. In fact, according to Bhatt (1997) there is a place for different kinds of microcredit programs. This view is also shared by Woller and Warner (1999).

RESEARCH FRAMEWORK, SAMPLE (DATA COLLECTION) AND VARIABLES

The analytical framework we have chosen to conduct our study is that of Middle East and North Africa (MENA) region while selecting ten countries: Egypt, Jordan, Lebanon, Morocco, Palestine, Sudan, Syria, Iraq, Tunisia and Yemen. We chose this framework because it is composed of developing countries where several successful experiments have been undertaken. As we mentioned previously, microfinance is the hope for these poor countries. Therefore, it is interesting to know whether in countries where microfinance plays an important role in the economy, MFIs are able to fulfill their dual mission and do not face a possible trade-off between profitability and social outreach.

The MFIs data are collected from individual institutions as reported to mix market (www.mixmarket.org), a non-governmental organization whose object is to promote the exchange of information on the microfinance sector around the world. This database collects information on 73 MFIs operating according to international standards from ten countries in the MENA region. This information, primarily financial in nature, is incomplete. Therefore, additional data were collected from the World Bank, World Development Indicators (WDI) and World Governance Indicators (WGI), the International Monetary Fund (IMF), various recent reports of Planet Rating, some additional reports of mix "Social Performance Standards" (SPS) and annual reports specific to MFIs.

We finally selected 64 MFIs with the highest levels of information transparency regarding their social and financial performance (three to five diamonds). The sample is composed of 14 MFIs from Egypt, 8 from Jordan, 10 from Morocco, 1 from Tunisia, 6 from Yemen, 3 from Lebanon, 8 from Palestine, 3 from Syria, 1 from Sudan and 10 from Iraq. It covers three North African countries and seven middle-east countries. The latest information for the selected microfinance institutions dates from 2008 to 2010. So our analysis will be done on this period of three years (Table 1).

From the selected sample, we will conduct an analysis of the relationship between depth of outreach and financial sustainability of microfinance institutions. The relationship between these two concepts will enable us to confirm whether or not MFIs face a trade-off. Thus, a negative link attest the presence of a trade-off in accordance with the Trade-off theory, which states that the inclusion of Corporate Social Responsibility (better social performance) involves additional financial costs, thus creating a competitive disadvantage (Friedman, 1970), which entail bad financial performance. However, a positive link may suggest a synergy and finally a neutral association refers to the absence of meaningful relationship.

Our study will be built on that made by D'Arcimoles and Trebucq (2002) in their article: The corporate social performance-financial performance link: evidence from France. We made a parallel between the FP-SP relationship in a corporate and the FP-DO relationship in MFIs. Indeed, in our research we aim to determine whether Middle East and North Africa MFIs can achieve together their two main objectives or a trade-off exists. Hence, to translate financial targets we use the financial

Table 1. Characteristics of surveyed countries in 2010.

Country	Population (millions)	Average GNI per Capita, PPP ($)	Population below national poverty line (%)*	No. of MFIs operating according to international standards	No.of borrowers in these MFIs (thousands)	Penetration rate
Egypt	83	5,690	16.7	16	795,306	24
Jordan	6	5,840	16.7	8	197,819	54
Iraq	31	3,340	N/A	12	74,359	3
Lebanon	4	13,230	N/A	3	37,647	12
Morocco	32	4,450	N/A	10	807,090	36
Palestine	4	N/A	N/A	8	34,782	10
Sudan	42	2,000	N/A	1	3,969	2
Tunisia	10	7,820	24.7	1	191,000	46
Yemen	24	2,340	41.8	8	32,895	3
Syria	21	4,620	N/A	3	38,999	3

N/A = Not available. Source: Benchmarking Arab microfinance, World Development Indicators, Human Development Report.

performance and for social goals we have chosen the depth of outreach (meaning the levels of poverty reached) rather than social performance. Indeed, the depth of outreach is defined as efforts to expand microfinance services to populations not served by financial institutions (Lafourcade et al., 2005).

As for social performance, rather they are defined as the effects of the institution on the social conditions of its customers: effect on living standards (poverty), housing, health, education, etc. (Lapenu et al., 2004). Therefore, the depth of outreach allows us to better understand the social objectives of MFIs (providing financial services to poor, excluded from traditional banking system).

To carry out our study, we have retained two social outreach indicators, three financial performance indicators and five control variables.

Social outreach indicators

The outreach indicators include the number and the type of clients that the MFI was able to reach. In this analysis, we focus on the depth of outreach, so on the type of clients served and their poverty level rather than the number of clients that have been reached. The proxies for depth of outreach used in various studies (Cull et al., 2007; Gonzalez and Rosenberg, 2006; Olivares-Polanco, 2005) are percentage of female borrowers and the average loan size per borrower / GNI per capita. Indeed, according to Hamed (2004), microcredits programs have a positive impact not only on the micro-enterprise income but also on the female borrowers. Through microcredit, women can achieve multiple productive activities and diversify their sources of income more than men (Soulama, 2005). Thus, a higher percentage of female orrowers also indicates more depth of outreach, because lending to women generally is related lending to the poor (Lensink et al., 2011).

As regard to the average loan size per borrower / GNI per capita, although it is relevant and can compensate for differences in monetary units, it is however debatable. Indeed, per capita GNP exceeds in some countries the poverty-line income (Schreiner, 2001). As a result, it no longer represents the correct proxy. To resolve this problem, we borrowed the index developed by Adair and Berguiga (2010) which consists of comparing the average loan size per borrower based on Gross National Income (GNI) per capita (AL) and the two poverty-lines income (1 and 2 $per day). Thus, this social outreach index, identifying more precisely the target clients of the MFI, is a qualitative variable with three modalities, which takes respectively 1 if AL <PL1: the MFI targets the very poor, 2 if PL1 <AL<PL2 AL: the MFI targets the poor and 3 if AL> PL2: the MFI targets the non-poor. Consequently, the lowest average loan size per borrower based on Gross National Income (GNI), the most a MFI is moving towards the very poor.

Financial performance indicators

Concerning the financial performance indicators, we will use three accounting variables used in banks and other commercial institutions and by extension in MFIs. The commonest measures of profitability are Return on Assets (ROA), which reflects organization's ability to use its assets productively and Return on Equity (ROE), which measures the returns produced for the owners as well as the operational self sustainability (OSS). A microfinance institution is profitable and sustainable if it has a positive return on assets and equity and an operational self-sufficiency over 100%. Moreover, it also means that the MFI has managed to have a positive net income, disregarding donor support to compensate

Table 2. Descriptive statistics.

Variable	Definition	Abbreviation	Mean	Min	Max
Social range index	Average loan size per borrower based on Gross National Income (GNI) per capita (AL) compared to the two poverty-lines income (1 $ and $ 2 per day)	SRI	1.45	1	3
Percentage of female borrower	Number of active women borrowers / Number of Active Borrowers	PFB	65	18	100
Return on assets	Net operating income, net of taxes/average total assets	ROA	9.32	-14.01	15.46
Return on equity	Net operating income, net of taxes/average total equity	ROE	14.34	-382.27	94.90
Operational self-sufficiency	Financial revenue/(financial expense + net loan loss provision expense + operating expense)	OSS	1.32	0.07	3.94
Portfolio at risk	Outstanding balance, loans >30 days overdue/GLP	RISK	6.32	-14.01	31.68
Age	Age of MFI in years	AGE	6.32	4	17
Type	NGO vs. NON NGO	TYPE	0.84	0	1
Size	MFI's total number of borrowers	SIZE	14887	448	368333
Lending methodology	Group Lending vs. Individual Lending	LM	0.89	0	1

potential operational losses. Larger values of these three accounting measures refer to more efficient institutions.

Control variables

As for control variables, we will consider the following: the MFIs size, measured primarily by the number of borrowers and the risk, measured by the quality of portfolio. The standard international measure of portfolio quality in banking is portfolio at risk (PAR) beyond a specified number of days. In microfinance, 30 days is a common breakpoint. Indeed, PAR> 30 is a key performance indicator for the MFI that reflects the *risk* associated with *non-repayment* of *loans* and determine future revenues and thus the ability of an institution to maintain and expand its services. Thus, the highest the PAR> 30 is low; the more portfolio quality is good. We will include three other variables: age, type of microfinance institution (NGO vs. non-NGO) and the lending methodology which are important data to consider as shown by Cull et al. (2007) and Olivares (2003) (Table 2).

RESEARCH METHODOLOGY

By performing this regression, we want to know whether or not alink (positive, negative or neutral) exists between the financial performance and the depth of outreach of MFIs and the presence of trade-off. In accordance with D'Arcimoles and Trebucq (2002), we will set two hypotheses while assuming the existence of a relationship between the financial performance and the depth of outreach. We formulate thus our first hypothesis while referring to the "slack resources theory" which states the positive impact of good financial performance on the social performance of a company. Our first hypothesis is:

H_1: Higher financial performance leads to a greater depth of outreach, ceteris paribus.

In order to test this hypothesis, we carry out a multiple regression including lags as in D'Arcimoles and Trebucq (2002) model to address the endogeneity problems. Endogeneity implies the existence of variables in the error term that are correlated with the explanatory variables previously assumed to be exogenous. This correlation false assumption of orthogonality of residuals, which biases the coefficients of these exogenous variables. To correct this bias we need to find instrumental variables that must firstly be correlated with the variables suspected of endogeneity and on the other hand, strictly orthogonal to the random deviation (Baltagi, 1995). Furthermore, these instrumental variables must not be directly correlated with the dependent variable. We have therefore adopted, as D'Arcimoles and Trebucq (2002) recommended, the theoretical solution that consists in taking as instrumental variables, the variables suspected of endogeneity delayed by a period. So, we will have only two years for each MFI. As regard to this limited period and number of MFIs, we are going to use pooled data. We will therefore assume that there is no specific effect of time. Thus our model should include 128 observations (64 MFIs observed in two consecutive years). Our estimates are more accurate resulting in a more robust model.

To test our first hypothesis, we considered as dependent variable the depth of outreach indicators (the percentage of female borrowers and the social range index). As for independent variables, they include return on assets, return on equity and operational self-sufficiency. Finally, the type, size, age, risk and

Table 3. Correlation matrix.

	OSS	ROA	ROE	PFB	SRI	RISK	SIZE	AGE	TYPE	LM
OSS	1									
ROA	0.465***	1								
ROE	0.340***	0.238***	1							
PFB	-0.362	-0.370	0.102	1						
SRI	-0.095	0.340	0.502	-0.245**	1					
RISK	-0.039*	-0.285***	0.085	-0.349	0.126	1				
SIZE	0.078	0.070	0.021	-0.542	-0.255	-0.174	1			
AGE	0.212	0.091	0.183	0.068	0.018	0.062	0.452***	1		
TYPE	0.034	0.305**	0.058	-0.234	0.285***	0.215	-0.143	0.476	1	
LM	0.315	0.258	0.114	0.191***	0.285	0.116	0.157	0.071	0.141	1

*Significant at 10% level, ** Significant at 5% level, *** Significant at 1% level.

lending methodology will be used as control variables.

The econometric model corresponding to our analysis, with t = 2009 and 2010 and i = 1 to 64 is:

$$OUTREACH_{t,i} = f(FP_{t-1,i}, RISK_{t-1,i}, SIZE_{t-1,i}, AGE_{t-1,i}, TYPE_{t,i}, LM_{t-1,i}) \quad (1)$$

Where: $OUTREACH_{t,i}$ = Proxies for the depth of outreach [Percentage of female borrowers (PFB) and the social range index (SRI)], $FP_{t-1,i}$ = Financial performance for the previous year, $RISK_{t-1,i}$ = Proxy for the MFI$_i$ risk in the previous year (PAR> 30: Portfolio at Risk> 30), $SIZE_{t-1,i}$ = Proxy for the MFI$_i$ size for the previous year (number of borrowers for the previous year), $AGE_{t-1,i}$ = Age of the MFI$_i$ in the previous year, $TYPE_{t,i}$ = Type of the institution (dichotomous variable: NGO vs. non-NGO), $LM_{t-1,i}$ = Lending methodology (dichotomous variable: Group vs. Individual).

As for our second hypothesis, it will be formulated while referring on the "good management theory", as in D'Arcimoles and Trebucq (2002) model. Our second hypothesis will be:

H_2: A greater depth of outreach leads to higher financial performance, ceteris paribus.

This second hypothesis will be tested in the same manner as the first but using financial performance measures as dependent variable and indicators of the depth of outreach as independent variable. Control variables will therefore remain the same.

The econometric model corresponding to our analysis with t = 2009 and 2010 and i = 1 to 64 is:

$$FP_{t,i} = f(OUTREACH_{t-1,i}, RISK_{t-1,i}, SIZE_{t-1,i}, AGE_{t-1,i}, TYPE_{t,i}, LM_{t-1,i}) \quad (2)$$

All models are estimated by generalized least squares (GLS) using the STATA software rather than ordinary least squares (OLS) since we have included panel data in our models.

RESULTS AND DISCUSSION

Before proceeding with the regression analysis we calculate the correlation coefficients to give us a first look at the relationship that may exist between our variables (Table 3).

The various measures of financial performance ROA, ROE and OSS are all positively related to each other (highly significant correlation coefficients ranging from 0.238 to 0.465). The two indicators of the depth of outreach are in contrast negatively related (correlation coefficient is negative: -0.245). This is justified by the fact that a higher depth of outreach is associated with a higher percentage of female borrowers but lower SRI. At first glance, there appears a linear neutral relation between financial performance and the depth of outreach. Indeed, we do not found significant correlation coefficients between the different indicators of financial performance and those of the depth of outreach. Regression allows us to test whether these initial results are sufficiently robust.

The purpose of the regression analysis is to detect the existence of a relationship between the financial performance and the depth of outreach. This will allow us to determine the mutual impact of these concepts and whether MFIs face a trade-off or not, between providing services to the poor and achieving financial sustainability. While testing our first hypothesis, we obtain the results presented in Table 4.

While using the percentage of female borrowers as an indicator of the depth of outreach, the P-value *(Prob> chi2)* is less than 0.05, the significance level chosen. Therefore, the models are significant overall and we reject our null hypothesis. So we cannot affirm that better financial performance lead to a higher depth of outreach. The impact of FP on the DO is not positive, but it is not necessarily negative since we did not found any significant coefficient that can attest. There is no significant relationship between depth of outreach indicators and financial performance measures.

The variables that are important in determining the percentage of female borrowers are the MFI size, MFI type and lending methodology (group lending). Thus, the MFI size has a negative impact on his desire to serve female borrowers. The largest MFIs (dealing with large number of active borrowers) would tend to be less anxious to serve female borrowers and therefore a

Table 4. Regression with outreach indicators as dependent variable.

		PFB			SRI	
ROA		-0.294			3.346	
ROE			0.096			0.489*
OSS	-0.804			-0.562**		
RISK	-0.007	-0.034	0.665	1.147	1.690	0.902
SIZE	0.348	-0.112*	-0.421**	0.009	0.018*	0.002
AGE	1.235	1.286	1.371	6.438	9.567	6.123
TYPE	21.511*	13.433*	16.453 *	12.392	5.642	29.132
LM	0.348***	0.876**	0.974**	0.298***	0.967***	0.459
Constant	68.314***	56.433***	49.208***	14.437	65.116	55.081
Prob>chi2	0.038	0.028	0.043	0.423	0.732	0.234
R^2	0.534	0.765	0.767	0.024	0.072	0.032

*Significant at 10% level, ** Significant at 5% level, *** Significant at 1% level

mission drift observed as the MFI grows. Indeed, these MFIs move towards a higher target market and away from reaching vulnerable populations. As for the positive link PFB / TYPE, it means that the NGOs status is consistent with the microfinance mission (Boye et al., 2006). The institutional type influences the MFIs orientation that target primarily poor households (mostly women) and seek for greater social impact. These results confirm the NGOs effect put forward by proponents of welfarists approach and identified by previous work such as Adair and Berguiga (2010), Cornée (2007) and Gutierrez-Nieto et al. (2005) employing different method. With regard to the lending methodology (group lending), a positive effect has been identified, reinforcing this technical innovation put forward by the welfarists.

Our results show an increasingly targeting of female borrowers across the group lending methodology. Through their groups usually composed of 3 to 10 people, MFIs become more efficient and socially able to reach the largest number of female borrowers and this because the group lending is usually considered as a 'female' method (D'Espallier et al., 2009). The basic argument behind lending to women is that they are good credit risks, are less likely to misuse the loan, and are more likely to share the benefits with others in their household, especially their children (Garikipati, 2008). The solidarity lending methodology appears to boost social cohesion among its women clients. In addition, this methodology implies economies of scale and influences the success of MFIs (Navajas et al., 2003). Most of the work that has studied the impact of the lending methodology on MFIs performance (Adair and Berguiga, 2010; Mersland and Strom, 2009; Cull et al., 2007 in Aghion and Morduch, 2005) have shown that group lending has a positive impact on the social performance.

When using instead the SRI as an indicator of the depth of outreach, the P-value *(Prob> chi2)* is well above 0.05. Therefore we do not reject our null hypothesis and the models are not also significant as a whole. The low values of R^2 confirm this fact. Models for which we use the SRI as a proxy for depth of outreach have low explanatory power.

Testing our second hypothesis gave the results shown in Table 5. When using OSS and ROE as measures of financial performance, the P-value models are well above 0.05. Therefore, we cannot reject the null hypothesis and the models are not also significant as a whole. In contrast, when we use ROA as an indicator of financial performance, the Prob> chi2 is less than 0.05. We therefore reject the null hypothesis which states that better financial performance generate a depth of outreach. Good financial performance did not have a positive impact on the depth of outreach. This impact is still negative because we did not find a significant coefficient that attests.

We detected the risk as the only variable that can strongly influence the financial performance of MFI (the correlation coefficient is negative and statistically significant at 1%). This negative relationship attests that a higher portfolio at risk (the risk measure used) would block good financial results. MFIs can therefore be concerned to improve the portfolio at risk to ensure their sustainability.

This reveals the existence of a trade-off between improving the portfolio at risk (which implies the search for better financial performance) and better targeting of the poorest populations (better depth of outreach). Indeed, by seeking to minimize the risk, MFIs move a part the poorest people because they are a priori more risky. However, this mission drift has no reason to be because we did not find significant relationship that can demonstrate a negative association between risk and the various indicators of depth of outreach.

Conclusion

This study attempted to answer an important question in the microfinance field: if there is indeed a trade-off

Table 5. Regression with financial performance indicators as dependent variable.

	OSS		ROA		ROE	
PFB	-0.041		-0.002		0.007	
SRI		-0.038		0.007		0.094
RISK	-0.532*	-2.180**	-0.315**	-0.356***	-1.226	-0.362
SIZE	-0.013	-0.017	-0.005	-0.002	-0.005	-0.006
AGE	1.325	0.855	0.234	0.005	2.664	7.125***
TYPE	9.852	5.548	5.122	4.865	-12.466	-8.765
LM	0.134	0.289	0.145	0.421	0.532	0.576
Constant	73.234***	97.535***	-3.457	-4.432	-41.834	-44.544***
Prob>chi2	0.345	0.243	0.004	0.002	0.479	0.176
R^2	0.018	0.115	0.434	0.556	0.045	0.088

*Significant at 10% level, ** Significant at 5% level, *** Significant at 1% level.

between financial performance and the depth of outreach (social performance) and therefore to know the validity of mission drift. The analytical framework chosen is that of the Middle East and North Africa (MENA) region, where it is crucial to know whether the hopes raised by MFIs in poverty reduction have its reason of being. To test our hypotheses on the MENA region data, we estimated two types of models while referring to D'Arcimoles and Trebucq (2002) study dealing with the link between corporate financial performance and social performance in a French context.

In accordance with the correlation coefficients we found, the results that flow from our regressions show a link neutral between the financial performance and the depth of outreach. Indeed, despite the fact that we have rejected all our hypotheses, we did not found significant negative relationship between the financial performance and the depth of outreach.

Nevertheless, we could detect the existence of a trade-off between these two concepts that can be done by the MENA region MFIs. Indeed, while seeking to improve their portfolio at risk to have better financial performance MFIs tend to deviate from the most disadvantaged populations. This mission drift is not justified. Our results did not prove that having good financial performance and serving the poorest were contradictory. Although the pursuit of a better portfolio at risk is laudable, we have not detected that it is associated with lower depth of outreach and therefore with poorer clients.

The variables that can influence the percentage of women borrowers are MFI size, MFI type and lending methodology (group lending). Our results indicate that the MFI size has a negative impact on his desire to serve female borrowers. The institutional type (NGOs) influences the MFIs orientation that target primarily poor households (mostly women) and seek for greater social impact. With regard to the lending methodology (group lending), our results show an increasingly targeting of female borrowers across the group lending methodology. Through their groups usually composed of 3 to 10 people, MFIs become more efficient and socially able to reach the largest number of female borrowers and this because the group lending is usually considered as a 'female' method (D'Espallier et al., 2009). Our study indicates also that risk plays an important role in determining social performance. The question is how to improve its portfolio at risk in order to show better financial results. As we have seen, remove the poorest people do not seem to be the only solution nor the best. Poor people can post good repayment rates. For example, in early 2007, Grameen Bank reported almost 7 million borrowers 96% of them poor, illiterate women from remote villages. And since 1976, it says, $6 billion has been lent, with a repayment rate of 98%.

Finally, although we recognize that the trade-off between financial performance and the depth of outreach (social performance) does exist, it does not mean that achieving the double bottom line, the ultimate promise of microfinance is impossible although it is difficult to achieve. Microfinance institutions can simultaneously achieve their financial goals (to be financially viable) and their social objectives (providing financial services to the poor, excluded from traditional banking system). These findings agree with those of Cull et al. (2007) that also attest the existence of a trade-off between profitability (financial performance) and serving the poor (depth of outreach). Their results showed that even though they are probably very few, some MFIs have been able to reconcile the good financial results with a good social impact.

REFERENCES

Adair P, Berguiga I (2010). Les facteurs déterminants de la performance sociale et de la performance financière des institutions de microfinance dans la région MENA: une analyse en coupe instantanée. Région et Développement. 32: 91-119.

Armendáriz B, Jonathan M (2005). The Economics of Microfinance. Cambridge. MA: MIT Press.

Baltagi BH (1995). The Econometrics of Panel Data. John Wiley &Sons.

Bhatt N (1999). Delivering Microfinance in Developing Countries:

Controversies and Policy Perspectives. Policy Stud. J., 29: 319-333.
Boye S, Hajdenberg J, Poursat C (2006). Le guide de la microfinance: microcrédit et épargne pour le développement. Paris : Éditions d'Organisation, p. 304.
Cornée S (2007). Une proposition d'évaluation conjointe des performances sociales et financières en microfinance. Document de travail SPI 3. CERISE.
Cull R, Demirguç-Kunt A, Morduch J (2007). Financial performance and outreach: a global analysis of leading microbanks. Royal Economic Society. 517: 107-133.
De Briey V (2005). Plein feu sur la microfinance en Regards Economiques, 28: 1-14.
D'Espallier B, Guérin I, Mersland R (2009). Women and repayment in microfinance. Working Paper. Available online at: http://www.microfinancegateway.org/gm/document1.9.40253/Women%20and%20Repayment%20in%20Microfinance.pdf.
Garikipati S (2008). The impact of lending to women on household vulnerability and women's empowerment: evidence from India. World Dev., 12: 2620-2642.
Gonzalez A, Rosenberg R (2006). The State of Microfinance. Outreach, Profitability and Poverty: Findings from a Database of 2600 Microfinance Institutions. Paper presented at the conference "Access to Finance: Building Inclusive Financial Systems" Washington D.C. World Bank Group Brookings Institution.
Gutierrez Nieto B, Serrano-Cinca C, Molinero CM (2005). Microfinance Institutions and Efficiency. Omega Int. J. Manage. Sci., 35: 131-142.
Hamed Y (2004). Microcrédit et financement de la microentreprise au Maghreb. Thèse de Sciences économiques. Université Paris 12.
Labie M (1999). La microfinance en questions : Limites et choix organisationnels. Bruxelles: Editions Luc Pire, p. 116.
Lafourcade AL, Isern J, Mwangi P, Brown M (2005). Etude sur la Portée et les Performances des Institutions de Microfinance en Afrique. Available online at: http://www.mixmarket.org/medialibrary/mixmarket/MIX Etude Afrique Fr.pdf.
Cécile L, Zeller M, Martin G, Chao-Béroff R, Koenraad V (2004). Performances sociales: Une raison d'être des institutions de microfinance et pourtant encore peu mesurées. Quelques pistes. Monde en développement, 126 : 51-68.
Mersland R, Strøm R (2009). Performance and governance in microfinance institutions. J. Bank. Financ., 4: 662-669.
Friedman M (1970). The Social Responsibility of Business is to Increase its Profits. The New York Times Magazine.
Morduch J (2005). The microfinance promise. J. Econ. Lit., XXXVII: 1579 -1614.
Morduch J (2005). The microfinance schism. World Dev., 4: 617 -629.
Navajas S, Conning J, Gonzales-Vega C (2003). Lending Technologies, Competition and Consolidation in the Market for MicroFinance in Bolivia. J. Int. Dev., 15: 747-770.
Olivares-Polanco F (2005). Commercializing microfinance and deepening outreach: Empirical evidence from Latin America. J. Microfinance, 7: 47-69.
Otero M, Rhyne E (1994). The new world of microenterprise finance: Building healthy financial institutions for the poor. West Hartford. CT: Kumarian Press.
Schreiner M (2001). Seven Aspects of Loan Size. J. Microfinance, 2: 27-47.
Soulama S (2005). Microfinance, pauvreté et développement. Agence Universitaire de la Francophonie. Archives contemporaines.
Trebucq S, D'Arcimoles CH (2002). The Corporate Social Performance-Financial Performance Link: Evidence from France. Univ. Bordeaux. pp. 02-01.
Von Pischke JD, Adams DW, Donald G (1983). Rural financial markets in developing countries: their use and abuse. Baltimore; London: Published for the Economic Development Institute of the World Bank by the Johns Hopkins University Press.
Woller GM, Dunford C, Woodworth W (1999). Where to microfinance. International J. Econ. Dev., 1: 29-64.
Yaron J (1994). What Makes Rural Finance Institutions Successful? World Bank Res. Observer, 9: 49-70.

Modelling daily value-at-risk using realized volatility, non-linear support vector machine and ARCH type models

Md. Ashraful Islam Khan

Department of Population Science and Human Resource Development, Rajshahi University, Rajshahi-6205, Bangladesh. E-mail: khan75ru@yahoo.com.

The aim of this paper is to compare the performance of the daily nonlinear support vector machines, the new semi-parametric tool for regression estimation, heterogeneous autoregressive (SVM-HAR)-ARCH type models based on the daily realized volatility (which uses intraday returns) with the performance of the classical HAR-ARCH type models by using different innovation distribution when the one-day ahead value-at-risk (VaR) is to be computed. The daily realized volatility is calculated using 5-, 15-min and optimally sampled intraday returns for Nikkei 225 index. This paper shows that the particular hybrid SVM-HAR-ARCH type model provides better performance when 15-min intraday returns are used. This paper also shows that the models based on a long memory skewed student distribution provide the better performance of one-day ahead value-at-risk forecasts.

Key words: Value-at-risk, HAR-RV model, nonlinear support vector machine-HAR-RV model, ARCH type models, Skewed student distribution, high frequency Nikkei 225 data.

INTRODUCTION

Value-at-Risk (VaR), a measure of how the market value of an asset or a portfolio of assets is likely to decrease over a specific time period under typical conditions, has become the standard tool for measuring and reporting financial risk. Due to the recent availability of high-frequency intraday data for the financial variables (stock indexes, exchange rates, bonds etc) most of the financial researchers are mainly concerned with modeling and forecasting volatility, which is the key input to VaR modelling, in asset returns to quantify the risk of financial instruments over a particular time period, which is taken to be equal to one day in this paper.

Researches on time varying volatility and risk measure using the time series models have been active ever since Engle (1982) introduced the ARCH model. The GARCH model, generalized by Bollerslev (1986), has been extended in various directions and these extensions recognize (based on the various researcher's empirical evidences) that there may be important nonlinearity, asymmetry, and long memory properties in the volatility process. The popular extensions can be referred to Nelson's (1991) EGARCH model, Glosten et al.'s (1993) GJR-GARCH which both account for the asymmetric relationship between stock returns and changes in variance (for e. g. Black 1976, the beginning study of the asymmetric effect and Engle and Ng 1993 for further discussion). Engle's (1990) AGARCH, Ding et al. (1993) APARCH; Zakoian's (1994) TGARCH; and Sentana's (1995) QGARCH models also have been developed for the flexibility of the models.

The recent literatures suggest the use of realized volatility, the square of intraday returns introduced in the literature by Taylor and Xu (1997) and Andersen and Bollerslev (1998) along with other researchers, as a measure of actual volatility and have quickly become popular after proposing the heterogeneous autoregressive realized volatility (HAR-RV) model of Corsi et al. (2001) and Corsi (2009) based on the HARCH (Heterogeneous ARCH) model of Müller et al. (1997b). Another recent development in the RV literature is the approach due to Barndorff-Nielsen and Shephard (2004, 2006), Andersen et al. (2003, 2007) of decomposing the RV into the contribution of continuous sample path variation and that of jumps. Extending the theory of quadratic variation of semi martingales, Barndorff-Nielsen et al. (2006) provided an asymptotic statistical foundation for this decomposition procedure under very general conditions.

This study is closer to Giot and Laurent (2004) and Clements et al. (2008). Giot and Laurent (2004) compare an ARCH-type model and a model using realized volatility in terms of forecasts of Value-at-Risk. They show better performance of Skewed student APARCH model. Clements et al. (2008) narrow their study to focus exclusively on models based on realized volatility and show comparatively better performance of HAR model for quantile forecasts. In this paper, the HAR-ARCH type models have been considered for one-day ahead Value-at Risk forecasts. The aim is to compare the performance of classical HAR-ARCH type models with the nonlinear support vector machine (SVM)-HAR-ARCH type models in terms of Value-at-Risk (VaR) forecasts, where the SVM is an efficient semi-parametric approach introduced by Vepnik, (1995) that guarantees to obtain globally optimal solution, (Cristianini and Shawe-Taylor, 2000), which solves the problems of multiple local optima in which the neural network usually get trapped into. The neural network (NN) and the SVM are being applied in different financial literatures. For example, Donaldson and Kamstra (1997) used neural network to model volatility based GJR-GARCH, Bildirici and Ersin (2009) fitted neural network based on nine different GARCH family models such as NN-GARCH, NN-EGARCH, NN-TGARCH, NN-GJR-GARCH, NN-SAGARCH, NN-PGARCH, NN-NGARCH, NN-APGARCH and NN-NPGARCH to forecast Istanbul stock volatility, McAleer and Medeiros (2009) proposed the NN-HAR model and estimated with Bayesian regul0061rization (BR) to forecast the daily volatility of the S&P 500 and FTSE 100 indexes, and more recently Dunis et al. (2010) applies higher order neural networks for modeling commodity Value-at-Risk of the Brent oil and gold bullion series with only autoregressive terms as inputs. In the very beginning, Müller et al. (1997a) applied SVM for time series forecasting to compare the performance of ϵ-insensitive loss and Huber's robust loss function. After that, Pěrez-Perez-Cruz et al. (2003) predicted GARCH (1,1) based volatility by SVM, Chen et al. (2008) proposed recurrent SVM as a dynamic process to model GARCH (1,1) based Volatility, Ou and Wang (2010) proposed GARCH-LSSVM, EGARCH-LSSVM and GJR-LSSVM hybrid models based on modification of Suykens and Vandewalle (1999) to forecast the leverage effect volatilities of ASEAN stock markets. These indicate that the hybrid models can also capture the stylized characteristics of time series. In this paper, the nonlinear SVM and HAR are combined as nonlinear SVM-HAR model. To the author's knowledge, this paper is the first to apply the nonlinear SVM-HAR model to RV literature in the daily VaR modelling context.

When ARCH type models are used, a well established result in the financial time series literature is that the standardized returns do not have a Gaussian distribution. Andersen et al. (2000a, b, 2001, 2003) showed that the distribution of the standardized exchange rate series was almost Gaussian when the realized volatility (RV) was used. Furthermore, the logarithm of the realized volatilities was also nearly Gaussian. Other literatures on realized volatility can be refer along with many researchers to Aït-Sahalia and Mancini (2006), Ghysels and Sinko (2006), Ghysels et al. (2006), Corradi et al. (2006). According to Giot and Laurent (2004), "the key issue is to use a daily ARCH type model that clearly recognizes and fully takes into account the key features of the empirical data such as high kurtosis and skewness in the observed returns." In this paper, the RiskMetrics, GARCH, GJR, EGARCH and APARCH models are being considered along with Gaussian, Student's t and Skewed Student distributions to capture the features of the empirical data.

REALIZED VOLATILITY, REALIZED BI-POWER VARIATION AND JUMP COMPONENT EXTRACTION

If we consider a simple diffusion process

$$dp(s) = \mu(s)dt + \sigma(s)dW(s)$$

where $p(s)dt$ is the instantaneous log-price, $W(s)$ is a standard Brownian process and $\sigma(s)$ is the standard deviation of $dp(s)$, which may be time-varying but is assumed to be independent of $dW(s)$. Then the volatility for day t is defined as the integral of $\sigma^2(s)$ over the interval $(t, t+1)$ that is, $\int_t^{t+1} \sigma^2(s)ds$, which is known as integrated volatility and it is unobserved. Let the discretely sampled Δ-period returns be denoted by, $r_{t,\Delta} = p(t) - p(t-\Delta)$. If the process (in our case the log of Nikkei 225 index level process) is a continuous semimartingale then under mild regularity conditions,

$$RV_t \equiv \sum_{j=1}^{1/\Delta} \left|r_{t+j\Delta,\Delta}\right|^2 \xrightarrow{p} \int_t^{t+1} \sigma^2(s)ds \text{ as } \Delta \downarrow 0$$

RV_t is the t-th day realized variance since t has the daily unit and $\left(\frac{1}{\Delta}\right)$ is integer. We will hereafter use the terms *realized volatility* or *realized variance* interchangeably, or their common abbreviation RV.

Again, if the process is semimartingale with finite-activity jumps, that is, only a finite number of jumps occurring in any finite time interval, such as Poisson jumps, then the realized variance converges to the quadratic variation, which can be decomposed as,

$$RV_t \xrightarrow{p} \int_t^{t+1} \sigma^2(s)ds + \sum_{t<s\leq t+1} k^2(s) \text{ as } \Delta\downarrow 0$$

where *k(s)* refers to the size of the jump occurring at time *s*. Andersen et al. (2007) proposed microstructure-noise-robust versions of the *bipower variation* as

$$BV_t \equiv \mu_1^{-2}(1-2\Delta)^{-1}\sum_{j=3}^{1/\Delta}|r_{t+j\Delta,\Delta}||r_{t+(j-2)\Delta,\Delta}|$$

where $\mu_1 \equiv \sqrt{2/\pi}$, holds under mild conditions and proposed to use $RV_t - BV_t \xrightarrow{p} \sum_{t<s\leq t+1} k^2(s)$ or $J_t \equiv max[(RV_t - BV_t), 0]$ as an estimator for $\sum_{t<s\leq t+1} k^2(s)$. J_t is known to take non-zero, small values very frequently due to measurement and possibly due to the presence of jumps infinite-activity types.

Data description and summary statistics

Calculation of intraday returns and RV measures from minute-by-minute Nikkei 225 data

We measure the realized volatility of the Nikkei 225 index for the sample of the period 11 March 1996 to 30 September 2009. Nikkei (Nihon Keizai Shinbun, Inc) computes and disseminates the Nikkei 225 index once every minute during the trading hours of Tokyo Stock Exchange (TSE). In this paper, we contract a "five-minute (percentage) returns" series by taking the five-minute log differences multiplied by hundred from the minute-by-minute data. This choice is made to mitigate the effect of microstructure related noise and increase the precision of volatility measures. (Ishida and Watanabe, 2009; Watanabe and Yamaguchi, 2007).

The Tokyo Stock Exchange is open only for 9:00-11:00 (Morning Session) and 12:30-15:00 (Afternoon Session). Our database includes every minute prices of the Nikkei 225 stock index for both sessions. We first extract prices for 9:01, 9:05, 9:10,........,11:00 in the morning session and for 12:31, 12:35, 12:40,.......,15:00 in the afternoon session. Sometimes, the last transaction price for morning (and/or afternoon) session is observed slightly after 11:00 (and/or 15:00). In such cases, we use the last prices instead of prices at 11:00 (and/or 15:00). Next, by using these prices, we calculate the five-minute returns as previously mentioned. There are 54 five-minute returns for a typical trading day in total, 24 from the morning session and 30 from the afternoon session.

Given the recent literature on the market microstructure noise effect on realized volatility estimation, the optimal choice of sampling frequency as studied by Bandi and Russell (2003, 2008) has been considered here. The sampling frequency M^{opt} (the number of observations per day) is calculated as (Zhang et al., 2005; Clements et al., 2008)

$$M^{opt} = \left(\frac{\bar{\hat{Q}}_i}{\hat{\alpha}}\right)^{\frac{1}{3}}$$

Where,

$$\hat{\alpha} = \left(\frac{\sum_{t=1}^{T}\sum_{j=1}^{M} r_{j,t}}{TM}\right)^2 \text{ and } \bar{\hat{Q}} = \frac{1}{T}\sum_{t=1}^{T}\hat{Q}_t, \hat{Q}_t = \frac{M_{15}}{3}\sum_{j=1}^{M_{15}} r_{j,t}^4.$$

M_{15} is the 15-min returns and M is the highest frequency at which data are available. In our case, it is 1-min returns. The 15-min intraday returns are being considered to calculate realized volatility as well.

We cannot calculate the 5-min, 15-min and optimally-sampled returns for the non-trading hours including lunch time and overnight period though we can calculate the lunch time and overnight returns by considering the last price of the morning session and the first prices of the afternoon session, and the last price of the afternoon session and the first price of the next morning session but following Hansen and Lunde (2005), we drop this idea and scale the realized volatility as follow,

$$RV_t \equiv C^* RV_t^{(0)}$$

Where,

$$C^* \equiv \sum_{t=1}^{T}(R_t - \bar{R})^2 \Big/ \sum_{t=1}^{T} RV_t^{(0)}, \text{ where } \bar{R} \equiv \sum_{t=1}^{T} R_t \Big/ T$$

and T is the number of complete trading days. In our sample period, the first trading in the second session from January 1, 2006 to April 21, 2006 observed at 13:01. Therefore, we remove these trading days along with the sessions from half trading days including the first and the last trading days of each year. The remaining number of complete trading days, T is 3279. We calculate RV_t and J_t by using this 3279 days data for the four series.

Properties of the realized volatility and related measures

The average daily optimal sampling frequency was observed 7.828 (≈8), that is, $\frac{1}{\Delta} = 8 \Rightarrow \Delta = 33.75$. 30-min returns are considered as optimally sampled returns here. The value of C^* for 5-, 15-min and optimally sampled returns were calculated as 2.02977, 1.78022 and 1.75065, respectively. Summary statistics of daily returns series, the daily logarithmic form of RV and jump series are presented on Table 1. In addition to the

Table 1. Summary statistics for Nikkei 225 daily returns, realized volatility and jumps logarithmic series.

Series		Mean	Std. dev.	Skew.	Kurt.	Min.	Max.	Jarque-Bera	LB(5)	LB(10)	LB(22)
Daily return		-0.024	1.621	-0.163	8.351	-11.953	12.912	3898.857	13.589	24.305	41.57
	5-min	0.609	0.817	0.030	3.719	-2.005	4.087	70.550	7710.639	13667.646	24950.93
lnRV	15-min	0.496	0.927	0.117	3.615	-2.614	4.246	58.760	6210.035	11092.093	20348.31
	Optimal	0.385	1.027	**0.087**	**3.635**	-3.220	4.706	58.809	4620.977	8306.383	15354.54
	5-min	0.792	0.426	1.262	6.220	0.067	3.302	2270.538	6669.961	11674.345	20728.59
ln(1+Jump)	15-min	0.724	0.496	1.558	6.509	0.035	3.631	2988.122	4549.871	7996.372	13955.17
	Optimal	0.673	0.550	1.923	8.672	0.009	4.623	6371.333	3082.669	5473.863	9818.06

The sample of the period 11 March 1996 to 30 September 2009, there are total 3279 daily observations. The 5% critical value for Jarque-Bera (that is,) is 5.991 (k = 2) and 5% critical values for LB (k) are 11.070 (5), 18.924 (10) and 33.924 (22), respectively.

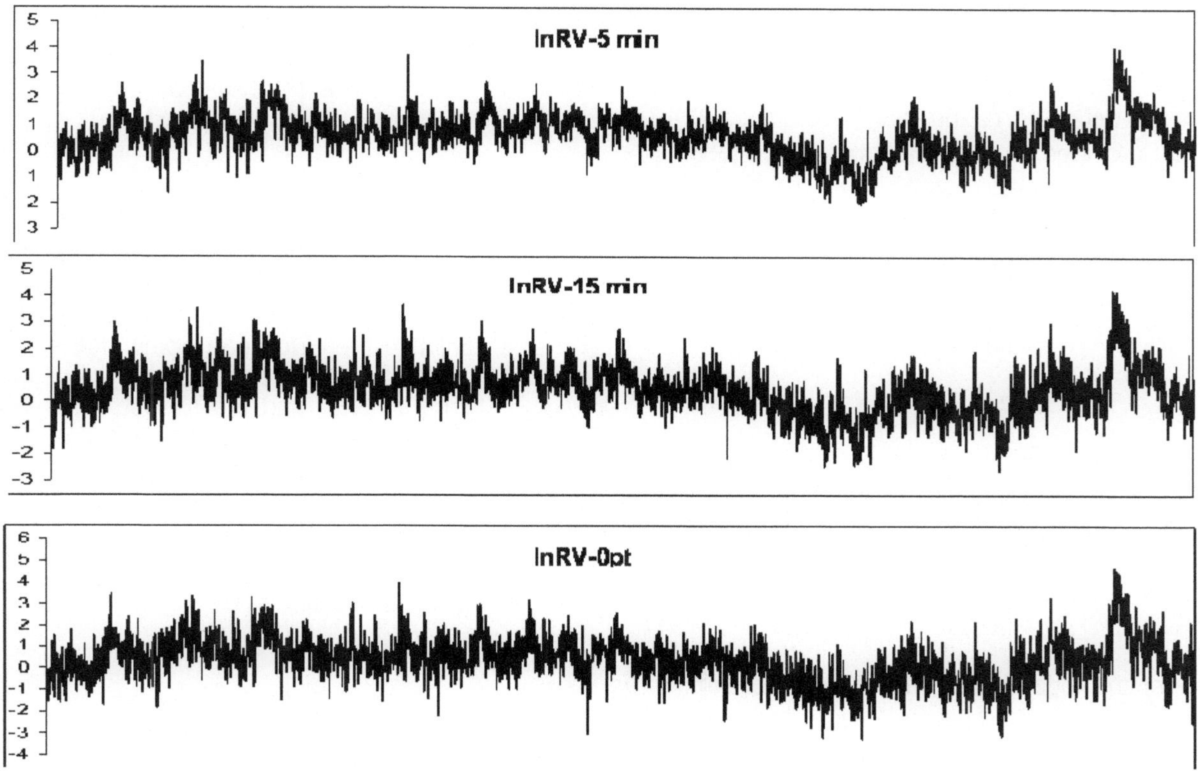

Figure 1. Log-realized volatility series. The top plot shows the daily log-RV series using 5-min intraday returns, the middle plot shows the daily log-RV series using 5-min intraday returns and last plot shows the daily log-RV series using 5-min intraday returns optimally sampled intraday return data. The sample period is 11 March 1996 to 30 September 2009. There are 3279 complete trading days.

sample skewness and kurtosis, the Jarque-Bera (JB) statistic for testing normality and the Ljung-Box statistics of order 5, 10 and 22 (corresponding to roughly one week, two weeks and a month) for testing serial correlations up to their respective order are also presented on the Table 1. It was observed that the unconditional distribution of the daily return series is negatively skewed but highly significantly nonnormal with high positive kurtosis. The LB statistics also indicated that the series are significantly serially correlated. It was also observed that the log transformation of RV's brings down the sample skewness and kurtosis values for all series but still significantly nonnormal. The value of skewness and kurtosis were close to zero (0.030) and three (3.719) for 5-min intraday returns while 0.117, 3.615 for 15-min and 0.087, 3.635 for optimally sampled intraday returns. All the transformed series remain highly significantly serially correlated. Figure 1 shows the daily lnRV for three intraday returns series.

COMPUTING MODELS

Realized volatility models

Heterogeneous autoregressive realized volatility (HAR-RV) model

The HAR-RV class volatility models proposed by Corsi (2001, 2009) on the basis of a straightforward extension of the so-called heterogeneous ARCH (HARCH) class of models is analyzed by Müller et al. (1997).

To sketch the HAR-RV model, define the multi-period realized volatilities by the normalized sum of the one-period volatilities,

$$RV_{t,t+h} = h^{-1}(RV_{t+1} + RV_{t+2} + \cdots + RV_{t+h})$$

Note that, by definition of the daily volatilities, $RV_{t,t+1} \equiv RV_{t+1}$. Also, provided the expectations exist, $E(RV_{t,t+1}) \equiv E(RV_{t+1})$ for all *h* (Andersen et al., 2003, 2007). Also *h* = *5* and = *22* will produce the weekly and monthly volatilities, respectively. The daily HAR-RV model of Corsi (2001), Corsi (2009) may then be expressed as:

$$RV_{t+1} = \beta_0 + \beta_D RV_t + \beta_W RV_{t-5,t} + \beta_M RV_{t-22,t} + \epsilon_{t+1}$$

where $t = 1, 2, \ldots\ldots\ldots\ldots, T$.

Andersen et al. (2003, 2007) included the jump component, which has been explained previously, as an explanatory variable to the above model and introduced the new model as

$$RV_{t+1} = \beta_0 + \beta_D RV_t + \beta_W RV_{t-5,t} + \beta_M RV_{t-22,t} + \beta_J J_t + \epsilon_{t+1}$$

In this paper the logarithmic form of the above model is used as

$$log(RV_{t+1}) = \beta_0 + \beta_D log(RV_t) + \beta_W log(RV_{t-5,t}) + \beta_M log(RV_{t-22,t})$$

$$+\beta_J log(1 + J_t) + \epsilon_{t+1}$$

e.g., (Andersen et al., 2003, 2007)

The support vector machines (SVMs)-HAR

The support vector machines (SVMs) were introduced by Vapnik (1995) based on the statistical learning theory, which had been developed over the last three decades by Vapnik, Chervonenkis and others (Vapnik, 1982, 1995) from a nonlinear generalization of the Generalized Portrait algorithm. SVMs were developed to solve the classification problem, but recently they have been extended to the domain of regression problems (Vapnik et al., 1997). The SVMs usually map data to a high-dimensional feature space and apply a simple linear method to the data in that high-dimensional space nonlinearly related to the input space. Moreover, even though we can think of SVMs as a linear algorithm in a high-dimensional space, in practice, it does not involve any computations in that high-dimensional space (Karatzoglou and Meyer, 2006). The terminology for SVMs can be slightly confusing in the literature. In few literatures, SVM refers to both classification and regression with support vector methods. In this paper, the tern SVM will be used for the nonlinear support vector regression (NL-SVR). The mathematical formulation of SVM is as follows.

In the ϵ-insensitive support vector regression of Vapnik (1995), our goal is to find a function $f(x)$ that has an ϵ deviation from the actually obtained targets y_t for all training data, and at the same time, is as flat as possible. Suppose $f(x)$ takes the following form

$$f(x) = k\langle \omega, x\rangle + b \text{ with } \omega \in X, b \in \mathbb{R}$$

where *X* is the space of the input patterns and $k\langle .,.\rangle$ denotes the kernel function. Flatness of the above model means need to find the small ω. One way to ensure this is to minimize the Euclidean norm, that is,$\|\omega\|^2$ (Smola, 1998). By applying the *soft margin* formulation of Cortes and Vapnik (1995), and the Karush-Kuhn-Tucker (KKT) conditions (Karush, 1939; Kuhn and Tucker, 1951) one can estimate the above model as

$$f(x) = \sum_{t=1}^{T}(\alpha_t - \alpha_t^*)k\langle x_t, x\rangle + \hat{b}$$

where b can be computed as

$$\hat{b} = y_t - k\langle \omega, x_t\rangle - \epsilon \; for \; \alpha_t \in (0, C)$$

$$\hat{b} = y_t - k\langle \omega, x_t\rangle + \epsilon \; for \; \alpha_t^* \in (0, C)$$

where, $C > 0$ determines the trade-off between the flatness of the $f(x)$ and the amount up to which derivations larger than ϵ are tolerated and $\alpha_t, \alpha_t^* \geq 0$ (Smola and Schölkopf, 1998). A several numbers (Kernlab in R, MATLAB, etc) of statistical software are available to handle SVM method.

According to Cortes and Vepnik (1995), any symmetric positive semi-definite function that satisfies the Mercer's conditions can be used as a kernel function in the SVMs context. The Mercer's conditions are

$$\int\int K(x,y)\, g(x) g(y) dx dy > 0 \text{ and } \int g^2(x) dx < \propto,$$

where $K(x,y) \equiv \sum_{t=1}^{\propto} \alpha_t\, \psi(x)\, \psi(y), \alpha_t \geq 0$

In this paper, the Laplacian kernel function $K(x,y) \equiv exp\left(-\frac{\|x-y\|}{\sigma}\right)$ has been considered.

The models that combines SVM technique, previously discussed, and HAR-RV models are known as SVM-HAR-RV models.

Now, when $\epsilon_{t+1} \sim N(0, \hat{\sigma}_{\epsilon}^2)$ then $exp(\epsilon_{t+1}) \sim logN(0, \hat{\sigma}_{\epsilon}^2)$, thus the conditional realized volatility can be computed according to

$$RV_{t+1|t} = exp\left(lnRV_{t+1} - \hat{\epsilon}_{t+1} + \frac{1}{2}\hat{\sigma}_{\epsilon}^2\right)$$

where $\hat{\epsilon}_{t+1}$ and $\hat{\sigma}_{\epsilon}^2$ are the estimated value and estimated variance of $\in_{t+1}$ respectively by HAR-RV-J model using both classical and SVM method separately. To compute the one-day ahead Value-at-Risk forecast, the ARCH type models will be applied on the conditional realized volatility series obtained from the aforementioned expression.

ARCH type models

An ARCH type model can be define as

$$y_t = \mu_t + \epsilon_t$$

$$\epsilon_t = \sigma_t z_t$$

$$\mu_t = c(\eta|\Omega_{t-1})$$

$$\sigma_t = h(\eta|\Omega_{t-1})$$

where $c(\eta|\Omega_{t-1})$ and $h(\eta|\Omega_{t-1})$ are functions of Ω_{t-1}, the information set at time $t-1$ and depend on an unknown vector parameters η, z_t is a i.i.d. process, independent of Ω_{t-1} with $E(z_t) = 0$ and $Var(z_t) = 1$. μ_t and σ_t are the conditional mean and conditional variance respectively.

In this paper, we fit an *AR* model for the conditional mean and five specifications for the conditional variance, which have been discussed as follows

GARCH model

Bollerslev (1986) proposed the GARCH model. We use GARCH (1,1) models as

$$\sigma_t^2 = \omega + \alpha\epsilon_{t-1}^2 + \beta\sigma_{t-1}^2, \omega > 0, \alpha, \beta \geq 0$$

where ω, β and α are the parameters, which are assumed to be non-negative to guarantee that volatility is always positive. This model is able to capture the volatility clustering. $|\beta + \alpha| < 1$, implies that the volatility is stationary and the speed for which the shock to volatility decays becomes slower as $\beta + \alpha$ approaches to one.

GJR-GARCH model

Glosten et al. (1993) proposed the GJR-GARCH model to capture the asymmetry. In this study, we use the GJR-GARCH (1,1) model as

$$\sigma_t^2 = \omega + \alpha\epsilon_{t-1}^2 + \beta\sigma_{t-1}^2 + \lambda\epsilon_{t-1}^2 I_{t-1}$$

where $I_{t-1}$is an indicator function with $I_{t-1} = 0$ if $\epsilon_{t-1} \geq 0$ and with $I_{t-1} = 1$ if $\epsilon_{t-1} < 0$. ω, β, α and λ are the parameters, which are assumed to be non-negative to guarantee that volatility is always positive.

EGARCH model

It has already established that the general GARCH model cannot capture the well-known volatility asymmetry phenomenon in stock markets. To capture this phenomenon, we use the Nelson (1991)'s EGARCH model. Specifically, we use the EGARCH (1,0) model as

$$ln(\sigma_t^2) = \omega + \phi[ln(\sigma_{t-1}^2) - \omega] + \theta z_{t-1} + \gamma(|z_{t-1}| - E|z_{t-1}|), |\phi| < 1$$

where $E|z_{t-1}| = \sqrt{2/\pi}$, since $z_{t-1}$is assumed to follow standard normal distribution. As EGARCH model specifies the logarithm of volatility, thus, it does not require any non-negativity constraints for the parameters. $\theta < 0$, implies the consistency with the volatility asymmetry in stock markets. In this model, $|\phi| < 1$, implies that the volatility is stationary and the speed for which the shock to volatility decays becomes slower as ϕ approaches to one.

APARCH model

The APARCH model is proposed by Ding et al. (1993) as an extension of Bollerslev's (1986) GARCH that nests at least seven GARCH specifications. In this paper, we use APARCH(1,1) model as

$$\sigma_t = \left[\omega + \alpha_1(|\epsilon_{t-1}| - \alpha_n\epsilon_{t-1})^{\delta} + \beta_1\sigma_{t-1}^{\delta}\right]^{\frac{1}{\delta}}$$

where $\omega, \alpha_1, \alpha_n, \beta_1$ and δ are the parameters to be estimated. $\delta > 0$, plays the role a Box-Cox transformation of σ_t. $\alpha_n, (-1 < \alpha_n < 1)$, refers the so-called leverage effect.

Focusing on the recent studies, we observe that the long memory skewed student distribution has frequently been used in VaR forecasting, for example Giot and Laurent (2003, 2004), Wang and Hsu (2006). Following

Giot and Laurent (2003, 2004) or Giot (2003), the standard version of the skewed Student distribution, introduced by Fernández and Steel (1998), has been used as innovation distribution along with the Gaussian and Student t distributions in this paper. According to Lambert and Laurent (2001), the innovation process z_t is said to have (standard) skewed Student distribution if

$$f(z_t|\xi,\vartheta)=\begin{cases}\frac{2}{\xi+\frac{1}{\xi}}sg[\xi(sz_t+m)|v]\text{ if } z_t<-\frac{m}{s}\\ \frac{2}{\xi+\frac{1}{\xi}}sg[\xi(sz_t+m)/\xi|v]\text{ if } z_t\geq-\frac{m}{s}\end{cases}$$

where $g(.|v)$, $v>2$ is a symmetric (unit variance) Student density and ξ is the asymmetry coefficient. Parameters $m=\frac{\Gamma\left(\frac{v-1}{2}\right)\sqrt{v-2}}{\sqrt{\pi}\,\Gamma\left(\frac{v}{2}\right)}\left(\xi-\frac{1}{\xi}\right)$ and $s^2=\left(\xi^2+\frac{1}{\xi^2}-1\right)-m^2$ are the mean and variance of the nonstandardized skewed Student (Lambert and Laurent, 2001)

Assessment of the VaR performance

Here, the application of the volatility models previously discussed to the Value-at-Risk application is focused on. The framework of VaR forecasts is to apply the classical and SVM techniques to the HAR-RV-J models to obtain the realized volatility forecast and compute conditional realized volatility. Two conditional realized volatility series will be found. The ARCH specification is being applied on these two series as an AR(2), where the lag was selected using AIC, model to estimate the conditional mean along with four different models with three innovation distributions (Gaussian, student t and skewed Student) to estimate the conditional variances, that is, (3×4) = 12 models for the conditional variance. These results were used as inputs to compute one-day ahead VaR.

When assuming a Gaussian distribution for the innovation process, the VaR for long trading positions (that is, the left tail of the returns density distribution) is $\mu_t+z_\alpha\sigma_t$ and for short trading positions (that is, the right tail of the returns density distribution) is $\mu_t+z_{1-\alpha}\sigma_t$, where z_α and $z_{1-\alpha}$ are the left and right quantile respectively at α% for the normal distribution. When the innovation distribution is Student t, the VaR for long and short trading positions are $\mu_t+t_{\alpha,v}\sigma_t$ and $\mu_t+t_{1-\alpha,v}\sigma_t$ respectively, where $t_{\alpha,v}$ and $t_{1-\alpha,v}$ are the left and right quantile, respectively at α% for the Student t distribution. And finally, for the skewed student innovation distribution, the VaR for long and short trading positions are respectively $\mu_t+skst_{\alpha,v,\xi}\sigma_t$ and $\mu_t+skst_{1-\alpha,v,\xi}\sigma_t$ with $skst_{\alpha,v,\xi}$ and $skst_{1-\alpha,v,\xi}$, the left and right quantile respectively at α% for the skewed Student distribution.

The performances of classical HAR and SVM-HAR models are tested by using Kupiec's(1995) likelihood ratio test and Engle and Manganelli's (1999) dynamic quantile test. Kupiec's likelihood ratio test is designed on computing the failure rate, the number of times realized returns exceed (in absolute value) the forecasted VaR, for the returns which is also known as the proportion if VaR violation (an occurrence of a market returns larger, in absolute value, than the forecasted VaR). If the VaR model is correctly specified, the failure rate should be equal to the prespecified VaR level, α. That is, $H_0\colon f=\alpha$ against $H_1\colon f\neq\alpha$. f, the failure rate, which is estimated as $f=1/T\sum_{t=1}^{T}I\left(y_t-VaR_t(\alpha)\right)$ is the sequence of yes/no observations, where $I(.)$ is an indicator function, y_t is realized return at time t and $VaR_t(\alpha)$ is the VaR forecast at time t and at %.

The Kupiec's likelihood ratio test statistic to test the aforementioned hypothesis is $LR=-2ln(\alpha^{T-N}(1-\alpha)^N)+2ln\left(\left(1-\left(N/T\right)\right)^{T-N}\left(N/T\right)^N\right)$, where N is the number of VaR violations, and T is the total number of observations. This LR test statistic is asymptotically distributed as $\chi^2(1)$.

Beside the failure rate, Engel and Manganelli (1999) consider the new variables as $Hit_t(\alpha)=I\left(y_t<VaR_t(\alpha)\right)-\alpha$ and $Hit_t(1-\alpha)=I\left(y_t>VaR_t(1-\alpha)\right)-\alpha$ on the basis of a relevant VaR model should feature a sequence of indicator functions that is not serially correlated and suggest to test jointly $A1\colon E\left(Hit_t(\alpha)\right)=0$ in case of long $\left(E\left(Hit_t(1-\alpha)\right)=0\right.$ in case of short) trading positions and $A2\colon Hit_t(\alpha)$ (or $Hit_t(1-\alpha)$) is uncorrelated with the variables included in the information set.

Engel and Manganelli (1999) show that testing $A1-A2$ can be done using the artificial regression $Hit_t=X\lambda+\epsilon_t$, where X is a $T\times k$ matrix whose first column is a column of one, the next q columns are $Hit_{t-1},\cdots\cdots,Hit_{t-q}$ and $k-q-1$ remaining columns are additional independent variables (including the VaR itself). This test is known as dynamic quantile test. Under the null $A1-A2$, Engel and Manganelli (1999) show that dynamic quantile test statistic is $\frac{\hat{\lambda}'X'X\hat{\lambda}}{\alpha(1-\alpha)}$, which is asymptotically distributed as $\chi^2(k)$.

EMPIRICAL RESULTS

In this paper, the computation procedure is conducted in two steps. In the first step, the R-2.12.0-win32's and R 2.12.0-win32's Kernlab package for filling the classical HAR and SVM-HAR models and computed the conditional realized volatility forecasts for both models. In the second step, estimation involved in Value-at-Risk (VaR) approach is carried out by calling G@RCH 5.0 in Ox. The R and Ox code are available upon request. Both Kupiec's likelihood ratio test and dynamic quantile test were used to assess the performance of the classical HAR and SVM-HAR models through the 12 aforementioned types of VaR forecasts with a level α that ranges

Table 2. VaR failure rate results for different models using 5-min intraday returns.

		In-sample										Out-of-sample									
		VaR for short positions					VaR for long positions					VaR for short positions					VaR for long positions				
α		5%	2.5%	1%	0.5%	0.25%	5%	2.5%	1%	0.5%	0.25%	5%	2.5%	1%	0.5%	0.25%	5%	2.5%	1%	0.5%	0.25%
GARCH-																					
Gaussian	HAR	0.189	0.000	0.000	0.000	0.000	0.000	0.000	0.000	0.047	0.522	0.528	0.031	0.000	0.000	0.000	0.000	0.000	0.001	0.089	0.000
	SHAR	0.584	0.005	0.000	0.000	0.000	0.000	0.000	0.000	0.000	0.019	0.027	0.000	0.000	0.000	0.000	0.000	0.000	0.045	0.019	0.000
ST-t	HAR	0.000	0.000	0.000	0.003	0.006	0.000	0.000	0.000	0.000	0.000	0.010	0.020	0.000	0.002	0.086	0.000	0.000	0.000	0.000	0.000
	SHAR	0.000	0.000	0.000	0.000	0.002	0.000	0.000	0.000	0.000	0.000	0.000	0.000	0.003	0.162	0.086	0.000	0.000	0.000	0.000	0.000
SKST	HAR	0.303	0.027	0.484	0.524	0.806	0.213	0.147	0.199	0.211	0.855	0.367	0.203	0.047	0.304	0.216	0.845	0.057	0.045	0.019	0.000
	SHAR	0.110	0.068	0.090	0.083	0.078	0.078	0.028	0.076	0.027	0.019	0.010	0.031	0.531	0.813	0.216	0.956	0.093	0.206	0.000	0.000
GJR-GARCH-																					
Gaussian	HAR	0.133	0.000	0.000	0.000	0.000	0.000	0.000	0.000	0.017	0.091	0.934	0.031	0.000	0.000	0.000	0.000	0.000	0.001	0.000	0.000
	SHAR	0.875	0.005	0.000	0.000	0.000	0.000	0.000	0.000	0.000	0.000	0.051	0.000	0.000	0.000	0.000	0.000	0.000	0.016	0.019	0.000
ST-t	HAR	0.000	0.000	0.000	0.006	0.006	0.000	0.000	0.000	0.000	0.000	0.005	0.008	0.013	0.006	0.030	0.000	0.000	0.000	0.000	0.000
	SHAR	0.000	0.000	0.000	0.000	0.001	0.000	0.000	0.000	0.000	0.000	0.000	0.000	0.003	0.002	0.216	0.000	0.000	0.000	0.000	0.000
SKST	HAR	0.403	0.433	0.778	0.728	0.522	0.524	0.657	0.423	0.107	0.855	0.825	0.729	0.084	0.304	0.216	0.825	0.402	0.016	0.019	0.000
	SHAR	0.653	0.294	0.059	0.142	0.160	0.812	0.147	0.294	0.211	0.255	0.068	0.147	0.474	0.162	0.470	0.720	0.143	0.045	0.000	0.000
EGARCH-																					
Gaussian	HAR	0.015	0.000	0.000	0.000	0.000	0.000	0.000	0.000	0.001	0.091	0.934	0.031	0.000	0.000	0.000	0.000	0.000	0.000	0.000	0.000
	SHAR	0.159	0.000	0.000	0.000	0.000	0.000	0.000	0.000	0.000	0.000	0.118	0.001	0.000	0.000	0.000	0.000	0.000	0.001	0.000	0.000
ST-t	HAR	0.000	0.000	0.000	0.001	0.015	0.000	0.000	0.000	0.000	0.000	0.019	0.031	0.025	0.015	0.086	0.000	0.000	0.000	0.000	0.000
	SHAR	0.000	0.000	0.000	0.000	0.001	0.000	0.000	0.000	0.000	0.000	0.000	0.000	0.006	0.002	0.216	0.000	0.000	0.000	0.000	0.000
SKST	HAR	0.953	0.978	0.778	0.728	0.806	0.890	0.703	0.294	0.211	0.855	0.934	0.470	0.363	0.079	0.086	0.720	0.297	0.045	0.089	0.000
	SHAR	0.402	0.702	0.090	0.083	0.160	0.812	0.467	0.023	0.005	0.019	0.443	0.203	0.085	0.304	0.646	0.934	0.526	0.045	0.000	0.000
APARCH-																					
Gaussian	HAR	0.000	0.000	0.000	0.000	0.000	0.000	0.000	0.000	0.000	0.000	0.000	0.000	0.000	0.000	0.000	0.000	0.000	0.000	0.000	0.000
	SHAR	0.000	0.000	0.000	0.000	0.000	0.000	0.000	0.000	0.000	0.000	0.000	0.000	0.000	0.000	0.000	0.000	0.000	0.000	0.000	0.000
ST-t	HAR	0.000	0.000	0.000	0.001	0.014	0.000	0.000	0.000	0.000	0.000	0.000	0.000	0.000	0.001	0.014	0.000	0.000	0.000	0.000	0.000

from 5 to 0.25% for three differently sampled intraday returns of Nikkei 225 index. Tables 2 to 4 reported the *P*-values for the Kupiec's (1995)

Table 2. Contd.

	SHAR	0.000	0.000	0.000	0.000	0.000	0.000	0.000	0.000	0.000	0.000	0.000	0.000	0.000	0.000	0.000	0.000	0.000	0.000	0.000	0.000
SKST	HAR	0.000	0.000	0.000	0.000	0.000	0.000	0.000	0.000	0.000	0.000	0.000	0.000	0.000	0.000	0.000	0.000	0.000	0.000	0.000	0.000
	SHAR	0.000	0.000	0.000	0.000	0.000	0.000	0.000	0.000	0.000	0.000	0.000	0.000	0.000	0.000	0.000	0.000	0.000	0.000	0.000	0.000

P-values for the dynamic quantile test statistic $\frac{\hat{\lambda}'X'X\hat{\lambda}}{\alpha(1-\alpha)} \sim \chi^2(7)$ both for long and short trading with α is successively equal to 5, 2.5, 1%, 0.5 and o.25% of 15 previously explained ARCH specifications for classical HAR-ARCH and SVM-HAR-ARCH type models. The left part presenting the results for in-sample forecasts while the right part, the out-of-sample forecasts using 5-min intraday returns of Nikkei 225 index. The in-sample period is 11 March 1996 to 29 December 2004 and the out-of-sample period is 5 January 2005 to 30 September 2009. $y_t = \mu_t + \sqrt{\sigma^2 RV_{t|t-1}}, z_t$.

Table 3. VaR failure rate results for different models using 15 min intraday returns.

α		In-sample										Out-of-sample									
		VaR for short positions					VaR for long positions					VaR for short positions					VaR for long positions				
		5%	2.5%	1%	0.5%	0.25%	5%	2.5%	1%	0.5%	0.25%	5%	2.5%	1%	0.5%	0.25%	5%	2.5%	1%	0.5%	0.25%
GARCH-																					
Gaussian	HAR	0.000	0.002	0.000	0.000	0.000	0.000	0.000	0.000	0.000	0.019	0.068	0.001	0.000	0.000	0.000	0.000	0.000	0.000	0.000	0.000
	SHAR	0.461	0.116	0.005	0.000	0.000	0.000	0.000	0.000	0.000	0.000	0.934	0.003	0.000	0.000	0.000	0.000	0.000	0.001	0.019	0.000
ST-t	HAR	0.000	0.000	0.000	0.000	0.015	0.000	0.000	0.000	0.000	0.000	0.000	0.008	0.013	0.521	0.216	0.000	0.000	0.000	0.000	0.000
	SHAR	0.000	0.003	0.269	0.047	0.000	0.000	0.000	0.000	0.000	0.000	0.000	0.002	0.013	0.162	0.086	0.000	0.000	0.000	0.000	0.000
SKST	HAR	0.189	0.150	0.023	0.083	0.160	0.147	0.311	0.199	0.005	0.019	0.019	0.103	0.085	0.521	0.216	0.633	0.143	0.005	0.000	0.000
	SHAR	0.031	0.515	0.623	0.083	0.015	0.009	0.041	0.883	0.047	0.019	0.193	0.020	0.047	0.304	0.216	0.178	0.033	0.005	0.089	0.000
GJR-GARCH-																					
Gaussian	HAR	0.403	0.000	0.000	0.000	0.000	0.000	0.000	0.000	0.000	0.000	0.118	0.001	0.000	0.000	0.000	0.000	0.000	0.000	0.000	0.000
	SHAR	0.524	0.150	0.002	0.000	0.000	0.000	0.000	0.000	0.001	0.000	0.367	0.020	0.000	0.000	0.000	0.000	0.000	0.001	0.019	0.000
ST-t	HAR	0.000	0.000	0.000	0.000	0.006	0.000	0.000	0.000	0.000	0.000	0.000	0.008	0.006	0.080	0.216	0.000	0.000	0.000	0.000	0.000
	SHAR	0.000	0.002	0.133	0.047	0.001	0.000	0.000	0.000	0.000	0.000	0.001	0.003	0.003	0.162	0.086	0.000	0.000	0.000	0.000	0.000
SKST	HAR	0.799	0.238	0.059	0.524	0.300	0.736	0.558	0.043	0.005	0.091	0.152	0.729	0.363	0.162	0.867	0.737	0.210	0.016	0.000	0.000
	SHAR	0.351	0.978	0.945	0.357	0.035	0.348	0.311	0.199	0.211	0.091	0.193	0.203	0.363	0.521	0.216	0.934	0.142	0.045	0.019	0.000
EGARCH-																					
Gaussian	HAR	0.403	0.000	0.000	0.000	0.000	0.000	0.000	0.000	0.000	0.000	0.243	0.001	0.000	0.000	0.000	0.000	0.000	0.000	0.000	0.000
	SHAR	0.049	0.089	0.000	0.000	0.000	0.000	0.000	0.000	0.000	0.000	0.956	0.071	0.000	0.000	0.000	0.000	0.000	0.000	0.019	0.000
ST-t	HAR	0.000	0.000	0.000	0.000	0.015	0.000	0.000	0.000	0.000	0.000	0.000	0.008	0.235	0.521	0.216	0.000	0.000	0.000	0.000	0.000
	SHAR	0.000	0.007	0.023	0.003	0.006	0.000	0.000	0.000	0.000	0.000	0.003	0.003	0.047	0.080	0.468	0.000	0.000	0.000	0.000	0.000

Table 3. Contd.

SKST	HAR	0.875	0.190	0.269	0.728	0.078	0.524	0.467	0.127	0.107	0.019	0.364	0.010	0.104	0.089	0.230	0.001	0.000	0.000	0.000	0.000
	SHAR	0.875	0.605	0.778	0,142	0.035	0.663	0.147	0.294	0.211	0.091	0.193	0.276	0.235	0.521	0.468	0.825	0.018	0.005	0.019	0.000
APARCH-																					
Gaussian	HAR	0.000	0.000	0.000	0.000	0.000	0.000	0.000	0.000	0.000	0.000	0.000	0.000	0.000	0.000	0.000	0.000	0.000	0.000	0.000	0.000
	SHAR	0.000	0.000	0.000	0.000	0.000	0.000	0.000	0.000	0.000	0.000	0.000	0.000	0.000	0.000	0.000	0.000	0.000	0.000	0.000	0.000
ST-t	HAR	0.000	0.000	0.000	0.000	0.000	0.000	0.000	0.000	0.000	0.000	0.000	0.000	0.000	0.000	0.000	0.000	0.000	0.000	0.000	0.000
	SHAR	0.000	0.000	0.000	0.000	0.000	0.000	0.000	0.000	0.000	0.000	0.000	0.000	0.000	0.000	0.000	0.000	0.000	0.000	0.000	0.000
SKST	HAR	0.000	0.000	0.000	0.000	0.000	0.000	0.000	0.000	0.000	0.000	0.000	0.000	0.000	0.000	0.000	0.000	0.000	0.000	0.000	0.000
	SHAR	0.000	0.000	0.000	0.000	0.000	0.000	0.000	0.000	0.000	0.000	0.000	0.000	0.000	0.000	0.000	0.000	0.000	0.000	0.000	0.000

P-values for the dynamic quantile test statistic $\frac{\hat{\lambda}\prime X\prime X\hat{\lambda}}{\alpha(1-\alpha)} \sim \chi^2(7)$ both for long and short trading with α is successively equal to 5, 2.5, 1%, 0.5 and o.25% of 15 previously explained ARCH specifications for classical HAR-ARCH and SVM-HAR-ARCH type models. The left part presenting the results for in-sample forecasts while the right part, the out-of-sample forecasts using 5-min intraday returns of Nikkei 225 index. The in-sample period is 11 March 1996 to 29 December 2004 and the out-of-sample period is 5 January 2005 to 30 September 2009. $y_t = \mu_t + \sqrt{\sigma^2 RV_{t|t-1}}, z_t.$

Table 4. VaR failure rate results for different models using optimally sampled intraday returns.

		In-sample										Out-of-sample									
α		VaR for short positions					VaR for long positions					VaR for short positions					VaR for long positions				
		5%	2.5%	1%	0.5%	0.25%	5%	2.5%	1%	0.5%	0.25%	5%	2.5%	1%	0.5%	0.25%	5%	2.5%	1%	0.5%	0.25%
GARCH-																					
Gaussian	HAR	0.890	0.020	0.000	0.000	0.000	0.000	0.000	0.000	0.000	0.000	0.068	0.001	0.000	0.000	0.000	0.000	0.000	0.000	0.000	0.000
	SHAR	0.091	0.000	0.000	0.000	0.000	0.000	0.000	0.000	0.000	0.019	0.737	0.203	0.000	0.000	0.000	0.000	0.000	0.000	0.000	0.000
ST-t	HAR	0.000	0.000	0.000	0.000	0.002	0.000	0.000	0.000	0.000	0.000	0.000	0.000	0.013	0.036	0.086	0.000	0.000	0.000	0.000	0.000
	SHAR	0.000	0.000	0.008	0.003	0.015	0.000	0.000	0.000	0.000	0.000	0.007	0.364	0.363	0.521	0.468	0.000	0.000	0.000	0.000	0.000
SKST	HAR	0.133	0.294	0.192	0.025	0.035	0.298	0.081	0.043	0.017	0.091	0.118	0.203	0.531	0.162	0.216	0.178	0.093	0.016	0.019	0.000
	SHAR	0.048	0.294	0.269	0.047	0.078	0.009	0.005	0.076	0.017	0.019	0.014	0.048	0.363	0.036	0.216	0.010	0.000	0.000	0.000	0.000
GJR-GARCH-																					
Gaussian	HAR	0.459	0.037	0.000	0.000	0.000	0.000	0.000	0.000	0.005	0.019	0.443	0.002	0.000	0.000	0.000	0.000	0.000	0.000	0.000	0.000
	SHAR	0.159	0.001	0.000	0.000	0.000	0.000	0.000	0.000	0.000	0.000	0.934	0.032	0.000	0.000	0.000	0.000	0.000	0.000	0.000	0.000
ST-t	HAR	0.000	0.000	0.000	0.000	0.035	0.000	0.000	0.000	0.000	0.000	0.000	0.000	0.025	0.079	0.030	0.000	0.000	0.000	0.000	0.000
	SHAR	0.000	0.000	0.000	0.003	0.015	0.000	0.000	0.000	0.000	0.000	0.007	0.203	0.737	0.848	0.468	0.000	0.000	0.000	0.000	0.000

Table 4. Contd.

SKST	HAR	0.159	0.433	0.090	0.142	0.300	0.890	0.311	0.076	0.107	0.019	0.300	0.203	0.235	0.303	0.216	0.535	0.057	0.045	0.019	0.000
	SHAR	0.519	0.868	0.623	0.357	0.078	0.348	0.028	0.294	0.364	0.522	0.019	0.147	0.145	0.080	0.216	0.100	0.000	0.005	0.000	0.000
EGARCH-																					
Gaussian	HAR	0.403	0.001	0.000	0.000	0.000	0.000	0.000	0.000	0.000	0.000	0.152	0.005	0.000	0.000	0.000	0.000	0.000	0.000	0.000	0.000
	SHAR	0.519	0.019	0.000	0.000	0.000	0.000	0.000	0.000	0.000	0.019	0.737	0.013	0.000	0.000	0.000	0.000	0.000	0.005	0.019	0.230
ST-t	HAR	0.000	0.000	0.000	0.001	0.006	0.000	0.000	0.000	0.000	0.000	0.242	0.592	0.104	0.252	0.230	0.000	0.000	0.000	0.000	0.000
	SHAR	0.000	0.000	0.003	0.025	0.006	0.000	0.000	0.000	0.000	0.000	0.007	0.147	0.786	0.848	0.468	0.000	0.000	0.000	0.000	0.000
SKST	HAR	0.653	0.605	0.366	0.524	0.300	0.953	0.193	0.043	0.005	0.019	0.068	0.103	0.145	0.162	0.216	0.135	0.010	0.045	0.019	0.000
	SHAR	0.663	0.247	0.778	0.524	0.015	0.592	0.110	0.199	0.005	0.019	0.118	0.031	0.363	0.304	0.216	0.292	0.000	0.000	0.000	0.000
APARCH-																					
Gaussian	HAR	0.000	0.000	0.000	0.000	0.000	0.000	0.000	0.000	0.000	0.000	0.000	0.000	0.000	0.000	0.000	0.000	0.000	0.000	0.000	0.000
	SHAR	0.000	0.000	0.000	0.000	0.000	0.000	0.000	0.000	0.000	0.000	0.000	0.000	0.000	0.000	0.000	0.000	0.000	0.000	0.000	0.000
ST-t	HAR	0.000	0.000	0.000	0.000	0.000	0.000	0.000	0.000	0.000	0.000	0.000	0.000	0.000	0.000	0.000	0.000	0.000	0.000	0.000	0.000
	SHAR	0.000	0.000	0.000	0.000	0.000	0.000	0.000	0.000	0.000	0.000	0.000	0.000	0.000	0.000	0.000	0.000	0.000	0.000	0.000	0.000
SKST	HAR	0.000	0.000	0.000	0.000	0.000	0.000	0.000	0.000	0.000	0.000	0.000	0.000	0.000	0.000	0.000	0.000	0.000	0.000	0.000	0.000
	SHAR	0.000	0.000	0.000	0.000	0.000	0.000	0.000	0.000	0.000	0.000	0.000	0.000	0.000	0.000	0.000	0.000	0.000	0.000	0.000	0.000

P-values for the dynamic quantile test statistic $\frac{\hat{\lambda}\prime X\prime X\hat{\lambda}}{\alpha(1-\alpha)} \sim \chi^2(7)$ both for long and short trading with α is successively equal to 5, 2.5, 1, 0.5 and o.25% of 15 previously explained ARCH specifications for classical HAR-ARCH and SVM-HAR-ARCH type models. The left part presenting the results for in-sample forecasts while the right part, the out-of-sample forecasts using 5-min intraday returns of Nikkei 225 index. The in-sample period is 11 March 1996 to 29 December 2004 and the out-of-sample period is 5 January 2005 to 30 September 2009. $y_t = \mu_t + \sqrt{\sigma^2 RV_{t|t-1}, z_t}$.

failure rate test whileTables 5 to 7 reported the *P*-values for Engel and Manganelli's (1999) dynamic quantile forecast test with $q = 5$ and $k = 7$ (that is, the contemporaneous VaR forecast is included as additional variable following Giot and Laurent (2004).

For both the tests, each table presented four panels successively the results for GARCH, GJR-GARCH, EGARCH and APARCH models. Each panel presented the results successively for Gaussian, Student t (ST-t) and skewed Student (SKST) distributions for both the classical HAR (HAR) and SVM-HAR (SHAR) models. The left part of each table presented the in-sample VaR forecasts results while the right part presents the out-of-sample VaR forecasts results for both short and long trading positions.

DISCUSSION

We first compared the results of GARCH and APARCH models for each of the Tables, that is, Tables 2 to 4 and Tables 5 to 7. The empirical results showed the same story for all intraday sampled returns and innovation distributions specifications. Almost all the *P*-values for both the tests are often smaller than 0.05. These three classes of models failed to forecast the one-day ahead VaR. Though we observe from Giot and Laurent (2004) that the Skewed-APARCH specification significantly improves the VaR forecasting performance where they use ARFIMAX model for volatility forecasts. The results for GARCH models

Table 5. VaR quantile regression results for different models using 5-min intraday returns.

α		In-sample										Out-of-sample									
		VaR for short positions					VaR for long positions					VaR for short positions					VaR for long positions				
		5%	2.5%	1%	0.5%	0.25%	5%	2.5%	1%	0.5%	0.25%	5%	2.5%	1%	0.5%	0.25%	5%	2.5%	1%	0.5%	0.25%
GARCH-																					
Gaussian	HAR	0.001	0.000	0.000	0.000	0.000	0.000	0.000	0.121	0.785	0.999	0.902	0.365	0.000	0.000	0.000	0.001	0.017	0.292	0.901	0.842
	SHAR	0.989	0.046	0.000	0.000	0.000	0.000	0.000	0.012	0.175	0.729	0.139	0.000	0.000	0.000	0.000	0.001	0.049	0.775	0.725	0.842
ST-t	HAR	0.000	0.000	0.000	0.000	0.000	0.000	0.000	0.043	0.175	0.490	0.079	0.281	0.000	0.014	0.631	0.000	0.001	0.089	0.485	0.842
	SHAR	0.000	0.000	0.000	0.000	0.022	0.000	0.000	0.003	0.092	0.490	0.012	0.000	0.012	0.810	0.631	0.001	0.017	0.089	0.485	0.842
SKST	HAR	0.001	0.006	0.016	0.030	0.000	0.215	0.633	0.923	0.963	0.999	0.851	0.684	0.151	0.948	0.907	0.668	0.530	0.775	0.725	0.842
	SHAR	0.643	0.414	0.385	0.594	0.634	0.091	0.410	0.802	0.629	0.729	0.113	0.102	0.945	0.999	0.907	0.309	0.150	0.956	0.485	0.842
GJR-GARCH-																					
Gaussian	HAR	0.021	0.000	0.000	0.000	0.000	0.000	0.000	0.043	0.629	0.904	0.714	0.177	0.000	0.000	0.000	0.000	0.017	0.292	0.485	0.842
	SHAR	0.828	0.084	0.000	0.000	0.000	0.000	0.000	0.012	0.0175	0.490	0.178	0.000	0.000	0.000	0.000	0.000	0.030	0.620	0.725	0.842
ST-t	HAR	0.000	0.000	0.000	0.000	0.000	0.000	0.000	0.024	0.175	0.490	0.031	0.076	0.074	0.051	0.289	0.000	0.001	0.089	0.485	0.842
	SHAR	0.001	0.000	0.000	0.001	0.005	0.000	0.000	0.001	0.092	0.490	0.001	0.000	0.011	0.014	0.907	0.000	0.001	0.089	0.485	0.842
SKST	HAR	0.088	0.333	0.023	0.020	0.000	0.535	0.862	0.522	0.899	0.999	0.669	0.909	0.451	0.948	0.907	0.073	0.009	0.620	0.725	0.842
		0.719	0.648	0.277	0.760	0.847	0.699	0.742	0.435	0.963	0.982	0.228	0.317	0.151	0.810	0.994	0.262	0.554	0.001	0.485	0.842
EGARCH-																					
Gaussian	HAR	0.000	0.001	0.000	0.000	0.000	0.000	0.000	0.043	0.299	0.904	0.660	0.165	0.000	0.000	0.000	0.000	0.017	0.089	0.485	0.842
	SHAR	0.594	0.003	0.000	0.000	0.000	0.000	0.000	0.006	0.175	0.490	0.353	0.018	0.000	0.000	0.000	0.002	0.030	0.292	0.485	0.842
ST-t	HAR	0.000	0.000	0.000	0.000	0.000	0.000	0.000	0.024	0.175	0.490	0.158	0.177	0.155	0.147	0.631	0.000	0.001	0.089	0.485	0.842
	SHAR	0.000	0.000	0.000	0.001	0.005	0.000	0.000	0.001	0.092	0.490	0.000	0.000	0.025	0.000	0.907	0.000	0.000	0.089	0.485	0.842
SKST	HAR	0.165	0.813	0.007	0.020	0.000	0.289	0.484	0.955	0.963	0.999	0.704	0.890	0.904	0.578	0.631	0.819	0.059	0.775	0.901	0.842
	SHAR	0.930	0.485	0.385	0.594	0.847	0.779	0.560	0.602	0.457	0.729	0.286	0.788	0.216	0.948	0.999	0.011	0.874	0.001	0.485	0.842
APARCH-																					
Gaussian	HAR	0.000	0.000	0.000	0.000	0.000	0.000	0.000	0.001	0.092	0.490	0.000	0.000	0.000	0.000	0.000	0.000	0.000	0.089	0.485	0.842
	SHAR	0.000	0.000	0.000	0.000	0.000	0.000	0.000	0.001	0.092	0.490	0.000	0.000	0.000	0.000	0.000	0.000	0.000	0.089	0.485	0.842
ST-t	HAR	0.000	0.000	0.000	0.000	0.000	0.000	0.000	0.006	0.092	0.490	0.000	0.000	0.000	0.000	0.000	0.000	0.000	0.089	0.485	0.842
	SHAR	0.000	0.000	0.000	0.000	0.000	0.000	0.000	0.001	0.092	0.490	0.000	0.000	0.000	0.000	0.000	0.000	0.000	0.089	0.485	0.842

Table 5. Contd.

SKST	HAR	0.000	0.000	0.000	0.000	0.000	0.000	0.000	0.001	0.092	0.490	0.000	0.000	0.000	0.000	0.000	0.000	0.000	0.089	0.485	0.842
	SHAR	0.000	0.000	0.000	0.000	0.000	0.000	0.000	0.001	0.092	0.490	0.000	0.000	0.000	0.000	0.000	0.000	0.000	0.089	0.485	0.842

P-values for the dynamic quantile test statistic $\frac{\hat{\lambda}\prime X\prime X\hat{\lambda}}{\alpha(1-\alpha)} \sim \chi^2(7)$ both for long and short trading with α is successively equal to 5, 2.5, 1, 0.5 and o.25% of 15 previously explained ARCH specifications for classical HAR-ARCH and SVM-HAR-ARCH type models. The left part presenting the results for in-sample forecasts while the right part, the out-of-sample forecasts using 5-min intraday returns of Nikkei 225 index. The in-sample period is 11 March 1996 to 29 December 2004 and the out-of-sample period is 5 January 2005 to 30 September 2009. $y_t = \mu_t + \sqrt{\sigma^2 RV_{t|t-1}}, z_t$.

Table 6. VaR quantile regression results for different models using 15-min intraday returns.

		In-sample										Out-of-sample									
α		VaR for short positions					VaR for long positions					VaR for short positions					VaR for long positions				
		5%	2.5%	1%	0.5%	0.25%	5%	2.5%	1%	0.5%	0.25%	5%	2.5%	1%	0.5%	0.25%	5%	2.5%	1%	0.5%	0.25%
GARCH-																					
Gaussian	HAR	0.010	0.003	0.000	0.000	0.000	0.000	0.000	0.043	0.175	0.729	0.005	0.006	0.000	0.000	0.000	0.000	0.009	0.089	0.490	0.842
	SHAR	0.801	0.174	0.020	0.000	0.000	0.000	0.000	0.006	0.092	0.490	0.213	0.016	0.000	0.000	0.000	0.000	0.001	0.292	0.725	0.842
ST-t	HAR	0.000	0.000	0.000	0.000	0.000	0.000	0.000	0.003	0.092	0.490	0.000	0.081	0.074	0.993	0.907	0.000	0.000	0.089	0.490	0.842
	SHAR	0.000	0.001	0.733	0.417	0.001	0.000	0.003	0.006	0.092	0.490	0.000	0.014	0.053	0.810	0.630	0.017	0.005	0.089	0.490	0.842
SKST	HAR	0.006	0.334	0.011	0.001	0.847	0.165	0.559	0.923	0.457	0.729	0.023	0.696	0.451	0.993	0.907	0.381	0.745	0.449	0.490	0.842
	SHAR	0.170	0.363	0.935	0.594	0.187	0.033	0.399	0.983	0.785	0.729	0.312	0.067	0.283	0.948	0.907	0.381	0.307	0.449	0.901	0.842
GJR-GARCH-																					
Gaussian	HAR	0.005	0.005	0.000	0.000	0.000	0.000	0.000	0.006	0.092	0.490	0.048	0.003	0.000	0.000	0.000	0.000	0.002	0.089	0.490	0.842
	SHAR	0.862	0.188	0.004	0.000	0.000	0.000	0.000	0.012	0.299	0.490	0.164	0.146	0.000	0.000	0.000	0.000	0.005	0.292	0.725	0.842
ST-t	HAR	0.000	0.000	0.000	0.000	0.000	0.000	0.000	0.001	0.092	0.490	0.000	0.138	0.031	0.578	0.907	0.000	0.000	0.089	0.490	0.842
	SHAR	0.002	0.029	0.505	0.417	0.005	0.000	0.000	0.006	0.092	0.490	0.001	0.010	0.011	0.810	0.631	0.004	0.005	0.089	0.490	0.842
SKST	HAR	0.182	0.702	0.017	0.030	0.963	0.147	0.702	0.108	0.457	0.904	0.108	0.540	0.904	0.810	0.999	0.268	0.638	0.620	0.490	0.842
	SHAR	0.963	0.783	0.976	0.957	0.386	0.292	0.314	0.343	0.963	0.904	0.043	0.407	0.904	0.993	0.907	0.881	0.610	0.775	0.725	0.842
EGARCH-																					
Gaussian	HAR	0.064	0.008	0.000	0.000	0.000	0.000	0.000	0.003	0.092	0.490	0.035	0.001	0.000	0.000	0.000	0.000	0.000	0.089	0.490	0.842
	SHAR	0.581	0.554	0.000	0.000	0.000	0.000	0.000	0.024	0.175	0.490	0.361	0.046	0.000	0.000	0.000	0.000	0.002	0.170	0.725	0.842
ST-t	HAR	0.000	0.000	0.000	0.000	0.000	0.000	0.000	0.001	0.092	0.490	0.000	0.081	0.792	0.993	0.907	0.000	0.000	0.089	0.490	0.842
	SHAR	0.000	0.096	0.127	0.030	0.072	0.000	0.000	0.001	0.092	0.490	0.000	0.002	0.065	0.578	0.994	0.003	0.002	0.089	0.490	0.842
SKST	HAR	0.294	0.608	0.017	0.000	0.000	0.054	0.708	0.873	0.899	0.729	0.180	0.396	0.889	0.901	0.982	0.040	0.001	0.089	0.490	0.842
	SHAR	0.875	0.980	0.962	0.760	0.386	0.561	0.591	0.955	0.963	0.903	0.223	0.710	0.328	0.993	0.994	0.480	0.338	0.449	0.725	0.842

Table 6. Contd.

APARCH-																					
Gaussian	HAR	0.000	0.000	0.000	0.000	0.000	0.000	0.000	0.001	0.092	0.490	0.000	0.000	0.000	0.000	0.000	0.000	0.000	0.089	0.490	0.842
	SHAR	0.000	0.000	0.000	0.000	0.000	0.000	0.000	0.001	0.092	0.490	0.000	0.000	0.000	0.000	0.000	0.000	0.000	0.089	0.490	0.842
ST-t	HAR	0.000	0.000	0.000	0.000	0.000	0.000	0.000	0.001	0.092	0.490	0.000	0.000	0.000	0.000	0.000	0.000	0.000	0.089	0.490	0.842
	SHAR	0.000	0.000	0.000	0.000	0.000	0.000	0.000	0.001	0.092	0.490	0.000	0.000	0.000	0.000	0.000	0.000	0.000	0.089	0.490	0.842
SKST	HAR	0.000	0.000	0.000	0.000	0.000	0.000	0.000	0.001	0.092	0.490	0.000	0.000	0.000	0.000	0.000	0.000	0.000	0.089	0.490	0.842
	SHAR	0.000	0.000	0.000	0.000	0.000	0.000	0.000	0.001	0.092	0.490	0.000	0.000	0.000	0.000	0.000	0.000	0.000	0.089	0.490	0.842

P-values for the dynamic quantile test statistic $\frac{\hat{\lambda}\prime X\prime X\hat{\lambda}}{\alpha(1-\alpha)} \sim \chi^2(7)$ both for long and short trading with α is successively equal to 5, 2.5, 1%, 0.5 and 0.25% of 15 previously explained ARCH specifications for classical HAR-ARCH and SVM-HAR-ARCH type models. The left part presenting the results for in-sample forecasts while the right part, the out-of-sample forecasts using 5-minute intraday returns of Nikkei 225 index. The in-sample period is 11 March 1996 to 29 December 2004 and the out-of-sample period is 5 January 2005 to 30 September 2009. $y_t = \mu_t + \sqrt{\sigma^2 RV_{t|t-1}, z_t}$.

Table 7. VaR quantile regression results for different models using optimally sampled intraday returns.

		In-sample										Out-of-sample									
α		VaR for short positions					VaR for long positions					VaR for short positions					VaR for long positions				
		5%	2.5%	1%	0.5%	0.25%	5%	2.5%	1%	0.5%	0.25%	5%	2.5%	1%	0.5%	0.25%	5%	2.5%	1%	0.5%	0.25%
GARCH-																					
Gaussian	HAR	0.564	0.071	0.000	0.000	0.000	0.000	0.000	0.006	0.092	0.490	0.121	0.003	0.000	0.000	0.000	0.000	0.002	0.170	0.490	0.842
	SHAR	0.173	0.003	0.000	0.000	0.000	0.000	0.000	0.024	0.175	0.729	0.389	0.480	0.000	0.000	0.000	0.000	0.001	0.089	0.490	0.842
ST-t	HAR	0.000	0.000	0.000	0.000	0.000	0.000	0.000	0.001	0.092	0.490	0.000	0.001	0.052	0.330	0.631	0.000	0.001	0.089	0.490	0.842
	SHAR	0.000	0.000	0.000	0.004	0.187	0.000	0.000	0.003	0.092	0.490	0.002	0.625	0.904	0.993	0.994	0.000	0.000	0.089	0.490	0.842
SKST	HAR	0.039	0.663	0.016	0.001	0.000	0.405	0.562	0.710	0.629	0.904	0.118	0.304	0.965	0.810	0.907	0.595	0.612	0.620	0.725	0.842
	SHAR	0.010	0.158	0.014	0.032	0.634	0.164	0.172	0.802	0.629	0.729	0.007	0.167	0.904	0.330	0.907	0.125	0.049	0.089	0.490	0.842
GJR-GARCH-																					
Gaussian	HAR	0.295	0.289	0.000	0.000	0.000	0.000	0.000	0.003	0.092	0.490	0.556	0.014	0.000	0.000	0.000	0,000	0.002	0.089	0.490	0.842
	SHAR	0.330	0.002	0.000	0.000	0.000	0.000	0.000	0.001	0.457	0.729	0.212	0.049	0.000	0.000	0.000	0.000	0.001	0.170	0.490	0.842
ST-t	HAR	0.000	0.000	0.000	0.000	0.386	0.000	0.000	0.001	0.092	0.490	0.002	0.000	0.150	0.578	0.289	0.000	0.000	0.089	0.490	0.842
	SHAR	0.000	0.001	0.000	0.000	0.187	0.000	0.000	0.003	0.092	0.490	0.001	0.339	0.989	0.999	0.994	0.000	0.000	0.089	0.490	0.842
SKST	HAR	0.167	0.844	0.253	0.044	0.962	0.061	0.581	0.171	0.899	0.729	0.549	0.593	0.793	0.948	0.907	0.668	0.636	0.775	0.725	0.842
	SHAR	0.649	0.380	0.275	0.957	0.634	0.647	0.189	0.426	0.000	0.000	0.006	0.101	0.632	0.578	0.907	0.559	0.041	0.449	0.490	0.842

Table 7. Contd.

EGARCH-																					
Gaussian	HAR	0.433	0.002	0.000	0.000	0.000	0.000	0.000	0.003	0.092	0.490	0.215	0.086	0.000	0.000	0.000	0.000	0.001	0.089	0.490	0.842
	SHAR	0.403	0.023	0.000	0.000	0.000	0.000	0.000	0.012	0.175	0.729	0.790	0.207	0.000	0.000	0.000	0.000	0.005	0.449	0.725	0.982
ST-t	HAR	0.000	0.002	0.000	0.000	0.000	0.000	0.000	0.001	0.092	0.490	0.410	0.431	0.889	0.981	0.982	0.000	0.000	0.089	0.490	0.842
	SHAR	0.000	0.000	0.005	0.022	0.072	0.000	0.000	0.001	0.092	0.490	0.000	0.143	0.998	0.999	0.004	0.000	0.000	0.089	0.490	0.842
SKST	HAR	0.790	0.849	0.012	0.000	0.000	0.221	0.636	0.108	0.457	0.729	0.078	0.310	0.632	0.810	0.907	0.250	0.396	0.775	0.725	0.842
	SHAR	0.793	0.082	0.724	0.989	0.187	0.108	0.170	0.336	0.000	0.729	0.000	0.019	0.904	0.948	0.907	0.920	0.119	0.170	0.490	0.842
APARCH-																					
Gaussian	HAR	0.000	0.000	0.000	0.000	0.000	0.000	0.000	0.001	0.092	0.490	0.000	0.000	0.000	0.000	0.000	0.000	0.000	0.089	0.490	0.842
	SHAR	0.000	0.000	0.000	0.000	0.000	0.000	0.000	0.001	0.092	0.490	0.000	0.000	0.000	0.000	0.000	0.000	0.000	0.089	0.490	0.842
ST-t	HAR	0.000	0.000	0.000	0.000	0.000	0.000	0.000	0.001	0.092	0.490	0.000	0.000	0.000	0.000	0.000	0.000	0.000	0.089	0.490	0.842
	SHAR	0.000	0.000	0.000	0.000	0.000	0.000	0.000	0.001	0.092	0.490	0.000	0.000	0.000	0.000	0.000	0.000	0.000	0.089	0.490	0.842
SKST	HAR	0.000	0.000	0.000	0.000	0.000	0.000	0.000	0.001	0.092	0.490	0.000	0.000	0.000	0.000	0.000	0.000	0.000	0.089	0.490	0.842
	SHAR	0.000	0.000	0.000	0.000	0.000	0.000	0.000	0.001	0.092	0.490	0.000	0.000	0.000	0.000	0.000	0.000	0.000	0.089	0.490	0.842

P-values for the dynamic quantile test statistic $\frac{\hat{\lambda}\prime X\prime X\hat{\lambda}}{\alpha(1-\alpha)} \sim \chi^2(7)$ both for long and short trading with α is successively equal to 5, 2.5, 1, 0.5 and o.25% of 15 previously explained ARCH specifications for classical HAR-ARCH and SVM-HAR-ARCH type models. The left part presenting the results for in-sample forecasts while the right part, the out-of-sample forecasts using 5-minute intraday returns of Nikkei 225 index. The in-sample period is 11 March 1996 to 29 December 2004 and the out-of-sample period is 5 January 2005 to 30 September 2009. $y_t = \mu_t + \sqrt{\sigma^2 RV_{t|t-1}}, z_t$.

go with the results of Ebens (1999), where he concluded that the GARCH model underperforms (when volatility must be forecasted) with respect to the model based on the daily realized volatility. We then compared the results for GJR-GARCH and EGARCH models for each Table. All the Tables showed almost similar empirical results. The skewed Student distribution specification produced better forecasts for both the classical HAR and SMN-HAR models while the Gaussian and Student t specifications failed to forecast one day ahead VaR. We observed that the optimally sampled intraday returns could not compute with 5 and 15 min intraday returns to estimate the daily realized volatility for both the skewed Student HAR and skewed Student SVM-HAR models. Finally, we consider the empirical results from 15-min intraday returns. We observed for the SVM-HAR-RV models that for the dynamic quantile test, all the *P*-values are greater than 0.05 for the SKST- EGARCH model and only one *P*-value is smaller than 0.05 for SKST- GJR-GARCH model out of 20 *P*-values (10 for in-sample and 10 for out-of-sample forecasts). Almost similar results were observed when 5-min intraday returns were used. The results for classical HAR-RV forecasts were also satisfactory but failed to compete with the SVM-HAR. The failure rate test results of SKST-GJR- GARCH and SKST-EGARCH were also satisfactory for both the classical HAR-RV and SVM-HAR-RV forecasts. Maximum of the *P*-values were greater than 0.05. Comparing all the results, we can conclude that the SVM-HAR-RV model performs better to forecast one day ahead VaR.

CONCLUDING REMARKS

In this paper, the Support Vector Machine (SVM) regression was combined with Heterogeneous Autoregressive (HAR) model as a hybrid (SMV-HAR) model to improve the VaR forecasting ability. We examined the VaR forecasting ability of the realized volatility based models for Nikkei 225 stock returns. The empirical results presented here are suggestive for several interesting extensions. First, we set the values $C = 1$ and $\epsilon = 0.1$ for the SVM-HAR-RV class models and observed better forecasting ability. The appropriate choice of the value C and ϵ could be helpful to improve the forecasting ability.

Second, we consider only the Laplacian kernel for the SVMs and observe better performances. The choice of other existing kernels in SVM literature or an appropriate new kernel could improve the forecasting ability.

Third, 5- and 15-min intraday returns were considered along with optimally sampled intraday returns to estimate daily realized volatility. The optimally sampled intraday returns as studied by Bandi and Russell (2003, 2008) were considered to mitigate the market microstructure noise but it failed to produce better VaR forecasting performance compared to 5- and 15-min intraday returns. It would be interesting to consider the two- scale estimators of Zhang et al. (2005) and kernel estimator of Barndorff-Nielsen et al. (2009a, b).

Fourth, since the long memory skewed Student distribution produces better performance, therefore, the long memory ARCH type model for conditional variance could be interesting.

REFERENCES

Aït-Sahalia Y, Mancini L (2006). Out of Sample Forecasts of Quadratic Variation. J. Econom., 109: 33-65.

Andersen TG, Bollerslev T, Diebold FX, Labys P (2003). Modeling and forecasting realized volatility. Econom., 71: 529-626.

Andersen TG, Bollerslev T (1998). Answering the skeptice: yes, standard volatility models do provide accurate forecasts. Int. Econ. Rev., 39: 885-905.

Andersen TG, Bollerslev T, Diebold FX (2007). Roughing it up: Including jump components in the measurement, modeling and forecasting of return volatility. Rev. Econ. Stat., 89: 701-720.

Bandi FM, Russell JR (2008). Microstructure noise, realized volatility, and optimal sampling. Rev. Econ. Stud., 75: 339-369.

Barndorff-Nielsen OE, Hansen PR, Lunde A, Shepherd N (2009a). Realised kernels in practice: trades and quotes. Econom., J. (In press).

Barndorff-Nielsen OE, Hansen PR, Lunde A, Shephard N (2009b). Subsampling realised kernels. J. Econom., (in press).

Barndorff-Nielsen OE, Graversen SE, Jacod J, Podolskij M, Shephard N (2006). A central limit theorem for realised power and bipower variation of continuous semimartingales, in: Kabanov Y, Lipseter R, Stoyanov J (Eds.), Stochastic Analysis to Mathematical Finance, Festschrift for Albert Shiryaev, Springer Verlag: Berlin.

Barndorff-Nielsen OE, Shephard N (2004). Power and bipower variation with stochastic volatility and jumps. J. Finan. Econom., 2: 1-37.

Barndorff-Nielsen OE, Shephard N (2006). Econometrics of testing for jumps in financial economics using bipower variation. J. Finan. Econom., 4: 217-252.

Bildirici M, Ersin OO (2009). Improving forecasts of GARCH family models with the artificial neural networks: An application to the daily returns in Istanbul Stock Exchange. Expert Systems with Applications. 36: 7355-7362.

Black F (1976). Studies of stock price volatility changes. Proceedings of the 1976 Meetings of the Business and Economics Statistics Section, American Statistical Association, pp. 177-181.

Bollerslev T (1986). Generalized Auto Regressive Conditional Heteroskedasticity. J. Econom., 31: 307-327.

Chen S, Jeong K, Hardle W (2008). Support Vector Regression Based GARCH Model with Application to Forecasting Volatility of Financial Returns. SFB 649 Discussion Paper of Economic Risk, Berlin.

Clements MP, Galvão AB, Kim JH (2008). Quantile forecasts of daily exchange rate returns from forecasts of realized volatility. J. Empir. Finan., 15(4): 729-750.

Corradi V, Distaso W, Swanson NR (2006). Predictive Inference for Integrated Volatility. Working Paper, Rutgers University.

Corsi F, Zumbach G, MÜller U, Dacorogna M (2001). Consistent high-precision volatility from high frequency data. Economic Notes., 30: pp. 183-204.

Corsi F (2009). A Simple Long Memory Model of Realized Volatility. J. Finan. Econom., 7(2): 174-196.

Cortes C, Vapnik V (1995). Support vector networks. Machine Learning 20: 273-297.

Cristianini N, Showe-Taylor J (2000). An Introduction to Support Vector Machines and Other Kernel-based Learning Methods, London, Cambridge University Press.

Ding ZC, Granger WJ, Engle RF (1993). A long memory property of stock market returns and a new model. J. Empir. Finan., 1: 83-106

Donaldson RG, Kamstra M (1997). An artificial neural network-GARCH model for international stock return volatility. J. Empir. Finan., 4(1): 17-46.

Dunis CL, Laws J, Sermpinis G (2010). Modelling commodity value-at risk with higher order neural networks. Appl. Finan. Econ., 20(7): 585-600.

Ebens H (1999). Realized stock index volatility. Working Paper No. 420.m Department of Economics, John Hopkins University, Baltimore. Value at Risk by regression quantiles. Working Paper, Mimeo, San Diego, Department of Economics.

Engle RF, Ng VK (1993). Measuring and Testing the Impact of News on Volatility. J. Finan., 48: 1749-1778.

Engle RF (1982). Autoregressive conditional heteroskedasticity with estimates of variance of UK inflation. Econom., 50: 987-1008.

Engle RF (1990). Discussion: Stock market volatility and the crash of 87. Rev. Finan. Stud., 3: 103-106.

Fernández C, Steel M (1998). On Bayesian modeling of fat tails and skewness. J. Am. Stat. Ass., 93: 359-371.

Ghysels E, Sinko A (2006). Volatility Forecasting and Microstructure Noise. Working Paper, University of North Carolina

Ghysels E, Santa-Clara P, Valkanov R (2006). Predicting volatility: Getting the most out of return data sampled at different frequencies. J. Econom., 131: 59-95.

Giot P (2003). The information content of implied volatility in agricultural commodity markets. J. Futures Mark., 23: 441-454.

Giot P, Laurent S (2003). Value-at-Risk for long and short positions. J. Applied Econom., 18: 641-664.

Giot P, Laurent S (2004). Modelling daily Value-at-Risk using realized volatility and APARCH type models. J. Empir. Finan., 11: 379-398.

Glosten L, Jagannathan R, Runkle D (1993). On the relationship between the expected value and the volatility of the nominal excess return on stocks. J. Financ., 46: 1779-1801.

Hansen PR, Lunde A (2005). A Forecast Comparison of Volatility Models: Does anything Beat a GARCH (1,1)?. J. Applied Econom., 20(7): 873-889.

Karatzoglou A, Meyer D (2006). Support Vector Machines in R. J Stat. Software, 15: 9.

Karush W (1939). Minima of functions of several variables with inequalities as side constraints. Master's thesis, Dept. of Mathematics, University of Chicago.

Kuhn HW, Tucker AW (1951). Nonlinear programming, in: Proceedings of. 2nd Berkeley Symposium on Mathematical Statistics and Probabilities, Berkeley, University of California Press, pp. 481-492.

Kupiec P (1995). Techniques for verifying the accuracy of risk measurement models. J. Deriv., 2: 173-184.

Lambert P, Laurent S (2001). Modelling financial time series using GARCH-type models and a skewed Student density. Working Paper, Mimeo, University de Liége.

McAleer M, Medeiros MC (2009). Forecasting Realized Volatility with Linear and Nonlinear Models. Discussion Paper Series, CIRJE, Faculty of Economics, University of Tokyo.

Müller KR, Smola AJ, Ratsch G, Schölkopf B, Kohlmorgen J, Vapnik V (1997a). Predicting Time Series with Support Vector Machines.

Proceedings of ICANN'97, Springer LNCS, 1327: 999-1004.
Müller UA, Dacorogna MM, Davé RD, Olsen RB, Puctet OV, von Weizs äcker J (1997b). Volatilities of different time resolutions: Analyzing the dynamics of market components. J. Empir. Finan., 4: 213-239.
Nelson DB (1991). Conditional Heteroskedasticity in Asset Returns: A New Approach. Econometric, 59: 347-370.
Phichhang O, Hengshan W (2010). Financial Volatility Forecasting by Least Square Support Vector Machine Based on GARCH, EGARCH and GJR Models: Evidence from ASEAN Stock Markets. Int. J. Econ. Finan. (Online), 2:1.
Perez-Cruz F, Afonso-Rodriguez JA, Giner J (2003). Estimating GARCH models using support vector machines. J. Quan. Finan., 3(3): 163-172.
Sentana E (1995). Quadratic ARCH models. Rev. Econ. Stud., 62(4): 639-661.
Shephard N (2005). Stochastic volatility: Selected Readings, Oxford University Press, Oxford.
Smola AJ, Schölkopf B (1998). A Tutorial on Support Vector Regression. NeuroCOLT2 Tenical Report Series, NC2-TR-1998-030.
Suykens JAK, Vandewalle J (1999). Least squares support vector machine classifiers. Neural Netw., 9: 293-300.
Smola JA (1998). Learning with Kernels. Ph.D. thesis, Technische Universität Berlin.
Taylor S, Xu X (1997). The incremental volatility information in one million Foreign Exchange quotations. J. Empir. Finan., 4: 317-340.
Vapnik VN (1995). The nature of statistical learning theory, Springer-Verlag, New York.
Vapnik V, Golowich S, Smola A (1997). Support vector method for function approximation, regression estimation, and signal processing, in: Mozer M, Jordan M, and Petsche T, (Eds.), Advances in Neural Information Processing Systems 9, Cambridge, MA, MIT Press, pp. 281-287.
Vapnik VN (1982). Estimation of Dependences Based on Empirical Data, Springer Verlag, Berlin.
Zakoian JM (1994). Threshold Heteroscedastic Models. J. Econ. Dyn. Control, 18: 931-955.
Zhang L, Mykland P, Aït-Sahalia Y (2005). A tale of two time scales: Determining integreted volatility with noisy high-frequency daya. J. Am. Stat. Assoc., 100: 1394-1411

Integrative funding and effective implementation of Universal basic education programme in Central Senatorial District of Delta State, Nigeria

E. D. Nakpodia

Department of Educational Administration and Policy Studies, Delta State University, Abraka, Nigeria.
E-mail: edwardnakpodia@yahoo.com.

This paper was an empirical study on the integrative funding of universal basic education (UBE) and effective implementation in Central Senatorial District of Delta State, Nigeria. The researcher adopted a descriptive survey design. Three research questions were posed. The study involved a population of 733 Principals and 1103 Head teachers in the public primary schools and junior secondary schools in the State. A sample size of 182 principals and 274 headmasters were used for the study. The validity of the instrument was based on face and content values. The reliability of the instrument was established through the use of test re-test method and the reliability co-efficient was 0.75. Mean and standard deviation were employed in the analysis of data. The study revealed that government contributed adequate finance towards effective implementation of UBE programme. The study also showed that parent teachers association (P.T.A) contributed immensely to the UBE programme towards its effective implementation. Also, that Non-governmental organizations (NGOs) equally contributed greatly in the provision of instructional materials, sports and health equipment, furniture, classroom blocks to the programme. Based on the findings, it was recommended that government should maintain the policy of making adequate budget for the funding of the UBE and a monitory supervisors be set up to see to the judicious expenditure of such funds. Similarly, that government should ensure that the contributed funds from the various agents are judiciously utilized. Government should also hold routine meetings with the various stakeholders.

Key words: Integrative funding, implementation, universal basic education (UBE), Nigeria.

INTRODUCTION

In Delta State, Nigerian parents, local communities and individuals assist in the funding and implementation of basic education programme. Parents deny themselves a lot of things to keep their children in schools. Local communities also often levied themselves to raise enough funds to provide facilities in both primary and secondary the schools like classroom blocks and dormitories. This is because education has been iden-tified by all in the economy as a dynamic instrument of change, hence developed countries and those aspiring to develop have adopted it as an instrument per excellence for effecting national development (Federal Republic of Nigeria, 2004). Nigeria, as a nation, needs the education of its citizens, in her onward march for technological development. It therefore needs the collective efforts of all concerned to reduce the illiteracy level to the barest minimum. Illiteracy is a dangerous, socially powerless and highly susceptible and vulnerable to exploitation.

However, Agada (2002) noted that education may not do the magic overnight but it would go a long way towards achieving global awareness whereby the populace would know the dynamics of what exists in their societies. This is true because educations has been regarded as the highest generation of democracy dividends. To enhance faithful compliance of the covenant and make the UBE programme relevant to the socio-cultural environment, the UBE has had its objectives defined. The universal basic education is a response to section 19 of 1989 Nigeria constitution which reads:

"Government shall direct its policy towards ensuring

that there are equal and adequate education opportunities at all levels".

It is pertinent to mention that the said 1989 constitution suffered a "still birth" as it was never put to use. However, that section was replicated as section 18(1) of the current 1999 constitution because the goals of the UBE programme are to universalize access to basic education, engender a conducive learning environment and eradicate illiteracy in Nigeria within the shortest possible time (Babalola, 2000).

In pursuance of these goals, the Ministry of Education organized a three-day mini summit on the implementation of the UBE in Abuja, Nigeria, between November 29th and December 1st, 1999. To enhance these goals and make the implementation of the programme relevant to Nigeria's socio-cultural background, Obenya (2000) stated that the UBE had its objectives redefined as follows:

a. Developing in the citizens a strong consciousness for education, a strong commitment to its vigorous promotion.
b. The promoting of free, universal basic education for every Nigerian child of school going age.
c. Reducing drastically the incidence of dropout from the formal school system through improved relevance quality and efficiency.
d. Catering for the learning needs of young persons who for one reason of another have had to interrupt their schooling through appropriate forms of complementary approaches to the provision and promotion of basic education.

To ensure that the objectives of the UBE programme are achieved, there are concerted efforts at publicizing it by way of implementing the programme. Ever since, Nigeria has always been convinced that education is a tool for empowering his people and also to the best legacy any nation can bequeath to its citizens. The universal basic education (UBE) programme is in fact, a response to the universal declaration of Human right (1948), which stipulated the rights of every citizen to education. Every member state of the United Nations is signatory to the declaration. In addition, there is a long list of international educational conlklklklkl on basic education to which Nigeria is committed. According to Obenya (2000), it includes amongst others:

a. The Jomtien (1990) declaration and framework for action on basic education for all.
b. The New Delhi (1991) declaration on the E-9 countries (that is, the nine countries with the largest concentration of illiterates of which Nigeria is a member) lately re-affirmed in Racife – Brazil (January, 2000) calling for a massive reduction of illiteracy within the shortest possible time span.
c. The Ouagadougou (1992) Pan-African declaration of the education of girls and women, and
d. The OAU decade of education in Africa (1997-2006) on Inter-African co-operation on education, with a strong emphasis on the vigorous pursuit of basic education.

In fact, Nigeria, as a predominantly illiterate society, needs a thickly populated educated citizens. For the masses to contribute meaningfully to the development of the country, education is needed as a panacea to eradicate all forms of ignorance likely to hinder effective national development. It is against this backdrop that the Federal Government of Nigeria is committed to the integration of the individual by the provision of equal educational opportunities for all citizens of the nation through the universal basic education scheme (UBE).

The Federal Republic of Nigeria (FRN) thus affirmed that education is the most important instrument for a fundamental change in an intellectual and revolutionary society. Dewey (1966) corroborated this, when he espoused that education itself is growth leading to further growth. This means that for development to take place, the educational process must be a continuous one. It is in consonance with the philosophy that the universal basic education (UBE) was introduced.

In contemporary times, there has been a growing interest in the funding of the universal basic education (UBE) in Nigeria. One of the reasons advanced for this development is the considerable growth in the volume of universal basic education activities and the huge financial expenditure which have become unbearable by the Federal government. This is because education is today one of the largest industries and the chief employer of highly skilled workforce. In sequel, Nwikina (2000) asserted that education is a vital social activity that is capital intensive. To actualize the short and long term plans of action on education, money provides the necessary ingredients for its implementation. Maduewesi (2005) corroborated Nwikina's assertion (2000) when he opined that money provides the essential power with which education acquires its human and physical inputs. In Central Senatorial District of Delta State, Nigeria, the mode of funding educational programme is expected to be a joint efforts of the Federal, State, local governments.

As a matter of fact, education is an expensive project in which the government alone cannot successfully handle it in the country. This is evidenced in the previous universal primary education (UPE), which collapsed because of poor funding, and it suffered multiple setbacks both under regional government and the federal military government in 1976. In an attempt to achieve the goals of the ill-fated UPE scheme, the present Universal Basic Education Programme was formally launched on the 30th of September 1999 in line with the constitutional provision of section 18 that the government shall as and when practicable provide:

1. Free, compulsory and universal primary education,

2. Free adult literacy programme amongst others to its citizens as a means of eradicating illiteracy in the country, and
3. Free secondary education.

The Universal Basic Education therefore, amid providing learners with basic skills within the first nine years of schooling, which includes reading, writing and numerical skills. Through this, they can competently contribute to the overall development of the society (Bassey and Archibong, 2001).

In sequel, there is no definite mode of funding the universal basic education (UBE) programme in Central Senatorial District of Delta State: hence, there is the need to codify an integrative funding system in the State:

The funding of UBE programme in Central Senatorial District of Delta State is a major problem both for the school managers/administrators and the general public. It has suffered a set back of decrees and edicts which have competed with policies to determine the budgetary allocations to the programme (UBE). The parent teachers association (P.T.A.) which should be another major source of funding the UBE programme lacks focus and coherence. PTA in the state has been bedeviled with records of poor management of its funds in project execution. Some executive members have not helped matters by their uncooperative attitude to assist the government to fund the UBE programme. The issue has been resented, as government is believed to have enough money from the gains of international marketers.

Statement of problem

There are many problems in the funding of the previous educational programmes, like the universal basic education (UBE), embarked upon by the Federal Government which now transcend to the UBE programme in Central Senatorial District of Delta State. There is the general outcry in Central Senatorial District of Delta State that her educational programmes have not produced the desired objectives as stipulated in the National Policy on Education due to lack of proper funding. It is on the basis of this, that there is the need for integrative funding of the UBE programme in order to enjoy its effective implementation. Government alone cannot properly fund the UBE programme. In order to avoid the bitter experience of failure in the previous educational programmes, there is the dire need to look into how the present UBE programme can be adequately funded for its effective implementation.

The increase in pupils' enrolment in schools without the corresponding increase in the needed number of professional teachers, the inadequate supply of instructional materials, the lack of financial commitment from the parent teachers association (PTA), the absence of curriculum development by the government, the poor funding of urban and rural schools, the non-challant attitude of the Non-governmental organizations (NGO's) and educational philanthropists in funding education have continued to plague the state's educational planning system. It is on the basis of these enumerated problems that the researcher saw it imperative to carry out this work. The major statement of problem therefore is to what extent does integrative funding affects the effective implementation of the UBE programme in Central Senatorial District of Delta State?

Research questions

The following research questions were raised to guide the study:

1. What are the financial contributions of government to the funding of universal basic education (UBE) programme in Central Senatorial District of Delta State?
2. What are the financial contributions of parents teachers association (P.T.A.) in the effective implementtation of the universal basic education (UBE) in Central Senatorial District of Delta State?
3. What are the financial contributions of Non-governmental organizations (NGOs) in the effective implementation of the UBE programme in Central Senatorial District of Delta State?

LITERATURE REVIEW

The UBE is an organization and integrated system of interdependent structures and functions in Nigeria. Also, the three tiers of government and Non-government organizations are related and interdependent. They work in unison towards the attainment of the goals of the programme in relation to the integrative funding and effective implementation of the UBE programme in Central Senatorial District of Delta State. The programme constituted of persons who know what others are doing. It is therefore essential to deal with different levels of insight when one seeks to understand and describe the phenomena. In this regard therefore, the choice of the unique features of the general systems theory aptly suit the integrative funding and effective implementation of the UBE programme in Central Senatorial District of Delta State. It is the responsibility of the different components to ascertain that the integrative funding and effective implementation of the UBE in Central Senatorial District of Delta State is sustained and achieved.

Teachers and the universal basic education programme

The teacher's position as a central figure in any

educational endeavour is universally recognized and as such it is agreed that "no educational system can rise above the quality of its teachers." Society therefore expects many things from the teachers. Students expect teachers to impact knowledge effectively, parents expect them to ensure discipline and sound moral values among students, development planners expect them to initiate ideas and actions towards community development, curriculum reformers expect them to adopt innovative technique of teaching, and also adult literacy planners expect them to help students imbibe positive attitude towards national unity and respect for the state. Years ago, many laudable educational programme like the universal primary education (UPE) failed mainly because they did not take due account of the teacher factor. Government is committed to ensuring the success of the universal basic education (UBE) programme and teachers are integral part of the process of its conceptualization, planning and execution. To this end, the on-going efforts to raise the level of their initial professional preparation is to be pursued, broadened and intensified (Ohwojeroh, 2010).

Moreso, the crucial issue of career-long professional development of serving teachers in areas of in-service programme like sandwich, weekend programme, seminars and workshops should be properly intensified for the actualization of the universal basic education (UBE) programme. The following accredited bodies such as National Teachers' Association (NUT), Universities, Colleges of Education, the National Teachers' Institute (NTI), the National Board for Technical Education (NBTE) are mobilized to develop a more systematic career improvement orientation and programmes for all categories of teachers.

In pursuance of the universal basic education (UBE) programme, the Federal Government has further charged the institute with the production of a large number of qualified teachers in the pivotal teachers training programme (PTTP). This programme prepares the beneficiaries for the specific teaching assignment in the universal basic education (UBE), and it was contracted to the National Teachers Institute, Kaduna. So far the pivotal teachers' training programme (PTTP) has produced about 30,000 additional teachers for the UBE programme. However, it is envisaged that the products of the PTTP will enter the teaching profession through continuing education programme up to the Nigeria Certificate in Education (NCE) level.

Corroborating the above view, Igborgbor (2000) assets that the right people at the right time and of course in the right place should be recruited for the UBE programme to make it effective and successful. He believes that the first step is staffing so to determine the present and future manpower needs for the UBE programme. He adds that the on-going efforts of training and re-training to raise the level of general education of teachers should be vigorously pursued, broadened and intensified for the survival of the programme. Employment of adequate number of well trained and qualified teachers who should be well motivated for improved teaching – learning process is essential for the effective implementation of the programme. That the teachers should be regularly trained and re-trained to improve their teaching methodology and competencies of instructional delivery. He concluded that the ultimate minimum qualification of teachers for the UBE programme should be the Nigeria Certificate in Education (NCE).

Integrative funding of the universal basic education in schools

The Nigeria National Policy on Education indicates that the financing of education is a joint responsibility of the Federal, State and Local Governments. In other words, education at the primary and junior secondary schools for the purpose of the universal basic education should be jointly funded, and the programme should have concurrent legislative jurisdiction for funding to actualize its objectives.

President Obasanjo (1999) noted that as far as funding of education is concerned the time has come for all Nigerian parents to appreciate the need to contribute to their children's education particularly at the elementary level. Presenting a financial flow model for education in Nigeria, Nwagwu (2002) stated that three groups of decision – makers are involved in the production of educational services in Nigeria. He listed them to include public sector, private sector and the rest of the world. The public sector includes the Federal, State, and Local Governments. The private sector is made up of companies and other firms that contribute to educational development, and the rest of the world involves international agencies like UNESCO and other bilateral and multi-lateral arrangements for funding of educational activities.

It has been argued that statutory allocation has been inadequate to meet the needs of the UBA programme (Enouch and Okpede, 2000). This calls for integrative funding to actualize its objectives. As noted in previous educational programme in Nigeria like the UPE of other years, government alone bears the burden of its financing and this situation makes such programmes not to succeed. In such situations, the government leaves the structures dilapidated, delay teachers salaries, while the classrooms lack seats and most of the used furnitures need rehabilitation. Also, there is no adequate supply of instructional materials, no development of teachers regarding retraining on the job as well as no proper attention on curriculum development to suit the educational objectives. All these, do not provide a conducive teaching and learning environments in the school system.

In the previous educational programmes in the country, emphasis on development in education is well placed in the urban schools where the governors (policy markers) have their interest than the rural areas where the citizens have almost drifted away to the urban. Today with the introduction of the UBE programme in the country, the rural schools are more cared for than the urban schools. The rural schools raise fund in various ways in funding the UBE programme. Some of the sources of raising fund for the UBE programme to succeed include launching of endowment fund, encouraging donations, schools engaging in commercial farming, fishing, organizing of sports and games, and support from parent teachers association (PTA). The old students/pupils association also supports the school financially. Local service organizations such as: Rotary Club of Nigeria also gives financial support for school programmes and development in their area of operation in assisting the inhabitants for their living. In the UBE programme local communities support the programme than in the urban areas where people see it as no man's land.

In addition, the local communities help the rural schools in the areas of land donation, supply of labour and security supply for the school properties as well as organizing themselves in raising fund for the school growth. All these are employed to complement government's efforts. The urban schools are mainly supported by government but with the integrative funding of the UBE programme, the situation has changed; because private individuals, foreign aids, endowment and religious organizations are now complementary to government's effort to achieve the goals of the UBE programme as entrenched in the 1999 constitution.

The provision of furniture and equipment is very important in the universal basic education programme. From the view of many scholars, provision of facilities especially in the rural area is far behind the expectation in line with the programme's determination. There is acute shortage of furniture in form of pupils and students seats and desks, teachers tables and chairs, books, teaching aids and instructional materials.

The supply of furniture in urban schools is fair except in a few cases where the supply is grossly inadequate because of unexpected increase in the schools population. A worse situation exists in the rural schools where both furniture and equipment were not provided when the schools were first built. Children have to carry their furniture form school each day. With increase in the enrolment rate in our primary and junior secondary schools today in view of the UBE programme. Government need to put the basic and necessary infrastructural and other facilities in place, with the fund from various stakeholders of the programme especially in the urban areas where majority of the population lived in other for the UBE programme to achieve her desired goals. This will also help to remove the disparity of the rate of infrastructural development in the rural and urban schools in view of the on-going universal basic education (UBE) programme in Central Senatorial District of Delta State.

Non-governmental organizations in the funding of UBE

A number of non-governmental groups participated in the funding of the Universal Basic Education in Nigeria. They include business enterprises, particularly the oil companies. Others include: the parents-teachers association, alumni and community development committees.

Nonetheless, the Nigeria government is categorical on a wide range of participation by government and non-governmental bodies in financing education. Thus: Education is an expensive social service and requires adequate financial provision from all tiers of government for a successful implementation of the educational programmes. In this connection, government welcomes and encourages the participation of local communities, individuals and other organizations. (NPE, 2004).

Nwagwu (2002) in his "Can Nigeria Survive" queries the national corporations in the development of the third world, when he stated that there activities are essentially those of underdevelopment. Agada (2002) also noted that these corporations have clandestine activities which are inimical to the interest of the developing world. He cited thanking insurance, construction and manufacturing as examples of the network of intrigue through which these multi-nationals operate. Their contribution he further argued are at best, illusory since they only service not transfer of technology and repatriate rather than reinvest their staggering profits. Essentially we expect business to contribute to the education system. After all, the product of the school system is utilized by the first as clerks, managers, engineers, economic analysis and accountants.

Maduewesi (2005) also asserted that companies could supplement government funding of education by paying the education tax. This is necessary because the business enterprises are also beneficiaries of the education acquired. In addition, community groups need to contribute because they also benefit from the education system. The community development committees as well as alumni of the primary and secondary schools who are gainfully employed can supplement government funding thereby promotion educational development in the area.

Ukeje (2002) argues that in the present circumstances, funds and facilities are very much limited and the school administrator is being asked to achieve maximum results with this limitation. He observed that there is increasing demand by the people for more and better education and the problem of rising cost, and concluded that there was crisis in the education system. Ukeje (2002) therefore argued that the way out of the financial malaise is to seek supplementary sources of funds. Such bodies from which to seek support includes: parent teachers association and alumni as well as community development committees and social clubs. Since education is now community based, there is need for considerable level of community support for the education system.

The argument above tends to contradict Okoye (2002), quoting that "school finance is public finance". Public finance according to Obanya (2006) is the spending on goods and services provided by the government for the generality of the people. The spending may be on wages/salaries, motor vehicles, housing, education, health subsidies and grants.

Framework for the implementation of universal basic education

Recruitment and training of new teachers

The successful implementation of the universal basic education in Delta State at the primary school level will require the recruitment of additional 7,109 teachers to the existing 10,520. The former figure of 7,109 was obtained based on projected figure of 40 pupils to classroom tied to the 284,332 expected enrolments. The figure of seven thousand, one hundred and nine teachers is quite an enormous one to locate at a stretch. Hence, the present effort of massive training of the would-be teachers through the National Teachers Institute specially designed for this scheme appears to be a viable means of addressing this problem. To actualize this dream, Akhaine (2001) reported that the federal government has mandated the National Teachers' Institute (NTI) to produce 30,000 teachers yearly for the scheme of which Delta State will be a benefactor. Caution should however be exercised as to the quality of the teachers being selected to participate in the programme. This advice is intended to avert incompetence in service delivery. Writing in support of this view, Harbison (1973) opined that those working in occupation which does not 'fit' their qualification are 'mal-employed', and therefore show incompetence at work. In another vein, the organizers of the programme should ensure that only competent hands are recruited to teach the would-be teachers. This is intended to alley the fear expressed by Chapman (1994) that poorly prepared teachers find it difficult to face the challenges of the classroom content, maintain classroom discipline and manages flow of class activities.

Retraining of existing teachers

The new scheme will entail retraining of existing teachers to acquaint them or create awareness at a general level and to highlight new additions to the various subject areas. On the whole, this programme of action can be attained through frequent seminars, workshops and professional contacts with other educators. This will reduce teachers' sense of isolation and build high professional morale. Throwing more light on this, Beaty and Schneller (1977), Casio (1978) observed that training and development activities were planned programmes of organizational improvement undertaken to bring about a relatively permanent change in an employee's knowledge skills, attitude or social behaviour. It is one method of improving performance and stability at the workplace.

Establishment of new schools

The present 817 public primary school spread in 25 local governments in Delta State is considerable adequate to cope with the existing number of students in the primary schools. It is in realization of this that the committee set up by the Delta State Government on school system data collection/collation (2000) recommended the establishment of additional 495 primary schools at the rate of 300 pupils per school. These projected schools, if established will go a long way in addressing the problems of school mapping currently in existence in the state, that is to say the existing schools are not evenly distributed.

Provision of infrastructure and equipment

Sequel to the establishment of new schools, there will be a need to adequately equip the schools. The existing number of libraries in the state primary schools is only 67 with 37 out of these in bad condition. The total number of benches was given as 44,238 while the number of toilets in usable condition is only 679. In light with the aforementioned data, it is imperative that something urgent should be done to redress the insufficient number these facilities.

Monitoring and evaluation

The human and material resources outlay involved in the universal basic education scheme calls for an effective monitoring and evaluation of the programme to ensure regular appraisal of the scheme. This will help to identify the progress made, areas of deficiency and what needs to be done. Ojedele (1998) had noted that the implementation had been a serious handicap to most genuine effort aimed at developing the educational system in Nigeria. He therefore upheld that:

> "If the Nigerian educational system is to develop and compare favourably with the advanced countries of the world, there is need to monitor and evaluate each stage of the implementation process so as to ensure that projects are being implemented".

Increased enrolment strategies

The projected figure for the universal basic education

scheme in the state is moderately high and therefore calls for sustainable strategy in ensuring a successful enrolment in the scheme. The entire exercise should not be abandoned at the well-wish level but some defined strategies as a viable publicity committee made up of churches, parent-teachers association, community development associations, village counsels and so on should be put in place to assist in creating awareness about the programme and its attendant benefit.

Insurance of school properties

The cost of rehabilitating existing school facilities, erecting new ones and providing necessary equipment is quite enormous and therefore, calls for an excellent school insurance programme. Commenting in support of this, Jordan (1969 maintained that a time has come when the school insurance programme should:

"Instead of being viewed as hedge against losses as a result of fire and other disaster, the insurance programme provides local school authorities with the opportunity to determine the values of school property, provide a plan through which the properties could be replaced or restored in case of loss and also develop an orderly systematic plan for proper care of the properties while they are used by the school".

The overriding importance of the school insurance programme apparently is a suggested new dimension in school facilities management intended to achieve Jordan's position, and hence save government huge losses incurred as a result of improper facilities management.

METHODOLOGY

Research design

The researcher uses the descriptive survey design. This is aimed at gathering information to describe the integrative funding and effective implementation of the universal basic education programme in Central Senatorial District of Delta State.

Population of the study

The population of the study consists of one thousand one hundred and three public primary schools (1103) with headmasters/headmistresses and seven hundred and thirty-three (733) public secondary schools principals in Delta Central Senatorial District.

Given a total population of one thousand eight hundred and thirty-six (1,836) both public primary and public secondary schools with the same population of principals and headmasters/headmistresses in Central Senatorial District of Delta State, Nigeria.

Sample and sampling technique

The sample of this study consists of four hundred and 456 representing 24.82% of the population. 182 public junior secondary schools principals and 274 public primary schools headmasters/headmistresses randomly selected by a means of stratified randomly sample technique. Six Local Government Areas in the Senatorial District were used for the study.

Instrumentation

The instrument used for data collection was the questionnaire. Titled: "Integrative funding and effective implementation of the universal basic education programme questionnaire (IFEIQ) in Central Senatorial District of Delta State.

The questionnaire consisted of 36 items distributed to reflect each of the research questions. Items 1-6 were structured to elicit information in relation to research question one. While items 7-13 were structured to elicit information in relation to research question two. Also items 14-20, were necessary to answer research question three. In the same vein, items 21-26 are required to answer research question four. Items 27-31 were also structured to elicit information in relation to research question five. And items 32-36 for research question six. It has four point likert interval scale, "strongly agree" (4 points) "agreed", (3 points), "disagreed", (2 points), and "strongly disagreed" (1 point).

Validity of the instrument

Two types of procedures were adopted by the researcher to establish the validity of the instrument. They include the face and content validity.

Reliability of the instrument

The reliability of the instrument was established by using the test-retest method. The questionnaire was administered to twenty (20) respondents not included in the sample size. After an interval of three weeks of the administration, the same sets of instrument were re-administered to the same group of respondents and the resulting test scores were correlated. The Pearson product moments correlation coefficient 'r' was used to correlate the responses obtained from the two separate scores. This yielded a reliability coefficient of 0.75 which shows that the research instrument has a high internal consistency, and therefore reliable.

Administration of the Instrument

The researcher administered the instrument personally to the respondents. At the end of the administration, four hundred and fifty-six (456) questionnaire were retrieved from the respondents.

Method of data analysis

Mean and standard deviation were the statistical tools used to answer the three (3) research questions. A mean of 2.50 was taken as the critical value for decision such that a mean response that falls below 2.50 was regarded as disagreed while a mean response on or above 2.50 was regarded as agreed.

PRESENTATION OF RESULTS

Research question 1

What are the financial contributions of government to the

Table 1. Mean and standard deviation of the financial contribution of government to the funding of universal basic education (U.B.E.) programme in Central Senatorial District of Delta State.

S/N	Statement	N	Mean	SD	Decision
1.	Provides money for payment of staff salaries and allowance regularly.	456	2.54	0.053	Agree
2.	Provides fund for development of new structures.	456	2.51	0.053	Agree
3.	Provides fund for Library and Laboratory equipment.	456	2.54	0.053	Agree
4.	Provides fund for maintenance and repair of building, equipment and furniture.	456	2.59	0.053	Agree
5.	Provides fund for the day-to-day running of schools.	456	2.54	0.052	Agree
6.	Provides fund for sports and health facilities.	456	2.52	0.053	Agree

Table 2. Mean and standard deviation of the financial contribution of parent teachers association (P.T.A.) in the provision of school facilities for effective implementation of UBE in Central Senatorial District of Delta State.

S/N	Statement	N	Mean	SD	Decision
1.	Renovates dilapidated structures.	4.56	2.48	0.052	Disagree
2.	Build classrooms.	4.56	2.73	0.051	Agree
3.	Provides writing desk and benches.	4.56	2.47	0.053	Disagree
4.	Buy books for the Library.	4.56	2.51	0.051	Agree
5.	Buy science equipment for the laboratory.	4.56	2.53	0.052	Agree
6.	Provides fund for toilet facilities.	4.56	4.56	0.052	Disagree
7.	Provides fund for potable water.	4.56	4.56	0.054	Agree

funding of universal basic education (U.B.E) programme in Central Senatorial District of Delta State?

Table 1, show that both principals and headmasters/ headmistress in public secondary schools and public primary schools agreed to items 1, 2, 3, 4, 5 and 6 with a mean ranging from 7.51 to 2.59 that government". Provides money for payment of staff salaries and allowances regularly; provides fund for development of new structures; provides fund for library and laboratory equipment; provides fund for maintenance and repair of building, equipment and furniture; provides fund for the day-to-day running of the schools; and provides fund for sports and health facilities to the funding of universal basic education (U.B.E.) Programme in Central Senatorial District of Delta State.

Research question 2

What are the financial contributions of parent teachers association (P.T.A.) in the provision of school facilities for effective implementation of the UBE?

Table 2, shows that both principals and headmaster/ headmistresses in public secondary and public primary schools agreed to items 8, 10, 11, and 13 with a mean ranging from 2.51 to 2.73 that parents teachers associations: Build classrooms, Buy books for the library, Buy science equipment for the laboratory, and provides fund for potable water for the effective implementation of UBE programme in Central Senatorial District of Delta State. While items 7, 9 and 12 with a mean ranging from 2.47 to 2.48 were disagreed by principals, and headmasters/headmistress of public secondary schools and public primary schools that parent teachers association do not contributes in renovating of dilapidated structures, provisions of writing desk and benches, and provision of fund for toilet facilities.

Research question 3

What are the contributions of Non-government organization (NGOs) in the provision of instructional materials to schools for the effective implementation of the UBE programme in Central Senatorial District of Delta State?

Table 3, indicates that both principals and headmasters/headmistresses in public secondary schools and public primary schools agreed to items 14, 15, 16, 17 and 19 with mean ranging from 2.50 to 2.71 that non-governmental organization contributes by: Build classrooms blocks for the schools; purchase science and laboratory equipment for the schools, provides furniture, provide books and writing materials and pay allowance to some special subjects teachers. While items 18 and 20 with a mean ranging from 2.03 to 2.49 were disagreed that non-governmental organizations to not provide funds for transportation of staff children and they do not provide fund for Sports/Health equipment for the effective implementation of UBE programme in Central Senatorial

Table 3. Mean and standard deviation of the contribution of Non-governmental organization (NGOs) in the provision of instructional materials to schools for the effective implementation of UBE programme in Central Senatorial District of Delta State.

S/N	Statement	N	Mean	SD	Decision
1.	Build classrooms blocks for the schools	4.56	2.62	0.053	Agree
2.	Purchase science and laboratory equipment for the schools.	4.56	2.50	0.053	Agree
3.	Provides furniture.	4.56	2.91	0.054	Agree
4.	Provide books and writing materials.	4.56	2.54	0.053	Agree
5.	Fund transportation of staff children.	4.56	2.49	0.052	Disagree
6.	Pay allowance to some special subjects teachers.	4.56	2.50	0.052	Agree
7.	Provide fund for Sports/Health equipment.	4.56	2.03	0.038	Disagree

District of Delta State.

DISCUSSION OF RESULTS

Financial contribution of government to the funding of universal basic education (U.B.E.) programme

The study in research question one revealed that government played an important role on adequate funding of UBE programme for its effective implementtation. The National Policy on Education (2004) indicated that the financing of "education" is a joint responsibility of the Federal, State and Local Government. Also in the words of President Obasanjo (1999) noted that as far as funding of "education" was concerned the time has come for all Nigeria parents to appreciate the need to contribute to their children's "education" particularly at the elementary level which is the first nine years of school age.

The implication of this finding was that there is integrative funding of UBE in Central Senatorial District of Delta State. That the government, individuals, parents, foreign aids, endowment and corporate bodies should contribute to the adequate funding of education to enhance the effective implementation of the UBE programme in Central Senatorial District of Delta State. This is to say that government alone cannot carry the responsibility of a funding the UBE programme in Central Senatorial District of Delta State.

Financial contributions of parents teachers association (P.T.A.) in the provision of school facilities for effective implementation of UBE

This study had discovered that parent teachers association (P.T.A.) funded UBE for its effective implementation. This is an indication of the various financial contributions made by this body towards the effective implementation of the UBE programme which came in form of provision of classroom buildings, schools halls, toilet facilities, furniture supply and sports equipment to mention but a few. It is also interesting to note that the two categories of respondents namely the principals and headmasters/headmistresses did not differ significantly with regard to the opinions on the financial contributions of PTA and effective implementation of universal basic education (UBE) programme in Central Senatorial District of Delta State.

In support of this finding, Nwikina (2000) opined that education in the urban areas are more emphasis than the rural areas in the previous years. Today, the rural schools raised fund in various ways in funding the universal basic education (UBE) programme. Some of such include: PTA supporting school projects through launching of endowment funds and donations for provision of furniture, building of classroom blocks, halls, toilets, urinaries, potable water etc.

Also, some of the parents provided school buildings sometimes called PTA block of classroom. Be that as it may, some communities do not have interest in the affairs of the school, they saw it as liability to them.

The contribution of Non-governmental organizations (NGOS) in the provision of instructional materials to school for the effective implementation of UBE programme

The study had as well revealed that NGOs financial contributions enhanced effective implementation of UBE programme in Central Senatorial District of Delta State. As disclosed by Nwagwu (2002) that "the era of over dependence on government for the funding of education in Nigeria is becoming over." In a free enterprise economy, he opined that educational institutions must find alternative means of generating revenue to supplement government budgeting. Thus:

Education is an expensive social service and requires adequate financial provision from all tiers of government for a successful implementation of the educational programme. In this connection, Government welcomes and encourages the participation of local communities, individuals and other organizations (NPE, 2004).

Okoye (2002) in support of this idea also asserted that companies could supplement government funding of education by paying the education tax (2% of their surplus). He also said that communities need to contribute as well as alumni of both primary and secondary schools who are gainfully employed need to contribute.

Ukeje (2000) was of the view that schools need to seek support from the parent teachers association and alumni association as well as community development committees and social clubs. In light of this, Non-governmental organizations contributed in various measures to the educational sector. These included provisions of charts, slide projectors, potable boards, laboratory equipment, sports equipment etc.

The petroleum trust fund (PTF) the UNESCO, UNICEF, UNDP, the parent teachers association (P.T.A.) made donations in forms of books, furniture, drugs, science equipment, sports and game equipment, organize workshops and seminars to pupils, teachers and students.

Consequently, in schools where these gestures are received, the administrators and the teachers are being encouraged to teach and the pupils and students are also encouraged to learn. There is very likelihood that the standard of education would be raised. It should be noted that not all parents make such contributions to the support of schools. Though some consider it a solely government efforts and others are ignorant of it and coupled with poverty.

Conclusion

Based on the findings of the study, the following conclusions were drawn:

1. That adequate funding led to effective implementation of UBE programme in Central Senatorial District of Delta State.
2. Parent teachers association's (P.T.A.) financial contribution in the provision of facilities of UBE programme enhanced effective implementation in Central Senatorial District of Delta State. And so parents should always strive to contribute their quota to the development of the programme. Similarly, Non-governmental financial contribution to the provision of instructional materials to schools for effective implementation of UBE programme in Central Senatorial District of Delta State need much desire.
3. The development of school curriculum for effective implementation of the UBE programme in Central Senatorial District of Delta State is viewed seriously on the order of the government in achieving the programme objectives.
4. Similarly, Non-governmental financial contribution to the provision of instructional materials to schools for effective implementation of UBE programme in Central Senatorial District of Delta State need much desire.

In line with the issues raided in the study, it could be concluded that integrative funding influenced effective implementation of UBE programme in Central Senatorial District of Delta State Nigeria. For Nigeria to attain the desired 100% national literacy rate, it is imperative that provision be made and actions taken to universalize basic education, enthrone a conducive learning environment and improve quality and standards. All these have demands on funding and implementation.

RECOMMENDATIONS

From the findings and conclusion of this study, the researcher made the following recommendations.

1. That the government should maintain the policy of making adequate budget for the funding of the UBE and a monitory supervisory team be set up to see the judicious expenditure of such funds. In the light of this, government should come out with a blue print on punishment to offenders on misappropriation of education fund. The government should intensify effort to over see the integrative funding of the UBE programme by the various educational stakeholders for its effective implementation.
2. The state government also should recruit more teachers into the primary and junior secondary schools in the state in other to enable the pupils to achieve permanent literacy and numeracy and the ability to communicate effectively.
3. Teachers should be allowed to attend seminars and workshop to acquaint themselves of new ideas and methods of teaching for the universal basic education programme.
4. Teachers should be sent for in-service training to enable them acquire more skills and competence in their job performances. The state ministry of education should intensify more efforts in the effective supervision, monitoring and evaluation of the universal basic education progrmme in the state. The welfare of teachers should be a priority.

REFERENCES

Agada LI (2002). The Strategies for the Effective Administration of Universal Basic Education (UBE) Programme in Enugu State. Unpublished M.Ed Thesis. University of Nigeria, Nsukka, p. 25.

Babalola SK (2000). Blue Print for the Management of the UBE at Secondary School Level, being a paper presented at the National Workshop organized by All Nigerian Conference of Principals of Secondary Schools.

Bassey UU, Archibong IA (2001). Planning and Managing Universal Basic Education (UBE) at the Primary School Level in Cross River State. In: Nwagwu, NA, Ehiametalor, ET, Ogunu, MA & Nwadiani, M (eds) Nigeria Association for Educational Administration and Planning (NAEAP), pp. 64-67.

Enouch EJ, Okpede EO (2000). The Meaning History Philosophy and Lesson of UBE. Proceeding of the 15th Annual Congress of the National Academy of Education. University of Benin: Ambik Press, pp. 61-64.

Federal Republic of Nigeria (2004). National Policy on Education Lagos: Federal Government Press.

Federal Republic of Nigeria (2004): Implementation Guidelines for the Universal Basic Education (UBE) Programme. Abuja Federal Ministry of Education. p. 17.

Igborgbor GC (2000). Implementation of the Universal Basic Education Programme. The Fate of the Nigerian Child. A keynote Address presented on the 2nd Quadrennial Delegates Conference of the Nigerian Union of Teachers Central Senatorial District of Delta State Wing at Sapele.

Maduewesi EJ (2005). Universal Basic Education: Lesson Problems and Prospects, in Benchmark and Global Trends in Education. Dasylvia Influence Enterprise, Benin City, pp. 256-258.

Nwagwu NA (2002). From UPE to UBE: Basic Planning Consideration for Effective Implementation of Programmers in Ajayi et al, (Ed) UBE in Nigeria Ondo: NIEPA, p. 20.

Nwikina CG (2000). Alternative Strategies for Funding Secondary Education in Rivers State. Unpublished M.E.d Thesis, University of Port Harcourt. p. 35

Obanya P (2006). Quality Dimensions of Universal Basic Education (UBE). Paper Delivered on the World Teachers Day Celebration, Millennium Celebration October 5, Nigeria Union of Teachers (NUT). p. 27

Obasanjo O (1999). Address delivered on the occasion of the Re-launching of the UBE programme in Sokoto 30th September. Strategies. A keynote Address presented on the occasion of International Conference on Basic Education held at University of Nigeria, Nsukka.

Ohwojeroh PO (2010). Integrative Funding and Effective Implementation of Universal Basic Education Programme in Delta State, Masters Dissertation, Delta State University, Abraka, Nigeria.

Okoye PN (2002). Funding of Secondary Education in Abia State: Implication for Educational Administration. Unpublished M.Ed Thesis, University of Port Harcourt. p.55

Ukeje BO (2000). UBE in Nigeria Logistics and Implementation Strategies. A keynote Address presented on the occasion of International Conference on Basic Education held at University of Nigeria, Nsukka, p. 4.

12

Determinants of financial performance of a firm: Case of Pakistani stock market

Sidra Ali Mirza[1]* and Attiya Javed[2]

[1]Shaheed Zulfiqar Ali Bhutto Institute of Science and Technology, Islamabad, Pakistan.
[2]Institute of Development Economics, Islamabad, Pakistan.

This paper examines the possible association between financial performance of the firm and economic indicators, corporate governance, ownership structure, capital structure, and risk management. It is also one of the very few examples, which attempts to test various determinant of firm performance in context of developing market (Pakistan). The present study examines the performance of firms in terms of profitability and its association with multiple determinants for 60 Pakistani corporate firms listed in Karachi stock exchange for the period of 2007 to 2011 and attempts to explain the observed behavior with the help of fixed effect model. The results consistently support the potential association between firm's financial performance and economic indicators, corporate governance, ownership structure, and capital structure although the intensity of relationship differs across different measures of performance. We find evidence in support of the hypotheses that a positive association exists between corporate governance, and risk management and performance while mixed results are observed for other variables.

Key words: Economic indicators, ownership structure, capital structure, risk management, financial performance, Pakistan.

INTRODUCTION

Performance of firms is of vital importance for investors, stakeholders and economy at large. For investors the return on their investments is highly valuable, and a well performing business can bring high and long-term returns for their investors. Furthermore, financial profitability of a firm will boost the income of its employees, bring better quality products for its customers, and have better environment friendly production units. Also, more profits will mean more future investments, which will generate employment opportunities and enhance the income of people. Many studies have been conducted to determine various financial and non-financial factors that can boost or have an adverse effect on the performance of firm. But still no single effective model has been established which captures maximum variation.

There is incomplete literature and an on-going debate on the issue of performance of firms. There is wider gap specifically in the case of growing economies like Pakistan, because most of the research done is based on the data from developed economies.

The purpose of this study is to empirically investigate the contribution of economy, ownership patterns, capital structure, and risk management towards financial performance, of firms in Pakistan. And also to find empirical evidence for contribution of economy, ownership patterns, capital structure, and risk management towards shareholders' return. It is important to conduct this study in Pakistan because it is a growing economy and there are a lot of differences in the situation faced by firms in developed and developing economies. Firstly, the difference of corporate governance affects the profit distribution policy. Weak corporate governance leads to ownership concentration ultimately increasing the power of owners to influence the policy decisions. Secondly, tax environment differences can lead to different investor behavior regarding the return. In Pakistan stock price appreciation is preferred mostly, but now capital gain tax has also been imposed which has lead to a slight change in the investor interests.

Effects of various factors on financial performance can be firm specific. This study will contribute to the limited literature on determinants of firm performance in Pakistan.

The rest of the study is organized as follows. First, the literature review and second the research methodology, and data were discussed. Also, empirical findings of the study are discussed, and finally, conclusion of this research is drawn.

LITERATURE REVIEW

Industrial revolution has divided the world economies into two categories; developed and under-developed. Those that are under-developed are struggling to get out of their present state and stand in line with those that are developed. To achieve this goal these countries have to work to decrease their resource unemployment, gradually reaching to full employment. More employment means higher productivity and better income which leads to a better life style. For employment of resources new and innovative projects have to be undertaken, industries need to be established, infrastructure has to be built and all this requires a lot of capital. Employment of resources requires investment in production activities that is, manufacturing industries. Private sector needs to play a supportive and sometimes leading role to establish the economy by investing in new projects (Kalirajan and Singh, 2009) and government should support these ventures by providing appropriate infrastructure for the industry to grow.

The basic motive behind any investment, made by the corporate sector, is to earn profit (Kyereboah-Coleman, 2007). It is among the goals of the organization to maximize shareholders' wealth and generate enough profits to continue the business and to grow further in future. Performance of the firm is affected by multiple external and internal factors. It is important to note here that the internal factors are firm specific while external factors can be same for all or most of the firms. The external factors include market preferences and perceptions, country rules and regulations, and economy of the country. The market and laws are same for similar businesses but different across industries. Economy impact is same for all industries but is nonetheless an important and un-ignorable determinant of firm performance.

Economic condition

Economic condition of the country can affect a firm's performance on multiple fronts. Cost of borrowings can negatively influence the firm's capability to generate finances and invest in projects (Ntim, 2009). Prices of utilities, high costs associated with plant and machinery due to either deterioration of currency or import costs, high inflation rate and low income level of people can decrease the demand for industrial goods and hence negatively impact the firm's performance (Forbes, 2002). This leads to our first two hypotheses;

H1: Inflation rate has a negative impact on firm performance.
H2: Per capita income has a positive impact on firm performance.

Corporate governance

Corporate governance practices are the structures and behaviors that guide how a business entity sets its objectives, develops strategies and plans, monitors and reports its performance, and manage its risk (Reddy, 2010).

Researchers are also of the view that good corporate governance practices enhance the performance of the firm (Chugh et al., 2009). There are two models of corporate structure shareholder model and stakeholder model. Shareholder model focuses on the wealth creation of owners while stakeholder model covers broader aspect and concerns the welfare of all stakeholders and overall firm performance (Maher and Andersson, 1999). There are five principles of corporate governance (Bocean, 2001);

(1) Protection of shareholders' rights
(2) Equitable treatment of shareholders
(3) Protection of stakeholders' rights
(4) Proper disclosure and transparency
(5) Fulfillment of responsibilities by board (IFC, 2009)

A study conducted by Javed and Iqbal (2007) explored impact of corporate governance on firm performance by creating indices for board characteristics, transparency and disclosure, and shareholder and ownership characteristics. Results of the study indicate a significant relation between indices and performance except for transparency and disclosure. Another recent research conducted by Yasser et al. (2011), tested for board characteristics, also support the previous findings. So we hypothesize;

H3: Better corporate governance practices lead to better firm performance.

Ownership structure

Division of Ownership into types rests on the dimension that is, separation of ownership and control. Berle and Means developed a dichotomy of ownership and identified two types namely, Owner-controlled firms and Managerially-controlled firms. McEachern found it to be insufficient for explanation of ownership structure and its impacts, so he identified three types adding Externally-controlled firms (cited by Ugurlu, 2000)

(i) Owner controlled firms are the ones where the managers are the dominant shareholders.
(ii) Externally controlled firms are the ones where the managers are not dominant shareholders.
(iii) Managerially controlled firms are the ones in which no dominant shareholder exists.

According to agency theory if managers of a firm also have ownership stake they are most likely to maximize shareholder wealth (Dutta, 1999). Managerial risk aversion and constraints on wealth, limit the ownership of managers. And ownership can become costly for more diversified managers (Jensen et al., 1992). Number of tradable shares is inversely related to inside ownership (Lin et al., 2011) as most of the shares owned by insiders are restricted from trading (Born, 1988).

Through greater monitoring the negative and positive impacts of ownership concentration can be equated, and some time benefits can over weigh the negativities (Kaserer and Moldenhauer, 2008). Insider ownership is negatively related to foreign institutional ownership (Ugurlu, 2000).

Agency conflict is an important problem associated with ownership structure. There are two agency problems, 1st agency problem is the one between managers and shareholders and is dominant in the firms having low inside ownership. Whereas, 2nd agency problem is between the large shareholders and small shareholders, this type is dominant in the firms where ownership is concentrated in blocks (Bohren et al., 2009). High inside ownership also reduces the agency conflict and information asymmetry (Ugurlu, 2000) which results in lower capital signaling needs.

According to a study in 2000 done by Ang et al. agency costs are higher when outsiders manage the firm, and are inversely related to inside ownership concentration but directly related to outside ownership. High inside ownership is associated with increased level of R&D, which leads to the 2nd agency conflict (Bathala et al., 1994 cited by Ugurlu, 2000). Institutional and concentrated outside ownership improves monitoring and helps reducing the agency conflict (Khan, 2006) but high R&D becomes more costly for external monitors (Jensen et al., 1992).

Ownership structure of a firm is influenced by some factors. Some scholars found that outside ownership concentration increases with the quality of law while others reported a varying relation between quality of law and size of inside ownership (Burkart and Panunzi, 2005). However there is a unified opinion regarding the impact of size of firm on the ownership structure (Jensen et al., 1992). Composition of board of directors also affects the type of major shareholders (Ugurlu, 2000). Short-term profitability of the firm is found to have a positive relation with institutional ownership (Ugurlu, 2000).

Ownership structure of a company is a very important factor which influences the company in multiple ways. Inside ownership concentration is directly associated with financial constraints of the firm, this association is weakened by institutional ownership (Lin et al., 2011). Some studies have found that outside ownership concentration leads to restructuring and downsizing of the firm (Ugurlu, 2000).

Inside ownership is also positively related to the growth of the firm (Bohren et al., 2009) but inversely related to its size (Jensen et al., 1992). Inside ownership positively affects corporate performance (Kaserer and Moldenhauer, 2007). Inside ownership has great impact on the financial choices of managers while individual ownership is unlikely to influence the choices (Dutta, 1999). The impact on the debt policy is still ambiguous because of conflicting findings of scholars. Some scholars report a positive relation between inside ownership and debt (Dutta, 1999) while others report a negative relation (Jensen et al., 1992) (Theis and Casey, 1999) and according to Ugurlu (2000), debt is not influenced by inside or institutional ownership. According to entrenchment hypothesis managerial controlled firms have lower debt ratios as compared to institutionally controlled firms (Ugurlu, 2000).

Ownership structure of firm is also found to have a great impact on the performance. The phenomenon has been empirically tested on various occasions that internal ownership results in long-term firm performance (Reddy, 2010). And concentrated ownerships and institutional ownerships lead to better control and monitoring of the board of directors and somehow force them to undertake profitable projects to ensure future earnings (Bhagat and Bolton, 2008). However small shareholdings by public do not support long-term plans, these owners are mostly interested in the short-term profits and not the overall growth of the company and same is the case for small or no internal ownership. So, the ownership structure should be carefully balanced for a firm to perform well. We hypothesize;

H4: Inside ownership negatively impacts firm performance.
H5: Blockholdings positively impact firm performance.

Capital structure

Every industry requires a substantial amount of

resources, whether it is land, labor or capital employment of all required finances. These finances can either be generated internally (retained earnings) or hired from outside sources (loans and bonds). The decision of selection of the source of finance is based on the cost associated with them and the capital structure of firm. These costs can be monetary or non-monetary.

Capital structure is also an important factor that determines the performance of a firm. Capital structure refers to the ratio of debt and equity financing. In case if more debt financing the company has to face certain bankruptcy risk, but there are also some tax and monitoring benefits associated with debt financing (Su and Vo, 2010). It also mitigates the agency conflict by reducing the free cash flow of the firm. There should be an appropriate capital structure that generates the maximum profit for the organization, as too less equity financing increases the control of the owners to a large extent (Abu-Rub, 2012).

In case of internally generated finances, it is said that these have the highest opportunity cost (Lewellen and Lewellen, 2004) for the firm because retainment of profits can affect share holder trust, because it would otherwise have been distributed as dividend. Dividend announcements have a significant impact on share prices (Akbar and Baig, 2010). As far as external borrowings are concerned they are considered to be the cheapest source of financing because of the tax benefits. But they do still have certain costs like interest payments and it is widely accepted that the cost of external funds is directly proportional to the amount of these funds also while borrowing the capital structure policy of the firm has to be kept in mind.

Another important factor which influences the generation of funds is the financial position of the corporation (Havemann and Webster, 1999). Firstly, to invest through retained earnings the corporation must generate enough profit that can satisfy its owners and fulfill the investment demands. Secondly, creditors like to invest in profitable corporations and projects (Amidu and Hinson, 2006); they tend to invest in corporations that can, to some extent, ensure the payment of their liability. This leads to our hypotheses;

H6: High ratio of debt leads to high performance.
H7: Short term debt is negatively related to firm performance.
H8: long term debt is negatively related to firm performance.

Risk management

Risk management of a firm may also impact its performance. Risky firms tend to attract only risk taking investors. The relationship of risk and returns has to be managed so that the investors do get the return associated and expected with the risk they are bearing.

Leading to our final hypotheses;

H9: Business risk has a positive impact firm performance.
H10: Firm risk is positively associated with firm performance.

Firm characteristics and policies

Certain firm characteristics are associated with high performance of firm. These include size (Love and Rachinsky, 2007), growth rate, dividends, liquidity (Gurbuz et al., 2010) and sales (Forbes, 2002). The forms that have better growth rate can afford better machinery, and then gradually the assets and size of the firm will increase. Large firms attract better managers and workers who in turn contribute to the performance of the firm. So, both firm and its people support each other's goals (Succuro) (n.d.).

Although many studies have been conducted on the individual determinants of firm but a very few have modeled all the factors. There is a much larger gap for the developing economies (Maher and Andersson, 1999). A few studies have been conducted in Pakistan on firm performance determinants; one was conducted in 2010 on the effects of capital financing patterns on firm performance. Another study was conducted by Yasser et al. (2011) which investigates the effect of board characteristics on firm performance. Wahla et al. (2012) analyzed the impact of ownership structure on firm performance. There is no study up till now to have modeled various determinants of firm performance for Pakistani firms, this study attempts to fill this gap of empirical research.

RESEARCH METHODOLOGY AND DATA

This section discusses the research and data collection methodology.

Method

We propose to analyze the non-financial firms listed in 100 index of Karachi stock exchange for five year period, 2007 to 2011. Empirical analysis will be done on panel data, according to researchers it controls for individual heterogeneity and multi-colliniarity (Kyereboah-Coleman, 2007). Fixed effect or random effects model whichever is appropriate will be used to find the results. Two models are estimated in the study, one for performance and other for shareholders' return:

$$ROE = \alpha + \beta1 Income + \beta2\ Inflation + \beta3\ Blockholding + \beta4\ Inside\ ownership + \beta5\ Debt\text{-}to\text{-}equity + \beta6\ Long\text{-}term\ debt\ to\ total\ assets + \beta7\ short\text{-}term\ debt\ to\ total\ assets + \beta8\ Firm\ size + \beta9\ Current\ ratio + \beta10\ Business\ risk + \beta11\ Firm\ risk + \varepsilon i \quad (Model\ 1)$$

$$SHR = \alpha + \beta1 Corporate\ governance + \beta2\ Blockholding + \beta3\ Inside\ ownership + \beta4\ Long\text{-}term\ debt\ to\ total\ assets + \beta5\ Firm\ size + \beta6\ Dividend\ yield + \beta7\ Business\ risk + \beta8\ Firm\ risk + \varepsilon i \quad (Model\ 2)$$

Here, α and $\beta 1$ to $\beta 11$ are coefficients, Income, inflation, corporate governance, Blockholding, inside ownership, leverage, long-term debt to total assets, short-term debt to total assets, firm size, current ratio, dividend yield, business risk and firm risk are set of explanatory variables, and εi is the error term.

Variables

Firm Performance: The dependant variable is measured using following variables.
Return on Equity (ROE): It is calculated as net income divided by common equity. The ratio is used to measure profitability of the firm in terms of its equity investments, as used by Yasser et al. (2011) for Pakistani firms.
Share holder Return (SHR): It is calculated by adding annual share price and dividend per share of the year. Dividend per share is calculated by dividing dividend paid by number of shares. And annual share price is calculated by averaging the standard daily returns of the firm. This variable is used to measure share holder return as done by Gregg et al. (2012) for firms of UK.
Economic condition: two economic indicators are included in this study as explanatory variable, as done by Forbes (2002).
Inflation: core annual inflation rate is taken to measure the impact of annual decline in the purchase power of currency.
Income per capita: constant factor per capita income is taken as a measure to analyze the impact of change in real income of people.
Corporate governance: dummy variable is created where registration with Pakistan institute of corporate governance is used as proxy for measuring corporate governance compliance, as done by Gurbuz et al. (2010).
Ownership structure: ownership structure is measured using two groups of variables, as done by Ugurlu (2000).
Blockholding: In the first group outside ownership concentration is measured. It uses percentage of ownership of shareholders with more than 10% holdings.
Inside ownership: The second group measures inside ownership as percentage of shares held by directors, CEO and their families.
Capital structure: we use three ratios to measure this variable.
Debt-to-equity: the ratio is obtained by dividing total debt by total equity. We use this measure to check the impact of debt ratio in a firm's capital on its performance as done by Ntim (2009).
Long-term debt to total assets: the ratio is calculated as long-term debt divided by total assets. We use this measure to check the impact of asset financing done through long-term debt on the performance of firm.
Short-term debt to total assets: the ratio is calculated as short-term debt divided by total assets. We use this measure to check the impact of asset financing done through short-term debt on the performance of firm.
Risk management: two variables are used in the study to as measures of risk;
Business level risk: it is calculated as standard deviation of return on asset of firm for past five years. The ratio is used by Reddy (2010).
Firm level risk: it is calculated as standard deviation of share price of firm for past five years. The ratio is used by Bhagat and Bolton (2008).
Firm policies and characteristics: four control measures are added to the study;
Dividend yield: the ratio is calculated as dividends divided by stock price. We use this ratio as a proxy to measure the dividend policy as used by Reddy (2010).
Size of firm: size is measured as natural log of total assets. Gurbuz et al. (2010) found that size of the firm is an important factor affecting the firms' performance.
Sales growth (SG): The value is obtained by subtracting preceding year's sales from current year's sales and dividing the figure by preceding year's sales. The variable measures the growth in sales of the corporation during the year. It is used to measure company growth as done by Peng (2004).
Current ratio: the ratio is calculated by dividing current assets by current liabilities. The ratio is used as measure of liquidity of firm as done by Gurbuz et al. (2010).
Market capitalization: the value is obtained by multiplying share price with the outstanding shares. It is used by Brav et al. (2008).

Data and sample

Sample of 60 was selected from the population of 100 firms listed in KSE-100. Only the non-financial firms were observed for the study and they were selected on the basis of data availability. The sample contained 9 firms each from oil and gas, and chemical industry, 5 each from general industries, food producers, electricity and personal goods industries, 4 from construction and materials industry, 3 from automobile and parts industry, 2 each from gas, water and multi utilities and pharma and biotech industries, and 1 each from leisure goods, tobacco, household goods, support services, media, fixed line communication, travel and leisure, Technology, hardware and equipment, electronic and electrical equipment.

Data was collected from Pakistan economic survey in 2011 for economic indicators. For corporate governance variable was obtained from PICG, and for ownership variables the values were calculated from the company annual reports, the data for the rest of the variables was taken from balance sheet and annual report analysis done by KSE.

EMPIRICAL ANALYSIS

The section presents the empirical findings and analysis of the data.

Descriptive statistics

The descriptive statistics of dependent variables and explanatory variables by using SPSS are reported in Table 1. It shows the average indicators of variable computed from the financial statements and deviations from those averages.

Average return on equity indicates that firms are earning 32.8% on their equity capital. While the average return a shareholder was getting was 322.7 rupees. On analyzing the economic indicators we find that the average inflation rate during the observed period was 14.03 and income per capita was 33725.43.

Mean of corporate governance dummy was 0.45, indicating that less than half of the analyzed firms were member of PICG (Pakistan institute of corporate governance).

Regarding the ownership structure we find that average inside ownership was 15.11% with standard deviation of 23.9 and average blockholdings were 45.51% with standard deviation of 31.82, indicating that most of the shares of firms in Pakistan are being held by blockholders.

After the analysis of capital structure we found that

Table 1. Means, standard deviations of variables (N=290).

Variable	M	SD
Return on equity	32.81	60.85
Shareholders' return	322.708	547.88
Income per capita	33725.432	681.16
Inflation	14.03	4.5
Corporate Governance	.4514	.477
Block holders	48.51	31.82
Inside ownership	15.11	23.96
Debt-to-equity ratio	1.40	3.42
Short-term debt to assets	99.75	138.64
Long-term debt to assets	72.066	196.19
Business risk	7.35	6.89
Firm risk	67.609	100.02
Sales growth	5.54	62.16
Size	9.73	1.65
Current ratio	2.02	3.46
Market capitalization	142393.63	1308323.28
Dividend yield	7.66	9.30

debt-to-equity ratio on average was 1.4 with standard deviation of 3.42, indicating that financing of firms is based on leverage rather than equity. Then we analyze short-term debt to total assets and long-term debt to total assets ratios and find that on average firms tend to use short-term debt as compared to long-term debt.

Business risk of firms on average was 7.35 with standard deviation of 6.89, while the firm risk average was 67.60 with standard deviation of 100.02.

Average firm size was 9.73, and average growth in sales was 5.54. The current ratio mean was 2.02, indicating that firms are keeping high liquidity. Average market capitalization was 142393.63 and mean of dividend yield was 7.66.

Correlation analysis

The correlation results are also reported in table 2. Matrix shows the relationship or association between the dependent variables and explanatory variable. The results of correlation matrix are as follows.

When return on equity is considered as performance measure, Pearson correlation test shows positive significant relationship between firm performance and income per capita, blockholding, debt-to-equity, business risk, firm risk, firm size and dividend yield. While the relationship of performance with inflation, inside ownership, long-term debt to total assets, short-term debt to total assets, and current ratio is negatively significant.

And the relationship of performance with other variables is insignificant. Where corporate governance and sales growth have positive impact on performance while market capitalization has a negative effect.

With shareholders' return as performance measure, the correlation between firm performance and corporate governance, blockholding, business risk, firm risk, firm size, sales growth and dividend yield is positively signifycant, while a negatively significant relation is observed between firm performance and income per capita, inside ownership, and long-term debt to total assets. Impact of inflation, and current ratio on performance was negatively insignificant. And the effect of debt-to-equity, short-term debt to total assets and market capitalization is positive on firm performance but is insignificant.

All the insignificant variables were excluded from further analysis.

Fixed effect model results

Haussmann test was conducted to decide between fixed effect and random effects models. For both the models the values for random effects model were insignificant, for model one the p-value of chi^2 was 0.08 and for model two it was 0.1, pointing towards the significance of fixed effects model. Fixed effect model was applied for both performance measures separately. Initially the test was conducted for all the variables showing significant correlation but later on the insignificant variables in the model were also excluded and only the significant variables were included in the final models.

Beta coefficients of model 1 are presented in Table 3. In this model return on equity was taken as the measure of firm's performance. Model r-square was 0.78 with an f-statistic of 14.09 significant at 0.00. According to the

Table 2. Correlations between independent and explanatory variables (N=290).

	ROE	SHR	CG	IN	INF	BH	IO	D-E	S-A	L-A	SG	S	CR	MC	DY	BR	FR
ROE	1																
SHR	0.42*	1															
CG	.01	.12*	1														
IN	.20*	.06	-.01	1													
INF	-.18**	-.01*	.00	.67**	1												
BH	.15**	.27*	.04	-.10	-.03	1											
IO	-.13*	-.23**	-.14	.12	.04*	-.67	1										
D-E	.63*	.05	.03	-.07	-.14	-.13	.05	1									
S-A	-.05*	-.10	-.06	-.01	.02	-.14	.15	-.00	1								
L-A	-.17*	-.14*	.01	.23	.11	-.08	.01	-.12	.36	1							
SG	.04	.04*	-.05	.06	-.00	.04	-.04	.00	-.06	-.03	1						
S	.08*	.20*	.42**	.01	-.01	.13	-.21*	-.11	.04	.12	-.10	1					
CR	-.01*	-.05*	.07	-.22**	-.14	-.18	.19*	.03	-.18	-.11	-.01	.04	1				
MC	-.02	.05	.10	.05	.11	.02	-.06	.01	-.06	-.02	-.01	.11	-.02	1			
DY	.26*	.63*	-.02	-.17	-.08	.20**	-.16	.03	.03	-.09	-.03	-.10	-.04	-.03	1		
BR	.14**	.15**	.03	.22	.12	-.05	.20	.04	-.02	.00	.01	-.01	.09	-.07	.03	1	
FR	.39**	.76**	-.16*	.04	.07	.18*	-.13	.06	-.11	-.16	-.03	-.29	.05	-.05	.48	.22	1

*$p \le .05$; **$p < .01$.
Here CG=Corporate governance, IN=Income per capita, INF=Inflation, BH=Blockholding, IO=Inside ownership, D-E=Debt-to-equity ratio, S-A=Short-term debt to total assets, L-A=Long-term debt to total assets, SG=Sales growth, S=Firm size, CR=current ratio, MC=Market capitalization, DY=Dividend Yield, BR=Business risk, FR=Firm risk.

Table 3. Fixed effect model analysis summary for income per capita, inflation, blockholdings, inside ownership, debt-to-equity ratio, short-term debt to total assets, long-term debt to total assets, business risk, firm risk and firm size predicting ROE (N=290).

Independent variable	B	SEB	β	Probability of t-stat
Constant	236.225		2.038	0.044
Income	.007	.167	2.042*	0.043
Inflation	1.012	-.021	-.285*	0.049
Blockholding	.146	.138	1.814*	0.045
Inside ownership	.202	-.021	-.264*	0.05
Debt-to-equity ratio	.026	.621	11.014**	0.00
Short-term debt to total assets	.027	.116	-1.868*	0.05
Long-term debt to total assets	.019	-.048	-.777*	0.05
Business risk	.525	.101	1.696*	0.048
Firm risk	.043	.336	4.745**	0.00
Size	2.417	.079	1.195*	0.03
Current ratio	1.069	-.066	-1.082*	0.038

Note. R2 =0.78; $F(11, 290) = 14.09$, $p < .05$
*$p \le .05$; **$p < .01$.

results income per capita boosts firm's performance by 2.04 times. This can be explained by the fact that whenever there is an increase in income level of people the demand for goods also increases which contribute to firm's profits. Inflation rate had a negative impact on performance, because when inflation rises so do the costs and expenses of firms reducing the income. The results are in line with research conducted by Forbes (2002).

When we analyze the impact of ownership structure we see that blockholdings have a positive impact while inside ownership negatively influences the firm's profits. Blockholdings increase monitoring and control which motivates firms to invest in more profit generating projects. The results are in line with studies conducted by Reddy (2010) and Ntim (2009).

Then we see the impact of capital structure on firm performance. It is evident from the results that debt-to-

Table 4. Fixed effect model analysis summary for corporate governance, block holdings, inside ownership, long-term debt to total assets, business risk, firm risk, firm size and dividend yield, predicting SHR (N=290).

Independent variable	B	SEB	β	Probability of t-stat
Constant	1865.058		1.205	0.13
Corporate Governance	6.15	-.035	.656*	0.046
Blockholdings	1.150	.030	.444*	0.05
Inside ownership	1.592	-.072	-1.029*	0.03
Long-term debt to total assets	.151	.015	-.285*	0.04
Business risk	4.145	.048	.929*	0.035
Firm risk	.340	.579	9.328**	0.00
Size	19.086	.004	.075*	0.05
Dividend yield	.001	.321	5.661**	0.00

Note. R2 = 0.67; F (8, 290) = 20.99, $p < .05$
*$p \leq .05$; **$p < .01$.

equity ratio has a positive impact on performance, referring to the fact that more debt pushes the firms' directors to develop more profit generating strategies in order to satisfy the existing creditors and also to attract new investors. The result is line with the study of Ntim (2009). Long-term debt to total assets and short-term debt to total assets had a negative influence on firm performance, indicating that in case of more financing of assets through these sources the firms' profits may suffer, because of heavy interest payments.

Business risk and firm risk both have a positive influence on firm performance. More risk leads to more return up to a point. For the observed period the firms have managed their risk so that it has not reached that limit. The results are supported by the study of Reddy (2010).

Firm size positively impacts its performance while the liquidity of firm's assets will negatively influence its performance. High liquidity means that too much assets are not being properly utilized, if this liquid were invested it may earn more profits. The results are supported by the research conducted by Gurbuz et al. (2010).

Beta coefficients of model 2 are presented in Table 4. In this model shareholders' return was taken as the measure of firm's performance. Model r-square was 0.67 with an f-statistic of 20.99 significant at 0.00. From the results of fixed effect model we find that corporate governance has a positive impact on firm performance. This indicates that firms listed in PICG have better profit distribution policies. The result is supported by the investigation of Gurbuz et al. (2010), which used the listing of corporate governance index as measure for corporate governance practices in their study.

After the analysis of impact of ownership structure on firm performance we find that blockholding had a positive while inside ownership had negative effect on performance of firms. This can be because of better monitoring from blockholders. And also due to the negative relation of inside ownership with dividends which directly contribute to shareholder return. The results are in line with studies conducted by Reddy (2010) and Ntim (2009).

For capital structure only long-term debt to total assets had a significant impact on shareholders' return. The reason for this negative influence is the long term compounding interest payment of debt, which reduces the company's profits and hence the return to shareholders.

Both business risk and firm risk have positive influence on return. Because proper risk management leads to higher profit for firms and hence better dividends to shareholders. Also the return for riskier investments is higher. The results are in line with the study of Reddy (2010). Firm size has a positive impact on shareholder return and dividend yield is also directly influential on the return. The results are supported by the research conducted by Gurbuz et al. (2010) and Reddy (2010).

Conclusion

Many researchers have conducted studies on financial performance of firms and have proposed various theories to explain the variation. But the issue is still under debate. We attempt to answer the following questions: what are the determinants of the financial performance of a firm?

Fixed effect model is applied on 60 non-financial companies listed in KSE 100-index of Pakistan. Our results show that economic factors, ownership structure and risk management have a major impact in determination of the financial performance of firms in Pakistan, if return on equity is considered as performance measure. Similarly if we consider financial performance in terms of shareholder return, which in most cases is the main concern of shareholders for it can also effect the share prices (Csanad, 2009), corporate governance, ownership structure, capital structure and risk management have major influence on firm performance. This means that firms having proper risk management and capital structure policies will be more profitable for too much financing done through long-term debt will reduce earnings by increasing the mark-up expenses. Similarly firms with well maintained ownership structures will also earn more than their counterparts because of a proper mix of monitoring and control. Economic factors are also important contributors to firm performance but are external to firms' control, so, proper measures should be taken while developing strategies and goals to minimize the negative impact of these factors and get maximum out of the positive ones. From the findings of this study we can say that firms having proper corporate governance structures and monitoring will be more profitable for shareholders. The results are in line with the previous studies. Overall we can conclude on the basis of the empirical findings of this study that firms having well governed ownership structure, capital structure, and proper risk management tend to have a better financial performance. Also corporate governance practices should be improved to increase the worth of the investors' wealth.

POLICY IMPLICATIONS

From the findings of the paper we can say that it would be advisable for the economic decision makers to consider the impact of their decisions on the corporate sector before finalizing them, especially the decisions related to the matter of inflation. And for the managers there are two important policy considerations. First, short term debt should be preferred over long term debt to minimize the negative impact of debt financing. And second, the negative impact of inside ownership on shareholders return should be analyzed before offering stock bonuses.

LIMITATIONS AND RECOMMENDATIONS

This paper contributes to the literature of determinants of firm performance, where we find significant effect of economic factors, corporate governance, ownership structure, capital structure and risk management on profitability of firms in case of emerging market of Pakistan. There is a need to further analyze with respect to effects and factors that can determine the performance of firm. Further researcher may extend the present study by the use of generalized model to examine the behavior of economic and other non-financial factors. From the findings of this paper it would also be useful to consider the future research on the share prices and their relation with corporate governance practices.

REFERENCES

Abu-Rub N (2012). Capital structure and firm performance; Evidence from Palestine stock exchange. J. Money Invest. Bank. 23:109-117.

Akbar M, Baig HH (2010). Reaction of Stock Prices to Dividend Announcements and Market Efficiency in Pakistan. Lahore J. Econ. 15(1):103-125.

Amidu M, Hinson R (2006). Credit risk, Capital Structure and lending decisions of banks in Ghana. Banks and Bank Systems, Volume 1.

Ang JS, Cole RA, Lin JW (2000). Agency Costs and Ownership Structure. J. Finance 55(1):81-105.

Bhagat S, Bolton B (2008). Corporate governance and firm performance. J. Corporate Financ. 14:257-273

Bocean CG (2001). Corporate governance and firm performance.

Bohren O, Josefsen MG, Steen PE (2009). Dividends and stakeholder conflicts: A cleaner test.

Born JA (1988). Insider Ownership and Signals: Evidence from Dividend Initiation Announcement Effects. Financ. Manage. 17:38-45

Brav A, Jiang W, Partnoy F, Thomas R (2008). Hedge fund activism, corporate governance and firm performance. J. Financ. 63(4):1729-1775

Burkart M, Panunzi F (2005). Agency conflicts, ownership concentration, and legal shareholder protection. J. Financ. Intermediation 15(1):1-31.

Chugh LC, Meador JW, Kumar AS (2009). Corporate governance and firm performance: evidence from India. Journal of finance and accountancy.

Csanad (2009). Earnings per Share-Interpreting EPS. Retrieved from http://hubpages.com.

Dutta AS (1999). Managerial Ownership, Dividend and Debt Policy in the US Banking Industry. Manag. Financ. 25(6):57-68.

Forbes KJ (2002). How do large depreciations affect firm performance? Palgrave Macmillan 49(1):214-238.

Gregg P, Jewell S, Tonks I (2012). Executive pay and performance: Did bankers, bonuses cause the crises? Int. Rev. Financ. 12 (1):89-122.

Gurbuz AO, Aybars A, Kutlu O (2010). Corporate governance and financial performance with a perspective on institutional ownership: empirical evidence from Turkey. J. Appl. Manage. Account. Res. 8:21-38.

Havemann R, Webster P (1999). Does Ethical Investment Pay?

IFC (2009). Corporate governance: the foundation for corporate citizenship and sustainable businesses. Global corporate governance forum.

Javed AY, Iqbal R (2007). The relationship between corporate governance indicators and firm value: A case study of Karachi stock exchange. MRPA Paper No.225, available at http://mpra.ub.uni-muenchen.de/2225.

Jensen GR, Solberg DP, Zorn TS (1992). Simultaneous Determination of Insider Ownership, Debt, and Dividend Policies. J. Financ. Quant. Anal. 27(2):247-263.

Kalirajan K, Singh K (2009). The Impact of Globalization on Employment Generation in India: The case of emerging 'Big Shopping Malls and Retailers'. The Foundation for Advanced Studies on International Development in Tokyo ASARC Working Paper 2009/18.

Kaserer C, Moldenhauer B (2008). Insider ownership and corporate performance: evidence from Germany, RMS (2008)DOI 10.1007/s11846-007-0009-3.

Khan T (2006). Company Dividends and Ownership Structure: Evidence from UK Panel Data. Econ. J. 116(510):C172-C189.

Kyereboah-Coleman A (2007). Corporate governance and firm performance in Africa: A dynamic panel data analysis. International conference on corporate governance in emerging markets. Sabanci University, Istanbul, Turkey, November.

Lewellen J, Lewellen K (2004). Taxes and financing decisions. AFA 2005 Philadelphia Meetings Paper.

Lin C, Ma Y, Xuan Y (2011). Ownership Structure and Financial Constraints: Evidence from a Structural Estimation. J. Financ. Econ. 102:416-431.

Love I, Rachinsky A (2007). Corporate governance, ownership and bank performance in emerging markets: evidence from Russia and Ukraine. Siteresources-worldbank. Working Paper, http://siteresources.worldbank.org/DEC/Resources/Corporate_Governnace

_Ownership_and_Bank_Performance.pdf.
Maher M, Andersson T (1999). Corporate governance: effects on firm performance and economic growth. OECD.
Ntim CG (2009). Internal corporate governance structures and firm financial performance: Evidence from South African listed firms. Department of accounting and finance, University of Glasgow.
Peng MW (2004). Outside directors and firm performance during institutional transition. Strateg. Manage. J. 25(5):453-471
Reddy K (2010). The relationship between corporate governance practices and financial performance in New Zealand: An empirical investigation. The University of Waikato.
Su G, Vo HT (2010). The relationship between corporate strategy, capital structure and firm performance: an empirical study of the listed companies in Vietnam. Int. Res. J. Financ. Econ., ISSN 1450-2887 Issue 50.
Succuro (n.d.). Does good corporate governance really make a difference? Available at www.succuro.com.au.
Theis J, Casey M (1999). An empirical investigation of agency relationships and capital structure of property management firms in the UK. Journal of property investment and finance. MCB university press.
Ugurlu M (2000). Agency costs and corporate control devices in the Turkish manufacturing industry. Journal of economic studies. MCB university press.
Wahla K, Shah ZA, Hussain Z (2012). Impact of ownership structure on firm performance. Evidence from non-financial listed companies at Karachi stock exchange. Eurojournals publishing Inc.
Yasser QR, Entebang H, Abu Mansur S (2011). Corporate governance and firm performance in Pakistan: the case of Karachi stock exchange (KSE)-30. J. Econ. Int. Financ. 3(8):482-491.

Financial inclusion by Zimbabwean commercial banks in a liquidity constrained environment

Chikoko Laurine[1]* and Mangwendeza Patrick[2]

[1]Department of Banking and Finance, Midlands State University, Zimbabwe, P Bag 9055, Gweru, Zimbabwe.
[2]FBC Microfinance, FBC House, 113 Leopold Takawira Street, Harare, Zimbabwe.

The study investigates the trends and challenges of financial inclusion by commercial banks in Zimbabwe after the adoption of the multiple currency regime. Results showed that some commercial banks made efforts to ensure financial inclusion. New innovations like cell phone banking and internet banking were positive steps towards ensuring financial inclusion by Zimbabwean commercial banks. The foreign owned commercial banks in Zimbabwe however were not doing much as compared to the locally owned commercial banks. A number of challenges to financial inclusion were identified, chiefly being the liquidity challenges and high bank charges. Based on the research findings, we recommend the structuring of sustainable financial products and establishment of supportive infrastructure to enable Zimbabwean commercial banks to mitigate the challenges of financial inclusion in a liquidity constrained environment.

Key words: Financial inclusion, commercial banks, liquidity constrained environment, strategies.

INTRODUCTION

Financial inclusion is the process of ensuring access to a full suite of quality financial services, provided at affordable cost, in a convenient manner, and with dignity to the entire population without discrimination of any type particularly against vulnerable groups such as weaker and low income groups (Rajan and Zingales, 2003; Personal Finance Research Centre 2007; Reserve bank of India, 2011). As banking services are in the nature of public goods, financial inclusion should therefore be viewed as availability of banking and payment services to the entire population. Gardeva and Rhyne (2011) highlighted the key factors that drive financial inclusion as illustrated in Figure 1.

The Centre for Strategy and Evaluation Services (2010) alluded that the objective of financial inclusion is to extent the scope of activities of the organised financial system to include within its ambit people with low incomes. This is only possible if an organisation is pursuing an appropriate business model. Devlin and Gregor (2008) concur that the services must meet requirements of individuals ranging from consumption to basic education, health and other services. This study then sought to investigate and evaluate interventions employed by Zimbabwean commercial banks in financial inclusion in a liquidity constrained environment.

The Zimbabwean banking sector underwent a period of impeded development in the 10 years to 2009 due to the hyperinflationary environment which prevailed in the economy. Regrettably the banking crisis of 2003/4 resulted in the closure of some of the newer banks and this resulted in a flight to quality by the investing public. This also increased the general risk aversion amongst average investors with most of them being wary of any financial product that was not generic. The hyper-inflationary environment also made investments meaningless with most people preferring to hold assets such as property to store value. In the second half of 2008, the world was hit by a financial services crisis whose systemic effects resulted in a worldwide economic crisis. Countries within the region, Zimbabwe included were not spared, although there were delayed effects. The impact was that inter-bank lending was ground to a halt, thereby freezing credit markets. Corporations and individuals found it difficult to use debt to finance

*Corresponding author. E-mail: chikokol@msu.ac.zw.

Figure 1. Key factors that drive financial inclusion. Source: Gardeva and Rhyne (2011).

purchases. For the banking industry, like other sectors of the economy, one of the consequences of the crisis was that organisations sought to streamline operations.

However, things took a turn following the adoption of multi currency in 2009. According to the Reserve Bank of Zimbabwe (RBZ) (2011), the Zimbabwean banking sector experienced a gradual improvement in its intermediation role since the introduction of the multiple currency regime in January 2009. In spite of the growth in the number of financial institutions, the bank penetration rate as measured by the collective number of accounts held by banks was not more than 20% of the entire adult population (RBZ, 2011). Geographical representation of branches was concentrated in major cities and towns. Accordingly, 70% of the country's population which is in the rural areas is served by only 11.7% of the banks' total branch network (RBZ, 2011). Rural communities and the informal sector continue to be shunned by some banks. The objective of the study is to ascertain if Zimbabwean banking institutions were taking adequate strategies that promote inclusive banking after the adoption of the multiple currency regime. The period covered is 2009 to 2011. The research also intends to establish the challenges to financial inclusion and to ascertain if the Reserve Bank of Zimbabwe created conducive regulatory framework that promoted financial inclusion.

RESEARCH METHODOLOGY

To achieve our objective, the research used a descriptive survey research design so that relationships between interventions used and level of financial inclusion achieved could be unraveled. The descriptive survey design was chosen because it allowed data obtained to be presented and analysed using both quantitative and qualitative methods. Given the divergences between the banks in terms of size, age, and organisational and environmental factors, there was a wide variation in terms of interventions employed and levels of financial inclusion outcomes as well. Thus, the adoption of the survey methodology with data collected from all banks allowed us to discern variations in the data gathered and find effects among variables as well as to verify the nature of theoretical relationships that had been proposed. Most of the information for this research was derived from primary sources but however secondary sources were also used. Data was collected using questionnaires and interviews. This helped to offset the weaknesses that each of the techniques carry. The study population had 16 institutions, with 15 commercial banks and the Reserve Bank of Zimbabwe. From each commercial bank, four participants were selected through use of judgmental sampling technique. For commercial banks, information was collected from management at head offices in Harare. Focus was on head offices because all information about branch networks and products on offer is available at head offices. Data from Reserve Bank of Zimbabwe was collected from management in the bank licensing, supervision and surveillance division. Questionnaires were sent to 64 participants. To compliment the questionnaires, interviews were done on 15 participants.

DATA PRESENTATION AND DISCUSSION

Response rate

From a sample target of 64 participants, there were 48 responses. This indicated an average response rate of 75%.

Strategies for reaching the unbanked and under banked public

To achieve the objective of the study, we investigated on

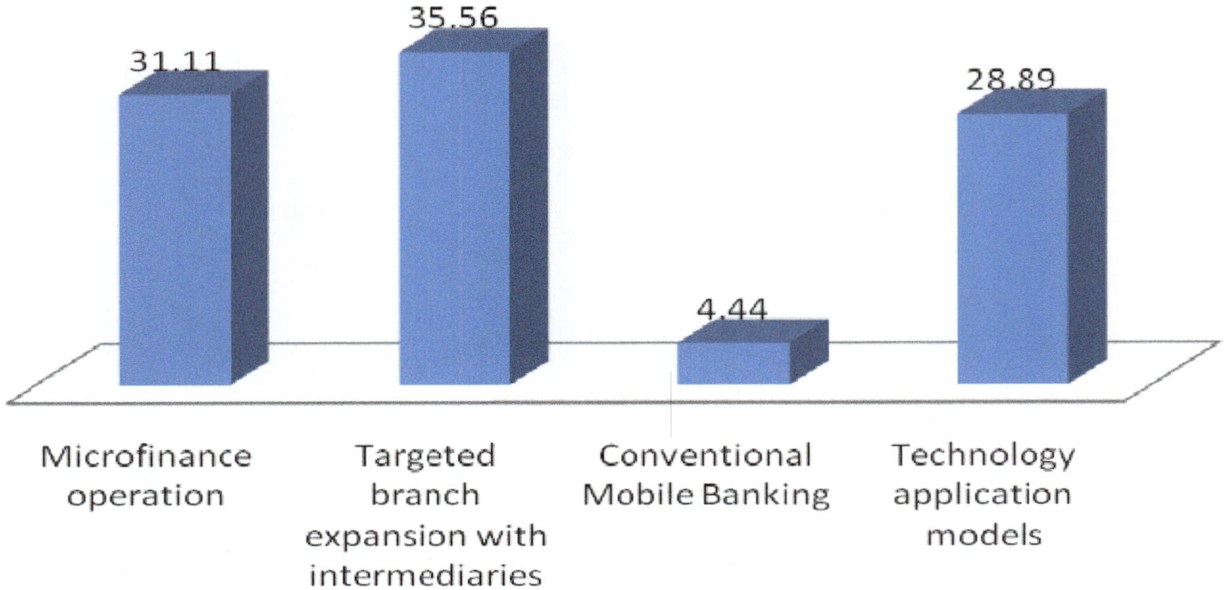

Figure 2. Models adopted by banks.

the models that were being used by banks on the unbanked sector. This focused on products offered and the distribution channels. From the survey, 60% of the respondents confirmed that their banks did not have the unbanked as their target market whilst 40% confirmed that their business models encompass the unbanked as a target market. This at least partly explains why a larger section of the rural communities remains excluded.

Models adopted by banks

The specific models Zimbabwean commercial banks adopted to reach out to the unbanked are presented in Figure 2.

From the survey, it is clear that many banks had moved away from the conventional mobile banking where banks would be moving around in mobile units to offer their services. 31% of the respondents indicated that their organisations had adopted a microfinance model, 36% indicated that their institutions were pursuing a targeted branch expansion model, 29% had adopted a technology application model. To compliment this, the breakdown of the commercial banks and the specific models they were using are presented in Table 1.

The study revealed banks that made a conscious decision to go into the unbanked space, reconfigured their models to encompass a microfinance wing to service this sector. The same banks also developed electronic banking channels given the geographic reach of the targeted segment. There were only 5 banks still undertaking the conventional mobile banking at strategic locations. The seemingly wide branch network with ATMs was resident in cities and not the rural areas. The survey also revealed that many banks had the technological capacity to deliver services to the unbanked but few had an appetite for this market. Reasons that were cited as barriers included high information, transaction and monitoring costs, inaccessibility due to poor infra-structure, dispersed and intermittent demand for financial services, seasonality of deposits and lack of collateral.

The research also revealed that the majority of banks had internet banking technology albeit accessibility was restricted to the affluent and established corporate clients. The delivery channel was the most appropriate for the unbanked segment in the far flung rural areas and other remote locations. The conventional mobile banking was wilting down given the attendant costs involved as compared to the cell phone banking route. These results conform to the results by Lyman et al. (2006, 2008). Table 2 gives a market comparison of cell phone banking products that were launched in by different players stampeding for a share of business in the unbanked and rural market space after the adoption of the multiple currency.

In the banking sector, Kingdom Bank and Tetrad Investment Bank were the first innovators with their virtual mobile-banking packages. Both the Kingdom Cell Card and Tetrad's E-Mali offered customers a platform to transact using cell phones. Despite this, the banks' small branch network in the country and market presence, the majority of the population did not have access to these products and did not know about them. But as pioneers, Kingdom and Tetrad laid a foundation for others to follow suit.

The launch in October 2011 of cell phone banking

Table 1. Adopted models broken down by institution.

Organisation	Microfinance	Electronic banking technologies	Mobile banking	Branch network/ATMs
ZB Bank	X	X	X	X
FBC Bank	X	X	X	X
TN Bank	X	X		X
Stanbic Bank				X
Standard Chartered		X		X
Barclays Bank		X		X
MBCA		X		X
Metropolitan Bank		X		X
ZABG				X
CBZ Bank	X	X	X	X
Agribank			X	X
BancABC		X		X
Kingdom Bank	X	X	X	X
NMB Bank		X		X
Premier Bank		X		X
Total	5	12	5	15

services by Econet Wireless Zimbabwe and Telecel Zimbabwe charted a new era in delivery of banking products to the public. With EcoCash from Econet Wireless, subscribers could send and receive money instantly through cell phones. The Telecel system was technically different from Econet's EcoCash and was cited as having the advantage of offering a wide range of products to its users due to its strategic partnership with ZimSwitch participating banks. Respondents cited it as an ecosystem, where they were exploiting the core competencies of ZimSwitch partners. ZimSwitch is a financial platform that was used to connect and carry out transactions amongst banks and has been operational for the past 15 years with 19 financial institutions connected through it. Together they had more than half a million customers, which is almost half the number of banked individuals in Zimbabwe (RBZ, 2011). It was expected that by end of 2011 about 85% of banks would be ZimSwitch ready. The greatest advantage of connecting through ZimSwitch for the mobile banking service was that the banks would enjoy synergies of being already connected to a web of institutions where users were able to send and receive money through any ZimSwitch-ready outlet, be it a bank or an agent (ZimSwitch Report, 2011). The survey also revealed that the most imposing of competitors was EcoCash whose major strengths were a powerful subscriber base, a very wide and growing agent network and a well funded and strategic advertising campaign. It was interesting to note that through this product, Econet was competing for deposits directly with financial institutions. The findings from this study clearly show the need for commercial banks to enter into strategic partner-ships with mobile phone operators. The biggest beneficiary of this innovation would be the unbanked market. Whilst the transaction fees were still considered high during the time the research was undertaken, it was expected that these would go down as competition sets in and make mobile banking services more affordable.

Challenges to financial inclusion in Zimbabwe

The other objective of the research was to ascer-tain the challenges being faced by commercial banks. A number of challenges to financial inclusion were identified. High bank charges and inadequate funding on the part of banks were cited as major challenges. Table 3 shows the challenges that were indentified and how partici-pants rated them.

The study revealed that liquidity or inadequate funding on the part of banks was the major challenge followed by high bank charges. Of the respondents, 73% indicated that inadequate funding was a very big challenge and rated it extremely high whilst high bank charges were rated high. These findings are in sync with Rutherford and Arora (2009) who concurred that high bank charges and lack of funding are barriers to financial inclusion.

Other challenges cited by the respondents included socio-economic factors (e.g. financial education, low and irregular income and geography), regulatory factors (stringent account opening requirements e.g. provision of identity documentation and proof of residence to open accounts) and product design factors (e.g., minimum account balance requirements and bank charges which are high). On the part of the banks, the respondents cited high information, transaction and monitoring costs, in-accessibility due to poor infrastructure, dispersed and

Table 2. Cell phone banking products.

Provider	FBC	Econet	Tetrad	Kingdom	CABS	NetOne
Product name	Mobile Moola	EcoCash	eMali	Cell Card	TextaCash	OneWallet
Attribute						
Transaction initiation	-POS -Mobile -ATM	Mobile	POS	- POS - Mobile	- POS - Mobile - ATM	- Mobile
Available functions	(Teller) Bal, Mini Stat, Dep, Withdraw, Send, Receive, Topup**, Bills, RTGS, PIN Change, HOT Card, Resey PIN (Merchant/Agent) Bal, Mini Stat, Send, Receive, Topup, Bills	Send, Receive, topup (Econet only), pay merchant (not on ZSW), Bal, Account Hist, PIN Change	Purchase, Deposit, Withdraw, Person to person transfer, Bills	Withdraw, Transfer, Topup, Bal, Change PIN, Mini Stat	Same as Mobile Moola	Send, Receive, Topup (Netone), NetOne bills
Limits	Min $5 and max $1,000	Up to $200			Min $10 and Max $1,000	Min $5 and Max $500
Access to networks	Receive from all networks, Send from Telecel**	Receive from all networks, Send from Econet	No mobile platform	Telecel	Receive from all networks, Send from Telecel**	NetOne
Access to banks	Potentially all banks on ZSW (currently POSB and CABS)	Partnership with TN; no function to transfer between wallet and bank	Tetrad	Kingdom	Potentially all banks on ZSW (currently POSB and FBC)	Partnership with FBC; no function to transfer between wallet and bank
Nature of ecosystem	ZimSwitch (ZSW) based – 19 banks and retail merchant network	Private	Private	Private	ZimSwitch (ZSW) based – 19 banks and retail merchant network	Private
Promotion and marketing	Introductory stage - press	Awesome! Direct and widespread – press, radio, TV	Press, radio, billboards, street campaigns	Good! Press, magazines, roadshows, street	Low tone. Introductory stage – press.	Strategic prime time radio campaign (albeit poor message), press
Future projection	Steady growth dependant on consistent message of shared platform advantage and creating access to remote parts.	Riding on subscriber base and market dominance. Its life will depend on how the ZSW based product will grow and how well it is marketed.	Private ecosystem not sustainable in the long run	Private ecosystem not sustainable in the long run	The future of mobile banking in Zim as more banks join the ecosystem.	Private ecosystem not sustainable in the long run. Least and dwindling subscriber base a huge negative.

Table 2. Cont

Agencies	Currently FBC branches. In future all FIs on the ecosystem. Needs aggressive agent partnering strategies.	Massive network across the country, presence in all provinces.	Reasonably wide including TM nationwide and Zimpost.	Branch network, TM, Community bankers	Currently CABS branches	NetOne shops

Table 3. Challenges in financial inclusion.

Rating	Extremely high	High	Moderate	Low
Challenge				
Financial literacy			X	
High bank charges		X		
Inadequate funding/liquidity	X			
Public mistrust of financial institutions			X	
Lack of interest by providers and policy makers				X
Poor infrastructure			X	
Political interference				X

intermittent demand for financial services, seasonality of deposits, lack of collateral and finding the regulatory space to innovate. For example, although there are 114 microfinance institutions, 98% of them were mere money lenders licensed under the Money Lending and Rates of Interest Act [*Chapter 14:14*], under which they were not authorised to take deposits, a key element necessary for deposit mobilisation to build capacity necessary for on lending.

Role of Central Bank in financial inclusion

Participants showed that RBZ had the role of ensuring financial literacy in Zimbabwe. It was also held that banks were direct beneficiaries of financial inclusion and were also to take the initiative for financial literacy. The study further revealed that RBZ was financially constrained and not in a position to provide adequate support to banks to ensure financial inclusion (Figure 3). The incapacity by RBZ to provide necessary support to banks was a major challenge to financial inclusion in Zimbabwe. This is because central banks naturally take a leading role in financial inclusion. Thirty participants (77.8%) agreed (both agree and strongly agree) that the Central Bank had the duty of educating public to foster financial literacy necessary for client protection. Fifteen participants (22.3%) (Jointly disagree and strongly disagreed) argued that commercial banks were the direct beneficiaries of financial inclusion and should take the initiative in ensuring financial literacy. Respondents from the central bank conceded that due to financial constraints, the RBZ was not discharging this duty. The RBZ was not visible particularly to the rural communities, the sector that requires education and protection most.

Strategies for reaching the unbanked and under banked public

All participants concurred that not all of the banks had products that were suitable for the poor and rural communities. The products that were identified include loans, micro insurance, and remittance facilities. It was also held that all banks had the capacity to provide high quality financial services to the poor. RBZ officials argued that commercial banks were required to have a minimum capital of US$12.5 million. Most banks had met the minimum capital requirements; implying that they had the capacity (financially) to provide high quality banking services.

On the issue of branch network, it was held that

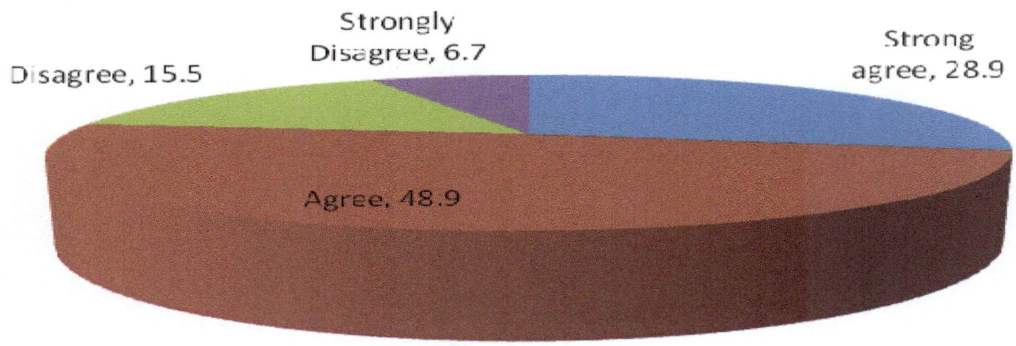

Figure 3. Central Bank's duty to educate the public.

few banks had branches at growth points and small towns. Participants also revealed that banks had developed innovative ways of reaching clients in remote areas.

These innovations included mobile technology and use of non banking agents. Nevertheless, RBZ officials shared the same sentiments with some respondents that the usage of mobile and internet banking were still very low.

Conclusions

Based on the above findings it can be concluded that;

Few banks, particularly the locally owned repositioned their business models to tap into the unbanked market. These had set up microfinance subsidiaries and introduced mobile banking technology in partnership with cell phone operators. The product offering however was still predominantly remittances and payment facilities which falls short of the full suite of financial services required in the unbanked space which include micro credit, micro insurance and financial advisory services.

Inadequate funding and high bank charges are the biggest challenges to financial inclusion in Zimbabwe. Other challenges identified were financial literacy, public mistrust of financial institutions and poor infrastructure.

The RBZ has the role of ensuring financial education of the unbanked and marginalised in Zimbabwe. Banks are direct beneficiaries of financial inclusion and should also take the initiative for financial literacy. Incapacity by RBZ to provide necessary support to banks is a major challenge to financial inclusion in Zimbabwe.

RECOMMENDATIONS

Based on the above conclusions, the following recommendations are made:

There is need for commercial banks to develop financial products that respond to the needs of diversified activities of the unbanked segment, giving due focus to loans, savings, insurance, remittance products and financial advisory services. The key to ensuring that the usage of financial products and services is sustainable is to make sure that these products and services address the real and very specific needs in their day-to-day realities. The development of banking institutions is at the sharp-end of increasing access.

Banks need to enter into strategic alliances with other support service providers like cell phone operators. Some players have gone on a frenzied rush to introduce mobile banking services as they battle to remain relevant due to the technology revolution sweeping across the globe that is redefining the way business is done. This has brought convenience and faster real-time transacting.

The RBZ has a key role to play in enabling policy and regulatory environment. This role is not in the delivery of services, but in laying out a clear policy direction and creating an enabling environment. The private sector players can then identify, invest and respond to opportunities in the market. Directly related to these policy moves, the commercial banks growing interest in new markets is demonstrated through product innovation and increased investment in new delivery channels in the form of branches, ATMs (Automated teller machine) and other electronic delivery channels. With the maturation of the micro-finance sub-sector, the RBZ should now move to provide a regulatory framework to license and regulate deposit-taking MFIs (money flow index). A number of institutions have now developed to the point where deposit taking from the public is a viable proposition. This will allow MFIs to broaden their product offer to include savings services – often the most important financial service demanded by low-income clients. This gradualist approach to regulation is important. Early regulation could have stifled an emerging industry.

There is need for ensuring, through the leadership and supervision of RBZ, that all players operate on a sustainable basis and are transparent in disclosing the results of their operations. Financial literacy is a pre-requisite for client protection. It is therefore recommended that given its critical role, the RBZ must be adequately resourced to discharge its functions.

REFERENCES

Centre for Strategy and Evaluation Services (2010). Study on the Costs and Benefits of Policy Actions in the Field of Ensuring Access to a Basic Bank Account.

Devlin JF, Gregor M (2008). From Access to Inclusion: An Evaluation of the Role of Basic Bank Accounts in Promoting Financial Inclusion, *Toynbee Hall.*

Gardeva A, Rhyne E (2011). Opportunities and Obstacles to Financial Inclusion, Survey Report, Center for Financial Inclusion, India.

Lyman T, Ivatury G, Staschen S (2006). Use of Agents in Branchless Banking for the Poor: Rewards, Risks and Regulation. Washington, D.C.: CGAP.

Lyman T, Pickens M, Porteous D (2008). Regulating Transformational Branchless Banking: Mobile Phones and Other Technology to Increase Access to Finance. Washington, D.C.: CGAP and DFID.

Personal Finance Research Centre (2007). Financial Services Provision and Prevention of Financial Exclusion, United Kingdom, Stage 2 Country Report, Personal Finance Research Centre, Bristol.

Rajan RG, Zingales L (2003). Saving Capitalism from the Capitalists. Unleashing the Power of Financial Markets to Create Wealth and Spread Opportunity. London: Random House.

Reserve Bank of India (2011). Taking Banking to the Common Man, Centre for Financial Inclusion .

Reserve Bank of Zimbabwe (2011) Monetary Policy Statement.

Rutherford S, Arora S (2009). The Poor and their Money. Second Edition, Practical Action Publishing.

Zimbabwe Zimswitch Report 2011.

Problems and prospects of electronic resources usage in Nigerian academic libraries

Famous Kose Dafiaghor

Department of Library and Information Science, Faculty of Education, Delta State University, Abraka, Nigeria. E-Mail:kosdaf80@yahoo.com.

This work dealt with the problems and prospects of electronic information resources in Nigeria. It was obvious from the review that the use of e-resources is not problem-free in Nigeria. Amongst others, it was pointed out that acquisition and maintenance cost, availability of electronic information resources gadgets, spare parts and experts, erratic power supply, are major problems militating against the effective use and usability of e-resources. It was also seen that though there are numerous problems plaguing the use of e-resources in Nigeria yet there are also numerous positive prospects; with emphasis that the use of e-resources will increase immensely; possibly, e-resources are likely to send print-resource on parking or the barest minimal use. These positive prospects were as a result of the numerous advantages that e-resources have over the print.

Key words: Academic library, e-resources, internet, information.

INTRODUCTION

The use of information technology in Nigerian academic libraries has been profoundly affecting all aspects of information acquisition, storage, and transfer. Its magnificent development has dramatically changed the mode of library operations and information services. Hundreds of thousands of monographic materials, journals, learning resources, databases, etc. are now available in electronic formats, and these materials can now be accessed from the remote corner of any country, thereby increasing the use of information and literature and the efficiency of information services in Nigerian tertiary institution. Users are now more independent than before; they can access to these electronic formats from their home computers and search databases according to their information needs. Students, teachers, researchers, information professionals, and employees are the user categories in tertiary institutions. Their needs vary, their information or literature-seeking behaviour also varies, and they need to be cared accordingly. Requirement of an individual needs to be individually addressed in an efficient way. Information resources also need to be accessed by them depending on their requirements – be they print materials and web-based resources.

Electronic resources imply information materials that require the use of electronic devices such as personal computers (PCs), laptops, palm-tops, Notebook-laptops, DVD-,VCD-,CD–players, projectors, phones, I-pods, I-phones, I-pads, internet-, WAN-, LAN- networks, etc for their usage. Some of the most used of these resources include flash-drives, memory cards, DVD-, VCD-, CD-ROMs, DVD-, VCD-, CD-RAMs, DVD-, VCD-, CD-R; DVD-, VCD-, CD-WR; DVD-, VCD-, CD+WR, etc.

Though there are numerous positive prospects to the use of these resources, yet there also are numerous problems militating against their sufficient use and usability.

PROBLEMS MILITATING AGAINST THE USE OF ELECTRONIC INFORMATION RESOURCES IN NIGERIA

According to Ali (2005), a sizeable number of users (almost 60%) are facing numerous problems while using electronic information resources, such as lack of knowledge about the resources, lack of trained staff and inadequate terminals. He also identified four barriers to the effective provision of electronic resources in those libraries, namely: lack of strategic planning: lack of adequate or reliable funding; lack of use of Internet to provide information services to users and a lack of consistent training for users in new information and communications technology (ICT) services.

Further, Wills (1990) also concur to these problems when he identified insufficient number of terminals available for use despite high demand and inadequate electricity supply; lack of information retrieval skills for exploiting electronic resources, thus making the level of usage of resources by students very low. In his study, he found that 57% of students sampled could not use a computer, that the use of database was poor, due to lack of awareness, lack of access to computers, insufficient training and the high cost of provision. From the foregoing, problems militating against the use of electronic resources could be outlined thus:

Acquisition cost

In the Nigerian context, the issue of acquisition of electronic information resources is not problem-free. This could be as a result of the poverty rate and economic meltdown, practically evident in every sector of the Nigerian economy; and the government's distress in financing projects in the society because these supposed monies have been carted away as a result of corruption that have eaten deep as a canker into the fabrics of the society. It is therefore obvious that most libraries in Nigeria are poor thus are not able to conveniently acquire electronic information resources for the use of their clients.

Maintenance cost

Unlike in the manual system, using electronic information resources in the Nigerian society entails high cost of maintenance of the facilities that are required for their use. For instance, the computer operator/engineer may need to create file backups, regularly update antivirus database, guide against power surge by the use of uninterrupted power supply (UPS) and stabilisers, etc otherwise, computer systems could crash and files lost at any time. Thus, the guiding against these eventualities lay great strain and demands on both human and financial resources of the economy.

Availability of electronic information resources gadgets and their spare parts

A times, the ready availability of the devices required for the use of electronic information resources and their spare parts pose to be more problematic than the very cost of their acquisition. In some cases, librarians and information experts may need to order these facilities and/or their spare parts from across Nigerian borders. This is also a distressing factor in the use of electronic information resources in Nigeria.

Erratic power supply

The devices that are required for the use of these resources require electricity to function, but in Nigeria electricity supply is epileptic and thus stands as a stumbling block to their by Nigerians. Even in some cases, when power generators are resorted to, the cost incurred is mind-blowing.

Lack of information retrieval skills for exploiting electronic resources

When access to information or materials depends on access to equipment, there will be problems for all individuals who cannot get to, or use, the necessary equipment. Similarly, for individuals to benefit from information in e-resources, they need to be able to know how to access them and be able to access them. There are also issues about what volume of information and teaching materials individuals can make use of. Most people welcome advice about what staff think are the most important or most useful materials for them to consult. Clearly, the more information and other materials that can be made available to individuals in a variety of ways, in a variety of environments, with advice about what to prioritise, the more helpful and accessible are those resources for all. Effective information retrieval skills can be demonstrated by: the ability to evaluate various bibliographic search strategies; the ability to select and justify the appropriate search techniques in order to carry out independent research, and the ability to critically evaluate search results.

Availability of experts

Electronic information resources gadgets are products of companies and individuals of high technologies so they require experts of high technologies as well for their manning and maintenance in the process of use. And since most of these high-tech companies are not found in Nigeria, in most cases many of the experts are not also readily available in Nigeria. This unavailability of experts hampers the rate of use of these resources.

The garbage in - garbage out phenomenon

This is one major feature of electronic information

resources. It is obvious that computers could easily spread error output when error input is made, compared with the manual system. This could also be a phobia of many Nigerians inhibiting the effective use of these materials. One obstacle to the use of a library's resources, and in particular its electronic resources, is that they are not seen as being straightforward. In contrast to an Internet search engine, where a single keyword search will usually result in thousands of hits, no matter what the topic, in the library, students have to choose a particular database and be more selective in the search words they use. Moreover, database subjects often overlap, with differences in dates, journal and subjects covered, and whether the material is full-text or not. In addition, the library may have a print subscription to a certain title that is not full-text electronically, or the title may be accessible full-text through another database than the one originally searched. Therefore, not only do students have to find the relevant citations, but they also have to know how to locate the article after that. This means juggling many screens, many technologies, multi-tasking electronic jobs, and of course, knowing where to look for all this necessary information. Lastly, there is the additional confusion that more and more library databases use Web-based technologies. Because the interface is seamless there does not seem to be a visible, on the screen, difference between Web-based library resources and general Web-based resources. All of the afore-mentioned also assumes the student is proficient in the use of computers. It is quite clear that searching for information has become "inexorably linked to computer technology" (Jacobson, 1991).

PROSPECTS OF ELECTRONIC INFORMATION RESOURCES USAGE IN NIGERIA

The use of electronic information resources in Nigeria is full of positive prospects. It is obvious from the way Nigerians get so attached to electronic resources gadgets such as GSM phones, computers, cyber cafés, TVs, VCD-, CD-, DVD-players, etc, that the use of electronic information resources will constantly or acceleratedly be on the increase. This view is supported by Bozimo (2010), when she opined that:

The use of technology will grow to fill the available capacity. Library information systems have the potential to provide access to tremendous amount of bibliographic and full text information to a large number of users. Many of who will operate in the library or remote areas. The success associated with introducing a new information system often leads to increased use of the system, and it is often difficult to estimate the increase in use. Thus, planning should be made to include expansion in the number of work stations and provision of high speed lines supporting external connectivity to end-users.

From the afore-mentioned excerpt, it could be deduced that convenience, success and sense of accomplishment that accompanies e-resources make it impossibly indispensable. Also, commenting on the prospects of electronic resources, Dadzie (2005) writes that electronic resources are invaluable research tools that complement the print – based resources, and possibly with time could even outdate the print formats. The advantages of electronic resources, according to her include: access to information that might be restricted to the user due to geographical location or finances, access to more current information, and provision of extensive links to additional resources related contents. She agrees that these advantages carve a positive future for electronic resources.

Furthermore, the importance and wide-ranging scope of electronic resources for general communication, information retrieval and instructional delivery to support teaching and research activities in tertiary educational institutions is acknowledged worldwide. Literature also shows that a number of relevant studies have been carried out on the use of e-resources by lecturers, research scholars and students, folks worldwide. General user opinion towards the use of electronic resources, in particular CD-ROM, has been positive, with individuals enjoying using these sources and finding relatively few problems while using them (Ray and Day, 2010). This is clearly confirmed in the case of a survey undertaken at Oakland University by Schultz and Salomon (1990) into students' satisfaction with CD-ROMs. The study according to Ray and Day (2010) found out that 83% of students surveyed felt that using this source saved them time, and found it relatively easy to use. Two thirds of those surveyed stated that if the CD-ROM was busy, they would wait for it to become free rather than use the print tool.

Studies have also been carried out on the use of electronic resources by teachers, students and research scholars of universities and research organizations. Seventy-eight percent (78%) of the respondents feel that the use of electronic resources has created high independency value on their research work, and they do not lack current article from these electronic resources (Madhusudhan, 2008).

In the Nigerian context, Okello-Obura and Magara (2008) investigated electronic information access and utilization at various academic libraries. He found out that of the 250 targeted students used for the study, 190 responded, giving a response rate of 76%. The study revealed that users derived a lot of benefits from electronic resources, gaining access to a wider range of information and improved academic performance as a result of access to quality information.

Jagboro (2003) had also emphasized the emerging reliance and attitude of users to electronic resources. In a study she conducted in some Nigerian Universities, it was found that 45.2% of respondents accessed electronic resources from cybercafés. Though this attitude, according to her is due to the proximity of cybercafés to user facilities.

In effect, all the studies reviewed so far are implemented on the assumption that uptake of electronic resources is highly desirable in that it leads to increased productivity of work, learning, teaching and research; thus electronic resources have come to stay and prosper.

In another perspective, young Nigerians are very spirited when it comes to information technology. They use their youthful strength in discovering phenomena that makes electronic resources indispensable in daily lives. Ray and Day (2010) supported this when they stated that:

Students entering higher education appear to have raised expectations about the capabilities of electronic resources. In some cases, they seem to think that there is a button they can press and it will write an essay for them.

This age is characterised by speed and accuracy; nobody wants to waste time anymore; people want whatever information at a push of a button. Thus, the advantages of electronic resources make them indispensable. With electronic resources, users could search more materials than when in print format.

Folks are now more sophisticated than their predecessors in using some of the basic functions of many electronic information systems. Both non-students and students use and like electronic resources, and most readily adopt them if the sources are perceived as convenient, relevant, and time-saving to their natural workflow. Experts in different subject disciplines (work fields) also have different usage patterns and preferences for electronic information resources.

Furthermore, another advantage that would make electronic resources usage increase in the future is its unlimited access both in time and space. Users could access more materials across the globe with the use of electronic resources in communication networks. This view is supported by Tiamiyu (2000) when he posited that:

Browsing large number of core journals is convenient with the use of electronic resources, especially for subject experts and for current awareness searching. Personal subscriptions to print-journals continue to decrease, so users rely more on electronic subscriptions subsidized by the library and on the Internet.

Valentine (1993) posited that individuals look for the fastest way that would lead to satisfactory results when doing research, going for electronic information sources first.

Ray and Day (2010) insinuated that there appears to be an emerging over reliance upon electronic information resources at the expense of the more traditional forms of information. In view of this, there exists debate over "access rather than holdings". This attitude amongst Nigerians may seem encouraging, considering the fact that electronic resources tend to bring about "access", regardless of time and space. Bozimo (2010) therefore lent credence to this when she concurred that "contemporarily, emphasis is shifting to *access* to information materials rather than *ownership*".

Jagboro (2003) is of the opinion that the prospects of e-resources could be outlined thus:

1) E-resources would be used unendingly in the classroom and lecture rooms of pre-primary, primary and secondary schools, and tertiary institutions respectively.
2) E-resources would likely be used to convert practically all manual system libraries to virtual libraries.
3) E-resources would be used by the Nigerian government to sensitise citizens of their programmes.
4) E-resources would be the backbone of communication.
4) E-resources would never replace print resources, though might put print resources to minimal use. This implies that paperless library would never be a reality but an illusion. This is supported by Spink (2003) when he concur that "even the e-journals, e-books, e-... are sometimes still printed for effective use".
5) E-resources would proliferate the academic, business, government, and all sectors of the Nigerian community.
6) There is even likely to be over-reliance upon e-resources.

Research questions

1) What are the problems militating against the use of electronic information resources in Nigerian academic libraries?
1) What are the prospects of electronic information resources usage in Nigerian academic libraries?

METHODOLOGY

Research design

In this study, a survey design is used and it is non- experimental.

Table 1. Academic libraries.

S/N	Academic libraries	Sample
1	University of Benin Library	20
2	University of Ibadan Library	20
3	University of Port-Harcourt	20
4	Delta State University Library	20
5	University of Abuja	20
Total		100

Population of the study

The population of this study includes all academic libraries in Nigeria.

Sample and sampling technique

The researcher randomly selected 20 subjects (both staff and users) each from five academic libraries for the study (Table 1).

Research instrument

The research instrument titled "Problems and Prospects of Electronic Information usage in Nigerian Academic Libraries (PPEIUN)" was designed by the researcher to generate data on the basis of the research questions formulated for this study. The questionnaire was made up of two sections, A and B respectively. The demographic variables on educational level and experience; and items on the main variables which were in line with the research questions formulated to guide the study.

Validity of the instrument

Two types of procedures were adopted by the researcher to establish the validity of the instrument. These include face and content validity.

Reliability of the Instrument

To ascertain the reliability of the instrument, the test-retest method was applied. The instrument was to a separate group of subject, and after a week's time, the same instrument was re-administered. It was found out that the responses remained the same. This showed that the instrument in reliable.

Administration of instrument

The research instrument was administered to respondents in person to the sampled academic libraries' patrons and staff by the researcher.

Method of data analysis

Simple percentage method was used to analyse the data gather with the instrument.

RESULTS

From Table 2, the respondents agreed that acquisition cost, maintenance cost, erratic power supply and lack of information retrieval skills for exploiting e-resources, are major problems militating against the use of e-resources in Nigerian academic libraries. This is shown in their "agree" responses of 65(65%), 73(73%), 95(95%) and 55(55%), respectively.

Also, the respondents do not see availability of electronic information resources gadgets and their spare parts, availability of experts and fear of spreading error input easily /speedily as problems militating against the use of e-resources in/by Nigerian academic libraries. This is evident in their "disagree" responses of 35(35%), 45(45%) and 23(23%), respectively.

From Table 3, the respondents agreed that E-resources would be used unendingly in lecture rooms; E-resources would likely be used to convert practically all manual academic libraries to virtual libraries; E-resources would never replace print resources, and that there is even likely to be over-reliance upon e-resources by Nigerian academic libraries. This is shown in the "agree" responses to the statements; 87(87%), 91(91%), 76(76%) and 56(56%), respectively.

DISCUSSION

The study has been able to ascertain that acquisition cost, maintenance cost, erratic power supply, and lack of information retrieval skills for exploiting e-resources, are major problems militating against the use of e-resources in Nigerian academic libraries. These findings are supported by Ali (2005) and Wills (1990) when they concur that a sizeable number of users are facing numerous problems while using electronic information resources, such as lack of knowledge about the resources, lack of trained staff and inadequate terminals; lack of strategic planning, adequate or reliable funding; lack of use of Internet to provide information services to users and a lack of consistent training for users in new ICT services; lack of information retrieval skills for exploiting electronic resources, thus making the level of usage of resources by students very low.

It was also found out that availability of electronic information resources gadgets and their spare parts, availability of experts and fear of spreading error input easily and speedily, are not problems militating against the use of e-resources in or by Nigerian academic libraries. Rather, prospectively, e-resources would be used unendingly in lecture rooms; e-resources would be

Table 2. The following are problems militating against the use of electronic information resources in Nigerian academic libraries.

Option	Agree (%)	Disagree (%)	Total (%)
Acquisition cost	65	35	100
Maintenance cost	73	25	100
Availability of electronic information resources gadgets and their spare parts	35	65	100
Erratic power supply	95	5	100
Lack of information retrieval skills for exploiting electronic resources	55	45	100
Availability of experts	45	55	100
Fear of spreading error input easily/speedily	23	77	100

Table 3. The following are prospects of electronic information resources in Nigerian academic libraries.

Option	Agree (%)	Disagree (%)	Total (%)
E-resources would be used unendingly in lecture rooms	87	13	100
E-resources would likely be used to convert practically all manual academic libraries to virtual libraries	91	9	100
E-resources would never replace print resources	76	24	100
There is even likely to be over-reliance upon e-resources by Nigerian academic libraries.	56	44	100

used to convert practically all manual academic libraries to virtual libraries; e-resources would never replace print resources, and that there is even likely to be over-reliance upon e-resources by Nigerian academic libraries. This discovery is supported by Bozimo (2010) when she stated that "the use of electronic resources will increase to fill the available capacity".

CONCLUSION AND RECOMMENDATIONS

E-resources usage in Nigeria is full of numerous bottlenecks. This notwithstanding, e-resources also have numerous positive prospects, not that there aren't any negative prospects but the positive outweighs the negative that the negative is so insignificant. It is therefore recommended that Nigerian governments and academic libraries at various levels should encourage and enhance the acquisition of skills required for the use of e-resources. Also, universities should instil in their students the concepts and importance of e-resources usage. These recommendations, if adopted, would put Nigeria in a significant position in the world globalisation trend in about three decades from now; this is because by then, every individual would have been an expert in handling e-resources for both individual and general advantage.

REFERENCES

Ali H (2005). The divide between virtual library and manual libraries, Warri: Jonakase Publishers.

Bozimo D (2010). Library Automation", Unpublished Lesson Note, Abraka: Department of Library and Information Science (LSE Unit), Faculty of Education, Delta State University.

Dadzie PS (2005). Electronic Resource: Access and usage at Ashesi University College, campus-wide Information Systems 22(5).

Jagboro KO (2003). A study of Internet usage in Nigerian Universityies: A case study of Obafemi Awolowo University, Ile-Ife, Nigeria", First Monday Vol. 8, No. 2. Retrieved 8th May, 2008 from: http://www.firstmonday.org

Madhusudhan M (2008). Use of UGC infonet-Journales by the Research Scholars of University of Delhi. Libr. Hi Tech., 26(3): 369-386.

Ray K, Day J (2010). Student attitudes towards electronic information resources", Inform. Res., 4: 2, October 1998. Retrieved 27th May, 2011 from: http://informationr.net/ir/4-2/paper54.html.

Schultz, K, Salomon, K (1990). "End-users' Response to CD-ROM", Libr. J., 1(1): 56-57.

Spink A (2003). Web search: Emerging patterns. Libr. Trends, 52(4): 299-306.

Tiamiyu MA (2000). Information technology in Nigerian federal agencies: Problems, impact and strategies. J. Inform. Sci., 26(4): 227-237.

Valentine B (1993). Undergraduate research behaviour: Using focus groups to generate theory. J. Acad. Librariansh., 19 (5): 300-304.

Publicly available information and the pricing of book built IPOs: Evidence from India

Neeta Jain[1]* and Anna Jain[2]

[1]Department of Management (Finance), NIMS University, Jaipur (Raj.), India.
[2]Department of Management (Finance), Centum Learning Centre, Jaipur (Raj.), India.

The pricing of initial public offering (IPO) plays a vital role for both the issuers and the investors. Therefore they also have a profound impact on the activities of primary and secondary capital markets. Extensive literature on pricing of IPOs has reported a significant mis-pricing across countries during different time periods. The present study analyzes the pricing of 207 book built IPOs listed on Bombay Stock Exchange (BSE) during the period from April 2004 to August 2009.The issuers provide rich information regarding their company and the issue pertaining to IPO before it gets listed. Therefore the study aims to find out how far the publicly available information about an IPO is affecting its pricing on the listing day. Furthermore the study identified the determinants of subscription pattern and opening returns on the listing day. It was found that different categories of investors do not subscribe independently. They instead look to the more informed investors to base their decisions. The results suggest that the issuers need to consider the impact of publicly available information before they decide the issue price.

Key words: IPO, Underpricing, overpricing, book building, subscription, market return, opening return.

INTRODUCTION

Financing is an imperative and major decision in any business organisation. The sources of finance thus become an important matter for any business. The sources of finance can be divided in two parts: Private sources and Public sources. Private sources are own wealth, earnings of the business, relatives, banks, financial institutions, etc. Public source is raising funds from the public. Going public is a very thoughtful decision for a company. Moreover, going public for the first time is an extraordinary event in any business. The first equity offering or issue by a company to the public is called initial public offering (IPO). On the event of IPO on the one side, the company reveals its value in the market and on the other side the market (investors) also decides the value of the company. Thus, determination of value of the company through determination of price of the IPO becomes a key aspect while going public. The international phenomenon is that valuation by the company differs from the valuation done by the market.

The valuation differs because these two players have opposite interests. The issuing firm wants to raise maximum funds from the market by selling the issue at maximum price while investors want to buy at least price. Moreover the effect of pricing of the initial public offerings is not limited to these two parties. The pricing of initial public offerings affects economy also. As public offering is a way of resource mobilisation from investors to business projects that implies the resource mobilisation from low growth opportunities to high growth opportunities. Therefore if issuing firms keep very high offering price then it discourages investors for buying the issue while if it is very low then it discourages the issuing firms because leaving money in the market in terms of low offer price is an indirect cost of fund raising for the company. Here, low and high price is the deviation from the true value of the issue. The true value of the share is determined by the secondary market forces on the first trading day.

Public offerings can be categorised into two broad categories: Initial Public offerings (hereafter, IPO) and Follow on Public offerings (FPOs). The pricing of the issue has different implication for these two kinds of

*Corresponding author. E-mail: jainneeta09@gmail.com.

public offerings. In case of IPO, investors have very little information regarding such companies, while they have good amount of information of companies issuing FPO. Similarly, IPO firms find it difficult to gauge market's perception on their IPO. Therefore the present study aims to empirically analyse the pricing of book built initial public offerings in India.

There are different methods of IPO pricing namely: Fixed price method, Book Building method, and Auction method. These methods differ on account of freedom given to the market to decide the price at which IPO is to be sold. In the fixed price method the issuer only decides the price of the issue without any involvement of the market or investors. In the book building method price is partially decided by the issuer and partially decided by the investors. While in the auction method the price is fully determined by the market. Therefore, theoretically the difference between market price and the price determined by the issuer is maximum in fixed price method and it is least in auction method.

If the price determined by the issuer is less than the price determined by the investors then it is called underpricing. High Underpricing of IPOs is unhealthy for three players: The IPO issuing firm, the Capital Market and the Economy. The Company loses the amount of funds which could have been raised if it was not underpriced. Thus high underpricing is a high indirect cost of fund raising for the issuing firms. Moreover high underpricing leads oversubscription and thereby high refunding cost for the issuing firm. Underpricing creates arbitrage activities in the capital market. For an economy it reduces the resource mobilisation because those companies which do not want or cannot afford leaving money on the table would not raise funds by initial public offerings. Thus underpricing becomes a problem for any country.

Now what happens if an IPO is overpriced? If issue is overpriced then investors will not buy the shares because market value of the issue is less than what they pay for buying it from the issuer. Therefore to avoid initial losses investors will not subscribe to the issue and company will not be able to sell the issue. Moreover, in India minimum ninety percent subscription of the offer is mandatory for getting listed on the stock exchange. In case of less than ninety percent subscription firms shall take the offering back. Thus overpricing will make loss to the investors who have bought the overpriced shares and the company gets listed. On the other hand if the issuing firm is unable to get minimum subscription then it will not get listed on the stock exchange and it will face a huge cost of calling back the issue and will not get listed and cannot raise funds. Thus underpricing and overpricing of IPO both are harmful.

In India SEBI (Securities and Exchange Board of India) makes certain disclosures mandatory for the IPO issuing companies. According to SEBI guidelines IPO issuing companies need to disclose certain information in the offer document. Moreover in the process of book building investors get a lot of information about the IPO issuing company. Therefore the present study aims to find out how publicly available information affects pricing in the book building method. Till now no study has been carried out on the said objective of present study. Thus the study fills the research gap and brings a contribution to the body of literature and practitioners.

In the present study we examine the pricing of IPOs in Indian capital market for the book built equity IPOs issued and listed between March 2004 and August 2009.

Review of literature on pricing of IPOs

Loughran et al. (1994) studied IPOs of several countries and found that underpricing is an international phenomenon but the degree of underpricing differs from country to country because each country has different binding regulations, contractual mechanisms, and the characteristics of the firms going public. In the said study the latest data (updated November, 2008) on 39 countries shows that still these countries are facing a problem of high average initial return. The given data shows that China is having the maximum average under-pricing of 164.5% during 1990-2005, in India it is 92.7% during 1990 to 2007 and in US it is 16.9% during 1960-2007. Thus It has been found that the Initial Public Offerings are underpriced worldwide (Loughran et al., 1994). There are many theoretical explanations to underpricing as well as it has been a favourite topic of empirical research for academicians across the world.

The underpricing and overpricing are the results of the difference between the price set by the investors and price set by the issuer. Therefore question arises: Why companies do not opt for auction method only? Sherman (2005) carried out a thorough analysis on trends of IPO pricing method across countries. The author reported that during 1980s, book building was being used by North America only, but by the end of 1990s it was a dominant method in Europe, Asia and Latin America. Fixed price method is being abandoned worldwide and it is being used only in smaller countries where retail investors are dominant. Auctions are used only where book building method has some regulatory restriction. The author, in contradiction to the popular belief found that auctions always do not lead to lower expected underpricing and that the issuers prefer book building regardless of the change in underpricing levels. The auction method has advantage if the investors are scattered and well informed about the issuing firm and industry. Auctions are not preferred where investors have to put efforts to learn about a new issue. The author mentions that the issuer incurs the cost of information acquisition from the investors in case of both auction method as well as book building method. But both the methods are different in the sense that in book building issuer has greater control over information expenditures than in auction. Moreover auction has high probability of under subscription and thereby lower expected proceeds. Book building allows the underwriter to coordinate the informed and uninformed investors and thereby ensuring enough investors to participate in the offering. In Indian capital market this advantage has different implications as the subscription information is available at every half an hour. Thus uninformed investors can follow informed investors' subscription pattern. The author reported one more advantage of discretionary power of the issuing firm in share allocation, which is not available in Indian regulatory framework of book building in India.

India is not the only country which is facing problem of underpricing. As Su (2004) studied 283 IPOs in China between January 1994 and December 1997 and found maximum underpricing of 692.60%, average underpricing of 129.36% and maximum overpricing of 36.64%.Thus IPOs' pricing is highly deviated from the true value. Further he concluded that firms with higher pre-IPO leverage are more underpriced .Moreover timing of offering also found to be important in China, if issue comes when the market fluctuations are high and market return are low surrounding an IPO then underpricing is higher. Thus underpricing differs with firm's capital structure and market conditions during an IPO.

Sehgal and Singh (2007) studied 438 IPOs in India between June 1992 and March 2006 and found that average underpricing during the study period is 101%, and maximum overpricing is 87.96%.They found that underpricing is not good for investors also because in the studied IPOs there is no relationship between initial return and long term return. That indicates that investors cannot get any signal from the initial return of IPOs, on long term performance of IPOs.

Sahoo and Rajib (2009) studied 43 IPOs during 2001-2005 and found average undervaluation of 46.63% and standard deviation of initial returns is 78.65% implying high degree of variations in initial returns. They found that the issues which are managed or priced by prestigious investment banks are less underpriced compared to issues priced by less prestigious investment banks. Because the prestigious investment banks are managing issues with the help of large number of syndicate members than their non prestigious counterparts. The said study also found that investment banks manage issues with larger size, old firms and higher promoters' holding in the post issue equity capital. This implies that investors in India can have a presumption about the listing day price on the basis of type of investment bank for a specific issue. Thus in India issue characteristics contributed to the degree of underpricing.

Kohli (2009) studied 499 IPOs from April 1994 to March 2006 and found that stock markets in India suffered from the excessive optimism and poor valuation because he found that high prices of new issues are not related with their future profitability and growth in the sample. Pande and Vaidyanathan (2009) studied 55 book built IPOs listed between 26th March 2004 to 31st October 2006. Average underpricing in the sample was 22.62%, maximum underpricing 82.50% and maximum overpricing was 33.40%. They found that issues with offer price towards upper end of the offer price band are more underpriced as compared to issues which are priced towards the lower end of the offer price band and listing delay is positively related with underpricing.

A recent study on IPO underpricing by Deb (2009) found out the evidence of on average underpricing in India during 2001 to 2009 for a sample size of 187 IPOs. Moreover the author found that in the aftermarket short run investors are not getting any excess return on mispriced issues. It shows that underpricing does not bring consistent benefits to investors also.

Thus from the prior research it is obvious that IPO underpricing is higher for fixed price issues than for book built IPOs. However on the other hand researches on book built IPOs' pricing still indicate high underpricing or overpricing. Therefore still pricing of IPO is a matter of research to get it fairly priced.

Regulatory framework for IPO pricing in Indian capital markets

Before May 1992 as per the Capital Issue (Control) Act, 1947, the office of Controller of Capital Issue (CCI) had full control over the pricing of new issues in India. In May 1992 CCI was abolished and Securities and Exchange Board of India (SEBI) was formed under the SEBI Act 1992. During the period 1992 to 1999 issuers were free to determine the issue price on the basis of own discretion .This method of free and fixed price suffered from high overpricing and underpricing because it was difficult for the issuer to decide appropriate price without any involvement of the market. Therefore book building method was introduced in October 1995 on the recommendation of an expert committee under the chairmanship of Mr. Y H Malegram appointed by SEBI. SEBI guidelines, 1995 define book-building as "a process undertaken by which a demand for the securities proposed to be issued by a body of corporate is elicited and built up and the price for such securities is assessed for the determination of the quantum of such securities to be issued by means of a notice, circular, advertisement, document or information memoranda or offer document". Thus book building is a process of determining price and gauging the market demand on the basis of bids received from the investors. The development of book building method in India has gone through many amendments in the guidelines. The first IPO through book building route was Hughes Software Systems Limited in September 1999. Though fixed price route is still available to the issuers, in the study period book built IPOs are more than fixed price issue. As Fixed price issues are around 25%

Table 1. Price discovery.

Bid quantity	Bid price (Rs)	Cumulative quantity	Subscription (%)
1000	40	1000	16.67
1500	39	2500	50.00
2000	38	4500	100.00
2500	37	7000	166.67
3000	36	10,000	250.00

of the total IPOs in the study period. Thus in India book building method of IPO pricing dominates the fixed price method.

Process of IPO pricing through book building

In book building mechanism price determination has a long process. In India book building starts with a price band decided by the issuer in consultant with the Book Running Lead Manager (BRLM). As per the SEBI rule the price band's upper limit should not be more than 120% of lower limit of the band. For instance if lower band is Rs. 100 then upper band would not be more than Rs. 120.But the issuer has freedom of deciding the upper band between 100 and 120 in the given example. If issuer decides price below than Rs.120 then it is the underpricing in the first phase of pricing. Suppose issuer decides upper end of Rs. 110. Then maximum permissible upper end is Rs. 120 and maximum upper end actually used is Rs. 110. Then First underpricing is the percentage difference between these two upper ends. It is [(120-110)/120]*100 = 8.33%. After deciding the price band issuer opens price band to the investors to gauge the market demand on various prices within the band. The permitted period for subscription is 3 to 7 working days and extendable by 3 days in case of any price revision. On the basis of bids received during subscription period issuer decides the maximum of the received prices where the issue is fully sold.

Illustration of book building and price discovery process

Bidders can bid at any price within the given price band. For instance, suppose a price band of Rs. 36 to Rs. 40 per share, issue size of 4,500 equity shares and receipt of five bids from bidders, details of which are shown in the Table 1.

The price discovery is a function of demand at various prices. The highest price at which the issuer is able to sell the desired number of shares is the price at which the book cuts off, that is, Rs. 38 in the above example. The issuer, in consultation with the Book Running Lead manager. finalizes the issue price at or below such cut off price, that is, at or below Rs. 38.

If this price decided on the basis of bids is less than the upper end of the price band actually used then it is underpricing in the second phase of pricing. The percentage difference between the actual upper end and the offer price is the underpricing. For instance, if actual upper end is 110 in the given example and the offer price is Rs. 105 then underpricing is [(110-105)/110]*100= 4.54%. The allocation of the issue is done within 15 days after closure of the issue. The bidding status during the subscription period is available on BSE/NSE websites on consolidated basis and on investors' category wise also.

The issued share gets listed on the exchange(s) within 3 weeks from the closure of the issue. The closing price on the listing day is considered as true value of the share because it is an equilibrium price in the open market .Therefore if on the listing day closing price is more than the maximum permissible upper end of the issue then it is called market underpricing of the share. If the closing price on the listing day is Rs. 125 then underpricing is [(125-120)/120]*100 = 4.17%. Thus first underpricing is done by the issuer while second pre-listing underpricing is partially controllable by the issuer because it depends on market demand/bids received from the investors and then a third type of underpricing is totally market determined excluding the underpricing done by the issuer. Now the total actual underpricing done by the issuer, investors and the market can be defined as [(125-105)/105*100] =19.05%.

The first attempt in bringing out the concept of three phases of underpricing of book built IPOs in India was by Khurshed et al. (2009).The present study aims to find out the impact of publicly available information on the pricing of book built IPOs.

The minimum allocation proportion of the issued shares into three categories of investors is regulated by the SEBI rule. The minimum 15% of net offer to public is to be allocated to retail investors, 35% to non institutional investors and 50% to qualified institutional investors. The allotment of shares to each category is done on the basis of these proportions.

Publicly available information

The following study variables are given in the sequence of availability of information to the investors:

1. Age of the firm: The period between incorporation date to listing date of the firm. Higher age shows long operating history of the firm therefore it gives good indication in the market. Therefore we assume that the investors give high value to an old firm's IPO than a young firm.
2. Issue Size: Issue size is defined as the number of shares offered through the offer document. The issue size

indicates supply of the shares therefore if supply is high then the price in the secondary market on the listing day would remain lower and hence market underpricing should be less if issue size is large.

3. Promoters' Holding: It is defined as percentage of promoters' holding in the post issue equity of the company. As per the SEBI regulation 20% of the post issue equity is mandatory for the promoters. This 20% holding has lock-in period of 3 years and promoters' holding in excess of minimum promoters' contribution has lock-in period of one year. Leland and Pyle (1977) argued that promoters' holding indicates issuer's willingness to invest in the project and thereby information about the future profitability of the project. Therefore high promoters' holding conveys good quality of the project.

4. Pre-IPO Leverage: It is defined as proportion of total debt in the total asset before IPO. The latest data on leverage available in the offer document was taken. Ross (1977) argued that high leverage indicates high financial distress costs, Jensen and Meckling (1976) stated that high leverage causes high agency costs and Myers and Majluf (1984) developed a model of capital structure in which lower profitable firms go for high leverage because highly profitable firms have enough internal funds to finance. Thus as per the capital structure theories high leverage does not convey good signal in the market.

5. Index Return: It is defined as average daily return on Sensex 30 days before an IPO opening. It shows the market condition surrounding IPO. If index return is high then market is highly attractive for investors. Therefore being highly optimism in good market investors gives high value to the issue in terms of high price in the secondary market.

6. Index Volatility: It is standard deviation of daily returns on Sensex 30 trading days before an IPO opening. It is an indicator of uncertainty/fluctuations in the market surrounding a new IPO. If market is highly fluctuating then the IPO gets less value in the market.

7. Subscription: It is number of times issue subscribed. It is defined as number of shares applied for divided by number of shares offered. It indicates high demand of the issue therefore high price in the secondary market can be expected if an IPO is highly subscribed.

In India as per SEBI regulations investors of IPO are categorised into 3 categories. Qualified Institutional Buyers (QIBs), Non Institutional Investors (NIIs) and Retail Individual Investors (RIIs).QIBs are institutional investors, NII is an individual investing more than Rs. 100,000 in the issue and RII an individual who can invest up to Rs. 100,000. The allocation of issue to these categories is fixed by SEBI. As not more than 50% of net offer to the public shall be allocated for QIBs, not less than 15% of net offer to the public shall be allocated to NIIs and not less than 35% of net offer to the public shall be available for RIIs, as bigger investors are supposed to be more informed about the issue than smaller investors. Therefore it is possible that QIBs are more informed than NIIs and RIIs and NIIs are more informed than RIIs. Thereby NIIs subscription may follow to subscription pattern of QIBs and RIIs subscription pattern may follow to NIIs subscription.

8. Listing delay: It is number of days between offer closing day and listing day. As the listing delay increases information dissemination about the IPO increases, therefore its impact on listing day price can be expected.

9. Opening return: It is defined as positive difference between opening price on the listing day and the offer price relative to offer price. This also can be used by the investors as signal of higher initial return and they become more optimistic about the issue till the closing on the listing day.

$[(OP_1 – OP_0)/OP_0*100]$

OP_1 = Opening price on listing day, OP_0 = Offer Price

After adjusting it for market return between offer closing and listing day, the formula is:

Market Return = $[(OS_1 - OS_0)/OS_0*100]$

Where, OS_1 = Opening Sensex on the listing day, OS_0 = Opening Sensex on the offer closing day.

Market Adjusted Opening return (MAOP) = Opening Return – Market Return

METHODOLOGY

Hypotheses

As per the research objectives of the study, the null hypotheses which are being tested in the study are given below:

H_1: The publicly available information does not affect the pricing of IPOs.
H_2: All the three categories of investors are equally informed about the issue and hence subscribe independently.

These hypotheses will provide us with a certain way to achieve the objectives of the study.

Materials and data

This study consists sample size of 207 book built equity IPOs listed on Bombay Stock Exchange (BSE) between April 2004 to August 2009 (Table 2). The sample proportion in the population is around 94%.

The data used in the study were collected from various authentic sources. The sources of data on IPOs which are available to the investors were taken for collecting the data for this study. The study aims to find out how far the publicly available information determines the degree of underpricing.

The source of data on price band, offer price, opening price on the listing day, closing price on the listing day, closing Sensex on the offer closing day and closing Sensex on the listing day, time delay between offer closing day and listing day is website of BSE, data on total assets, total loans, promoters' holding in the post issue equity, issue size, age of the firm were taken from the final offer documents filed with ROC/SEBI by the issuing firms available on website of Securities and Exchange Board of India (SEBI), data

Table 2. Sample size of 207 book built equity IPOs listed on Bombay Stock Exchange (BSE) between April 2004 to August 2009

Year (Financial year)	IPOs	Amount (Rs Crore)	Book built sample IPOs
2004 to 2005	23	13,749	13
2005 to 2006	79	10,936	44
2006 to 2007	77	28,504	64
2007 to 2008	85	42,595	64
2008 to 2009	21	2,082	18
2009 to 2010 (April to Aug.)	7	9,664	
Total Book built IPOs	292-72(fixed price issues) = 220		207 (94.09%)

Source: SEBI Bulletin (September, 2009) and Website of BSE.

on subscription was collected from the Basis of Allotment documents available on web. Data on index return and index volatility before one month of IPO was taken from Prowess a CMIE database, though CMIE database is not available to all the investors but we assume that these data indicates market conditions surrounding IPO which is known to the investors.

Formulae of the variables used in the study

Thus underpricing in the above discussed book building process can be broken into the following categories:

First pre-Listing underpricing (Price band_ UP)% = [(MAXP-MAXA)/MAXP*100]

Second pre-Listing underpricing (Offer Price_ UP)% = [(MAXA-OP)/MAXA*100]

Where, MXAP = Maximum Permissible Price, MAXA =Maximum Actual Price and OP =Offer Price.

Market underpricing (Market _UP) % = [CP-MAXP)/MAXP*100]

Where, MXAP = Maximum Permissible Price, MAXA =Maximum Actual Price and CP= Closing Price

Adjusted Market_UP(%) = (Market_UP) – (Market Return)

Or

[CP-MAXP)/MAXP*100] - [(CS_1-CS_0)/CS_0]*100

Where, CS_1 = Closing Sensex on the listing day, CS_0 = Closing Sensex on the offer closing day.

Initial Return (%) = [(CP_1-OP_0)/OP_0]*100

Where, CP_1=closing price on the listing day and OP_0 =offer price of the share

These returns after adjusting with the market returns are the market adjusted initial return as

Adjusted Initial Return= Initial Return – Market Return.

Market Return (%) = [(CS_1-CS_0)/CS_0]*100

Where, CS_1 = Closing Sensex on the listing day, CS_0 = closing Sensex on the offer closing day.

Market Adjusted Opening Return (MAOR)% = [{OP_1-OP_0)/ OP_0}*100] - [{OS_1-OS_0)/ OS_0}*100]

Where, OP_1 = listing price or opening price on the listing day, OP_0= offer price, OS_1 = Opening Sensex on the listing day and OS_0 = Opening Sensex on the offer closing day.

Natural logarithm transformation of the variables

To get the normality of the variables natural logarithm of the variables were taken. Normal curves before and after natural logarithm can be seen in the Histograms with normal curve in the Appendices (Figure 1A).

In Adjusted Market_UP = ln (CP/MAXP) –(CS_1/CS_0)
In Adjusted Initial Return = ln (CP/OP) – (CS_1/CS_0)
In MAOR =ln (OP_1/OP_0) – (OS_1/OS_0)
In Issue Size
In Index Volatility
In Total Subscription
In QIBs, In NIIs, In RIIs

Models used in the empirical analyses

Determinants of market underpricing

In the model market underpricing adjusted for market return depends on the variables available at the time of listing day closing.

Model 1(a)

Ln Adjusted market _UP = β_0 + β_1 Price band_UP + β_2 Offer price_UP + β_3 Age+ β_4 Listing delay+ β_5 ln Issue size + β_6 Index return + β_7 ln Index volatility + β_8 Leverage + β_9 Promoters' holding + β_{10} ln Subscription .

Model 1(b)

Ln Adjusted market _UP = β_0 + β_1 Price band_UP + β_2 Offer price_UP + β_3 Age+ β_4 Listing delay+ β_5 ln Issue size + β_6 Index return + β_7 ln Index volatility + β_8 Leverage + β_9 Promoters' holding + β_{10} ln MAOR.

Table 3. Minimum, maximum, mean and standard deviation for sample of 207 book built IPOs in India during 2004 to 2009.

	Minimum	Maximum	Mean	Std. deviation
Adjusted Total_UP (%)	-36.60	334.93	**28.17**	49.74
Price band_UP (%)	0.00	13.81	4.62	3.66
Offer Price_UP (%)	0.00	16.67	2.17	4.47
Adjusted Market_UP (%)	-38.42	302.34	20.04	47.96
QIBs (No. of times)	0.02	252376.00	1247.17	17539.43
NIIs (No. of times)	0.05	306.63	33.77	50.14
RIIs (No. of times)	0.13	125929.00	647.96	8758.41
Age (years)	0.08	99.83	15.60	13.35
Listing delay (Days)	14.00	34.00	19.66	2.62
Issue size (Lakh Shares)	5.00	8658.30	266.06	818.84
Total subscription (No. of times)	0.91	145.57	22.98	28.24
Index return (%)	-20.15	23.72	2.96	7.36
Index volatility (%)	0.29	16.79	2.42	2.67
Leverage (%)	0.00	89.39	32.14	20.77
Promoters Holding (%)	22.57	92.45	60.23	15.84
Valid N (listwise)	207.00			

Determinants of opening return on listing day

Model 2

In the model market adjusted opening return depends on the variables available at the time of issue opening.

Ln Market adjusted opening return(MAOR) = $\beta_0 + \beta_1$ Price band_UP + β_2 Offer price_UP + β_3 Age+ β_4 Listing delay+ β_5 ln Issue size + $\beta_6$ln Subscription + β_7 Index return + β_8 ln Index volatility + β_9 Leverage + β_{10} Promoters' holding .

Determinants of subscription pattern

Model 3(a)

We regress QIBs subscription on the information available at the time of their subscription.

Ln Qualified Institutional Buyers(QIBs) = $\beta_0 + \beta_1$ Price band_UP + β_2 Age+ β_3 ln Issue size + β_4 Index return + β_5 ln Index volatility + β_6 Leverage + β_7 Promoters' holding .

Model 3(b)

In the model specification NIIs subscription depends on the information available at the time of their subscription.

Ln Non Institutional Investors(NIIs) = $\beta_0 + \beta_1$ Price band_UP + β_2 Age+ β_3 ln Issue size + β_4 Index return + β_5 ln Index volatility + β_6 Leverage + β_7 Promoters' holding + β_8 ln QIBs.

Model 3(c)

In the model specification RIIs subscription depends on the information available at the time of their subscription.

Ln Retail Individual Investors(RIIs) = $\beta_0 + \beta_1$ Price band_UP + β_2 Age+ β_3 ln Issue size + β_4 Index return + β_5 ln Index volatility + β_6 Leverage + β_7 Promoters' holding + β_8 ln QIBs + β_9 ln NII.

RESULTS AND ANALYSES

This chapter covers data analysis and interpretations of empirical results.

Descriptive statistics

Table 3 shows the minimum, maximum, mean and standard deviation for the whole sample of 207 book built IPOs in India during 2004 to 2009. The average adjusted initial return is 28.17% and maximum is 335% that implies that on average in India issuers left 28% of money which could have been raised if issues would have been priced at true value. Higher Standard deviation 49.74% indicates larger variance in underpricing, which can also be seen in the wide range of minimum and maximum. The minimum of adjusted initial return is -36.60 which shows overpricing of the issue that is, issuers could raise up to 37% in excess from the market than the true value of the issue. It discourages the investors to invest in IPOs.

In the sample 138 IPOs are underpriced and 69 IPOs are overpriced, which implies that either issuers left money on the table or investors faced the initial losses on their investments in IPOs. The total underpricing dissected into three categories as discussed in the section of book building process. By seeing maximum 14% price band_UP it can be concluded that on average underpricing is being done by the issuers also. In the sample 178 IPOs have positive price band_UP and only 29 issuers used MAXA=MAXP. Thus 86% of the issuers decided MAXA<MAXP.

The maximum of offer price_UP shows that issuers

Table 4. Regression analysis (Determinants of market underpricing).

In Adjusted Market_UP	Model 1 (a)			Model 1(b)		
	B	p-value	VIF	B	p-value	VIF
Constant	-0.05	0.781	-	-0.027	0.884	-
Price Band_ UP (%)	-0.01	0.234	1.25	-0.007	0.22	1.25
Offer Price_UP (%)	-0.02	0*	1.32	-0.021	0*	1.352
Age (years)	0.00	0.879	1.08	0.001	0.419	1.087
Listing delay (Days)	0.01	0.319	1.09	0.009	0.212	1.096
In Issue size	-0.01	0.474	1.14	-0.024	0.169	1.166
Index return (%)	0.00	0.357	1.51	-0.002	0.534	1.489
In Index volatility	0.01	0.618	1.44	0.011	0.656	1.44
Leverage (%)	0.00	0.379	1.13	-0.001	0.585	1.145
Promoters holding (%)	0.00	0.334	1.13	6.90E-05	0.956	1.129
In subscription	0.12	0*	1.33			
In MAOR	-	-	-	0.846	0*	1.361
	R^2 = 42.5% F = 14.490(0.000) df =196			R^2 = 42% F = 14.118(0.000) df = 196		

*Significant at 1 % level.

decided offer price below the MAXA up to 17%. In the sample 187 IPOs 'offer price was set below to MAXA and only 20 IPOs' offer price was equal to MAXA.

It can be seen that maximum adjusted market_UP is 302.34 % which is very high than the 14 and 17% of price band_UP and offer price_UP. In the sample 125 issues have positive adjusted market_UP and 82 issues having negative adjusted market _UP indicates that IPOs are either underpriced or overpriced in the market. But underpriced IPOs are more than overpriced IPOs. Average of adjusted market_UP also showing underpricing of around 20%. Thus on average still problem of underpricing is more serious than overpricing. If we compare the subscription pattern of different investor categories then the mean subscription is highest for QIBs and it is minimum for RIIs. The other variables like age, issue size, subscription, leverage and promoters' holding are having a wide spread between minimum and maximum. It indicates a large variance between the issues or issues differ extensively on their characteristics. Therefore any analysis will be practical by considering these publicly available information also.

Determinants of market underpricing

In Appendix, Table 1A presents bivariate correlation among variables used in the model. It shows high correlation between opening return and subscription. To avoid the multi-collinearity problem in the model separate models for each of these two variables were taken.

In Table 4 models 1(a) and (b) aimed to find out the determinants of adjusted Market_UP. These models consider the information that is available to investors at the time of closing on the listing day. Model 1(a) considers total subscription with other variables excluding opening return while model 1(b) considers opening return with other variables excluding total subscription. The multiple regression result of model 1(a) and (b) shows that adjusted opening return, offer price_UP and total subscription are significant variables of adjusted market underpricing. The negative sign of coefficient of offer price_ UP indicates that market underpricing is high for those IPOs which have offer price close to upper end. This may be attributed to good quality perception by the investors if offer price is high and therefore theses IPOs are highly valued in secondary market on the listing day. The positive sign of subscription coefficient indicates that as total subscription increases market underpricing increases. The positive sign of opening return coefficient indicates that issues having higher return on opening are more underpriced in the market than IPOs having low opening return. Among the significant variables all three variables are not directly controllable. But if we can find out features of the firm/IPOs which are more having high return on opening, offer price closer to upper end and high total subscription then those findings may help in controlling market underpricing.

Determinants of opening returns on listing day

Table 5 shows that offer price UP, age and total subscription are significant determinants of opening return. Opening return is high for the IPOs with offer price close to upper end of the price band. Opening return is

Table 5. Regression analysis (Determinants of opening returns on listing day): Model 2.

ln Market Adjusted Opening Return (MAOR)	B	p-value	VIF
Constant	0.093	0.339	
Price Band_UP(%)	0.001	0.738	1.25
Offer Price_UP(%)	-0.007	0.005	1.32
Age (years)	-0.001	0.074	1.08
listing delay (Days)	-0.003	0.411	1.09
ln Issue size	0.018	0.041	1.14
ln subscription	0.081	0.000	1.33
Index return (%)	0.001	0.516	1.52
ln Index volatility	-0.010	0.447	1.44
Leverage (%)	-0.001	0.099	1.13
Promoters Holding (%)	-0.001	0.088	1.13

R^2 = 53.2%; R^2 = 53.2%; F = 22.287 (0.000).

high for large issues than for smaller issues. It is high for the firms with high subscription because it indicates high demand of the issue. These three variables explain around 53% of the variance in opening return.

Thus subscription is a significant variable of opening returns also therefore now we go for analysing determinants of subscription for different categories of investors.

Determinants of subscription

In Appendix: Table A2 shows that subscription of three categories of investors is having different correlation (sign as well as degree) with other characteristics of the offerings therefore we expect different determinants of each category. As discussed QIBs are bigger investors than other two categories and NIIs are bigger investors than RIIs.

Determinants of QIBs' subscription

Table 6 shows that subscription of QIBs significantly depends on index return, index volatility, leverage and promoters' holding. The positive sign of index return coefficient implies that QIBs subscribe more when market return surrounding IPO is high. The negative coefficient of index volatility implies that QIBs subscribe less if index returns are highly fluctuating surrounding IPO. The negative sign of leverage coefficient implies increase in QIBs subscription with any decreases in leverage. Similarly positive sign of promoters' holding coefficient indicates increase in QIBs' subscription with an increase in promoters' holding.

Thus firms with higher promoters holding, low leverage get more subscription from the QIBs than the firms with low promoters' holding and high leverage. Similarly issues in the time of high market return and less fluctuations in the market returns get high QIBs subscription.

Determinants of NIIs' subscription

Table 7 shows that NIIs subscription depends on subscription of QIBs and promoters' holding. Surprisingly, in contrast to QIBs, subscription, NIIs subscription is negatively related with promoters' holding. Interestingly, NIIs subscription increases with an increase in QIBs' subscription because QIBs are more informed than NIIs, therefore they follow more informed investors.

Determinants of RIIs' subscription

In Appendix; Table A2 correlation matrix shows high correlation between NIIs and QIBs subscription, therefore stepwise regression can give a better model fit.

The result of stepwise regression in Table 8 shows that RIIs subscription depends on subscription of NIIs, index return and issue size. As NIIs subscription increases, RIIs subscription increases. And like QIBs, RIIs also subscribes more when market return is high. For small issues RIIs subscribes more .This is possible because in small issues investors expect high initial return due to low supply. Independent Variables which are excluded due to low partial correlation with dependent variable (RIIs) are given in (Appendix: Table A3).

DISCUSSION

1. Empirical results of the study show that when market return is high and less fluctuating then QIBs and RIIs subscription in an IPO increases and thereby results in high closing price on listing day. Therefore high market underpricing can be seen on any IPO if market conditions are good.
2. Pre-IPO leverage has negative impact on QIBs subscription. If it is high then QIBs subscription gets reduced and thereby market underpricing is lower in terms of lower closing price on listing day.
3. Promoters' holding has positive impact on QIBs' subscription and negative on NIIs subscription. With promoters' holding QIBs subscription increases while NIIs decreases.
4. Issue size has negative impact on RIIs subscription but it has positive impact on opening return. NIIs follow to QIBs and RIIs follow to NIIs subscription pattern. Therefore null hypothesis which says investors subscribe independently is rejected.
5. If offer price is close to upper end of the price band actually used (MAXA) then market under-pricing is high it implies that investors value high those firms which decide offer price close to upper end of the price band.

The finding of significant variables implies that the publicly

Table 6. Determinants of QIBs' subscription: Model 3 (a).

Dependent : ln QIBs	B	p value	VIF
Constant	0.872	0.211	
Price Band_UP (%)	0.030	0.405	1.179
Age (years)	0.005	0.559	1.041
ln Issue size	0.139	0.215	1.133
Index return (%)	0.056	0.004	1.355
ln Index volatility	-0.388	0.016	1.395
Leverage (%)	-0.013	0.044	1.086
Promoters holding (%)	0.016	0.044	1.071

R^2 = 16%; F = 5.452 (0.000); df = 199.

Table 7. Determinants of NIIs' subscription: Model 3 (b).

Dependent : ln NIIs	B	p value	VIF
Constant	1.45	0.012	
ln Price Band_UP	0.030	0.308	1.18
Age	-0.001	0.868	1.04
ln Issue size	0.055	0.551	1.14
Index return (%)	0.015	0.362	1.41
ln Index volatility	-0.100	0.450	1.44
Leverage (%)	-0.007	0.180	1.11
Promoters holding (%)	-0.016	0.014	1.09
ln QIB	0.682	0.000	1.19

R^2 = 48.6%; F = 23.381(0.000); df =198.

Table 8. Stepwise Regression model: Model 3(c).

Dependent variable :- ln RIIs				
Model		**B**	**p value**	**VIF**
1	Constant	0.39	0.001	
	ln NII	0.63	0.000	1.00
2	Constant	0.36	0.002	
	ln NII	0.59	0.000	1.07
	Index return (%)	0.04	0.000	1.07
3	Constant	1.09	0.000	
	ln NII	0.59	0.000	1.08
	Index return (%)	0.04	0.000	1.07
	ln Issue size	-0.17	0.009	1.01

Model	R^2	Adjusted R^2	df	F	Sig.
1	0.551	0.549	205	251.744	0.000[a]
2	0.584	0.581	204	143.136	0.000[b]
3	0.598	0.592	203	100.478	0.000[c]

available information of an IPO affects its pricing. The information which has significant affect on pricing of an IPO is promoters' holding, pre-IPO leverage, Subscription pattern of informed investors and size of the issue. Thus findings entail rejection of second null hypo-thesis which argues that publicly available information does not affect pricing of IPOs.

Conclusion

Initial public offerings are important source of corporate financing. It is used worldwide as a source of financing. The phenomenon of pricing and use of book building method is also not new and is widely used. However its application differs from country to country. Moreover in one market with the same method issues are priced differently. This kind of situation made us to search out the reasons of it. This study found that pricing in book built IPOs in India is inclined more towards underpricing. Book building has three phases of pricing in which it is found that on average issuers are also underpricing. But this study found that underpricing is high in the third phase of pricing where issue is priced in secondary market.

The empirical analysis found that publicly available information is making sense in Indian capital market. Therefore after disclose of the information its impact should also be considered. Issuers should decide the price with the prediction of impact of publicly available information. As underpricing harms to issuers and in long term to investors also while overpricing harms investors and in long term to issuers also when they come again in the market for follow on offerings. Therefore for win-win situation IPOs should be priced fairly.

The present study leaves immense scope for further studies which can be carried out by industry wise analysis, comparing with fixed price issues and searching some more important variables explaining market underpricing. It leaves the scope to find out why issuers decide price band below maximum permissible limit and the offer price below upper end of the price band actually decided. In the literature no study was carried out to find out the relevance of publicly available information and its impact on the pricing, thus present study bridges this research gap.

REFERENCES

Deb SG (2009). Some insights into IPO underpricing in India.Vilakshan 6(2):1-14.

Jensen MW, Meckling H (1976).Theory of the firm: Managerial behavior, agency costs and ownership structure. J. Financial Econ. 3(4):305-360.

Khurshed A, Pande A, Ajai KS (2009). A dissection of bookbuilt IPOs: Subscriptions, Undrepricing and Initial Returns. March, University of Manchester. Available at SSRN: http://ssrn.com/abstract=136191

Kohli V (2009). Do stock markets allocate resources efficiently? An examination of initial public offerings. Econ. Poll. Weekly 44(33):63-72.

Leland HE, David HP (1977). Informational asymmetries, financial structure, and financial intermediation. J. Financial 32(2):371-387.

Loughran Tim, Jay RR, Kristian R (1994). .Initial public offerings: International insights. Pacific-Basin-Finance J. 2: 165-199. June

Myers SC, Nicholas SM (1984).Corporate financing and investment decisions when firms have information that investors do not have. J. Financial Econ. 13(2):187-221.

Pande A, Vaidyanathan R (2009). Determinants of IPO underpricing in the National Stock Exchange of India. ICFAI J. Appl. Financial 15(1):14-30.

Ross SA (1977). The determination of financial structure: The incentive-signalling approach. Bell J. Econ. 8(1):23-40.

Sahoo S, Prabina R (2009). Investment bank prestige and IPO underpticing: An empirical study.*IIMB* Mgt. Rev. 21(3):189-204.

Sehgal S, Balwinder S (2007). The Initial and Aftermarket Performance of Indian IPOs. ICFAI J. Appl. Financial 13(11):16-36.

Sherman AE (2005). Global trends in IPO method: Book building versus auctions with endogenous entry. J. Financial Econ. 78(3):615-649.

Su D (2004). Leverage, insider ownership, and the underpricing of IPOs in China. J. Int. Financial Markets, Institutions and Money 14(1):37-54.

Websites

http://www.bseindia.com/
http://www.sebi.gov.in/
http://www.cmlinks.com/moneypore/ipo/ba.asp

APPENDICES

Table 1A. Correlation analysis (a)

	In adjusted Market_UP	Price band_UP (%)	Offer price_UP (%)	Age (years)	listing delay(Days)	In Issue size	In subscription	Index return (%)	In Index volatility	Leverage (%)	Promoters Holding (%)	Ln MAOR
In adjusted Market_ UP	1	0.034	-0.471(**)	0.065	0.078	-0.020	0.579(**)	0.161(*)	-0.113	-0.173(*)	-0.080	0.582(**)
Price band_UP(%)		1	-0.177(*)	-0.077	0.046	-0.261(**)	0.023	-0.174(*)	-0.247(**)	-0.206(**)	0.025	-0.0035
Offer price_UP(%)		1		-0.131	-0.051	0.023	-0.397(**)	-0.238(**)	-0.146(*)	0.167(*)	0.077	-0.421(**)
Age(years)		1			0.101	0.151*	0.092	0.083	0.014	0.017	0.120	-0.0011
Listing delay(Days)			1			0.004	0.002	0.107	0.035	-0.095	-0.185(**)	-0.014
In Issue Size			1				.068	0.049	-0.089	0.157(*)	0.168(*)	0.103
In Subscription				1				0.323(**)	-0.262(**)	-0.121	0.059	0.688(**)
Index Return (%)				1					-0.506(**)	0.075	0.027	0.273(**)
In Index Volatility					1					-0.101	-0.021	-0.235(**)
Leverage (%)					1						0.159(*)	-0.176(*)
Promoters Holding (%)											1	-0.063
Ln MAOR						..						1

** Correlation is significant at the 0.01 level (2-tailed); * Correlation is significant at the 0.05 level (2-tailed); a List wise N=207.

Table A2. Regression analysis (Determinants of QIBs' subscription).

	Price band_UP (%)	Age	In Issue size	Index return (%)	In Index volatility	Leverage (%)	Promoters Holding (%)	In QIB	In NII	In RIIs
Price band_UP (%)	1	-0.077	-0.261(**)	-0.174(*)	0.244(**)	-0.206(**)	0.025	-0.019	0.027	0.027
Age	1		0.151(*)	0.083	-0.060	0.017	0.120	0.091	0.042	0.030
In Issue Size		1		.049	-0.089	0.157(*)	0.168(*)	0.105	0.059	-0.067
Index Return (%)		1			-.506(**)	0.075	0.027	0.304(**)	0.260(**)	0.368(**)
In Index volatility			1			-0.101	-0.021	-0.282(**)	-0.237(**)	--0.318(**)
Leverage (%)			1				0.159(*)	-0.078	-0.142(*)	-0.068
Promoters Holding (%)				1				0.145(*)	-0.040	-0.104
In QIB					1				0.674(**)	0.557(**)
In NII					1					0.742(**)
In RIIs						.1				

Table A3. Excluded variables.

Model		Beta In	t	Sig.	Partial correlation	Collinearity statistics		
						Tolerance	VIF	Minimum tolerance
1	Price band _UP (%)	0.007(a)	0.144	0.886	0.010	0.999	1.001	0.999
	Age (years)	-0.001(a)	-0.016	0.987	-0.001	0.998	1.002	0.998
	In Issue size	-0.111(a)	-2.388	0.018	-0.165	0.997	1.003	0.997
	Index return (%)	0.187(a)	4.006	0.000	0.270	0.932	1.073	0.932
	In Index volatility	-0.150(a)	-3.183	0.002	-0.218	0.944	1.060	0.944
	Leverage (%)	0.038(a)	0.806	0.421	0.056	0.980	1.021	0.980
	Promoters Holding (%)	-0.074(a)	-1.588	0.114	-0.110	0.998	1.002	0.998
	In QIB	0.103(a)	1.640	0.103	0.114	0.546	1.831	0.546
2	Price Band _UP (%)	0.042(b)	0.916	0.361	0.064	0.964	1.037	0.900
	Age(years)	-0.014(b)	-0.318	0.751	-0.022	0.993	1.007	0.927
	In Issue size	-0.117(b)	-2.626	0.009	-0.181	0.995	1.005	0.930
	In Index volatility	-0.080(b)	-1.513	0.132	-0.106	0.732	1.367	0.723
	Leverage (%)	0.017(b)	0.367	0.714	0.026	0.966	1.035	0.906
	Promoters holding (%)	-0.081(b)	-1.806	0.072	-0.126	0.997	1.003	0.930
	In QIB	0.061(b)	0.985	0.326	0.069	0.528	1.893	0.528
3	Price band_UP (%)	0.012(c)	0.254	0.800	0.018	0.899	1.113	0.899
	Age(years)	0.003(c)	0.062	0.951	0.004	0.971	1.030	0.926
	In Index volatility	-0.090(c)	-1.725	0.086	-0.120	0.728	1.373	0.723
	Leverage (%)	0.037(c)	0.815	0.416	0.057	0.940	1.064	0.901
	Promoters holding (%)	-0.063(c)	-1.399	0.163	-0.098	0.968	1.033	0.927
	In QIB	0.075(c)	1.226	0.222	0.086	0.525	1.906	.525

Predictors in the Model: (Constant), In NII; Predictors in the model: (Constant), In NII, Index return (%), Predictors in the model: (Constant), In NII, Index return (%), In Issue size; Dependent variable: In RIIs.

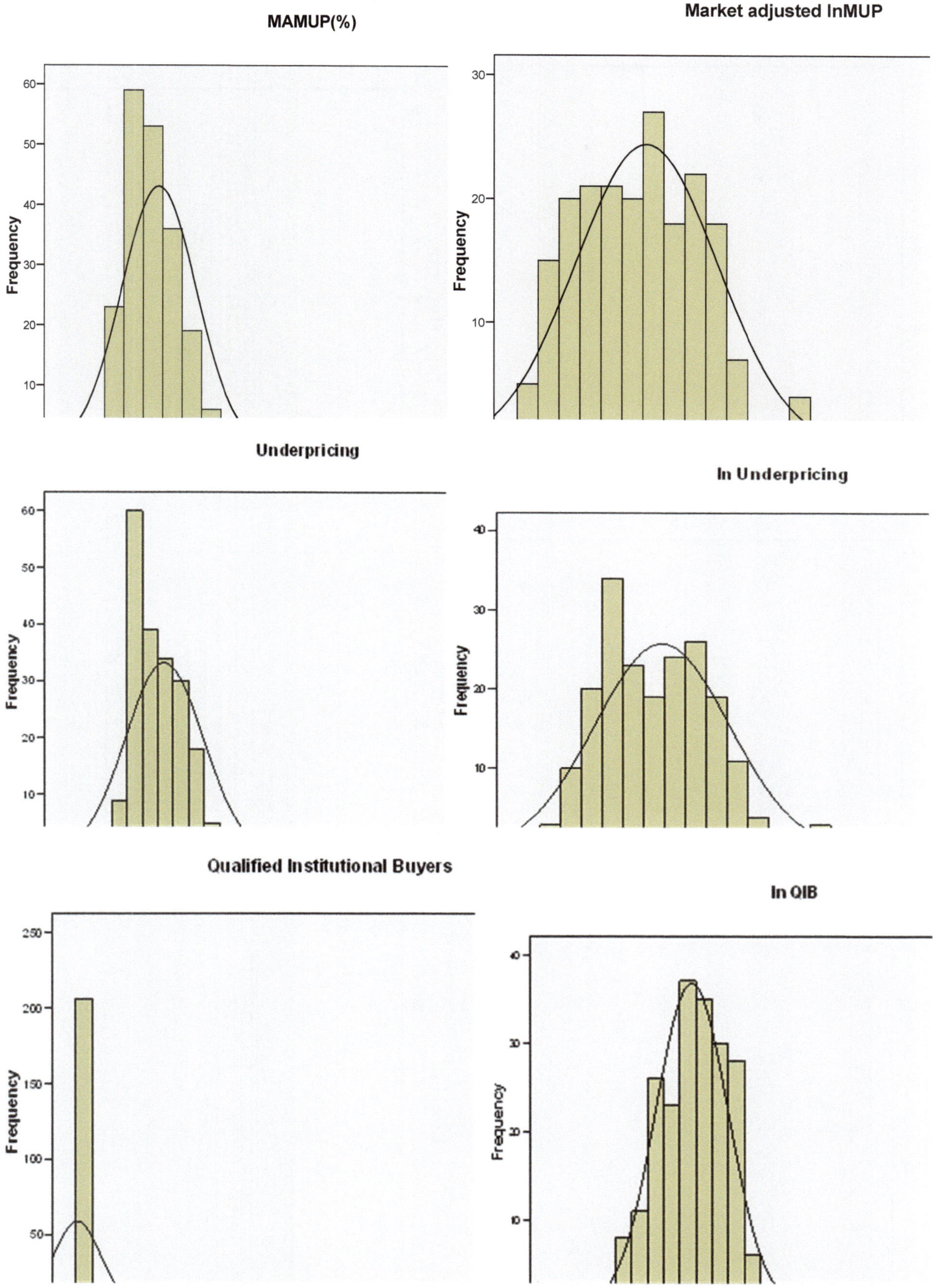

Figure 1A. Histograms with normal curve.

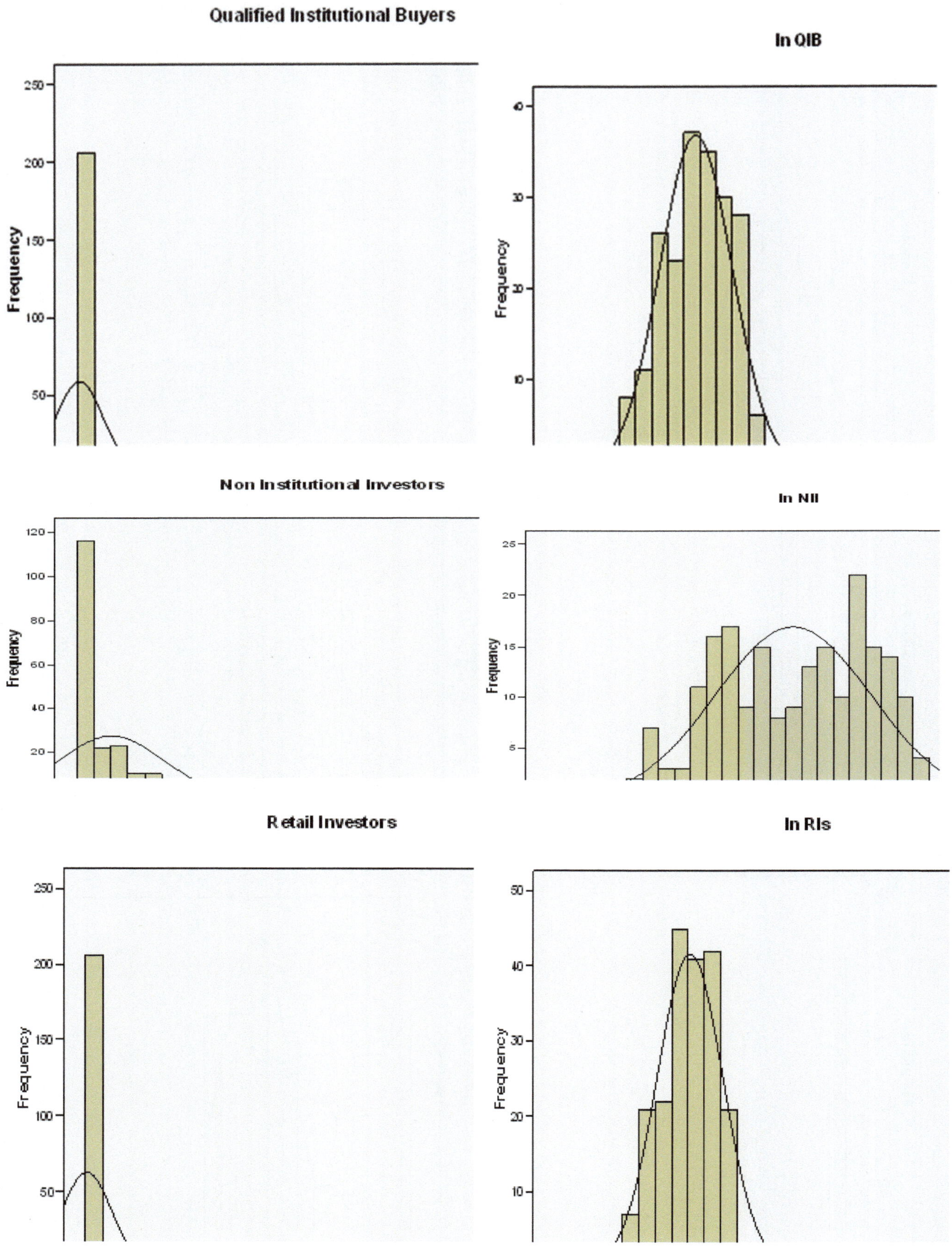

Figure 1A. Contd.

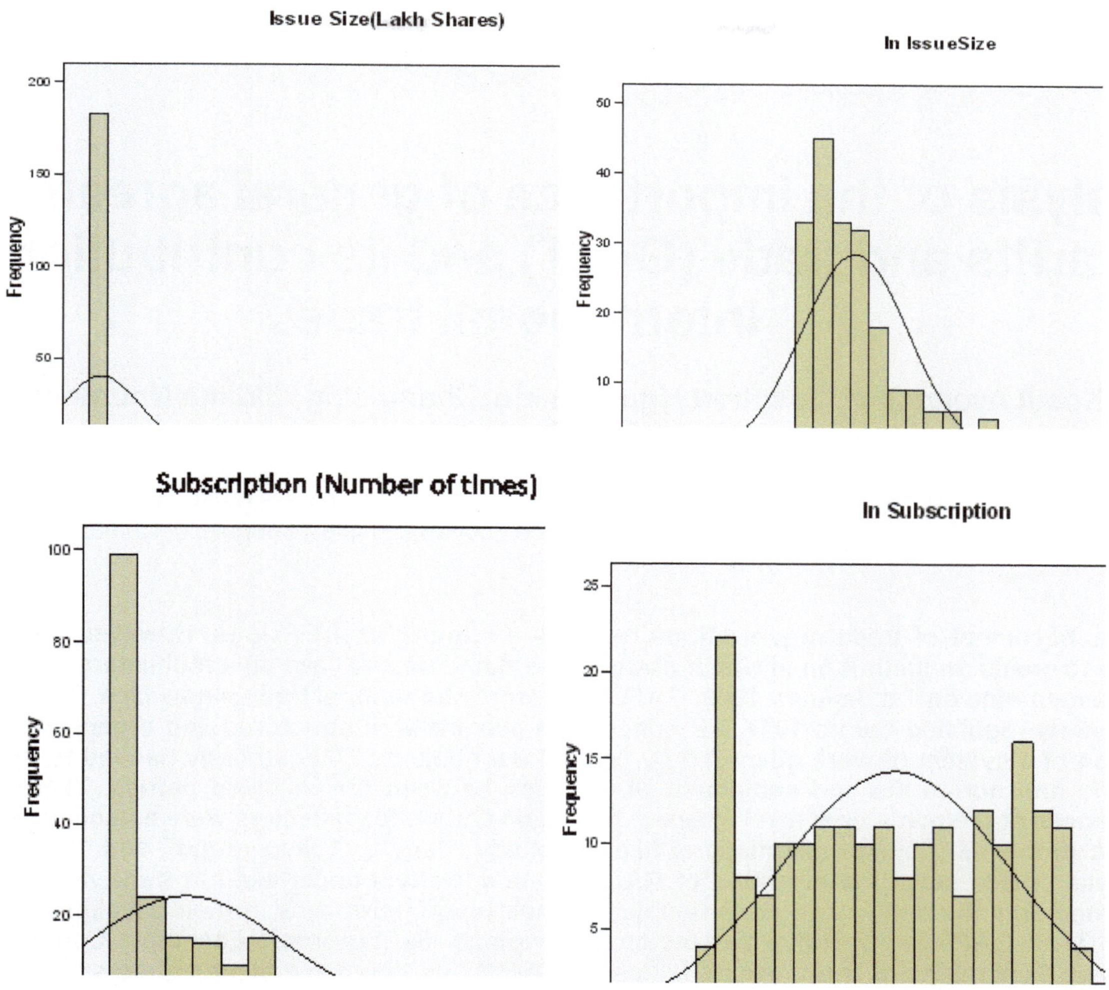

Figure 1A. Contd.

Analysis of the importance of general agreement on tariffs and trade (GATT) and its contribution to international trade

Kossi Ayenagbo*, Josphert Ngui Kimatu, Zhang Jing, Sidime Nountenin and Wang Rongcheng

College of Urban and Environmental Sciences, Northeast Normal University. No. 5268 Renmin Street, Changchun, Jilin Province, Post Code 130024, Peoples Republic of China.

The establishment of trade organizations requires a number of provisions. However, the negotiators wanted to create an institution in which trade issues could be analyzed on a multilateral basis. Since its enforcement date on 1st January 1948, GATT has given international trade a new face. The international trade barely regulated before 1947, has since then become well structured and organized through the adoption of a system of work governed by general negotiations. This strategy has led to the reduction of tariffs and non-tariffs and settlement of disputes between the involved parties. There have been conferences at the ministerial level where experts and committee meetings were established to address specific problems. Several negotiations like "Kennedy round", "Tokyo round" and "Uruguay round" have taken place since the inception of GATT. Some decisions undertaken in trade negotiations have concerned only the developing countries due to their unique problems in their development. However, Article 24 of GATT treaty authorizes regional groupings like European Economic Community (EEC), Economic Community of West African States (ECOWAS), as they are constituted as a free trade area, a customs union or community, provided only that these groups do not impose trade barriers with the rest of the world.

Key words: General agreement on tariffs and trade GATT, international trade, free market, developing countries, tariffs.

INTRODUCTION

International trade rules are not as easy as those governing domestic trade. Indeed the international trade was governed by the laws and regulations in force in the country .The rules of international trade are far more complex. This complexity is due to the urgent need for each country to protect its national economic space. The absence of supranational authority capable of imposing obligations on states with respect to international trade has prevented the evolution of this trade until recently. States which look only to their own self-interests, have always opposed any kind of barriers based on international trade. These barriers are of tariff and non-tariff types such as prohibitions and quantitative restrictions. After the great economic crisis of 1929 and the Second World War which disrupted the world, some large-economy countries like the United States, Britain and others took care of the reorganization of the postwar world. Thus, the UN was created with its specialized agencies, each branched out for dealing with an activity. Among these agencies, we can distinguish those with a purely economic characteristic, such as the international monetary fund (IMF) and international bank for reconstruction and development (IBRD), now called the World Bank. The Havana Charter which was supposed to lead to the creation of the international trade organization (ITO) has never been ratified. Hence, the general agreement on tariffs and trade (GATT) remained the only multilateral code governing international trade. Based on this framework, this review highlights some of the contributions of the GATT 1947 after throwing light on the

*Corresponding author. E-mail: ayenagbo@yahoo.fr.

institution itself.

PRESENTATION, ORIGIN AND THE FOUNDATION OF GATT

The GATT was a specialized institution which has economic and technical features. It is a multilateral treaty that establishes a common code of conduct for international trade and which provides a mechanism to reduce and stabilize tariffs and other trade barriers and to hold consultations on issues related to trade. In the 1930s, when the world was suffering from a serious economic depression, many states tried to find refuge behind various forms of barriers to protect their economies like high protective tariffs, quantitative restrictions on imports, exchange controls. During Second World War, it became clear that these restrictions would weigh constantly on the world unless vigorous attempts are made to dismantle and ban them. Along with the creation of IBRD (currently the World Bank) and the IMF, various governments considered the establishment of an institution designed to regulate trade: the international trade organization (ITO).

Despite the fact that this institution has never emerged, a group of twenty-three countries (eleven for developed countries and twelve for developing countries according to WTO; FOCUS, 1998) began negotiations on tariffs, reaching at an agreement on a set of standards, intended to liberalize their trade. These standards have resulted in the general agreement on tariffs and trade (GATT), which entered into force in January 1948 (Geneva, since 1945). The GATT remained the only multilateral instrument governing international trade until 1995, the time when the world trade organization (WTO) was formed. The GATT was the tangible result of all efforts in this direction, otherwise stated in the resolution of international trade problems. The starting point lies in the Atlantic Charter and other treaties concluded between the Allies themselves during the war to seek together a trading system based on non-discrimination and aiming at achieving high standards through free and fair trade of goods and services. Pursuing this goal, even long before the end of the war, the United States, United Kingdom and other major trading powers of the time discussed the establishment of international organizations to tackle problems of post-war regarding the movement of capital, investment and trade. The foundations of the GATT can be summarized as follows: a) rates should normally be the only instrument used to protect domestic industries; b) quantitative restrictions (prohibitions / limitations) are generally prohibited (GATT Art. xi) ... but may in certain circumstances be permitted; c) tariffs should be transparent, predictable and stable; d) commitments tariffs comprise of a "list of concessions" (Sergio, 2008).

The GATT was originally considered an interim arrangement, pending the entry into force of the Havana Charter and the establishment of the ITO as a specialized institution of the United Nations. But circumstances have been such that the GATT, since 1948, remained the only international instrument which laid down rules of conduct for international trade and employing a large proportion of world trade. Only originally twenty-three, the number of contracting parties has rapidly grown over the years. In 1988, it is an exhaustive list of these countries. Among real contracting parties, they were (South Africa, Federal Republic of Germany, Antigua and Barbuda, Argentina, Bangladesh, Botswana, Brazil, Burkina Faso, Burundi, Cameroon etc). Tunisia remained the only country which has acceded to the GATT provisionally (Christian, 2006).

As regards to countries applying the GATT right away or immediately, among them they were (Algeria, Angola, Bahamas, Bahrain, Brunei Darussalam, Cape Verde, Dominica, United Arab Emirates, Fiji, Grenada, Guinea Bissau, Equatorial Guinea etc). Most of these countries (real contracting parties, country which has acceded to the GATT provisionally and countries applying the GATT right away or immediately) became members of WTO from 1995 to 1997 while others have remained observers until May 1998 as Algeria, Cape Verde, Seychelles and Tonga (WTO, FOCUS, 1998). The highest decision-making structure in GATT was the session of contracting parties usually held once a year. Decisions were made by consensus and not by vote. But on rare occasions when the vote should take place, each contracting party had one vote. Decisions were then taken by simple majority, except for important issues where the two-thirds majority is required. Between sessions of the contracting parties, the Council of Representatives was responsible for sending current matters and pressing problems. It meets at least six times a year. Committees are established to handle technical problems. The GATT secretariat is the administrative system by excellence. Most of meetings that the GATT organizes were done at its headquarters in Geneva.

Principles of GATT 1947

The GATT 1947 was a multilateral treaty with rights and obligations. It is based on the following fundamental principles: a) Non-discrimination. This principle involves the provision of most favored nation (MFN) under which each contracting party must give any other contracting party the same benefits as those that it gives to another party or country. It also implies prohibition to disadvantage any party to the detriment of other parties. In addition, signatory countries promise not to subject imported products to more severe treatment than national treatment in tax and regulation, b) the obligation on parties to consider tariffs as only permissible means of protecting domestic production. Thus, the use of quantitative restrictions is generally condemned; c) consultation between the contracting parties is a rule that relates to all the arrangements. It prohibits measures published by surprise without taking into account the interests of others. So there are rules of procedures which notably include information exchange, consultation and dispute settlement.

Exceptions to the principles

Export subsidies are contrary to fundamental principles of GATT. Concessions have historically yet been made in this area, particularly the European community, but it wrapped up its common politics in the 1960s (Jean-Marie Boisson, 1964). The text of the GATT treaty contains provisions which expressly waive some of these principles. Thus, the general agreement authorizes the establishment of regional groupings on the sole condition that these groups do not pose trade barriers with the rest of the world. These clusters can be formed as zones of free trade, customs union and community. The GATT taking account of different levels of development, has installed to the benefit of developing countries special measures to enable them to raise their standard of life. Thus, these countries are allowed to use measures other than tariffs to protect their domestic production. These measures may be quantitative restrictions, quotas and even prohibitions. But as we have already said, these measures should not be unilateral and edited by surprise. They must be taken in agreement with other contracting parties.

The sub-regional groupings listed are subject to the provisions of Article 24 of the GATT treaty. Indeed, this article highlights the interest of closer integration of national economies to achieve the establishment of free trade. Therefore, it allows these groups to derogate from the principle of most favored nation, provided it meets strict criteria under which the arrangements must facilitate trade between countries without creating barriers against other countries. It is in order to achieve fixed goals that, the GATT has laid down the principles which we have discussed above.

OBJECTIVES OF THE GATT

In general terms, the goals and objectives of a treaty have always been considered of special relevance given that they express the common wishes and aspirations of those who reach a formal agreement at an international level (Reuter, 1970). The aims and objectives of general agreement have played a vital role as the only reference for limiting the reach and jurisdiction of such an Organization. These objectives and goals not only limit its contents but also decide on the directives to follow during its development. The central objective of the general agreement is therefore progressive trade liberalization (Cobb, 1994).

The objectives of the general agreement are set forth in the preamble, where the contracting parties recognize that "... their relations in the commercial and economic matters should be directed towards raising standards of living, ensuring full employment and a large and steadily growing volume of real income and effective demand, the full utilization of global resources and increased production and trade of products and to the progressive development of the economies of all contracting parties." This sentence of the preamble of the GATT treaty, is sufficient in itself to demonstrate how ambitious the mission that the general agreement has set. Let us examine in detail some of these objectives.

RAISING OF STANDARDS OF LIVING

The basic objectives of the GATT are to have higher standards of living and progressive development of all contracting parties (Part IV of GATT). Therefore, from the initiative of UNCTAD, the Generalized System of Preferences (GSP) has been brought on to take account of imbalances in development between countries (Jacques, 2006). The general agreement aims, through trade liberalization, at providing access to all productions worldwide. The removal of tariff and non-tariff barriers allows any producer, wherever it is, to export its products as it sees fit. It also allows any consumer to supply his needs from any market.

Unimpeded exports and imports can only contribute to raising standards of living of individuals. But it should be noted that this only benefits countries with high export capacity. Developed countries that have large unbeatable industries are the only masters. So a basic factor in setting the objectives and goals of GATT and which therefore should always be borne in mind when mention is made of them is that, this agreement forms part of a body of treaties which emerged between 1945 and 1950 which looked to design a new economic order for post-war international society.

ACHIEVING FULL EMPLOYMENT

The achievement of full employment being closely linked to that of the full use of world resources cannot be achieved, unless there is a further trade liberalization. Indeed the situation is hurting autarkic development, in that the capacities and potentials of each producing countries are constrained by its boundaries. This also implies that, every country should have every possible variety of industries. But the reality is that, no country has all the factors of production. Some countries, rich in raw agricultural and mining, do not have trained manpower and appropriate technology.

On the contrary, a country that possess advanced technology is lacking (or almost) of raw materials. The implementation of full use of global resources must necessarily pass through the liberalization of trade. This liberalization is hampered by national or regional considerations. Indeed all states have the duty to protect their national economic space. It is this desire to protect the national economic space which prevents the development of trade. Therefore, this is why the GATT was established as a key objective of trade liberalization for reducing or removing tariffs and non-tariff barriers.

PROGRESSIVE DEVELOPMENT OF ECONOMIES OF CONTRACTING PARTIES

Since the contracting parties agree to exchange among themselves their products, their capabilities and producing potential will therefore be developed. There will thus be a large global market in which all countries can freely sell their products. Countries can increase their production, if they want because they will have no more problems from lack of opportunities. It should be noted that the development of trade arrangements only benefits countries with a high production capacity. Countries which do not have large capacities are relegated to the last place because they are forced to export only raw materials whose prices fluctuate, according to the willingness of the developed countries. Therefore, the parties have taken special measures to develop the economy and trade in developing countries.

MULTILATERAL TRADE NEGOTIATIONS

Since its inception, the GATT has organized several multilateral negotiations. According to WTO (WTO, FOCUS, 1998), the first meeting took place in Geneva, Switzerland in 1947, the second at Annecy in France in 1949 where the contracting parties exchanged some 5,000 tariff concessions, the third in Torquay, England, in 1950 during which the contracting parties exchanged some 8,700 tariff concessions, which have reduced by 25% the tariff levels of 1948, the fourth in Geneva between 1955 and 1956 (this round was completed in May 1956 and resulted in tariff cuts representing about 2.5 billion U.S. dollars), the fifth round of GATT negotiations has been so named in honor of Deputy U.S. Secretary of State who proposed the opening: Douglas Dillon. Launched in 1960 and completed in 1962, they led to tariff concessions on international trade worth 4.9 billion dollars and have also included negotiations related to the creation of the EEC, the sixth in Geneva 1964 to 1967 (Kennedy round), the seventh in Tokyo in 1973 to 1979 (Tokyo round), eighth in Uruguay from 1984 to recent (Uruguay round). Among all these negotiations, the last three are the most important. So our study here would focus on the last three negotiations.

KENNEDY ROUND (1964-1967)

Named in honor of U.S. President, the sixth round of GATT negotiations began in 1964 and ended in 1967 with tariff reductions on international trade worth 40 billion dollars (WTO, FOCUS, 1998). The experience gained during the tariff negotiations of 1960 to 1961, which, like all previous negotiations had been conducted on the principle of negotiating a product, led contracting parties to the conclusion that traditional techniques of tariff negotiations were no more adapted to changing conditions of world trade and the possibility of adopting new techniques including that of the general linear reduction could be envisaged. When trade ministers launched the "Kennedy round" trade negotiations in May 1963, they were able to ask directions aiming at the reduction of tariff and non-tariff trade barriers on a large scale and with a broader scope. The ministers agreed, among other things: i) the overall negotiations were to take place starting in 1964 with the widest possible participation; ii) negotiations should cover all kinds of products, including agricultural products and raw materials; iii) negotiations should cover both tariff barriers and non-tariff barriers; iv) the negotiations should provide acceptable conditions of access for agricultural products to world markets; v) for most industrialized countries, the tariff negotiations in the industry sector should be based on a plan for substantial reductions linear with minimal exceptions that are prone to confrontation and justification. But where the differences between tariff levels are significant, the reductions will be based on the special rule of general and automatic application; vi) efforts should be made to reduce barriers on exports from developing countries.

The Ministers also agreed that negotiations between the developed countries are based on the principle of reciprocity and that developed countries should not expect such reciprocity from developing countries. When negotiations opened in May 1964, the rate of 50% was accepted as a hypothesis for the working of determining the overall rate of linear reduction. They were fifty states to take part in the work which constituted the majority of developing countries. The EEC, now EU, attended the conference and negotiated as a single entity. In mid-May 1967, the Director General was able to announce that the essential elements have been negotiated successfully. The final conclusion was reached June 30, 1967 when the participants had signed the Final Act, authenticating legal instruments arising from the conference. These legal instruments specified the international obligations that the participating governments committed themselves to respect. Apart from tariff concessions, separate agreements were negotiated (agreements on grain, chemicals and the anti-plumping). Protocols which were signed, authorizing the accession of four new countries to GATT, they were: Argentina, Ireland, Iceland and Poland. Like the case study: Promoting trade interests through

GATT/WTO negotiations; the "Kennedy round" of trade negotiations marked the beginning of defensive strategies orchestrated by many developing countries.

The Round, which began in 1964 and ended in 1967, eschewed the item by item approach of the previous five rounds, preferring instead to adopt, for the first time, across the board percentage tariff reductions. This approach was perceived by many developing countries, the Caribbean among them, as a direct threat to their protected, assured market. This perception among the Caribbean countries - later to become the "C" in the African, Caribbean and Pacific (ACP) countries - was to exert an overwhelming influence on all future negotiations where success meant defending turf to avoid further erosion of preferences. After the closing of the "Kennedy round" in 1967, it was only in1973 that the new negotiations will begin in Tokyo, Japan. It was the "Tokyo round".

TOKYO ROUND (1973-1979)

The multilateral trade negotiations under the auspices of GATT was opened in September 1973 at a meeting of Ministers held in Tokyo. The seventh round, launched in the Japanese capital, saw the GATT addressing not only tariffs but also non-tariff barriers. One hundred participants have exchanged concessions in the form of tariff reductions on international trade in excess of 300 billion dollars. Agreements have been concluded, inter alia, in the fields of subsidies, import licensing, the valuation and the fight against dumping. Ninety-nine countries, whose levels of development and economic systems are very different and who are not all GATT members, have participated in these negotiations. These are the industrialized countries of Western Europe and North America, the relatively less industrialized countries like Australia and New Zealand, countries of Eastern Europe and the entire range of developing countries, from least developed to more developed ones.

These negotiations, called "Tokyo round" were more extensive and detailed than any that preceded them. They were designed not only to reduce or eliminate tariffs and non-tariff barriers to trade, but also to shape the multilateral trading system and international trade relations during a period that would spill well into the next decade. Other differences also distinguish the "Tokyo round" negotiations: the relative weight of major powerful economic in international trade have indeed significantly changed. The European Communities became the main business entity in the world, and economic progress of Japan was such that it became one of the top three trading nations. Also, the "Tokyo round" negotiations saw three economic powers, namely the U.S., the European Community and Japan, take the lead in negotiations and largely determine the direction, pace and content.

The big difference compared to earlier negotiations concerned developing countries. For the first time in multilateral negotiations of GATT, the problems of these countries played a prominent role commensurate with their growing economic and political international affairs, as well as their own importance and weight of participation in the negotiations. Participants focused on issues such as agriculture, tropical products, tariff, non-tariff measures, subsidies and countervailing duties, technical barriers to trade, technical assistance to developing countries and others. The "Tokyo round" was preferentially treating tariffs and non-tariffs, which may be granted to developing countries so that they can agree between themselves a legal permanent element of the system of international trade. The "Tokyo round" negotiations had the credit for having proposed a new definition of customs value. Since long, every country had their conception of the customs value. This was detrimental to international trade because all these countries do not have the same idea. Therefore, the GATT gave itself the duty to harmonize the concept of value. After the "Tokyo round", the "Uruguay round" occurred in 1984.

URUGUAY ROUND (1984)

The trade ministers of member countries of GATT launched the eighth round of multilateral negotiations in Punta del Este (Uruguay); negotiations have never ever covered such an important amount of themes. The successful negotiation of the "Uruguay round" in December 15, 1993 and the opening of markets resulting from this latest round of GATT negotiations, which is also the most ambitious, were expected to boost global income by $ 500 billion up in the year 2005 (WTO, FOCUS, 1998). Begun in 1984, trade negotiations called the "Uruguay round" are moving now to the final conclusions. Mr. Arthur Dunkel (Director General of GATT) recognized during the month of April 1990 that, it is difficult at this stage to find points of convergence on the actual substance of trade negotiations under the "Uruguay round" in eight months prior to their conclusion. But he tempered his verdict by two findings: one hundred countries, parties transacting worldwide, have pledged to negotiate seriously, and the activities of each other showed that, there was now a very good collection of parameters that govern the negotiations. "There is therefore no place neither for satisfaction or pessimism," Mr. Dunkel said during a press conference after a two-day meeting of the Trade Negotiations Committee (TNC) which oversees the two strands of the "Uruguay round" goods and new sectors (services, intellectual property, investments).

The Director General of GATT has confirmed that the two most difficult issues of bargaining were those of textiles and agriculture, areas where he was ironic about trading nations of the world "sinning for 35 and 40 years" and where the stakes were enormous. Agriculture opposes supporters of the abolition of all production support and export, including the United States and those who consider this approach unrealistic as the current EU /EEC. Washington and Brussels swallow in those supports sums estimated globally at some 60 million dollars a year. As for textiles, some producers in the Third World call for the early repeal of the agreement of the protectionist MFA (multi-fiber arrangement), which strictly governs the past 16 years, half of world trade. To Mr. Dunkel, another point is vital for the survival and strengthening of multilateralism: the development of a "system on certain and solid dispute resolution". It is obvious that the vulnerabilities that exist in this area are often the pretext for the use of reprisals of unilateral measures or attempts for bilateral regulations.

In his approach, the Director General of the GATT has had at least two reasons to be encouraged: i) there is "total Agreement" between the negotiators to sketch before July 1990, which he called "the profile of the overall package". The remaining time should be devoted to refine the details and translate the acquired in clear and legal texts. He did not rule out that in case of deadlock on certain points, the trade negotiations committee would be convened in special session; ii) the significant economic changes occurring in the world, both in the East as that in some Latin America and Africa, accentuate the need for a strong multilateral system and give more depth to the "Uruguay round". Mr. Dunkel said that at least forty countries around the world consider that, the strengthening of this system is essential to their growth and development (Statement by the Director General of GATT reported by AFP, April 12, 1990). The goal pursued by the GATT negotiations is to foster the emergence of international trade through the reduction or elimination of tariff and non-tariff barriers.

Agriculture has played a decisive role in the initiation and the extension of the "Uruguay round" beyond the deadlines originally set (Jean-Marie Boisson, 1994). After the failure of negotiations in Montreal (1990), then in Brussels (December 1991), while the theoretical maturity of the "Uruguay round" is fast approaching, the Secretary General of GATT, Arthur Dunkel, proposed a draft of an agreement on agriculture made up of twenty items, which should serve as a basis for final negotiations of the "Uruguay round" (Dunkel, 1991).

CONSOLIDATION AND REDUCTION OF TARIFFS

One of the main activities of the GATT, which is laid down in Article 28 bis of the agreement, was to organize conferences in order to negotiate the reduction and stabilization of tariffs. These conferences are intended to promote international trade by substantially reducing the level of tariff protection and allowing some trade organization with the assurance that the rights trading will not suddenly be increased. They have resulted in a reduction or consolidation of duties applied by most developed countries on industrial products (including many of particular interest to developing countries). While many developing countries have agreed during the negotiations on tariffs to reduce or consolidate some of their costs, most of the concessions have been, as it was in the nature of things, granted by developed countries. The clause of most-favored nation enshrined in Article I of the general agreement, however, has the effect of extending the benefits of these concessions to all contracting parties. Negotiations between the developed countries were formerly based on the principle of full reciprocity of concessions. Developing countries were granted on a reciprocal basis a number of concessions, particularly in the initial tariff conferences. However, it is also widely accepted that the principle of reciprocity as applied between developed countries is not appropriate in respect of developing countries and at the meeting at the ministerial level of May 1963 which launched the idea of the "Kennedy round", it was formally recognized that "no effort be spared to reduce barriers to exports from developing countries but developed countries cannot expect to receive reciprocity from the developing countries".

Until now, the technical basis for tariff conferences was mainly product by product trading. But there is reason to believe that the performance of this method will diminish. Accordingly, ministers agreed, when they launched the "Kennedy round", that their appearance in tariff negotiations would be based on a method for reducing general linear rights with limited exceptions and special rules where there is significant disparity in tariff levels. To prepare a plan for tariff negotiations that meets these conditions, it was agreed to take as a working hypothesis, a rule of linear reduction of 50%. Its application would lead to halving the rights of the majority of tariffs in industrialized countries, the reduction of which would benefit the developing countries. It should be noted that this would be a futile effort to try to reduce the tariff rights, if there is no consensus on the concept of value. Also the GATT gave a definition of customs value to allow international trade to speak the same language. Article 7, which was the starting point, states that "the customs value of imported goods must be real, that is, the value at which they are sold". A declaration of intent was signed in 1973. In this statement, it was stated that the new value not to be based on arbitrary or fictitious values, but on criteria consistent with commercial practices. Finally, the agreement was signed in 1979, during the trade negotiations of the "Tokyo round" and implemented in June 1980, in the countries of the EEC under the current reference EEC Regulation 1224/80. Currently, the regulation is signed by most trading partners of the current EU/EEC. For developing countries, a number of safeguards are provided and a transitional period of development adjusted. One of the main objectives of the

Cotonou Agreement signed between the EEC/EU and African, Caribbean and Pacific is to achieve the progressive harmonious integration of these (EU-UN).

However, the ECOWAS countries, meeting in Cotonou in 1983, did not accept the new definition because it remained in favor of developed countries, suppliers in most cases, having at their disposal large industries (production series) capable of giving unbeatable prices. Customs in developing countries would not recognize the customs value of the transaction value without having thoroughly and before analyzed their effects on their economies and finances. The new definition of value has remained unheeded in the ECOWAS countries which still use the value defined by Regulation 803/68. For the general agreement, the customs value of imported goods is the transaction value, that is, the price actually paid or payable by the buyer to the seller. This price is only increased by some elements listed in Article 8 of Regulation namely: commissions, brokerage fees, transportation costs, license fees etc[1]. Only after the harmonization of the definition of customs value, that the GATT may claim to act positively on tariffs. Otherwise, it would purely and simply fall on deaf ears.

REMOVAL OF NON-BARRIER TARIFFS

One of the fundamental provisions of general agreement is the general prohibition of quantitative restrictions under Article 11. It is clear from the provisions of Article 11 that, quantitative restrictions are in principle prohibited. It should be noted however that this prohibition is not absolute. The rule has some exceptions. The main exceptions to this rule are those that allow countries, under well defined conditions (and more rigorous in developed countries), to resort to restrictions on imports to protect their reserves in case of difficulties relating to their balance of payments. In addition, for example when it is impractical to use tariff measures, developing countries can make use of quantitative restrictions to protect developing industries. The provisions applicable to the case (Article 18 section C) stipulate that any developing country, that has notified its intention to apply such restrictions to products that are not subject to tariff concessions, has the faculty to apply within thirty days of notification, unless the contracting parties invite it to enter into consultations with them. In this case, they will give their approval in the proposed measure, if it is established that there is no further action consistent with the normal rules of the general agreement for achieving the development goal target.

Countries that apply import restrictions for balance of payments reasons are required under the agreement to enter into consultations with the contracting parties (each year in the case of the developed countries and every two years in the developing countries) about the nature of the difficulties associated with their balance of payments, alternative corrective measures among which they can choose and the potential impact of these restrictions on the economies of other contracting parties. These import restrictions, widespread in the aftermath of the Second World War, are today less and less used. The GATT has worked hard to get rid, from the contracting parties, all discriminatory measures which hindered international trade.

FAVORABLE MEASURES FOR DEVELOPING COUNTRIES BY THE GATT

The increasingly urgent character of problems relating to economic development and trade in developing countries, which has been highlighted in the Haberler report prepared at the request of the GATT, had been recognized by trade ministers at the meetings held in 1957 and 1958. An emphasis was made to examine these problems in the program for the expansion of international trade, that contracting parties had launched immediately after the ministerial meeting of 1958. Three committees were established to implement the program. They had to deal with, first, the issue of new multilateral negotiations, the second, of the problems of agricultural trade and finally, the third, of the increase in export earnings of developing countries.

Among these three committees is the third committee that comes to exclusively look after the problems of developing countries on a systematic and increasingly open method with the key milestones being: i) identification of barriers to trade by processing product by product; ii) continuing efforts to remove these barriers; iii) parallel extension of the product by product approach to the general study of development plans and potential export; iv) consideration of other measures to increase exports (e.g., preferences, business information services and trade promotion). Many people rejoice the initiatives taken by Europe in international trade. As the Secretary General of UN, Kofi Annan has welcomed the EU's initiative "Everything but Arms", which proves to him that Europe is really a system of international trade fair in which poor countries are given a real possibility to export to get out of poverty[2]. Total imports from all beneficiary countries increased by 8.9%, since the entry into force of the initiative (from 12.9 to 14.1 billion Euros). The commercial benefits that Commonwealth developing countries obtain from "imperial preferences" vary according to their economic structure and composition of their trade flows. These benefits, which one tends to undervalue the importance, were brutally illustrated during the first attempts by Britain to join the European Economic Community (EEC). It is thus, for example, the preferences agreed by Great Britain - and to a large extent by Canada on imports of sugar, bananas, citrus

[1] FC Course of Customs procedures

[2] Article by General Secretary Kofi Annan in the Financial Times March 5,2001

and rum which are important to the Caribbean, those of cocoa for Ghana and Nigeria, those of tobacco for the Malawi, those products of light industry, including textiles, for India and Pakistan. Also Ghana, India, Pakistan and Nigeria have experienced serious concerns for their exports, due to the possibility that Great Britain eliminates Commonwealth preferences to adopt the common external tariff of the EEC (Common Market, 1961).

Under the pressure of events, however, such as the accession of many Third World countries (over 70) to the GATT and the creation of the United Nations conference on trade and development (UNCTAD), which for a time seemed to become the latter's great rival, Western countries have accepted the principle of non-reciprocity in their trade relations with the Third World. Thus one of the rules for the conduct of the "Kennedy round" (1964 to 1967) took the form of a special effort of developed countries to reduce tariffs on products of particular interest to exporters from developing countries without waiting for an equivalence in reciprocal concessions (Basic instruments and Miscellaneous Documents, 13th supplement). These tariff reductions were, however, to be extended on a non-discriminatory basis with all countries benefiting from the treatment of the most favored nation. Significant progress has been made in this direction during the "Kennedy round", especially as regards to tropical products and industrial raw materials. Preferences should be granted, within the possible extent, without discrimination for all countries in developing items for all semi-finished and manufactured goods. As for existing preferences, they should be removed gradually, as other international measures would provide beneficiary countries with at least equivalent benefits (General principle No. 8, UNCTAD, 1964). The objectives of the new preferential arrangements as set by Resolution 21 (JOHNSON, H.G.) and adopted at the second UNCTAD Conference in New Delhi in 1968, are increased export earnings, industrial promotion and the acceleration of economic growth of developing countries.

In fact, since the developed countries agreed to enforce their national systems, despite their persistent disagreements on the basic elements of a generalized, issue of preferences is becoming an integral component of business strategy of major economic powers. Thus, the U.S. administration hoped to apply its tariff proposals, to forget somewhat the growing protectionism at home. Unfortunately, these same protectionist pressures in the Congress are likely to seriously delay the implementation of, or otherwise just jeopardize, the existence (Journal of Commerce (March 29, 1971)). For its part, the EEC decided to take this paralysis of the American administration to create the image of a liberal business entity, outward looking and aware of its responsibilities towards the Third World (Europe, 1971 and The Journal of Commerce, 1971). Thus, it seems that the preferential generalized community offer can be put into effect in July, 1971 without requiring parallelism from the United States. It would be same in Japan.

The GATT rules recognize that the governments of developing countries, in implementing their programs and economic development policies, may be required to provide assistance to new industries and emerging or expanding existing industries and, that this can take the form of safeguard measures temporarily restricting imports. Because the application of such restrictions could have a negative effect on the interests of exporting countries, it is subject to strict conditions (GATT, 1994, Article XVIII: Section C). Some preferential arrangements exist between Spain, Portugal and its overseas territories as well as between the United States and the Philippines (whose phase is planned for 1974), the Canal Zone and Panama Trust Territories in the Pacific. Australia, meanwhile, implemented a system of limited preferential tariff quotas for developing countries in 1965 (GATT, Basic Instruments Miscellaneous Documents, 14th Supp.).

REMOVING OBSTACLES OF TRADE

The third panel focused its main efforts on increasing the export earnings of developing countries. In doing so, it has accumulated an extensive literature on trade barriers and trade flows and, incidentally, helped to identify areas where export potential is being formed in developing countries. The approach of the Third Committee was to examine the products in groups. The committee examines a particular group of products, makes recommendations and then tries to remove barriers to trade that have been identified. It then proceeds to another group. In this way, products that are of interest to developing countries are come in and come in still more numerous amount in the field of examination of the third committee which was able to study the obstacles to trade affecting a range of more broader articles. The Committee's investigation is now spread to hundreds of tariff of the Brussels Nomenclature.

The two parties have discussed the first report of the Third Committee at the meeting they held in Tokyo in November 1959 and recommended that, "the contracting parties, especially developed countries, review customs duties, fiscal duties and the charges, quantitative restrictions and other measures they are applied to, in order to facilitate a rapid expansion of export earnings of developing countries; this expansion would allow developing countries to be less dependent on foreign aid, strengthen their economies and accelerate their development". The Third Committee has continued to direct its attention to trade barriers and has added new products to the list of those it examines. At the same time, it began to broaden its scope, to introduce other issues such as trade promotion and study of development plans. Towards the end of 1961, it presented to the contracting parties a special report which was submitted to Ministers when they met in November 1961. The most important outcome of the meeting of Ministers is the declaration concerning the promotion of trade in developing countries. The contracting parties agreed that their governments would commit themselves to observe the extent possible the principles underlying the Declaration, to reduce in the near future barriers to exports from developing countries. These principles and certain facts relating to tariff and non-tariff barriers affecting access to markets are set forth in the Declaration under the following headings: quantitative restrictions, tariffs, tax law nature, trade commodities.

Remember that, it is difficult to assess the effects of generalized tariff preferences on the export earnings of countries in the developing world. These effects depend largely on the psychological and economic impact on the volume of investments in those countries. Some economists have calculated that these exports could increase by about $ 1 billion per year (John PINCUS, 1968). The implementation of decisions of the contracting parties and the search for practical measures to that end have led to the establishment, towards the end of 1962, of a program of action in eight points that the Ministers adopted in general, subject to certain points in their meeting in May 1963.

EIGHT-POINT PROGRAM ESTABLISHED BY THE GATT

The first major concerted efforts by member countries of GATT to promote, on a multilateral basis, the expansion of trade in country development, led to the adoption by the Ministerial meeting in May 1963 of a «Program of action» in eight points. The main recommendations relating to tariffs aimed: duty-free tropical products, the elimination of tariffs on primary products, the reduction and elimination of tariff barriers that hinder exports of semi-products and products manufactures from less developed countries. The results of this « program action » have largely disappointed the hopes it had created (GATT, 1963).

The agenda has significantly contributed to enhancing trade liberalization. It revolves around eight points which are: i) Developed countries should not introduce any new tariff or non-tariff barrier to trade export of developing countries for products which it is established that they are of interest particularly for those countries ; ii) Quantitative restrictions on imports of products from developing countries that are contrary to the provisions of the general agreement will be abolished within one year; iii) Admission free of tropical products in developed countries must occur before December 31, 1963 ; iv) The developed countries which must eliminate tariffs on primary products occupy an important place in the trade of developing countries; v) The industrialized countries must also adopt an urgent timeline for reduction and elimination of tariff barriers to exports of semi-finished manufactured products from developing countries, providing that current tariffs will be reduced by at least 50% within three years to come ; vi) Developed countries should gradually reduce import duties and internal taxation on products derived wholly or mainly in developing countries, in order to be removed by December 31, 1965; vii) Developed countries that maintain the above obstacles will have to report to the GATT Secretariat in July of each year, on the measures they have taken the previous year, to implement these decisions and measures they intend to take over the next twelve months to expand access to markets for developing countries; viii) The contracting parties should also, urgently consider adopting other measures to facilitate the efforts of developing countries to diversify their economies, strengthen their capacity export and increase revenue from their sales abroad.

For developing countries, the first seven points of the program only provide a minimum program and the eighth point demands, to achieve the common objective which is the strongest and fastest increase in export earnings of all developing countries, affirmative action other than removing barriers to trade (The Role of GATT in the Field of Trade and Development, Geneva, March 1964, p. 26). The GATT has also taken action on some tropical products, especially cotton.

TROPICAL PRODUCTS

Tropical products hold a predominant place on the list of products studied by the Third Committee. The committee conducted a detailed examination of the obstacles facing the expansion of exports of these products and it has highlighted in this regard, the adverse effects of high tariffs and heavy internal taxes which are levied in the importing country. Since then, the GATT has paid particular attention to the study of trade in tropical products. To this end and following the proposed duty-free tropical products that Nigeria was presented at the Ministerial Meeting in November 1961, it established a panel in early 1962. The group's mandate was: "Given all the factors relating to current problems and future international trade in tropical products, it is necessary to consider ways of overcoming the difficulties faced by least developed country exporters of these products and of making appropriate proposals" (The Role of GATT in the Field of Trade and Development, Geneva, March 1964, p. 27).

The task of the panel reflects the way the GATT considers issues that trade in commodities in general poses to developing countries. Its approach to these problems is broad, and takes into account all relevant factors relating to trade and economic development. The panel discussed these issues in their broader aspects, linking the price considerations and conditions of access to considerations relating to production and consumption, future prospects, the obstacles to trade, the effects of the abolition of preferential agreements on the countries that are currently enjoying it and the opportunity to offset the adverse impact, such a measure would lead to those countries, such as providing financial assistance and encouraging other types of production for export. The GATT has studied very carefully the issues relating to certain tropical products like cocoa, coffee, bananas, oil-seeds and vegetable oils, tea, tropical timber.

TRADE IN COTTON TEXTILES

Given the evolution of international trade in cotton textiles, this sector of world trade has been the subject of special attention. A long-term agreement came out on international trade in cotton textiles. This agreement aims at allowing the growth of international trade in cotton textiles while avoiding the effects of disruption in a vital sector of the economy of developed and developing countries. The importing and exporting countries have welcomed the idea of a long-term agreement and have considered it preferable to any alternative. The agreement provides opportunities when there is disruption of market or threat of market disruption, according to the definition given in an annex to the agreement. The mitigation measures must include some annual growth of imports. All current restrictions in importing countries must be phased out. Developing countries attaching greater importance to the provisions of the agreement, including those concerning the disruption of markets, are strictly observed. When in December 1963, the committee of cotton textiles has conducted its first comprehensive review of the implementation of the agreement; it adopted conclusions on this and other issues relating to the interpretation and the implementation of the agreement.

In the case of GATT and textiles, the first thing to bear in mind is that these legal systems mainly obey the interests of those states which bring about such regulations and which in a given moment had sufficient strength to achieve their proposals without hardly adjusting them. These states as can be seen from both the negotiations and the texts themselves, did not have the application of economic theories such as the interests of the free market as their goal in furthering the development of international society. This can be seen not only from the GATT text but also from the maintenance and in some cases the improvement of privileged positions in the sphere of international trade with the ideological function of law used as a useful sub-product. In the case of textiles where developed countries had lost their competivity in the majority of products, the objective was exactly the reverse: to cancel the effects that a policy based in these comparative advantages could produce, given that they would bring about an end to its non-competitive industries in that sector. On this point, Robertson correctly states that:

> "experience since the 1950s has shown that, any developing country that achieves success in exporting to industrial countries must expect to find that access to these markets will be restricted" (Patterson, 1966; Kojima, 1977).

REGIONAL GROUPINGS FAVORED BY THE GATT

In Article 24 the text of the general agreement recognizes the need for the integration of national economies to better yields. These groups promoted by the GATT may take the form of a zone of free trade, a customs union or a community. Since the inception of the GATT, these groupings were formed here and there, meeting the aspirations of each region. These groups are now in large numbers. They are not very detailed and have different legal characteristics. For clarity and brevity, we shall not discuss all these programs. Rather we will focus only on the study of some examples.

EUROPEAN ECONOMIC COMMUNITY: EEC

After the Second World War, the American Secretary of State for Foreign Affairs George Marshall, launched a vast program of recovery in European countries ruined by war. The plan known as the Marshall plan was the source of the EEC. But the Soviet Union and other popular democracies had refused that American aid.

The treaty establishing the European Economic Community was signed in Rome in 1957 and thus, became known as the Treaty of Rome. Initially, only six states, members of the community increased to twelve. They are Belgium, Luxembourg, France, Netherlands, the Federal Republic of Germany, Italy, United Kingdom, Portugal, Greece, Spain, Ireland and Denmark. The treaty came into force on 1 January 1958 and was submitted for consideration by the contracting parties at the twelfth session, which was to decide on the conformity of the treaty to the provisions of Article 24 of the general agreement. It is recognized that the details of many important features of the Treaty of Rome are to be decided by the institutions of the community and it is impossible at this stage to consider the terms in relation to the provisions of the general agreement.

The contracting parties have therefore agreed that multilateral consuls could be of necessity between the community and the contracting parties who feel aggrieved by the specific measures taken by the community. A working committee was established to study problems that may arise from the combination of overseas territories with the EEC, which such problems would hinder the trade of other contracting parties of the GATT. At each session of the contracting parties, the representative of the community commission shall report on the development of community activities and decisions taken in trade. It was also noted that all future arrangements between the EEC and other states were subject to the review of the contracting parties.

Objectives and functioning of the EEC

By establishing the EEC, the signatory countries of the treaty were intended to promote harmonious development of economic activities throughout the community. The treaty of the EEC aims to create a homogeneous economic entity - it was planned to create a common market and the gradual approximation of economic policies of member states. Regarding the customs legislation in particular, the constitution of the community based on the formation of a customs union comprising: i) Elimination between member states of customs duties and quantitative restrictions; ii) The establishment of a common customs tariff; iii) The establishment of a common agricultural policy; iv) the establishment of a common commercial policy; v) The approximation of national legislation and the creation of a community law; vi) The approximation of tax laws.

In the years that followed the creation of the common market, the community has entered into various association agreements with many countries, mostly European. These association agreements have resulted in the implementation of new very important custom regulations. In the same vein, the establishment from 1st July 1971 of the system of tariff preferences for developing countries has changed to considerably trade relations between these countries and the EEC, and leads the implementation of a new regulation. There are areas in which the common market has brought profound changes in the laws and custom regulations. Without going into details, we will only see the legal acts issued by the council and commission of the community which are the resources available to those bodies to achieve the objectives set in particular by the Treaty of Rome.

To achieve the progressive harmonization of laws, regulations and administrative provisions, member states of the council and commission of the community, shall adopt regulations and guidelines. Regarding regulations, they are of legal community by excellence. The regulations which supplement the provisions laid down by the treaties are directly applicable throughout the territory of the community without any intervention by national authorities. In each of the member states, utilities and individuals are subject to two legal systems: national legislation and regulatory community. The most important rules are made by the Council of Ministers proposed by the commission. The latter in turn adopts the regulations. As regards to the guidelines, they pose no directly applicable rules. They define the goals and commit the members to amend their national legislation in the direction indicated, but leaving to them the choice of means. Other categories of legal acts less important than the preceding can also apply the customs. They are decisions, recommendations and opinions, judgments and resolutions: i) the decisions are sent to a government, a company or an individual. They fulfill a very specific situation and have the force of law; ii) advice and recommendations: these acts give a solemn character to the steps taken by the council or the commission, but they are not legally binding on member states; iii) judgments of the court of justice ensure compliance with the law. The court interprets and applies the treaty provisions, regulations and guidelines; iv) resolutions of the council are the views of the council on a given problem. They are not binding on member states and these can only be inspired from.

The community has concluded with many countries of the association, agreements to promote trade by reducing tariffs on imports in each contracting party. These agreements may establish between the community and the states concerned either a customs union or a free trade agreement. Yet some large power countries worry about preferential arrangements negotiated by the EEC with a large number of African and Mediterranean countries. The trend towards regionalization of trade among Third World countries and industrialized countries has contributed to increased feelings of frustration and protectionist forces in the United States who have not hidden on some occasions their intention to have resort to trade retaliation against the EEC (The Journal of Commerce, 1969; Duty, 1970). For its part, Canada is becoming more worried about the prospects of increased isolation and the risk of being drawn completely into the American orbit. In November 1970, the Minister of Industry and Commerce, Jean-Luc Pepin, said: “we are concerned about the proliferation of preferential arrangements negotiated by the EEC with a large number of African and Mediterranean countries. There is a serious risk that the eventual accession of the United Kingdom to the EEC will give rise to similar discriminatory arrangements with many developing Commonwealth countries. A discrimination on the hemispheric basis would lead to a concentration of economic activity that would benefit only a few blocks in extending their sphere of economic influence” (Minister of Industry and Commerce, Canada, 1970). In some measures, industrialized countries have not benefited from their proposals to the Third World to settle their old scores as noted by Jeune (1969).

For some superpowers, it is actually the use of an instrument of generalized trade discrimination to limit or eliminate selective and regional trade discrimination. This, however, does not question the legal basis of relations between Western countries and the Third World, since it is an autonomous act with no contractual obligation, even if the legal framework of the GATT should be adapted because of an exception to the principle of non-discrimination. The Director-General of the GATT considers that this development will lead to a multilateral trading system at two levels: "I see a situation now developing where, for some time; a kind of two-stage system of non-discriminatory treatment may exist in the trading world. As a foundation would remain the generalized most favored-nation tariff treatment for ailing GATT countries and, built upon this as a kind of temporary superstructure, basically non-discriminatory tariff preferences by developed for developing countries measures of this sort, represent an important new element in international trading relationships which the multilateral system of trade must accommodate in a positive and realistic way. They should help the phasing out of discriminatory preferential arrangements between developed and one of a few developing countries. Such arrangements run counter to the purposes of the generalized scheme of preferences. They provide a potent source of friction and disharmony among developing countries" (Olivier, 1970). Like the countries of Western Europe, the West African states have created a common market as large and ambitious as the EEC: the ECOWAS.

ECONOMIC COMMUNITY OF WEST AFRICAN STATES (ECOWAS)

The phenomenon of regional integration is nowadays widespread. All states of the world, are aware that solitary actions are always doomed to failure in this world of economic turmoil, seek refuge behind regional groupings. Africa is not an exception. It was established in Africa several regional groupings that met the wishes of leaders in order to prevent an extreme balkanization of the continent to be an obstacle to economic expansion. These groups include the ECOWAS, ECCAS and others. We will put special emphasis on ECOWAS, not only because it has the largest number of States but also because it presents itself to all the diversities of the continent (it includes small and large Francophone, Anglophone and Lusophone states).

The ECOWAS with Mauritania, this group has 243 million inhabitants in 2003 (UN, 2004) and represents 35% of the population of Sub-Saharan Africa. The treaty establishing ECOWAS was signed in May 28, 1975 in Lagos at the initiative of Togo and Nigeria. Member states, at first sixteen in number, which went to fifteen today. These are: Benin, Burkina Faso, Cape Verde, Cote d'Ivoire, Gambia, Ghana, Guinea, Guinea Bevel, Liberia, Mali, Niger, Nigeria, Senegal, Sierra Leone and Togo. Among them Nigeria played an important role. Nigeria contributed in every way to assist the ECOWAS to realize its objective of integrating West African Countries, in order to consolidate the regional peace and security and to free the people of the Community from poverty and marginalization (Olusegun, 2007). The member states have decided to overcome their linguistic distinctions by addressing geographic, economic and political barriers, which exist and which complicate the problem of the ECOWAS, which is yet intended to be a privileged instrument of economic cooperation by creating a vast market more than 150 million consumers. The administration of ECOWAS is ensured by the Executive Secretariat and the Presidency by one of the heads of state for a period of two years.

Objectives and functioning of the ECOWAS

West Africa has to take up significant challenges "to contribute in a sustainable way to satisfying the food needs of the population, to economic and social development and to reducing poverty in the member states and the inequalities between territories, areas and countries" (ECOWAP and ECOWAS, 2005). ECOWAS has set a goal to "promote cooperation and development in all areas of economic activity, particularly in the fields of industry, transport, telecommunications, agriculture, natural resources, trade, monetary and financial issues, as well as social and cultural context in order to improve the standard of living, increase and maintain economic stability, to promote the reinforcement of the relations between member states and contribute to the progress and development of Africa".

To achieve these objectives, the action of ECOWAS is done in stages: i) elimination between member states of customs duties and other charges having equivalent effect ; ii) the abolition of quantitative restrictions and administrative trade between member states; iii) the establishment of a common customs tariff and a common commercial policy towards third countries; iv) the abolition among member states of barriers to the free movement of people, services and capital ; v) harmonization of agricultural policies and promotion of community projects including member states in the field of marketing research and that in the agro-industrial vi) harmonization of the system on the proper functioning of the monetary policies of member states.

At the same time, especially nowadays, we must admit that the functioning of an agreement requires a long-term stability to guarantee individual economic partnerships and foreign direct investment. The operation to maturity of a preferential agreement comes after a period of investment or running in routines of operating providers. For example, European importers argue that the introduction of the generalized system of preferences for specific countries fighting against drug trafficking had taken 4 to 5 years (Gallezot and Bureau, 2005). In other words, to take the path of an incompatible agreement (and which can be appealed to the DSB) poses a significant threat to the viability of the project and business. ECOWAS is now faced with problems such as: i) commercial food-deficit and food addiction. The degradation of the food trade balance corresponds to increases in imports (Gallezot, 2006) which were even stronger in volume since import prices have fallen. This situation is quite paradoxical in view of the place of agriculture in the ECOWAS; ii) a difficult regional integration. A too strong opening of foreign markets could destabilize the trade relations of proximity and have serious consequences on the coherence and stability of the regional union. A recent study emphasized the correlation between the rise of conflicts being associated with the degradation of local exchanges, and vice versa, of stability when trade relations are important (Martin et al., 2006). The presence of similar products is highlighted in the literature to explain the structural reasons for failure of regional integration (Cadot et al., 2005); iii) the weak border protection of ECOWAS. The weak protection of markets of ECOWAS in the framework of the implementation of EPAs must be put into perspective with the cycles of multilateral negotiations. Although the timing of the Doha Round is being compromised, a resumption of multilateral liberalization will lead to a mechanism of erosion of preferential margins (Bouët et al., 2005).

ECOWAS appears to be an organization with multiple dimensions. The elimination of tariffs and quantitative restrictions in intra-community relations is one of the cornerstones of the treaty of Lagos. ECOWAS, despite some difficulties in applying the legislation and decisions taken by different bodies, is the only economic grouping of hope for West African States. It is now a well established truth that, the development of any country must necessarily go through a consolidation at the regional level. Thus, every country in the world is struggling to form regional groupings.

Other regional groupings favored by the GATT

We do not intend to attempt studying all regional groupings around the world. Indeed, some of these groups comprise a very small number of countries and therefore, have a negligible importance. Some instead grouping a large number of states weigh all their weight in international trade relations. We will discuss some of them.

ACP-EEC

The African, Caribbean and Pacific countries associated with the EEC through agreements known as the ACP-EEC Convention. These agreements are intended to focus on trade between the ACP and the EEC. Under the agreements, products originating in ACP countries and transported directly to the ECE countries, subject to production of certificate of exemption, benefit from customs duties and abolition of quantitative restrictions (except agricultural products which are the common organization of markets). In contrast, the ACP states retain the right to receive, during the import of EU products on their territory, customs duties to promote the development of their economy. Agreements with ACP countries impose no obligation of reciprocity. The EU products have nevertheless benefit from the provision of most favored nation.

Begun with the Arusha Conference and Yaoundé, the ACP-EEC reached its full development phase at the Lomé agreements. Among the Lomé agreements are included those of Lomé signed in February 1975, the Lomé II signed October 31, 1979, the Lomé III signed December 8, 1984, the Lomé IV, signed December 15, 1989. Measures are taken to compensate the losses suffered by the ACP because of the trade with the EEC. That is what justifies the agreement of the financial envelopes. Special provisions are taken for stabilizing the prices of certain products (e.g. STABEX). These agreements, despite some difficulties, remain a privileged part of the North-South dialogue.

EFTA

On November 20, 1959, seven European countries signed a convention of the Stockholm Convention establishing the association of European free trade association (EFTA). These countries are Austria, Denmark, Norway, Portugal, Sweden, Switzerland and the United Kingdom. The objective of the convention, which would enter into force on 1 July 1961, is to establish a free trade by phasing out tariffs on key industrial products and reduction of quantitative restrictions.

LAFTA

The Montevideo Treaty which created the Latin American Free Trade Association was signed on February 18, 1960 by Brazil, Chile, Peru and Uruguay. Argentina, Mexico and Paraguay have subsequently acceded to this Treaty and in 1961 Colombia and Ecuador have made their entry into the association. At the seventeenth session of the GATT in 1960 that the Treaty of Montevideo had a deep consideration by the contracting parties to ensure compliance with the treaty provisions of Article 24 of the general agreement.

However, when periods of recession come along, the very same states who were theoretically interested in respecting the trade system which they had set up in 1945 turned without fail to protectionist measures and moved away from the main objectives of GATT (SAPIR, op.cit., p. 423). Thus the GATT was replaced in January 1995 by the world trade organization (WTO) in order to respond to the insufficient of this institution (GATT). In order to solve specific problems of developing countries, UNCTAD was created in 1962 with the aim of improving the conditions of trade between developing countries in establishing a new world economic order. The problem of preferential treatment was always in the study of UNCTAD, as well as in the context of multilateral trade negotiations which are held under the GATT (Document:-A/CN.4/L.268, 1978).

Organization and functions of WTO

It has a permanent administrative structure which gives it great stability and institutional continuity. It has three major bodies: i) the Ministerial Conference: This is the body which brings together members of the WTO. It meets at least every two years, sets the general policy of the WTO and decide all issues related to multilateral trade agreements; ii) the General Council: It is the permanent body to exercise the powers of the Ministerial Conference when it is not sitting in plenary iii) Dispute Settlement System (DSS): it is the great innovation compared to the GATT.

Indeed, the litigation is characterized by its non-jurisdictional nature. The WTO implements mechanisms of law. The DSS will review disputes by panels, shall have the power to adopt the reports of these groups and the appellate body and finally will be responsible for overseeing the implementation of the decisions. The WTO must fulfill three essential functions: i) monitor compliance with the agreements between members; ii) organize the settlement of trade disputes between members; iii) continuity of negotiations with the aim of further liberalizing trade especially services.

Progress of WTO compared to the GATT

The progress of the WTO compared to the GATT are enormous and are without any doubt to be at the credit of the WTO: i) the WTO is a truly international organization, responsible for ensuring compliance with standards accepted by its members; ii) the WTO is responsible for arbitrating commercial disputes that oppose the countries. For this, it has structures to achieve this arbitration (DSS); iii) the WTO is the blueprint of a genuine international trade law; iv) in theory, countries are on an equal footing. The WTO gives smaller countries the opportunity to turn against the majority; v) the rich countries have a means to require from the South to open their markets; vi) the powers of the WTO have expanded to new areas: services, intellectual property right. Free trade promotes the GATT by the successive elimination of trade barriers which had originally no universal vocation. However, the collapse of the Soviet system, the globalization of the economy and the creation of the WTO now seem to create a global free trade (Sandrine, 2002/2003).

It is essential to note that, it finds the limits of current WTO namely: i) the bilateral practice did not disappear; ii) the United States continues to use the threat of the famous sections 301 and super 301 of U.S. trade law to deal with trade practices deemed unfair and continues to threaten a sanction of companies that do business with Cuba, Iran, Libya and Iraq. It can also wonder whether the DSS has really the means to enforce its recommendations. The WTO is now an institution in crisis: the Doha Round which began in 2001 is still not completed in 2009. The crisis of this institution stems from conflicts between major developed powers, including on agriculture, but also with developing countries on the role of services (GATT, 1947 to 1995). Finally, the DSS has a misleading name: it facilitates the settlement of disputes rather than the rule itself. It is therefore an administrative, not judicial, assistance in implementing the obligations of members[3] (Julien, 2005).

Conclusion

When highlighting the achievements of the GATT, the first aspect to be pointed out is the fact that, the system has managed to survive up until its recent substitution by the WTO. In its regulatory role of international trade (Jackson and Winhan) it has, at least in theory, controlled more than 80% of world trade (MAGRO MAS, op.cit., p. 200) and has also settled multiple economic conflicts by coercing those contracting parties which wanted to adopt certain measures contrary to the established rules, through consulting and even through tolerating conduct of dubious legality (such as GATT's position). A second and undeniable achievement has been the continuous expansion of international trade, which began to take place from the moment that the arrangement was applied (especially among the developed countries) (Jaenicke, 1983) thanks to tariff reductions in those manufacturing sectors not considered as "sensitive" and with considerable access in these areas especially from the incorporation in the "Kennedy round", of the lineal system (Jackson, 1967: p. 137) in substitution for the product by product system. From then on and until the "Uruguay round", such a system has been used with notable success. The GATT is both a collection of agreements and negotiations center (Olivier, 1976).

The GATT had probably played a predominant role in the international trade. This idea is corroborated by Olivier Long, who said "in this world full of uncertainty and innovation, the GATT is one of the oldest and most known institutions. Therefore, it must be prepared to

---

[3] On this point santulli, supra note 102 at P. 82

comply with a critical analysis and to provide adequate follow-up. This analysis is now underway. It might well reveal flaws that should be corrected. But I firmly believe that the GATT has altogether proved its great value for all trading countries, both developed, in developing or socialist. As a code of agreed principles of international trade, live and in constant evolution, it is the essential feature in which members operate and develop their trade and commercial relations. As a place of meeting, it gives way to solve trade problems as at when they arise, to prevent any relapse into protectionism that all nations would suffer greatly, and develop the international trading system as given necessities. Finally, today, where countries require development of imaginative measures to meet their needs of trade, the GATT is the effective tool with which governments seek to make agreement on measures to meet these needs".

The GATT remained since the end of the Second World War as the only multilateral code governing international trade and for more than 40 years, several changes were made in trade relations between the different nations of the world. The GATT has, during this period, risen concrete positive actions; but in some areas, it remains to be done.

This conclusion will be a somewhat hasty review of the GATT at the period of its evolution. In the assets of the GATT, it must include the multilateral negotiations which allow several nations to express their views on issues of international trade. The GATT has devoted special attention to the problems of developing countries and has established a special procedure for resolving disputes between contracting parties. Enormous efforts are made to facilitate access for developing countries to markets of industrialized countries. Some measures are taken regarding the trade of some products of strategic interest to developing countries. The GATT has prevented the international trade in the fall of bilateralism and the pre-war period, and has released several tariff and non-tariff barriers.

It should be noted that one of the main objectives of the GATT is to promote development, and raise living standards in developing countries which is far from being achieved. There is, however, the opposite phenomenon. GATT is responsible for the deterioration of terms of trade of developing countries. The GATT Agreement shall, to maintain its credibility, address the critical issue of deteriorating terms of trade. The recommendations must have the force of law and become directly enforceable in member states. Given these shortcomings of the known role of GATT (entered into force in 1948) in international trade, it was replaced by the WTO in January 1995. Despite the significant progress of the WTO in resolving problems of international trade, this new organization is currently experiencing limitations. Since the gap in many economic areas in general, and particularly in international trade, is very wide between the developed and developing countries, problems will not be lacking in the management of commercial disputes.

ACKNOWLEDGMENTS

We thank the Chinese Scholarship Council and the Togolese government for their assistance in the preparation of this paper. In addition, we are also grateful to the comments and suggestions made by Dr Tang-ke, Dr Mawunou Zinse and Dr T. Alphaeus Koroma.

REFERENCES

Bouet A, Fontagné L, Jean S (2005). Is Erosion of Tariff Preferences a Serious Concern? "mimeo, CEPII Paris.
Cobb J (1994). The new GATT agreement "Regulation, 2: p. 11.
Common Market (1961). A monthly Review of European. Integr. Econ. Dev., p. 9.
Conclusions and resolutions adopted at the Ministerial Meeting of GATT Contracting Parties (1963). Basic Instruments and Selected Documents, p. 12.
Cadot O, De Melo J, Olarreaga M (2005). Regional integration in Africa: where are we? Asymmetric Regionalism in Sub-Saharan Africa: Where Do We Stand? Working Paper.
Chirstian D (2006). WTO / WTO Pol.4470.
Document:- A/CN.4/L.268 (1978). Nation clause most-favored: statement by the representative of the UNCTAD secretariat at the 1497th meeting, at the request of the Commission. Extrait of the Yearbook of the International Law Commission, II: 2.
Dunkel A (1991). The Uruguay Round Agreement on Agriculture Proposals. Text on Agriculture, MTN-TNC/W/FA, p. 22.
Europe International Information Press (1971). News Series No. 777 (30 mars1971), and "EEC Preferences Held has MajorForce Widening in World Trade", J. Comm., p. 1.
Gallezot J (2006). Challenges and flexibilities of ECOWAS and the challenge of agricultural negotiations, "ROPPA, July, p. 47.
Gallezot J, Bureau JC (2005). "Preferential Trading Arrangements in Agricultural and Food Markets. The Case Of The European Union and the United States", OECD ed, p. 183.
GATT (1947-1995). The role of GATT in international trade "
GATT (1964). The Role of GATT in the Field of Trade and Development, Geneva ".
Jean-Marie B (1994). The agricultural negotiations in the Uruguay Round.
Jacques G (2006). For sustainable development in West Africa: Food sovereignty.
Jackson (1967). op.cit., and Winham, op.cit. pp.160-797.
Jaenicke (1983). op.cit., p. 27.
Julien B (2005). Effectiveness Of Dispute Settlement Mechanism Of The Wto: Towards A Better The Multilateral Trading System Predictability.
Kojima K (1977). Japan and a New World Economic Order, Croom Helm, London, quoted in Robertson, p. 25.
Martin P, Mayer T, Thoening M (2006). Make Trade not War ", Working, p. 37.
Olivier L (1976). GATT (Geneva), an instrument for multilateral negotiations, Mr. LONG delivered the text of the speech before an audience gathered at the Pakistan Institute of International Affairs (Karachi).
Olusegun O (2007). The Challenge Of Democracy And Development In Africa, Interview.
Pincus J (1968). Trade, Aid and Development, McGraw-Hill Book Company, pp. 225-230.
General Principle (1964). of the Final Act adopted by the first UN Conference on Trade Dev., p. 8.
Patterson G (1966). Textile and Clothing Industries: Structural problems and policies in OECD Countries, OECD, Paris.
Reuter P (1970). La Convention de Vienne du 23 mai 1969 sur le Droit

des Traités, Paris, p. 17.
Revue Jeune Afrique (1969).
Sergio D (2008) .Organisation Mondiale du Commerce, ACCÈS AUX MARCHÉS DANS LE GATT/OMC.
Sandrine D (2002/2003). Les relations entre les règles des accords multilateraux sur l'environnement et celles de l'OMC.
US Lagging Behind on Préférences Plan » (1971). United Nations Juridical Yearbook (1964). J. Comm., p. 1.
WTO/OMC (1998). .FOCUS, Bulletin d'information N, p. 30.

Consequences of fiscal deficit

Artan Nimani

Faculty of Applied Business Sciences in Peja, University of Prishtina, Republic of Kosovo.

The main objective of this paper is to understand and to evaluate recently expressed popular anxiety about fiscal deficits. The paper begins with a discussion of problems involved in measuring the fiscal deficit. A general conclusion is that all interesting measures of the federal fiscal deficit have increased substantially over the past eight presidential terms and are likely to increase further in the near future. The paper goes on to analyze possible connections between fiscal deficits and inflation, economic growth, and fluctuations in the level and composition of economic activity. Fiscal deficit is the difference between current and capital expenditure and current receipts the debt trap. The fiscal policy is intended to play a key role in the prospective economic growth. It is not merely because of the fact that fiscal situation is a major component that determines the macroeconomic stability. Important conclusions are that of the monetary policy, inflation, and aggregate economic activity are all largely independent of the fiscal deficit, but that of the fiscal deficit can have major effects on the division of output between consumption and investment. Key elements in the analysis are the effects of taxation on consumption and investment demands and the relations between real and financial developments.

Key words: fiscal deficit, real exchange rate, financial integration, fiscal sustainability, EU, panel co integration.

INTRODUCTION

Economic problems as consequence of fiscal deficit

Fiscal deficit is the difference between current plus capital expenditure and current receipts. When a government spends more than it receives in taxes and other revenues in a given year, it has a budget deficit (Stiglitz and Walsh 2008) commonly referred to as the fiscal deficit. If a government runs a deficit; it borrows on financing the gap between expenditure and taxation; as a result, the stock of outstanding debt is increased. It is necessary to analyze the cause of fiscal deficits to see when such can or cannot cause economic problems. Investment expenditures such as those on infrastructure yield returns that exceed the interest paid. These expenditures will improve future government revenues e.g. $100 spent to finance the construction of a stretch of highway may yield additional revenue of $5 additional revenue to government every year. Likewise, it represents an increase in revenue greater than the Revenue Consequences of Capital Expenditure (RCCE). The fiscal deficit is justified in such a case. Fiscal deficit to finance capital expenditures on building of bridges, roads, dams, railway lines, water supply systems, etc. can also be justified due to inter-generational distribution of costs so that later generations will also use such services. When deficit is used to finance a revenue deficit, aggregate consumption increases as the government uses the money for consumption expenditure, while there is fall in investment. This will lead to decline in the GDP growth and the growth rate of economy will fall. In such case, the government will spend all its revenue on interest payments leading to potentially serious political and economic problems. However, it is a risk if there are long term deficits and ultimately countries risk falling into the debt trap.

In addition, governments may run deficits due to higher defense spending during wartimes such as in U.S. during the 1970s Vietnam war when it was 8.4% of GDP. Increased social sector spending such as on elderly, and health care expenditures cause higher deficits as well. Similarly, expenditures on healthcare were rising rapidly in 2003, China and India proclaimed increased fiscal deficits compared with previous year, of 5.6 and 3% of GDP, respectively. In both cases, deficits were used mainly finance increased infrastructure, defence and social sector spending. However, increased government borrowings such as through issuance of bonds increase the interest rates. Thus, the deficit financing of the revenue deficit causes crowding out of potential flow of investment resources to the private sector and also reduces private welfare by reducing private consumption enabling the government to consume more. It is clear that governments running deficits accumulate debt, as the fiscal deficits to finance investment expenditures for future revenues may be justified and those to finance revenue deficits may cause economic problems.

SIGNIFICANCE OF SOURCES COVERING GOVERNMENT DEBTS

When the government runs a deficit, it must borrow to finance the difference between expenditure and revenues. Subsequently, due to borrowings, the government accumulates debt.

Domestic/national debt

Governments may accumulate national debt by issuing bonds that are subscribed to by the private sector in the country. In this case of national debt, there is no subtraction from the net wealth of the nation as the assets of the government are owned by the citizens themselves. Furthermore, national debt also has redistributive effects when only relatively well-off people with savings may be able to subscribe to the bonds and have claims to national debt, considering here crowding out and impact on interest rates.

The national debt can either be repaid through increased taxation or through cuts in expenditure. As mentioned by Stiglitz and Walsh 2008, taxation affects risk taking, the allocation of resources to research and development, and long run rate of growth of economy. Further, taxation affects behaviour of individuals and firms and can lead to changes between pre-tax and post tax decisions. National debt can have inter-generational implications. With the fast increasing population of those eligible for social security and medical care and increasing health care costs in U.S and Europe, the financial costs for social sector is increasing. In addition, some people in Europe criticize, the selfish sixties (1960s) and those who enjoyed benefits of free education and healthcare financed by debt that burdens the present generation. Thus, in most countries, governments are reluctant to incur debt for welfare and social spending on grounds of such claims about inter-generational inequity.

External/foreign debt

Implications of increasing foreign debt may lead to flow of resources outside of the country due to increased interest payment and therefore reduction in GDP growth. When a government incurs foreign debt, it leads to reduction in the net wealth of the government. Nepal's fiscal deficit stood at 8.4% of GDP and the external debt stood at 6.0% of GDP in 1990. These reduced to 5.7 and 4.0% of GDP, respectively, in 1997. In Nepal nearly 28.6% of the total fixed (capital) investment during the five year plan is through foreign assistance. Foreign borrowings to fund infrastructure can lead to rapid economic growth, but inappropriate and excessive foreign borrowing generate debt service obligations that will constrain future economic policy and growth

In addition, excessive foreign borrowings may lead to debt trap for example, when Africa as a whole pays more to rich countries as way of interest and debt repayments than it receives in foreign aid and loans. When a country is not able to repay borrowings from its own sources, it has to borrow to repay loans. Thus, external debt is more serious problem than national debt as it can impoverish a country. Secondly, external debt is also subject to risk of exchange rate fluctuations that increases external debt repayment when a currency is reduced in value while the external debt is denominated in a foreign currency.

DEFICIT REDUCTION TECHNIQUES

As governments borrow to finance deficit, they are under pressure from external sources such as IMF and World Bank and also through legal agreements such as Gramm-Rudman-Hollings Law of 1985 in U.S and Maastricht Treaty of 1992 in European Union to reduce deficit. The Gramm-Rudman-Hollings Law of 1985 in U.S. had two main provisions – it sets budget deficit targets and automatic series of cuts if the targets were not met. Secondly, any new spending programmed must be explicitly financed either by cutting other programmers or by raising revenues. The Act was later ruled to be unconstitutional, but its two main provisions stayed in force and caused reduction in budget deficit. Maastricht Treaty of 1992 in EU had the budget deficits constrained at 3% of GDP, the gross public debt constrained at 60% of GDP and inflation rate within 1.5% of the three EU countries with lowest inflation rates which ruled out inflationary methods of funding deficits. To reduce deficit governments, either under external pressure (mostly in developing countries) or under legal agreements such as US and EU as shown above, use various means such as dissimulation of assets through privatization, reduce public investments, reduce operation and maintenance (O and M) spending, shift revenue and expenditure over time and run implicit liabilities.

Privatization

William Easterly (1999; pp 58) underlined that governments in developed and developing countries used privatization receipts to cut deficits e.g. Nigeria by selling equity shares in upstream oil ventures for US $ 2.5 billion due to IMF stand-by agreements and two World Bank adjustment loans during 1989 - 93. And United States due to fiscal rule of Gramm-Rudman-Hollings Law of 1985 had $7 billion of asset sales in 1987 (Easterly, 1999; pp 58). Easterly, further notes that there is strong correlation between privatization revenues as a percentage of GDP and IMF/WB adjustment loans, although governments forced to reduce liabilities will reduce assets [through privatization (Easterly 1999 pp 68). Privatization receipts in euro countries after Maastricht Treaty more than quadrupled while it fell in non-euro countries.

Further, Germany reclassified public hospitals into corporate sector in 1997, thereby taking these debts out of general government debt to reduce deficits (Easterly, (1999) Fiscal Illusion: Taking the Bite Out of Budget Cuts, Economic Policy, April 1999; pp 58). Thus, privatization when done for financial reasons rather than efficiency, leads to illusory fiscal adjustment.

Public investment reduction

In periods of restrictive fiscal policies, capital expenditures are the first to be cut. Regarding this issue, during fiscal adjustment, governments cut capital spending (about 35%) by far more than other categories like wages (about 10%). Further, the African countries lowered their budget deficits during 1981-6 to 1990-1 mostly through cuts in capital investments (Easterly, 1999; pp 59). In euro countries, seven of the Euro countries reduced public investments as percentage of GDP, two left it unchanged while only two increased it after Maastricht Treaty.

Further, estimated rates of return on public investments such as infrastructure during 1983-92 by World Bank ranged from 19 (in telecommunication) to 29% (in highways) even State Owned Enterprise (SOE) investments can be profitable. However, due disinvestment by Zambian government in state copper company ZCCM to reduce deficit, the revenues from mining fell from 10.8 of GDP in 1970-4 to 1.6% of GDP in 1990-4 (Easterly, 1999; pp 59). Thus, cutting public investment to reduce deficits may be false economy.

Operation and maintenance (O and M) spending cut

Governments use this technique to reduce deficits e.g. in Philippines-cuts of about 40% in O and M expenditures to reduce deficit during 1983-5 and cuts by about 80% of O and M in Costa Rica during fiscal adjustment 1980s. There were cuts in O and M even in USA, in order to meet Gramm-Rudman-Hollings targets in 1980s (Easterly, 1999; pp 59). Delaying payment to government workers or suppliers to reduce the cash deficit and explicit debt is another technique although the accrual based net-worth remains same. Postponements of addressing financial crises, unfunded pension liabilities are themselves a hidden form of liability accumulation. Some governments ask the pension funds to lend to them on preferential rates that redistributes the expenditure over time although cutting deficit today (Easterly (1999) Fiscal Illusion: Taking the Bite Out of Budget Cuts', Economic Policy, April Easterly, 1999; pp 61).

The above section shows various techniques used by governments on reducing deficits due to external and internal pressures. These may be illusory as they can shift expenditures over time, increase implicit government liabilities, lead to reduction in growth of GDP and even reversal of fiscal improvements in future. As William Easterly (1999; pp 62) points out, the government maximizes the present value of the stream of present and future utility, subject to budget constraint. Further 'since the government is indifferent about the composition of net value, any externally imposed constraint on a subset of its components (e.g. explicit liabilities) can immediately be substituted by other components of net worth, and has no effect on the optimal path for consumption and net worth. The apparent fiscal adjustment is entirely illusory.

FACTORS ON REDUCING POVERTY

All these data serve on promoting a debate on the role of fiscal policies for poverty reduction. The following main issues need to be addressed and are the focus of the discussions.

BUDGET REVENUES

Economic growth and income generation

The fiscal policy is intended to play a key role in the prospective economic growth. It is not merely because of the fact that fiscal situation is a major component that determines the macroeconomic stability. The essential argument consists on the fact that the capacity of the Albanian economy to generate revenues remains highly limited. Although, in terms of economic growth performance, Albania has developed relatively well compared to the economies of the region, data indicate that the budget revenues are at a lower level compared to the GDP. At the end of 2001, budget revenues in relation to the GDP for some of the countries of the region are as the following:

(1) Albania 23 percent,
(2) Romania 31.5 percent,
(3) FYROM 35.3 percent,
(4) Bulgaria 40 percent.

Customs revenues continue to play an important role in

Table 1. Income Structure and Potential Growth.

Country	Total of revenues from taxes % of GDP*	Personals income taxes	Income taxes	Social insurance contributions	Goods and service
Albania	19.3	1.1	1.7	3.8	10.8
Bulgaria	30.8	4.7	3.3	8.0	12.8
FYROM	25.0	3.9	0.8	9.2	11.1
Rumania	30.1	4.1	3.0	9.1	10.0
Hungari	38.7	6.5	2.2	13.9	15.1
Italy	42.7	10.7	3.0	12.2	13.0

*note: the total of tax income in the above table includes also the social insurance contributions.

the total revenues of Albania in relation to the other countries with which it compares: At the end of 2001, customs revenues in relation to the GDP and the total budget revenues for some of the countries of the region are the following:

(1) Albania 2.2, 9.4%,
(2) FYROM 4.0, 11.2%,
(3) Romania 1.1, 3.5%,
(3) Bulgaria 0.9, 2.2%.

The implications of these developments are pointed out in Albania's perspective of the reduction of customs tariffs both in its perspective of free trade with the countries of the region (Table 1). From this analysis, it results that it is necessary to examine the alternatives for the increase of the revenues.

Income structure and potential growth

When analyzing the income structure at the end of 2001 according to the main categories we see: From the analysis of the tendencies noted as of 1997, we notice the following trends:

(i) Overall, the budget revenues from taxes have grown from 16.6 - 19.3% of the GDP; however, their level is much lower than that of the other countries surveyed in this analysis (obviously this ratio is much lower compared to the economies of the developed countries).
(ii) Indirect taxes account for the main share of this category of budget revenues: VAT (30.8% of the total tax income), customs revenues (9.4%) and from excises (7%). The growth of revenues in this category of income has come particularly from the increase of VAT revenues, mainly from the increase of its rate from 12 - 20%. Even though this is a slight tendency, the fact is that the revenues from the customs are declining, while the revenues from the excises have grown compared to 1997 and remain almost constant as of 1998. The VAT rate for some countries is as follows: Bulgaria - 20%; Croatia - 22%; FYROM - 19%, (5% farming products, energy, and transport); Romania - 19% (0% for goods and investments in the free zones).
(iii) The tax on the companies' revenues accounts for 7.6% of the total tax income, as against 4.6% in 1998. The rate of the profit tax 2 that is applied in Albania has been reduced from 30% in 2001 to 25%. This rate is 15% in FYROM, 18% in Hungary, 25% in Romania, 20% in Croatia, etc.
(iv) PERSONAL income tax has marked an increase of about 1% of the total income in 97-98 to 4.6% in 2001. Albania applies a progressive system of personal income tax system. In other countries, this tariff varies from 20% in Yugoslavia to 35% in Hungary and FYROM. Since 1998, Albania began application of taxes over the revenues created from the investments of the depositors (revenues from bank interest rates) and capital investments (over dividends).
(v) Revenues from social and health insurances make up 16.6% of the total income (or 3.8% of the GDP), marking a slight increase during all the period from 1996. The rates of social insurance contributions are much higher than the personal income taxes; on an average, the employers and the employees pay 35 - 45% of the salary fund in contributions.
(vi) Non-tax revenues which are composed almost entirely of the transfer profit of the Bank of Albania are another source of financial support to their country and also at the end of 2001, this category of income ranks third in terms of its size (after VAT and the revenues from customs taxes) with 8.1% of the total budget revenues, or 1.85% of the GDP. Resulting mainly from the high bank interest rates, this category of income will tend to go gradually down (0.5% of the GDP in the developed countries).
(vii) The levels of taxes or contributions in all the categories of income seem to be within the possible limits.
(viii) The level of consumption taxes (regressive taxes which weigh more heavily on the poor strata) are not differentiated.
(ix) Macroeconomic consolidation of the country and the integration trade processes will account for the flow out of a considerable share of budget revenues (tax and non

tax).

Informal economy

A major obstacle on increasing budget revenues is the spread of informal economy. In various documents, its figures vary from 40 - 60% of the GDP. There is no complete study of the informal economy in all its dimensions so far. Studies on the informal labour market indicate a figure which is approximately 25% that is relatively considerable in terms of the dimensions of the total labour market. Bearing in mind that these assessments describe only the informal employment and that it is much more difficult to make a comprehensive assessment of it, because of the under reporting of the level of wages of the employees employed in this system. The author might say that this phenomenon must be more widely spread. Hence, it is also an important source for the increase of revenues from social insurance, which have drawn a considerable part of state, transfers (about 2% of GDP), such funds might be reallocated to other fields of social sector and social protection.

Fiscal evasion - (avoidance by private entities of paying taxes and customs dues), apart from having major implications in upsetting the economic structure of the country and deforming the market, has also created an incalculable outflow for the country's finances. It is estimated that figure of fiscal evasion can be as high as about $ 500 million a year, a figure which is about 50% of the total revenues of the state budget. As can be seen from such data, the chance for increasing the supplementary revenues to the budget from the reduction/ elimination of the informal economy is a major source, and, given the current tax rates, probably the only one.

Tax system administrative aspects

Considering the legislative aspect, efforts have been focused on the establishment of a legal fiscal network. This is why there has been no equality among entities in the payment of taxes.

(i) Tax inspectors do not have the required authority to establish equality among tax entities and have not developed the necessary mechanisms to ensure this equality, also for the registered companies, while the number of unregistered companies that exercise economic activity is still very high. Although, it is hard to quantify it in figures, the fact that the media continue to publish reports on the actions (though sporadic) of the tax police and their sequestering of the assets of such companies are evidence to the fact that we do not yet have developed sustainable mechanisms of control. The companies themselves complain that the payment of taxes is more often based on the plan of budget revenues and not on the real indicators of the profitability of their activity. The reimbursement of the VAT still remains a chronic problem, placing the activity of various subjects in difficulties regarding their liquidities.

(ii) The auditing system of the accounting balances has constantly been a source of abuses, creating difficulties for the tax authorities. Auditing by the tax authorities cannot cover all the registered companies. On the other hand, the responsibility of the accounting experts in certifying the balance sheets of the companies is very undeveloped.

(iii) The customs procedures leave great opportunity for subjectivism by the customs agents, which incur supplementary costs to businesses.

In general, the climate of cooperation among these tax and customs institutions and businesses continues to remain distrustful. On the one hand, entities appeal that they are prevented in their activity by the fiscal authorities through subjective, arbitrary and discriminatory procedures and on the other hand, many companies carry out economic activities outside the fiscal system.

Government budget expenditures

The low level of budget revenues and the considerable increase of the public debt have brought pressure on the fiscal adjustment and have had an impact on the continuous reduction of government expenditures. In real terms, the increase of these expenditures began only after year 2000. Similar to the budget revenues, the expenditures also stand below the average level of the economies in transition. This has dictated the need for a reduction of expenses in all the categories, of which the only item that has grown is the payment of interests (25.3% of budget expenditures in 1998, dropping to 12.7% in 2001), due to the high bank interest rates. Since 2001, the Medium-Term Budget Program (MTBP) began to applied regarding from the point of view of a more effective and strategic management of government expenditures (Table 2). This document serves as an important orientation for preserving fiscal discipline, prioritizing public expenditures, and linking them better with the government policies and encouraging greater technical effectiveness in the allocation and use of financial resources.

(i) Personnel expenses - Employment in the public services has been constantly reduced as a result of the public administration reform. Hence, the expenses for salaries have marked a decline until the end of 2000, although if we see the analysis of figures, we will notice that payments have increased (in nominal terms) by about 50% in 2000, as against 1996. The growth after year 2000 in this category is linked, besides the reform in the increase of salaries, (with more marked increases in the sectors of defense, justice and police) also with the

Table 2. Spending structure.

Total expenditures, % GDP	1998	1999	2000	2001
	30.8	**32.7**	**31.6**	**31.5**
Main categories of expenditures in relation to total expenditures (% of GDP)				
Current expenditures	82.9 (25.5)	79.1 (25.9)	78.1 (24.7)	75.7 (23.8)
Personal	20 (6.2)	18.8 (6.2)	19.5 (6.2)	21.1 (7)
Interests	25.3 (7.8)	21.1 (6.9)	17.3 (5.5)	12.7(4)
Operational and maintenance expenditures	13.1 (4)	12.1 (4)	11.3 (3.6)	8.5 (2.7)
Subsidies and social insurances	17.2 (5.3)	20.5 (6.7)	21.9 (6.9)	23.4 (7.4)
Capital expenses	17.1 (5.3)	20.6 (6.7)	21.3 (6.7)	23.3 (7.4)

(Ministry of Finances, 2001)

reclassification of 'bonuses" (about 0.5% of the GDP) which in the past was included in the operational and maintenance expenses.

(ii) In the budget projections was included for the increase of salaries in the sectors of health and education, both considered priority sectors for the reduction of poverty, because the pace of their growth must be higher. Compared to the payments in the other sectors of civil service, the pays in these two sectors continue to be lower. The levels of salaries in these sectors have been identified by the GPRS as critical elements among the causes that have led to the decline in the educational level and the lack of medical treatment, particularly in the rural zones.

(iii) Maintenance and operational expenses - Even though expenses for the categories of the MTBP have been expected to grow (with the growth of GDP rate), their levels are considered insufficient to cope with the maintenance of infrastructure due to the imbalance between and maintenance expenses account for less than 15% of the current expenses.

(iv) Subsidies and social insurance services are affected by the lack of facilities and the necessary basic materials. This is becoming a critical issue also in terms of maintaining physical infrastructure repaired by the donors' funds. For this reason, the MTBP envisions an increase of up to 3.9% in 2004, which will address mainly the sectors of education, health, and physical infrastructure.

(v) Subsidies and social protection transfers - Subsidies have covered textbooks, railway and urban transport, the drainage system (in agriculture), and the programs for the promotion of employment (for employers). Although, subsidies have accounted for only 0.4% of the GDP in 1996, due to the energy crisis (subsidies for the imported energy price) they amounted to 1.2% of GDP in 2001. There has been taken some measures by the Albanian Energy Corporation [KESh] in order to improve the situation of receivables from the debts, but even the public utilities enterprises, (particularly the water enterprise) are debtors to KESh. This may result in an increase of subsidies for them. In general, this category of expenses is expected to be reduced up to 0.3% of the GDP up to 2004. The social protection transfers are linked mainly with the pension schemes. The financial sustainability of KESh has been depending for a long time mostly on the fiscal transfers. The number of contributors is very low, and the number of contributors of the private farming sector accounts for less than 20% of the total number of contributors in the system. The two measures taken recently by the government (the increase of the pension age and the reduction of the measure of contributions, combined with the increase of the threshold of salary for the calculation of the pension contribution are expected to give results in the improvement of the performance of the insurance scheme. These measures along with the promotion of participation in the voluntary insurance schemes are expected to reduce the share of budget transfers to about 1.4% of the GDP up to the end of 2004 (as against 2% which is at present). There is yet opportunity for improvement also to better target the families benefiting from the economic assistance. The best check systems and their gradual decentralization and transfer to the local authorities, have made it possible to reduce the number of the beneficiary families and increase the amount of benefits for the strata that are really in need.

(vi) Public investments - Public investments have marked a sustainable increase estimated to be 7.4% in 2001. The inclusion of foreign funding in the budget system remains a constant problem. It is estimated that about 30% of the foreign financing remain unreported, which creates problems regarding their financial management, the postponement of the projects (due to the non allocation of the funds as local share, compensation for the VAT, etc.) as well as the lack of transparence. Nevertheless, the main problems in public investments are:

(a) Lack of professional capacities in the ministries line for the planning and budgeting of projects,

(b) The inherited practices of the division of budgets on an annual basis and not according to the total cost of projects,

(c) Lack of consolidated information for projects with foreign and domestic funding,
(d) Investment projects do not have clear and transparent cost procedures and techniques of calculations. Therefore, there are possibilities for reducing the costs of individual projects and increasing the number of projects,
(e) The projects monitoring mechanisms, particularly the infrastructure projects still remain very weak, and as consequence is the postponement of projects' implementation within the set deadlines.

Such disadvantages were also obvious during the process on drafting of the GPRS, where in general the line ministers were unable to provide the budget implications for the measures proposed as government actions included in the program. The education expenses of approximately 3.2% of the GDP are lower than those in countries with income under the average level (4.8% of the GDP). In health, public expenditures are calculated to be around 2% of the GDP, or 2/3 of this level in the countries with income levels below average.

FISCAL DECENTRALIZATION

The fiscal decentralization process and the transferring of responsibilities to the local authorities is a new phenomenon that has been developed after 1999. The revenues of the local authorities accounted for only 0.35% of the GDP in 2001 and were raised mainly by the central fiscal authorities and were given to local authorities in the form of unconditional grants. Some local taxes are currently in the process of the transition to the local authorities to be collected by them as taxes on small businesses, on the farming land. A positive impact on revenues is supposed to have the shifting of this function to the local authorities. At any rate, the transition of these functions should be done parallel with the training of the future local administration to be capable of taking over these responsibilities.

The main economic sources on exercising their exclusive functions (maintenance of local roads, lighting of roads and public services, urban planning, transport, collection and processing of waste, water supply, cultural and sport activities and the services of local economic growth) have been ensured mainly through the allocation of funds from the central budget. In this respect, the problems have to do with undeveloped local capacities to estimate the financial requirements based on the real needs. Another aspect of decentralization includes also the development of common functions between local and central authorities in the field of education, health, social protection, public order, and protection of environment. The development of these functions can be done mainly through sectional initiatives and the line ministries should cooperate with the local authorities to develop joint programs.

REFERENCES

Easterly W (1999). Fiscal Illusion: Taking the Bite Out of Budget Cuts', Economic Policy p.63
Easterly W (1999) 'Fiscal Illusion: Taking the Bite Out of Budget Cuts', Economic Policy pp.70-71.
Easterly W (1999). Fiscal Illusion: Taking the Bite Out of Budget Cuts', Economic Policy p.61.
Gramm-Rudman-Hollings (1985). Act on Federal Budgetary Outcomes " J. Pol. Anal. Manage. 11(2).
Maastricht Treaty (1992). Provisions amending the treaty establishing the european economic community with a view to establishing the european community maastricht. Feb, 1992
Stiglitz JE, Walsh CE (2008). The seven deadly Deficits. Special Reports, the New Economy.

Medical tourism: The new favorite tourist market

Guojinga F. A. N.[1,2] and Zhijun L.[3*]

[1]Hunan Agriculture University, Changsha 410128, China.
[2]School of Culture and Tourism, GanNan Normal University, GanZhou 341000, JiangXi, China.
[3]Department of Sociology, Zhejiang University, Hangzhou 310058, China.

Medical tourism, a new form of tourism industry flourishing around the world, holds a huge market potential in China. Its definition and related issues are under the way of being carefully examined with quite a concern on its development conditions and strategies. China, a late boomer in medical tourism, is in a total different social and economical situation and in urgent need to get close scrutiny in its new favorite tourist market. Thus, a SWOT (Strengths, Weaknesses, Opportunities, and Threats) analysis is conducted in Chinese tourism development strategies and conditions.

Key words: Medical tourism, strengths, weaknesses, opportunities, and threats analysis, China.

INTRODUCTION

In the process of globalization, Medical Tourism (MT), which focuses on the combination of medical services and traveling, is flourishing around the world. As a new form of tourism industry, MT originated in 1980s in Europe. In recent years, many countries have seized the opportunity to discover resources of MT and to expand market in their own countries as well as abroad. As for China, the emergence of both "Traditional Chinese Medicine Care Tourism" in San ya and "Medical Health Care Tourism" (Xian, 2010) indicates that the MT has become the new favorite of Chinese tourism market.

So far, Chinese hospitals are still in lack of comprehensive knowledge on the essence and working mechanism of MT. Theoretical studies on MT are relatively weak and put a lot of emphasis on techniques and the market. Besides, there is confusion between the conception of MT and Recuperative Tourism. The existing academic controversy about the definition of the essence of MT resulted in unclear boundary of MT industry and the lack of international standards of this industry. Therefore, the practice development and theory research of Chinese Medical Tourism is still in isolated phase.

The definition of MT

Tourism industry and theoretic researches on MT share no unanimous definition. According to the World Tourism Organization, MT is a tourism service themed with medical care, disease and health, recovery and recuperation. Goodrich proposed double features of MT, defining it as attracting tourists not only by local sceneries but also by intentional promotion of medical health service equipments in some tourism facilities or destinations (e.g. hotels). In a research report on Global Medical Tourism, MT in Tourism Research and Marketing is defined as: going to an alien place (especially foreign countries) and spending over 24 h there with the purpose of medical treatment (including medical nursing and surgery). Thus, MT turns a new "gold ore" for hospitals. Meng (2008) put forward that MT is a new industry formed by the combination of recreational travel and those who go abroad for better health care service due to the expensive or imperfect medical service in their own settlements. These definitions reflect the ideas and ways of MT from the view of market suppliers and demanders.

It is obvious that this perspective from which MT is defined does not equalize Recuperative Tourism, Pharmaceutical Tourism and Health Tourism for their differences and connections are embodied in their similarities. For example, Sun and Liu (2007), from the view of content and way of Traditional Chinese Medicine travelling, thought that Traditional Chinese Medicine travel could include Medical Tourism, Pharmaceutical Tourism, Visiting and Learning, MICE tourism and so on. Li et al (2008), however, believed that medical treatment was one of the major seven demands of health tourist products for health tourist customers.

According to the above different points of view, in broad sense, MT should include both Medical Tourism and Health Tourism, the purpose of which is mainly for health and recreation and disease treatment, including surgery and medical cosmetic spa, aroma spa and mountaineering tour.

BRIEF ANALYSIS OF RELEVANT ISSUES ON MT

Benefits of Medical Tourism

International Medical Tourism industry gives a great highlight on the benefits in economy, society and tourism during its development. MT facilitates the win-win situation between medical treatment and tourism which is beneficial to the people and the country. Economical benefit from the World Medical Tourism industry, according to the report by RNCOS (a sector specializing in the tourist economics research in America), has showed rapid growth in the past few years. In 2000, Medical Tourism industry around the world grossed less than ten billion U.S. dollars, while it reached 20 billion U.S. dollars by 2005, and it is estimated 23 to 24 billion U.S. dollars in 2007. The above data showed the astonishing development of global MT. In many countries, MT has become the backbone of the tourism industry. Due to the interrelated dependences, MT needs the support of many related industries and promotes their development at the same time. In addition, the target markets of international MT, whose development is conducive to increasing foreign exchanges, are mainly the international markets instead of the native ones. Thus, MT will be one of the industries that offer tremensdous economic benefits throughout the world and promote economic development.

Social benefit, on one hand, through medical tourism development contributes to the further communication and cooperation between countries through personnel communication and economic exchanges so as to drive comprehensive development of health and tourism at home and promotes the national image abroad. On the other hand, MT development is beneficial to reducing regional wealth gap and maintaining social stability by adding employment opportunities.

For environmental benefit, MT, an industry based on medical technology and tourism resources, has special benefits which mainly focus on the tourism resources and ecological environment protection, infrastructure construction and maintenance. Therefore, it contributes to the establishment of the new way of sustainable development in tourism, ensuring the sustainability and scalability in medical tourism.

Causes of rapid development of the international MT

Tourism is a kind of comprehensive phenomena in regard to many aspects, such as society, economy, culture, etc. For over half a century, tourism activities are in constant changes and development along with social and economic development, scientific and technological progress and changes of people's values. Besides, there are many other aspects which are helpful for promoting the development of MT (Liu, 2008).

Firstly, the transformation in people's concept of medical tourism consumption is the first cause. With the development of tourist environment and people's growing mature concept on consumption, their consuming patterns gradually transform from extensive type to comfortable and healthy one. That's to say, people pay more attention to physical and mental relaxation. Therefore, MT just caters to the consuming trends of the healthy, comfortable travel.

Secondly, differences in the development of international medical industry are the second aspect. The differences are mainly reflected in medical price, resource and service. The first point should be price. Generally speaking, medical cost in developed countries is higher than that in developing countries. Coupled with restrict on medical insurance, the expensive medical cost in developed countries is a heavy burden for part of the population. Thus, the difference on price is one of the major causes that cause patients in developed countries to have medical travels in developing countries. A heart replacement surgery in the United States , for instance , people with and without medical insurance need to pay respectively the minimum fee of 7.5 times and 16.7 times of that in India , 6.8 times and 15.2 times in Thailand, and 5.5 times and 12.3 times in Singapore. For the resources, including supply and demand of medical resources, many developed countries, who are with heavy burden of their medical security system resulted from aging and the socialized medical treatment, are of shortage of medical resources, while other countries might leave many advanced medical equipments unused. Besides, a number of unique medical technologies in developing countries have great attraction for consumers from developed countries, for example, the specialized medical equipment of Indian robots, cosmetic technology of South Korea and traditional Chinese medical care in China. People's increasing demand for new medical projects also became an impetus of the international MT development. The last is the difference of services, which also resulted from the aging and socialized medical treatment. Apart from restricted medical cost, the decrease of service quality is also an important cause of driving patients in developed countries to receive treatment in other countries. In the UK, a patient needing knee transplant have to wait for 18 months in order to get the treatment of UK National Health Service, while it takes only 5 days in India. The long wait may delay the best time for treatment. However, with the medical standards and service quality improving significantly, developing countries can provide patients with specia-lized treatment programs and full range of services like accommodation and translation at the same time.

Thirdly, the promotion of globalization and government support can be regarded as the third factor. Tourism is a social phenomenon worldwide. Medical and tourism industry is increasingly internationalized with the accele-rated process of cross-country integration. Therefore, the international economic environment has greater impact on medical tourism. In recent years, as world economy has developed and people's living standards have improved, more and more people choose international tourism. Meanwhile, driven by tremendous economic and social benefits of medical tourism, many countries release policies to encourage medical tourism develop-ment, such as the "international medical plan" made by Singapore government and a 5-year plan by Philippines for MT. These policies and measures played a positive role in regulating medical tourism market, maintaining the legitimate interests of participants, and promoting the MT development effectively.

Fourthly, the impetus of tourism development could be the last factor. Stimulated by tremendous benefits in the tourism industry, more and more countries give the priority to developing tourism. On one hand, they develop special tourism products to establish brand image by fully developing and using their native tourism resources and advantages. On the other hand, they strengthen infra-structure construction and enhance the capacity of recep-tion and service. These measures are helpful to attract international medical tourists and guarantee the medical tourism activities will proceed smoothly.

In addition, the development of technology communi-cation like the network and air traffic is also an important factor to promote the development of international medical tourism.

Moving patterns and market positioning of international medical tourism

The positioning of tourism product is of important mea-ning on choosing marketing mix, and it determines whether tourists of target market will receive the product and concerns the status of tourism product for tourists. Therefore, we need to have a clear understanding of target market and know about tourists' demand for tourism product. Product requirements orientation of international medical tourists are largely reflected in the flow law of the international medical tourism.

On the research of the flow law, Zhang and Yang (2007) put forward constructive conclusion in which they believe that the flow law of international medical tourism mainly reflects in three aspects: Firstly, from the less developed countries to developed countries, which mainly happens in the primary period, the fundamental cause of this phenomenon is the wide difference in the international medical standards. The second point is that from developed countries to developing countries, which is the main direction at present. It mainly exists in the modern period, during which medical standards in developing countries improved significantly and some have reached the world's top medical standards level. Meanwhile, some traditional medical items in developing countries can satisfy certain special needs of tourists whose main purpose is to seek high quality and in-expensive or personalized medical service. Third, a special flow direction, which means international medical tourists flow from developed countries to developed countries and from less developed countries to less developed countries, is relatively special. On one hand, tourists flow from developed countries to developed countries because destination countries have some special medical items and technology. On the other hand, tourists flow from less developed countries to less developed countries because in the recent half a century, medical technology and standard in these countries have risen fast and even reached advanced world level and the medical cost is appropriate. Therefore, medical tourists in less developed countries do not have to spend high price to get the same medical care and travel service in developed countries. Meanwhile, some special medical tourist items and technology in less developed countries are also important factors to attract international medical tourists, and this trend exists in each period. However, tourists flowing from less developed countries to less developed countries mainly exist in the modern and future period of development.

Therefore, the international MT market mainly targets at consumers in three kinds of countries: the countries with expensive medical cost and restricted medical insurance; the broad consumer groups in the countries that need special medical items and technologies and those with low medical technology standards.

Motives and needs of medical tourism

People have medical tourism on the premise of their understanding of its content, which is all about the needs that starting point is the tourist motivation.

Behavioral science believes that various human acts are caused by certain motives that produced in the inhe-rent needs among people. Modern scholars on Manage-ment Psychology believe that behaviors that can inspire people and cause action to meet certain needs of desire, aspirations, ideals, beliefs and other psychological factors should be called motives. Maslow made his famous "hierarchy of needs", ranking physiological needs, safety needs, social needs, esteem needs and self-actualization needs in order of importance. They can all become a motive, and one or two of them may become tourists' motivation. Therefore, medical tourism motivation is closely linked to consuming demand for it.

Medical tourists have the following five demands for the products: firstly, cheap and fine medical service; secondly, save waiting time for treatment; thirdly, advanced or unique medical technology; fourthly, unique exoticism and tourism environment; fifthly, the symbol of status.

Tourists have motives for MT after confirming their needs. Consuming steps like information gathering, program evaluation and purchase of decision, travel, assessment will thus proceed.

Features of MT product

As the component of tourism market, MT products have the general fundamental properties of tourism products such as non-portability, invisible, aftereffect as well as their own uniqueness.

The first feature is its high degree of internationalization. MT is the product of the internationalization of medical and tourism. The main target market is the international market, therefore, it requires international features of the product from design to sales, and even to the services.

The second feature is its distinct health cares. To receive treatment in alien places is one of the main purposes of medical tourism. As the combination of medical and tourism, health care is exclusive for medical tourism.

The third one is the certain regional differences. The attraction of medical tourism destination is usually its superior treatment or exoticism, which would inevitably contribute to the spatial movement of tourists due to spatial differences in resource distribution.

The fourth one is the temporal spirit and high-income. MT rises with the world economy development and the change of people's values on medical and tourism consumption. Its character of time is notable. Due to changes about consumption, more and more consumers are choosing compound or first-rate service, which MT just sized up. As an overall tourism product, MT has powerful promotion and also can produce great economic benefits.

Fifthly, the richness and diversity of the product type and form should be concerned. The types of MT product are abundant and cover a wide range, involving dental, cosmetic, medical care and so on. International MT providers provide different tourists with different products, both single-function services and the integrated one.

STATUS QUO AND FORECAST FOR MT IN CHINA

Background: Status quo of MT development in Asia

Among the seven major MT industry markets, Asia occupied four which are Thailand, Singapore, Malaysia and India. The most common services are the dental, plastic surgery, joint replacement surgery, cardiac surgery, cancer treatment, artificial reproductive technologies and health checks.

Medical tourism industry in India developed early and has developed fast in recent years. According to Indian Ministry of Commerce and Industry, it is reported that the annual growth rate of medical tourism reaches up to 30%. Last year, about 600,000 foreign patients came to India for surgery or treatment. Thailand has the second largest medical tourism industry in Asia, which is only next to India. As Thailand has beautiful scenery and beaches in Asia (also around the world), the foreigners travelling to Thailand has been increasing year by year. Moreover, the number was estimated over one million last years. It shows that 25% of who came to see the doctor, bringing hundreds of millions of dollars revenue for Thailand every year. Malaysia is also one of the early Asian countries that developed medical tourism. This country is rich in tropical tourism resources. Due to its abundance in oil reserves, Malaysian financial situation is much better than other countries in Southeast Asia and its medical equipment of hospitals is said to be the first in Asia. Therefore, it has excellent conditions to offer treatment to foreign tourists. Recently, it is learned that there has been an increasing number of patients coming from western countries and rich countries in Arab to Malaysia year by year. Malaysian tourism sources for treatment is second only to India and Thailand. Singapore is an English-speaking country in Asia, and almost all of its citizens that have received secondary or higher education can speak English, it means that there is no language barrier for them to talk to westerners. With first-class hospital in Asia, Singapore has been striving to develop medical tourism industry in recent years. According to the latest report abroad, Singapore Government has already set up offices in 15 countries and strongly recommended Singapore's tourism and medical resources to these countries. In the next few years, Singapore Government intends to attract at least one million foreign tourists to travel and receive medical treatment in their country every year .And thus 5.9 billion us dollars can be added to its GDP.

Apart from these four countries, South Korea, Jordan and China's Hong Kong, Macao and other countries and regions are also striving to develop medical tourism. Most foreign patients go to South Korea to seek medical services like dental, plastic surgery and physical examination. According to other reports, more and more females in Japan, China and other Asian countries came to South Korea for cosmetic surgery. From this year, on the South Korean capital Seoul has started the work to contact the Seoul cosmetic surgery hospitals for "foreign cosmetic tourists". Among the local autonomy groups, the City of Seoul will, for the first time, set up the support center for cosmetic plastic surgery to attract medical tourists. Since 2004, Jordan has attracted medical tourists with a steady growth of 10% each year. Last year, patients from Iraq reached 45,000, both Palestine and Sudan reached 25,000. As for Occident, over 1,800 patients were from America, 1,200 from British and 400 from Canada. Currently, Jordan has 58 private hospitals, of which 44 are members of PHA. In order to promote the medical tourism market, the Jordan Investment Bureau (JIB) will send representatives to attend this year's international conference on medical tourism held in America, and there will be over 1,000 representatives from 50 countries. Jordan will seek cooperation opportunity with American Medical Assurance Company. It is estimated that about 500,000 people in the United States have gone abroad each year for medical tourism so far and this number is expected to be doubled by 2012.

Taiwan also joined this field of competition and will seek markets in the mainland. On July 30, 2007, Taiwan authorities Mainland Affairs Council passed the draft "Guidance Notice on Document to Mainlanders applying the project of receiving medical services in Taiwan", which stipulates that since August 1, 2007, the mainlanders can apply for receiving medical service in Taiwan of a maximum stay for three months. Extension can be applied for individual medical needs. On July 20, 2007, Ma Ying-jiu delivered a speech entitled "the international view of modern leaders", stating that "if the KMT return to power, the law would be amended to promote the development of Taiwan's medical tourism industry". Ma said that Taiwan's artificial joint transplant costs only one-tenth of that in the United States, and teeth transplant costs only a third of that in Japan. Taiwan's medical quality is of considerable potential, it is estimated that 3 billion RMB (renminbi) market in one year is possible if combined with sight-seeing. On July 30, the Taiwan authorities announced that mainlanders could come to Taiwan and receive medical services like Living donor liver transplantation, craniofacial reconstruction, artificial reproduction, joint replacement, cardiovascular invasive treatments and surgery.

Chinese MT Development Strategy research based on SWOT analysis

In recent years, SWOT analysis is widely used in the study of tourism product development environment and prerequisites. It can provide favorable market position for the tourism product and image position with scientific basis to enhance the possibility of success and competitiveness in tourism product development, thereby improving benefits of product development constantly.

SWOT analysis of Chinese development in medical tourism

The analysis is shown in Table 1. The advantages of China's development in MT outweigh its disadvantages, the opportunities found in external environment are greater than its threats, and Chinese medical tourism has great potential. Therefore, China has bright prospects in developing medical tourism. According to national circumstances, the suggestions are as follows.

Firstly, the measures should contain four aspects: to bring the development of medical tourism into the overall planning of China's tourism development; to establish sound management system; to improve relevant laws and regulations; to regulate the market to create favorable macroscopical condition and environment for medical tourism development. Meanwhile, the Government should guide hospitals' theme of medical Tourism in an active and correct way and change the development concept to promote transformation of marketization among medical tourism organizations.

Secondly, as to the aspect of product developing, China should establish creative consciousness, focus on the series products and project development, integrate the resources and advantages of medical treatment and tourism, form integrated advantages of products and the optimal combination of projects and face the broad international medical tourist market together so as to develop and upgrade this industry. Meanwhile, China should also focus on the formation of products' core competence, fully excavate feature resources and use the comparative advantages, especially resources and advantages in Chinese medicine and nursing.

Thirdly, we propose to promote the overall quality of medical tourism employees, especially in health care, foreign language ability, etiquettes and other aspects of knowledge and skill so that they can provide better service for tourists.

Fourthly, to improve the degree of internationalization in medical tourism should be concerned. Comparing with other countries developing medical tourism, internationalization of China is relatively insufficient, which is mainly reflected in reception areas, airports and scenic spots without clear guidance of foreign language because their staff are not good at foreign languages. Among hospitals that running well in medical tourism development, 20% of their service and 80% of the patients are international, which requires China to strive to improve its degree of internationalization, especially to improve the products' competitiveness in the world.

Fifthly, to strengthen exchanges and cooperation with the pioneering countries and Hong Kong and Macao regions and Taiwan regions is also suggested. China is a latecomer in MT field and lacks development experience.

Therefore, strengthen international cooperation, master breakthrough point and highlight China's comparative advantages are not only good for international co-

Table 1. SWOT analysis of Chinese development in medical tourism.

Internal condition	External condition
S1: Rich and high quality medical tourism resources: high quality and low price medical service and rich tourism resources in China, including many cultural and natural tourism resources with the potential for medical tourism development. S2: Exclusive in traditional Chinese medicine nursing, unique in methods, rich in content and great value in use for developing medical tourism. S3: Close to pioneering medical tourism countries such as Malaysia and Thailand, which avails China to learn from their experience and strengthen exchanges and cooperation with them. S4: Medical tourism season can be free from restrictions. S5: the speeding up of Chinese reform and opening up makes Chinese medical tourism organizations better use international resources and open international markets.	O1: Success of Beijing Olympic Games further improved the overall image of Chinese tourism. O2: The deepening exchanges and cooperation between China and other countries, especially the neighboring ones created favorable external conditions and provided wider market for Chinese development in medical tourism. O3: Chinese medical projects, especially projects related to Chinese medicine are getting trusted and popular among the international community.
W1: Chinese medical service is not well-known and its international image has not been established. W2: Non-standard management, imperfect relevant policies and regulations. W3: Late start, weak supporting infrastructure, the lack of strength in product development and its core competitiveness. W4: Small scale, low level , inappropriate marketing strategies and the lack of publicity W5: Obsolete ideas, imperfect market mechanisms and the low overall quality of medical tourism employees.	T1: RMB appreciation and the global financial crisis results in great pressure on the development of inbound tourism in China. T2: After joining WTO, some overseas medical tourism institutions with international influence entered Chinese market and intensified the competition. T3: Many neighboring countries have taken more open policies in the development of medical tourism, which confronted China with fierce competition in attracting international tourists.

operation but also helpful for the healthy development and realization of mutual benefit and win-win result of international medical tourism.

Sixthly, to increase publicity and speed the brand and image building is in need. In order to make Medical tourism product as the customer's first choice, China should increase the building of product and develop scientific marketing strategies such as increasing the scope of propaganda through different channels and analyzing the tourists' sources of information in order to provide customers with the information they need. Most medical tourists are foreigners and, as a result, Internet as the source of latest information is suggested to build a comprehensive network information service to promote international medical tourism. Apparently, the international community has not been impressed by ever advancing medical technology in China but the impression still stays in Chinese medicine treatment and basic health and epidemic prevention, which indicated that Chinese medical service, quality and image need more investment in marketing. Therefore, Chinese need to fully discover its feature resource in Chinese medical and tourism, that is while strengthening the construction of hardware and software, China should also develop special medical tourist product and publicize it.

REFERENCES

Li C, Pengcheng D, Jie Z, Yan L (2008). Research on Status of International Medical Tourism development. Inner Mongolia Science Technology and Economy 4:32-38

Liu BX (2008). Study on Related Issues of Medical Tourism. Modern Bus. Trade Ind. 6:68-72

Meng XM (2008). Management experience of American national park system: Lesson for Chinese National Park management. World Forest. Res. 20:75-79.

Sun Y, Liu D (2007). Primary Research on traditional Chinese Medicine Tourism. Market Modernization 5:165-169.

Xian Y (2010). "medical tourism is becoming a global tourism attraction. J. Tour. 3:19-21

Zhang W, Yang X (2007). International Medical Tourism probing. J. Guilin Institute Tourism 10:96-100.

Evaluation of the current higher education funding model in Rwanda using Higher Education Students' Loans Department (HESLD-REB) as a case study

Alfred Nuwagaba

Mount Kenya University-Kigali Campus, P.O. Box 5826, Kigali, Rwanda.

Higher education funding in Rwanda uses a costs sharing approach. This has been analyzed to ascertain its suitability for Rwanda. This research looked at other funding methods that can be applicable for the higher education sector in Rwanda. These included use of PPP, tuition fees, bank loans and internally generated funds by higher learning institutions. It was found in this research that costs sharing approach is ą good model in Rwanda but it has faced the challenge of using financial means testing (FMT) to identify potential beneficiaries. There FMT is viewed by most respondents as unfair and that in some cases, financial assistance has not been given to those that deserve it due to corruption in the system. The other funding methods mentioned above have also been analyzed and appropriate conclusions arrived at in the research findings. It was also found out that a failed higher education system would impact on the economic development of the country and also if the higher education sector is underfunded, this will impact on the quality of the graduates and the sector as a whole. There is need for policy change by government of Rwanda towards funding of its higher education.

Key words: Costs sharing, financial means testing (FMT), higher education funding model, public private partnerships (PPP).

INTRODUCTION

A good higher education system is a driver for social economic development of an economy. This is one of the vision 2020 priorities for Rwanda. A well educated workforce is more productive when compared to an uneducated one. It is therefore crucial that adequate funding is provided for the higher education sector. Failure to provide adequate funding may lead to weakening the sector and this will impact the social economic development of the country as there will not be enough well educated manpower. The research aims to; analyze higher education funding options of using bank loans, setting up of industries, cost sharing, tuition fees, and public-private partnerships arrangements. There is an issue that the Government of Rwanda is slowly phasing out of funding higher education and hence the above options have been proposed (MINEDUC, 2011). The evolution of the higher education system has been discussed, stretching from 1994 to 2012. This includes the statistics on students' enrolment and higher learning institutions. Statistics show that in 1994, there was only one university in the country, with a total students' enrolment of 3,261 students, and this has grown overtime to 73,674 students in the current year, 2011/2012, with 31 higher learning institutions in Rwanda (MINEDUC,2011). This reflects a 95% increase of the number of students in higher learning institutions. Such increase most likely comes with increased financial requirements for students and government has to take on the financial burden for these increased numbers. An analysis has been done in this study that links higher education funding to quality of education for the achievement of 2000 Millennium Development Goals on higher education in Rwanda (Millennium Development Goals, 2000). This chapter finally gives the motivations that led to the analysis of the higher education system in Rwanda since 2009 to date.

This study scope is chosen because it was when higher education funding started reducing considerably that the need to find ways of generating funding for higher education in Rwanda arose. The higher education budget in 2008 amounted to USD 42,737,627.42 and this reduced to 43. 1% in 2009, and then increased by 60% in 2010; it then reduced by 6% in 2011 and it went up by 9.5% in 2012 (MINICOFIN, 2012). The problem here is that the increment in funding in 2011 may not be considered realistic since student numbers have gone up to 73,674 as seen in Table 1.

Statement of the problem

Government funding of higher education in Rwanda has been reduced by 25% every year, starting from financial year 2010/2011 (MINICOFIN, 2011). Therefore, there is the need for Government of Rwanda and higher learning institutions to find ways of financing their activities as per the government proposed funding models. These models include the use of students' bank loans, funding through public/private partnerships, tuition fees charges, setting up of commercial companies at higher learning institutions to generate income, and costs sharing which the researcher has analyzed in this study (MINEDUC, 2011; Semugaza, 2005). The researcher has to ascertain their applicability and sustainability for the higher education sub-sector in Rwanda.

Objectives

1. To analyze the current higher education funding model and also analyze the other government higher education funding methods.
2. To assess the relationship between higher education funding and quality of education.
3. To analyze the link between a well functioning higher education system and its effect on economic development.

Research questions

1. Is the government of Rwanda current and other higher education funding methods suitable for this sector?
2. Does reduced higher education funding affect the quality of higher education in Rwanda?
3. Does reduced higher education funding affect the economic development of Rwanda?

OVERVIEW OF HIGHER EDUCATION SUBSECTOR IN RWANDA

The higher education funding in Rwanda since 1963 to 1994 was fully done by the Government of Rwanda, and at the time there was only one state university called National University of Rwanda. The country was only having 3,261 students by 1994 accessing higher education and this was not so much of a funding budget burden to the state. There was only 3,261 students in the academic year 1994/1995 and this has since increased to 73,674 students in 2011/2012 (MINEDUC, 2011). This increment in number of students justifies the need for increased student funding which has unfortunately been going down overtime (Semugaza, 2005; MINEDUC, 2011).

Table1 shows that higher education in Rwanda has been growing since the end of genocide in 1994. There is currently student's enrolment of 73,674 and 31 institutions of higher learning. The academic year of 1993/1994 was dead year due to the war that was in the country at the time and there was no students' enrolment. There was only one university in Rwanda in 1994, though, there were other small existing higher learning institutions (6 in number); the total number at that time was 7 (MINEDUC, 2011). Overall, during the periods of 1994 to 2011, there has been a 95.57% student increment in higher learning institutions. This has put the Government of Rwanda on enormous task in finding resources needed to fund the requirements of the increased number of students.

HESLD (2011) analyzed higher education funding models namely the use of tuition fees, student bank loans, public-private-partnerships, and setting up of firms at higher learning institutions to generate funds. There is a correlation between higher education funding and service delivery at higher learning institutions and looking at Rwanda where government higher education funding is being cut by 25% every year (MINEDUC, 2011). This would mean that in about a few years, the Government of Rwanda will pull out completely of funding higher education. There are some effects on service delivery at higher learning institution and achieving set government target of quality education if higher education funding is not adequate (Barr, 2004). Reduced higher education funding affects the country in achieving its target of having a pool of quality educated workforce as envisaged

Table 1. Higher education student enrolment statistics and number of higher learning institutions in Rwanda since 1994-2012.

Academic year	Higher Learning Institutions (HLIs)	Students in HLIs	Percentage change in students enrolment (%)
93/94	7	Dead year	
94/95	7	3,261	100
95/96	1	3,948	17.40
96/97	6	4,665	15.36
97/98	8	5,751	18.88
98/99	8	3,045	11.11
99/00	10	9,357	67.45
00/01	10	12,802	26.91
2-Jan	10	15,940	19.68
3-Feb	9	20,393	21.83
4-Mar	20	27,243	25.14
2005	18	26,800	-1.65
2006	18	37,149	27.85
2007	20	41,013	9.42
2008	20	47,406	13.48
2009	28	55,213	14.14
2010	30	62,734	11.98
2011	31	73,674	14.84

Source: MINEDUC, 2011 (Rwanda)
Note: Dead year of 1993/1994: This means that, there were no student enrolments done in higher learning institutions in Rwanda during that academic year. This was due to the liberation war at the time.

in the vision 2020 targets to help in the development of the economy. If higher education funding keeps reducing, this will have an effect on institutional capacity of higher learning institutions as physical and infrastructure development will stall and institutions will be losing a lot of its staff who opt out to look for better working conditions elsewhere.

Evolution of higher education in Rwanda since 1994

Higher education sector in Rwanda has since independence grown with a total of 31 higher learning institutions of which 17 are public owned and 14 are privately owned (NCHE, 2011). The current student population in higher learning institutions totals 73,674 which reflects a 96% students' enrolment increase since 1994 to 2012. Rwanda has a liberalized higher education system encouraging the participation of private investors in the higher education sector.

The dynamics of higher education funding in Rwanda changed after the 1994 genocide. Rwanda wants an educated workforce and in the process, a number of people requiring higher education increased with support from government and so was the number of state owned higher learning institutions totaling 17 in number (MINEDUC, 2011). The government of Rwanda overtime has faced budget constraints causing a challenge in sustaining the required funding for higher education institutions and hence, the need by government and higher learning institutions to find other ways of funding higher education in Rwanda.

Higher learning institutions in Sub-Saharan countries are generally faced with budget constraints as government vote allocations tend to be inadequate and this calls for a need to find other sources of supplementing incomes allocated to these institutions (Oghenekohwo and Abu, 2011). The Government of Rwanda is considering using higher education funding through student loans from commercial banks, setting up of a government bank that only handles student loans, adoption of public private partnership initiatives. Higher learning institutions are being asked to set up companies that will help them generate funds, costs sharing and tuition fees charges (MINEDUC, 2011).

The importance of quality higher education in Rwanda is a pillar for its social economic development especially if training is matched with the needed skills in the market. This is a critical issue for the Government of Rwanda and one would guess that this should be crucial for all economies (Barr, 2004). Barr (2004) argues that very good quality education is very expensive and calls for adequate funding, which should not be only shouldered by governments.

The government of Rwanda currently gives a student pursuing arts and humanities courses USD 1,423 per annum, and on study completion the student pays back 50% plus 5% interest. Science students are given USD 2,093 per annum, and on completion of studies, the student pays back 25% plus 5% interest as a cost sharing model; though, the government has proposed that a student should pay back 100% of grant provided plus interest (MINEDUC, 2011). The point here is that affordability of the costs may be an issue for some students and this will impact on higher education accessibility. This means that qualifying students may not get access to higher learning institutions, and this may cause skills shortage in some sectors of the economy thus impacting on the social economic development of the country.

This method comes with challenges as it may prove very expensive for the recipients; the government's thinking here is that these funds will come from say commercial banks or from other sources of which the student takes full responsibility of servicing the loan obligation and the government would use budget allocation to higher education for development purposes (Barr, 2004; MINEDUC, 2011).

The Government of Rwanda in pursuit of higher education funding options is considering public-private-partnership, especially on infrastructure development; for instance, some universities like National University of Rwanda, Umutara Polytechnic. Quiet a good percentage of higher learning institutions in Rwanda have tried these options and they have faced challenges on their operationalization hence the need to analyze them further to ascertain their suitability for Rwanda (MINEDUC, 2011; Jonathan and Peter, 2011).

A number of public higher learning institutions in Rwanda have set up companies to do private work for income generation; examples being School of finance and banking (SFB), National University of Rwanda (NUR), ISAE Busogo, Kigali Institute of Education (KIE), Kigali Institute of Science and Technology (KIST) among others (MINEDUC, 2011). The results show that, private companies owned by higher learning institutions can generate income internally, but one needs to understand their efficacy and sustainability in Rwanda (Millett, 1955).

The Government of Rwanda has allowed public higher learning institutions to admit private students who pay tuition, which can be used to support their financial requirements. Privately sponsored students admitted in higher learning institutions are not supported by the government to meet their tuition and leaving allowances. The challenge here is that admission of private students could lead to enrolment explosion. Atuahene (2011) argues that when numbers of students are increased in a higher learning institution, it should be able to use the proceeds from students' paid tuition to develop infrastructure and other learning material needed for students learning. The researcher has to analyze how tuition fees collections can be used to contribute to funding higher education in Rwanda. The issue is that charging of tuition fees to students makes higher learning institutions get some cash. The problem, however, is that Rwanda is a poor country and therefore, without the help of the government, some students may miss out on attaining higher education qualification. Higher education in Rwanda is key to its economic development and hence, if higher learning institutions were to be allowed to charge tuition fees to students, the government should put limits on such charges. There is need to analyze the mechanics of how tuition fees charges by institutions help to narrow their funding gap.

Rwanda has a number of private financial institutions, which can provide student loans and some more funding needed by higher learning institution and the beauty here is that those individual higher learning institutions and students would be responsible for financing their loan obligations (MINEDUC, 2011). This will especially force institutions to find ways of generating income from consultancies, research, students' fees and others ways to meet loan repayments. However, universities have to be careful in these circumstances to ensure value for money when making investment decisions and the advantage here is that government is relieved of this financial burden of financing higher education (Devarajan et al., 2011; MINEDUC, 2011).

Funding of higher education in Rwanda has gone through a transformation from full government funding to costs sharing between government and the students, use of public private partnership arrangements, use of student loans from financial institutions, internally generated incomes by higher learning institutions and tuition fee charges. The researcher has evaluated all these options in this study to ascertain their feasibility and sustainability and their effects on quality of service delivery at higher learning institutions in Rwanda.

LITERATURE REVIEW

This is a review of the numerous sources that supports or does not support the study topic as previous published work on higher education funding. The analysis of their findings is done and from that, study gaps are identified and these will shape and support the main research question and sub-research questions of this study. On completion of the literature review, it would be clear how the research study would help in dealing with the gaps that would have been identified. Quality education can be achieved with adequate funding and this is mainly because institutions will be able to access the needed resources to support the educational system. There is need to analyze this assertion to help Rwanda understand the relationship between higher education funding and its quality as the findings will aid policy formulation on higher education funding in the country. Resources allocation to different sectors in an economy is done through parliament. It is therefore, vital that politicians give due consideration to resources allocated to higher education subsector. Analysis of higher education funding models is vital since it is the only way that the funding mechanism of the sector can be under-stood and implemented. Any failures would lead to a non functioning sector.

This chapter also looks at higher education funding and its effect on social and economic development of Rwanda. Higher education is a good catalyst to economic development of a country as it would bring out the needed manpower resources. The manpower produced from universities will fill the skills gaps that may be existing in an economy. The researcher has to analyze all these funding models for their suitability for Rwanda based on the research questions that have been set in the previous chapter. It is important that the country gives adequate funding to higher education since it is a great pillar for achieving its economic development. A good funded higher education aids in producing graduates that are of good academic standing and comparable internationally and this is a dream that Rwanda strives to achieve as one of its 2020 goals (MINEDUC, 2011). Research is very fundamental in a university for achieving new innovations and inventions in a country. This is what enhances a country's economic development.

Funding of higher education

Higher education funding in Rwanda is a real challenge as the government ponders its withdrawal completely from funding recurrent budget of higher learning institutions, and provision of tuition fees and leaving allowances to students (HESLD, 2011). The government wants the expansion of the tertiary sector to be able to achieve its social economic development, and whereas this is the government's wish; its budget allocation to the sector has been going down and more funds tend now to go to 9 year basic education. The implication of this is that, more students will access primary and secondary education and they may get problems accessing higher education as its funding keeps reducing. This may not be regarded as a good move since primary and secondary education by its self does not provide enough skills to facilitate the functionality of an economy. It may be vital if followed with some form of vocational training to get practical skills.

Rwanda is faced with a challenge of its unit cost in that comparatively, both a private and public sponsored students may be doing the same course but paying different tuition fees. For instance for a science course, a private student would pay $526 and a public sponsored student is paying $2,192 and there has been questions surrounding such disparities. The Government of Rwanda is beginning to think that, it would be cheaper if higher education is made private where students have to take financial responsibilities for their university studies. They could get financial help from government in form of loans, where the student would have to pay back to the government 100% of the loan plus an interest of 8% per annum (HESLD, 2011). Initially, students would only pay back a certain percentage of tuition back to the government interest free. Science students would only pay back to government 25% and Arts and humanities would pay 50%. This is cheaper when you compare it with paying back to government 108%. The argument here is that all students will have to pay back the 100% of principle amounts of loans given and an additional 8 %payment in interest. This may not be affordable to a lot of students especially those from deprived financial backgrounds and this would affect students' loans recovery.

Loans recovery from students has not been good in Rwanda and this could be attributed to poverty levels and lack of employment for some students. Another theory could be that employers may not be deducting agreed loan repayments from salaries of loan beneficiaries from Higher Education Student Loans Department. The loans distributed by HESLD are USD 115,261,894 and the loans recovered are just about USD 1,754,385. This rate of loans recovery is so low and it could lead to costs sharing approach unattainable in the long run for the country since there will be no revolving funds to sustain it (HESLD, 2011). Higher education funding has suffered cuts in Rwanda mainly because, the ministry of education and the government think that basic education is a fundamental right for every Rwandan. So, the Government of Rwanda has made it free for every Rwandan and it has devoted most of the budget vote allocated to ministry of education to this sub sector (MINEDUC, 2011). The researcher, however, feels that there is a contradiction on policy of achieving a robust higher education in the country and yet it is gradually having its resources allocation going down. It is a good policy to have free universal basic education in Rwanda, but this may not be good enough in developing its economy since the country will need to have them trained further in higher education institutions. The Government of Rwanda ought to continue supporting higher education through the cost sharing approach introduced in 2008 as a way to achieve its 2020 vision of producing enough manpower for the economy. All the funding approaches as suggested in this study should be explored for adoption and implementation. The government could decide to invest a portion of its resources in the primary sector and seek support from donors who are willing to support the sector. Rwanda has a number of partners investing in the primary and secondary education sectors. This policy approach could be given more support by the government.

According to Hayman (2007), adequate higher education funding is vital for a country's economic growth, as poor funding for higher education would impact its potential for growth since it would have shortage of educated manpower. It is good to appreciate that having basic education is crucial as it raises literacy rates in a country. This allows for successful students to proceed to polytechnics to study practical courses that are vital for job creation and this is a step in the right direction. The government, however, does not have enough financial resources to cater for construction of good physical and social infrastructure for students' learning. The government has set one of its priorities to have basic education provision for all and donors and government have pumped in a lot of resources. The government does not view higher education as a priority for the moment and its budget vote will depend on what the government can afford and not what is needed for the sector.

The Government of Rwanda has seen an expanded higher education sector with 17 public higher learning institutions and 13 private higher learning institutions. As highlighted previously, public higher learning institutions draw their budget from the state for infrastructure funding and students' tuition and considering the science tuition fee per student of USD 2,093 and USD 1,423 (MINEDUC, 2011). Private institutions in Rwanda are fully funded privately from investor's equity and tuition fees collections from students, whereas public institutions are funded by the government through budget allocation. The current cost sharing approach could be made better if the financial means testing approach for one to qualify was reviewed to ensure that it is corruption free. This will help widen access and recoveries from recipients and more so, the interest charge could be waived to make repayments affordable for students. The catch, however, is that private higher learning institutions in Rwanda charge less compared to public institutions. Again, private students enrolled in public institutions pay less compared to government sponsored students. Private institutions in Rwanda charge less by about 50% when compared with public ones. This is one of the reasons why the government is of the view that it would be cheaper if higher education funding in terms of tuition fees payment and leaving allowances was left as the responsibility of the learner.

A good number of private higher learning institutions have been set up in Rwanda (MINEDUC, 2011). These institutions have been recognized for providing quality education in the country at affordable costs. These institutions are well recognized and regulated by government to ensure provision of quality education in the country. The government should consider encouraging admission of private sponsored students at public higher learning institutions. This would increase financial resources of universities and foster competition, which leads to raising of standards to the benefit of students. The government would wish to gradually phase out in providing students' tuition fees and also reduce funding for other activities in higher learning institutions, a situation that will create funding gaps (MINEDUC, 2011), and hence a call on institutions to look for funding sources like use of public-private partnership (Jonathan and Peter, 2011). The current per capita income of Rwanda is about $1,600 having improved from $291 in 1998 (NBR, 2012). There is a big income disparity between the rich and the poor. People with some relatively stable income leave in the urban centers whereas village dwellers have very low incomes. The presupposition here is that, the people with stable incomes will afford to fund their children's higher education while those in poor backgrounds will face some challenges. This may bring imbalances in economic development and levels of literacy.

Rwanda uses a cost sharing approach for funding its higher education. This approach apportions financial responsibilities to both the students and the government. This approach needs the corporation of provincial, district and other local leaders who help to determine potential beneficiaries of government assistance. Currently, HESLD (2011) asserts that there has been challenges since poor assessments are done by the local leaders. This leads to poor decisions being made in facilitation of students. This system could be improved with strengthening of the assessment mechanism for the potential beneficiaries. Higher education funding could be done using public-private partnerships funding mechanism as has worked in sub-Saharan African countries (Jonathan and Peter, 2011). This approach could work for Rwanda if the necessary infrastructure has been created for interested investing firms in the higher education sector. Organizations like UNESCO among others have been at the fore front of funding higher education in Sub-Saharan countries and it is therefore vital to find whether or not such avenues can be used in Rwanda and hence the justification for the study on funding higher education in Rwanda. The government of Rwanda would have to negotiate with financial institutions in the country that would provide study loans to students on favorable terms. This would ease accessibility of the loans. It would also help if the government in its capacity can provide the loans at 0% interest rates as opposed to the 8% charge on the leaving allowance support given to the students supported by the government. This higher percentage has led to slow collections and bad debts (HESLD, 2011).

Funding higher education through cost sharing

Cost sharing could be one of the ways to fund higher education in Rwanda and this is to say that governments could give higher learning institutions some funds for students' support and the rest generated by individual students or institutions. Cost sharing involves shared responsibility for higher education funding. This approach was adopted in Rwanda in 2008 (HESLD, 2011). It was adopted as good policy and financial assistance is given after a financial means testing (FMT). This has not worked successfully in Rwanda as it is riddled with many challenges like corruption in doing the financial means testing to identify those who are financially able and those that are not. This leads to leaving out potential beneficiaries and this denies a chance to some people in accessing higher education. Another example of this type of approach was presented by the study developed by Adeniyi and Taiwo (2011) that analyzed higher education cost sharing in Nigeria and their finding showed a positive response, though they did not analyze other methods of funding. Therefore, it is vital to contextualize the cost sharing to the Rwandan situation and explore its applicability and this is what the researcher has done. The findings showed that the continued survival of higher education in Nigeria will depend on the mutual contributions between the parents and the government in pre-determined proportions by the government.

Cost sharing is good due to sharing of financial responsibility between the learner and the government, which reduces the government financial burden, though a challenge is associated with parents in accepting this kind of arrangement. It was adopted in Rwanda in 2008. The government has been honoring its part of the bargain, but students have not been forthcoming in repayment of the loan percentage (25 and 50% given to students for arts and science courses respectively). The Government of Rwanda gives priority to science education and that is why it allocates students more funds compared to arts and humanities. However, lack of employment has been cited as a major reason as to why loans recovery from student beneficiaries has not been good (HESLD, 2011). There is also a belief that employers have also not been forthcoming in deducting some funds from employee's salaries to cater for their loan obligations received from the Higher Education Students' Loans Department. Students' loans in Rwanda are recovered through deductions from an employee's salary by an employer and credited directly to Higher Education Students' Loans Department.

The Government of Rwanda has emphasized the teaching of science and technology in the country (MINEDUC, 2011). This is a government policy and its emphasis has been zeroed on the argument that, it is science and technology that helps in jobs creation and quick development of the economy. Arts and humanities students also get appropriate funding from government; the difference is that, they pay more back to the government compared to sciences students. The argument, however, would be that it takes long to train a science students and they need to do a lot of practical work and in a sense, they will need more financial resources when compared to arts students who train for a short period and may not need to do a lot of practical work.

Teferra and Altbach (2004) argue that cost sharing is inevitable if the higher education funding is to be realistic; for instance in Tanzania, the policy provides for cost sharing between the government and the students. Under this arrangement the government has to deal with financing direct costs of higher learning institutions and then costs in form of leaving allowances should be met by students with the help of their families. The current situation in Rwanda puts a student at a line of paying their full tuition and leaving allowances and this will financially strain them. The higher education funding has been reduced by 25% putting less development budget for institutions and this will constrain physical infrastructure development in form of lecture halls, laboratories, etc. Yet, students' enrolment has increased to about 65,000 based on the 2010/11 statistics (MINEDUC, 2011).

Increased students' enrolment in higher learning institutions is a good outcome for the country. The numbers could have probably been higher if the costs sharing approach in the country was regarded as fair and affordable and the financial means testing was adopted efficiently and effectively. The reliance on local leaders to do the financial means testing for the beneficiaries has so far not worked as expected. The definition of financially able parents in the villages has not been done well by the local leaders due to lack of definable and proper indicators. This has caused a lot of grief to parents who are considered financially able and yet they are not. Children of such parents are being denied financial support on faulty financial assessment. The Government of Rwanda has realized this problem and is moving in to find ways of how the financial means testing can be made more efficient and reliable. There is a need to strengthen the Higher Education Students' Loans Department such that its officers are facilitated to work with other government agencies at district levels to ensure a fair assessment. At the moment, HESLD (2011) estimates that disbursements are higher when compared to recovery; since the introduction of costs sharing in higher education funding in 2008, about USD 102,249,488.8 has been disbursed and only about USD 1,573,069.058 has been recovered. This puts question marks on the success of this students financing approach in Rwanda.

According to Rwanda's vision 2020, one of its priorities is to produce graduates that are internationally comparable in terms of quality and the argument here is that quality education comes with costs attached; for example, heavy investment in employing high qualified personnel, construction of lecture halls, good library, construction and equipping of laboratories etc. Funding for higher education should be adequate and more to say is that once higher education funding reduces, this will have an impact on quality of education. A study done by Culkin and Mallick (2011) indicates that producing ready employable graduates in the United Kingdom was vital and yet higher education funding keeps going down and would reduce to £4.2 billion by 2012 to 2015. A comparison here can be made to Rwanda, which aspires to produce graduates of international credence and comparability and yet, it is continuously reducing funding for the sector. The aspiration is to produce practical graduates ready for the job market but this may not be possible if investment is not done in the teaching of the practical subjects that are hands on and vital for job creation. It is therefore fundamental that this study explores the link between higher education funding and the quality of graduates from Rwandan higher learning institutions as the findings would help the government revise its higher education funding decisions accordingly.

Political role in higher education funding

The allocation of government resources is done with the approval of parliament. Parliament has the power to approve and reject proposed government budget allocations. These politicians may decide, support and approve allocation of more funds to the higher education sector. It is clear that once a sector is considered crucial and a priority for the government, it will have the power to allocate it more financial resources which will have the support of cabinet and parliament. The education sector has a big budget vote from government; it should be at ministry of education level to allocate a big part of it to higher education provided there is good political will (MINEDUC, 2011). Political influence is deemed to have a role in funding of higher education. For instance, McLendon et al. (2009) talk about higher education funding in the US that tends to have a lot of support from politicians and if this is linked to the situation in Rwanda, for the country to transform its economy through producing quality graduates, there are needs of political support in allocation of state funding to the higher education sector and generally the study explores this assumption. The findings by McLendon et al. (2009) indicate that states in the US with powerful politicians lobby for good funding allocations to their states from the central government and the individual states themselves to ensure that a good percentage of their budget is allocated to higher education. The point here is that in Rwanda, some sectors with strong politicians would have a good budget allocation. The education sector gets a huge budget allocation, but the problem is that the higher education sub sector is not allocated enough resources, a factor that has constrained service delivery at higher learning institutions.

The Government of Rwanda is considering having one state university system called the University of Rwanda and this has been done to monitor quality of higher education in Rwanda and to ease resource mobilization in form of research grants, gifts, etc. And looking at universities in countries like Germany and the Netherlands, funding is linked to the quality of education provided by higher learning institutions (Ingo, 2003). It is assumed that the operation of one state university system would among other issues ease resource mobilization for higher learning institutions in Rwanda and this research has been on it to ascertain the correlation between the two as stated in this hypothesis. Examples of developing countries that have seen success in the proposed funding models include Uganda that has successful implemented cost sharing approach at its public higher learning institutions; it has also succeeded in generating a lot of funds through tuition fees charges (Ssempebwa, 2011). Kenya higher education system has been successful in implementing a cost sharing approach and it has had successes in its loan recovery. Rwanda can learn from the Kenyan experience especially on what it has been done to make Kenyans believe in cost sharing in funding their higher education system and its efficient system of loans recovery from students. Tanzania has seen a success story on costs sharing funding mechanism and it has been successful on public- private partnership as a method of funding higher education (Teferra and Altbach, 2004). There is evidence that funding higher education through public- private partnerships has not been successful in Rwanda; for instance it failed at National University of Rwanda and Umutara Polytechnic. There is need to analyze the reasons for such failures and yet there have been successes in other developing countries.

Higher education funding in some selected developed and developing countries

Developed countries like US, Netherlands, UK, Germany and most of European countries have been successful in funding their higher education systems using tuition fees, costs sharing, public- private partnerships, scholarships and grants (Ingo, 2003; Newfield, 2010). The issue of funding higher education in some countries has been met with increased tuition fees. For example, in the US in the state of California, there has been persistent tuition fees increment since 2004 to 2011 (Newfield, 2010). The issue is whether or not this can be adopted in Rwanda and the way to find out is if this is test driven on Rwanda higher education system. This has been done by analyzing different higher education funding options in Rwanda. The stakeholders or interest groups have an influence on the funding of higher education in a country (Tandberg, 2009) and this could be through lobbying, which will affect the funding allocated to the sector by the state. Rwanda is a country that is looking forward to sustained social economic development and this can be achieved with good quality higher education system that is adequately funded and not necessarily from state funding. Other avenues have to be explored as long as the policy favors government higher learning institution to be flexible in search for funding; for example Makerere University in Uganda can be singled out where 80% of students pay privately their tuition fees and this relieves the government of the financial burden (Teferra and

Altbach, 2004).

The current situation in Rwanda is lack of enabling environment to allow higher learning institutions to be given autonomy to find ways to generate and manage its cash resources which the researcher has evaluated. The idea here is that even if the institutions were successful in generating resources, the bureaucracy in government would make it difficult to spend swiftly in having quality education in the country. Developed countries have efficient and transparent systems and they have given their universities some good levels of financial and academic autonomy; for example the US has adopted AFT-American funding model in form of public -private partnerships and a big part of its higher education funding mostly comes from the private sector (Newfield, 2010). Public- private partnership has worked well in countries like Tanzania and Uganda Higher learning institutions but it came with its challenges; for instance some underfunding of research work since private investors would mostly be interested in infrastructure development where they can easily and quickly realize their returns. Universities like MIT gets most of its funding from research grants, endowment income, tuition fees, contracts etc; it never gets any direct funds from government. This has made the university center of excellence which has helped to create alliances with funding organizations (Ingo, 2003). This could be a learning lesson for Rwanda if it is to adopt public-private partnership and or any others like use of tuition fees, bank loans and costs sharing. This will allow higher learning institutions to generate supplementary financial resources and spend on resources needed for uplifting higher education academic quality in the country. Universities in Netherlands like University of Twente and University of Bristol in the UK get part of their funding annually from their respective governments, but they must generate additional funds by themselves through research grants, tuition fees, and other contracts etc. (Ingo, 2003). Bristol University is given by the government only 36% of its budget every year and it must strive to raise the remaining percentage by itself and this would not be possible if it is not academically and financially autonomous. These universities are empowered by their respective countries to find their own funding and this is what is needed in Rwanda for universities to be able to generate their own funds internally.

Higher education funding models in Rwanda

This sub-section deals with current higher education funding model in Rwanda, and those which have been proposed by the government which include charging of tuition fees to students, public- private partnerships, and using internally generated funds by higher learning institutions. An analysis has been made on the link between HE funding and quality of HE, and the effect of poorly funded higher education on Rwanda's development.

Current higher education funding model in Rwanda

The current higher education funding structure in Rwanda is based on cost sharing depending on the unit costs of science and arts subjects. The determination of the beneficiaries of financial support depends on the financial means of families. The Government of Rwanda through Higher Education Students' Loans Department (HESLD) and district leaders used FMT (Financial means testing) to determine the beneficiaries of government's support for their higher education. FMT is based on family incomes and what they own in form of assets. For instance, the number of houses owned, cows, goats, monthly earnings etc. Local leaders help central government officials in making the analysis in the FMT construct. Students from families that lack assets and live on daily incomes of less than $1 are beneficiaries of government sponsorship at higher learning institutions. The government, having seen and experienced the challenges with this method, has proposed other funding mechanisms namely use of tuition fees, loans, incomes generated internally by higher learning institutions and the use of public -private partnerships.

Funding higher education using tuition fees

It is argued in developed European states that acquiring higher education should be free since those economies would use the trained manpower to develop their economies. This could be applicable where demand for higher education is low but where it is high, it puts pressure on governments to find resources for financing this sector. This may lead to a decision to charge increased tuition fees to students which may not be afforded by everyone hence leading to limited access to higher education (Vandenberghe and Debande, 2007). The reality of charging tuition fees at higher learning institutions in Rwanda seems to be based on the principle that the recipient of higher education benefits should be able to pay for it personally. The danger here is that those who cannot afford the tuition fees charged will miss out and this will affect accessibilty and the country will not be able to realize its ambition of creating a pool of quality educated workforce to transform the economy (MINEDUC, 2011; Vandenberghe and Debande, 2007). The argument developed by Barr (2004) is that quality education is not cheap, and therefore, it should not be left to only the state; owing to the importance of higher education in attaining economic development, countries like United Kingdom have made some reforms allowing for charging of tuition fees ranging from £0 to £3000 per annum and this leads to financial boost of higher learning institutions in the country. The issue, however, in Rwanda is that mechanism for admitting private fee paying students in higher learning institutions is there and the tuition is in the range of USD 1,574 per annum. The challenge however, is that most eligible students are not able to afford such amounts and this would call for need of access to loans which can be provided by financial institutions or even the state; such option of private tuition fee loans for students is not currently readily available in Rwanda. The students' tuition loan facility should be enough to cover the tuition and leaving allowances of students at higher learning institutions; though it should be appreciated that loans can be risky as they are security free and there is a danger of non–payment. And this may explain why the Government of Rwanda would need to be cautious enough in adopting a policy of loans advance to students that have to pay back when they complete their education and get a job (Gwosc and Schwarzenberger, 2011; MINEDUC, 2011).

Funding higher education using public -private partnerships

Public- private partnerships in education involve having private players helping in supporting funding of education. A good example where public- private partnership has been successful is Nigeria where the University of Ibadan had arrangement with Mac Arthur Foundation that provided the university with a grant of $100,000 in 2001 and in 2002, it gave the university a grant of $3,000,000 for strengthening its operations, research and ICT (Jonathan and Peter, 2011). Rwanda could learn some good lessons from such a country and encourage its universities to solicit for such arrangements from the international arena. Rwanda has to realize that it is good higher education system that drives economic development and earning potential of its citizens.

Funding higher education using internally generated funds

This is a really good option if the right environment is created for higher learning institutions. A good example of an institution in Rwanda that was able to generate in 2002 about 35% of its incomes internally is KIST (Kigali Institute of Science and Technology) and the percentage has since gone up; by 2008, it was projected to be more than 50% (Butare, 2004). This is a good case in point that other higher learning institutions in the country could emulate and overtime, the government could even pull out of funding completely recurrent expenditure and dedicate its efforts to funding only capital expenditure. KIST, having realized that its budget allocation by the government is not enough to support its activities, devised ways to generate its own resources and started projects in ICT like selling of internet services to the general public, and providing general IT solution to the public, in order to generate some money (Butare, 2004). These are some of the projects among the many being undertaken at Kigali Institute of Science and Technology (KIST). National University of Rwanda (NUR) has projects like a radio station, houses for rent, consultancy firm, etc which provide some additional income for it (NUR, 2012).

Effect of reduced higher education funding on the quality of higher education in Rwanda

Lack of enough HE funding has been the cause of low levels of research in higher learning institutions in Africa and the problem has been compounded by poor pay for lecturers. This could lead to low motivation and can have an effect on higher education since students will not get the best recent research materials from their instructors (Devarajan et al., 2011). Carrying out research makes tutors abreast with current developments locally and internationally vital for students' learning. It is quite unfortunate in Rwanda that most lecturers do not engage in research due to lack of financial support and this really does not develop them intellectually to make them current with their ideas; and this means students will not get up-to-date knowledge. The student population in Africa is projected to be 18 to 20 million by 2015 in about 10 countries in Africa including Rwanda whose student population currently stands at 73,674, showing that it has been going up since 1994/1995 when it was 3,261 representing about 96% increment (MINEDUC, 2011 and Devarajan et al., 2011). The increment in student population is a good thing for Rwanda provided that, adequate facilities are put in place to ensure good learning environment for students, which is not the case. Rwanda strives to ensure that it gets a pool of quality graduates from its higher learning institutions as they will have a lot to offer in terms of skills needed in the economy to transform itself and better the lives of its citizens; and again it is true that better qualified graduates get better pay for their services which increases their disposable incomes and tax base (Demange et al., 2008). Researchers like Ssempebwa (2011) argue that higher education in African countries like Uganda tends to be commercialized in a sense that public and private higher learning institutions recruit large numbers of students without considering the available physical and social infrastructure that aids learning, and this affects quality of education. Rwanda has been conservative in its students' enrolments in public higher learning institutions, only attracting government sponsored students. This trend has changed and private students are being enrolled in all the 7 public universities. This has led to numbers shooting up while facilities like university building have not been expanded, there is shortage of ICT equipment, well equipped laboratories, etc, and definitely these create negative effect on the quality of higher education. Higher learning institutions in Rwanda depend mostly on academic staff sourced from neighboring countries like Uganda, Kenya, Tanzania, Zimbabwe and India. The problem, however, is that salaries offered are not attractive and this leads to attract-tion of less qualified staff. Higher learning institutions do not put enough research funds for staff and there is also shortage of publishers and access to international journals. The Ministry of Education has urged higher learning institutions in Rwanda to facilitate their academic staff to do research as this improves a university's rating and career development of the researcher. The problem of shortage of funding in Rwanda higher learning institutions is in both private and public ones.

The socio-economic transformation of a country has a lot to do with the quality of graduates or the quality of higher education (Ajakaiye and Kimenyi, 2011). Now, the issue is that good quality education depends on the available resources to offer it, and in Rwanda, there are financial resource constraints from the state budget. Because of this challenge, institutions have been urged to generate resources internally through research and consultancy to fill the financing gap and there is also a need to understand its feasibility. It is good for universities to generate resources internally. Universities can engage in applied research such that their new inventions can be sold to governments and other corporations. This would help generate additional financial resources. Consultancy can also be a good source of income for universities; and letting out some of the un utilized facilities like building to the public could also be another good source of income among other possibilities. The problem, however, is that potential sources for such revenues are limited in the country. There is need to develop and expand the private sector from which the higher learning institutions can harness some funding from as the public sector is not rich enough to provide for consultancy opportunities for universities. Economic development of a country may not be attained with poorly educated work force. South Africa is a good example of an economy that is doing well or developing because of its well educated workforce and this could be a good learning model for most African countries, and Rwanda should not be an exceptional case (Ouma, 2010). The United States of America has been commended for its quality higher education leading to quite a number of technological innovations, and generally its economic success has been attributed to its highly educated workforce (Newfield, 2010). An analysis is needed to ascertain lessons that can be learnt by the Government of Rwanda from such model countries as this could help in forging a way to improve the quality of its workforce that is vital for her economic development.

Effect of reduced higher education funding on the social and economic transformation of Rwanda

A country's social economic transformation depends on the quality and not the quantity of its labor force graduating from higher learning institutions. According to a study by Rangel (2004), Mexico has invested heavily on this sector and its graduates have a key role in its economic development. The country's population is more than 97,483,412 and it has eligible work population of 34,154,854 and out of these, 33,730,210 are working; though 15.8% are in the primary sector, 27.8% in the secondary sector and a big number of 53.4% work in the tertiary sector. This should be attributed to education attained at different levels (Rangel, 2004). Mexico is a developing country and so is Rwanda. What Rwanda can learn from Mexico is that, for a country to develop, it must invest substantially in its higher education sub-sector and ensure that it has a well educated workforce. Educated people are able to fend for themselves locally and internationally and even when they get jobs, the returns are better than those that never got higher education.

Rwanda targets to have for example 275,000 graduates in the construction sector, 235,000 in transport and communication, 75,000 in mining and quarrying, 520,000 in manufacturing by the year 2020. Rwanda is heavily constrained with these skills because universities in the country have not been training people in these sectors and this leads to reliance on imported manpower from other countries, which is not enough. Lack of knowledge leads to deficiencies and Rwanda has had these sectors underdeveloped due to lack of professionals. Higher learning institutions have started training people to work in these sectors and the government hopes that such shortages will be no more as per its vision 2020. Training in such skills is quite expensive and needs to be financially supported by government through adequate funding which is currently not the case; otherwise such skills will remain in short supply and this will deter the country's economic growth and hamper attainment of its vision 2020. There is a body of knowledge by Taylor and Machado-Taylor (2010), which asserts that higher learning institutions training should relate to the social and economic skills required in an economy. The idea is a formidable one but a country like Rwanda will need to train adequate number of engineers in its higher learning institutions which obviously comes at a high cost; but its economy may not sustain since there are also other sectors' priorities that need funding. There is need for balance in resources allocated for training in different fields and skills so that there will not be surplus skills in some areas and shortage in others. Given this kind of situation, the higher education sector has to find resources to complement those provided by the state through, for instance, students' fees, philanthropists, public -private partnerships and income generating activities which the government has to champion policy-wise and through other governments' supported forum.

The Government of Rwanda in collaboration with international universities has overtime been offering students grants in form of tuition fee waivers. The government through HESLD provides leaving allowances to students, which they must pay back with interest. The collaborating universities are mostly in US through the presidential scholarship schemes as well as South African universities; the financial responsibilities for study tuition and leaving allowances are shared between the Government of Rwanda and sponsoring universities. Partner universities give tuition waivers to students and the Government of Rwanda only pays for student's accommodation and leaving allowances (HESLD, 2011). This has helped many students from Rwanda to access quality higher education abroad at affordable costs. Rwanda as a country has different categories of people in terms of their social and financial status. Mostly people in the rural areas are the ones prone to failing to get tuition fees for their children due to limited incomes and hence a requirement for governments' support. Financially able parents in town are able to pay tuition fee for their children in universities. The researcher has to explore the affordability to borrow funds from private institutions, which may not be easy for people without collateral for such loans. This means that parents without collateral will have their children miss out on pursuing higher education. This could lead to imbalances in economic development in terms of regional development in a country. The state has to ensure such borrowing is affordable by all potential beneficiaries and this should be guaranteed by the sitting government. Higher education system in the United Kingdom allows for universities to look for funding to complement contribution from the government and this has enabled the higher education system to produce credible graduates needed in the economy (Scott, 2009). Scott states that an average university in the UK has £200 million turnover annually of which some is raised privately by an institution from fees, and users of the university services and such amounts would keep the university functioning properly. Rwanda has to borrow a leaf from such systems, though from advanced countries. They can be tailored to Rwanda environment and adopted accordingly as the reality is that the Government of Rwanda cannot adequately fund higher education sector in the country and hence it should encourage alternative sources of funding by higher learning institutions.

RESEARCH METHODOLOGY

Research methodology is about designing ways systematically on how research questions can be solved or how the researcher intends to do his research. Alternatively, it could also be called the work plan; procedures to be followed by the researcher in conducting research study (Rajasekar et al., 2006). It is crucial that the researcher understands and presents clearly the techniques to be used during the research study and how the collected data are to be analyzed so as to provide answers to the outlined research questions. Appropriate data must be collected using the right methods depending on the study method.

This research has adopted a qualitative research and especially survey questionnaires and interviews to collect both primary and secondary data. The qualitative approach was adopted because of its ability to help the researcher to form a holistic and narrative understanding of the problems associated with higher education funding models in Rwanda. This approach is quite appropriate when collecting data from population that require use of instruments like document reviews, observations and interviews employed in this research as supported by McMillan and Schumacher (1993).

Quite a number of secondary sources (MINEDUC Higher Education Action Plans, 2011; MINICOFIN Higher Education Budget Estimates, 2010) have supported this study. The analysis of information from secondary sources has helped to supplement primary data collected from the field. The study outcomes are coming up with a research report that gives analysis about higher education funding sources in Rwanda, and also analyze the impact of reduced higher education funding on the quality of education in and its impact on achieving millennium development goals especially on education. The researcher has adopted a qualitative research study methodology because it allows working without specific boundaries and hence inclusion of new concepts, innovation in the study and ability to find reliable answers to the research question and it allows for realistic findings as argued by Toloie-Eshlaghy et al. (2011).

The study data sample of 45 respondents from the central province was chosen purposively and randomly such that, reliable information could be got from the respondents. This sample was divided into two subsamples. The first subsample focused on 15 employees from HESLD and the second subsample on 30 students that have benefited from HESLD financing their higher education. It is argued by Marshal (1996) that small samples are appropriate for qualitative research studies and what should matter should be the quality of the chosen sample and the richness of the information obtained from them. Russell and Gregory (2003) also argue that small samples could be adopted in a qualitative study provided that the research questions can be fully answered and provocative issues could be generated and call for further research and again the researcher should have to exercise adequate judgment in identifying the study sample. This is why the researcher has used a smaller sample in this study with the view of generating credible findings since the respondents are rich with the information and experience about higher education funding in Rwanda. A qualitative study has been adopted because it allows for reasoning during the study investigation. This really helps for the analyzing of the reliable data used during the research study (Jahoda et al., n.d). Data were collected in this study, using questionnaire due to its appeal in collecting reliable data and also gives the respondents time to respond at their own will. Interviews were also used for this study bringing the respondents face to face with the researcher; and this helped in getting answers to structured questions by the researcher. Generally, a survey approach was adopted and instruments also included use of interviews and case studies.

A pilot study was done to make sure that the designed questionnaire was appropriate and basically, it was about understanding its weaknesses in collection of appropriate data, such that it can be improved on with the help of the targeted respondents. It was found to be appropriate and it was adopted without any changes made on it. The study results had to be verified to ensure reliability. The reliability test has been done using triangulation and generalization of research findings as these are considered vital tests in qualitative research (Johnson, 1997). If the findings can be used as a basis for other researchers, this means they are reliable and if similar or related studies can be made by other researchers, and they obtain nearly or almost similar findings, this becomes a good test on reliability of findings. Also to ensure reliability of the study findings, data were collected with full understanding of research ethics as per the University of Liverpool guidance.

Qualitative research study

Qualitative research method has been adopted for this study

because of its appropriateness to investigate the research questions stated. Data analysis was done continuously as information was being gathered from the field, and is possible under qualitative research as supported by Clissett (2008). Information collected from field survey was tabulated for interpretation using Excel worksheet software, and Ms Word for tabulation to facilitate easy analysis. Analyzing the higher education current funding model in Rwanda is a crucial question, which could have different variables involved; for instance, the argument that quality of higher education depends on adequate funding. Increased higher education funding may lead to high number of graduates needed in the market. It is vital that funding is channeled to training of skills that are needed in the country. The statistical tools that can be used in assessing and measuring this can be the SPSS, Excel and others. Use of these tools helps to understand and process the data accordingly. This kind of approach is crucial in improving reliability of research findings. A systematic study inquiry has been used in this study since it is supported under qualitative research method so as to get a holistic view on higher education funding in Rwanda and basically this method has been adopted because, it is fundamental when doing research on social issues in a country (McMillan and Schumacher, 1993). Data were collected in this study from natural setting especially from records on higher education form, MINEDUC, MINICOFIN and HESLD. Data collection methods like interviews, observations, review of documents or records, questionnaires, case studies were considered appropriate due to their appropriateness to collect reliable and massive data for such a study (Wiersma, 1995).

Data collected for the study

The data collected from the field were about the current higher education funding model based on a costs sharing approach in Rwanda. Specifically, primary data were collected on the perception of the model by the respondents, its successes and failures, funds disbursements and collections under this method and what can be done to improve the model. Data were also collected on the perceptions of the targeted respondents on the other government proposed higher education funding models, which use of loans from private banks, internally generated resources by higher learning institutions, and public- private partnerships. Secondary data were collected through document reviews on higher education, HESLD budgets and analysis of funds disbursements and collections by HESLD and government new proposed higher education funding models (MINEDUC, 2011 and MINICOFIN, 2012).

Data sample

The data sample was chosen as a judgment sample targeting departments involved in funds allocation in the higher education of Rwanda, and these are loans disbursement and recovery at Rwanda education board where HESLD agency falls. These two departments have been sampled because they are the ones that deal with funding of higher education and so the researcher considered them appropriate for this study. From this data obtained from the selected samples, the researcher is able to understand the suitability of current higher education funding model in Rwanda after analyzing its advantages and disadvantages and also to understand the implication of adopting the other government proposed higher education funding models. The government would therefore need to step in and act accordingly on the appropriate model if it is to make its higher education vibrant so as to avert the disadvantages of a failed higher education system, which could impact on its economic development.

Study period

The period considered for this study is 2009 to 2011. Higher education financing in Rwanda during this period underwent through reforms in terms of higher education financing. The government was faced with heavy financial burden of supporting students going to public higher learning institutions. The dilemma here was that many students were qualified to join universities but the capacity of the state to financially support them was not enough. This the same period that the Government of Rwanda opted for costs sharing such that the state and the learners share the financial responsibilities (HESLD, 2011). This is the same period that the Government of Rwanda vigorously started urging higher learning institutions to look for alternative sources of financing. Among the options were public private partnerships, generating funds internally by higher learning institutions through research and consultancy and engaging financial institutions in the country to support higher education funding in Rwanda (MINEDUC, 2011).

Data collection instruments and design

Data were collected from both primary and secondary sources in this study. For secondary sources, the research reviewed budget documents from HESLD, disbursements and loans recovery documents, and Rwanda higher education policy documents (MINEDUC, 2011). This was done through observation by reading and analyzing the contents therein those documents. Primary data were collected from HESLD using questionnaires and group interviews. Primary data in this case are regarded as first hand collected data from the field. The research held two group interviews: one with loans disbursement department, and the second one with the loans recovery department of HESLD.

The researcher also held individual interviews with the Director General of HESLD and the statistician of the agency. The questionnaires had both open and closed ended questions with multiple choice questions. The questions were about the advantages and disadvantages of costs sharing, use of internally generated funds, public private partnerships, and use of bank loans in funding higher education in Rwanda. The questionnaire also had questions about the relationship between higher education funding and quality of education and economic growth of Rwanda, and what can be done to improve current higher education funding in Rwanda. The structure of the questionnaire is addressed in the next section.

These instruments were adopted for use in this study because of their easy applicability. Questionnaires were adopted because they allow the respondents freedom to give information without disclosing their personal details. There is no fear of being reprimanded by superior colleagues. This allowed for high response rate of about 90 percent. The respondents were preselected with the help of administration at HESLD and 10 workers in the two departments were selected to give information about the study problem. Out of the 10 questionnaires distributed to the respondents, 9 were received back by the researcher. This represented 9/10 response rate on the side of HESLD employees and a good response rate from the students was achieved (26/30 response rate). This kind of response allowed the researcher to give representative findings about the research topic, which is about higher education funding in Rwanda. The respondents had to be knowledgeable in the subject to ensure reliability of responses. The respondents fortunately were workers and students who were once also beneficiaries of funding from HESLD. This also helped in improving reliability of the information. The nature of sample organization-HESLD and its sensitivity deal with financial matters and students' financial affairs; the respondents were comfortable with the group interviews divided into two. Higher education loans department has only two functional departments.

Questionnaires and their design

The questionnaires composed of both open and closed ended questions. The questionnaire design was based on literature from secondary sources of information especially from ministries of education and finance published documents (MINEDUC, 2011; MINICOFIN, 2012). The information that was particularly useful was that on higher education financing and the models used. The closed ended questions took the form of multiple choice questions based on 1 to 5 scale. This Likert scale helped in understanding the feelings, attitudes and opinions of the respondents on the subject matter (Brown, 2000). The reason was to identify the support levels given to current and government proposed higher education funding models. The open ended questions were aimed at understanding the respondent's perspective on how they look at higher education funding in Rwanda against her economic development and how a failed higher education funding system affects the HE quality. This was an appropriate data collection instrument as it allowed for easy data collection from the respondents, questions were clear and easy to understand and respond to. The structure of the questionnaire consisted of two sections: A had questions about the current and proposed higher education funding models in Rwanda and their appropriateness and suitability. The section B of the questionnaire had questions about the relationships between higher education funding and quality of education in the country and how higher education funding impacts the economic growth of Rwanda. This kind of approach was adopted because it helped to collect the required data about the major research question, which is about analyzing the current higher education funding model of costs sharing in Rwanda and the other government higher education proposed funding models. The link in the quality of higher education as a result of adequate funding had to be analyzed and this also goes with the economic development of the country resulting from a vibrant higher education system. The questionnaire is attached as an appendix and it contains questions to respondents on this point.

Interviews and their design

The targeted study population at HESLD was its two departments of loans disbursement and recovery. HESLD has only two departments. They were all considered for this study. This was because the loans disbursement department is responsible for identifying and giving out funds to the student beneficiaries and the loans recovery department is responsible for collection of the loans disbursed to students during their study. For interview purposes, each department was interviewed as a group. The researcher used group interviews in the study and this was mainly because it is a good method for understanding the feelings and thoughts of the respondents about the research problem (Kothari, 1985). Four staff members from the loans recovery department formed one group and three staff members from loans disbursement formed another group. The group's interviews were good since they helped in avoiding controversy in answers given to the interview questions. The groups would not agree when a wrong answer was given to a question posed by the researcher. This helped the researcher in getting reliable information during the data collection.

Observation and design

This instrument was used by the researcher to observe higher education financing trend, which has been turbulent under the 2009 to 2011 period considered for this study. It was done through documentary reviews from the ministries of education, finance and economic planning. There was no particular design for this research instrument. This approach enabled the research to collect primary data by observing situations, actions and people at HESLD and this helped to collect data that respondents were not able to reveal especially on their attitude towards the current costs sharing on funding higher education in Rwanda. Some respondents were not willing to freely criticize it due to some fears. Again, through observation, it was clear from the respondents that they had reservation on the government proposed higher education funding models especially on the use of commercial loans and PPP, which they felt could be expensive in the long run in form of interests payments and the hidden costs that may be associated with public-private partnerships in higher education.

Data analysis

As regards the analysis of collected data, this has been done using Excel and Ms Word as they have features for analyzing the collected data and more so it is easy to come up with information that can be graphically presented for illustration purpose and understanding of the end users of the project report. The process involved editing the raw data to remove errors and ambiguities; the data were classified into groups depending on the questions asked and answers obtained. Tabulation of data was done to help explain the findings from the research. Since this is a qualitative study, there has been a content analysis of the information obtained from the survey as codes were assigned to different questions and responses from the survey based on the themes; and from this, a study analysis is made to make some recommendations on the findings of the study. The data collected from the survey using questionnaires, group interviews were done using SPSS to find frequencies. This helped in explaining the findings logically.

Validity and reliability of research results

The study questions were fully answered since the survey method, which employed use of questionnaires, group interviews, and observation used to collect data was reliable. Johnson (1997) argues that as long as the study findings can be generalized to different circumstances and wider groups, this becomes a good test for the validity of study findings. The findings from this study can be generalized to different wider groups and the trustworthiness of the source of information increases the validity of the study results. Triangulation is also a vital test on reliability of study findings (Mathison, 1988) as different methods are used in collecting data and analyzing them. The researcher has use questionnaires, interviews, observation and review of past literature about higher education in Rwanda as the use of such various techniques increases reliability of the study findings.

The questionnaires, interviews, and observations were done appropriately by the researcher to ensure research was well done. The study gaps identified in the literature that shaped the research questions for this study have to be narrowed since the findings from this study have come up with some answers and the way forward. Patton (2002) argues that reliability and validity of a study are paramount as the audience needs to be convinced of the research findings and the argument here is that the researcher has to trust his sources of information for the qualitative study. The source of information for this study is trusted and hence the results are reliable. There cannot be reliability if the information is not valid; there is some argument that validity of information in qualitative research is not crucial (Creswell and Miller, 2000). However, there is need to find some ways on how research findings should be measured and to check out for its correctness depending on the rigor involved in the study. This qualitative study approach involves rigor, quality procedures that ensure the findings are valid and reliable and can be depended on for further research in the area.

RESULTS AND DISCUSSION

This chapter gives details about the research findings from this study. The study is about the evaluation of the current HE financing model in Rwanda. It is vital to have a good higher education system in Rwanda if the country is to achieve economic development that is sustainable (MINEDUC, 2011). Rwanda aspires to achieve an educated middle class of entrepreneurs who are knowledgeable and equipped with business skills needed for making investments in the country as laid down by MINICOFIN (2012). A good higher education system in the country can help to achieve its dream of creating a middle class who would for instance take risks based on the projected returns which have to be compared with risks and then understand how the risks can be mitigated. It is through taxes paid by such investors that the government uses to set up other infrastructure needed to support economic growth for instance setting up of hydro power projects for electricity needed to run factories and other business installations.

This may not be possible if a country has its higher education sector underfunded and this is the case in Rwanda (HESLD, 2011). Rwanda currently uses the system of costs sharing where the financing responsibility is shared between the government and the student. This has been proven to be quite expensive and unsustainable since the financial means testing (FMT) being used is seen as unfair when selecting the potential beneficiaries who are supposed to be from poor backgrounds (MINEDUC, 2011; HESLD, 2011). There is need to have this model improved and if possible to look at and analyze other possible funding models like PPP, tuition fees and internally generated funds. This study has sought views from the respondents about the costs sharing approach employed for funding higher education in Rwanda, analysis of the use of tuition fees, PPP, bank loans and internally generated funds funding models for higher education in Rwanda. The other research questions are to find if there is a link between higher education and economic development of Rwanda, and also if there is a relationship between higher education funding and its quality. The chapter is structured as follows: cost sharing in Rwanda, various other funding models, effect of higher education funding on quality of higher education, and higher education funding and its impact on economic development of Rwanda.

Cost sharing in Rwanda

This is the current higher education funding model used in Rwanda (HESLD, 2011). This method is viewed by respondents as one where the parent and the state both make financial contribution for a student pursuing her/his studies at Rwandan higher learning institutions. Findings from the study showed that Rwanda uses a costs sharing approach to fund its higher education system since 2008. From the 67% questionnaires received from respondents, 60% of them rated it as excellent, 20% as a very good system, 10% rated it as good and 10% also rated it as poor (Figure 1). No respondent rated as fair. This means that, whereas it may be a good funding policy, its method of implementation is not good. It may also seem to suggest that, the model receives different supports from the respondents and one would think that the respondents were rating it on how fair or unfair it is as a policy instead of just giving it weight based on Likert scale rating. The majority rated it as excellent giving reasons like; it is a government policy and therefore, it should be adopted and thus make a parent and state both responsible for funding higher education in the country. This finding compares well with those of Adeniyi and Taiwo (2011) on costs sharing in Nigeria where this method has been used for quite a long time. Whereas the findings from the rating of current higher education model by respondents showed excellent support, there is a need to look at affordability by parents and students. This approach could be excellent for countries that have attained some good level of economic development and parents have enough savings, which they can use to support their children at higher learning institutions in Rwanda. The FMT approach used in selecting beneficiaries of funding support from government should be reviewed and strengthened to ensure support goes to those that deserve it. This may also help to close the gap between the rich and the poor and in the long run, this may bring about balanced regional economic development. As regards the FMT, the government could think of employing a neutral private firm that could do the assessment of all applicants for financial support from the government; one would think that this is fairer than just using politicians at districts who may not do well in this regard.

The questionnaire had a question seeking for views from the respondents on how they rate the current cost sharing system of funding higher education in Rwanda. Guidance was given on the rating where an excellent rating score was 5, very good was 4, good was 3, fair was 2, and poor rating was 1. Figure 1 shows that a total number of 60% respondents at HESLD gave cost sharing system funding model of funding higher education system an excellent score and this means that, they view it as a good model. Only 20% respondents view it as very good, 10% as good, 10% as poor and none rated it as fair. Such rating disparity shows that the model is good and what the Government of Rwanda might need to do is to improve loans assessment methods and recovery mechanisms from students. This could be done by

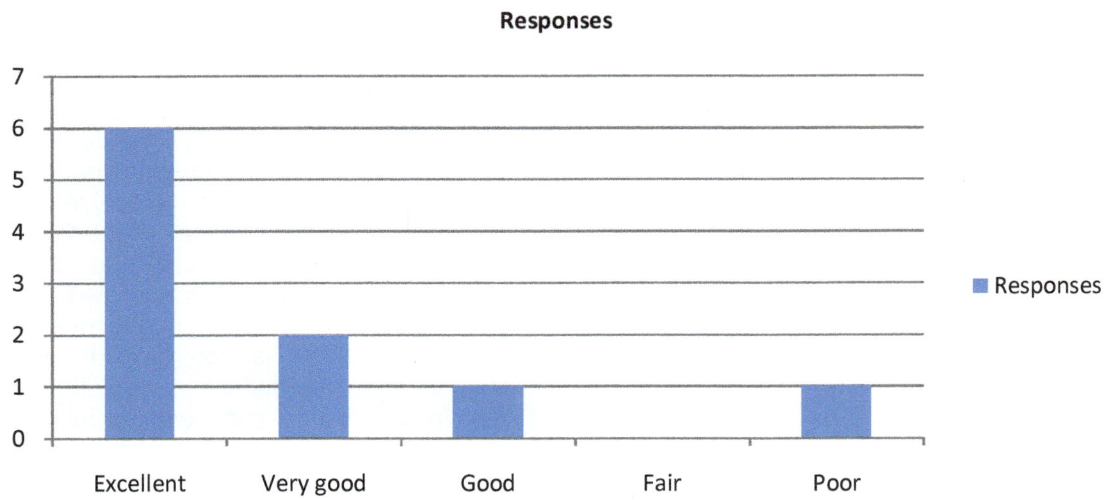

Figure 1. Graphical illustration of responses from HESLD.
Source: Author.

automatically giving financial assistance to all students who meet the cut off points of entering the higher education institutions (HEIs) in Rwanda and also putting up a system that compels the student to pay back the loans upon employment without any difficulties. It is clear from Figure 1 that the majority of respondents from HESLD support costs sharing as a policy and what needs to be done is to improve on it and also the Government of Rwanda should make steps to educate parents on why this policy should be supported. The state could argue that, they are trying to ensure that students from poor backgrounds get financial support and those from rich backgrounds are individually supported by their parents. It should be clear that what is being discussed here is the leading allowances and memoir fees. Regarding the tuition fees, every student who meets the government cut off point for entering HEIs gets it and the contentious issue is only the monthly allowances for students, which support during their stay in the universities. The rating of poor should not be dismissed as what should be done is to address the loopholes in the model as a way forward; instead of using politicians, the government could opt to use teachers and head teachers that may know the economic background of these students since they would have interacted with them at high school.

Rating of costs sharing model of funding higher education in Rwanda by students

The student respondents almost gave the opposite rating of the current higher education funding model of costs sharing whereby, of the 83% responses received from student respondents to the questionnaire, 40% respondents rated it as poor, 36% gave it a fair rating, 16% rated it as good, and 8% rated it as very good. The argument advanced by students for this poor rating is attributed to unfairness in the evaluation process which uses the FMT (financial means testing). This makes some eligible students to miss out due to miss evaluation by some corrupt government officials. The students in their responses are not sure whether or not the errors in the evaluation process are innocent or intentional. The other reason for not giving costs sharing a good rating is that people in Rwanda are poor and they may not be able to meet their financial obligations or contribution to their higher education funding since they may not be employed as this makes the situation economically worse (MINEDUC, 2011; MINICOFIN, 2011). When one looks at a similar study in Tanzania by Teferra and Altbach (2004), it was argued that costs sharing can only be possible if the parents are economically empowered and this compares appropriately with situation in Rwanda where this policy might not receive a lot of support from students since they are fully aware of their poor economic positions, which makes them run to seek for government's support on their study leaving allowances and memoir fees.

As seen in Figure 2, students do not find costs sharing an attractive funding model, and hence the reason for this very poor rating, with 0 as excellent and 10 as poor. The rating is based on the information from the field and these are students' responses to the question that requests students to give a rating of cost sharing model of funding higher education in Rwanda from excellent, very good, good, fair and poor and the assigned scale was 5, 4, 3, 2, 1 respectively based on the Likert scale. Though, from 0, the rating keeps going up in terms of number of respondents who rate from excellent to poor. This means that virtually, this model is not well rated by students and the logic here is that students may not want the financial obligation attached to their studies where they have to contribute and also, they may be seeing it as unfair in

Figure 2. Graphical representation of students' responses.
Source: Author.

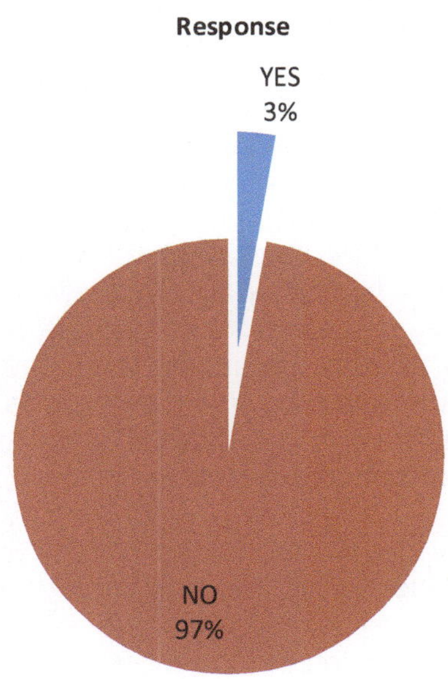

Figure 3. Graphical representation of students' support level of costs sharing.
Source: author.

terms of its implementation by the state. Again if the students never fairly benefitted from it, they would give it a bad rating and more so, students may have issues with funds recovery from them where they may not wish to have their salaries deducted to cater for the loans received from government when they were in the universities.

Support for cost sharing findings

Respondents were asked in the questionnaire on whether or not they support the current cost sharing model of funding higher education in Rwanda. The responses from HESLD showed this pattern: 90% answered NO, and 10% answered YES. The reasons advanced for NO is that Rwandan students are not able to financially support their studies, and that students should instead get full tuition and leaving expenses loans which they can pay when they get employment after completing their studies. The YES response came with a reason that a student must somehow also take some financial responsibility as this would make them more serious with their studies and responsible students. All the 100% student respondents do not support costs sharing and the argument advanced by students is that it is expensive for them and it is not fair. They feel the government should take full responsibility for funding higher education in the country as a way of providing a social service to its citizens. Figure 3 shows that 97% of respondents do not support the current system of funding higher education, which is based on costs sharing between the government and the students.

However when one looks at these responses, one wonders whether or not the policy on higher education funding adopted by government is fair to its beneficiaries; and according to MINEDUC (2011), costs sharing is the way to go and it is the policy that was eventually adopted by government in 2008, but it has come with challenges especially with application of FMT and high poverty levels in the country. The major issue with student respondents is that the country is poor and does not adequately make students and parents able to meet their contribution for students to be able to attain their higher education degrees. Barr (2004) argues that it is crucial for students and parents to contribute to their higher education financing as nothing comes cheap in this sector. Students should not hide under the veil of arguing that it is expensive. In any case, it is the state that pays all the funds and the student pays only upon getting employment and really it is a small percentage that is deducted from the salary of the beneficially and this is done for a reasonable period time that will not financially hurt them (HESLD, 2011).

Figure 3 shows that 97% do not support costs sharing and 3% support it. It would be squarely clear from the students' perspective that the government could have better options or be fair still; it could improve this model and say offer 0% interest loans and then to ensure that beneficiaries of the scheme are fairy chosen based on merit only. The 3% support could be improved if such mentioned issues herein are addressed and again one would think that, it would be fair to combine the costs sharing approach with other funding models like use of bank loans and PPP etc.

Other higher education funding models in Rwanda

HESLD responses

Respondents from HESLD were asked about other government proposed funding methods of using tuition fees, bank loans, setting up firms to generate funds internally and use of PPP. The responses took this pattern: of the total 67% responses, 20% support use of tuition fees and 80% do not support use of tuition fees for funding higher education. The reason identified for not supporting using tuition fees charges is that Rwandan students or parents may not be able to afford it due to high levels of poverty in the country. Those who answered yes believe that as the country is not rich, it should be the burden of the students to find ways to support or fund their higher education. The responses for internally generated funds as a source of funding higher education had 30% yes and 70% no; and the reason advanced for high rate of disapproval is that the government would still slow them down due to its bureaucracy and those that support it advance an argument of relieving the government some financial burden and such funds can be allocated to other sectors of the economy. Bank loans as a proposed form of funding higher education in Rwanda is the one that received a lot of support from respondents as out of 67% responses, 0% respondents support it and only 100% did not support it. This is because bank loans can be expensive in interest payment and they may not be readily available on the market. This makes it unattractive for the majority of students.

The responses received about use of PPP were with mixed reactions, where 20% respondents believe that use of this method is good especially for infrastructure development. The rest of the 80% responses did not show support. The reason advanced for this is that, the Rwandan Government may not have the expertise to deal with such arrangements and again they believe that such arrangements have been tested in Rwandan higher learning institutions and have failed especially at NUR and Umutara Polytechnics. The issue here is lack of understanding of how PPP works, and they had failed to make prior studies on where such arrangements had been successful. They were adopted by these institutions and the financing arrangements became a problem making their services unaffordable by students and also became difficult on the side of these institutions. Jonathan and Peter (2011) argue that PPP is good provided the arrangements have been negotiated well between the players and the service user should be able to afford the cost; but this seemed not to be the case at NUR and Umutara where these initiatives were adopted.

Figure 4 shows that, bank loans are not a favored option to HESLD respondents. All the 67% respondents gave it a NO, 80% responded NO to using of tuition fees and using of PPP and 70% responded NO to use of internally generated funds. When one looks at this trend of responses, it leaves one thinking that all these options may not work well in Rwanda; for instance, the banking sector is not well developed and prepared to offer student financing as they may fear the risks involved. HEIs may also abuse the tuition fees policy by charging high fees. For the case of PPPs, these may be difficult to find and manage and may be abused by some investors. As far as use of internally generated funds is concerned, this may not be a very feasible funding model as the sources for such a model may not be many and hence rendering it not sustainable and unsuitable long term higher education funding model in Rwanda.

Students' support of the various funding models

The situation illustrated in Figure 5 shows that of all the proposed funding models, use of internally generated funds is highly supported by students as compared to other options and this is generally fine as it puts higher learning institutions on the lime light of not depending on the vote from government. Butare (2004) argues that it is great for higher education institutions (HEIs) to generate their own resources which they can use for the operations of the institutions. It is clear from his study at KIST that such resources are instrumental in the development of the institution and the general welfare of its human resources as they get 50 %top up on their salaries and this improves the morale of lecturers as well as having a knock on effect on their service delivery. There is no

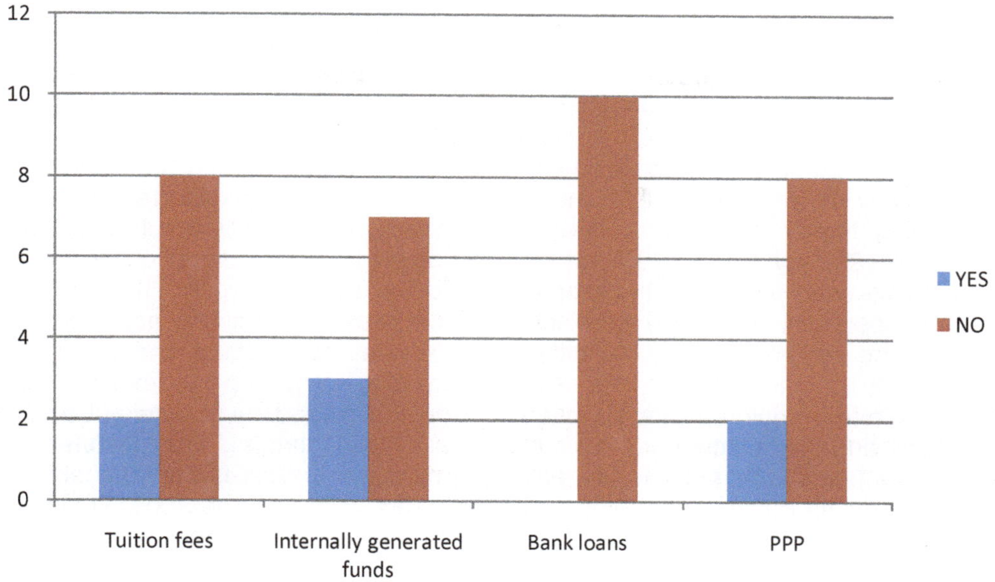

Figure 4. Graph showing hesld support of various funding models.
Source: Author.

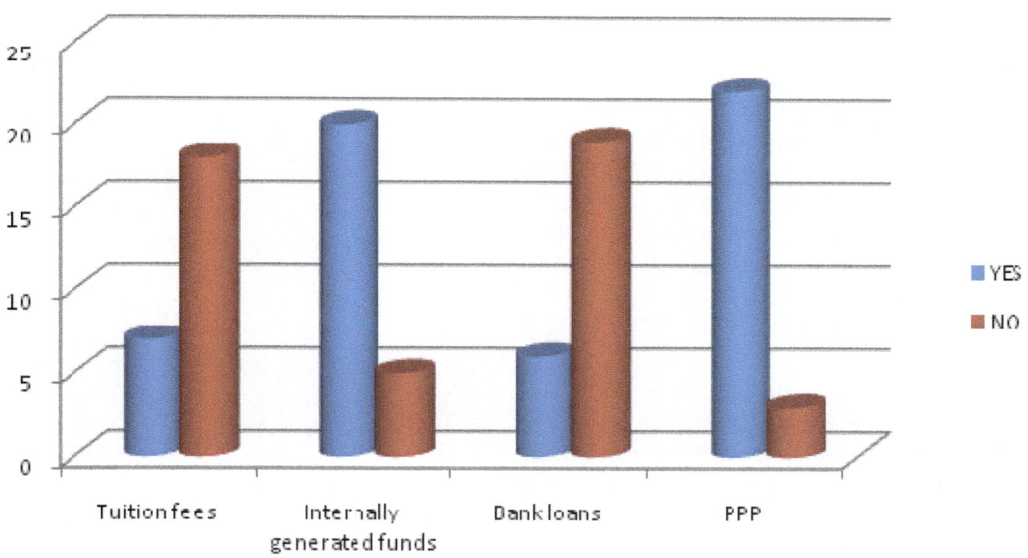

Figure 5. Graphical illustration of students' support for other funding models.
Source: author

support for bank loans as an option for funding higher education because they are not affordable; this is valid given the poor economic situation in the country.

Discussing students' support for proposed higher education funding models

The student respondents strongly believe that use of PPP is a very attractive option for funding higher education in Rwanda. The support given is 88% for yes and 12% for no. The issue here should be to get the arrangement right and to ensure that the benefits from this arrangement outweigh the costs and there is also need to understand that this arrangement could be good for capital project development and not for say equipping of laboratories and buying of books which the HLIs should be responsible for. The other huge support was on use of internally generated resources; it had 80% support and 20% no. This method makes the institution responsible for generating resources through say consultancy work, research and other activities as argued by Butare (2004).

Here, the government has to be cautious not to lock the generated funds into unnecessary bureaucracy. This might not help to make the situation better for HLIs if such red tape on government institutions spending is not addressed even if the funds are generated. In other words, higher learning institutions should be given some level of financial autonomy by the government. There is little support for funding higher education in Rwanda using tuition fees where 72% say no and 28% say yes. The disapproval could be associated with the fear that HLIs could use it as an opportunity to charge high fees to students and this will be unaffordable by majority of Rwandan students. Vandenberghe and Debande (2007) argue that charging tuition fees could be used as long as it is done right and fairly and the student does not suffer some much loss. The point here is that tuition fees policy should be clear and fair to all parties and it should be used solely for funding higher education. The use of bank loans is also not supported and it has received 76% no responses and 24% yes; and arguable, this could be attributed to the weak banking sector in Rwanda. The existing banks may not all be ready to provide education loans to students without some form of guarantee from government and some other institutions (MINICOFIN, 2012).

Figure 5 shows there is high support for adoption and need for use of public- private partnerships and use of internally generated resources to fund higher education in Rwanda. A question in the questionnaire requested student respondents to support or not support the current cost sharing and other proposed funding models; the responses received are indicated in Figure 5. The least supported models by students are the use of tuition fees and use of bank loans. The fear here is that both models can be misused by HEIs and financial institutions to exploit students.

Higher education funding and its effect on quality education in Rwanda

The findings indicated that 100% respondents agree that when higher education is poorly funded, it will affect its quality. No response was against it. All the 67% responses received from HESLD show that, they all believe that higher education subsector in Rwanda is underfunded and this is also the belief of all the 100% responses received from students. The arguments for the support are that, it is vital to give adequate funding for research, infrastructure development, equipping of learning facilities, and paying lecturers and other employees. This all leads to provision of quality learning. Devarajan et al. (2011) believe that to have a quality education, all the necessary study apparatus and all functions in the HLIs should adequately have all the necessary resources. The findings from this study show that quality is just not achieved, it must be sought for; and it would require some heavy financial investment; for example capacity building and putting up infrastructure and other systems that support quality development and enhancement. The Government of Rwanda should inject some more funds in the sector for this to be realized.

From Figure 6, one can easily say that the Government of Rwanda has to start rethinking its strategy of ensuring the higher education sub-sector is given adequate funding as a poorly funded one will impact service delivery at universities. However, the government ought also to understand that quality achievement is a responsibility for all the stakeholders and for it to be achieved, it will require some support from the top management of the institution and the Ministry of Education.

The scenario in Figure 7 showed that quality is affected by funding. This is the view shared by student respondents where all the 100% responses concur that poor funding of higher education affects quality. It is against such a background that government could review the HE budget upwards if it is to achieve an internally comparable higher education (HESLD, 2011).

Higher education funding and economic development of Rwanda **students' responses**

The study findings from questionnaires reveal that 90% of respondents agree that once you reduce higher education funding, this will have an impact on the economic development of the country. Those that do not agree are 10% as reflected in Figure 8 and their argument is that, they do not understand how higher education funding is linked to economic development. Those that agree that economic development can be hampered by a poorly funded higher education have advanced these reasons. The country will lack well educated workforce to help build the country. Also, the earning capacity of poorly educated workforce may not be good and this will deny the economy some taxes essential for her development. For a country to develop, it should have a well functioning higher educa-tion sector according to Rangel (2004). It is an educated workforce that helps to drive an economy, therefore, Rwanda has to provide funding for this sub sector such that, it will be able to have required manpower in all the key and no key areas in an economy. Arguably, it may not be possible to achieve social and economic transformation with lack of vibrant higher education that feeds different sectors of the economy with the required manpower (Ajakaiye and Kimenyi, 2011).

The analysis of the information in Figure 9 shows that 92% of respondents believe that a good education in an economy is paramount for its economic development and 8% think that there is no relationship between them. The emphasis of the government should be to provide quality of education to produce quality graduates that will work in service and non service sectors of Rwanda. This will enhance development, as argued by Sempebwa (2011)

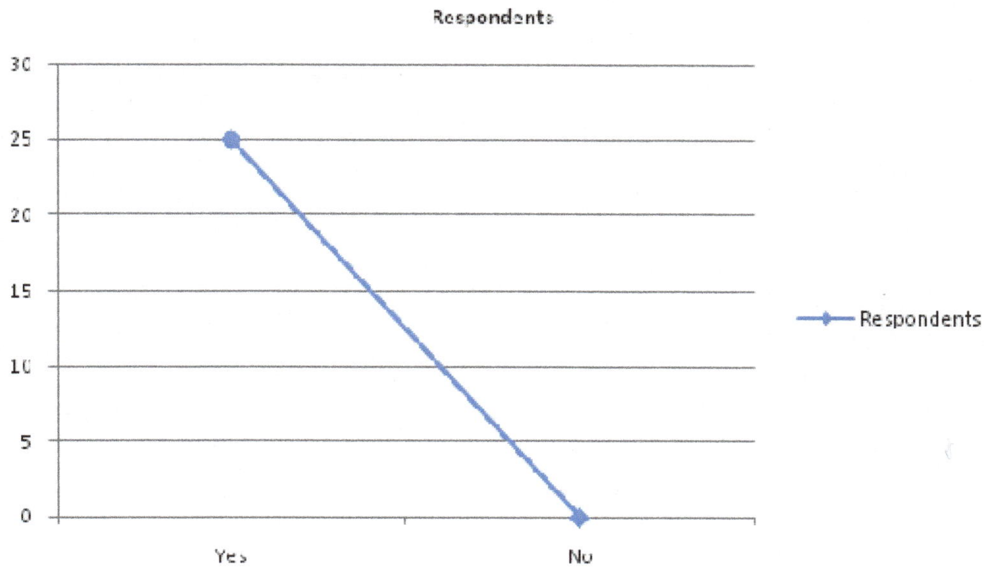

Figure 6. Student respondents' view on effect of funding on quality education.
Source: Author.

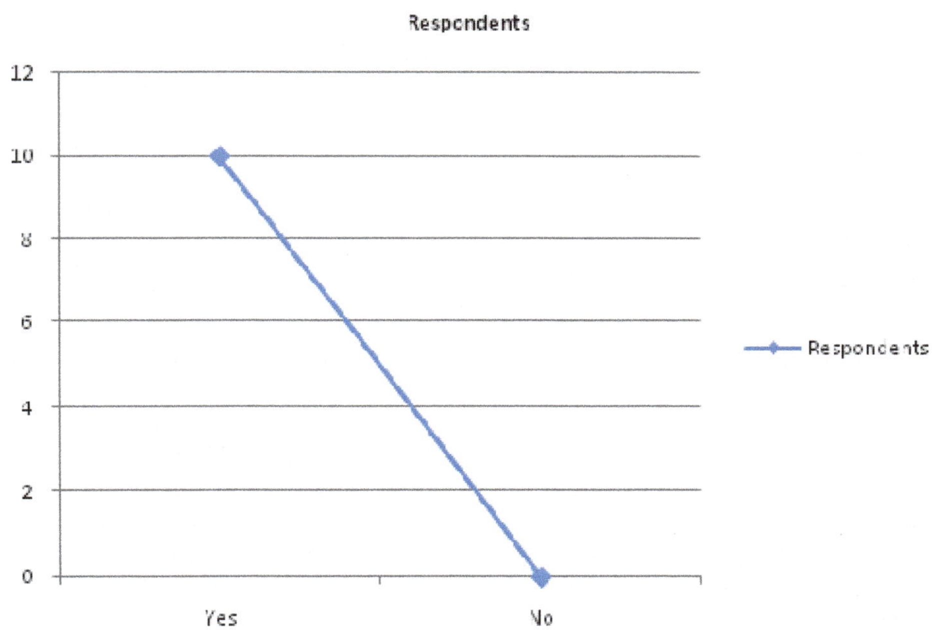

Figure 7. HESLD respondents' view on effect of funding on quality education.
Source: Author.

that higher learning institutions should strive to produce well qualified graduates and this may not be achieved with inadequate funding of the sub sector.

Findings from research interviews and review of documents

The results from the interview conducted in the two departments of loans recovery and loans disbursement about the current higher education funding model yielded the responses as follows. Respondents were asked about the evolution of higher education funding in Rwanda. The responses received are discussed as follows.

Evolution of higher education funding in Rwanda

Students were only getting living allowance of $19 per

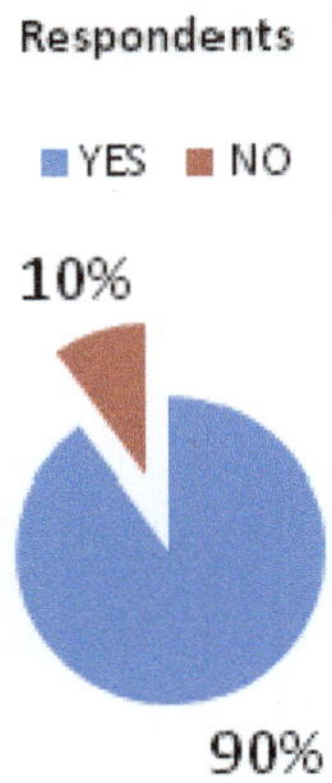

Figure 8. HESLD responses on funding and economic development of Rwanda.
Source: Author

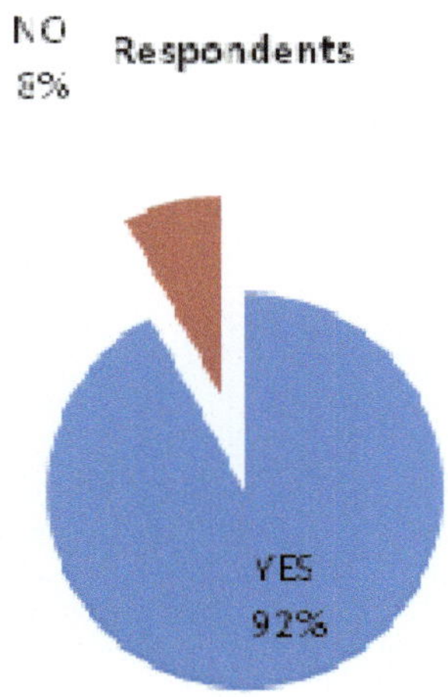

Figure 9. Student responses on funding and economic development of Rwanda.
Source: Author.

month (Student financing agency of Rwanda) during 1994-95. This was a small amount for a whole month. However, this was something and at the time there was only one university and this amount at least was paid to student's satisfaction (HESLD, 2011). This amount at the time was justified since the government did not have enough revenue to increase this figure and it was paid to all the beneficiaries as long as you qualified to enter the university. From 2001-2002, students were getting from SFAR $19 per month as living allowance plus $173 for dissertation. This now is a good improvement of the situation and it showed that the government was committed to improving quality and higher education funding in the country and this was really a step in the right direction taken by the government. Students started getting $43 dollars as living allowances per month plus $173 for dissertation from 2003-2007 and further still, this was an improvement of the higher education funding situation in Rwanda. The emphasis at this point should have been on effective disbursement of these funds to students. It is from 2008, that costs sharing began with government and students' contribution. Unit cost was introduced. For science and technology courses, $2,590 is provided to students per year. Here the student makes a contribution of 25% and the government makes a contribution of 75%. For non science courses and education, the unit cost is $2,072 per year where government contributes 50% and the students contribute 50% as well. For education, the student contributes 25% and the government contributes 75%. All these initiatives are intended for the good of the students but the problem of non compliance from student in meeting their financial contribution still persists because due to lack of credible sources of income to support their educational investment (MINEDUC, 2011). FMT (Financial means testing) started in 2011 to help identify potential beneficiaries of financial support from government for their education. This means that funding was only given to those that are financially unable to fund their education or those from poor families. The ones from rich families do not qualify for financial support for HESLD to support their education. This kind of arrangement could work effectively if the government employees qualified FMT assessor who can do the work efficiently and competently. Until this is done, the FMT will keep riddled with inefficiencies and this will exacerbate the problem of loans disbursement and collections by HESLD. Cost sharing approach will continue facing challenges unless the parents and students are thoroughly educated on it such that all the parties make their contributions effectively.

Student group interview

The groups were asked about the $43 per month leaving allowance paid to qualifying students on whether or not they thought it was enough. They all agree that, it is not enough and what makes matters worse is that students do not sometimes get it on time. This leads them to run out of essentials that they may need during their studies. The interviewees agreed that in some, there is selective payment of leaving allowances. They argued that because, the FMT is not fairly done as a result of corruption by local government officials as supported by HESLD (2011), financial assistance, in some cases, is given to the would be non-qualifying beneficiaries. About funding memoir, it was revealed in the interview, that, this ended in the year 2011. This means that the students at higher learning institutions no longer get $173 to facilitate their research work.

RECOMMENDATION AND SUGGESTIONS

This study has analyzed the costs sharing approach of

funding higher education in Rwanda. This is the current funding model used in Rwanda since its adoption in 2008 (HESLD, 2011). This study also looked at other funding models as proposed by the government of Rwanda, which include using tuition fees, PPP, internally generated funds and use of banks. These models need to be analyzed further to ascertain clarity and their suitability for adoption in Rwanda. This study also tried to look at the relationship between higher education funding, quality of higher education and economic development. This is an area that can be analyzed further by future researchers. The findings from such a study would direct policy making by different stakeholders on how best they can find adequate resources to inject in the sector. The Government of Rwanda is committed to developing its higher education sector based on quality that can be compared to other international higher education systems (MINEDUC, 2011).

The current higher education funding model of costs sharing should be maintained since it is clear from the findings that once the FMT is done right and fairly, then the model is excellent. This model has worked well in Uganda and Tanzania and with the right approach, it would work also well for Rwanda since one would also argue that all these countries almost have the same economic realities as also argued and supported by Teferra and Altbach (2004).

The creation of a state bank for funding education could work successfully provided that it has full support of the government. The Education Bank in Nigeria established in 1993 by decree no. 50 has been a success (Chuta, 1998). It has been able to support higher education funding successfully. Rwanda could set up such a bank and make it specific for the education sector and to make it more interesting, it should take a business model approach such that, it remains liquid and solvent. The use of internally generated resources by HEIs would be a good funding option if the institutions could get the right opportunities and funds are efficiently utilized by the HEIs with no corruption and embezzlement. Rwanda has zero tolerance for corruption and this means that, this option can be best suited model for funding higher education in Rwanda. Discussed here is an example where internally generated funds can be misused by HLIs if there are no proper financial controls put in place to safe guard the generated resources. One University called Maseno in Kenya lost about US$660,000 in the 1995/96 financial year in financial malpractices according to Teferra and Altbach (2004). It is such vices that would make this model inappropriate in countries where people do not have good work ethics and skills in managing funds of an institution. Rwanda is a country where financial resources can be generated by HLIs and used for their intended purpose as corruption is heavily condemned.

Higher learning institutions should be allowed to charge tuition fees to students and the policy on this should be very clear (Adeniyi and Taiwo, 2011). The point is such fees should be regulated by the responsible government for them to be affordable by parents and students. Government's higher learning institutions in Rwanda charge tuition fees to privately sponsored students. This has proven a success in generating funds, which they use to fund university activities (MINEDUC, 2011). This higher education funding model works well for Rwanda since regulations in Rwanda are closely respected by the institutions. Public- private partnerships are only good for funding higher education if they are properly negotiated and arranged by both the government and private investors and what is done should be to the interest of the education system. If one takes an example of the University of Bristol, it gets its 36% funding from the government and the rest of the funding is generated through PPP and tuition fees according to Ingo (2003). This is probably because the university is in a rich country and it has also built its reputation overtime and it can easily be supported and trusted by investors. The situation in Rwanda is different where most universities are young and the country is still poor. Such issues may not attract the interest of investors in the sector. This model may not currently work for Rwanda as the country and HEIs would need to grow their capability to deal with PPP.

Conclusion

The study is about analyzing the current (costs sharing) higher education funding model in Rwanda so as to understand its suitability for the country. Other funding models analyzed in this study are use of internally generated funds by HEIs, bank loans, PPP, and tuition fees. This kind of analysis would influence a policy change on how the Government of Rwanda can best use the suited models to fund its higher education sector. Rwanda stands a high chance of attaining economic development if it develops and adequately funds this sector. Higher education funding methods in Rwanda have been changing since 1963 when funding was solely the responsibility of the state. Currently, the model used by the Government of Rwanda is based on the costs sharing method (MINEDUC, 2011). This is where both the Government of Rwanda and students make financial contributions towards Higher Learning Institution (HLI). The HLIs student population in Rwanda has increase from 3,216 in 1994 to 73,674 in 2011 (MINEDUC, 2011). The higher education sector in Rwanda has been growing from one university in 1994 to 31 HEIs at present (NCHE, 2011). The funding of higher education in Rwanda has not been enough and this has in most cases slowed down funding of activities and infrastructure needed by HEIs.

The funding models namely tuition fees, bank loans, public private partnerships and internally generated resources are being considered to fund its higher education system in Rwanda (HESLD, 2011). All these models are being considered for adoption in Rwanda. Rwanda has been spending a lot of money on funding higher education through student financing and infrastructure development at HLIs and this has been a huge financial burden on the government's budget (MINEDUC, 2011). It is this situation that has taken the government to start looking at other models that can be used to fund higher education in Rwanda. There is also need to understand why the cost sharing has met a lot of challenges in Rwanda. The Government of Rwanda gives out a lot of loans to students, which are not properly recovered; for instance between 2008 to 2011, USD 115,261,894 was given out as loans and USD 1,754,385 is the only amount that has been recovered to-date (HESLD, 2011).

This is the current operation model or system used in funding higher education in Rwanda and it was introduced in 2008 (HESLD, 2011). The responses from the study showed that this approach is ranked favorably by staff of HESLD where 60% respondents rated it excellent; whereas students do not rank it favorably as 40% respondents rated it as poor, and 90% gave it a fair rating and none rated it as excellent. The approach has been used in countries like Tanzania according to Teferra and Altbach (2004). This approach to funding higher education can function properly in Rwanda if the HESLD was to review its operation efficiency by ensuring that students are selected fairly and their funds disbursed on time and students are sensitized on the essence of having their loan repayments commence upon getting employment. This helps to create some sort of revolving fund, which other student beneficiaries can benefit from.

This model is about using private funds to develop and complement investment made by the public sector into the higher education system (Jonathan and Peter, 2011). A number of HLIs in Rwanda like Umutara and NUR have tried using PPP and they have not been very successful. The 80% responses from the staff responses showed lack of support for this model and 88% student responses support use of PPP to fund higher education in Rwanda. The conclusion on adoption of this model in funding higher education can only be made after the Government of Rwanda and its other agencies have fully understood every detail necessary in adopting the model. This is because a wrong decision made can be very expensive for the government and the private investors. The adoption of this funding method in Rwanda should only be considered based on the principle that, it will not be abused by higher learning institutions to charge high fees to students which they may not be able to afford as argued by Vandenberghe and Debande (2007). The responses from the study showed that 72% do not support it and 80% HESLD staff do not support use of tuition fees as higher education funding model. The use of this model should depend on the ability of the government of Rwanda to regulate and be able to set an upper limit on how much fees higher learning institutions are allowed to charge. This will help to protect students from high fees charges that may affect student's accessibility to higher education institutions.

Funding higher education using bank loans is the model that would require students to access funding privately from commercial banks in Rwanda at favorable interest rates (HESLD, 2011). This model has 0% support from HESLD responses and it received 76% no responses from student respondents. The pattern in these responses shows you that such an option is not currently suitable for Rwanda.

This approach call for higher leaning institutions to look for avenues of generating their own funds internally which they can use to fund their activities that help promoting and developing their individual institutions (Butare, 2004). Findings from this study indicate that 80% students showing support and 70% respondents from HESLD do not support it. There is need for the Government of Rwanda to appreciate that, the development of its higher education sector will depend on how well funded it is and in this regard, the higher learning institutions should be given some financial autonomy which allows them to source for funding needed by their institutions. Quality of higher education in a country is premised on accessibility to material required to enhance it (Devarajan et al., 2011). The higher education sector must be fully or adequately funded if tutors are to be able to do for instance research and publications, capacity building, developing education infrastructure and other facilities needed in advancing quality education. The economic development of a country depends partly on the quality of its manpower produced in its higher learning institutions (Rangel, 2004). The country can build a manpower pool if it has a well functioning higher education system. This means it will not lack human resources to work in different sectors of the economy.

SCOPE FOR FURTHER RESEARCH

The FMT testing appraisal method should be studied further to ascertain on how best it can be done. This is a precursor to success of costs sharing model of funding higher education in Rwanda. The analysis of the PPP model is also crucial especially linking it to the developing economies to ascertain how they can effectively work there to the benefit of service users and the countries concerned.

The Government of Rwanda should look at how it can set up a specialized bank to fund education at higher level. This would involve the engagement of the right personnel who are knowledgeable in banking and higher education funding. The government has to put in place an enabling legislation for this to happen. As regards tuition fees charges by HLIs, the threshold and ceilings should be determined by government and legislated such that no any institution is able to overcharge students. This will enable the government to get a well organized higher education system. There is need to explore all these in future research to ensure the right policies are set up by the government.

ACKNOWLEDGEMENTS

I would like to thank HESLD-REB staff for the assistance given to me during this research. I quite appreciate the agency for allowing me to do this research there. My thanks also go to my wife who was very supportive during this study. I also thank Lucie Morales who was very instrumental throughout this research work.

ABBREVIATIONS

HE, Higher education; **HLI,** Higher learning institutions; **HEI,** Higher education institutions; **PPP,** Public private partnerships; **FMT,** Financial means testing.

REFERENCES

Ajakaiye O, Kimenyi MS (2011). Higher Education and Economic Development in Africa: Introduction and Overview, J. Afr. Econ. 20: iii3-iii13, Oxford journals (Online). Available from: http://jae.oxfordjournals.org.ezproxy.liv.ac.uk/content/20/suppl_3/iii3.full.pdf+html (Accessed April 13, 2012).

Atuahene F (2011). Re-thinking the missing mission of Higher Education: An anatomy of the research challenge of African Universities, J. Asian Afr. Stud. 46:321-341, Sage Pub (Online). Available from: http://jas.sagepub.com.ezproxy.liv.ac.uk/content/46/4/321.full.pdf+html (Accessed February 28, 2012).

Adeniyi EO, Taiwo SA (2011). Funding Higher Education in Nigeria through Cost Sharing: Perceptions of Lecturers, Students and Parents, Eur. J. Soc. Sci. 24(4):524-536, ebscohost (Online). Available from: http://ehis.ebscohost.com.ezproxy.liv.ac.uk/eds/pdfviewer/pdfviewer?vid=3&hid=124&sid=9a48245d-1b42-4573-8745-5fb06410cb36%40sessionmgr111 (Accessed January 13, 2012)

Butare A (2004). Income-Generating Activities in Higher Education: The Case of Kigali Institute of Science, Technology and Management (KIST), JHEA/RESA, 2(3):37-53.

Barr N (2004). Higher Education Funding, Oxford Review of Economic Policy, 20(2):264-283, Oxford Journals (Online). Available from: http://oxrep.oxfordjournals.org.ezproxy.liv.ac.uk/content/20/2/264.full.pdf+html (Accessed February 28, 2012).

Brown JD (2000). What issues affect Likert-scale questionnaire formats, Testing and evaluation, Jalt (Online). Available from: http://www.jalt.org/test/bro_7.htm (Accessed June 5, 2012).

Culkin N, Mallick S (2011). Producing work-ready graduates, Int. J. Market Res. 53(3):347-368, ebscohost (Online). Available from: http://ehis.ebscohost.com.ezproxy.liv.ac.uk/eds/pdfviewer/pdfviewer?vid=3&hid=124&sid=9a48245d-1b42-4573-8745-5fb06410cb36%40sessionmgr111 (Accessed January 13, 2012)

Chuta EJ (1998). New dimensions in educational financing: The Nigerian Education Bank. Higher Educ. 35:432-433.

Creswell JW, Miller DL (2000). Determining validity in qualitative inquiry. Theory Practice 39(3):124-131.

Clissett P (2008). Evaluating qualitative research, J. Orthopaedic Nurs. 12(2):99-105, Science direct (Online). Available from: http://pdn.sciencedirect.com.ezproxy.liv.ac.uk/science?_ob=MiamiImageURL&_cid=272461&_user=822084&_pii=S1361311108000459&_check=y&_origin=search&_zone=rslt_list_item&_coverDate=2008-05-31&wchp=dGLbVlk-zSkWb&md5=b56e0df89b70ea394970aa62775a0dcc/1-s2.0-S1361311108000459-main.pdf (Accessed January 23, 2012).

Devarajan S, Monga C, Zongo T (2011). Making Higher Education Finance Work for Africa, J. Afr. Econ. 20:133-154, Oxford Journals (Online). Available from: http://jae.oxfordjournals.org.ezproxy.liv.ac.uk/content/20/suppl_3/iii133.full.pdf+html (Accessed February 28, 2012).

Demange G, Fenge R, Uebelmesser S (2008). The Provision of Higher Education in a Global World-Analysis and Policy Implications, CESifo Econ. Stud. 54:248-276, Oxford Journals (Online). Available from: http://cesifo.oxfordjournals.org.ezproxy.liv.ac.uk/content/54/2/248.full.pdf+html (Accessed April 13, 2012).

Gwosc C, Schwarzenberger A (2009). Public/private cost-sharing in higher education: an in-depth look at the German system using a comparative study, J. Higher Educ. Policy Manage. 31(3):239-249, ebscohost (Online). Available from: http://ehis.ebscohost.com.ezproxy.liv.ac.uk/eds/pdfviewer/pdfviewer?vid=7&hid=22&sid=bb2b9e39-94d4-498d-93e5-0841f3086041%40sessionmgr11 (Accessed April 13, 2012).

Hayman R (2007). Are the MDGs enough? Donor perspectives and recipient visions of education and poverty reduction in Rwanda, Int. J. Educ. Dev. 27(4):371-382, ebscohost (Online). Available from: http://www.sciencedirect.com.ezproxy.liv.ac.uk/science?_ob=MiamilmageURL&_cid=271756&_user=822084&_pii=S0738059306001210&_check=y&_origin=search&_zone=rslt_list_item&_coverDate=2007-07-31&wchp=dGLzVlt-zSkWA&md5=769ecf93f378ad8f57e4a96f974638b1/1-s2.0-S0738059306001210-main.pdf (Accessed January 13, 2012).

HESLD (2011). Higher education proposed funding models, REB

Ingo L (2003). Funding, Resource Allocation, and Performance in Higher Education Systems, Higher Educ. 46(4):469-489, ebscohost (Online). Available from: http://ehis.ebscohost.com.ezproxy.liv.ac.uk/eds/pdfviewer/pdfviewer?vid=3&hid=124&sid=9a48245d-1b42-4573-8745-5fb06410cb36%40sessionmgr111 (Accessed January 23, 2012)

Jonathan E, Peter B (2011). Public-Private Partnership in Higher Education Research, The Nexus of Mandate, Challenges, and Opportunities for Sustainable Development in Africa, Eur. J. Soc. Sci. 24(1):116-120, ebscohost (Online). Available from: http://ehis.ebscohost.com.ezproxy.liv.ac.uk/eds/pdfviewer/pdfviewer?vid=12&hid=124&sid=9a48245d-1b42-4573-8745-5fb06410cb36%40sessionmgr111 (Accessed January 13, 2012).

Jahoda M, Deutsch M, Cook WS (n.d). Research Methods in Social Relations p.4.

Johnson BR (1997). Examining the validity structure of qualitative research. Education 118(3):282-292.

Kothari CR (1985). Research Methodology- Methods and Techniques, New Delhi, Wiley Eastern Limited.

MINEDUC (2011). Rwanda Education Sector: Long-term strategy and financing framework 2006 -2015 (LTSFF), (online). Available from: www.mineduc.gov.rw (Accessed January10, 2012).

Millett JD (1955). Recent Developments in Financing Higher Education, the Annals of the American Academy of Political and Social Science, 301:205-210, sage pub (Online). Available from:http://ann.sagepub.com.ezproxy.liv.ac.uk/content/301/1/205.full.pdf+html (Accessed February 28, 2012).

McLendon MK, Hearn JC, Mokher CG (2009) Partisans, Professionals, and Power: The Role of Political Factors in State Higher Education Funding, J. Higher Educ. 80(6):686-713, ebscohost (Online). Available from: http://ehis.ebscohost.com.ezproxy.liv.ac.uk/eds/pdfviewer/pdfviewer?vid=3&hid=124&sid=9a48245d-1b42-4573-8745-5fb06410cb36%40sessionmgr111 (Accessed January 23,2012).

Millennium development goals (2000). Millennium development goals, 8th goal, UN, (Online). Available from: www.un/org/millenniumgoals/index.shtm (Accessed January 10, 2012).

MINICOFIN (2010). Budget estimate, (Online). Available from: www.minicofin.gov.rw (Accessed January10, 2012).

MINICOFIN (2012). Budget estimate, (Online). Available from: www.minicofin.gov.rw.

Newfield C (2010). The End of the American Funding Model: What Comes Next?, American Literature 82(3):612-635.

McMillan JH, Schumacher S (1993). Research in education: A

conceptual understanding. New York: HarperCollins.
Mathison S (1988). Why triangulate? Educ. Res. 17(2):13-17.
Marshal MN (1996). Sampling for qualitative research, 13(6):522-525, Oxford University press (Online). Available from: http://fampra.oxfordjournals.org/content/13/6/522.full.pdf (Accessed July 17, 2012).
NBR (2012). National bank of Rwanda, (Online). Available from: www.bnr.rw (Accessed 3 May 2012).
NUR (2012). National University of Rwanda, (Online). Available from: www.nur.ac.rw (Accessed 9 May 2012).
Oghenekohwo JE, Abu PB (2011) Public-Private Partnership in Higher Education Research: The Nexus of Mandate, Challenges, and Opportunities for Sustainable Development in Africa, European Journal of Social Science, 24 (1) pp. 116-120, ebscohost (Online). Available from: http://ehis.ebscohost.com.ezproxy.liv.ac.uk/eds/pdfviewer/pdfviewer?vid=12&hid=124&sid=9a48245d-1b42-4573-8745-5fb06410cb36%40sessionmgr111 (Accessed January 10, 2012).
Ouma GW (2010) Funding and the attainment of transformation goals in South Africa's higher education, Oxford Review of Education, 36 (4), pp.481-497, ebscohost (Online). Available from: http://ehis.ebscohost.com.ezproxy.liv.ac.uk/eds/pdfviewer/pdfviewer?vid=3&hid=124&sid=9a48245d-1b42-4573-8745-5fb06410cb36%40sessionmgr111 (Accessed May 2, 2012).
Patton MQ (2002). Qualitative evaluation and research methods(3rd ed.). Thousand Oaks, CA: Sage Publications, Inc.
Rajasekar S, Philominathan P, Chinnathambi V (2006). research methodology, arxiv, pp.1-23 arxiv (Online). Available from: http://arxiv.org/pdf/physics/0601009.pdf (Accessed June 5, 2012).
Rangel E (2004). Policies for Employment and Higher Education in Mexico: an Approach to Human Resource Development as Policy, Adv. Dev. Hum. Resour. 6:374-381, Sage pub (Online). Available from: http://adh.sagepub.com.ezproxy.liv.ac.uk/content/6/3/374.full. pdf+html (Accessed April 13, 2012).
Russell KC, Gregory MD (2003). Evaluation of qualitative research studies, evidence based nursing, EBN (Online). Available from: http://ebn.bmj.com/content/6/2/36.full (Accessed June 17, 2012).
Semugaza A (2005). Funding Higher Education in Rwanda through Loans or Grants: efficiency and equity arguments, Educate J. 5(2):11-18, (Online). Available from:http://www.educatejournal.org/index.php?journal=educate&page=article&op=view&path[]=64&path[]=60 (Accessed February 9, 2012).
Ssempebwa J (2011) Evaluating the utilization of resources in higher education institutions: The case of teaching space at a Ugandan university, Evaluation 17:247-259, Sage pub (Online). Available from: http://evi.sagepub.com.ezproxy.liv.ac.uk/content/17/3/247.full.pdf+html (Accessed April 13, 2012).
Scott P (2009). Higher Education: Social Mobility, Economic Development and Cultural Transformation, local economy, the journal of the local economy unit, 24:681-686, Sage pub (Online). Available from: http://lec.sagepub.com.ezproxy.liv.ac.uk/content/24/8/681.full.pdf+html (Accessed April 13, 2012).
Toloie-Eshlaghy A, Shahrzad C, Karimian L, Charkhchi R (2011). A Classification of Qualitative Research Methods, Res. J. Int. Stud. 20:106-123, ebscohost (Online). Available from: http://ehis.ebscohost.com.ezproxy.liv.ac.uk/eds/pdfviewer/pdfviewer?vid=5&hid=23&sid=78e3a9b4-82c7-4b85-a163-61441725cc86%40sessionmgr4 (Accessed 6February 2012).
Tandberg D (2010). Interest Groups and Governmental Institutions: The Politics of State Funding of Public Higher Education, Education policy, 24:735-778, Sage pub (Online). Available from: http://epx.sagepub.com.ezproxy.liv.ac.uk/content/24/5/735.full.pdf+html (Accessed April 13, 2012).
Teferra D, Altbach PG (2004). African Higher Education: Challenges for the 21st Century, Higher Educ. 47(1):21-50, ebscohost (Online). Available from: http://ehis.ebscohost.com.ezproxy.liv.ac.uk/eds/pdfviewer/pdfviewer?vid=4&hid=22&sid=bb2b9e39-94d4-498d-93e5-0841f3086041%40sessionmgr11.
Vandenberghe V, Debande O (2007). (Deferred and Income-contingent Tuition Fees: An Empirical Assessment using Belgian, German and UK Data, Education Economics, 15(4):421-440, ebscohost (Online). Available from: http://ehis.ebscohost.com.ezproxy.liv.ac.uk/eds/pdfviewer/pdfviewer?vid=3&hid=22&sid=bb2b9e39-94d4-498d-93e5-0841f3086041%40sessionmgr11 (Accessed April 13, 2012).
Wiersma W (1995). Research methods in education: An introduction (6th ed.). Boston: Allyn and Bacon.

APPENDICES

Appendix 1: Questionnaire

This questionnaire is about funding of higher education in Rwanda. HESLD has been chosen as a case study by the researcher. The information obtained will only be used for this academic research which is a partial fulfillment to attain an MSc corporate finance of the University of Liverpool.

Section A

The government of Rwanda has proposed the following models for funding higher education;

A) Student bank loans
B) Tuition fees
C) Public private partnerships (PPP)
D) Cost sharing
E) Setting up private firms at HLIs for income generation.

Please, tick as appropriate
Qn. 1. How would you rate government proposed funding methods on a scale of **1-5.**
1-Poor; 2-Fair; 3-Good; 4-very good; 5-Excellent

A)	Student bank loans;	1	2	3	4	5
B)	Tuition fees	1	2	3	4	5
C)	Public private partnerships (PPP)	1	2	3	4	5
D)	Cost sharing	1	2	3	4	5
E)	Setting up of firms by HLIs	1	2	3	4	5

Qn. 2. Would you support using tuition fees for funding higher education?
A) Yes B) NO

If yes; Why?---

If NO; Why?---

Qn. 3.Would you support using Student bank loans for funding higher education?
A) Yes B) NO

If yes; Why?---

If NO; Why?---

Qn. 4. Would you support using public private partnership for funding higher education?
A) Yes B) NO

If yes; Why?---

If NO; Why?---

Qn. 5. Would you support using cost sharing for funding higher education?
A) Yes B) NO

If yes; Why?--

If NO; Why?--

Qn. 6. Would you support setting up of firms by HLIs for funding higher education?
A) Yes B) NO

If yes; Why?--

If NO; Why?--

Section B

Qn. 7. Do you think reduced higher education funding has an impact on quality of higher education?
A) Yes B) NO
If yes; why?--

If No; Why?--

Qn. 8. Do you think a failed higher education funding will impact on economic development of Rwanda?
A) Yes B) NO
If yes; why?--

If No; Why?--

Qn. 9. What do you think the government of Rwanda can do better to facilitate improved higher education funding;
1-Increase budget vote for higher education
2-Get more funds from private investors
3-Empower HLIs to generate their owns funding
4-Pull out of funding higher education completely

Thank you for filling this questionnaire

Corporate disclosure, transparency and firms' cash holdings: Evidence from the Emerging capital market of Ghana

Godfred A. Bokpin

Department of Finance, Business School, P. O. Box LG 78, University of Ghana.

The paper documents the monitoring effect of corporate disclosure and transparency on cash holdings on the Ghana Stock Exchange (GSE). The paper employs the Fama and French (1998) valuation model by relating firm level variables to firm value with panel data covering a period from 2002 to 2007 for 23 firms. It builds further on the agency theory and its relevance to emerging markets. We find that the relationship between corporate disclosure, transparency and cash holdings is economically significant and inversely related. We provide that a 1% increase in the composite disclosure and transparency index decreases cash holding by 0.0338 with the market also discounting the value of such firms by 0.0522. Additionally, we provide that firm size, profitability, financial leverage and investment needs are economically significant determinants of cash holdings. The sample refers to only Ghana and the extent of generation of the findings could be affected. We argue that further research should be carried out using other country data to confirm or contradict our findings. The paper includes implications for the management of cash resources on the GSE and builds on the mechanism of aligning the interest of shareholders with managers. It further provides implications for the development of the capital market in Ghana and argues that further research should be carried out using other country data to confirm or contradict our findings

Key words: Corporate disclosure, transparency, cash holdings, emerging market, Ghana.

INTRODUCTION

Generally, holding cash aggravates the agency problem as in the spirit of Myers and Rajan (1998) liquid assets can be turned into private benefits at lower cost than other assets and therefore represent a promising opportunity to investigate the implications of agency theories (Pinkowitz et al., 2006). Though Acemoglu et al. (2003) contend that countries in which the appropriation of private benefits is easier are also typically riskier, and therefore firms in these countries may hold more cash simply because they require a larger buffer to protect themselves against adverse shocks (see Pinkowitz et al., 2006), holding cash exacerbates the agency problem. This is because according to Dittmar et al. (2003) agency costs and information asymmetries are expected to have a significant impact on the value of cash resources. With improved governance leading to enhanced disclosure and transparency, holding cash should significantly add to shareholder value. Corporate disclosure and transparency impacts the agency problem through reduction in information asymmetry (information effect leading to reduction in cost of capital (Botosan and Plumlee, 2002) improved liquidity and stock performance (Healy et al., 1999)) and monitoring effect (moral hazard effect of corporate disclosure and transparency). Whilst the former (disciplinary effect of corporate disclosure and transparency) has received considerable research attention, the latter has not received as nearly an important place in the literature. According to Huang and Zhang (2008) no research to date has unambiguously isolated the monitoring effect from the information effect of corporate disclosure activity and therefore there is the need to examine the monitoring effect of corporate disclosure on cash holdings. This is particularly important as Jensen (1986) argues that conflicting interests between investors and managers are especially severe when managers stockpile cash to grow their firms beyond the optimal size to pursue their private control benefits. It is imperative then to separate the information effect of corporate disclosure and transparency from the monitoring effect. This according to Huang and Zhang (2008) will help to understand the sources of value derived from corporate disclosure activity more precisely. Empirically, Harford (1999) documents that firms with stockpiles of cash tend to undertake value-decreasing acquisitions. Later, Harford et al. (2005) find that firms with weak shareholder rights dissipate cash quickly through acquisitions because shareholders in such firms are particularly concerned with mounting cash reserves. According to Mitton (2002) improved transparency mitigates management's proclivity for investing in assets that destroy investor value, which in turn improves shareholder protection. Bushman and Smith (2001) posit that when companies engage in higher disclosure quality and greater transparency, investors can effectively monitor firm performance and contractual commitments thus emphasizing the monitoring effect of corporate disclosure and transparency.

The paper argues is consistent with Huang and Zhang (2008) that greater transparency limits insiders' capacity to accumulate liquid assets for their private benefits because they have little to conceal from outsiders. Ghana`s stock market has gained momentum since its establishment a little over two decades ago, being judged the best performing stock market in 2004 and the most innovative African stock market in 2010 by the New York Exchange. Ghana has also experienced significant changes in corporate governance since the establishment of the GSE. Corporate governance has gone through transformations both at the firm level and the political governance level following reforms principally led by the World Bank and IMF. Empirically, corporate governance has received a considerable attention both by academicians and industry practitioners (Abor, 2007; Kyereboah-Coleman et al., 2006), but corporate disclosure and transparency has not received much empirical attention. Extant literature on corporate disclosure has focused on disclosure level and determinants (Tsamenyi et al., 2007); corporate disclosure and foreign share ownership (Bokpin and Isshaq, 2009) but the monitoring effect (essentially meant to reduce moral hazard component of information asymmetry) of corporate disclosure has remain under studied as has also been noted by Huang and Zhang (2008) at the international level. The paper seeks to contribute to extant literature using an emerging market data. Empirical evidence focused on international comparative data and we argued their results can better be understood with country-specific findings because as Klapper and Love (2004) suggest that firms can adopt firm-specific shareholder protection to distinguish themselves from other firms in the same country (Durnev and Kim, 2005) and even in the same industry. This is because La Porta et al. (1998) had earlier opined that countries that include more disclosure items in firms' annual reports generally have better legal protection for investors (Levitt, 1998). There is considerable bias in sample selection in recent international comparative studies relating corporate disclosure and transparency to cost of capital (Huang and Zhang, 2008) as most authors focus on country level studies. But, more detailed within-country studies can complement the results of cross-country investigations and this would enable specific policies to be fashioned out that takes into consideration institutional and cultural differences. Using emerging market data will further buttress or refute the argument that international findings are not attributed entirely to the level of countries` stock market development or the sophistication of investors or number of analyst following.

THEORETICAL FOUNDATION AND EMPIRICAL EVIDENCE

Empiricists underscores that perhaps no other theory has had profound impact on the world of business as the agency theory. The theory is predicated on the premise that organisations should be seen as no more than a set of implicit and explicit contracts with associated rights. Jensen and Meckling (1976) defined an agency relationship as "a contract under which one or more persons (the principal(s)) engage another person (the agent) to perform some service on their behalf which involves delegating some decision making authority to the agent". The premise of agency theory is that self-interested managers hold motives that often conflict with organizational goals and shareholder expectations and hence will only disclose information to their advantage; accordingly, self-interested managers need to be monitored and sufficiently motivated (Fama, 1980). Firms hold cash for a number of reasons including transactional, precautionary, speculative and compensating balance purposes. Thus, how much liquid balance is held by a corporation is influenced by factors such as transaction costs, opportunity costs and informational asymmetries (Bruinshoofd and Kool, 2004). Cash is the life blood of the firm and it enables the firm to turn itself around especially in the short run in terms of meeting its short term financial obligations as and when they fall due.

Thus, consistent with Pinkowitz et al. (2006) we do not expect that controlling shareholders or managers transform a firm's liquid assets into private benefits in such a way that the firm is always starved for cash. But holding cash also presents challenges for expropriation by managers or controlling shareholders. The presence of cash exacerbates this agency problem. This is because according to Dittmar et al. (2003), agency costs and information asymmetries are expected to have a significant impact on the value of cash resources. This is against the backdrop of the prepositions of Keynes (1936) who argues that cash hoardings can add value to firms in which asymmetric information increases the cost of external financing and thus exacerbates the underinvestment problem (Myers, 1984). Acemoglu et al. (2003) contend that countries in which the appropriation of private benefits is easier are also typically riskier, and therefore firms in these countries may hold more cash simply because they require a larger buffer to protect themselves against adverse shocks (Pinkowitz et al., 2006). According to Myers (1984) the precautionary motive of cash reserves requires that financial slacks can reduce underinvestment costs because information asymmetries inherent in capital markets often make outside funds prohibitively expensive. Jensen (1986) reports that liquid assets aggravate agency conflicts because managers often over invest cash in negative NPV projects whilst to Myers and Rajan (1998), it is easier for managers to steal cash than fixed assets. With the separation of the ownership of companies' resources from their control, corporate disclosure is a potentially important means of communication between management and outside investors (Hassan et al., 2009). This will significantly reduce the information asymmetry (agency problems) between ownership and control that leads to adverse selection and moral hazard. Stiglitz and Weiss (1981) relate that greater information flows can mitigate the principal-agent problem, which in turn improves resources allocation in financial markets.

Later, Harford et al. (2005) find that firms with weak shareholder rights dissipate cash quickly through acquisitions because shareholders in such firms are particularly concerned with mounting cash reserves. Berger and Hann (2007) affirm that managers conceal segment information to obscure their firms' underlying agency problems, suggesting that greater disclosure reduces agency costs. Black (2001) contends that extensive disclosures on matters regarding governance mechanisms, ownership structures, and financial reports improve external monitoring, thereby reducing agency costs. Kanodia and Lee (1998) further argue that company disclosure facilitates external discipline, thereby preventing managers from expropriating the wealth of investors. Healy and Palepu (2001) posit that disclosure of relevant information allows investors to closely monitor firms' operations and thus effectively evaluate whether managers have utilized the resources in the best interests of shareholders. In this same spirit, Bushman and Smith (2001) relate that when companies engage in higher disclosure quality and greater transparency, investors can effectively monitor firm performance and contractual commitments.

DATA AND MODEL SPECIFICATION

The study used data mainly from the Ghana Stock Exchange (GSE) FactBook for the various years (2002-2007) and the annual reports and financial statements of the firms listed on the GSE. The market data namely dividend yield, share prices were extracted from the GSE FactBook whilst Tobin`s Q was calculated by the author from the FactBook. Contacts were made with the GSE library and the Securities and Exchange Commission for the annual reports. Missing figures were filled by making contact with the specific firms for the annual reports and financial statements. There are six financial institutions on the GSE today. These financial services companies such as banks and insurance companies were excluded because of their specific financial characteristics, affect their information disclosure (Hassan et al., 2009) and liquidity requirements. For corporate disclosure and transparency, we adapted the S&P's overall transparency and disclosure rating which is categorized into three dimensions: ownership structure and investor rights, financial transparency and information disclosure and board and management structure and processes. The index is adjusted for non-applicable items and reconciled with the Ghana National Accounting Standards for conformity and compliance. Ghana however adopted the IAS in 2007 though implementation did not start immediately and therefore significant variation is expected which should significantly increase the marginal contribution of corporate disclosure and transparency to cash holdings, which makes it also easier comparing Ghana`s disclosure practices at the international level. The disclosure and transparency index was arrived at bearing in mind the disclosure and governance framework as enshrined in the Companies Code 1963 (Act 179). The Securities Industry Law, 1993 (PNDCL 333) as amended by the Securities Industry (Amendment) Act 2000, (Act 590), which provides among other things for governance of all stock exchanges, investment advisors, securities dealers, and collective investment schemes licensed under by the Securities and Exchange Commission (SEC) and the Membership and Listing Regulations of the Ghana Stock Exchange (GSE, 1990). It is supported by the Ghana National Accounting Standards and the codes of professional conduct imposed by the Institute of Chartered Accountants (Ghana) on its members. A score of 1 is assigned to an item if it is disclosed (disclosure index), and a score of 0 otherwise.

The total score of a company is obtained as:

$$TDS = \sum_{i=1}^{m} di$$

Where di is 1 if item i is disclosed, and 0 if otherwise; m is the maximum number of items (m=106).

Paper mirrors the Fama and French (1998) valuation model by relating firm level variables to firm value. The basic regression model is specified as

$$Y_{it} = B`nX_{it} + ni + \varepsilon_{it} \quad (1)$$

where Y_{it} is the dependent variable for firm *i* at time *t*, $B`n$ is a vector of independent variable and coefficients, X_{it} includes a

Table 1. Symbol and variable definition.

Symbol	Definition
$LIQRAT$	Cash and cash equivalent scaled by net assets
$LOGLIQ$	Logarithm of cash and cash equivalent
TDS	Corporate Disclosure and Transparency Index
$SIZE$	Firm Size (Logarithm of Total Sales)
ROA	Cash Flow (EBIT/Total Assets)
$FINLEV$	Total Liabilities Scaled by Total Assets
$ASSTANG$	Investment in Fixed Assets Scaled by Total Assets
$DIVBIN$	Dividend Binary (1 if dividend is paid and 0 if otherwise
$RISK$	Firm specific three-year rolling standard deviation of ROA

constant as well as independent variables (see table 1), ni and ε_{it} are firm-specific and stochastic term.

Proceeding from the above, we estimate the following specific model;

$$LIQRAT_{it} = \chi TDS_{it} + \delta SIZE_{it} + \gamma ROA_{it} + \lambda FINLEV_{it} + \zeta ASSTANG_{it} + \phi DIVBIN_{it} + \sigma RISK_{it} + \varepsilon_{it} \quad (2)$$

$$LOGLIQ_{it} = \partial TDS_{it} + \wp SIZE_{it} + \int ROA_{it} + \wp FINLEV_{it} + \ell ASSTANG_{it} + \lambda DIVBIN_{it} + \sigma RISK_{it} + \varepsilon_{it} \quad (3)$$

$$TOBIN!SQ_{it} = \int TDS_{it} + \chi SIZE_{it} + \infty ROA_{it} + \iota FINLEV_{it} + \partial ASSTANG_{it} + \eta DIVBIN_{it} + \sigma RISK_{it} + \varepsilon_{it} \quad (4)$$

Our main liquidity variable ($LIQRAT$ in model 1) is cash ratio defined as the ratio of cash and cash equivalents to net assets, which are total assets net of cash and cash equivalents expressed mathematically as $\frac{Cash + CashEquivalent}{NetAssets}$, $LOGLIQ$ measured as the logarithm of cash and marketable securities (model 2) is included for robustness test. Consistent with La Porta et al. (2002), the paper employs Tobin s Q to measure market valuation of the firm, measured as the ratio of the book value of total assets less the book value of equity plus the market value of equity to the book value of total assets (Nohel and Tarhan, 1998 as in model 3).

In the case of the explanatory variables, disclosure and transparency index is as explained above, Firm size is measured by the logarithm of total sales. This is also included to test for the transactional demand on firms and economies of scale rather than as a measure of antitakeover deterrent as the market or firms in general are subject to little or no takeover threat in Ghana compared to the case of Huang and Zhang (2008). Cash flow is measured as as earnings before interest, taxes, depreciation, and amortization less interest, taxes, and common dividends scaled by net assets. Financial leverage is measured as the ratio of total debts to total assets to gauge the level of external monitoring and a test of financial and interest commitment of firms as firms are still largely reliant on financial institutions, asset tangibility is included to test for the investment demand of firms. The dividend binary variable is included to assess the presence of financial constraints and it takes the value of 1 if the company pays dividend and 0 if otherwise. The seemingly unrelated regression approach was adopted.

RESULTS AND DISCUSSION

This section presents the descriptive summary statistics (Table 2) and the results and discussion of the regression (Table 3).

Liquidity ratio records overall mean of 5.8058 but varies both between and within firms over the sample. Using the logarithms of cash and cash equivalent, we record average mean of 0.1539 but shows overall variation of 1.0876 over the sample period across the firms. Inferring this at the international level though with different time period and institutional differences and different samples, firms in Ghana maintain slightly higher (15.39%) cash level than Germany (11.6%) and minimally below US (16.4%) and Japan (19.0%) (Pinkowitz and Williamson, 2001 for other country statistics). Dittmar et al. (2003) contend that corporations in countries where shareholders rights are not well protected hold up to twice as much cash as corporations in countries with good shareholder protection. Though, the level of corporate disclosure and transparency is low in Ghana as compared to developed markets (Tsamenyi et al., 2007) we did not confirm their evidence in the Ghanaian case as the level of cash holdings is slightly above that of Germany and below US and Japan reputed to have higher investor protection compared to Ghana. Given the level of the financial market development including the

Table 2. Descriptive statistics.

Variable	Obs	Mean	Std. Dev.	Min.	Max.
LIQRAT	138	5.8058	1.0876	1.2006	8.2985
LOGLIQ	138	0.1539	0.1772	0.0001	0.9353
TOBIN`SQ	138	0.1876	0.2041	0.0008	0.9502
TDS	138	0.4835	0.9278	0.3333	0.6889
SIZE	138	4.4243	0.7796	3.0410	6.3610
ROA	138	0.0694	0.0832	-0.1676	0.2965
FINLEV	138	0.7785	0.4915	0.0063	2.5064
ASSTANG	138	0.4328	0.2149	0.0000	0.8551
DIVBIN	138	0.5579	0.4984	0.0000	1.0000
RISK	138	0.1070	0.1509	0.0013	0.9468

Source: Author`s Compilation, 2011.

Table 3. Regression results of cash holding on disclosure.

Variable	Model 1	Model 2	Model 3
TDS	-0.0338(0.0201)	-0.1259(0.1660)	-0.0522(0.1837)
SIZE	-0.2994(0.1115)	-0.0578(0.0188)	0.0401(0.0208)
ROA	0.2385(1.0769)	-0.0597(0.1816)	-0.0066(0.2010)
FINLEV	-0.4424(0.1737)	0.0305(0.0293)	-0.0996(0.0324)
ASSTANG	-0.9957(0.3881)	-0.2465(0.0655)	0.2701(0.0724)
DIVBIN	-0.4519(0.1757)	0.0163(0.0296)	-0.7103 (0.0328)
RISK	-1.2050(0.5566)	-0.0462(0.0939)	0.1607(0.1039)
CONSTANT	8.2668 (0.6903)	0.5453(0.1164)	0.0188(0.1288)
Obs	138	138	138
Parms	7	7	7
RMSE	0.9495	0.1602	0.1772
"R-sq"	0.2322	0.1773	0.2403
Chi2	41.74	29.75	43.64
P	0	0.0001	0

Consistent with Fama and French (1998), we report the coefficients and the standard errors as we are more interested in the marginal contribution of the explanatory variables. Standard errors are in parenthesis.

stock market (GSE) as well the level of corporate governance, it is expected that firms will hold more cash to compensate for the deficiencies in the system but that is not the case perhaps due to firms' inability to generate more cash hence the low level of cash holdings. Tobin`s Q registers overall mean of 0.1876 and ranges from 0.0008 to 0.9502. Disclosure and transparency index registers overall mean of 0.4835 and ranges from as low as 0.3333 to 0.6889. The standard deviation reveals considerable variation over the period across the firms and over the sample period. The level of information disclosure on the GSE is low. Size registers overall mean of 4.4243 indicating majority of the companies are not large companies and are perhaps in the range of small to medium size companies. Averagely firm profitability hovers around 0.0694 and ranges from a negative of -0.1676 to 0.2965. Financial leverage (debt ratio) records 0.7785 suggesting firms relay heavily on the financial institutions for financing. Investment in fixed assets changes minimally over the period see standard deviation whilst only 56% of the firms on the average pay dividend with some level of exposure to operating uncertainties.

Empirically, Pinkowitz et al. (2006) document that the relationship between cash holdings and firm value is much weaker in countries with poor investor protection than in other countries and Fresard and Salva (2008) report that governance environment that requires stricter disclosure requirements save to limit managers ability to squander liquid balances. We mirrored their findings with majority of disclosure items from the S&P disclosure and transparency index instead of their investor rights index (Pinkowitz et al., 2006). In economically significant manner, we document a negative relationship between cash holdings and TDS suggesting that the level of cash holdings dips by 0.0338 when the a firm`s disclosure and transparency index increases by 1%. Perhaps with general improvement in the governance and information disclosure managers' propensity to build financial slack is reduced and could limit managers' desire to squander the firms' cash resources. Whilst cash and cash equivalent when scaled by total assets dips by 0.0338 with a 1% increase in the composite disclosure and transparency index, the logarithm of cash and cash equivalent decreases by 0.1259 with investors also marking down the market value of the firm (Tobin`s Q) by 0.0522. We affirm the findings of Huang and Zhang (2008) that corporate disclosure and transparency continues to be negatively related to cash holdings at economically significant levels (mostly significant at 5% in our case whilst significant at 1% in their situation) and consistent with Fresard and Salva (2008) who document that governance environment that requires stricter disclosure requirements save to limit managers ability to squander liquid balances. Corporate disclosure and transparency is important in holding the leash on management use of cash resources consistent with Dittmar et al. (2003) who documented that strong and well-enforced outsider rights prevent controlling managers from hoarding high cash reserves to acquire private benefits. We find direct link between their paper and this article even in the face of different measures; investor rights in their case with La Porta et al. (1998) providing the mediating channel that countries that include more disclosure items in firms' annual reports generally have better legal protection for investors (Levitt, 1998).

To avoid misspecifications as a result of omitted variables consistent with Huang and Zhang (2008) we controlled for other firm level factors affecting firms` cash holdings (Dittmar et al., 2003; Pinkowitz et al., 2006). To test for Keynes (1936) transactional motive of cash holdings which has been applied to firms also by Bruinshoofd and Kool (2004), we included the logarithm of total sales and we find an economically significant relationship (inverse) with cash holdings. Consistent with the transactional motive, cash holdings respond inversely with firms` transactions and are at statistically significant level of 5%. A 1% increases in sales (a measure of transactional demand on firms` cash holding) significantly decreases cash holdings by 0.2994 when scaled by total assets but decreases cash holdings (logarithm of cash and cash equivalent) by 0.0578. But 1% increases in firm size sends its market value upwards by 0.0401 and economically significant at 10%. There is a statistically significant positive relationship between profitability and cash holdings. More profitable firms hold more cash than less profitable firms. But, we found negative relationship between profitability and cash holdings (log of cash and cash equivalent) and the market value of the firms perhaps the direction and magnitude of profitability is sensitive to the measures of cash holdings. Huang and Zhang (2008) find that the level of leverage is negatively related to cash balances at the 1% significance level, which according to them supports the agency theories that highly levered firms retain less cash because they are more subject to capital market monitoring. We mirrored their findings in the Ghana`s case reporting that 1% increase in the debt level of firms, decreases cash holdings by 0.4424 and such firms suffer a mark down in their market value by 0.0996. Borrowing brings other financial commitment on the firm by way of interest payment (demand on liquidity to service interest payment) and the repayment of the principal and this decreases cash available to managers. Firms carrying high debt levels also suffer from downward valuation. We further document a negative and statistically significant relationship between investment demands (fixed assets) of firms and levels of cash holdings. Increase in the investment opportunities of firms in fixed assets reduces the cash available for hoarding. Also commitment to dividend payment reduces cash available to firms perhaps for hoarding. Huang and Zhang (2008) report that coefficient on the dividend indicator variable is negative and significant at the 5% level, suggesting that commitment to dividend payout forces firms to disgorge cash, we mirrored this evidence in Ghana. Uncertainties in earnings forces firms to hold less cash though economically insignificant.

Conclusions and Implications

Reasons for holding cash dates back to Keynes (1936) and since then many researchers have looked at the demands on the cash holdings of corporations (Opler et al., 1999) from different angles. Empirical, the agency theory has been used extensively in investigating the susceptibility of cash to expropriation (Dittmar et al., 2003; Pinkowitz et al., 2006). Holding cash exacerbates the agency problem because according to Dittmar et al. (2003), agency costs and information asymmetries are expected to have a significant impact on the value of cash resources because according to Myers and Rajan (1998), liquid assets can be turned into private benefits at lower cost than other assets and therefore it is easier to make cash disappear than to make plant disappear. With improved governance leading to enhanced disclosure and transparency, holding cash should significantly add to shareholder value. Corporate disclosure and transparency impacts firms through its disciplinary (reduction in information asymmetry (Botosan and Plumlee, 2002)) and monitoring effect (Huang and Zhang, 2008). But, Huang and Zhang (2008) contend that the former (information effect) of corporate disclosure and transparency has received its place in the literature much to the neglect of the monitoring effect. According to them, no research to date has unambiguously isolated the monitoring effect from the information effect of corporate disclosure activity and therefore there is the need to examine the monitoring effect of corporate disclosure and transparency on cash holdings. Our paper builds on the premises of Huang and Zhang (2008) by providing first hand empirical evidence on the monitoring effect of corporate disclosure and transparency on cash holdings from a developing country perspective. Though, the Ghana Stock Exchange (GSE) has been around for just a little over two decades, the paper posits that the level of corporate disclosure and transparency of firms listed on the GSE ought to be examined as well as its monitoring effect on cash holdings. Whilst employing the Seemingly Unrelated Regression approach for 23 non-financial firms, we provide that a 1% increase in the composite disclosure and transparency index decreases cash holding by 0.0338 in economically significant level. We further report that though the direction of the impact of corporate disclosure and transparency is the same, the magnitude of the reduction in the level of cash holdings is sensitive to the measurement of cash holdings; slightly higher for logged liquidity (0.1259) than when scaled by net assets (0.0338). But firms with low disclosure and transparency do not suffer from a lower valuation by the market with 1% increase in the composite disclosure and transparency index recording a mark down of 0.0522. Consistent with the transaction motive, cash holdings respond inversely with firms` transactions and are at statistically significant levels. There is a statically significant positive relationship between profitability and cash holdings. More profitable firms hold more cash than less profitable firms. Mirroring Huang and Zhang (2008) in the Ghanaian case we report that 1% increase in the debt level of firms, decreases cash holdings by 0.4424 and such firms suffer a mark down in the market by 0.0996. Huang and Zhang (2008) find that, the level of leverage is negatively related to cash balances at the 1% significance level, which according to them supports agency theories that highly levered firms retain less cash because they are more subject to capital market monitoring.

The findings of the paper present implications to managers of firms on the GSE and regulators. Corporate managers should look at the results with the understanding that adjusting their corporate disclosure will be rewarded by the market though a negative relationship is reported in the case of market valuation. Running an opaque company will not only be discounted by the market but it significantly destroys firm value. Agreeing with the preposition that Shareholder wealth maximization is not a simple task and the fact that management cannot directly influence or control the firm's stock price but can only act in a way that is consistent with the desires of shareholders, corporate disclosure and transparency remains one of the viable option of maximizing shareholder wealth and other stakeholder concerns. Further studies are needed to investigate the negative relationship between corporate disclosure and market valuation, perhaps the characteristics (timeliness, reliability, its predictability, value relevance) of the information being provided ought to be looked at together with other factors.

REFERENCES

Abor J (2007). Corporate governance and financing decisions of Ghanaian listed firms. Corp. Gov. 7:83-92.

Acemoglu D, Johnson S, Robinson JA, Thaicharoen Y (2003). Institutional causes, macroeconomic symptoms: Volatility, crises, and growth. J. Monet. Econ. 50:49-123.

Berger PG, Hann R (2007). "Segment Profitability and the Proprietary and Agency Costs of Disclosure", Account. Rev. 82(4):869-906

Black BS (2001). The legal and institutional preconditions for strong securities markets. UCLA Law Rev. 48:781-856.

Bokpin GA, Isshaq Z (2009). Corporate Governance, Disclosure and Foreign Share Ownership on the Ghana Stock Exchange. Manag. Auditing J. 24(7):688-703

Botosan CA, Plumlee MA (2002). A Re-examination of disclosure level and the expected cost of equity capital. J. Acc. Res. 40(1):21-40.

Bruinshoofd WA, Kool CJM (2004). Dutch corporate liquidity management: new evidence on aggregation. J. Appl. Econom. 7(2):195-230.

Bushman R, Smith A (2001). Financial accounting information and corporate governance. J. Account. Econ. 32:237-333.

Dittmar A, Mahrt-Smith J, Servaes H (2003). International corporate governance and corporate cash holdings. J. Financ. Quant. Anal. 38:111-133

Durnev A, Kim H (2005). To steal or not to steal: Firm attributes, legal environment, and valuation. J. Financ. 60:1461-1493.

Fama E (1980). Agency problems and the theory of the firm. J. Polit. Econ. 88:288-307.

Fama EF, French KR (1998). Taxes, financing decisions, and firm value. J. Financ. 53:819-843.

Fresard L, Salva C (2008). The Value of Excess Cash and Corporate Governance: Evidence from US Cross-Listings. Vlerick Leuven Gent Management School Working Paper Series (accessed 1-03-2011).

Ghana Companies Code (1963). Ghana, Companies Code, (Act 179), Act of Parliament, Accra.

Harford J (1999). "Corporate cash reserves and acquisitions", J. Financ. 54:1969-1997.

Harford J, Mansi S, Maxwell W (2005). Corporate governance and a firm's cash holdings. Working paper, University of Washington

Hassan OAG, Romilly P, Giorgioni G, Power D (2009). The value relevance of disclosure: Evidence from the emerging capital market of Egypt. Int. J. Account. 44:79-102

Healy PM, Palepu KG (2001). Information asymmetry, corporate disclosure, and the capital markets: A review of the empirical disclosure literature. J. account. & econ. 31(1-3):405-440.

Healy PM, Hutton AP, Palepu KG (1999). Stock performance and intermediation changes surrounding sustained increases in disclosure. Contemp. Account. Res. 16(3):485-520.

Huang P, Zhang Y (2008). Does enhanced disclosure really reduce agency costs? Evidence from the value of corporate cash holdings and dividends. Working Paper.

Jensen M (1986). Agency costs of free cash flow, corporate finance, and takeovers. Am. Econ. Rev. 76:323-329.

Jensen MC, Meckling WH (1976). Theory of the firm: managerial behaviour, agency costs and ownership structure. J. Financ. Econ. 3:305-360.

Kanodia C, Lee D (1998). Investment and disclosure: The disciplinary role of periodic performance report. J. Acc. Res. 36:33-55

Keynes JM (1936). The general theory of employment. in: interest and money, Harcourt Brace, London.

Klapper L, Love I (2004). Corporate governance, investor protection, and performance in emerging markets. J. Corp. Financ. 10:703-728

Kyereboah-Coleman A, Adjasi KDC, Abor J (2006). Corporate governance and firm performance. Evidence from Ghana listed firms. Corp. Own. Control J. 4(2):123-132.

La Porta R, Lopez-de-Silanes F, Shleifer A, Vishny R (1998). Law Finance. J. Appl. Econom. 106:1113-1155.

La Porta R, Lopez-de-Silanes F, Shleifer A, Vishny R (1998). Investor protection and corporate valuation. J. Financ. 57:1147-1170.

La Porta R, Lopez-de-Silanes F, Shleifer A, Vishny R (2002). Investor protection and corporate valuation, J. Fin. 57(3):1147-1170. http://dx.doi.org/10.1111/1540-6261.00457.

Levitt A (1998). The importance of high quality accounting standards. Account. Horiz. 12:79-82.

Mitton T (2002). A cross-firm analysis of the impact of corporate governance on the East Asian financial crisis. J. Financ. Econ. 64:215-241.

Myers SC (1984). The capital structure puzzle. J. Finance 39:575-592.

Myers SC, Rajan RG (1998). The paradox of liquidity. Q. J. Econ. 108:733-771.

Nohel T, Tarhan V (1998). Share repurchases and firm performance: new evidence on the agency costs of free cash flow. J. Financ. Econ. 49:187-222.

Opler T, Pinkowitz L, Stulz R, Williamson R (1999). The Determinants and Implications of Corporate Cash Holdings. J. Financ. Econ. 52:3-46.

Pinkowitz L, Stulz R, Williamson R (2006). "Does The Contribution Of Corporate Cash Holdings And Dividends To Firm Value Depend On Governance? A Cross-Country Analysis" J. Financ. 61(6):2725-2751.

Pinkowitz L, Williamson R (2001). Bank power and cash holdings: Evidence from Japan. Rev. Financ. Stud. 14:1059-1082.

Stiglitz JE, Weiss A (1981). Credit rationing in markets with imperfect information. Am. Econ. Rev. 71:393-410.

Tsamenyi M, Enninful-Adu E, Onumah J (2007). Disclosure and Corporate Governance in Developing Countries: Evidence from Ghana. Manag. Auditing J. 22(3):319-334.

21

High credit rating IPOs and determinants of underpricing

Rohit Bansal and Ashu Khanna

Indian Institute of Technology, Roorkee, Uttrakhand, India – 247001.

In this paper, we declare that such objective, autonomous and exogenous certifying mechanism provides a better opportunity to test the well-established credit rating hypothesis, especially in the context of emerging markets with institutional voids. Employing a sample of 142 Indian IPOs (January 2007 to December 2012), we also experiment Ex-ante uncertainty with the efficacy of IPO (Initial Public Offerings) grading mechanism. We procure; grading decreases IPO underpricing and positively influences demand of retail investors, issue size, earnings before interest and dividend, long-term debt-equity equity ratio and profit to the book value ratio. Grading diminishes the number of share offered, a debt-equity ratio, and earnings before interest, dividend and tax, fixed to assess ratio and is having much impact on Ex- Ante uncertainty. Notwithstanding, grading does not affect subscription rate, offer timing (difference in days between offer days and listing days), firm's age, debtors turnover ratio, creditor payment method, cash to price earnings ratio, PIPH (post issue promoter's holding), interest coverage ratio, inventory turnover ratio, market capitalization, price earnings ratio, return on capital employed and return on net worth of the IPOs. IPO grading is prominent to capture firm size, business group affiliation and firm's quality of corporate governance. Our findings put forward that, in emerging markets, regulator's role to signal the quality of an IPO contributes with respect to the market welfare.

Key words: Initial Public Offerings, underpricing, credit rating, ownership structure, Ex-ante uncertainty.

INTRODUCTION

Initial Public Offerings (IPOs) are distinguished by high levels of information asymmetry. Many Firms are planning to go public, often use various certification mechanisms such as high-quality underwriters, venture capital affiliations, high-quality auditors and lockup agreements to reduce information asymmetry and to signal their quality to potential investors. The pricing and performance of initial public offerings (IPOs) is one of those experimental is sued that attract attention from many researchers in finance. The empirical evidence on the pricing of IPOs provides a puzzle to those who in other respects believe in efficient financial markets. Even though there is the extensive amount of studies on the abnormal initial returns provide d by IPOs there is not even a single study to speak on the price cap phenomenon during the first days of trading. The pre-eminent purpose of this study is to fill this gap using not one but three regulations changes over the covered period. Regulations and listing requirements have played a major role of the life of IPOs. A request for a stock exchange listing is the basis of an introduction prospectus whose contents are subject to regulations and, which is generally filed a few months before the admission date. In order to compile the IPO prospectus, lawyers, together with the underwriting bank examines the company regarding its legal, financial and commercial aspects. The process of a firm's IPO is characterized by the expansion of its ownership structure (Pham et al., 2003) to include a much larger number of outside investors. This leads to higher trading liquidity (Fidrmuc et al., 2006) which curtails transaction costs in future equity raising (Ibbotson and Ritter, 1995) and increases the firm value (Amihud and Mendelson, 1986). Promoting trading consist with general perception that the large trading volume in initial public offerings is mostly due to flipping activity and Rating IPOs by Deb and Mariestty (2010), certification grading (Arif et al., 2011), ownership structure at BSE by Bansal and Khanna (2012). Pricing mechanism at BSE tested by Bansal and Khanna (2012).

LITERATURE REVIEW

Several papers discussed the vital role played by underpricing in achieving the desired ownership structure. Among these papers, LaPorta (1999) point out that for emerging market countries, ownership structure plays a very important role in corporate finance. Kim et al. (2004) study the relationship between managerial ownership and firm performance using Thai IPO firms. Yong (2001) suggested that ownership has a positive relationships between managerial ownership and the change in performance. Stoughton and Zechner (1998) indicates that IPO companies use underpricing to create a more practical ownership structure. As a result, how underpricing affects ownership structure is a question and we, provide direct evidence in this present study. However, underpricing may affect liquidity directly without the link of a broad ownership structure. It can be said that underpricing attracts investor attention and creates a broad base of possible traders. We endeavor to find the answers of these all questions.

Financial theories suggest that underpricing can be used to affect ownership structure. Booth and Deli (1996) examine that small investors are preferred and underpricing is used to help achieve a dispersed ownership. Reese (1998) reveals that, there is a significant positive relationship between under-pricing and post-listing trading volume for up to three years after listing. He suggested the level of investor interest in each IPO, which is represented by the extent of financial media coverage, to be a possible explanation for this relationship. He also states that this relationship is formed through the mediation of owner ship structure formed after the allocation process.

Pham et al. (2003) discover that underpricing is positively related to the breadth of shareholding base and negatively related to blocking holder ownership in Australia. He also put forward that the main motivation of achieving a broad initial ownership through underpricing is to increase secondary market liquidity. Results evoke that in the U.S. market, underpricing appears to improve liquidity throughout another dimension of ownership structure: the number of non-block institutional shareholders.

According to Arif et al. (2011), India has the unique distinction of grading its IPOs and demonstrating the IPO Book building process to investors. In the context of this backdrop we investigate the certification role of these mechanisms in bookbuilt IPOs in India. We find that contrary to the expectations, grading does not affect the underpricing of IPOs. We also find that though grading was introduced to help retail investors, it is instead being used by informed institutional investors to make their investment decisions in Indian IPOs. However, the benefits of grading do pass on to the retail investors, albeit indirectly. We show that the transparency of the IPO book building process offers a much stronger certification signal to retail investors as compared to that of IPO grading. Known certification mechanisms such as the reputation of the sponsor or VC affiliation are of limited importance in the Indian IPO market.

IPO grading regulation

The primary market for equity in India gained momentum after the liberalization initiative taken by the government in the early 1990s. Following the improvement in the growth rate of the economy of that time, there were a large number of IPOs, particularly during the period, 1990-2004. Unlike the US market, which is the basis for many IPO studies, the Indian IPO market has been dominated by retail investors. The dominance of retail investors can also be observed in the secondary market. During the last fifteen years, the Indian IPO market has undergone many changes that are widely seen to have improved its transparency and efficiency.

In particular, the initial years of liberalization, after 1990 to 1991, witnessed a boom in the Indian IPO market. With fewer regulations during this period, many entrepreneurs used the primary market as the main vehicle to raise capital (Khanna and Palepu, 1997, 2000). A majority of the IPOs in our sample were made during the first five years of liberalization (1990 to 1995). The spurt in interest in the equity markets also witnessed several instances of "fly-by-night" entrepreneurs who eroded investors' wealth. During 1995 to 1996, the new security's regulator, the Securities and Exchange Board of India (SEBI), introduced more regulations on IPO pricing and enforced other restrictions on promoters, such as the lock-in period for their holdings. This resulted in a slump in the IPO market immediately following this period. For encourage equity participation after the 1995 to 1998 slumps, between 1999 and 2000 the SEBI tried to shore up investor confidence by tightening its norms for public issues of equity. Some of the main changes are related to

(1) Financial reporting norms (For example, the eligibility

Table 1. Magnitude of Initial public offering listed at Bombay stock Exchange.

Year	BSE	BB	FPO	BB-Under	BB-Over	FPO-Under	FPO-over	% BBU	%BBO	% FPOU	% FPOO
2000	67	11	56	6	5	30	26	21.96	-46.87	191.32	-32.3
2001	10	2	8	0	2	2	6	0.00	-62.00	47.50	-52.0
2002	5	1	4	0	1	4	0	0.00	-50.93	16.07	0.0
2003	11	4	7	3	1	5	2	90.16	-87.41	97.86	-85.3
2004	25	17	8	9	8	6	2	54.43	-45.45	74.10	-56.0
2005	67	48	19	26	21	14	5	31.47	-51.75	60.37	-63.8
2006	89	68	21	36	32	14	7	36.75	-46.33	38.91	-25.0
2007	105	91	14	58	32	7	7	51.54	-21.42	113.67	-3.3
2008	38	33	5	16	17	2	3	36.45	-26.36	18.06	-32.3
2009	21	21	0	14	7	0	0	19.09	-14.52	0.00	0.0
2010	73	71	2	47	24	2	0	22.35	-12.85	60.77	0.0
2011	39	38	1	19	19	0	1	47.36	-33.32	0.00	-70.4
Total	550	405	145	234	169	86	59	34.29	-41.6	59.88	-35

Source: http//www.bseindia.co.in.

criterion for making a public offer was changed from "actual dividend payout" to "distributable profit"; the resulting emphasis on profitability ensured that only companies with a track record of financial performance enter the IPO market.)

(2) Allotment norms (For example, the minimum allotment to Qualified Institutional Buyers (QIBs) was reduced from 60 to 50%, giving greater scope for retail investor participation. Moreover, a minimum allotment of 25% was reserved for the retail public (investors with an investment below Rs. 50,000).

(3) Cost/efficiency norms (For example, the secondary market infrastructure of the stock exchanges was used for the primary market also, and the number of collection centers for investor applications for new issues was reduced to cut issue costs).

(4) Transparent book building procedures: (Bids were invited from investors to aid price discovery). Consequently, there have been three distinct regimes in the Indian primary market, namely, (1) the immediate post-liberalization regime (1990 to 1995), (2) the initial regulated regime (1996 to 2000), and (3) the reformed regulated regime (2001 to 2004).

DATA AND METHODOLOGY

Data description

The study examines the initial performance of 168 IPOs listed in the Bombay Stock Exchange both in Main and Parallel board during the period from January 2007 through to December 2011 (Table 1). The sample contains only common and ordinary stocks. Preference stock as well as transfer from Parallel to Main market is excluded. All data are mainly extracted from IPOs prospectuses, daily press, SEBI reports (History of BSE, Fact Books, Annual and Monthly Statistical Bulletins), Annual Reports of Reserve bank of India, SEBI and some special internet sites.

Measure of underpricing

Consistent with the standard methodology, underpricing is calculated as the percentage change from the offer price to the closing price in the secondary market.

$$\text{Traditional underpricing} = ((\text{Closing price} - \text{Offer price})/\text{Offer price}) * 100 \quad (1)$$

$$\text{Log underpricing} = \ln (P1\text{-}P0/P0)^{*}\ 100 \quad (2)$$

Log underpricing = ln (closing price/ offer price) is used to determine the level of underpricing and to make standard practice and to avoid heteroscedasticity. The initial return is adjusted for market changes, taking into account movements of the Bombay Stock Exchange (BSE) between the offer price closing date and the end of initial day of trading. Raw initial return, which is calculated using equation 1, does not consider time lag symptoms between the offer price closing day and the first day of trading in the stock exchange. During this period, many changes in market conditions may occur. As a result, the initial return measured may be a result of changes in market conditions. So the raw introductory return is adjusted for market changes and variances.

Market adjusted rate of return (MAARO)

We tested marketed adjusted returns on securities (MAARO) as a benchmark to find out the degree of underpricing. Firstly, we calculated the return on, i security, where we used Ri = (P1-P0) / P0 where, Ri = return on i = security, P1 = Price of i security on first listing day, P0 = offer price of i security.

$$Ri = (P1\text{-}P0)/\ P0 \quad (3)$$

Secondly, we calculated index return on corresponding days, where we used Mi = (Ii - I0)/I0 where Mi = market return on ith day, Ii = closing index at listing day, I0 = closing index at offer day.

$$Mi = (Ii\text{-}\ I0)/\ I0 \quad (4)$$

Finally, we premeditated market adjusted return on security, where we have taken Ri from equation (1) and Mi from equation (2). The

Table 2. Details for the IPO determinants by low and high grading.

Variables / IPO grading	Rank 1 to 2 (low grading)	Rank 3 to 5 (High grading)
Subscription	17.75	31.17
Issue size	222.25	1119.59
Market cap (Cr.)	1778.42	11885.25
PIPH	71.69	69.44
No. of shares	21269959	77031050

Table 3. Details for IPO credit ratings.

Grade agency	Grade					Total
	1	2	3	4	5	
CARE	7	20	23	13	1	64
CRISIL	6	11	9	11	1	38
ICRA	5	24	19	8	0	56
FITCH	1	3	4	2	0	10
Total	19	58	55	34	2	168

market adjusted initial return is calculated as follows:

$$MAARO = \{100*[(1+Rit)/ 1+Mit)1]\} \quad (5)$$

$R_{i,t}$ = Raw initial return of company 'i' at period t
$M_{i,t}$ = Market adjusted (excess) initial return of company 'i' at period t
$R_{i,0}$ = IPO offer price as per prospectus of company 'i'
$R_{i,1}$ = Closing price of IPO of company 'i' at the end of the first trading day
$MI_{i,0}$ = BSE Index at the date of prospectus company 'i'
$MI_{i,1}$ = BSE General Index at the close of first trading day of company 'i'

Hypothesis model

Based on several empirical studies, we constructed various hypotheses for the IPOs underpricing including all independent variables. We tested several hypotheses related to our research problems, research objectives and variables. One tailed hypothesis test has been soiled to determine the significant association between different variables at the 5% significance level. Nonetheless, we formulated several alternative hypotheses.

Null hypothesis: H0: There is no significant disagreement between independent variables with the dependent variable that is level of underpricing.

These are several alternative hypotheses:

H1: The degree of IPO underpricing should curtail in the post-grading regime compared to the pre-grading regime.
H2: IPO underpricing is supposed to be lower for highly graded IPOs compared to low graded IPOs.
H3: IPO grading should positively impact post issue promoters holdings demand in primary market.
H4: Grading should reflect firm's health, both in terms of financial stability and management quality.
H5: High IPO grading declining Ex- Ante uncertainty variables (such as subscription rate, market capitalization, issue size, number of shares offered and offer timing).

Data and descriptive statistics

Magnitude of IPOs

Table 2 summarizes the statistics of the variables used in this study are re-ported in Table 4. Average initial return for the entire sample is 34.9%. Marisetty and Subrahmanyam (2010) report underpricing of more than 100% during 1991 to 2006. Therefore our result indicates that the IPO market in India has matured post year 2006. Table 2 reveals the magnitudes of IPOs after the Indian stock market crisis since October 2000 to December 2011. It is divided based on IPO that listed via book build and fixed price option. It also discloses the percentage of underpricing and overpricing in different years. It differentiates issue that is priced through the book build, and that is price through fixed price option. Data is collected with BSE websites and Capitaline database.

Detail of the IPO grading

Table 2 integrates the credit rating 1 and 2 on one column and rank 3, 4 and 5 in second columns. High credit ratings (3 to 5), reveals more subscription rate, more issue size of IPOs, highest market capitalization of issuing firms and maximum number of issue shares. Nevertheless, Low credit rank 1 and 2, expresses the low subscription rate, less issue size, fewer market capitalization amounts and fewer numbers of issued shares. In our sample, average issue size of the high graded IPOs is (1119.59) and post-issue promoter's holding is (69.44) respectively as compare to low grading issue size (222.25) and PIPH (71.69) correspondingly. The difference in the total subscription ratio between these two sub samples is very elevated; the mean values of total subscription are almost different. It is noticeable that QIB subscription is quite high for the graded IPOs (31.17 times) compared to the low graded IPOs (17.75 times). Numbers of shares are offered in high-grade IPO are much elevated as compare to low grade IPO (77031050) to (21269959) relatively.

Details of the IPO credit rating or IPO grading

Table 3 contains distribution of graded IPOs in our sample across different grades and various grading agencies. Table 3 reports details about the composition of our final sample. Our sample covers 168 graded IPOs. About 85% of the IPOs in our sample are offered through Book-Building method and rests of them are Fixed-Price IPOs. Table 3 shows details of the IPO grades in our sample. Only one IPO in our sample is graded by grading agency FITCH. It rests of graded issues are divided among three rating agencies – CARE, CRISIL and ICRA.

A probit regression model using the impact of higher grading IPOs at Ex-ante uncertainty variables, several sectors and IPOs

Table 4. Descriptive results for IPO underpricing and Ex-Ante uncertainty.

Variable	Mean	Median	Maximum	Minimum	Std. Dev.	Skewness	Kurtosis	Jarque-Bera	Probability	Sum	Sum Sq. Dev.
IPO_GRADING	2.65	3.00	5.00	1.00	0.97	0.06	2.25	4.03	0.13	446.00	155.98
IPO_CODE_3_TO_5_1	0.54	1.00	1.00	0.00	0.50	-0.17	1.03	28.01	0.00	91.00	41.71
LGNOOFSHARE	16.27	15.80	21.24	14.56	1.40	1.35	4.22	61.79	0.00	2733.32	326.24
LOGCEPS	2.45	2.41	7.63	-0.56	1.18	0.73	6.28	80.68	0.00	368.17	205.76
LOGISSUESIZE	5.07	4.67	9.65	1.79	1.54	0.84	3.27	20.43	0.00	852.00	394.41
LOGMKTCAP	6.81	6.50	12.28	2.98	1.86	0.73	3.01	14.74	0.00	1144.71	578.55
LOGPBV	0.42	0.56	2.98	-3.22	1.01	-0.71	3.88	18.25	0.00	64.91	158.35
LOGPIPH	4.25	4.34	4.61	3.26	0.32	-0.98	3.37	26.48	0.00	684.40	16.79
LOGROCE	2.31	2.72	4.55	-1.14	1.34	-0.91	2.71	23.54	0.00	387.56	297.75
LOGRONW	2.47	2.83	4.60	-1.83	1.35	-1.07	3.26	32.68	0.00	414.74	305.57
LOGMAARO	2.95	3.25	5.65	-0.49	1.42	-0.58	2.61	10.64	0.00	496.40	337.74

underpricing are presented as follows:

LOG CREDIT_ RATING = A + B1 DEB-EQ + B2 INVENTRY + B3 LOG NO. OF SHARE + B4 LOG DIFF IN AGE + B5 LOG AGE + B6 DEBTORS + B7 LOG MARKET CAPITALIZATION + B8 LOG ISSUE SIZE + B9 LOG EBIDTM + B10 LOG EBAPTM + B11 LOG PERE + B12 LOG PBV + B13 LOG PIPH + B14 LOG SUBSC + B15 LOG CEPS + B16 LOGEBIDTAM + B17 LOG INRTC + B18 LOG ROCE + B19 LOG RONW + B20 LOG MKTCAP + Ē (6)

Wherever, the dependent variable higher IPO grading or high credit ratings consults to initial return of the IPOs calculated as (IPO grading by several rating's agencies to IPOs, FITCH, CRISIL, ICRA and CARE). Elevated Grade_Dummy takes value 1 to indicate high graded IPOs (ratings 3 to 5) otherwise 0 in the sample. Number of shares offered to issuers is the natural logarithm of the number of shares issued to investors. Ln(Difference in age is the), distinctions in days between IPO offer date and IPO listing days, natural logarithm taken to make that value in standard practice. Age applies to age of the firm (in number of years) at the time of the IPO. Ln(Issue_size) is the natural logarithm of the issue amount in Rs. Crores; Ln (subscription) of the IPOs is symbolized by entire subscription; cash to price earnings ratio is measured to acquire the value of earning per share by investors. Market capitalization refers to market capital of the issuing firms. Ln(mktcap) is the natural log of the amount in Rs. Crores; P/BV is the profit to the book value ratio, pre IPO return on net worth is RONW and natural logarithm of return on net worth Ln(RONW).

DESCRIPTIVE RESULTS

Summary statistics of the variables used in this study are given as; therefore our result indicates that the IPO market in India has matured post year 2006. Mean value of initial return for ungraded sample is marginally (2.95%) higher than the graded IPOs 1.95 (Bansal and Khanna, 2012), this difference is higher in median initial return. Standard deviation are maximum at (2.03), (1.42), (1.44) for Institutional non promoters, Log maaro and sub-scription respectively. Skewness is under 0 to 3 for all variables used in our models.

The impact of high IPO grading at the level of underpricing and Ex-ante uncertainty by Logit regression are model as follows:

Log Credit_rating = α + β1 DEB-Eq + β2 LOG No. of share + β3 LOG age + β4 LOG market capitalization + β5 LOG Issue size + β6 LOG EBIDTM + β07 LOG EBAPTM + β08 LOG PERE + β09 LOG PBV + β10 LOG PIPH + β11 LOG Subsc + β12 LOG CEPS + β13 LOG INRTC + β14 LOG ROCE + β15 LOG RONW + Ē (7)

The dependent variable higher IPO grading or high credit ratings consults to initial return of the IPOs is calculated as (IPO grading by several ratings agencies to IPOs, FITCH, CRISIL, ICRA and CARE). High Grade_Dummy takes value 1 to indicate high graded IPOs (ratings from 3 to 5) otherwise 0 in the sample. IPO_ Type method is dummy variable, which obtains the value 1 for book-building IPOs and 0 if the offer is the fixed price. Number of shares offered to issuers is the natural logarithm of the number of shares issued to investors. Ln(difference in age) is the distinctions in days between IPO offer date and IPO listing days, natural logarithm taken to make that value in standard practice. Age refers to age of the firm (in number of years) at the time of the IPO. Ln(Issue_size) is the natural logarithm of the issue amount in Rs. Crores; Ln(subscription) of the IPOs is symbolized by entire subscription;

Table 5. Binary Logit results for high IPO grading and its impact on Ex- ante uncertainty.

Dependent variable: IPO_CODE_3_TO_5_1
Method: ML - Binary Logit (Quadratic hill climbing)
Included observations: 134
Convergence achieved after 6 iterations
Covariance matrix computed using second derivatives

Variables	Coefficient	Std. error	z-Statistic	Prob.
C	3.786981	3.956841	0.957072	0.3385
LGNOOFSHARE	-0.307404	0.193092	-1.692007	0.1014***
LOG_DEBEQ	-0.942290	0.436094	-2.160751	0.0307**
LOGAGE	0.297042	0.245042	1.212207	0.2254
LOGAPATM	1.108457	0.673982	1.644640	0.0870***
LOGCEPS	-0.663264	0.800181	-0.828892	0.4072
LOGCPM	-0.837434	1.069131	-0.783285	0.4335
LOGFIXDAST	-0.292659	0.176615	-1.657047	0.0975***
LOGISSUESIZE	0.803242	0.517515	1.552115	0.1206
LOGMKTCAP	0.179074	0.404095	0.443149	0.6577
LOGPBV	0.954233	0.338100	2.822341	0.0418*
LOGPIPH	-0.596519	0.479640	-1.243679	0.2136
LOGROCE	-0.211715	0.416779	-0.507978	0.6115
LOGRONW	-0.255899	0.434399	-0.589088	0.5558
LOGSUBSC	1.097918	0.142437	0.687447	0.4918
LOGTERMDEBTE	0.830736	0.392272	2.117755	0.0342**

McFadden R-squared	0.219607	Mean dependent var	0.321388
S.D. dependent var	0.401373	S.E. of regression	0.404314
Akaike info criterion	1.076566	Sum squared resid	14.81825
Schwarz criterion	1.017207	Log likelihood	-51.82990
Hannan-Quinn criter.	1.196265	Deviance	97.6598
Restr. deviance	185.4947	Restr. log likelihood	-12.74735
LR statistic	87.83490	Avg. log likelihood	-0.401716
Prob(LR statistic)	0.000000		
Obs with Dep=0	78	Total obs.	168
Obs with Dep=1	90		

1% significance level (*), 5% significance level (**), 10% significance level (***).

cash to price earnings ratio is measured to obtain the value of earning per share by investors. Market capitalization refers to market capital of the issuing firms. Ln(mktcap) is the natural log of the amount in Rs. Crores; P/BV is the profit to the book value ratio, pre IPO return on net worth is RONW and natural logarithm of return on net worth Ln(RONW). We obtain firm's age ln(ag) and offer timing (difference in listings days and offer days) in our model.

LOGIT RESULTS

Model-A exhibits the impact of IPO high grading at the level of underpricing. Table 5 report estimated parameters to the model described in Equation (7), simultaneously with the z-statistics, P-value, Std. errors and R^2 value from the model. The models are appraised over a sample of 134 IPOs issues over the period of Jan 2007–December 2012. The dependent variable high IPO grading relates to high grades of the IPOs considered as per the details provided in Table 3. We additionally investigate how different investor classes acknowledge to IPO grading. Basic intention behind IPO grading is that it furnishes information on the fundamentals of fewer known private firms, and as a consequence investors can make informed decision. We investigate whether investors' demand significantly varies across the different grades of IPO. We experiment the equation characterized in the model-A, over the sub-sample of graded IPOs. The

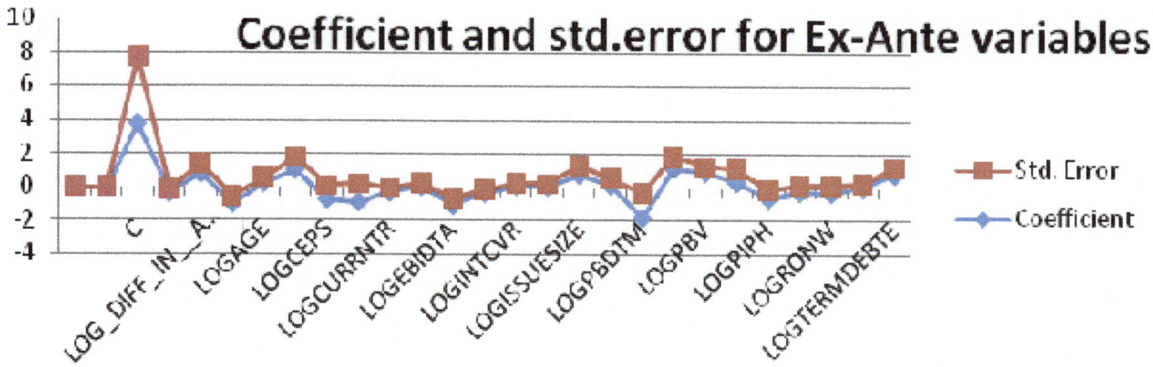

Figure 1. Coefficient and standard deviation for Ex- ante variables are used in regression model.

estimated parameters of these models are furnished in Table 5 and Figure 1. It examinations primary market demand from retail investors/non institutional investors and as the results, investigates the demand of the institutional investors. Outcomes from Model A indicate the demand of the retail investors, which are positive and significantly related to IPO grades. Accordingly, Results also display that no. Of shares offered, Debt-equity Ratio, Profit after tax management, Earning before tax, dividend, fixed assets ratio, issue size, Profit before interest, depreciation and tax, Profit to book value and long-term debt equity ratio are a prominent determinant of retail demand in primary market. All other variables that are included in our models, the difference in age, firm's age, CPM, cash to price earning ratio, current ratio, debtor turnover ratio, interest coverage ratio, inventory turnover ratio, market capitalization, profit before interest and dividend, price earnings ratio, post issue promoters holding, return on capital employed, return on net worth and subscription ratio are not significant in explaining the impact at the high IPO grading. Following Brennan and Franks (1997), he concludes high IPO grading positively and significantly affects primary market demand of the retail investors. It consequence is equivalent weight to Marisetty and Subrahmanyam (2010). There is no significant association between CEPS, CPM, current ratio and debtor turnover ratio at the high grading IPO. Nevertheless, issue size, profit before interest and dividend, profit to book ratio and, long-term debt equity indicate a pessimistic relationship at the high IPO grading (5% significance level).

Summary

In order to safeguard retail investors' wealth from low-quality IPOs, for the first time in the world, Indian stock market regulator SEBI introduced grading of initial public offerings and made it mandatory since May 2007. In this study, we investigate whether IPO grading provides information on the IPO quality and more specifically helps retail investors in their investment decisions. We also investigate whether better graded IPOs exhibit higher liquidity and lower risk in the post-issue secondary market. We determine that underpricing is lower in the post-grading regime compared to a pre-grading regime, and underpricing is low for high-grade IPOs compared to the low-grade ones. Retail investors' interest on IPO turns on the quality of the IPO. Better graded IPOs attract higher interest from the retail investors. These results indicate that retail investors believe IPO grading provides credible certification. On the other hand, our results reflect that institutional investors' subscription does not depend on IPO grading. We look for that the demand of the institutional investors is primarily deter-mined by profitability and financial risk of the firm.

Our analysis on the Ex- ante uncertainty suggests that, to a certain extent, mandatory IPO grading has reduced short term post listing risk and improved secondary market liquidity. Highly graded IPOs enjoy lower risk in the periods immediate after listing in the stock ex-changes. Finally, we analyse whether IPO grading really captures firm characteristics. We find that, among other factors, firm size and board independence explain IPO grading. In summary, we conclude that, in markets where credible institutions that provide certification for IPOs are less prevalent, regulator's role to certify the quality of an IPO adds value to the market welfare.

Conclusion

The results obtained from this study reveal that fresh issues on the BSE are subject to underpricing, consistent with developed and other emerging markets. In this respect, prospective investors should pursue the strategy of buying the fresh issues at the offer and selling them immediately on the first day of trading. Nevertheless, the study also exposes that investors should not hold new issues very long as the highest component of the introductory returns is found on the initial day of trading and that the average initial returns turn negative on the fourth day of trading. We determine that IPO underpricing is positively related to post-IPO growth in sales and EBITDA, but is not significantly related to growth in earnings. Our evidence recommends that accrual reversals or earning's management may cause this inconsistency.

The results obtained from this study indicate that fresh issues on the BSE are subject to underpricing, consistent with developed and other emerging markets. In this respect, prospective investors should pursue the strategy of buying the fresh issues at the offer and selling them according to their need. The study provides useful insights into which firm specific ratios or market-related ratios are important in determining the extent of underpricing of IPOs We explain the ROCE, PER, PBV and EBITDA as measures of firm quality, and conclude that our evidence supports the notion that IPO firms with greater efficiency and profitability are of better quality and lesser the level of underpricing.

REFERENCES

Amihud Y, Mendelson H (1986). Asset pricing and the bid–ask spread. J. Financ. Econ. 17:223-249.

Arif K, Stefano P, Alok P, Silvio V (2011). IPO certification: The role of grading and transparent books. Draft: 31 March 2011.

Bansal R, Khanna A (2012). Pricing mechanism and explaining underpricing of IPOs, evidence from Bombay stock exchange India", Int. J. Res. Financ. Mark. 2(2):205-216.

Bansal R, Khanna R (2012). "Post Indian stock market's crisis and its impact on IPOs underpricing: Evidence from 2008-2011". Asian J. Manage. Res. ISSN- 2229-3795, 3(1):1-11.

Bansal R, Khanna R (2012). "IPOs underpricing and money "left on the table" in Indian market". Int. J. Res. Manage. Econ. Commer. 2(6):106-120.

Booth J, Deli D (1996). Factors affecting the number of outside directorships held by CEOs. J. Financ. Econ. 40:81-104.

Brennan M, Franks J (1997). "Underpricing, ownership and control in initial public offerings of equity securities in the UK". J. Finan. Econ. 45:391-413.

Deb SS, Marisetty VB (2010). Information content of IPO grading. J. Bank. Financ. 34(9): 2294-2305.

Fidrmuc JP, Goergen M, Renneboog L (2006). Insider trading, news releases and ownership concentration. J. Financ. 61:2931-2973.

Ibbotson RG, Ritter JR (1995). Initial Public Offerings. Chapter 30 of North-Holland Handbooks in Operations Research and Management Science, Vol. 9: Finance. Edited by R. Jarrow, V. Maksimovic, and W. Ziemba.

Khanna T, Palepu K (1997). Why focused strategies may be wrong for emerging markets? Harv. Bus. Rev. 75:41-51.

Khanna T, Palepu K (2000). Is group membership profitable in emerging markets? An analysis of diversified Indian business groups. J. Financ. 55:867-891.

Kim KA, Kitsabunnarat PJR, Nofsinger JR (2004). "Ownership and OperatingPerformance in an Emerging Market: Evidence From Thai IPO Firms". J. Corp. Financ. 10(3):355-381.

LaPorta R, Lopez-De-Silanes F, Shleifer A (1999), "Corporate Ownership Aroundthe World". J. Finan. 54(2):471-517.

Marisetty VB, Subrahmanyam MG (2010). Group aliation and the performance of IPOs in the Indian stoke market. J. Financ. Mark. 13:196-223.

Pham PK, Kalev PS, Steen AB. (2003). Underpricing, stock allocation, ownership structure and post-listing liquidity of newly listed firms. J. Bank. Fin. 27(5):919-947.

Reese W (1998). "IPO Underpricing, Trading Volume and Investor Interest", Working paper, Tulane University.

Stoughton N, Zechner J (1998). IPO Mechanism, monitoring and ownership structure. J. Financ. Econ. 49:45-77.

Yong O (2001). Initial public offerings: the Malaysian experience 1990 – 1994. In: Bos T, Fetherston T (Eds.), Advances in Pacific-Basin Capital Markets, JAI Press, Connecticut 3:177-188

Tenant eviction in property management practice in Ilorin Metropolis, Nigeria

Ibrahim Tajudeen Akogun[1*] and Olatoye Ojo[2]

[1]Moshood Abiola Polytechnic, Abeokuta, Ogun State, Nigeria.
[2]Department of Estate Management, Obafemi Awolowo University, Ile – Ife, Osun State, Nigeria.

This paper examines the causes and methods of tenant eviction in property management practice in Ilorin metropolis, Nigeria with a view to suggesting measures aimed at reducing its incidence. The 16 registered estate surveyors and valuers in the study area were surveyed with a structured questionnaire. Data collected were analysed using descriptive statistics. The study's result revealed that rent default which accounted for 57.66% of the reasons for evictions was the most important. The most significant method adopted for evicting tenants was quit notice. This paper provides a basic guideline for policy makers to seek a solution to eviction problems. It also provides an alternative method of eviction which is relatively less expensive and time consuming.

Key words: Property management, tenant, tenant eviction, summary possession, premises recovery, tenancy, Ilorin, Nigeria.

INTRODUCTION

The term 'eviction' describes the practice of involuntary removal of person(s) from their homes. It is frequently associated with a range of related terms such as premises recovery, ejection, forced removal, relocation, dislocation, expulsion and displacement. The consequences of eviction are highly disturbing, particularly when we look more closely at its local impacts – on individuals, families and communities (Leckie, 1995; Momah, 2011; Landlord and Tenant Board, 2012; Moneke, 2009). Also of great concern is the impending eviction of thousands of families living in various categories of rental properties across the country.

Although the causes of tenant eviction can be varied, in most instances, it arises as a response of landlords to violation of the lease term by tenant. A lease is a contract between a landlord and tenant which contains the terms and conditions of the rental. It cannot be changed while it is in effect unless both parties agree (Boulder, 2012). Both landlord and tenant have some obligations to respect under the tenancy agreement. Whenever there is a conflict between the landlord and tenant arising from breach of lease terms, eviction may be inevitable especially when other forms of settlement are not feasible (Ojo, 2007). Different methods have been used in different places. While tenant eviction raises a lengthy series of human, social, economic and political considerations, this study will examine the practice primarily within the purview of property management.

A very important aspect of the activities involved in property management is dealing with leases and most importantly, dealing with tenants to facilitate a good landlord-tenant-manager relationship.

Property management problems would reduce considerably if all tenants comply with the rules, covenants and conditions of a tenancy. Even where this is possible, some other reasons would make it imperative to terminate some tenancies. In property management, tenant eviction is almost inevitable although some precautions may be taken to avoid it. It is a global phenomenon, occurring in all parts of the world, both developing and developed countries (COHRE, 2004). A Landlord who wants to terminate a tenancy and recover possession of his property from a tenant for whatever reason must observe due diligence and lawful procedure to achieve his objective. Self-Help is an extra-judicial remedy to enforce or protect a right, where the Landlord employs self-help, it must be lawful otherwise he will be criminally liable for his actions (MBIE, 2013; Momah, 2011; Moneke, 2009).

In Nigeria and particularly in the study area, most tenants, landlords as well as property managers have suffered untold hardship, tremendous financial loss, social stigma, and various degrees of disgrace from the problems that culminated in tenant eviction. The main thrust of this paper is to identify and examine the causes and methods adopted for tenant eviction in residential and commercial property markets in order to improve upon property management generally and more specifically in Ilorin metropolis.

LITERATURE REVIEW

Concept of tenant eviction

Ordinarily, eviction means removing a tenant from the premises in which they live by legal proceedings, for a particular reason known to the Landlord. Its professional meaning is given as "a legal proceeding by a lessor (landlord) to recover possession of property" (Friedman et al., 1997). When a tenant fails to comply with the lease agreement, the landlord may seek eviction of the tenant to terminate his rights to use the property. The Wikipaedia (2011) defined eviction as "a legal process by which a landlord forces a tenant to move out of the landlord's property involuntarily and usually permanently". Texas Low Income Housing Information Service (2006) refers to eviction as "a lawsuit filed by a landlord to remove persons and belongings from the landlord's property". In Texas law, these are also referred to as "forcible entry and detainer" or "forcible detainer" suits. There are hundreds of cases filed every day with Texas justice courts (also called justice of the peace or J. P. courts). In British Colombia Canada, eviction, also known as "unlawful detainer", "summary possession", or "forcible detainer" in some jurisdictions, is the removal of a tenant from rental property by a law enforcement officer. Before a tenant can be evicted, a landlord must win an eviction lawsuit (Wikipedia, 2011). In Australia, Residential Tenancies Act 1995 and Regulations described eviction as a legal process to force the tenant to leave the rented premises (South Australia Central, 2006). "An eviction is a court action a landlord must use to remove a tenant from an apartment or room". [The Legal Assistance Resource Center of CT, 2006).

In some areas, landlords can evict their tenants without cause. In other areas, the law requires landlords to have a "just cause", which usually includes non-payment of rent or damaging the property. There is a general trend towards requiring just cause for eviction and this portends danger for efficient housing delivery (Carroll, 2008). In Nigeria, just cause is necessary for an eviction suit to favour the landlord (ACN, 2011; Lagos State Government, 2011; Nigeria Property Centre, 2012).

Eviction can be actual, constructive, partial or retaliatory in nature (Friedman et al., 1997; RHOL, 2006): Actual eviction exists where one is removed from the property either by force or process of law. When it is by the process of law it is called Legal eviction (Aaron, 2003). It requires that a proper notice is served requiring the tenant to vacate the apartment within a specified time interval, and court process is used to follow up when the tenant dishonors the notice. Constructive eviction exists when, through the fault of the landlord, physical conditions of the property renders it unfit for the purpose for which it was leased. A tenant who has been constructively evicted has a number of legal recourses. He may be able to terminate the lease, order constructive eviction, and end liability for future rent payments (Burke and Snoe, 2008). Partial eviction exists where a tenant is deprived of a portion of the property for example, where a substantial modification is required on one side of the building, the landlord and the tenant may agree to a partial eviction from the property because of the disruption to be caused by the work. The tenant's rent will be reduced accordingly. Retaliatory eviction according to Aaron (2003) and RHOL (2006) occurs when a landlord attempts to evict a tenant in response to some (legal) action taken by the tenant. Eviction suit could be dismissed if the tenant provides reasons to convince the court that it is retaliatory.

Reasons for tenant eviction

Although the reasons for evicting tenants can be varied, some of the common factors identified from literature as grounds for tenant eviction in real estate practice are non-payment of rent, violation of other lease covenants, health and safety issues, criminal acts, unruly behaviour and requisition of the premises for personal use by the landlord (Aaron, 2003; Amos, 2006; Ojo, 2007; Lagos State Government, 2011; Land Registry for England and Wales, 2012; Nigeria Property Centre, 2012; e-How, 2013; Department of Commerce, 2012; Minnesota Judicial Branch, 2013). These are common to all countries and states.

Non-payment of rent

On any day following the day the rent was due, when the tenant failed to pay, the landlord can serve a termination notice to be effective ten days after the date the notice was served. The tenant may within five days after receipt of the notice pay all rents due and the notice of termination is then void (University of British Columbia, 2004). If the tenant refuses to pay or move out, eviction procedure may commence. Rent arrears is the commonest of all the reasons for tenant eviction (ACN, 2011; Nigeria Property Centre, 2012; Topham, 2012; Land Registry for England and Wales, 2012; MBIE, 2013; Michigan Legal Aid, 2012; Hartman and Robinson, 2006; Mitchell, 2003; Amos, 2006).

The vast majority of residential evictions are for non-payment of rent, which are usually treated as a summary proceeding and do not require a trial of fact (RHOL, 2006).

Regarding rent arrears in Scotland, non-payment of rent for a period exceeding three months is sufficient grounds for a Sheriff Court to grant a repossession order whether the lease is an assured tenancy or a short assured tenancy (The Housing (Scotland) Act, 1988). However, the law in England and Wales regarding private sector tenancies, the Housing Act (1988) provides that if the tenant owes more than two months or eight weeks rent, then the Judge must award a repossession order (HowToBooks, 2006). For non-payment of rent, the tenant must be fourteen days in arrears before a landlord serves the notice.

Eviction for cause

The identified grounds on which a landlord can terminate a tenancy agreement for cause are disturbance of other tenants, extraordinary damage to the property, abuse of the property, failure of tenant to pay security deposit within 30 days of signing tenancy agreement, knowingly misrepresented the property to a prospective tenant or purchaser, serious infringement on safety and other lawful right or interest of landlord or other tenants, unreasonable number of people occupying the premises, breach of reasonable term of agreement, frustration of the agreement, assignment or subletting of premises without landlord's consent, break a serious law like prostitution, or buying and/or selling drugs; and government's order to vacate the premises relative to safety, health, fire prevention or zoning (University of British Columbia, 2004; Spitzer, 2006; Chavis, 2006; U. K. Deputy Prime Minister, 2005; Kyle and Kennehan, 1979; Carroll, 2008). Where there is a breach of the agreement by the tenant, he must be given at least seven days to remedy the breach and then at least a further seven clear days to vacate, if the breach is not remedied.

Requisition of premises for personal use by the landlord

Whenever the landlord requires the property for his personal purpose, the tenant may be required to vacate the property. A landlord may terminate the tenancy agreement on the ground that he requires the property for his personal use but proper notice must be given to the tenant (Aluko, 1998; University of British Columbia, 2004).

Holdover

Where the term granted under a lease expires, the tenant is expected to vacate the premises, or renew the tenancy with the consent of the landlord. In absence of any of these, the tenant overstays so the landlord may evict to recover possession (Spitzer, 2006).

THE STUDY AREA – ILORIN

Ilorin is located on Latitude $8^{0}30'$N and Longitude $4^{0}35'$E. It lies in the transitional zone of the middle belt and serves as a gateway city between the north and south-western part of the Nigeria. It is the capital of Kwara State and lies along the Lagos – Kaduna highway, 306 km from Lagos, 600 kilometres from Kaduna and about 500 kilometres from Abuja. The 2006 population census figure revealed that there are 2,371,089 people in Kwara State with growing rate of 6.2% (NPC, 1991, 2006; Odeniyi, 2007). Out of this, 1,012,894 representing 42.72% of the state total population lives in Ilorin. The state capital is experiencing a very high rate of population growth over the time. The metropolis is divided politically to form parts of five local government areas. One urban – Ilorin West Local Government, and four rural – Ilorin East, Ilorin South, Moro and Asa Local Government Authorities.

The Ilorin property market can be classified into three viz: the residential, commercial and industrial property markets. The residential property market is characterised by various types of houses present all over the city. The traditional centre of the city (Oke – lele, Pakata, Adangba, Omoda, Ajikobi, Oloje, Gegele, Sanni-Okin, Eruda, Balogun Fulani, Alanamu, Ita – Adu, etc) comprises mainly old compound and tenement houses interspersed with block of flats all of high-density category. Medium density housing estates are found at Oloje, Kulende, Adewole, Irewolede and the Mandate estates. They are characterised by two, three and four – bedroom bungalows, and extensions and modifications to create extra spaces to accommodate more people. Low-density areas are found in the GRA, Taiwo and parts of Adewole areas where the houses are mainly detached bungalows of two to five bedrooms, duplex and maisonettes.

Commercial properties consist mainly of shops, open markets and offices. Shops are generally available at all locations and neighbourhoods to provide shopping facilities. They however, attract higher values at the city centres and main business districts. They range from small cubicles or kiosks patronised by small-scale traders, to open markets and stores. Office refers to buildings that provide ample room spaces and facilities to support a good working condition for people. They include those occupied by private professional offices of lawyers, chartered accountants, surveyors, consultants, hospitals, etc and corporate organisations like banks, insurance companies, etc.

Commercial buildings dominate the properties along Taiwo, Yoruba, Murtala and Unity Roads. Most of the buildings that were hitherto designed for residential purposes along these roads have been converted to either offices or shops. Multi-purpose built offices and shopping complexes are also very common. Along other roads are found residential, convenience shops and stores. Although there are owner-occupied properties, the commercial and residential property markets are active in Ilorin. This is evidenced by the number of quacks apart from professionals engaged in real estate business.

There is little concentration of industrial properties as industrial development in the city is very low. Few industrial premises are found along Asa Dam Road, Gaa – Imam along Ajase – Ipo Road and Western Reservoir Road. Examples of the available industries are Global Soap and Detergent, Dangote Flour Mills, Sawmills, Kwara State Metal and Chemical Industries, Delta Cables, 7-UP and Coca Cola plants. Cases of isolated small-scale industries (food, drink, leather and furniture products) are also found scattered all over the city. Most of the industrial premises are owner-occupied and there are few cases of tenancy in industrial property, so the market is not quite active.

RESEARCH METHODOLOGY

The study was conducted in Ilorin metropolis in 2010. The focus group for the research work was the 16 practising firms of estate surveyors and valuers who are custodians of properties and are often involved in management of landed properties. They are the real estate consultants professionally recognized in Nigeria to conduct property management activities (FGN, 1975). Essential primary data for this study include the socioeconomic characteristics of respondents, causes and methods adopted for evicting tenants. The primary data were collected through self-administered questionnaires from the practising estate surveying firms in the city. The questionnaires were a combination of closed and open-ended questions.

Each respondent was asked to complete a questionnaire by answering questions concerning their socioeconomic status including qualifications, scope of practice, experience of property management practice, reasons for evictions and methods adopted for evicting tenants. Data were analysed mainly with descriptive statistical techniques such as frequency distribution tables and percentages.

Sample characteristics of respondents

The sampling characteristics for the practising firms of Estate Surveyors and Valuers that were surveyed are shown in Table 1. A total number of 16 firms that were practising in Ilorin were all considered for the study.

All the 16 questionnaires administered were duly completed and returned giving 100% response rate. 56.25 % of the respondents were over 50 years old, 21% average 41 to 50 years while 18.75 were less than 40 years old. 62.5% were the principal partners in their firms, 25% were estate officers while 12.5% were branch managers. 37.5% have more than 15 years experience of the practice, 31.5% have between 11 and 15 years, 18.75% have 6 to 10 years while 12.5% have less than 6 years experience in the practice of estate surveying. 50% had BSc degree, 31.25% had HND while 18.75% had additional qualifications at masters level. 62.5% were associates, 31.25% were fellows while only 6.25% were probationer members of the Nigerian Institution of Estate Surveyors and Valuers. The scope of practice of the respondents indicated that all (100%) engaged in property valuation, management, estate agency, 50% engaged in feasibility appraisals and 43.75% engaged in property development.

RESULTS

Causes of tenant eviction

Overall, the main causes of eviction revealed by the study were rent default, breach of covenant, holdover and owner's intention to use the property. As presented in Table 2, the estate surveyors indicated that out of a total of 2,147 evictions that occurred during the period under review, the majority of eviction 1,238 (58%), were prompted by rent default; 415 (19%) tenants were evicted because they breached covenants involving repairs, subletting without consents, misuse of property and other terms of their tenancies. 262 (12%) tenants were evicted because the landlord wanted to use the property, holdover accounts for 103 (5%) while 130 (6%) tenants were evicted for other reasons like the need for renovation and change of ownership.

In the residential property sector as shown also in the Table 2, eviction of 870 (60%) tenants were caused by rent default, breach of covenant caused 252 (17%) evictions, while 163 (11%) tenants were evicted because the landlord wanted to use the property. Furthermore, 65 (5%) tenants were evicted on account of holdover and 96 (7%) tenants were evicted for other reasons. In the commercial property sector, breach of covenant accounted for the largest proportion of eviction. It was responsible for evicting 368 (53%) tenants. Moreover, 163 (23%) evictions were due to rent default; owner's intention to use the property accounted for 99 (14%) evictions, holdover accounted for 37 (5%) while other reasons accounted for evicting 34 (5%) tenants. Rent default was discovered to be the most significant cause of tenant eviction in residential properties while breach of covenant was the most prominent reason in commercial property sector.

Table 1. Sample characteristics for estate surveyors (16).

Characteristic	Value	Percentage
Age	Less than 40 Years	18.75
	41 – 50 Years	25.00
	Over 50 Years	56.25
Positions in their firms	Principal	62.50
	Branch Manager	12.50
	Estate Surveyor	25.00
Years of experience	3 – 5 Years	12.50
	6 – 10 Years	18.75
	11-15 Years	31.25
	16 – 20 Years	18.75
	Over 20 Years	18.75
Academic and professional qualifications	B.Sc	50
	HND	31.25
	M.Sc / MBA	18.75
	Probationer	6.25
	ANIVS	62.50
	FNIVS	31.25
Professional services	Property valuation	100
	Property management	100
	Estate Agency	100
	Feasibility study	50
	Property development	43.75

Source: Author's field survey, 2010.

Table 2. Reasons and methods adopted for eviction.

Reasons for eviction	Residential	Commercial	Total
Rent default	870 (60.17%)	163 (23.25%)	1033(48.11%)
Breach of other covenants	252 (17.43)	368 (52.50%)	620 (28.88%)
Holdover	65 (4.5%)	37 (5.28%)	103 (4.80%)
For owner's use	163 (11.27%)	99 (14.12%)	262 ()12.20%
Others	96 (6.54%)	34 (4.85%)	130 (6.06%)
Total	1,446 (67.35%)	701 (32.65%)	2,147 (100%)

Methods adopted for eviction	Residential	Commercial	Total
Quit notice	856 (59.20%)	365 (52.07%)	1221 (56.87%)
Court action	338 (23.38%)	183 (26.11%0	521 (24.27%)
Inter-personal resolution	252 (17.43%)	153 (21.83%)	405 (18.86%)
Self-help	0	0	0
Total	1,446 (67.35)	701 (32.65)	2,147 (100%)

Source: Author's Field Survey, 2010.

Methods of tenant eviction

The responses shown in Table 2 also reveals that majority of the tenants were evicted by conventional methods of eviction that is, court action and or notice to quit. Of all the evictions, quit notice accounts for the largest proportion 1,221 (57%) while court action accounts for 521 (24%). Evictions effected by negotiation also amounted to 405 (19%). In the residential property sector, 856 (59%) tenants were evicted by quit notice, 338 (23%) by court action, and 252 (18%) by negotiation. Furthermore, the responses also revealed that 365 (52%) commercial property tenants were evicted by quit notice, 183 (26%) by court action and 153 (22%) by negotiation. Eviction by quit notice is the most prominent during the period under review for residential and commercial properties.

The court action and quit notice are much related. Before the eviction procedure can get to court, quit notice must have been served appropriately. Most tenants will vacate the premises latest by the expiration of quit notice. However, the other tenants that refuse to respect the stipulations of the quit notice are dragged to court. Notice to quit and court actions are the legal methods supported by statutory provisions for tenant eviction and that is the reason why they are most commonly employed by the professionals.

IMPLICATION OF FINDINGS AND CONCLUSION

The implications of the above findings are many. First, the qualitative and quantitative housing problems remained substantial in Nigeria. Eviction is a hidden problem that confronts many and constitutes a major problem for most productive men and women in the society. The implication here is that most people live in constant fear of eviction and this represents traumatic living condition which will have negative impact on real productivity of average persons involved. Rent default is the most prominent cause of eviction especially in residential property sector. Whether any downward trend in evictions can be achieved depends largely on the future trend of rent arrears and this could be significantly affected by the level of income. To a very small extent, the future trend of evictions is also dependent on the changing incidence of other causes of eviction and how they are addressed. The professional property managers should continue to embrace the legal methods of eviction (as is done in developed countries of USA and UK) notwithstanding they are expensive and time consuming in Nigeria. To enhance the efficacy of these methods in Nigeria, government should ensure that the problems associated with court method of eviction are removed to make them relatively less cumbersome, inexpensive and speedy. It is also necessary to organize at the state and local levels, improved legal system that will create policies to reduce the impact of involuntary moves on the most vulnerable tenants and prompt determination of eviction cases within short period. This will encourage landlords and managers to adopt court process whenever it is necessary to evict a tenant. The estate surveyors should also be mindful of proper selection of tenants for properties. Careful screening of tenants before giving possession will eliminate bad tenants and reduce drastically incidence of eviction for all categories of properties. While evictions may be inevitable in certain circumstances, they should be undertaken only as a last resort, and adequate care must be taken to avoid waste of resources.

REFERENCES

Aaron L (2003). "Being Evicted? Tips for Tenants". Expertlaw articles, Retrieved February 17, 2007, from http://www.expertlaw.com/library/real-estate/evicted-tenant.html.

ACN (2011). What the New Lagos Tenancy Law Says Accessed on 30/9/2012 at http://actioncongress.org/category/news/article.

Aluko O (1998). The Law of Real Property and Procedure. Spectrum Law Publishing; Ibadan; Nigeria.

Amos J (2006). "The Unpleasant Process of Tenant Eviction". *EzineArticles*. Retrieved February 19, 2010, from http://ezinearticles.com/?The-Unpleasant-Process-Of-Tenant-Eviction&id=360372.

Boulder (2012). Landlord-Tenant Handbook. Accessed on 17/03/2013 at http:www.bouldercolorado.gov/index.php?//.

Burke DB, Snoe JA (2008). Disturbed Tenant: A Constructive Eviction in Property: Examples & Explanations - Page 312 - Google Books Aspen Publishers, Retrieved March 25, 2013, from *books.google.com.ng/books?isbn=0735570310.*

Carroll AB (2008). International Trend Toward Requiring Good Cause for Tenant Eviction: Dangerous portent for the US; Seton Hall Law Review, 38:427. Available at SSRN: http://ssrn.com/abstract=1401605.

Chavis BM (2006). "Finding the Blue Chip Tenant and Putting a Stop to the Majority of Landlord Tenant Problems". Retrieved October 18, 2006, from http://www.landlording101.com/docs/BlueChipTenant Jan2006.pdf.

COHRE (2004). "Housing Rights for Everyone, Everywhere". Evictions Monitor Vol. 1 No. 2 December. Retrieved March 03, 2010, from http://www.cohre.org.

Department of Commerce (2012). When Things go Wrong; Accessed on 23/03/2012 at http;//www.wa.gov.au/consumerprotection/contents

e-How (2013). What to Do When a Tenant Will Not Vacate?. Accessed on 23/03/2012 at www.ehow.com.

FGN (1975). Estate Surveyors and Valuers Registration Board of Nigeria (Registration, etc) Act, Chapter III of the Laws of the Federation of Nigeria 1990, Lagos.

Friedman JP, Harris JC, Lindeman JB (1997). Dictionary Of Real Estate Terms; 4th Edition; Baron's Education Series; New York.

Hartman C, Robinson D (2006). "Evictions: The Hidden Housing Problems"; Volume 14; Issue 4; Faniemae Foundation; USA. Retrieved October 18, 2010, from www.fanniemaefoundation.org

HowToBooks (2006). "Tenant Eviction: How to Evict a UK Tenant". Retrieved February 19, 2007, from www.howtobooks.co.uk/property/buy-to-let/evi ction.asp.

Kyle RC, Kennehan AM (1979). Property Management. Real Estate Education Company; Chicago; USA.

Lagos State Government (2011). Lagos Tenancy Law 2011; Ikeja. Accessed on 12/02/2013 at http://www.nigeria-law.org/Legislation /Laws of the States.

Land Registry for England and Wales (2012). Practice guide 26-Leases Determination. Accessed on 12/01/2013 at http://www.landregistry.gov.uk/.

Landlord and Tenant Board (2012). How a Tenant Can End Their Tenancy, accessed on 29/09/2012 from Http://www.ltb.gov.on.ca/key_information

Leckie S (1995). When Push Comes to Shove: Forced Evictions and Human Rights. Habitat International Coalition; Utrecht, Netherlands.

MBIE (2013). Ending Tenancies Frequently Asked Questions; Accessed on 30/02/2013 at http://www.dbh.govt.nz/tenancy-index.

Michigan Legal Aid (2012). Evictions for Termination of Tenancy. Accessed on 30/02/2013 at http://www.michiganlegalaid.org/library

Minnesota Judicial Branch (2013). Eviction Actions. Accessed on

30/02/2013 at http://www.mncourts.gov/.
Mitchell QC (2003). Eviction and Rent Arrears – A guide to the law in Scotland (electronic edition). Shelter Scottish Housing Law Service, Edinburgh. Retrieved March 10, 2006, from http://www.jonathanmitchell.info/uploads/Eviction.pdf.
Momah CN (ed.) (2011). Recovery of Premises In Nigeria: A Summary Review, The Legal Luminary; Volume 1, Issue 10 September. Accessed on 30/02/2013 at www.ndic.org.ng/../luminary-September
Moneke F (2009). Nigeria: Landlord & Tenant - the Right to Shelter and Statutory Protection of Tenants. Accessed on 30/02/2013 at www.allafrica.com.
Nigeria Property Centre (2012). How to Recover Residential Premises from Tenants in Lagos State, Nigeria. Accessed on 30/02/2012 at www.nigeriapropertycentre.com/blog/author/administrator
NPC (1991). Provisional Census Figures; Lagos.
NPC (2006). Provisional Census Figures; Abuja.
Odeniyi P (2007). "Census 2006: North is 75m, South 64m". In The Nation Newspapers, Volume 1, No 0164, January 10.
Ojo O (2007). "Tenant Eviction Methods in Residential Property Market in Ibadan Metropolis". In Fadare W. and Adesanya A. (eds.) ("2007): Towards a Sustainable Built and Natural Environment; Faculty of EDM Conference Paper, OAU, Ile-Ife.
Rental Housing Online, http://www.rhol.org/rental/KURLTA.htm (last visited March 6, 2006).
South Australia Central (2006). "Residential tenancies Act 1995 and Regulations" Retrieved February 02, 2007, from www.thelpa.com/pa/landlord/ tenant-law/australia- landlord/tenant-law html
Spitzer E (2006). "Tenant's Rights Guide". Office of the New York State Attorney General, New York. Retrieved February 17, 2007, from www.oag.state.ny.us.
Texas Low Income Housing Information Service (2006). "Texas Tenant Advisor: Know your rights as a tenant in Texas". Retrieved February 17, 2007, from www.texastenant.org/rights/eviction/process.
The Housing Act (1988). In: HowToBooks (2006) "Tenant Eviction: How to evict a UK Tenant" Retrieved February 19, 2007 from www.howtobooks.co.uk/property/buy-to-let/eviction.asp.
The Housing (Scotland) Act (1988). In: HowToBooks (2006) "Tenant Eviction: How to evict a UK Tenant" Retrieved February 19, 2007 from www.howtobooks.co.uk/property/buy-to-let/eviction.asp
The Legal Assistance Resource Center of CT (2006). "Tenants' Rights: Eviction". Retrieved February 19, 2010, from www.larcc.org/pamphlet/ housing/tr-eviction.htm.
Topham AF (2012). Termination of a Lease In "Real Property, An Introductory Explanation of The Law Relating to Land", Accessed on 13/01/2013 at http://www.chestofbooks.com/Real-PropertyLaw/Section-III-Termination -of-A-Lease.html.
UK Deputy Prime Minister (2005). "Possession Actions and Evictions by Social Landlords". Housing Research Summary Number 219, 2005 Retrieved February 19, 2007, from http://www.renewal.net/Documents/ RNET/Research/Possession actionsevictions.pdf.
Wikipedia (2011). "Eviction Procedures". Retrieved February 19, 2012, from http://en.wikipedia.org/wiki/Image:Eviction_ process_bc_canada .JPG.

Evaluating profit organizations' financial tools development strategy for managing crises

Abdullah Ibrahim Nazal

Department of Finance and Banking, Faculty of Economics and Administrative Sciences, Zarqa University, Jordan.

The purpose of the present study is to evaluate profit organizations' financial tools development strategy in order to find limits. These limits can help the strategy to organize development internationally and locally without solving crises with negative effect. The study found out that there were negative outcomes because profit organizations were ignorant of their responsibility and were revenue oriented without considering the balance between their aims and that of their countries. This leads to weak monetary and financial policies. Islamic profit companies (as a case study) avoid interest with bad effects, being ignorant of one's responsibility and negative effects on countries' aims, by applying fixed and flexibility rules. Limits can speculate dealing and stages of financial tools life cycle. But this is not enough; there must be fixed and flexibility rules decided by law in addition to rules that control economic sectors for protection of communities. It is suggested that development be controlled up by contract conditions, which must be practical as Islamic companies share their account.

Key words: Crises, profitable organizations, developing financial tools, limits.

INTRODUCTION

Background

Budget management gives idea about changes of economic. Financial managers must try to understand the economic framework and be alert about the consequences of varying levels of economic activity and changes in economic policy; they must also use economic theories as guidelines for efficient business operation. Financial decisions should be made and actions taken only if there would be added benefits that exceed the added cost (Lawrence, 2000). Profit organization aims to make great net profit even in limited time or to increase their assets value. Some organizations can make their sales in other countries to avoid sales tax, increase their sales price or reduce currency risks. When producing goods, costs need to be decreased. There may be increase in price of inter goods during production. Developing financial tools gives way to keep inter goods price in suitable price. Rather than storing entering goods, options or future contracts can be made to reduce cost. The problems come in two ways: first, options or future contract give right to make deal in future, but there will be no deal at the time of making the contract. Second: there is speculation on these rights without owning goods. Selling one's rights to another leads to ignorance.

The problem

The problem is profit organizations want to achieve revenue as much as possible within a limited time by developing financial tools strategy. This strategy can be affected by the monetary policy or financial policy of the country on its possible revenue. Rapid development is more than covering rules. This problem can be cleared by these questions:

1. Can profit organizations' financial tools development strategy (with negative and positive effects) be evaluated at suitable time?
2. Can profit organizations' negatives effects be limited and its positives effects be increased?
3. How can we manage profit organizations' economic crises up to standards and practically control their account?

The importance

At this time, it is important to find the problems of developing financial tools which culminate to crises. This study discusses standards for achieving three aims which are social responsibility, aims of financial policy and monetary policy in order to limit negative effects and direct development to make crises have positive effects. It helps to balance the aims of profit organization and social responsibility, financial policy aims and monetary policy in the country. Also it shows the ways of balancing profit organizations with their countries' aims or to avoid bad effects by creating standards and controlling account.

Objectives

The main objectives of this paper are,

1. To find positive effect of developing financial tools.
2. To find negative effect of developing financial tools.
3. To limit developing financial tools effects in order to increase positive effects and reduce negative effects as a way to solve crises.

PREVIOUS STUDIES

Pedro and Erwan (2010) show that there is a strong statistical relationship between financial development and economic development. This is often presented as evidence that financial development causes economic development by promoting investment and making allocation of resources more efficient (Thomas, 2011).

Center bank decides that monetary policy must agree on assets development or improvement in banks because it is important to save in own country than migrating to other countries. Jean et al. (2011) cleared the relation between company's decision and financial policy. As private companies decide their cash holding policies and dividend payment up to market expectation, if countries increase their expenses amount as aids to people, this would encourage companies to get payments in cash more quickly.

Some other studies concentrated on the importance of social responsibility; like Mc Kinsey (2010) who found that corporate social responsibility contributes positively to long term shareholders' value and helps their companies to build strong reputation. Chatterji et al. (2009) found poor social responsibility leads to sell outs of companies' shares by large investment fund which decreases companies' financial performance. David (2012) studied the effect of investors' relations and firms' news on stock prices. It affects returns and media coverage. Nestlin et al. (2006) found that retaining customer is key drive of profit firms. So he recommended that it is important for profit firms to build predictive model for customers' real needs.

On the other hand, some studies showed conflict between some countries' aims and their companies' aims. Other studies concentrated on solving deficit problems affecting citizens; an example is Ahmad (2003). He aims to analyze general budget by correcting economic policy. He found that reducing of current expenses, obligating price on essential products produced by local company and increasing tax besides encouraging foreign companies were not successful. It makes local companies weak and increases deficit. There were many studies that tried to apply Islamic economic rules to avoid negative effect of developing financial tools; like Ahmed (1998) who aims to study budget deficit in order to find solution. From his result, Ahmad suggested integration with other countries and using solutions from Islamic economic system as rules to organize companies' aims and countries' policies. Abdullah (2006) studies Islamic standards of developing financial tools. He found that standards can overcome effect if interest is equal to zero, ignorance is avoided and if there is no unfair pricing and damaging of individuals or community rights. This can be if fixed rules are applied to any dealing like selling, leasing and sharing and other flexibility rules which take care of companies' environment.

POSITIVE AND NEGATIVE EFFECTS OF PROFIT ORGANIZATION'S FINANCIAL TOOLS DEVELOPMENT STRATEGY

Studies of Holzach (1985) and David (1985) encourage that developing financial tools should concentrate on banking. It is the base for developing services and goods. Banks may develop their services which relate to financing or investing by improving steps of services, producing some services as one or making new service (Midan, 1988). Developing or improving products has advantages; it is just like increasing quality to make it similar to competitors' products or solving clients' problems; it could involve giving unique benefit to client or establishing standards better than that of other competitors. As profit organizations work in open environment their financial tools face changes. Life cycle stages show tools pricing with their risks (Zeithaml and Bitner, 2000) (Table 1).

Profit organizations use resources to produce products. If there is increase in tax in their country, profit organizations would face this by many ways. They include reducing workers, leaving the country or developing financial tools to make cost suitable. These solutions will affect the country negatively. Reducing worker will decrease workers' income and increase country's expenses to help these workers. Leaving the country makes the country lose its tax returns. Derivatives have two sides: it can reduce cost and can lead to ignorance especially in speculation. It may give high price just because of speculation demand for future expectation. This means losing investment and savings. By developing financial tools, profit organizations finance their assets. It can get loan for long time by selling bonds, can get loan from banks, can finance its needs by sharing with other shareholders or it can buy on credit from other companies. Every way has positive and negative effect (Table 2).

As selling of debts is possible, there is way to make unusual return because of speculation. It can be increase demands by increasing bond return or guarantee or increasing of bond currency price. Financial tools can control expected risk. Mortgage crisis, as an example, is developing of loans dealing. Banks get loan interest as profit. It can increase profit by developing loan contract to be bond. This increases flexibility to get liquidity and makes other profits by speculation. Speculation demand can be increased to get other profits by increasing the international credit rating up to grantees. Other profits can be got by increasing asset evaluation which is financed by loan. Bonds mortgage price can be changed to interest rate, assets price and grantee value. These lead to ignorance. Fast dealing and amount of demand increase expected profit until bonds' real value is discovered. The crises came after creditors had preferred to lose mortgage to buy in debts.

LIMITS OF ACCEPTING DEVELOPING FINANCIAL TOOLS

Limits are important to control and direct developing financial tools. Profit organizations have ability to improve or develop financial tools to meet their aims. But due to its negative effect on countries, developing financial tools have to be controlled by law. This is important to make direct investment in different economic sectors successful. As development has positive effect, a country can direct it to solve economic or financial crises. It can use developing financial tools as tools for its monetary policy or financial policy. It can also use limits to control or direct development. There are limits to increase the advantages of developing financial tools and reducing disadvantages. It is important to relate profit organizations to growth of economic sector and countries' international relationship. Therefore, foreign profit organizations' loss could lead to bad relation between countries. There are many limits to complex environment changes. Limits may lead to the acceptance of tools in the market or may lead to dealing with tools. Using one of the developing financial tools means there are legal duties and rights that must be done in any contract. Steps and procedures of contract must be made clear to dealers for them to know the rights or duties to apply. Contract can be done manually or by machines such as using internet. Buying bonds from financial market shows the importance of knowing the steps of buying and selling. All dealers must evaluate bonds price, risks and legal way to manage risk. This helps to turn sellers' duties to buyer's debts and interest in future. Every profit organization has resources, life cycle and products life cycle. Therefore, as it develops its product to meet customers' need, it faces the problems of making profit and having the ability to indulge in competition.

Case study: Evaluating profit organizations' financial tools development strategy to manage stocks speculations crises by Islamic companies

Stocks speculations crises come as a result of ignorance, interest and loss of responsibility. Ignorance leads to increased speculations crises because of gambling with the possibility of future increasing or decreasing price. There must be interest on debts even if a company makes loss. Some gaps in law lead to the problem of losing responsibility, which makes transfer of duties an option. Option like buying of shares with limited price to avoid increasing price in the future gives dealers the right to continue with or cancel the contract. Also, options contract can be selling of right regardless of the owners of the shares. These things lead to unstable standard used in dealings (Abdullah, 2006). Common shares in Islamic economic have rules. Every Islamic profit company has to apply these rules. Therefore, Islamic profit companies apply company's law of the country but without neglecting any Islamic rule. It does not establish what if the company's law goes against the Islamic rules. Its common shares mean sharing in investment. Selling common shares means sharing in a company's investment. It may be involved in managing share like Moushraka or not managing like Modaraba. Also if it shares by Moushraka, then it will be for long term known as permanent Moushraka or for short term called decreasing Moushraka. This means Islamic companies can sell common shares for long term and short term due

Table 1. Asset lifecycle stage and banks strategy.

Asset lifecycle stages	Banks strategy
Introducing stage	Expansionism: as it will produce new asset If there is possible needs in market, enough resources, competition, and possibility to reduce cost.
Growth stage	Permeation: as it will promote the advantages of the assets to keep growth of profit
Maturity stage	Defense: as improving assets to keep profit
Fall stage	Reparation: as releasing loss assets

Table 2. Affects of profitability organization developing financial tools to finance their assets.

	Negative affect	Positive affect
Selling bonds	*Possibility of transferring rights of loan and interest to competitors. *Affected by negative affect of speculation. *Financial marketing rules not allow the organization to sell bonds.	Any unusual return will own by the organization
Banks	*Possibility of transferring rights of loan and interest to competitors *Affected by negative speculation. *Affect of increasing cost as changing of interest. *Bank rules not allow the organization to get loan.	Any unusual return will own by the organization
Sharing with other shareholders	Any unusual return is shared with shareholders	Any loss will be shared with shareholders
Buy by credit	*Possibility of transferring rights of loan and interest to competitors *Companies rules against buying by credit	Any unusual return will own by the organization

to the possibility of buying these shares in limited time. In spite of the similarity among traditional stock companies, the differences come as a result of Islamic rules which are:

First: Effect of fixed rules:

1- Shareholders must not sell their common shares more than par value until liquidation of capital change from cash to other assets. It is a way to protect currency value by avoiding creation of money.
2- Managers can get wages but not part of net profit or can get just part of net profit; but for other shareholders who manage share they must take part of net profit. It is a way of protecting almost all shares by ordering the manager to do his best or not get revenue.
3- Any amount of net profit got by a company would be one of the rights of shareholders. This means undistributed profit must be given to shareholders. Therefore, every equity items are owned by shareholders making them to deserve part of the net profit.
4- Loss must be divided among all shareholders but not the amount of shares. This makes loss to be distributed among all sharers.
5- Net profit is distributed by the percentage the shareholders agree on. It takes sharers with different abilities to manage it.
6- Percentage of net profit distribution is decided during the signing of the contract of selling common shares. It prevents ignorance which may lead to problems.
7- Shareholders have the right to get revenue due to increasing value of net profit and asset up to market price regardless of historical value.
8- Interest is prohibited because of its negative effects.
Example: Suppose a company has common 300,000 shares and its value is up to net profit and market assets value; and other revenues are equal to $3,000,000. In order to finance new assets, it decides to sell new common shares of 300,000 to get $3,000,000. Every share will get 30% of revenue. Distribution of revenue will be as follows:
First: If the sharing is not limited by time (Permanent Moushraka) (Table 3).
Second: If the sharing is limited by time (Decreasing Moushraka):

Table 3. Permanent Moushraka calculated revenue.

Year	All capital	Capital of old shareholders	Capital of new shareholders	Yearly revenue as profit and assets market price increasing	Revenue for new shareholders 30%	Revenue for old shareholders 70%
2010	6,000,000	3,000,000	3,000,000	1,000,000	300,000	700,000
2011	6,000,000	3,000,000	3,000,000	500,000	150,000	350,000
2012	6,000,000	3,000,000	3,000,000	600,000	180,000	420,000
Ect---	----	---	---	---	----	---

Table 4. Decreasing Moushraka calculated revenue at case no loosing.

Year	All capital	Capital of old shareholders	Capital of new shareholders	Yearly revenue as profit and assets market price increasing	Revenue for new shareholders 30% × Revenue	Revenue for old shareholders 70% × Revenue	Old shareholders will buy from their revenue 80%
2010	6,000,000	3,000,000	3,000,000	4,000,000	1,200,000	1,700,000	1,360,000 which minuses from new shareholders capital and add to old shareholders capital
2011	6,000,000	4,360,000	1,640,000	3,000,000	900,000	2,100,000	1,680,000 which minuses from new shareholders capital and add to old shareholders capital as it will be more than 1,640,000 which it is the right of new shareholders. Old shareholders just buy 1,640,000 to own all capital
2012	6,000,000	6,000,000	Zero	6,000,000	zero	6,000,000	Zero

Table 5. Decreasing Moushraka calculated revenue at case there is losing.

Year	All capital	Capital of old shareholders	Capital of new shareholders	Yearly revenue as profit and assets market price increasing	Revenue for new shareholders 30% ×Revenue	Revenue for old shareholders 70% ×Revenue	Old shareholders will buy from their revenue 80%
2010	6,000,000	3,000,000	3,000,000	4,000,000	1,200,000	1,700,000	1,360,000 which minuses from new shareholders capital and add to old shareholders capital
2011	6,000,000	4,360,000	1,640,000	(- 3,000,000) Loosing divide up to sharing in capital not as agree between shareholders	zero	zero	zero
2012	3,000,000	2,180,000	820,000	6,000,000	1,800,000	4,200,000	But they just buy 820,000
2013	3,000,000	3,000,000	zero				

Ex: suppose a company sells common shares as decreasing Moushraka in a limited time. This means to buy new common shares from old shareholders' revenue. This has to be the percent of buying 80% of old shareholders' revenue (Table 3,4).
This means old shareholders had owned all capital after two years.

Third: If the sharing was limited by time and was lost (Table 5).
New shareholders will lose from their capital:
(New shareholders' capital/ all capital) × Loss (1,640,000 /6,000,000)= 819,999.9 × 3,000,000
Therefore, their capital becomes 820,000
Old shareholders will lose their capital: (New

shareholders' capital/ all capital) × Lose (4,360,000 /6,000,000)= × 3,000,000

Therefore, their capital becomes 2,180,000
This mean rules may come from companies managing them. Practically, these rules will direct management of/ and accounting for profit.

Conclusion

The study showed that the problem came as a result of profit organizations developing financial tools strategy to maximize profit in open environment regardless of the community's rights and country's aims. Negative effect came as a result of ignorance of responsibility. This leads to weak monetary policy and financial policy. There is a way to increase the strategy advantage of organizations and reduce their disadvantages through limits. Limits can be used to decide speculation dealing and stages of financial tools of life cycle. But this is not enough. There must be law. Islamic profit companies as case study avoid bad effects of interest, responsibility ignorance and negative effects on country's aims by applying fixed and flexibility rules. Practically, Islamic profit companies apply these limits to sell their common shares. These limits have directed their accounting revenue, making it possible to control balance between all aims, practically.

RECOMMENDATION

The researcher recommended the studying of the effect of financial tools using Islamic profit companies as a case study. Then limits should be made to avoid negative effects, and practical rules should be made to avoid deflection between organizations with legal aims using strategy of profit organizations. This will lead to economic growth. This can be applied in accounting revenue either through net profit or by increasing assets. The researcher suggests model for controlling developing financial tools used in contract dealing with the following questions:

1- What are the fixed rules of contract that cannot be changed in developing financial tool? This will make contract legal and determine the rights and duties needed in any kind of contract in any environment.

2- What are the flexibility rules used to develop contract either by adding or reducing environmental risk conditions if the fixed rules of contract accept these conditions? This will make possible adjustment on the contract if the conditions are accepted.

3- What are the rules that control economic sectors for the protection of any community? This will give any country the ability to develop its financial tools in order to help its monetary policy or financial policy.

REFERENCES

Ahmad M (2003). Analyses study about general budget in Jordan up to economic correctly policy. Econ. Horizons J. 24:94.

Ahmed Y (1998). Solving general budget deficit between modern opinion and Islamic opinion: comparative study. Kingdom of Saudi Arabia, Publ. Manag. J. 38:1.

Abdullah N (2006). The Effect of Sharia Controls on Development of Banking Services-A Theoretical Empirical Study, Ph.D. Dissertation, College of Banking and Financial Sciences, Amman, Jordan.

Chatterji A, David L, Micheal WT (2009). How well do social ratings Actually Measure corporate Social Responsibility? J. Econ. Manag. Strategy 18:1.

David HS (2012). Selective Publicity and stock Prices. The American Finance Association, U.S.A. J. Finan. 67:2.

David LR (1985). Developing New Bank Services. Bankers Mag. 154:4.

Holzach R (1985). New Challenges to Bank Management. Bankers Mag. 168:5.

Jean-Paul D, Thomas M, Jean CR, Stephane V (2011). The American finance Association Free cash flow, Issuance Costs and Stock Prices U.S.A. J. Finan. 66:5.

Lawrence JG (2000). Principles of Managerial Finance ,ninth edition, Addison Wesley Publishing Company, U.S.A, Chapter 5, Chapter 16 and Chapter 17.

Midan A (1988). Bank Marketing Management, 2ND Edition, Machmillan Education LTD, London, England.

Pedro SA, Erwan Q (2010). Limited Enforcement, Financial Intermediation, and Economic development: A Quantitative Assessment, International Economic Review, Economic Department of University of Pennsylvania and the Osaka University Institute Soc. Econ. Res. Assoc. 51:3.

Thomas H, Zieseme W (2011). Saving finance emigration and worker remittances serve to make staying rather than migrating possible UK. Int. Econ. J. 25:3.

Zeithaml VA, Bitner MJ (2000). Services Marketing International Customer Focus Across the Firm, Second Edition, McGraw-Hill Companies, Inc, U.S.

Permissions

All chapters in this book were first published in JEIF, by Academic Journals; hereby published with permission under the Creative Commons Attribution License or equivalent. Every chapter published in this book has been scrutinized by our experts. Their significance has been extensively debated. The topics covered herein carry significant findings which will fuel the growth of the discipline. They may even be implemented as practical applications or may be referred to as a beginning point for another development.

The contributors of this book come from diverse backgrounds, making this book a truly international effort. This book will bring forth new frontiers with its revolutionizing research information and detailed analysis of the nascent developments around the world.

We would like to thank all the contributing authors for lending their expertise to make the book truly unique. They have played a crucial role in the development of this book. Without their invaluable contributions this book wouldn't have been possible. They have made vital efforts to compile up to date information on the varied aspects of this subject to make this book a valuable addition to the collection of many professionals and students.

This book was conceptualized with the vision of imparting up-to-date information and advanced data in this field. To ensure the same, a matchless editorial board was set up. Every individual on the board went through rigorous rounds of assessment to prove their worth. After which they invested a large part of their time researching and compiling the most relevant data for our readers.

The editorial board has been involved in producing this book since its inception. They have spent rigorous hours researching and exploring the diverse topics which have resulted in the successful publishing of this book. They have passed on their knowledge of decades through this book. To expedite this challenging task, the publisher supported the team at every step. A small team of assistant editors was also appointed to further simplify the editing procedure and attain best results for the readers.

Apart from the editorial board, the designing team has also invested a significant amount of their time in understanding the subject and creating the most relevant covers. They scrutinized every image to scout for the most suitable representation of the subject and create an appropriate cover for the book.

The publishing team has been an ardent support to the editorial, designing and production team. Their endless efforts to recruit the best for this project, has resulted in the accomplishment of this book. They are a veteran in the field of academics and their pool of knowledge is as vast as their experience in printing. Their expertise and guidance has proved useful at every step. Their uncompromising quality standards have made this book an exceptional effort. Their encouragement from time to time has been an inspiration for everyone.

The publisher and the editorial board hope that this book will prove to be a valuable piece of knowledge for researchers, students, practitioners and scholars across the globe.

List of Contributors

Ronald Chibuike Iwu-Egwuonwu
Department of Business Administration, University of Abuja, Nigeria
Managing Partner Stride Associates Consulting, Nigeria

Isola Oluwabusuyi
4370 Peachtree Road N. E. Atlanta, Ga 30319, USA

P. O. O. Nto
College of Agribusiness and Financial Management, Michael Okpara University of Agriculture, Umudike, Nigeria

J. A. Mbanasor
College of Agribusiness and Financial Management, Michael Okpara University of Agriculture, Umudike, Nigeria

J. C. Nwaru
College of Agribusiness and Financial Management, Michael Okpara University of Agriculture, Umudike, Nigeria

Matthias Nnadi
School of Management, Cranfield University, Bedfordshire, UK

Samet GÜNAY
Anadolu BİL Vocational School, İstanbul Aydin University, Florya Campus, İstanbul, Turkey
İstanbul University, İstanbul, Turkey

Gökberk CAN
Anadolu BİL Vocational School, İstanbul Aydin University, Florya Campus, İstanbul, Turkey
İstanbul University, İstanbul, Turkey

E. D. Nakpodia
Department of Educational Administration and Policy Studies, Delta State University, Abraka, Nigeria

Vincent N. Ezeabasili
Department of Capital Market Studies, Anambra State University, Igbariam Campus, Anambra State, Nigeria

Joseph N. Mojekwu
Department of Actuarial Sciences and Insurance, Faculty of Business Administration University of Lagos, Nigeria

Hussain Ali Bekhet
College of Business Management and Accounting, Kampus Sultan Haji Ahmad Shah, UniversityTenaga Nasional, Pahang, Malaysia

Nor Salwati bt Othman
College of Business Management and Accounting, Kampus Sultan Haji Ahmad Shah, UniversityTenaga Nasional, Pahang, Malaysia

BEN SOLTANE Bassem
Faculty of Economics and Management of Sfax-Tunisia

Md. Ashraful Islam Khan
Department of Population Science and Human Resource Development, Rajshahi University, Rajshahi-6205, Bangladesh

E. D. Nakpodia
Department of Educational Administration and Policy Studies, Delta State University, Abraka, Nigeria

Sidra Ali Mirza
Shaheed Zulfiqar Ali Bhutto Institute of Science and Technology, Islamabad, Pakistan

Attiya Javed
Institute of Development Economics, Islamabad, Pakistan

Chikoko Laurine
Department of Banking and Finance, Midlands State University, Zimbabwe, P Bag 9055, Gweru, Zimbabwe

Mangwendeza Patrick
FBC Microfinance, FBC House, 113 Leopold Takawira Street, Harare, Zimbabwe

Famous Kose Dafiaghor
Department of Library and Information Science, Faculty of Education, Delta State University, Abraka, Nigeria

Neeta Jain
Department of Management (Finance), NIMS University, Jaipur (Raj.), India

Anna Jain
Department of Management (Finance), Centum Learning Centre, Jaipur (Raj.), India

Kossi Ayenagbo
College of Urban and Environmental Sciences, Northeast Normal University. No. 5268 Renmin Street, Changchun, Jilin Province, Post Code 130024, Peoples Republic of China

Josphert Ngui Kimatu
College of Urban and Environmental Sciences, Northeast Normal University. No. 5268 Renmin Street, Changchun, Jilin Province, Post Code 130024, Peoples Republic of China

Zhang Jing
College of Urban and Environmental Sciences, Northeast Normal University. No. 5268 Renmin Street, Changchun, Jilin Province, Post Code 130024, Peoples Republic of China

Sidime Nountenin
College of Urban and Environmental Sciences, Northeast Normal University. No. 5268 Renmin Street, Changchun, Jilin Province, Post Code 130024, Peoples Republic of China

Wang Rongcheng
College of Urban and Environmental Sciences, Northeast Normal University. No. 5268 Renmin Street, Changchun, Jilin Province, Post Code 130024, Peoples Republic of China

Artan Nimani
Faculty of Applied Business Sciences in Peja, University of Prishtina, Republic of Kosovo

F. A. N. Guojinga
Hunan Agriculture University, Changsha 410128, China
School of Culture and Tourism, GanNan Normal University, GanZhou 341000, JiangXi, China

L. Zhijun
Department of Sociology, Zhejiang University, Hangzhou 310058, China

Alfred Nuwagaba
Mount Kenya University-Kigali Campus, P.O. Box 5826, Kigali, Rwanda

Godfred A. Bokpin
Department of Finance, Business School, P. O. Box LG 78, University of Ghana

Rohit Bansal and Ashu Khanna
Indian Institute of Technology, Roorkee, Uttrakhand, India - 247001

Ibrahim Tajudeen Akogun
Moshood Abiola Polytechnic, Abeokuta, Ogun State, Nigeria

Olatoye Ojo
Department of Estate Management, Obafemi Awolowo University, Ile - Ife, Osun State, Nigeria

Abdullah Ibrahim Nazal
Department of Finance and Banking, Faculty of Economics and Administrative Sciences, Zarqa University, Jordan